Proceedings of the World Bank Annual Conference on Development Economics

1994

Supplement to The World Bank Economic Review and The World Bank Research Observer

Introduction — 1
Michael Bruno and Boris Pleskovic

Opening Remarks — 7
Lewis T. Preston

Keynote Address — 9
Development Issues in a Changing World: New Lessons, Old Debates, Open Questions
Michael Bruno

Transition in Socialist Economies

Macropolicies in Transition to a Market Economy: A Three-Year Perspective — 21
Leszek Balcerowicz and Alan Gelb
Comment, *Anders Åslund*
Comment, *János Kornai*
Floor Discussion

Russia's Struggle with Stabilization: Conceptual Issues and Evidence — 57
Jeffrey D. Sachs
Comment, *John Williamson*
Comment, *Maxim Boycko*
Floor Discussion

Establishing Property Rights — 93
Andrei Shleifer
Comment, *Olivier Jean Blanchard*
Comment, *Roman Frydman*
Floor Discussion

How Industrial Reform Worked in China:
The Role of Innovation, Competition, and Property Rights 129
Gary H. Jefferson and Thomas G. Rawski
Comment, *Athar Hussain and Nicholas H. Stern*
Comment, *Shahid Javed Burki*
Floor Discussion

NEW INSTITUTIONAL ECONOMICS

The Institutions and Governance
of Economic Development and Reform 171
Oliver E. Williamson
Comment, *Robert D. Putnam*
Comment, *Peter Murrell*
Floor Discussion

The Impact of Constitutions on Economic Performance 209
Jon Elster
Comment, *Adam Przeworski*
Comment, *Pranab Bardhan*
Floor Discussion

ECONOMIC GEOGRAPHY—
DYNAMICS OF DISPARATE REGIONAL DEVELOPMENT

Urban Concentration: The Role of Increasing Returns
and Transport Costs 241
Paul Krugman
Comment, *Andrew M. Isserman*
Comment, *J. Vernon Henderson*
Floor Discussion

Interaction between Regional and Industrial Policies:
Evidence from Four Countries 279
Ann Markusen
Comment, *William Alonso*
Comment, *Michael E. Porter*
Floor Discussion

INTERNATIONAL MIGRATION PRESSURES

European Migration: Push and Pull 313
Klaus F. Zimmermann
Comment, *Julian L. Simon*
Comment, *Xavier Sala-i-Martin*
Floor Discussion

Frontier Issues in International Migration 361
Oded Stark
Comment, *Michael J. Greenwood*
Comment, *Mark R. Rosenzweig*
Floor Discussion

LABOR MARKETS UNDER SYSTEMIC CHANGE

Labor Market Responses to a Change in Economic System 405
Robert J. Flanagan
Comment, *Richard Layard*
Comment, *John Pencavel*
Floor Discussion

ROUNDTABLE DISCUSSION 439
Employment and Development
Nancy Birdsall, Paul Collier, Richard B. Freeman, and Christopher A. Pissarides

Introduction

Michael Bruno and Boris Pleskovic

The papers in this volume were presented at the sixth World Bank Annual Conference on Development Economics, held April 28–29, 1994, in Washington, D.C. The conference series seeks to expand the flow of ideas among development policy researchers and practitioners around the world and to open the Bank to the views of outside experts who can challenge or expand our knowledge of the theories and practice of development. Each year the topics selected for the conference represent either new areas of concern or areas we believe will benefit from a review of existing knowledge and identification of areas for further research.

The sixth conference addresses five themes: transition in socialist economies, new institutional economics, economic geography, international migration pressures, and labor markets under systemic change. The 1994 conference continues the tradition of holding a roundtable discussion related to the subject of the next *World Development Report*—in this case, employment and development.

In his opening remarks Lewis T. Preston, president of the World Bank, reflecting on the Bank's nearly fifty years of experience, emphasizes that in many ways its real value added lies in ideas. He stresses the importance of knowledge and research at the World Bank and the value of advice and technical assistance based on the lessons learned from working in more than 140 countries. Preston notes that the challenge of transition also deals with the power of ideas and involves not just a change in economic systems but a change in thinking as well. He outlines what we know about reform and what we still need to learn, emphasizing such important areas as poverty, environmental degradation, and change in economic systems, where improved knowledge and good ideas are more important than ever.

Michael Bruno notes in his keynote address that the development agenda has changed significantly in the past twenty-five years. Drawing on the experiences of recent decades, Bruno sets out three necessary conditions for development: sustainable growth is necessary for a sustainable reduction in poverty, adjustment is necessary for the resumption of growth, and fiscal and monetary restraint is a nec-

Michael Bruno is chief economist and vice president, Development Economics, at the World Bank. Boris Pleskovic is deputy administrator, Research Advisory Staff, at the World Bank.

Proceedings of the World Bank Annual Conference on Development Economics 1994

essary component of adjustment. However, these conditions may not be sufficient. Bruno discusses three areas in which experience has provided insights, but in which further work remains to be done. First, he points out that growth may not be sufficient for poverty reduction; investment in human capital, notably in basic education and health, is an essential complement. Second, he considers the links between macroeconomic stability and microeconomic reforms such as privatization and financial sector reform. Additional research is required to understand the appropriate sequence for reforms and new regulatory needs. Finally, Bruno considers institutions and the transferability of policies. Bruno concludes that the research agenda should aim at reducing the area of ignorance between what we know to be necessary and what we suspect to be sufficient, by deepening our knowledge of institutions and political factors and by drawing on the Bank's extensive operational knowledge.

Leszek Balcerowicz and Alan Gelb analyze three elements of transition to a market economy: macroeconomic stabilization; the liberalization of prices, markets, and entry; and institutional change. They point out that initial stabilization has been most successful when radical programs have been launched during an early period of "extraordinary politics" following a political breakthrough. A reversion to "normal politics" and business-as-usual complicates further stabilization by raising inflationary expectations, slowing reform, and reducing the propensity of state enterprises to adjust. Country experience suggests that there are no adverse medium-run tradeoffs between stabilization and either output or the speed of transition to a private economy. Failure to stabilize wastes valuable time and delays recovery. For countries that are grappling with stabilization in the absence of a major political breakthrough the authors recommend that, even without a formal program, they proceed with liberalization and institutional changes as rapidly as possible to strengthen the constituency for future stabilization.

Jeffrey Sachs describes the deep crisis facing Russia and argues that highly unstable political and economic conditions could trigger a collapse of that country's nascent democracy. He points out that the situation could unravel in a spiral of self-reinforcing destructive responses: criminality, regional separatism, tax evasion, and flight from the currency. To overcome these risks, the Russian government should embark on a rapid program of stabilization, backed by large-scale assistance. Reviewing the role of international assistance to Russia during the past three years, Sachs concludes that assistance has fallen far short—in speed, direction, and magnitude—of real need. The concerns he raises apply not only to Russia, but more generally to weak states in acute financial crisis. The current methods of delivering aid are typically too slow and too oblivious to the risks of a "contagion" of state collapse. Throughout the world weak, newly democratic states are grappling with an inheritance of high indebtedness and failing public institutions. These countries can overcome their bitter inheritance, but only if the world community responds with urgency and support. Sachs argues that a combination of restrictive monetary policy, an early pegging of the exchange rate, and large-scale international assistance offers Russia the most realistic chance of avoiding political catastrophe.

Andrei Shleifer argues that establishing property rights in developing countries and the transition economies of Eastern Europe amounts to solving two problems: inefficient structures of control rights over assets, and unenforceable contracts. The allocation of resources is inefficient in transition economies because politicians and bureaucrats have control over too much of the economy, thus discouraging investment by entrepreneurs. The most obvious way to get around excessive bureaucratic control is corruption, but this strategy is of limited usefulness as an efficiency-restoring mechanism given the general unenforceability of corruption contracts between politicians and entrepreneurs. Shleifer discusses three alternative approaches for establishing property rights: giving bureaucrats equity ownership, reforming the civil service, and eliminating bureaucratic control rights politically, through privatization. Equity ownership might not be politically feasible because equity contracts are not enforceable, while weakening the control of bureaucrats through civil service reform requires a very effective government or a very effective press, and so may be an option only in countries with advanced political institutions. Using the example of Russia, Shleifer shows how privatization, combined with equity incentives for insiders, transfers control rights from bureaucrats and stimulates political and economic pressures for the genuine protection of private property rights.

In another exploration of transition in socialist economies, Gary Jefferson and Thomas Rawski compare China's gradual and partial implementation of reform with other approaches. The authors explore the mechanisms through which initial attempts at partial reform unleashed forces that, fifteen years later, have brought China's economy to the brink of a market system. Their analysis highlights the participation of tens of thousand of enterprises and millions of administrators, managers, and workers whose decisions over the years of reform eventually built a constituency for market-directed change that was far stronger than any official announcement could have produced. This process, though very different from that in Western parliamentary democracies, has produced a durable reform constituency that easily rebuffed high-level efforts to roll back reform in the wake of the inflation scare and political repression of 1989. The authors conclude that China's industrial economy, despite its divergences from textbook ideas, is looking increasingly like a market system.

Oliver Williamson explores the reasons why the ambitions of economic development practitioners are so often disappointed. He says that one answer is that development policymakers and reformers are congenital optimists. More to the point, though, is that good plans are regularly defeated by those who occupy strategic positions. Williamson suggests that these negative outcomes reflect the fact that institutions are important for carrying out the intentions of government, and yet they are a persistently neglected aspect of the planning process. The author suggests that useful work can be accomplished by the new institutional economics. He notes in this connection that the predilections of both optimistic planners and cynical implementers are features to which institutions should be expected to respond. Williamson takes a bottom-up, microanalytic approach that examines the efficacy of the de facto (as against the de jure) institutional environment with respect to credible commitments. According to Williamson, institutional economists are in effect cast in the role of archaeologists of economic development and reform: they uncover and decipher the lessons of the past that bear on shaping better programs for the future.

Also on the theme of institutional economics, Jon Elster examines the interaction between constitutions and economic performance. He distinguishes between two core provisions of modern constitutions: those that regulate the machinery of government and those that guarantee the basic rights of citizens. These components are so basic that they cannot be changed by the ordinary legislative process but require a more stringent amendment procedure. The author discusses two polar positions of economic performance. The first pertains to economic efficiency, and the second to well-being, or security. Because neither the pure efficiency-oriented view nor the pure security-oriented view is satisfactory, Elster discusses the impact of constitutional provisions on both efficiency and security. He concludes that constitutions matter for economic performance to the extent that they promote the values of stability, accountability, and credibility. While emphasizing the idea that constitutions can be useful by serving as precommitment devices, the author also underlines the dangers of rigidity and the need for flexibility.

Pursuing the topic of economic geography, Paul Krugman claims that very large urban centers are a conspicuous feature of many developing economies, yet development economists have neglected the subject of the size distribution of cities. He argues that some important insights into urban concentration, especially a tendency in some developing countries toward very large cities, can be derived from recent approaches to economic geography. Krugman compares three approaches: the well-established neoclassical urban systems theory, which emphasizes the tradeoff between agglomeration economies and the diseconomies of city size; the "new economic geography," which attempts to derive agglomeration effects from the interactions among market size, transportation costs, and increasing returns at the level of the firm; and a nihilistic view that cities emerge out of a random process in which there are roughly constant returns to city size. Krugman suggests that the desire to reduce the size of these large cities, or at least slow their relative growth, may be met indirectly by the kinds of economic policies currently in favor—liberal trade, less government intervention, and decentralization of power.

In another exploration of economic geography Ann Markusen argues that national governments are turning increasingly to sectoral and technology policies as strategies for economic growth and competitiveness. Such policies are often fashioned simultaneously as regional initiatives to decentralize economic activity from large metropolitan areas and to stimulate laggard regions. Using evidence from Brazil, the Republic of Korea, Japan, and the United States, Markusen concludes that industrial policy was essentially compatible with regional policy over the postwar period but has become less so in recent years as the emphasis shifted toward innovation-intensive export sectors. A key element in the shift has been a preference for locating in primate cities, undermining efforts at regional decentralization. As conflict between industrial and regional policies intensifies, governments appear to favor industrial policy initiatives and to deemphasize centralized regional planning. The increasing devolution of economic development powers to local governments in all four countries is seen as an indicator of this trend. Markusen argues that the emphasis on high-technology industrial sectors will reinforce the advantages of regions with already high per capita incomes and relatively faster rates of regional growth, slowing progress toward eliminating differentials in regional growth and income.

On the topic of international migration Klaus Zimmermann notes that the heightened interest in European migration is a reflection of increased tensions about foreigners in countries of the European Union. For decades migration was seen as benefiting the host country by supplying needed labor. But in the 1970s immigration policies became more restrictive as social tensions and fear of recession mounted. Considering Europe's long experience with immigration after World War II, Zimmermann suggests that this new concern has more to do with recent flows of asylum seekers and persistently high and increasing unemployment rates than with migration as such. New econometric evidence suggests that immigration after World War II was driven by business-cycle effects as well as by family migration patterns but that the processes changed after 1973, when many countries acted to halt the recruitment of workers. Zimmermann argues that neither the families of earlier waves of migrants nor ethnic networks in sending countries were affected by the economically motivated immigration policies. His analysis shows that ethnic and family migration networks can counteract policy measures to induce return migration.

Writing on frontier issues in international migration Oded Stark presents the results of an analysis that, although not conclusive, is sufficiently advanced to suggest a number of concrete testable implications. His analysis addresses three issues: return migration, migrants' remittances, and migrants' market performance. Stark asks why and which migrants return home, why and how much migrants remit, and what explains migrants' market performance. Building on the assumption that information is imperfect, Stark traces return migration to the lagged ability of employers at destination to distinguish between skilled and unskilled workers, which results in the return of less-skilled workers. The motive for remittances is seen as self-interest: remittances protect the wages of high-skill workers from being eroded by the entry of low-skill workers into the same pool. To account for the fact that migrants often outperform native-born workers, Stark suggests that perceived group attributes rather than individual abilities and skills determine how migrants fare, absolutely and relative to the indigenous population.

Robert Flanagan addresses the employment problems in Eastern Europe and concludes that the transition to a market economy has led to a contraction in aggregate labor supply and the beginnings of a reallocation of labor from activities favored by central planners to those favored by consumers. Flanagan observes that the expansion of the private sector has reversed—if not eliminated—many of the labor market distortions established under central planning. Thus the first years of economic transition recorded increasing returns to human capital. But there is little evidence of a tight connection between growth of the private sector and development of more rational wage structures. Labor market programs in the region seem ill-suited for facilitating restructuring. In particular, the emphasis on "passive" measures, such as unemployment compensation, may extend joblessness. Would a change to "active" labor market policies designed to improve the skills of job seekers reverse the decline in employment? Not likely at this point, the author observes. Training and related measures do not create vacancies; they help to fill them. Only when job vacancies and unemployment are more closely aligned would a reorientation away from passive measures and wage subsidies toward training programs for modern production seem desirable. Flanagan finds little evidence that labor unions and minimum wage legislation have inhibited the objectives of restructuring, but he argues that incomes policies appear to have retarded adjustments in wages and other aspects of labor restructuring in state enterprises.

The roundtable discussion on employment and development was designed to address some of the issues central to the forthcoming *World Development Report 1995*. The panel brought together four experts, each of them drawing attention to different aspects of the topic. Nancy Birdsall talked about growth, inequality, and the labor market. Paul Collier discussed African labor markets. Richard B. Freeman discussed global market issues. Christopher A. Pissarides compared the performance of European and U.S. labor markets and presented lessons for the developing world. The panelists' presentations were followed by a floor discussion chaired by Michael Bruno.

As in previous years, the planning and organization of the sixth conference was a joint effort. We would like to thank Shahid Yusuf, the acting administrator of the Research Advisory Staff, for his guidance on the conference. Particular thanks for their support are due to Gregory Ingram, Paulo Vieira Da Cunha, and Mark Baird. We would also like to thank other staff members, in particular the conference coordinators, Jean Gray Ponchamni, Mantejwinder Jandu, and Evelyn Alfaro, whose excellent organizational skills kept the conference on track. Finally, we thank the editorial staff, especially Meta de Coquereaumont, Paul Holtz, Patricia McNees, and Bruce Ross-Larson.

Opening Remarks

Lewis T. Preston

Good morning, and a warm welcome to the sixth Annual Bank Conference on Development Economics. As you may know, the World Bank is approaching the fiftieth anniversary of its establishment at Bretton Woods. As we reflect on our past experience—and, more important, as we look to the future—the role of knowledge and research in what we do looms large.

Yes, the Bank is a development institution *and* a financial institution. But it is also a knowledge-based institution. Indeed, in many ways, our real value added lies in our ideas.

Over the past five decades the Bank has supported more than five thousand development projects with financing totaling more than $300 billion. Along with the money came advice based on the lessons learned from working in over 140 countries in many different sectors.

We continue to learn today. That is one reason why this event is so important. It allows us to listen and exchange ideas with our colleagues in the development economics community. In short: your coming here offers us the opportunity to learn.

The Transition Theme

This year's conference addresses one of the biggest stories of the century: economic transition in the socialist economies. Again, we are dealing here, fundamentally, with the power of ideas. The transition phenomenon involves not just a change in economic systems, but also a change in thinking.

Our collective experience so far with the transition process is relatively limited. But already we have learned that moving from state to market is very different in each country—and that issues of timing and sequencing need to be customized.

- We have learned that reforms reinforce each other—one without others will not work.
- We have learned that social safety nets and adequate external support are essential to ease the pain of transition.

Lewis T. Preston is president of the World Bank.

Proceedings of the World Bank Annual Conference on Development Economics 1994

- And we have learned, perhaps above all, that without strong internal political commitment to reform, foreign assistance can achieve little.

And yet notwithstanding these early lessons, we find ourselves at the steep end of the learning curve. There is much that we do not know about how to achieve successful transition. Your discussions over the next two days should help shed further light on the road ahead:

- About institutional economics, and how best to build the financial, legal, and political frameworks that provide the critical underpinning for markets.
- About the adjustment of labor markets in countries where "full employment" has traditionally been seen as a basic right.
- And about how the process of transition affects economic geography, substantially altering the pre–cold war map—from industrial patterns to migration pressures.

The challenge of transition has added urgency to our analysis of these issues. But the lessons to be learned—and, let us not forget, to be applied—go beyond the transition economies. The issue of jobs, for example, is of vital interest to every country—developing or industrial. The same can be said of migration. These are issues that represent the practical realities of interdependence because they affect us all.

Ideas and Development

The familiar division of our world into East and West or North and South has vanished. But as the curtain that once distorted global economic and political relationships has been raised, the imperative of development has become even more visible:

- Over a billion people still live in absolute poverty.
- Environmental degradation threatens the earth.
- Numerous countries are struggling to reinvent their economic systems.

In this new world where the scope of peoples' needs is ever more obvious, resources for development are ever more scarce—and good ideas are at an ever greater premium.

Generating those ideas is a challenge facing the World Bank, the development economics profession, and everyone participating in this conference.

KEYNOTE ADDRESS

Development Issues in a Changing World: New Lessons, Old Debates, Open Questions

Michael Bruno

The 1960s look like the golden age of economic development. GDP in Latin America, East Asia, and the OECD countries was growing at about 5 percent a year. South Asia and Sub-Saharan Africa were trailing close behind. Predictions for the future were frankly optimistic and—interestingly—rosier for Africa and somewhat bleaker for East Asia. Growth would continue (if not accelerate) and poverty would be sharply reduced.

But the next twenty years were turbulent—with many setbacks. During the 1970s and 1980s the interregional growth gap widened dramatically. Roughly half the wider gap came from the unexpectedly fast growth in East Asia (including China). The other half came from the plummeting drop to negative growth rates in Latin America and particularly in Sub-Saharan Africa.[1]

Growth has now resumed for the developing countries as a group. Will it last, and will it spread? Do past failures of prediction imply that we have learned no general lessons about the sustainability of the development process, its fundamental components, its distributional consequences? Do we understand when and why some countries—facing the same world environment—got into the wrong growth and poverty track and stayed there for a long time? What rises from the wreckage and the reform process as the correct blend of government and market? And what pieces of our acquired knowledge are generalizable, and what institution-specific or country-specific? In short, how have our old ideas about some of these questions been modified with experience? What robust lessons have we learned? In what areas are new ideas (or rigorous testing of existing ones) most needed? All these questions are important for shaping future development policy.

Modified Perceptions of Growth's Fundamentals

Most striking about the comparative developments of the past twenty years is the diversity of regional experience in a common turbulent environment. The East

Michael Bruno is chief economist and vice president, Development Economics, at the World Bank. The author is grateful to Masood Ahmed, Mark Baird, Miguel Kiguel, Lyn Squire, Paulo Vieira Da Cunha, Michael Walton, and Shahid Yusuf for helpful comments on an earlier draft.

Asian "miracle" countries emerged with an apparent long-run model of development, seeming to have done almost everything right. Against them, one can contrast other countries and ask what went wrong.

There is very broad agreement about their remarkable shared growth—with rapid growth and poverty reduction reinforcing each other. The most interesting and compelling part of the story (it featured less in the development literature of twenty years ago) is the role of basic education in enhancing the quality of labor—complemented on the demand side by a pattern of export-led growth that made productive use of labor, the poor's most important asset. The emphasis on the health and education of mothers reduced fertility rates and increased the time they spent at home on the education of the next generation of children. Supplementing this was an increased slice of basic education spending in an expanding resource pie.

The effect was substantial. Based on a cross-country regression estimate, if Korea had Pakistan's low school enrollment rate in 1960, its GDP per capita in 1985 would have been 40 percent lower than what it actually attained.[2] The role of educating mothers can also be decomposed. Between 1965 and 1985 Korean mothers' enhanced primary education and the resulting drop in their fertility rates doubled their estimated gap with Kenyan mothers in the time (weighted by education) they devoted to their children. Similarly, Korea's lower birth rate kept a more or less stable number of children eligible for basic education over the period—in Kenya the number eligible almost doubled. Combining the effect of a larger percentage of GDP spent on basic education and the much faster growth rate gives a startling result: in 1985 Korea's public expenditure per child was twenty-seven times Kenya's, up from being only three times as high in 1970.[3] This stronger performance on education plus a high savings rate (cause or effect?) provided the bulk of the supply-side capital and labor accumulation for Asia's "miracle." Exports, meanwhile, delivered the demand side—along with the discipline of market prices.

Technological spillovers, contrary to what is sometimes claimed, do not appear to explain much of the rapid East Asian growth. Measured total factor productivity for many of the East Asian countries does not account for more than 20 to 30 percent of GDP growth.[4] And the part of this residual attributable to technological progress could be much smaller.

Consider instead that the East Asians responded to the thick and thunder of the 1970s and 1980s with better macroeconomic policies. The departures from rapid growth were shorter and the margins of underused capacity were smaller. Better macroeconomic policy may thus account for a big part of the observed difference between East Asia and the rest of the world in the growth of total factor productivity.[5]

Amid Diversity—Salvaging Necessary Conditions

Among the factors that may account for varying country performance over the past two decades, domestic responses to external shocks may be most important. The protracted crises and their different resolutions have highlighted growth as a path-dependent process. The shocks and the different responses were not predicted. But the unfolding of the crises vindicated the importance of macroeconomic fundamentals and highlighted the importance of market-oriented microeconomic reforms—salvaging some major common policy lessons amid the diversity of country experience.

It is useful, and conventional, to distinguish two elements of the adjustment package to rescue an economy from a crisis and move it to relative price stability and the resumption of growth.[6] One is stabilization, necessary to correct the underlying macroeconomic imbalance. The other is structural reform centering on the supply side, necessary to change incentives and restructure the distorted microeconomy. This usually encompasses a series of market-oriented reforms, such as trade liberalization, public sector reform, and financial sector reform.[7] These also fundamentally redefine the role of government.

Three nested necessary conditions link growth with poverty reduction and with the two elements of adjustment:

- Fiscal and monetary restraint is necessary for adjustment.
- Implementing an adjustment package is necessary for resumption of sustainable per capita growth.
- Attaining sustainable average growth in per capita income is necessary for sustainable reductions in poverty.

All three, in addition to basic education, are necessary—but by no means sufficient—for more rapid growth, and narrowing the gap between necessity and sufficiency remains a major research task. But even the three conditions have been—and sometimes still are—subjects of heated dispute, especially the links between growth and poverty reduction.

Links between Growth and Poverty Reduction

The controversy on the "tradeoff" between growth and equity endures, though its intensity and form have varied. In the golden age of growth at the end of the 1960s and in the early 1970s, the debate was over "redistribution with growth." Policy actions, often misguided, led to an undifferentiated increase in public social spending that largely bypassed the poor. Higher spending enlarged public sector deficits and deepened macroeconomic imbalances when worldwide shocks impinged on country performance.[8]

In the adjustment to new external shocks (such as the debt crisis), the attack has centered on the social consequences of adjustment. One form of the attack implies that poverty can be reduced only by direct targeted policies. The rhetoric comes close to denying any link between growth and sustainable poverty alleviation. By implication, it belittles the view that adjustment is in turn a fundamental step toward renewed long-term growth after a crisis.

It is hard to see how a given (or diminishing) pie can be redistributed in favor of the poor and yet make them absolutely better off in income or wealth.[9] The evidence on this is clear, and here again recent research has helped clarify and solidify our understanding. The incidence of poverty, defined as the proportion of the population living below the poverty line, falls rapidly with growth in consumption. Across several countries, the elasticity is about –2: that is, each percentage point of growth in mean per capita consumption is associated with a reduction in the incidence of poverty of 2 percentage points (Ravallion forthcoming).

East Asia's shared growth shows that growth and poverty alleviation can go together, though estimates differ about the strength of the two-way causal link between them.[10] Experience elsewhere in Asia and more recently in Latin America shows that poverty measures are strongly correlated with the ups and downs of growth. But this evidence is silent on two crucial aspects. It does not argue that growth is sufficient for poverty alleviation. Nor does it support the view that pro-poor government policies, other than those that enhance growth, are not important for poverty reduction. On the contrary, patterns of growth can clearly be shown to be more or less poverty-enhancing, depending on initial conditions.

World Development Report 1990 has already stressed the importance of primary education and basic health care both for the benefits they confer and for their role in promoting labor-intensive growth. Moreover, the experience in Latin America and elsewhere shows that growth can falter and become increasingly inequitable when policy is biased against the rural sector through mistaken pricing and protection policies,[11] overvalued exchange rates, or the neglect of rural infrastructure.

Adjustment need not hurt the rural poor even when it reduces short-term aggregate output. The result depends on the economy's openness: in more open economies the adjustment costs are significantly lower. The result also depends on the choice of public expenditure cuts and on the efficiency of public spending in improving the terms of trade for the rural sector (as producers versus consumers). Costa Rica and Indonesia show adjustment with reduced social costs. Argentina, the Philippines, and Venezuela show the opposite. Venezuela's recent policy reversals attest to the dangers of a reform program whose fruits are not widely shared, as do recent events in Mexico. More widespread household survey data—particularly panel data—should provide further evidence on this important issue, especially for the most controversial and least-researched region of Sub-Saharan Africa. Note that none of this refutes the basic premise that sustainable per capita growth is a necessary, though by no means sufficient, condition for sustainable poverty reduction.

A new consensus on the roles of the private and public sectors is influencing the design of policies aimed at poverty alleviation. With a more neutral structure of microeconomic incentives, price stability and growth work in favor of the poor on two important counts. First, the poor benefit from increased demand for labor and thus from greater private consumption. Second, with incomes growing, governments are more capable of financing (and arguably more willing to do so) public action that is pro-poor.

One key question, requiring much more study, is how to make public action on poverty more cost-effective, especially in the provision of infrastructure and social services. Unresolved is the issue of programs targeted to groups (such as women, families with many children, or poverty-stricken regions) compared with universal provision of social services. This issue raises difficult questions of political economy and is fraught with problems in implementation. There is also difficulty in evaluating the effectiveness of proposed policies.[12] Much is known about poverty, about how to measure it, and about its relationship to growth and macroeconomic policies—much less is known about developing effective policies and institutions for optimal poverty reduction.

Macroeconomic Fundamentals and Microeconomic Reforms

Macroeconomic fundamentals and the reform of microeconomic incentives work together in adjustment and in the resumption of growth after a prolonged crisis—and the past twenty-five years vindicate some old and by now well-honed ideas.

High inflation in Latin America (as well as in Israel and Eastern Europe) has dealt a mortal blow to the bubble theory of inflation—that nonmonetary and nonfiscal means could be used for stabilization.[13] Orthodox fiscal and monetary components have become a necessary and generally accepted part of any stabilization package. But there are some important new modifications. Since the mid-1980s there has been an added twist for countries that have had prolonged inflationary inertia—the multiple anchor approach. This calls for a wage and exchange rate freeze (with or without price controls) to accompany the orthodox parts of a stabilization package, making it heterodox. First successfully used in Israel in 1985, it was followed by Mexico in 1988 and later applied in several Eastern European countries. Another relatively new emphasis calls for bolstering the independence of central banks, a stabilization tool with a structural reform element.

The other important legacy of recent reform experience has to do with the microeconomy of market incentives and the redefinition of the role of government and the private sector. Here again are old elements and new. The advantage of trade-determined market discipline for reasons of efficiency and distribution (political economy) was well established more than twenty-five years ago. It proved effective for the Asian newly industrializing countries, for isolated Latin American countries (Colombia), and for Israel.

The crises of the past two decades produced additional hard evidence on the resilience of an outward orientation in the face of external shocks.[14] And the very recent brand of reform experiments in Latin America (Argentina, Chile, Mexico) and Eastern Europe (the former Czechoslovakia, Poland) incorporates an even more extreme form of quick-fix import liberalization. Indeed, in these later approaches the pace of liberalization is clearly more heavily influenced by political economy than by economic arguments alone.[15]

Government divestiture is providing new lessons about its two main aspects: the divestiture of production (mainly through privatizing state-owned enterprises) and the demonopolization of finance. A new paradigm is emerging from the pervasive mismanagement of public enterprises and political patronage in both industrial and industrializing countries, culminating in the extreme in the collapse of the centrally controlled economies. Private ownership of the means of production—except in a diminishing share of infrastructure investment, natural monopolies, and so on—is the new ideal.

Changes in ownership do matter in the long run. And in the transition economies privatization is the only way to move from central state control to a market economy with a private sector. But hard budget constraints and market disciplines are critical even in the short run. These forces can work—or fail—under either government ownership or private ownership.

In the intermediate stage of commercializing state-owned enterprises, the credible imposition of market discipline even before the transfer of ownership, as in China and Poland, creates the incentives for productivity and profit through better management.[16] In Poland managers (and workers) may change their behavior either because they have a stake in future profits under an impending privatization program or because they are signaling their value as managers in a future market for their services.

But a mere formal change of ownership does nothing to change incentives when the budget faucet stays open. Consider an authoritarian ruler distributing ownership of enterprises to cronies or close family associates (the Philippines under Marcos). Or consider quasi privatization in Russia, where ownership passes into the hands of managers and workers—yet the enterprise may for a time continue to milk the state budget. There are also many examples of private enterprises that are mismanaged under soft budget constraints. Redrawing the boundary between the public and the private sector as part of structural reform may thus start with the clear demarcation of future ownership of enterprise debt even before proceeding on the asset side.

With time, more will be learned from the varying restructuring experiences in Eastern and Central Europe. For example, to resolve bad debts, the most advanced restructuring economies in transition have opted for different channels. The Czech Republic expects private owners to take responsibility. Poland relied on the banking system. And Hungary is relying on liquidation and bankruptcy procedures.

On the importance of financial reform and the restructuring of banks, lessons are coming from both Latin America and Eastern Europe. Governments with large deficits tend to sequester private savings through monopolies of the financial system. But even with more prudent fiscal behavior, the philosophy of central control over investment and lending invariably segments credit markets. Privileged sectors obtain credit at low—and often negative—real interest rates, while the much smaller free market segment is exposed to usurious rates. In times of high inflation the allocative distortions usually mount, and the microeconomic counterpart of public sector reform becomes a necessary complement of the adjustment package.

Two issues require more research. First, what is the correct sequence of reforms in the financial and production sectors? Experience in Latin America and Africa suggests that financial reform fails when public enterprises are not restructured at the same time (as they continue to be a drag on the bad loan portfolio of the banks). But commercial banks may help induce changes in the corporate governance of nonfinancial enterprises in the immediate postprivatization stage of a transition economy. For that matter, what is the relevant model for banks? Should they be allowed to hold equity, as in the continental or Japanese models? When and where is one or the other argument dominant?

What are the appropriate regulatory mechanisms for newly liberalized economies? (Again, what is the best sequence?) The fact that greater microeconomic market liberalization has to go hand in hand with tougher supervision at the government level, especially for the financial sector, is a paradoxical lesson that not just the newly reforming countries are learning (see the recent major financial supervision failures in the Japan, the United Kingdom, and the United States).

Can microeconomic adjustment precede macroeconomic stabilization? The standard answer used to be that macroeconomic stabilization has to come first. From the perspective of the 1990s the answer may be somewhat less straightforward. It still seems correct to say that without macroeconomic stabilization no sustainable growth is possible because price instability usually yields large distortions in relative prices. Even Brazil, where growth continued for a long time despite high inflation, seems to have fallen into the familiar low-growth pattern in the past ten years. Yet Brazil managed to privatize amid high inflation. Argentina failed in its stabilization attempts and managed to get its act together only after a substantial tax reform, suggesting that microeconomic restructuring had to precede macroeconomic stabilization. The most recent case in which stabilization has not—or could not have—been achieved before substantial microeconomic change is Russia, which has gone through mass privatization amid high inflation. For the subsequent restructuring stage, however, greater price stability becomes crucial. The upshot: some years and more country experience will have to accumulate before we can rewrite the macroeconomic-microeconomic adjustment sequencing paradigm.

Second, what are the necessary and sufficient conditions for adjustment that leads to sustainable growth? Put differently, what is the minimum package of reforms? We seem to understand the issues, but we know little about how to handle them for policy design. Even when macroeconomic fundamentals are in place, and structural reforms are under way, sustainable growth takes a long time to resume.

We know that stabilization from high inflation may yield fairly immediate output dividends—but that investment is very slow to resume. The resumption of profit-motivated, real long-horizon private investment (as against portfolio investment or speculation) depends on how investors evaluate the future of an economy that is emerging from a crisis and that has a bad track record. The irreversibility of reforms—both economic and political—plays the dominant role in forming investor's speculations.

Governments can help to some extent by providing complementary infrastructure, covering start-up costs, and alleviating the worst social hardships. But the most important—and hardest—service for a government to deliver is the irreversibility of a new policy environment and the credibility of the reform effort. A supposed positive-sum game (with society in the aggregate standing to gain) is not enough. Government resolve and the widespread shared ownership of a reform effort are the great imponderables. Experience is accumulating from the successes and failures in more and more countries, yet evaluation for policy purposes escapes precise assessment.[17]

Institutions and the Transferability of Policies

Institutions matter, and they may vary substantially, as recent cross-country experience demonstrates. So, similar policy advice (as for the introduction of regulatory agencies and rules) can result in different policy outcomes in different institutional settings.

Progress in economic theory does not always conform to progress in policy practice. Practitioners and policymakers reared in the cultural and political traditions of a particular country know the importance of institutions in shaping what is feasible (that is, both the enhancing and constraining factors) for recommended policies. The problem arises with attempts to replicate policy lessons in another setting, naturally tempting for the emissaries of a multilateral institution. Not all policy applications are institution-sensitive, but many are.[18]

Is there a general institutional theory that could be empirically applied or used as a tool kit for predictive modeling? Not yet. But this does not mean that the study of institutions and organizations should not be taken seriously. At a minimum, the economics agenda should involve a careful and systematic comparative study of markets and the institutional constraining factors in different countries. The normative implication of this agenda would then—in the absence of generally distilled theories—bring cumulative international experience to bear when advice is given for the application of a policy in a country.

Consider three very different recent lines of inquiry. Much progress has been made in recent years in understanding the relationship of central bank independence and price stability.[19] One interesting finding is the difference between legal independence (based on an index derived from formal statutes, that is, the written "rules") and actual independence (measured by, say, the rate of turnover of central bank governors).[20] Legal independence is a good predictor of price stability for industrial countries but a very poor one for developing countries. Actual independence turns out to be a much better predictor for developing countries. This is consistent with the intuition that the enforceability of legal rules (including their social and political acceptance) is what matters.[21]

Another example is a recent World Bank comparative study of regulatory agencies in the telecommunications industry, from which some general lessons can be drawn about the applicability of different regulatory institutions depending on the commitment mechanisms and the complexity of regulations in different country settings (Levy and Spiller 1995).

Third is a study comparing the efficiency of the civil service, in terms of the different rates of mobility and rules of promotion, as observed in the irrigation systems of India and the Republic of Korea (Wade 1993). A good understanding of the rules governing the behavior of those in charge of policy implementation in any country should be a prerequisite for giving advice. For example, irrespective of the results of the debate about the role of microeconomic interventions in East Asia, it would be of small practical service for Sub-Saharan Africa unless it can explicitly tackle the different institutional foundations of the civil service in these countries.

Between Necessity and Sufficiency

Basic education is necessary for rapid growth. Growth is necessary for a persistent reduction in poverty. Adjustment is necessary for the resumption of growth. And fiscal and monetary restraint are necessary components of adjustment. These conditions, met in the success stories of the past twenty-five years, cut across diverse experiences and have withstood the test of time. But the necessary conditions are not sufficient. The definition of adjustment remains ambiguous. And several questions raised here call for additional research, especially on the role of government.[22]

Because development and adjustment are inherently uncertain and complex, it is futile to attempt to get at necessity and sufficiency for the general case. A less ambitious and more realistic research agenda would reduce the area of ignorance that lies between the two poles and sift out from theory and empirical evidence all that is general and invariant.

There should be an attempt to minimize the residual country-specific or situation-specific factors (recognizing that they will always be there to qualify the efficacy of our policy prescriptions). For a better understanding of the difference between necessity and sufficiency in prescribing development policy, we need deeper knowledge of institutions and political factors. And we have to make this knowledge operational across a broad array of countries and experiences.

By all indications world trade will grow considerably faster than output. The demise of the Council for Mutual Economic Assistance, the successful completion of the Uruguay Round, and the trade-increasing regional trade arrangements all point to a better harmonization of institutions and regulations. Flows of private capital and of ideas have increased rapidly, and the global business environment is increasingly competitive. This observation is also applicable to the World Bank. As a major player on the world scene, what mix of capital and ideas is it best equipped to deliver? The reality is likely to continue to induce very unequal responses by developing countries. This likelihood will continue to make the comparative country approach to policy all the more important.

Will the current upbeat assessment of a stable and competitive world economy prove to be more accurate than the earlier ones? Is there indeed a better capacity to prescribe and implement policies that lead to sustained growth and reduced poverty? A sober assessment of past predictions should instill humility. But a hard core of knowledge—small but increasing—has been sustained and buttressed through the turbulence. There is also the comforting thought that it is surprises that make the worlds of development research and policy design so challenging.

Notes

1. Since 1973 per capita growth rates in the industrial countries, and particularly in Europe, have fallen to what looks like a permanently lower rate—roughly half the postwar quarter-century average.

2. The estimates are based on Birdsall, Ross, and Sabot (1994). Summers (1992) also has provided very pertinent analysis.

3. Based on the same study the figures for Brazil and Pakistan are intermediate: 8.5 times Kenya's number and 3.5, respectively.

4. The theoretical argument for the role of technological spillover effects was made by Lucas (1993) and the empirical estimates appear in World Bank (1993) and in Young (1993).

5. This fact is not brought out clearly in World Bank (1993), where short-term macroeconomic policy and long-run growth are treated separately even though during this turbulent period they should really have been considered jointly both in the East Asian context as well as in other regions of the world. Quantifying this element of path-dependence remains a task for further study.

6. The presumption is that in an open economy internal imbalance may express itself in either inflation (open or repressed) or external imbalance or, very often, in both.

7. Admittedly the term is somewhat flexible. Other elements like fiscal and labor market reforms would also be included here. Long-run fundamentals like education or health, mentioned earlier, or the very basic pillars of a market economy (property rights, payment systems) that are crucial components of reform in the transition economies would normally be considered complementary to the adjustment package.

8. This is not to deny the importance of supplementing growth-targeted policies with pro-poor public expenditure programs within a balanced budget framework.

9. Direct action on health, education, and nutrition could always improve the quality of life for the poor, even if their improved human capabilities may not translate into higher income or wealth (see Dreze and Sen 1990). Even that, however, requires public expenditure, which is unlikely to come out of a diminished aggregate pie.

10. The argument is that initial conditions, in terms of both existing human capital and greater equality at the outset, help explain post-1960 growth at least as much as growth accounts for subsequent better distributional outcomes. Better distribution enhances political stability, which in turn makes for less political disruption of sound macroeconomic policies (see also Alesina and Rodrik 1994). For a detailed evaluation of the two-way links in the East Asian case see Birdsall, Ross, and Sabot (1994).

11. For measurement of the effects of protection in agriculture see, for example, Schiff and Valdes (1992).

12. An interesting study just launched at the World Bank attempts to build the evaluation methodology into the household survey prior to the intervention itself so as to enable a structured "before" and "after" comparison.

13. It was relatively easy to fall into this trap because of the apparent empirical existence of multiple inflationary equilibriums—the fact that different inflation rates may be consistent with the same budget deficit. It is interesting that countries hardly ever learn from other countries' past mistakes and have to repeat the same painful experience before they turn around; Russia may be no exception.

14. Even in Israel's extreme crisis, the fact that its export sector was kept immune from external shocks helped keep growth from dropping to negative rates.

15. The replacement of quantitative restrictions with relatively high tariffs and a preannounced across-the-board gradual removal of tariffs may have employment and fiscal revenue advantages (if the right long-term signals to investors are maintained) as compared to a 'big bang' removal of all restrictions at once. Weak commitment capability and the danger of reversal may dictate the second approach.

16. In this context one should also mention the variety of ways in which the market is gradually entering the provision and financing (helped by the surgence of capital flows) of infrastructure services, a central subject of *World Development Report 1994*.

17. The natural bias of economists against any arguments that are not quantifiable often results in a less than optimal approach to policy and project planning. Suppose an effort were made to attach to each project loan (money) or piece of policy advice (ideas) some ex ante probability of successful implementation involving such nonquantifiable attributes as good governance, degree of social consensus, and ownership of reform. Could this be a first step in the right direction?

Getting to know more on these seemingly nonquantifiable attributes is important both in the context of the political economy of sustainable reform, from the reforming country's point of view, and in the context of assessing the effectiveness of development assistance, from the donors' point of view. How can one give operational content to the dictum "offer help only to those that help themselves?"

18. Inflationary processes, for example, are remarkably alike in different countries and their elimination requires very similar standard therapies (including our third necessary condition) in different countries. Ability to implement the same medicine will of course be institution-dependent.

19. I believe that the typical role of a central bank goes considerably beyond commitment to a monetary rule—that is, successful central banks take care of the efficient regulation of financial activity, provide independent and credible macroeconomic policy assessment and advice (through a high-level research department), and so on. But we abstract from these aspects here.

20. For example, prior to 1990, the Central Bank of Argentina ranked high according to any formal index, but was extremely low on actual revealed independence, with governors changing at the average of one a year.

21. Similar statements could be made to invoke the comparative importance of informal rules. For example, the governor of the Bank of England's "raised eyebrows" may play the role that only the credible threat of imprisonment would bring about in another country.

22. The questions are far from exhaustive. Not mentioned, but important, are research on the environment, on urban issues, and on the new international environment.

References

Alesina, Alberto, and Dani Rodrik. 1994. "Distributive Politics and Economic Growth." *Quarterly Journal of Economics* 109: 465–90.

Birdsall, Nancy, David Ross, and Richard Sabot. 1994. "Inequality and Growth Reconsidered." Draft.

Boycko, Maxim, Andrei Shleifer, and Robert W. Vishny. 1993. "Privatizing Russia." *Brookings Papers on Economic Activity*. Washington, D.C.: The Brookings Institution.

Cukierman, Alex. 1992. *Central Bank Strategy, Credibility, and Independence: Theory and Evidence.* Cambridge, Mass.: MIT Press.

Dixit, Avinash. 1992. "Investment and Hysteresis." *Journal of Economic Perspectives* Winter (6): 107–32.

Dornbusch, Rudiger. 1991. "Policies to Move from Stabilization to Growth." In Stanley Fischer, Dennis de Tray, and Shekhar Shah, eds., *Proceedings of the World Bank Annual Conference on Development Economics 1990.* Washington, D.C.: World Bank.

Dreze, Jean, and Amartya Sen. 1990. *Hunger and Public Action.* Oxford: Clarendon Press.

Leijonhufvud, Axel. 1973. "Life Among the Econ." *Western Economic Journal* 11 (3): 327–37.

Levy, Brian, and Pablo Spiller, eds. 1995. *The Institutional Foundations of Regulatory Commitment: A Comparative Analysis of Telecommunications Regulation.* Cambridge: Cambridge University Press. Forthcoming.

Lipton, Michael, and Martin Ravallion. Forthcoming. "Poverty and Policy." In Jere Behrman and T.N. Srinivasan, eds., *Handbook of Development Economics,* Vol. 3. Amsterdam: North Holland.

Lucas, Robert. 1993. "Making a Miracle." *Econometrica* 61: 251–72.

Pindyck, Robert, and Andres Solimano. 1993. "Economic Instability and Aggregate Investment." Massachusetts Institute of Technology, Cambridge, Mass.

Pinto, Brian, Marek Belka, and Stefan Krajewski. 1993. "Transforming State Enterprises in Poland: Evidence on Adjustment by Manufacturing Firms." *Brookings Papers on Economic Activity*. Washington D.C.: The Brookings Institution.

Ravallion, Martin. 1993. "Growth, Inequality, and Poverty: New Evidence on Old Questions." Policy Research Department, World Bank.

———. Forthcoming. "Growth in Poverty: Evidence for the Developing Countries." *Economic Letters.*

Schiff, Maurice, and Alberto Valdes. 1992. *The Political Economy of Agricultural Pricing Policy*, Vol. 4. Baltimore: Johns Hopkins University Press.

Squire, Lyn. 1993. "Fighting Poverty." *American Economic Review* 83 (2): 377–82.

Summers, Lawrence H. 1992. "Investing in All the People." Policy Research Working Paper 905. World Bank, Office of the Vice President, Development Economics, Washington, D.C.

Wade, Robert. 1993. "The Operations and Maintenance of Infrastructure: Organizational Issues in Canal Irrigation." Institute of Development Studies, Sussex University.

World Bank. 1993. *The East Asian Miracle: Economic Growth and Public Policy.* New York: Oxford University Press.

———. 1994a. *Adjustment in Africa: Reforms, Results, and the Road Ahead.* New York: Oxford University Press.

———. 1994b. *World Development Report 1994.* New York: Oxford University Press.

Young, Alwyn. 1993. "The Tyranny of Numbers: Confronting the Statistical Realities of the East Asian Growth Experience." NBER Working Paper. National Bureau of Economic Research, Cambridge, Mass.

Macropolicies in Transition to a Market Economy: A Three-Year Perspective

Leszek Balcerowicz and Alan Gelb

Countries in transition to market economies have had to implement macroeconomic stabilization programs at the same time that they were engaged in massive changes of their political institutions and the systemic frameworks of their economies. What has been the interaction of stabilization with economic liberalization and deep institutional reform in the countries of Eastern Europe, in particular, the relations among initial conditions, political developments, reform strategies, and outcomes? Experience in Eastern Europe suggests that when there is a political breakthrough (as in the countries under review) a radical stabilization-liberalization strategy is probably the least risky approach to reform and will not constrain output or structural reform over the medium term. Even stabilization that is initially successful in containing inflation will later come under pressure because of social policies and the structural transitions impelled by reform. Several factors are identified that affect the credibility of reforms, and lessons are derived for countries that have stabilized and those that yet face this task.

The collapse of party and state domination of society and the economy left the countries of Eastern Europe and the former Soviet Union facing a daunting dual challenge: to move toward competitive market economies while at the same time maintaining and strengthening newly gained democracies. The economic transition in these countries is viewed here as having three elements: macroeconomic stabilization; liberalization of prices, markets, and entry; and deep institutional change. This article focuses on the problem of achieving macroeconomic stability and sustaining macroeconomic balance through the transition.

Countries in transition must implement stabilization policies in the midst of deep changes in political institutions and in the systemic frameworks of their economies. In the context of such large changes outcomes usually ascribed to macroeconomic policies can strongly influence systemic and political developments. Conversely,

Leszek Balcerowicz is professor of economics at the Warsaw School of Economics. Alan Gelb is division chief, Transition Economics Division, at the World Bank. The authors gratefully acknowledge the contributions of staff of the World Bank, the International Monetary Fund, the Bank for International Settlements, and Planecon and the assistance of Raquel Artecona and Nikolay Gueorguiev. Responsibility for errors and shortcomings is that of the authors alone.

Proceedings of the World Bank Annual Conference on Development Economics 1994

macroeconomic policies can have a large impact on outcomes traditionally attributed to structural or institutional policies. We therefore emphasize the pattern of interaction between macroeconomic policies, systemic changes, and political developments—rather than the details of individual programs and outcomes, which are, in any event, subject to unusually large measurement problems. The core countries in the analysis are those in Eastern Europe with longer post-1989 reform experience—Bulgaria, Czechoslovakia and its successors, Hungary, Poland, and Romania—but comparisons are made with other countries as appropriate.

"Destroyed Capitalism": Initial Conditions and Measurement Problems

> "There's no use trying," she said, "one can't believe impossible things."
> "I daresay you haven't had much practice," said the Queen ... "Why, sometimes I've believed as much as six impossible things before breakfast."
>
> —Lewis Carroll, *Through the Looking Glass*

The Common Legacy...

After forty or more years of communism the "destroyed capitalism" of Eastern Europe and the Soviet Union differed from both the temporarily "suspended capitalism" of postwar Germany and the "distorted capitalism" embraced by Latin American and other dirigiste economies. In the economies characterized by destroyed capitalism, institutions reflected a fundamentally different system of organization and incentives (Kornai 1992). With few exceptions private activity was severely repressed, and private ownership of assets was limited to savings deposits and part of the housing stock.

The restricted role of the private sector had important implications for economic institutions, including the operation of factor markets. Medium-size and large state enterprises dominated output and employment. Industry was overbuilt, especially machine building and heavy industry; services, particularly trade and distribution, were underdeveloped and highly constrained. Government played a major financial role, intermediating between enterprises and between households through subsidies and transfer programs, and spending accounted for more than half of gross domestic product (GDP). Much of the revenue base was provided by the enterprise sector, where surpluses were concentrated among relatively few firms (in contrast, in market economies state enterprises are usually a fiscal drain).

The features of destroyed capitalism shaped many institutions and professions, including those of the legal system. Statistical systems were not adapted to dealing with large numbers of small firms or individual taxpayers, and enterprises had primitive marketing and accounting capabilities. But nowhere was the legacy of destroyed capitalism more pronounced than in the financial sector. Banking systems may have been "deep" (as measured by the ratio of balances to output), but financial flows accommodated decisions on the real economy. There was no experience of indirect, market-based monetary policy. Payments systems were primitive. Passive, monopolistic state banks lacked the capability to evaluate creditworthiness, and risk was socialized.

Foreign trade was dominated by a few monopolistic organizations. Autarkic trade patterns emphasized bilateral exchange between the members of the Council for Mutual Economic Assistance (CMEA), with increasingly adverse implications for product quality, as shown, for example, by the low prices of Soviet automobiles on Western markets (Roberts 1993). Relative prices were distorted; prices of energy and essential goods and services were heavily subsidized so that cash wages (subject to centralized norms) could be kept low and investment levels high. Official trade margins were tightly controlled.

Repressed inflation was widespread, reflecting an absence of broad commodity markets and a "shortage" economy, where demand for goods (and labor) often exceeded supply at controlled prices. Queuing, rationing, and hoarding were common responses, although use of these practices differed among countries and over time. The prevalence of "seller's markets" had profound implications for behavior. Enterprise managers set production goals to meet the requirements of bureaucratic bargaining processes (including spurious quality improvements) rather than those of markets and clients. Parallel prices often were multiples of official prices. Input stocks were hoarded, and inventories of unfinished investments were large.

...and Its Implications for Measurement

Even in established market economies standard statistical data provide only an incomplete description of economic reality, but in countries in transition data deficiencies and biases are much more serious (for more extensive discussions, see Lipton and Sachs 1990; Berg and Sachs 1992; Berg 1993a,b; Bratkowski 1993; and Balcerowicz 1993a). The statistical system inherited by the transition countries focuses on the contracting public sector rather than on the expanding private sector, and while output was overreported before transition, now there are strong tax incentives to underreport. Conventional statistics fail to reflect the sharp improvement in the quality and range of goods and in the composition of output stemming from market-oriented reform, instead applying the same "welfare weights" to pre- and postreform aggregates. And when prices are freed, conventional statistics overstate increases in the price level relative to an initial situation with unsatisfied demand at official prices. This bias distorts all deflated variables, particularly wages, which appear to fall more, relative to a consumer price index (CPI), than do real purchasing power and consumption. And conventional statistics do not measure welfare gains from the elimination of queuing, which may be considerable.

Reported unemployment data also are problematic. They are heavily influenced by incentives to report and typically are smaller than true labor redundancy, including that hidden within enterprises; indeed, the relation between unemployment and redundancy may vary a great deal among countries.[1] Cross-border transactions are poorly reported, giving rise to sometimes massive errors in trade data; there is still no perfect way to compare ruble and hard currency trade, and so to distinguish the impact of the collapse of CMEA markets from that of the reforms themselves. Reported fiscal deficits can seriously understate true consolidated government deficits, particularly where the central bank supports enterprises with cheap credit (although, at the same time, enterprises may assume some functions of government, including providing unemployment benefits and social services) for an extended period. Finally, such basic statistics as stock-building and enterprise markups and profits are severely distorted by inflation and rapid disinflation, and bank profits can be spurious because of inadequate loan-loss provisioning.

These data biases are not neutral with respect to types of reform program. Although many benefits of reform will be more seriously underreported the faster the economy moves away from the inherited statistical system, the swifter are the reforms the more rapidly will the inefficiencies of the old economic system be revealed. These inefficiencies include hidden unemployment, inefficient investments, excessive input stocks, repressed inflation and the associated costs of queuing, and "purely socialist" output for which demand can be maintained (if at all) only in a socialist economy. Instituting market-based monetary policies will make subsidies and losses more transparent. Invariably, the fiscal budget becomes the repository for the losses of the previous system.

Country-Specific Factors and the Stabilization Problem

Despite the commonalities of their heritage, the transition economies inherited very different macroeconomic, structural, and systemic conditions. These conditions determined the environment in which these countries began reform and thus the relative difficulty of achieving stabilization. The differences in those conditions reflect longstanding differences in policies and in the political developments that preceded—and followed—the breakdown of the one-party state.

Even with conservative macroeconomic policies all socialist countries were plagued by shortages resulting from supply rigidities and forced substitution in demand at administratively fixed prices. Resolving such microeconomically induced shortages is part of the liberalization problem, and a one-time correction of the price level will be needed to accommodate large changes in relative prices, along with sufficient macroeconomic discipline to preserve stability in the liberalized environment. Countries also faced macroeconomically induced imbalances, reflected in a mix of shortages and open inflation (depending on the degree of price control) and, to the extent that overexpansive policies had been externally financed, high external debt.

Only some of the core countries faced an urgent internal stabilization problem at the start of reform. In Bulgaria, Poland, and Romania the weakening of the communist regime was manifested in progressive loss of economic control and increasing macroeconomic imbalances driven by growing consumption. But Czechoslovakia, in keeping with a long tradition of macroeconomic conservatism, preserved spending discipline throughout its political transition. The stabilization problem was also less urgent in Hungary, where both the political and the economic transitions began in a more stable and liberalized environment and involved far more continuity than the transitions in the other countries. Like Bulgaria and Poland, however, Hungary had accumulated large foreign debts. In contrast, Czechoslovakia was essentially debt-free, and Romania had repaid previously contracted foreign debts by the end of the 1980s.

The magnitude of the initial stabilization problem the core countries faced is suggested by the strength of open and repressed inflation in their economies. Open inflation was most serious in Poland, and repressed inflationary pressures were strong in Bulgaria, Poland, and Romania. Czechoslovakia's economy was macroeconomically balanced yet microeconomically distorted, with key relative prices way out of line and a large foreign exchange premium on a small parallel market.

The core countries faced structural problems of varied seriousness that were reflected particularly by dependence on CMEA trade and the size of industry's share in the economy. Other conditions shaping the reform environment included the extent to which the old economic system had been reformed and the strength of the labor movement after reform: a strong labor movement tended to produce a wage push, which complicated the stabilization effort. In addition to external debt Bulgaria inherited perhaps the most difficult structural problem: its high dependence on CMEA trade implied losses of 16 percent of GDP or more with the collapse of that trade. The trade collapse was a large external macroeconomic shock for all countries, with particularly severe effects for sectors that depended on the Soviet market. Romania's industry was unusually concentrated, with a hydrocarbon-based complex dependent on imports from the Soviet Union. Poland too had serious structural problems, as well as high foreign debt and strong trade unions; however, following reform, its private agricultural sector outperformed state-dominated systems elsewhere. Other than dependence on CMEA trade the main liability of Hungary's relatively open and reformed economy was its high level of foreign debt. At the other end of the spectrum, debt-free Czechoslovakia had a weak trade union movement, and the Czech Republic would later be able to separate away its most serious problems of industrial structure with its split from Slovakia.

Also vital for the reform environment are political developments during economic transition. Hungary has been close to a model of political stability, with a smooth transition and the government freely elected in March 1990 still in power in 1994. Czechoslovakia's far more radical political transition involved elections in June 1990 and June 1992, both held according to a predetermined timetable. The country's split in early 1993 was a serious political shock, resulting in fiscal gains to the Czech Republic and losses to Slovakia, yet in the Czech Republic the same economic team has functioned since December 1989.

The other countries have experienced far less political stability. Poland formed its first noncommunist government in September 1989 and launched its reform program three months later. Following presidential elections in late 1990, a new government was seated in early 1991. Nevertheless, essentially the same basic team was responsible for the economy until December 1991. After the parliamentary elections in October, however, the pace of political change visibly quickened. By April 1994

Poland had gone through three governments and five ministers of finance; three of the ministers resigned. In Bulgaria, where a coalition government initiated an economic program in early 1991, the period up to February 1994 saw two parliamentary elections and three governments. Since early 1991 Romania has had as many governments, and it held parliamentary elections in September 1992. Romania has been the only country in which the government was forced to resign (in September 1991) under the pressure of widespread industrial unrest and riots.

For a stabilization plus transition program, perhaps even more than for stabilization in a nontransition economy, political developments form an important part of the conditions for implementation. Elections in an early stage of implementation tend to raise inflationary expectations and reduce the propensity of state enterprises to adjust because of expectations of a change of direction in economic policy. Frequent turnover of governments and ministers slows the implementation of structural and institutional reforms. Thus the political framework for stabilization has been less favorable in Bulgaria, Poland, and Romania than in Hungary and the former Czechoslovakia. As discussed below, experience shows that the period of "extraordinary politics" that follows a major political breakthrough and the discrediting of the old order can create conditions conducive to effecting a determined stabilization. A vital element of that breakthrough in Eastern Europe (as in the Baltics) was undoubtedly the sense that the long period of Soviet domination was at an end.

Economic Policy and Political Breakthrough

Given initial conditions, whether economic policy can shape outcomes in a controlled way depends on political developments. Extreme political instability may render economic policy uncontrollable, so that the outcome is a product of initial conditions, external factors, and political chaos. With that in mind, consider three important dimensions of economic policy:

- Launching speed: the interval between a political breakthrough and the launching of a coherent economic program.
- Phasing: the timing of the launching and implementation of the main components of the program.
- The implementation rate for each main component.

The importance of launching speed becomes clear when we analyze economic transition from the perspective of political economy. The period following a great political breakthrough, such as those experienced in Eastern Europe and the Baltics, is characterized by a special mass psychology. In the interval between the discrediting of the old political elite and the coalescing of new interest groups, conditions are especially favorable for technocrats to assume positions of political responsibility. There is also a greatly increased probability that the population will accept difficult, normally controversial economic policy measures as necessary sacrifices for the common good (Balcerowicz 1994b). But the experience of Eastern Europe suggests that this period of "extraordinary politics" usually lasts no longer than one to two years. Then, "normal politics" reemerges, when political groups are much less willing to accept such measures—or their distributional implications. The timing of difficult economic measures can therefore be expected to affect their acceptance.

With respect to phasing, consider the three sets of policy reform measures: macroeconomic stabilization, microeconomic liberalization, and deep institutional restructuring. Stabilization policy involves fiscal and monetary restraint, exchange rate management, and possibly wage or other controls. Liberalization policy eliminates legal or bureaucratic restrictions on economic activity, including price controls, quantitative restrictions on foreign trade, limits on foreign exchange convertibility, rationing and the command mechanism, and barriers to setting up and developing private firms.[2] Liberalization policy primarily supports a rapid shift toward a market economy and spontaneous growth of the private sector. Institutional restructuring policy, which involves, for example, privatization of state enterprises and reform of legal codes and tax administration, creates the fundamentals of a capitalist economy and makes possible well-functioning financial and labor markets. As discussed below, single policies alone do not determine economic outcomes. Stabilization outcomes, for example, are the result of liberalization and institutional restructuring as well as the stabilization policy.

The implementation rate is the rate at which reformed policies are effected relative to the maximum possible speed for that type of change. We term rapid policies as more radical and more gradual policies as less radical.[3] Gradualism may reflect initial conditions. For example, if a government had earlier undertaken substantial price liberalization or started reform from a balanced macroeconomy, only limited further decontrol or macroeconomic tightening may be needed. Or the initial economic situation may allow radical approaches, but the actual policy may be gradualist by design or because of political drift. Radical reforms, in contrast, are invariably introduced deliberately.

Clearly, stabilization and liberalization policies can be implemented much faster than most deep institutional changes. A radical strategy thus involves a two-stage transition to a market economy. In the first stage the economy is largely "marketized," thanks to liberalization policy, and stabilized, thanks to stabilization policy, but it remains market socialist rather than capitalist. In the second stage, if stabilization and liberalization policies are successful, their gains are consolidated and deep institutional change is completed under macroeconomic stability. Alternative scenarios involve delaying or interrupting stabilization or liberalization, or both, or implementing them over a longer period during which deep institutional change might be effected.

A comparison of the economic reform policies of the core countries, focusing on the speed with which reform packages were launched and the scale of changes achieved, suggests some general observations:

- Bulgaria and Poland responded to severe macroeconomic imbalances with radical programs introduced soon after the political breakthrough (three months afterward in Poland but a year afterward in Bulgaria). Private sector liberalization and institutional change advanced much more slowly in Bulgaria, however, and by the end of 1993 growing fiscal imbalance and rising enterprise losses and arrears threatened to derail reform. Romania, inheriting a less severe macroeconomic situation, adopted a less consistent, stop-go macroeconomic policy but launched a renewed stabilization and liberalization program at the end of 1993.

- With a far smaller stabilization problem but distorted relative prices, Czechoslovakia implemented radical liberalization safeguarded by tough macroeconomic policy.
- Hungary responded to a moderately difficult macroeconomic situation with more gradualist stabilization and liberalization policies. The response largely reflected initial conditions, including a more liberalized price system, but it was also a deliberate choice; the government could have opted for a more radical program, which the main opposition parties favored. In contrast, Romania's gradualism did not reflect favorable initial conditions but was dictated by political factors.
- The countries that adopted radical stabilization policies also adopted radical price liberalization, raised many administered prices, and largely liberalized foreign trade. In contrast, Romania implemented a much more stepwise liberalization and delayed decisive price and interest rate adjustments.
- Countries undertaking radical reforms also tended to take a radical approach toward external debt inherited from the old regime. Among the heavily indebted countries, only Hungary continued to fully service its debt.

Stabilization Outcomes

What were the outcomes of these moderately heterodox stabilization programs for inflation, internal and external balance, and the restructuring of the economy? None of the countries implemented an orthodox stabilization program that relied solely on fiscal and monetary restraint. The severity of initial distortions ruled out broad reliance on price controls (as in some of the heterodox programs implemented elsewhere). But the dominance of the state sector and the absence of owners who would resist excessive wage pressures called for temporarily maintaining, or even strengthening, inherited wage controls. All countries maintained tax-based wage controls, at least through the initial phase of transition. Among the countries facing severe macroeconomic problems, Poland devalued its currency and pegged the exchange rate, Bulgaria floated its currency, and Romania floated its currency but intervened heavily in foreign exchange markets and restricted convertibility. Czechoslovakia devalued and pegged its exchange rate; Hungary devalued and moved to a crawling peg. Thus there were two variants of the somewhat heterodox programs: one with wage controls and one with both wage controls and pegged exchange rates.

Disinflation and Elimination of Shortages

In Bulgaria, Poland, and Romania, where repressed inflation was strongest, prices and exchange rates might have been expected to overshoot longer-run equilibriums at the start of reform; in the event, initial price increases greatly exceeded projections (Bruno 1993). Czechoslovakia's price increase also exceeded projections. But perhaps because inflationary expectations had not become deeply institutionalized, except in Romania, the initial inflationary burst lasted only a few months. Nevertheless, only Czechoslovakia—where initial macroeconomic imbalances had been least serious—managed to bring inflation to below 20 percent after a year. Hungary kept inflation moderate in 1990 and 1991 as it further decontrolled its already relatively liberalized price system and raised administered prices.

Continuing to exert upward pressure on price levels, however, were the need to finance fiscal deficits that reemerged after the first year of reform, the introduction of new indirect taxes (notably valued added taxes), and the adjustment of key administered prices (rents, energy, public transport) (Orlowski 1993a,b). Although no country fully adjusted prices in one step, Poland effected especially large adjustments at the beginning; Czechoslovakia and Hungary adjusted prices more gradually. At the end of 1993 most countries still subsidized residential rents and household utilities, however.

Romania's inflation profile was an outlier. Despite an apparently tight macroeconomic program and far slower price liberalization than in the other countries, inflation remained above 200 percent after 1990 and reaccelerated after 1991. An initial phase of decontrol in 1990 stalled and partially reversed in 1991; liberalization was resumed in 1992 but became pervasive only in May 1993 with the lifting of restrictions on trade margins. Romania also maintained a number of export restrictions.

Price and trade liberalization and the elimination of restrictions on private business, combined with restrictive macroeconomic policies, were remarkably effective in eliminating shortages. Agricultural markets in Poland, for example, swung from chronic shortage to excess supply in little more than a month as households and farmers dishoarded stocks and food ceased to be used for animal fodder. Food aid and export controls added to food surpluses (Kwiecinski and Quaisser 1993). Business surveys and interviews with managers of industrial state enterprises in several countries suggest that a demand barrier rapidly replaced input shortages as the main constraint on output, at least for established firms. Surveys in Poland show that most managers saw the new environment as credible and not as a short interlude before a return to "business as usual." Sharp increases in nominal interest rates in January 1990 appear to have played an important signaling role, even though real rates did not immediately become positive. Many state enterprise managers began to take initiatives toward restructuring, despite high uncertainty about the macroeconomic outlook, constraints on corporate governance set by enterprise councils and trade unions, and limited information about their options (Gelb, Jorgensen, and Singh 1992; Pinto, Belka, and Krajewski 1993). Whether managers in other countries took such initiatives is less clear.

Fiscal Deficits, External Financing, and Monetary Policy

Reform initially led to sharp reductions in reported fiscal deficits, particularly in Bulgaria and Poland, where deficits had been large before reform. The largest turn-around, more than 10 percent of GDP, came in Poland, which ran a sizable surplus in 1990. In 1992, however, large fiscal deficits reemerged in all the countries except Czechoslovakia, which, along with Hungary, initially maintained a conservative fiscal stance. But Hungary's deficit widened sharply in 1992 and 1993, to more than 7 percent of GDP. The increase reflected mainly an unexpectedly large decline in corporate taxes—a surprising result considering that Hungary had by far the most reformed tax system. Bulgaria saw its deficit explode to 13 percent of GDP in 1993. The reemergence of serious fiscal deficits reflected depressed economic activity, as well as longer-run processes of systemic change and costly social policies.

Current accounts, like fiscal balances, were at first unexpectedly strong. Bulgaria, Czechoslovakia, Hungary, and Poland all ran surpluses in the early stages of reform, although Bulgaria and Poland would not have been able to had they been fully servicing their foreign debts. By 1993, however, for all but the Czech Republic (which gained a fiscal benefit of some 4 percent of GDP on the separation from Slovakia), current accounts had swung back into deficit. The deterioration was especially sharp for Bulgaria and for Hungary, which in 1992 had been able to finance its deficit domestically because a sharp rise in household financial savings coincided with a sharp fall in net domestic credit to enterprises.

Romania again followed a different pattern. A demand explosion combined with a contracting economy to worsen the current account by 14 percent of GDP between 1989 and 1990. Current account deficits continued through 1993 even though the budget was in ostensible surplus until 1992; current account deficits and sharply higher inflation therefore preceded an open fiscal deficit by three years. Romania's failure to stabilize after 1990 reflected mainly a self-fulfilling monetary policy failure that helped to undermine the credibility of the reform program and made subsequent stabilization far more difficult. At the start of reform Romania had a command, rather than a market-socialist economy, and strong ties between industrial ministries and enterprise managers continued after 1990. Far more than in the other countries, industrial lobbies, representing heavy and petrochemical industries and *regies autonomes* (strategic sectors that were not to be commercialized) exerted great political power, as did the agricultural lobby. Firms continued to have access to credit at interest rates far below inflation. Real rates on bank loans averaged about –58 percent in 1991–93, and National Bank rediscounts were available even more cheaply until the end of 1993. National Bank losses contributed to a real consolidated government deficit of about 21 percent of GDP in 1992, which was financed in part by monetary expansion.

In Romania, as in the other countries, deflated monetary aggregates and credit to enterprises contracted at the start of reform. The enterprise sector responded to the cut in real bank credit by increasing interenterprise borrowing, which soared to 190 percent of bank credit by the end of 1991. Surveys of Romanian enterprises left little doubt about their payment priorities: wages first, suppliers last (Calvo and Coricelli 1993). That ranking of priorities suggests that weak credibility—not involuntary lending—caused the credit explosion. In contrast, interenterprise credit actually declined relative to bank credit in Poland in 1990, as the credibility of the hardened budget constraint and the high real cost of borrowing made enterprises less inclined to extend such credits. Interenterprise credit was contained at 20 percent of bank credit in Czechoslovakia and Hungary. At the end of 1991 Romania eliminated the overhang of interenterprise debts, which had made evaluating creditworthiness impossible, through a global compensation scheme. Canceling out the net debt required the injection of heavily subsidized credits from the National Bank, which added to inflationary pressures and undermined the credibility of future stabilization policies. Further compensations have since been needed, suggesting a "low-discipline arrears equilibrium."[4]

In addition to continued credit subsidies from the National Bank, Romania's inflation in 1992 reflected the need to finance an open fiscal deficit of 7 percent of GDP. This deficit was caused in large part by fiscal subsidies, which increased from 8.6 percent of GDP in 1991 to 11.4 percent in 1992 (subsidies in the other countries had by then been cut to an average 3.6 percent of GDP). By 1993 fiscal balance ostensibly had been restored by sharp spending cuts, but off-budget interventions were still significant, and the inflation tax was being levied on rapidly shrinking leu balances. Romanians were building up foreign exchange deposits (a third of M2 by early 1994) and fleeing the leu. Until initiation of its stabilization program in late 1993, Romania's monetary policy, and the erosion of its financial balances, was not unlike that of Russia after 1992 (Easterly and Vieira Da Cunha 1994). Both countries formally "deregulated" deposit rates, but their state- and enterprise-dominated banking systems have temporarily benefited from inflationary expropriation of householders' deposits.

In contrast, the radical stabilizers that raised deposit rates to positive real levels soon after the first shock of price liberalization saw sustained remonetization and conversion of foreign exchange deposits into domestic assets as their currencies reappreciated from initially very devalued levels. The cumulative dollar return on Bulgarian deposits for the two years after May 1991 was about 60 percent.

Stabilization and Restructuring

What did the financial side of stabilization imply for the restructuring of the real economy? In the three radical reformers—Bulgaria, Czechoslovakia, and Poland—real interest rates were negative during the sharp initial spike of price liberalization, so that the real burdens of domestic debt were suddenly written down (much like external debt in Bulgaria and Poland). In Hungary, where price liberalization had been under way far longer and reform involved more gradual adjustment in the price level, the writedown was more modest and was soon reversed, but external debt service was sustained, at heavy fiscal cost. Real borrowing rates subsequently averaged about 15 percent in Poland and Hungary and 8 percent in Czechoslovakia.

With modest growth in deflated credit volumes net of enterprise deposits and large interest rate spreads,[5] the net resource transfer from banks to enterprises (defined as the expansion of net credit less the net interest bill due from the enterprises to the banks) was negative. Enterprises therefore had to proceed with physical restructuring in a highly resource-constrained financial environment and to rely on cash flows for new investments. The main question about the banking system, then, is how it redistributes scarce resources between firms: efficiently—toward profitable, growing (private sector) firms—or perversely—rolling over loans to loss-makers and postponing adjustment? This question is taken below.

Net transfers followed a different pattern in Romania. Negative real interest rates offset the contraction of real credit, particularly in 1991, the year of the global compensation. The net resource transfer from banks to firms was therefore positive but unsustainable because of the erosion of leu deposits.

Exchange Rate Outcomes

Although the three radical reformers pursued different exchange rate management, their exchange rate profiles after reform showed strong parallels. The initial devaluations in Czechoslovakia and Poland set their newly unified rates at about 4 times the purchasing power parity (PPP) level; Bulgaria, with low reserves, saw the freely floating lev briefly devalued to almost 10 times PPP.[6] Nevertheless, independent of whether exchange rates were pegged or floating, real rates converged within a year toward levels of between 1.8 and 2.5 times PPP, with Czechoslovakia maintaining a more competitive rate than Poland. The lev reappreciated strongly toward a market to PPP ratio of 2 until October 1993, when the widening fiscal imbalance and an increasingly chronic buildup of tax, social security, and interest arrears helped to provoke a foreign exchange crisis and a series of devaluations that halved the lev's external value. The expected ratio of market to PPP rates for countries with real per capita incomes comparable to those of Eastern Europe is about 2, according to 1985 data of the United National International Comparison Programme (Ahmad 1992); in this sense the exchange rates were converging toward "normal" levels.

Hungary's real exchange rate had slowly depreciated by 25 percent over the period 1985–90. More so than the other countries, Hungary pursued a deliberate exchange-rate-based stabilization after 1990. It encouraged foreign borrowing and foreign direct investment to offset its heavy debt service burden and at the same time to build reserves. Hungary's policy of limiting devaluations considerably dampened inflation, particularly for industrial goods (Solimano and Yuravlivker 1993), but resulted in steady real appreciation, with the forint reaching a value of 1.6 times PPP by early 1993.

In real exchange rate movements Romania again displayed a distinctive pattern. With continued heavy intervention in goods and foreign exchange markets, the exchange rate moved erratically, and the official rate tended to depreciate relative to PPP rather than to firm at levels close to expected longer-run values. By 1993 the official rate was still more than 3 times PPP. Grey and black foreign exchange markets were active, however, with the National Bank allocating limited foreign exchange on a pro rata basis on the official auction and with premia between 25 percent and 40 percent. The real effective exchange rate was therefore even higher than the official rate. Strong depreciation of the leu reflected the partial and contradictory nature of Romania's reforms, particularly the subordination of monetary policy to cushion loss-making firms rather than to reestablish confidence in the currency. In late 1993 Romania initiated renewed stabilization efforts, including sharp increases in interest rates to positive real rates and exchange rate unification. These efforts led to a substantial decline in inflation, to 5 percent a month by early 1994, and a considerable firming of the leu.

Was Radical Reform Too Radical?

Monetary and fiscal policies thus have been powerful tools in containing inflation and stabilizing exchange rates, possibly because inflationary processes were not deeply institutionalized at the start. But were the radical programs too tough? Not only were the initial price increases higher than projected, but deflated credit aggregates and measured output levels were lower, and current accounts considerably stronger, than expected (Bruno 1993). Considering data lags and the uncertainty accompanying the programs, deviations from projections are not surprising. How should policies have responded to new information? Should they have been relaxed to take advantage of space on the external account? Or should they have been maintained (or tightened further) to reduce the likelihood that the unexpectedly strong surge in prices would translate into sustained high inflation?

Such conundrums are endemic in stabilization programs. Both options have risks that cannot be considered in isolation from the political situation. Policies could indeed appear too tough to be credible, particularly if there is no major political breakthrough. But relaxation poses risks of rising inflation, progressive indexation, loss of credibility, and costlier (and politically less acceptable) stabilization in the future. The transition economies generally were not highly indexed; that could argue for speedy relaxation once the initial price spike had dissipated. But maintaining macroeconomic stability in a liberalized economy requires fundamental changes in behavior, particularly for enterprise managers long used to an accommodating budget constraint and a passive banking sector. This problem is compounded by the inevitable lag of institutional reforms, including privatization, behind radical stabilization and liberalization. Because the phase of current account improvement was short, and because all the countries (with the possible exception of Czechoslovakia) faced an external balance constraint again by 1992, the risks of relaxation far outweighed any temporary benefits.

Liberalization, Relative Prices, and Competition

After price and trade liberalization, most relative price ratios appear to have approached world levels relatively rapidly in Bulgaria, Czechoslovakia, Hungary, and Poland (Berg 1993a). In some cases policy slowed the transmission of international prices; in other cases, notably agricultural marketing and input supply, domestic monopolies in processing and distribution prevented a full pass-through of world prices. Although the ratio of market to PPP exchange rates is only a rough indicator, it suggests that prices for a wide range of goods should have converged to close to their long-run levels within about a year of the start of radical reforms; comparative costs would then play a more important role in determining real exchange rates. The elimination of temporary "exchange rate protection" exposed firms to the full pressures of domestic and international competition, squeezing industrial enterprises' margins and creating pressures for selective protection (Schaffer 1993; ACED 1993).

The persistent undervaluation of the leu seems to have limited competitive pressure from abroad in Romania; although data are inadequate, the pattern of reported profitability in the *regies autonomes* and the commercialized sectors suggests that price controls were more important than foreign competition in determining markups and profits.

Large formal devaluations did not simply imply a relative price shift in favor of sectors producing traded goods. Exchange rate unification reduced the relative prices of many goods (especially high-quality consumer durables and foreign travel) that had been obtainable only through parallel exchange markets with high premia. Not surprising, consumption of high-quality consumer durables increased sharply at the same time that the corresponding domestic industries faced a demand barrier. Thus consumers benefited from unification, while state enterprises that had purchased commodities at official prices and sold at artificially high market prices lost.

Interpreting inflation rates and exchange rate movements in transition is further complicated by the divergence between consumer and producer prices in most transition economies. In Bulgaria, Hungary, and Poland consumer prices rose more rapidly than industrial producer prices, while Romania showed, if anything, the opposite tendency. In addition to indirect taxes and technical factors that can cause price indexes to diverge,[7] the relative rise in consumer prices appears to reflect two transitional processes. First, relative prices of previously heavily subsidized essential services are realigned, and second, trade and distribution margins widen from previously repressed levels as the service sector is privatized and Western marketing patterns take hold. Indeed, the service sector has often led to CPI inflation. In contrast, service prices lagged behind the CPI in Romania until May 1993, when margins were freed. Romania was also the only country in which budgetary subsidies increased as a share of GDP after reform. These important differences in pricing policies show up in household budgets, where the share of nonfood essentials rose sharply in the other countries after 1989 but fell in Romania despite a possibly deeper decline in living standards (Cornia 1994; UNICEF 1993).

A widening wedge between industrial producer prices and the CPI has several implications. Part of the CPI inflation in the period following an initial stabilization comes from a relative price adjustment in favor of previously suppressed or heavily subsidized nontraded sectors. This price adjustment increases financial pressures on industry and agriculture—the traditional tradables sectors—which must contend with wage demands boosted by rising consumer prices. Increases in the prices of nontradables offset, in part, the impact of an initial devaluation on competitiveness. To the extent that price increases reflect cuts in consumer subsidies, higher wages represent a progressive monetization of the overall consumption bundle; to the extent that they reflect growing trade and distribution margins, they are part of the process of shifting resources away from state-dominated industry to build private wealth in the service sectors. For these reasons, as well as the fiscal consequences of systemic changes, it is unrealistic to expect inflation rates to fall to levels typical in OECD countries immediately after initial stabilizations. They need to be sufficiently high for a period to accommodate relative price shifts.

Is Stabilization Sustainable? Feedbacks from Systemic Change

The larger process of transition involves many interrelated transitions: from public ownership toward private, from industry toward services, from an economy dominated by large enterprises to one with many small firms, from seller's markets to buyer's markets (including the labor market, where open unemployment replaces hidden unemployment), and from CMEA product standards toward world market standards (Kornai 1993). Another fundamental change is to transform the financial sector from a passive player to an active one and to desocialize risk-bearing.

Eastern Europe already has seen huge changes along these lines. The private sector's recorded shares in the economy have increased especially rapidly in the Czech Republic and Poland, at first in trade and services but later in other sectors (Rostowski 1993). Little of this private sector growth is directly attributable to the privatization of state enterprises. Although private sector development has lagged in Bulgaria and Romania, thriving private economies have nevertheless arisen in these countries too. The share of industry in output and employment has fallen sharply in all the countries in favor of services and, in Romania, agriculture. Layoffs and breakups are transforming the structure of industrial employment; for example, employment in Hungary's largest industrial firms fell by half between 1989 and 1991 while small firms multiplied.

What do such structural and institutional transitions imply for the sustainability of macroeconomic stabilization? We consider three areas important for the credibility and sustainability of stabilization programs: the supply response, fiscal sustainability, and banking reform.

Supply Response

The asymmetric response of private and public sectors to reform argues for a dual-sector framework for explaining the supply response (Aghion and Blanchard 1993; Berg 1993c; Chadha and Coricelli 1993).[8] Because of the composition of its output the state sector became demand constrained after markets were liberalized, competition emerged, and CMEA trade collapsed. But the private sector has benefited both from demand substitution effects and from the recognition and guarantee of private property rights, which is equivalent to a growth-enhancing supply shock.

Cross-country comparisons suggest two possibly surprising conclusions. First, radical stabilization is not associated with lower measured output over a period of two to three years. Indeed, the association is positive in our sample, where the largest cumulative contraction is in Romania, the least successful stabilizer, and the smallest in Poland, the most successful stabilizer. Second, stabilization does not seem to slow the transition to a private economy. Indeed, some supply-side stimuli to the private sector have been directly related to the severe financial squeeze on the state sector. In addition to freeing up labor for the private sector, cash-strapped public enterprises have sold and leased assets to private firms. Where state firms have not responded to a tightened budget constraint (as in Bulgaria), the private sector has tended to be crowded out.

These two observations are related. Although Poland shows that state industry can recover under credible hard budget constraints (Pinto, Belka, and Krajewski 1993), one clear message of the past three years is the importance of private sector growth for the initial stage of output recovery and job creation—and hence for the sustainability of stabilization.

Fiscal Sustainability

Before reform, fiscal revenues came mainly from three taxes collected through the state enterprise sector: the profits tax, the turnover tax, and the payroll tax, which funded social payments. Together these taxes accounted for almost 80 percent of tax receipts in Czechoslovakia and Poland and about 50 percent in Hungary. Because the enterprise sector concentrated surpluses and employment in large units, governments did not need to develop the capacity to tax large numbers of individuals and small businesses. But with competition, constrained demand, and an end to cheap credit, enterprise sectors could no longer concentrate fiscal resources for governments.[9] Meanwhile, widespread private sector underreporting is encouraged by high profit tax rates and payroll and wage taxes that can cause gross labor costs to be double net pay. As would be expected, transition has eroded tax revenues.

Fiscal sustainability is not essentially a revenue problem, however. For the core countries, excluding Romania (which followed a different fiscal profile), the average ratio of government expenditure to GDP was 61 percent in 1989. Of this, 16 percent represented subsidies and 13 percent social transfers, so that redistributive current spending accounted for half of total government expenditure. Ratios of government spending to GDP normally are far lower for market economies at comparable levels of PPP income: about 21 percent of GDP for revenue and 22 percent of GDP for expenditure (Krumm, Milanovic, and Walton forthcoming). Recent research suggests that, allowing for the level of income per capita, an increase of 10 percentage points in the ratio of fiscal expenditures to GDP is associated with a 1 percentage point drop in the growth rate (Easterly and Rebelo 1993). That suggests a high premium on constraining fiscal spending—beyond simply containing the deficit—during the transition.

Between 1989 and 1992 fiscal expenditure fell relative to GDP only in Bulgaria and Czechoslovakia. The considerable increase in Romania can be attributed to rising producer and consumer subsidies. In the other countries subsidies declined sharply, so that the average ratio of nonsubsidy spending to GDP rose by 5 percentage points. Social spending accounted for almost all of this increase, rising on average from 13 percent to 17 percent of GDP between 1989 and 1992. Although the fiscal costs of registered unemployment have been limited, other social expenditure programs are comprehensive, with pensions by far the largest component. Transition generally has led to a retirement boom; only a small part of the sharp increases in the ratios of pensioners to population after 1989 has been due to demographic factors. Some early retirement has substituted for unemployment, but much has occurred under the many special regimes offering full pensions far earlier than even the low official retirement ages. As the number of pensioners increases, the number of contributors to pay-as-you-go state pension schemes shrinks, raising dependency ratios in Bulgaria to a high of 87 percent by 1992. Ratios of average pensions to wages also have tended to rise; in Poland they climbed from 43 percent to 63 percent between 1989 and 1992.

With minimum wages little above poverty lines and a need to drastically restructure employment, transition countries face a huge challenge in designing affordable social protection systems that avoid perverse incentives for workers. Moreover, because of low retirement ages and slow population growth, pensioners and aspiring pensioners weigh heavily in voting-age populations. No country except Estonia has been able to achieve radical reform of the benefit system, perhaps because reformers did not see it as an early priority.

Transition also raises the issue of intergenerational equity. The time horizons of the older generations since the onset of reform are short, and opportunities to accumulate (nonhousing) wealth largely bypass them in favor of younger entrepreneurs, often well educated, skilled in foreign languages, and able to earn high incomes in the private sector. The age-specific distribution of wealth arising from transition will thus differ markedly from the long-run equilibrium distributions in market economies, where wealth tends to be concentrated among older generations. Transition thus increases the need for intergenerational income transfers through the state for several decades. This need will be greatest in countries that have failed to stabilize, because of the erosion of household savings by inflation.

Banking Reform and the Enterprise Sector

At the start of stabilization programs banks were typically passive and inexperienced creditors. Rollovers of loans and capitalization of unpaid interest have led to a dual financial system in which loans are heavily concentrated among a few, usually less profitable enterprises. But considerable learning-by-doing in the banking sectors of the more advanced reformers has resulted in a progressive tightening of financial constraints on loss-making firms, although loan quality probably is still deteriorating in the other countries.

In addition to improving banking services, one major objective of financial reform is to resolve the allocation of the stock of bad debt. After stabilization this stock of debt is no longer eroded by inflation but tends to expand because of positive real interest rates. A second major objective is to ensure that new credits flow to solvent, growing firms, to avoid creating another serious loan portfolio problem.

The two objectives are closely related. Incentives for prudent commercial lending cannot be established in the absence of properly capitalized banks: solving the flow problem requires addressing the stock problem. Conversely, recapitalization, if repeated as part of the process of unearthing and provisioning against bad debt, threatens to undermine the credibility of the hard budget constraint. Some argue for a third objective: to give banks an active role in corporate governance of the enterprise sector—not because they are an ideal choice but for want of other plausible outside strategic owners and because they have the most knowledge of the enterprises—and, through this arrangement, an active role in resolving the bad debt problem.

Countries are addressing this complex set of interrelated problems through various strategies, usually including a mix of debt transfers to special institutions, debt-equity swaps, and bank recapitalization and provisioning financed in part by government and in part by large spreads.[10] The ultimate fiscal costs of resolving problem loans still are not known, but they will be considerable for all countries (Dittus forthcoming; Gomulka 1993). In Hungary, for example, the costs of provisioning against bad loans accounted for 4 percentage points of the 10 percentage point spread between lending and borrowing rates in 1992, and the effect of new provisioning rules on banks' profitability cut profit tax revenues by 2 percent of GDP.

Hardening budget constraints and moving to sound finance is not likely to be achieved quickly. The institutional change in the banking sector and other financial markets needed to fully privatize commercial risk will take time. Risk will remain high, in part because of the preponderance of new firms (including those split off from old firms) without a track record in the new economic environment. In addition, in most countries in transition legal processes still favor debtors over creditors. Necessary yet abrupt measures to fully decentralize risk could encourage banks to hold excess liquidity and lead to the withdrawal of credit from many potentially viable clients. As a practical matter, government budgets therefore probably will have to bear some of the costs of problem loans for some time, if spreads are not to be so large as to inhibit good firms and further weaken bank portfolios.

Ten Lessons

From the perspective of stabilization, postsocialist countries now fall into two groups. Except for Romania, the core countries, together with Albania, Slovenia, and two of the Baltic states, have had some success in containing inflation following price liberalization and now must consolidate macroeconomic stability while deepening institutional reforms. Most of the others, many with new currencies, have not yet succeeded in holding inflation at even moderate levels. The experience of the more advanced reformers offers lessons for both groups of countries.

A general lesson is that, in addition to economic policy, what matters in determining outcomes are initial conditions, political developments, and external factors. On balance, the core countries that faced the most serious macroeconomic problems may also have inherited the most difficult structural conditions for stabilization, as well as high foreign debt and powerful trade unions. It is not clear that countries that had earlier undergone a phase of market socialism were at an advantage. Their institutions may have been somewhat better adapted to market conditions, but decentralization of management to enterprises created difficult political problems for further reform in Poland, and an apparently less urgent need for reform may have encouraged policy drift in Hungary.

1. *Radical is less risky.* The countries of Eastern Europe and the former Soviet Union that have managed to contain inflation to low or moderate levels have all experienced major political breakthroughs combining democratization and renewed national independence. The record suggests that when there is both high initial macroeconomic imbalance and a major political breakthrough of this kind, a radical approach involving forceful stabilization measures and rapid liberalization is almost surely the least risky option. Initial stabilization has been most successful when radical programs have been launched during an early period of extraordinary politics following the breakthrough. The reversion to normal politics after an initial hiatus complicates further stabilization by raising inflationary expectations, slowing the implementation of structural and institutional reforms, and reducing the propensity of state enterprises to adjust—Bulgaria is an example. Normal politics is especially problematic if it involves extreme political fragmentation. Successful stabilization requires fundamental behavioral and institutional changes in an economy still dominated by state enterprises. One function of radical reform is to signal the need for such change through a fundamental shift in regime. If that change is not achieved, chronic financial indiscipline and mounting arrears can rapidly erode a reform program and destroy the credibility of a financially disciplined equilibrium.

2. *There is no simple link between type of reform and political stability.* Contrary to popular opinion, the degree of political instability does not appear to have a simple relationship to the type of economic program: consider, for example, the Czech Republic and Hungary (both stable but with different political transitions and very different economic programs) or Poland and Romania (both unstable, but one sustaining a radical program and the other not).

3. *Don't fine-tune at the start.* It is better to err on the tight side than to try to fine-tune policies in the early stages to take advantage of the temporary balance of payments relief that appears as inflation is brought under control. Failure to stabilize initially will lead to a need for further attempts, but from weakened economic and political bases and with lower credibility. In any case, the inevitable uncertainty makes successful fine-tuning impossible.

4. *Monetary and fiscal policy can stabilize in transition.* Monetary and fiscal policies can be powerful instruments for containing inflation to moderate levels (very low inflation may be difficult to reconcile with the need for continued price realignment) and for stabilizing exchange rates, possibly because inflationary processes are not deeply institutionalized at the start. Conversely, stabilization can be elusive after initial price liberalization if financial policies fail to support the holding of domestic financial assets. The main failure in Romania (and in Russia and other countries)

has been monetary and interest rate policy; lack of credibility in this area may encourage arrears. Minimum interest rate targets may be needed for an extended period to protect uncompetitive, state-dominated banks from decapitalizing household balances.

5. *Wage controls are vital.* All the countries relied on wage controls, which become important as privatization inevitably lags behind stabilization and liberalization policy. The enterprise sector needs to preserve retained earnings to finance its restructuring and is likely to have to effect a net resource transfer to the banking system as stabilization is consolidated. Some countries, such as Romania and Russia, have temporarily continued positive transfers to their enterprises, but these transfers become unsustainable as financial balances erode. And because the transfers are related to political pull rather than to performance, they also are likely to be inefficient.

6. *Liberalization reinforces stabilization.* In theory a government could achieve stabilization while retaining extensive state control of the economy. But in practice there has been a close relation between stabilization and liberalization except on the wage front. Policymakers who valued stabilization also valued liberalization. Cutting fiscal subsidies and avoiding large central bank losses due to subsidized credits (a major weakness in Romania and many countries of the former Soviet Union) have been important elements of macroeconomic adjustment. Most fundamental, stabilizing a heavily controlled economy that retains extensive price controls and strong institutional links between government and enterprises is very difficult even for a strong state because the enterprises can blame these controls for their losses. In addition, the enterprises always have better information than the government and can take advantage of their lack of autonomy to claim subsidies. Romania shows how problematic this option is.

7. *The importance of exchange rate pegs depends on the nature of inflationary expectations.* Some of the transition countries pegged their exchange rates to provide another nominal anchor. The experience of Bulgaria, as well as that of Latvia and Slovenia, suggests that the importance of fixing the exchange rate is a more open question than the need for wage controls. It may hinge on whether deeply embedded inflationary expectations concern price increases (as in Latin America) or mostly shortages.

8. *Radical stabilization and liberalization policy encourages recovery and transition to a private economy.* Country experience suggests no adverse medium-run tradeoffs between stabilization (with its accompanying liberalization) and either output or the speed of transition to a private economy. Failure to stabilize wastes valuable time and will delay recovery. Measures to promote private sector development, including privatizing small assets and providing access to commercial real estate, should be essential components of a stabilization package because of their importance for the supply response.

9. *After initial stabilization, credible, sustainable reform will require a strong growth response by the private sector; fiscal reform, especially on the spending side, and probably some external support; and resolution of bad debts without reducing*

the credibility of budget constraints. The inevitable lag of institutional reform behind stabilization and liberalization suggests that an extended phase of fiscal pressure is to be expected in a radical reform program. In theory a fiscal balance condition can set an upper limit to the speed of transition from a public to a private economy. Although this tradeoff is appealing, in practice the aim of preserving tax receipts is a poor argument for deliberately slowing this transition because revenues are in any case not sustainable. It is counterproductive to try to maintain fiscal revenues by supporting public enterprises with quasi-fiscal subsidies through the banking system: rampant fiscal deficits will shatter the credibility of reform. On the other hand, very high (actual or anticipated) taxation will slow the private economy, which will need to finance rapid growth mostly out of retained earnings. Slow private sector growth also will undermine reform.

The main fiscal reforms must, therefore, center on spending. Even after the elimination of subsidies, ratios of expenditure to GDP are far above those usual in middle-income countries, largely because of social transfers. Severe resource constraints will prevent economies from rapidly growing out of these ratios, particularly if the budget also has to bear the costs of previously hidden inefficiencies. Spending analyses, including detailed studies of the incidence of social benefits, are needed to show where adjustments will be less painful. But it is difficult to cut expenditures abruptly (especially after the end of "extraordinary politics") when trying to preserve a democratic consensus in favor of reform. Unlike in nontransition stabilizing economies, fiscal deficits in transition economies must be seen in a medium-term perspective, with greater emphasis placed on reducing government spending and improving its composition. In the interim external finance will be needed to allow larger fiscal deficits than conventionally acceptable to be financed without excessive monetary expansion. For the same fiscal reasons, reductions in debt service obligations are critical to the success of radical reform in heavily indebted countries.

Especially because financial systems can transfer few resources to borrowers in the stabilization phase, measures to limit credit rollovers to loss-making state firms and to encourage lending to private firms need to be put in place relatively quickly, even if banks cannot immediately assume a leading role in initiating bankruptcies. It is also vital to "activate" at least part of the banking system as fast as possible, to support the reorganization of the enterprise sector without, however, creating expectations of bailouts that weaken the credibility of reform. How best to resolve the bad debt problem depends on the country's conditions; the Czech Republic, Hungary, and Poland offer a range of experience suggesting that progress is possible. Across-the-board debt relief is problematic, however, and a simple one-off resolution of the bad debt problem is probably unrealistic.

10. Failure to stabilize at first does not argue against continuing institutional restructuring and liberalization. Consider countries still grappling with major stabilization problems in the absence of a major political breakthrough (or having failed to stabilize initially in the aftermath of a breakthrough). How should these countries proceed? Clearly, their task is difficult because of continued economic weakening and the likelihood that indexation mechanisms will be strengthened. One lesson is to exploit the credibility imparted by any major political discontinuity to implement a determined stabilization program. Even while not yet stabilized, however, these countries should proceed with liberalization and institutional reforms as rapidly as they can. These reforms will not realize their full potential until macroeconomic stability is achieved. But they can improve the underpinnings for future stabilization and may strengthen a constituency in support of a future stabilization effort.

Notes

1. For example, in 1992 a third of Hungary's registered unemployed workers (12 percent of the labor force) may have been working, but in Russia, where registered unemployment is only 1 percent, actual unemployment has been estimated at 10 percent.

2. For a more detailed breakdown of policies, see Fischer and Gelb (1991).

3. The term *radical* is preferred to the more emotive *big bang* because the second term implies a possibility of effecting all changes immediately; see Balcerowicz (1994a,b).

4. The countries that have needed to resort to global compensation (Romania and Russia) have also achieved less policy credibility for stabilization. Bulgaria's experience in 1993 supports the view that decreased credibility of reform (in Bulgaria's case, the stalling of institutional restructuring after initial stabilization and liberalization) leads to explosive growth of arrears of all types (ACED 1993); if sufficiently widespread, these arrears create a low-discipline equilibrium (see Rostowski 1992).

5. Large spreads in transition countries reflect four factors: limited competition, costly reserve requirements, the banking system's need to generate resources for modernization, and the need to provision against loan losses and recapitalize the banks.

6. Because historical indicators of real exchange rates are not a useful guide to long-run equilibrium market rates, a ratio of nominal exchange rates to estimated purchasing power parity (PPP) rates is used to suggest the level of the real exchange rate.

7. The consumer price index (CPI) is a Laspeyres index, and weighting may be inaccurate; the producer price index (PPI) is a Paasche index, and coverage of industrial products may be limited. The continued divergence between CPI and PPI, especially in Bulgaria, suggests that measurement anomalies are serious.

8. Extensive discussion of the relative importance in explaining output of measurement errors, demand shocks, supply shocks (including those effected through credit contractions), trade disruption, decline in "information capital," and increased uncertainty due to the change in economic system is beyond the scope of this article (but see, for example, Blejer and others 1993).

9. This effect has been somewhat offset in the early stages of reform by cuts in subsidies and deficient inflation accounting, which sustained taxes by decapitalizing enterprises (Schaffer 1993; Barbone and Marchetti forthcoming). For an extensive treatment of fiscal issues in transition, see Tanzi (1993).

10. It is not yet clear how well the strategies have worked; for reviews of the strategies that different countries have adopted, see Pleskovic (1994); *Transition* (1994); BIS (1993); Dittus (forthcoming).

References

ACED (Agency for Economic Coordination and Development). 1993. *Bulgarian Economy in 1993.* Annual Report. Sofia.

Aghion, Phillippe, and Olivier Blanchard. 1993. "On the Speed of Transition in Central Europe." Working Paper 6. European Bank for Reconstruction and Development, London.

Ahmad, Sultan. 1992. "Regression Estimates of per Capita GDP Based on Purchasing Power Parities." Policy Research Working Paper 956. World Bank, International Economics Department, Socioeconomic Data Division, Washington, D.C.

Balcerowicz, Leszek. 1993. "Common Fallacies in the Debate on the Economic Transition in Central and Eastern Europe." European Bank for Reconstruction and Development, London.

———. 1994a. "Economic Transition in Central and Eastern Europe: Comparisons and Lessons." *Australian Economic Review* (first quarter): 47–58.

———. 1994b. "Poland." In John Williamson, ed., *The Political Economy of Policy Reform.* Washington, D.C.: Institute of International Economics.

Barbone, Luca, and Domenico Marchetti Jr. Forthcoming. "Transition and the Fiscal Crisis: Crisis in Central Europe." *Economics of Transition.*

Berg, Andrew. 1993a. "Does Macroeconomic Reform Cause Structural Adjustment? Lessons from Poland." International Monetary Fund, Washington, D.C.

———. 1993b. "Measurement and Mismeasurement of Economic Activity during Transition to the Market." In Mario I. Blejer, Guillermo A. Calvo, Fabrizio Coricelli, and Alan H. Gelb, eds., *Eastern Europe in Transition: From Recession to Growth?* World Bank Discussion Paper 196. Washington, D.C.

———. 1993c. "Supply and Demand Factors in the Output Decline in East and Central Europe." Paper presented at the International Conference on Output Decline in Eastern Europe, November, Vienna, Austria.

Berg, Andrew, and Jeffrey Sachs. 1992. "Structural Adjustment and International Trade in Eastern Europe: The Case of Poland." *Economic Policy* (April): 117–73.

BIS (Bank for International Settlements). 1993. *Sixty-Third Annual Report.* Basel.

Blejer, Mario I., Guillermo A. Calvo, Fabrizio Coricelli, and Alan H. Gelb, eds. 1993. *Eastern Europe in Transition: From Recession to Growth? Proceedings of a Conference on the Macroeconomic Aspects of Adjustment, Cosponsored by the International Monetary Fund and The World Bank.* World Bank Discussion Paper 196. Washington, D.C.

Bratkowski, Andrzej. 1993. "The Shock of Transformation or the Transformation of the Shock? The Big Bang in Poland and Official Statistics." *Communist Economies and Economic Transformation* 5 (1): 5–28.

Bruno, Michael. 1993. "Stabilization and Reform in Eastern Europe: Preliminary Evaluation." In Mario I. Blejer, Guillermo A. Calvo, Fabrizio Coricelli, and Alan H. Gelb, eds., *Eastern Europe in Transition: From Recession to Growth?* World Bank Discussion Paper 196. Washington, D.C.

Calvo, Guillermo A., and Fabrizio Coricelli. 1993. "Inter-Enterprise Arrears in Economies in Transition." Paper presented at the International Conference on Output Decline in Eastern Europe, November, Vienna, Austria.

Chadha, Bankim, and Fabrizio Coricelli. 1993. "Fiscal Constraints and the Speed of Transition." International Monetary Fund and World Bank, Washington, D.C.

Cornia, Giovanni A. 1994. "Poverty, Food Consumption, and Nutrition during the Transition to the Market Economy in Eastern Europe." *American Economic Review* 84 (2): 297–302.

Dittus, Peter. 1994. "Corporate Governance in Central Europe: The Role of Banks." BIS Economic Papers 42. Basel, Switzerland.

Easterly, William, and Sergio Rebelo. 1993. "Fiscal Policy and Economic Growth: An Empirical Investigation." World Bank, Transition and Macro-Adjustment Division, Washington, D.C.

Easterly, William, and Paulo Vieira Da Cunha. 1994. "Financing the Storm: Macroeconomic Crisis in Russia, 1992–93." Policy Research Working Paper 1240. World Bank, Macroeconomics and Growth Division and Europe and Central Asia Country Operations Division II, Washington, D.C.

Fischer, Stanley, and Alan Gelb. 1991. "The Process of Socialist Economic Transformation." *Journal of Economic Perspectives* 5 (1): 91–105.

Gelb, Alan, Erika Jorgensen, and Inderjit Singh. 1992. "Life after the Polish 'Big Bang': Episodes of Pre-Privatization Enterprise Behavior." In Arye Hillman and Branko Milanovic, eds., *The Transition from Socialism in Eastern Europe: Domestic Restructuring and Foreign Trade.* Washington, D.C.: World Bank.

Gomulka, Stanislaw. 1993. "The Financial Situation of Polish Enterprises (1992–93) and Its Impact on Monetary and Fiscal Policies." Eastern Europe Research Paper Series 28. World Bank, Transition and Macro-Adjustment Division, Washington, D.C.

Kornai, János. 1992. *The Socialist System: The Political Economy of Communism.* Princeton, N.J.: Princeton University Press.

———. 1993. "Transformational Recession: A General Phenomenon Examined through the Example of Hungary's Development." Paper presented at the François Perroux Lecture, Collège de France, June, Paris.

Krumm, Kathy, Branko Milanovic, and Michael Walton. Forthcoming. "Transfer and the Transition from Socialism: Is a Radical Alternative Necessary?" World Bank, Europe and Central Asia Regional Office and Transition Economics Division, Washington, D.C.

Kwiecinski, Andrzej, and Wolfgang Quaisser. 1993. "Agricultural Prices and Subsidies in the Transformation Process of the Polish Economy." *Economic Systems* 17 (2): 125–54.

Lipton, David, and Jeffrey Sachs. 1990. "Creating a Market Economy in Eastern Europe: The Case of Poland." *Brookings Papers on Economic Activity* 1. Washington, D.C.: The Brookings Institution.

Orlowski, Lucjan T. 1993a. "Destabilizing Factors in the Economic Transition in Central Europe." Paper presented at the Conference of the European Association for Evolutionary Political Economy: The Economy of the Future Ecology, October 28–30, University of Barcelona.

———. 1993b. "Problems of Corrective Inflation in the Transformation from Central Planning to a Market Economy: The Experience of Poland." Sacred Heart University and Kiel Institute of World Economics, Kiel, Germany.

Pinto, Brian, Marek Belka, and Stefan Krajewski. 1993. "Transforming State Enterprises in Poland: Evidence on Adjustment by Manufacturing Firms." *Brookings Papers on Economic Activity.* Washington, D.C.: The Brookings Institution.

Pleskovic, Boris. 1994. "Financial Policies in Socialist Countries in Transition." Policy Research Working Paper 1242. World Bank, Research Advisory Staff, Washington, D.C.

Roberts, Bryan. 1993. "What Happened to Soviet Product Quality? Evidence from the Finnish Auto Market." University of Miami, Miami, Fla.

Rostowski, Jacek. 1992. "The Inter-Enterprise Debt Explosion in the Former Soviet Union: Causes, Consequences, Cures." *Communist Economies and Economic Transformation* 5(2): 131–59.

———. 1993. "The Implications of Rapid Private Sector Growth in Poland." Discussion Paper 159. London School of Economics and Political Science, Centre for Economic Performance.

Schaffer, Mark. 1993. "The Enterprise Sector and Emergence of the Polish Fiscal Crisis, 1990–91." Policy Research Working Paper 1195. World Bank, Transition and Macro-Adjustment Division, Washington, D.C.

Solimano, Andrés, and David E. Yuravlivker. 1993. "Price Formation, Nominal Anchors, and Stabilization Policies in Hungary: An Empirical Analysis." World Bank, Policy Research Department and Europe and Central Asia Country Department II, Washington, D.C.

Tanzi, Vito. 1993. *Transition to Market: Studies in Fiscal Reform.* Washington, D.C.: International Monetary Fund.

Transition. 1994. World Bank, Policy Research Department, Washington, D.C. January.

UNICEF (United Nations Childrens Fund). 1993. *Public Policy and Social Conditions.* Regional Monitory Report 1. New York.

Comment on "Macropolicies in Transition to a Market Economy: A Three-Year Perspective," by Balcerowicz and Gelb

Anders Åslund

As the transition from socialism to capitalism has proceeded from Central Europe to the Balkans and the former Soviet Union, it has proved to be more difficult than many had expected, and the focus has moved back from the details to the fundamentals. Richard Portes makes a telling comment: "The results of economic transformation so far have been remarkably similar. The stabilizations have been relatively successful. The initial jump in the price level is always greater than expected, sometimes so much that significant inflation persists; but the rate does come down rather than taking off into hyperinflation" (1993, p. 40). In fact, nine of fifteen new states of the former Soviet Union were in hyperinflation last year, and the results of economic transformation have been remarkably different.

Balcerowicz and Gelb provide a good reflection of the state of the art in macroeconomic policies in the transition to a market economy. They bring out several of the fundamental new insights. One such insight is that it is better to act fast and hard than to try overly sophisticated fine-tuning of policy. Another insight is that the political dynamics of transition dictate that reformers must fully utilize the period of extraordinary politics following a democratic breakthrough.

Many economic arguments favor a swift transition, and now we seem to have the empirical evidence to support that view: compared with a more gradual approach, radical stabilization has led to less decline in output over a three-year period. In the most striking comparison Romania's measured GDP declined about 25 percent more than Poland's over the past three years. Similarly, stabilization does not harm the development of the private sector, because the financial squeeze is directed primarily against the state sector which, under loose monetary policy, tends to crowd out private enterprises. As the authors argue, failing to stabilize wastes valuable time and delays recovery.

The article introduces two useful concepts. One is the distinction among destroyed capitalism in the countries of Eastern Europe and the former Soviet Union, suspended capitalism in postwar Germany, and distorted capitalism in Latin America. This distinction helps us understand why the transition in the formerly socialist countries is so much more fundamental. Another is the definition of radi-

Anders Åslund is senior associate at the Carnegie Endowment for International Peace.

Proceedings of the World Bank Annual Conference on Development Economics 1994

cal and gradualist policies in relation to the maximum speed possible for a given change, avoiding truisms about certain changes being by necessity time-consuming.

Balcerowicz and Gelb divide postsocialist countries into two groups: the nine in which inflation was below 60 percent last year and those in which it was not—eighteen, if we limit ourselves to Eastern Europe and the countries of the former Soviet Union. I would suggest subdividing the group of eighteen between the ten that have entered hyperinflation and those that have not, leaving such countries as the Kyrgyz Republic, Lithuania, Romania, and Russia in an intermediate category that may still avoid hyperinflation.

A look at the details of the transition in Romania suggests the political explanation of the high inflation. Romania's poor performance can be traced to several main causes: the issuing of credits at interest rates lower than inflation, the favoring of agrarian and heavy-industry lobbies, and the cancellation of net interenterprise arrears with injections of heavily subsidized credits. When both the state and civil society are weak, narrow vested interests can grab untold fortunes. That is what we are seeing in Romania and even more dramatically in most countries of the former Soviet Union.

To build state structures and to mobilize society against the narrow vested interests of the old regime, democratization is needed. It is difficult to discuss macroeconomic policies and institution-building without considering the success of democratization, which appears to explain more than political stability. The kind of government a country has is more important than whether that government is stable.

Romania's debacle is clear and instructive, but it also warrants a look with a newly critical eye. In 1990 Hungary, the most advanced reformer, was widely expected to be the great success story of Eastern Europe. But Poland, then crisis-ridden, has since turned itself around and has suffered less decline in GDP than Hungary. While Poland's growth has steadily met projections, similar growth projections for Hungary have consistently proved overly optimistic. Hungary's failure is becoming evident enough to merit comment.

Although total public expenditures remain high throughout Eastern Europe, in the range of 50 to 60 percent of GDP, Hungary is at the top of that range and Poland at the bottom. Because the budget deficit must be kept in check, Hungary's high expenditures are reflected in high taxes. Only Sweden has a higher tax burden as a share of GDP. Hungary's taxes are high in large part because it reformed its tax system before the demise of communism. Although early reform has been widely considered an advantage, in light of the current situation I would argue the opposite. Having a less reformed tax system would have forced Hungary to cut expenditures much earlier, resulting in a much more liberal economy providing better incentives and thus more growth. It is better to reform the tax system later in the transition, as Poland did. First it becomes necessary to cut public expenditures drastically. Later, in the poststabilization period, the strain on revenues will be great, and the additional revenues that a more rational tax system can provide are badly needed.

There is a similar problem on the expenditure side. The foremost cause of the Eastern European countries' unusually high public expenditures compared with other middle-income countries is large social transfers, as the article points out. In Hungary and the former Czechoslovakia, which had the most reformed social welfare systems, much of the social welfare spending was transferred from state enterprises to the state. Social welfare provided directly by the state has turned out to be far more difficult to cut than that provided by enterprises; enterprise welfare was seen as connected with employment and therefore naturally ceasing with departure from a job. Moreover, reform communism seemed to have unrealistic ideas about what the state could provide. The experience in Hungary and the former Czechoslovakia suggests that social welfare reforms before the transition to a market economy lead to excessive public expenditures and distortion of incentives.

In general, quasi-fiscal deficits have turned out to be far more difficult to handle than straightforward fiscal deficits. The most obvious problem has been credits given at interest rates lower than inflation, which appear to be the primary reason for high inflation. The article correctly points out that the main failure in Romania and other laggards has been in monetary policy. A litmus test is how a country handles interenterprise arrears. These arrears appear in every postsocialist country, because socialist enterprises were not used to demanding payment and money suddenly became scarce. Countries that have failed with gradualist reform, such as Romania and Ukraine, typically have given in to demands from state enterprises for credits to net out interenterprise debts. This response has given rise to a situation of moral hazard in which state enterprises continue not to demand payment, convinced that the state will pay them for what no customer is prepared to buy with real money.

A more complex problem is what to do with bad commercial bank debt. All the Eastern European countries have banking systems dominated by old state banks with old bad debts that are recurring issues of negotiation with the state. The risk is great that this stock problem is being transformed into a flow problem with the renewal of bad debts. That development has been particularly pronounced in Hungary, where the state has spent heavily to keep the banking system afloat. In stark contrast, Estonia has let its three biggest commercial banks, accounting for 40 percent of M2, go bankrupt (Hansson 1994).

Commercial banks in Eastern Europe operate under very different circumstances than do those in the West. Many of these commercial banks have few or no deposits from the public. Since deposit rates vary greatly in less stable economies and banks in Eastern Europe adhere to few ordinary banking standards, bank deposits must be interpreted in those countries as higher risk. It would be natural to let depositors lose money if a bank goes into bankruptcy. The postsocialist state is weak and poor and cannot be expected to spend substantial amounts that would benefit primarily either the old or the new elite.

Balcerowicz and Gelb bring out nicely the contrast between the success of radical policies—as in Poland—and the disappointing results of gradualist policies—as in Romania. But with time the disadvantages of the moderate and more responsible gradualist policies of Hungary have also become apparent. The focus moves to the need to cut both social transfers and taxes in order to improve incentives and thus supply, and to the problem of bad debt in old commercial banks.

References

Hansson, Ardo. 1994. "Reforming the Banking System in Estonia." Stockholm Institute of East European Economics, Stockholm.

Portes, Richard. 1993. "From Central Planning to a Market Economy." In Shafiqul Islam and Michael Mandelbaum, eds., *Making Markets: Economic Transformation in Eastern Europe and the Post-Soviet States.* New York: Council on Foreign Relations.

Comment on "Macropolicies in Transition to a Market Economy: A Three-Year Perspective," by Balcerowicz and Gelb

János Kornai

Few contributions to the growing literature on transition are as comprehensive as this article, provide such a rich, subtle, and balanced review of macroeconomic policy, or draw on so broad a range of experience. I take little issue with the authors on most of the topics they discuss. Instead, I will describe the lines along which their study has prompted me to reflect further on the problems of transition.

The authors are preoccupied by the problem of launching the process: What is the best launching speed? How radical should the first measures be? What should the first package of reforms contain? That these questions recur throughout the article is understandable; Balcerowicz was responsible for directing the first such program, which can now be declared a success. No one is better qualified to talk about these issues.

The collapse of the communist system and the creation of new democratic institutions provided a unique opportunity for implementing tough, bold economic policy that caused trauma to much of the population but promises to be beneficial in the medium and long term. Politicians committed to radical reform could explain their position to the people in terms like these: "We are opening a new chapter in our country's history. The legacy of the previous regime is a heavy burden. The break with the past and the transition will inevitably entail grave sacrifices, but we must put our joint efforts into making them."

Every postcommunist country had a chance to move forward quickly while the euphoria of the change in government lasted. Czechoslovakia and Poland—and perhaps the German Democratic Republic—seized that historic opportunity. In the other countries political leaders either missed or misused this opportunity, which will never recur. Russia tried to take advantage of this contingency but failed because of a number of factors. My own country, Hungary, is among those that made no real attempt to seize the opportunity.

I am not implying that every country ought to have copied the Balcerowicz program. Hungary's situation differed from Poland's in many ways—to Hungary's advantage in most economic respects. The new democratic government should have

János Kornai is Allie S. Freed Professor of Economics at Harvard University and a Permanent Fellow of Collegium Budapest.

Proceedings of the World Bank Annual Conference on Development Economics 1994

used the opportunity to give a frank account of the grave economic problems the country faced and to call for the necessary sacrifices then, when people would have been far more willing to make them. But Hungary's economic policymakers could not bring themselves to take the necessary measures—tax reforms, public spending cuts, exchange rate devaluation, wage policy reform—that would have been politically feasible at the time but that will now encounter much greater resistance. With regard to welfare spending and real wages, for example, Hungary's government was far more timid than its counterparts in Poland or Czechoslovakia (and later the Czech Republic).

What this part of the world failed to do during 1990–92 cannot now be accomplished under the political conditions of that time. But there is a lesson here for countries in which the communist party maintains its political monopoly: China, Cuba, the Democratic People's Republic of Korea, and Viet Nam. The political structure in these countries may not undergo transformation under conditions like those in Eastern Europe or the Soviet Union in the early 1990s. But if there comes a heroic first stage that the people recognize as the collapse of communism, linked with staggering symbolic events (like the velvet revolution in Prague, the mass meetings favoring German reunification, or the first free elections), this juncture must be utilized for economic policy reform.

The passage of time since the crucial moment means that measures must now be taken by the second or third democratic government, not the first, and laws must be passed by the second parliament, not the first. The political environment has changed. Opinion polls show that many people have become disillusioned and bitter. Domestic political conflicts have sharpened. Where elections have been held again, many people have voted for the opposition. Parties stemming from the reform wing of the communist party have gained ground. If these successor parties take office, it is unlikely that they will try to restore the old political system, but they may try to avoid or delay the drastic steps necessary for economic stabilization, such as cutting state spending or curbing wage inflation.

To its credit, this article—unlike many other studies prepared under World Bank auspices—takes account of the interaction between politics and the economy. That interaction is worth examining further. The macroeconomic policy choices that the transition countries face cannot be addressed in a discussion devoid of politics, using the sterile language of academic economics. In this context I would like to raise an issue that Balcerowicz and Gelb did not cover, although each has dealt separately with it in earlier work. That issue is the choice that must be made between two main historical courses. By choice I do not mean simply the decisions of a country's citizens and political parties, but also those of outside experts who take a position on these matters.

One course is that taken by Pinochet's Chile, in which a tough administration tolerates no opposition and entrusts its economic policy to specialist advisers. The other is the democratic course, in which the people can freely criticize the government, in which laws—not presidential decrees—govern, and in which the passage of laws requires a parliamentary majority. This second course involves discomfort. It entails much debate, protracted decisionmaking, and, sometimes, impasses and parliamentary incompetence. Politicians' competition for the favors of the electorate influences their views. Compromises must be patiently sought and concessions made, which can pull policymaking away from "pure," rational economics.

Each of these courses must be conceded to have advantages and drawbacks. Let each economist from the international financial organizations and each expert in postsocialist transformation decide which course he or she endorses. A position cannot simply be taken on the grounds of economic expediency, because the dilemma becomes one of fundamental choices between values. I respect the choices that people make, so long as they are made consistently. But I do not deny being irritated by the peculiar inconsistency in the views of those who airily recommend the historical course of China, Singapore, Taiwan (China), or the postwar Republic of Korea to these harassed transition economies. For there are U.S. or Western European experts who think like this: "It is important for *us,* back in the United States or Western Europe, to uphold democracy, of course, because that is our due, but it would certainly be better for *them* if they were pushed for a good while along the road to a market economy by a strong hand, with an element of force behind it."

As an observer of history I acknowledge that in some communist countries autocratic administrations inclined toward reform can play a big part in transforming society while the totalitarian system is breaking down. That was the case in Kádár's Hungary and Tito's Yugoslavia, and it is the case now in Deng Xiaoping's China. As an analyst I try to grasp the reasons for this situation. As an adviser who draws up normative proposals, however, I am not prepared to recommend any such course to postcommunist countries of Eastern Europe and the former Soviet Union struggling with stagnation or anarchy. I do not want to see, for example, an iron-fisted, "enlightened absolutist" reformer in charge of Russia. In fact, I feel a duty to warn of the perils and drawbacks of an enlightened absolutist or reformist dictatorship.

Those who attach intrinsic value to democratic institutions must calculate into their proposals the existing political power relations and the rules of parliamentary democracy. We will achieve little if we rely on advice based on a formula such as this: "It's our job to advise you about what's good for your country and yours to take our advice. If you don't, that's your problem. We can't help it if your politicians turn out to be stupid or malicious."

One requirement for reaching consensus is thorough clarification of the advantages and disadvantages of possible measures. Here I would like to take issue with a statement in the Balcerowicz and Gelb article: "Country experience suggests no adverse medium-run tradeoffs between stabilization...and either output or the speed of transition to a private economy. Failure to stabilize wastes valuable time and will delay recovery" (p. 40). This statement may have been valid for Poland in January 1990, for example; the monetary stabilization and liberalization undertaken then certainly aided the development of the private sector and, after a lag of a few years, the growth of real output. But from Poland's experience at that time there follows no universal rule applicable in every political and economic situation. Nor does there follow an absolute time sequence or an eternally valid ranking of priorities in economic policy.

If policy measures had no adverse effects, either immediate or after a lag, on the attainment of other economic policy targets—that is, if there were no tradeoffs—reaching political compromises would be easy indeed. But that is not the case. On the contrary, the postsocialist transition creates serious tradeoffs and poses dilemmas with marked political consequences for legislators and those executing the laws. And even the most fortunate postcommunist countries display a range of grave macroeconomic problems: moderate or more rapid inflation, a very high budget deficit, stagnant or falling production (with the exception, perhaps, of Poland), high unemployment that threatens to persist as the normal level, serious foreign debts, and difficulty in increasing exports. Beyond the well-known "inflation-unemployment" tradeoff, these problems present many others. A few examples:

- Several countries need to devalue more than they have done in order to improve their trade and current account balances, but that will certainly accelerate inflation.
- An effective way to halt the decline in production and stimulate recovery would be to use fiscal means, ranging from tax concessions for private investment projects to publicly financed investment, but that could increase the budget deficit.
- Improving the fiscal balance and encouraging financial discipline both call for a hard budget constraint, with no bailouts for persistent loss-makers, but consistent refusal to rescue these nonviable enterprises contributes to higher unemployment, lower aggregate demand, and lower output and slower growth in the short run.

These examples of tradeoffs are limited to macroeconomic policy. To these can be added the tradeoffs between macroeconomic policy and political stability. Many measures that would reduce budgetary spending (for example, cutting social transfers), relieve inflationary pressure (curbing nominal wages), or tighten financial discipline (closing down loss-making state enterprises) would keenly affect the financial position and sense of security of huge numbers of people.

These examples suffice to show that there are no universally valid rules for setting priorities for economic policy. Each country needs to find the point on each tradeoff curve that is politically feasible while allowing for the retention of democratic institutions. One task for economists is to make the tradeoffs clear to the politicians.

But even if we economists do not point out the tradeoffs, they soon will become apparent, along with the political responses to them. For the winners and losers in each tradeoff both have their spokesmen and their political advocates—perhaps even within the government, but if not there, certainly among the parties, the professional organizations, and the pressure groups. And that is precisely why it is so difficult in a democracy—even a mature democratic market economy—to formulate coherent economic policy. Nor will it be easy for the postsocialist countries to learn to manage this process. So, if only for this reason, it is important to examine the experiences of the transition countries very carefully. This thought-provoking article provides much help in doing so.

Floor Discussion of "Macropolicies in Transition to a Market Economy: A Three-Year Perspective," by Balcerowicz and Gelb

A participant from Italy expressed surprise that after almost five years nobody was discussing the major changes taking place in the distribution of income, wealth, or opportunities in these countries. What role has such redistribution played, he asked, and what role will it play in the future? He suspected this redistribution was an underlying cause of current difficulties in the transition economies.

Gelb said he wished he had more time to respond to this interesting question. Information on changes in the distribution of income in these countries, he said, was just beginning to become available, but we could begin to form impressions about relative changes in wages and income. The structure of relative earnings will probably come to resemble patterns in market economies, said Gelb, with premiums on skills and education and with declining earnings for such groups as blue-collar workers in the manufacturing sector. To some degree what happens will probably be a compression of what has happened in market economies over the past forty years. The only study Gelb had seen on the distribution and social effects of the transition was a UNICEF study, which indicated that income distribution had not deteriorated as badly as many think, partly because governments have maintained social transfer programs.

It is hard to judge what is happening to assets in the transition economies, said Gelb, but a new class of asset owners is probably developing. Gelb suspected that the distribution of assets would resemble that in capitalist countries—with a concentration of wealth among a relatively small segment of the population—but with differences. The age-specific distribution of wealth is likely to be different, for one thing. In market economies wealth is often concentrated among older cohorts; in the transition economies it is more likely to be concentrated in the hands of younger, more educated people, such as managers with access to the service sectors.

It is important, added Balcerowicz, to distinguish between equality of chance and equality of situation. Everyone agrees that the more equality of chance, the better. But as for equality of situation: obviously a gross income differential, for example, is undesirable, but what is the norm? One norm could be taken from the justice the-

This session was chaired by Wilfried P. Thalwitz, vice president, Europe and Central Asia Regional Office, at the World Bank.

ory, that the optimum income differentials are those that ensure the highest rate of improved growth for the poor. But in applying this to real-life situations, do we then say that every increase in income differential is bad?

Another distinction must be made in the countries of transition, said Balcerowicz. People confuse true growth with what he calls the "visibility effect." There has been a shift in the mass media from the controlled system, which featured a propaganda of success, to a free system, which features a propaganda of failure. People are now seeing television images of poor people at Warsaw's central station, just as they have seen images of poor people in New York, and they conclude that income differentials have grown enormously. Perhaps differentials in income and wealth have grown, but one must disentangle apparent growth from true growth.

In commenting on tax reform, Balcerowicz continued, Anders Åslund (discussant) raised an interesting question that could be broadened: was market socialist reform a liability or an asset? Many are inclined to say it was an asset, but that may not be true. In Poland, for example, workers councils are very strong within enterprises, because previously it seemed that only market socialist reform was feasible. Now the workers councils tend to be factors of resistance in the transition to markets.

A former World Bank economist asked the speakers about the importance of enterprise reform. Enterprise reform had been an essential part of reform in Brazil and Portugal in the past, and currently in China, he said. Balcerowicz, referring to the deep institutional trench in which it can get stuck, responded that enterprise reform means two things: it can mean the privatization of state enterprises or it can mean making state enterprises perform more efficiently within the state sector. Recent experience provided two lessons, said Balcerowicz. First, if you inherit a huge public sector, there is no substitute for privatization. Second, there is no substitute for radical stabilization and liberalization programs for inducing state enterprises to improve their behavior. You cannot get them to improve their behavior simply by creating state holdings or new structures for supervising the huge state sector, as Italy tried to do.

A participant from the United Nations who did not necessarily agree that there is no substitute for privatization asked: assuming that there is no substitute, and accepting the evidence that privatization does not happen quickly, what do we do until we can privatize? Do we abandon state enterprises, allowing their bad debts to return to the state? Or do we provide an interim substitute for corporate dominance of state enterprises?

When saying there was no substitute for privatization, said Balcerowicz, he had meant that there was no substitute if your objective was rapid economic growth, which is important for countries in transition. Privatization—together with other conditions—is essential for such growth, and if it does not happen then you must accept a lower growth rate. Meanwhile, searching for a better corporate structure within the framework of a large state sector is futile if you define the state sector in a way that has any meaning.

One participant asked if countries such as Hungary and Ukraine, which missed the boat on the first round of reform, would be able—assuming political will—to seize a later window of opportunity under more favorable political conditions. Or did the speakers think that the window of opportunity was lost forever?

One sad conclusion to be faced, responded János Kornai (discussant), is that we missed the boat on the shift from communism to postcommunism, and that that unique opportunity will not recur. On a less grand level many opportunities become available every time a parliamentary democracy has a new parliament and a new government, but there is no universal rule about how to take advantage of confidence, events, and opportunities. In countries like Hungary the socialist party will probably become part of the new government—maybe even a leading part of that government. No one is in a better position than that party, with its base of support among trade unions and workers, to initiate a move toward voluntary wage restraint and to restrain the drift toward higher nominal wages (the high partial indexing of nominal wages) and hence toward permanent inertial inflation. Don't base expectations on what happened in 1990, said Kornai, because this is a new situation, which presents new opportunities.

A university participant asked Kornai to elaborate on the lessons that he thought Russia could learn from China's experience. Kornai warned that the history and initial conditions of the two countries were different in so many ways that to suggest transplanting the Chinese experience to Russia was so simplistic as to be almost meaningless. Chief among these differences is the political structure of the two countries. One reason for the smoothness of the Chinese transformation, Kornai said, was the continuing monopoly of the communist party; its power might be getting weaker, but in China there is no competition among political forces. In Russia, on the other hand, there is debate and competition among different political forces. One could make value judgments about such differences in approach to the transition, but one should not assume that the Chinese experience could be easily translated to the Russian environment.

Russia's Struggle with Stabilization: Conceptual Issues and Evidence

Jeffrey D. Sachs

The most important question about Russian economic reform is how to avoid a collapse of Russia's nascent democracy in the face of highly unstable political and economic conditions. The precarious situation could unravel in a spiral of self-reinforcing destructive responses: criminality, regional separatism, tax evasion, and flight from the currency. A combination of monetary tightening, an early pegging of the exchange rate, and large-scale international assistance to support stabilization offers Russia the most realistic chance of avoiding political catastrophe. International assistance to Russia during the past three years has been inadequate in amount and without a proper conceptual framework. The article offers a strategy for Russian stabilization and Western assistance based on theoretical and empirical analysis. The concerns raised apply not only to Russia, but more generally to weak states in acute financial crisis, for which the current methods of delivering aid are typically too slow and too oblivious of the risks of state collapse.

Russia faces at least three fundamental economic challenges. The first is to overcome the state insolvency that is a legacy of the defunct Soviet regime. The second is to establish a market system on the ruins of central planning. The third is to manage the profound problem of structural adjustment, as workers and resources move from heavy industry to light industry and services. And it must manage these three enormous tasks while attempting to consolidate democracy and transform itself from empire to nation-state.

Any one of these economic tasks would challenge a society's stability and forbearance. The combination of all three is historically unprecedented in scale and extent. It is not surprising, therefore, that Russia has lived perilously close to hyperinflation and social instability during the first three years of post-Soviet reform and adjustment. This article discusses the design of macroeconomic policies that are most appropriate in the face of Russia's extreme economic crisis.

Jeffrey D. Sachs is Galen L. Stone Professor of International Trade at Harvard University. The author thanks Richard Cooper, Bill Easterly, Alan Gelb, and Christine Wallich for useful comments. Mark Nagel provided useful assistance in analyzing budgetary trends and issues related to fiscal federalism. Some parts of the article were updated after the conference.

Proceedings of the World Bank Annual Conference on Development Economics 1994

My thesis is that the "shock therapy" approach to stabilization—a clearly announced, comprehensive program including an abrupt tightening of monetary conditions, an early pegging of the exchange rate, and large-scale international aid to support the stabilization—is desirable because it is the least-cost and least risky form of stabilization.[1] Rapid, decisive, comprehensive reform reduces uncertainty, aligns public expectations in support of stabilization, and adds credibility to government policies. Such credibility is extremely important in highly unstable conditions such as Russia's. When governments are politically and financially fragile, adverse expectations can become self-fulfilling, so that economic reforms fail even when fundamental conditions are adequate.

The risks facing Russia exist in large part because of grave weaknesses of the Russian state in the aftermath of communism. Political instability and financial distress are making it extremely difficult for the Russian government to provide the basic public goods required of a functioning economy and society: law and order, public administration, a fiscal system to pay for the army and vital social services, and a working monetary system to support the division of labor among enterprises. A key element of radical market reforms, particularly shock therapy stabilization, is to severely restrict the domain of state activity in economic life, so that the government can focus its limited capacities on its core responsibilities of monetary stability and social protection. The most positive recent news in Russia has been that the new constitution adopted by referendum in December 1993 seems to have contributed to an institutionalization of democratic political life, which has strengthened the capacity of the state to pursue its basic functions, including macroeconomic stabilization and law enforcement.[2]

Stabilization Crises in Weak States

Russia is similar to many countries in the world over the past twenty years in emerging from authoritarian rule in the midst of financial crisis. Russia's crisis is far more complex, however, by virtue of the scale of its problems, its previous history, the size and diversity of the country, and the need to create completely new state institutions. It is notable, therefore, that even countries whose position was easier—Argentina, Bolivia, Brazil, Nicaragua, Peru, and Yugoslavia—have succumbed to hyperinflation in the midst of the democratic transition.

New democracies that inherit a financial crisis are especially susceptible to hyperinflationary collapse. When states are financially weakened and the political rules of the game are unclear, the government can be overwhelmed by various kinds of contagious antisocial behavior, such as massive tax evasion or a flight from the domestic currency. Abnormal behavior spreads rapidly through contagion as the public comes to expect that the state will be unable to enforce normal behavior. Almost always, these contagions occur only after the state has already been gravely weakened by poor fiscal conditions.

The key to contagion is that pessimistic expectations about state power can prove self-fulfilling. Once unshakable regimes can collapse when undermined by profound financial weakness that creates adverse public expectations. The normal monopoly of state power can disappear, and executive authority may become helpless in the face of civil disorder and violent challenge. Society can be thrown into a Hobbesian war of all against all, until a new (and often brutal) central authority is reestablished. The population may accept a new tyrant not because of a preference for tyranny but because of a preference for order over a brutal state of nature.

The risk of a vicious circle of a weakening state and growing instability has important implications. It may not be enough for foreign donors to demand that the government pull itself together as a precondition for large-scale assistance. Foreign assistance may be necessary at the very start of reforms to halt the downward spiral of government collapse and to change expectations about the outcome of reforms.[3] Up-front assistance may make it possible to achieve early visible results—such as currency stabilization and an end to high inflation—that become a prelude to more fundamental changes, such as overhaul of the fiscal system.

Fiscal Weakness and State Collapse

Several simple examples of immediate relevance to Russia illustrate the risks of state collapse. The Russian state is threatened by at least six types of contagious antisocial behavior: a flight from the ruble, tax evasion, criminality, regional separatism, foreign debt overhang, and panic by government creditors. For each case there is a "good" equilibrium that permits the government to function normally and a "bad" equilibrium in which basic state functions collapse. These models are deliberately very simple (technicalities are generally left to the endnotes) but nonetheless illustrative of the general problems of a weak state. Later, explicit dynamics are added to show that whether society reaches the good or bad equilibrium depends on initial conditions (determined by a country's history) and expectations.

Money demand. Suppose that domestic firms hold rubles or black market dollars for transaction purposes. If they hold rubles, they enjoy lower transaction costs because there is no need to resort to the black market. On the other hand, they must bear the inflation tax on ruble holdings. Suppose that the government is raising a given percentage of GDP through seigniorage, which is shared among enterprises holding rubles. If all firms are using rubles, the inflation tax is spread widely and the inflation rate and the inflation tax paid by each firm are low. If most firms have fled into dollars, the inflation tax would fall only on the few remaining firms holding rubles. The inflation rate would be higher, and the cost of using rubles would be higher as well. The more firms that flee to the dollar, the higher is the incentive for the remaining firms to flee to the dollar as well. (Boone forthcoming also offers a model of a self-fulfilling collapse of money demand in the context of postcommunist market reforms.)

Tax evasion. A firm can choose to go underground to evade taxes. In doing so, however, the enterprise loses some of the public goods provided by the government, such as police protection, enforcement of contracts, and ready access to the banking system (which exposes the enterprise to greater risk of detection). A firm should balance the benefits of the public good against the cost of tax payments. Its decision depends on what *other* firms are doing. If other firms are paying their taxes, the government is able to provide a significant scale of public goods. In that case, it pays to remain legal. But if the other firms have stopped paying their taxes, the state is in near-collapse and cannot provide public goods on a significant scale. The firm sees no reason to keep paying taxes and goes underground. Formally, there are two equilibriums: one in which all firms pay their taxes, and one in which no firms pay their taxes.[4]

Law enforcement. Criminal behavior can spread for another reason: the probability of getting caught and of being prosecuted drops as criminal activity rises. If most firms are violating the law, law enforcement authorities must divide their scarce enforcement resources among a large number of cases, so the chances of any particular firm being caught and punished are low. If most firms are obeying the law, however, the chances of catching and punishing a violator are much higher. So, if all other firms are breaking the law, the remaining firm will do so as well, and if all other firms are obeying the law, the remaining firm will also obey the law (Sah 1991). Therefore the rate of criminality may be subject to multiple equilibriums.

Fiscal federalism. In a loose confederal state like Yugoslavia in 1989, the Soviet Union in 1990–91, and Russia today, the federal government must collect taxes from regions that may have incentives to delay or underpay their federal tax obligations. Regional leaders may withhold tax payments intended for the federal government at the risk of being punished in the future (for example, at the end of the fiscal year). But withholding taxes reduces the political strength of the central government and the likelihood that it can effectively punish the region. Again, two equilibriums are possible: one in which most or all regions pay their taxes so that the real threat of retaliation makes illegal withholding too dangerous, and another in which tax withholding is so widespread that the center is weakened to the point of being impotent. This kind of behavior undermined the Yugoslav federal government in 1989 and the Soviet Union in 1991. It could still threaten the Russian Federation.[5]

Foreign government debt. Suppose that there is a foreign debt burden that is greater than the government's immediate capacity to repay and that there are many potential creditors. If each creditor makes a new small loan, the government could undertake enough profitable additional investments to pay back the original debt plus the new debt. But if most creditors decide not to make a loan, the government is unable to undertake the new investments and so remains unable to repay the original debt. In this circumstance no single small creditor should extend a new loan, since a small loan will not solve the problem but will merely get added to the stock of unpaid debt. The government is thereby forced into outright default (Sachs 1984).[6] One remedy to a creditor panic of this sort is to let the new investors lend on a priority basis, so that their repayments are guaranteed ahead of existing debt. This arrangement is common in domestic bankruptcy proceedings, but there are no agreed mechanisms in the international arena for assigning priority to incremental credits.[7] An alternative is a large international line of credit from official sources.[8]

Domestic government debt. In the case of an overhang of domestic debt, which unlike foreign debt can be partially "repudiated" through inflation, a panic among domestic debt holders can lead to inflation in the same way that a panic among foreign creditors can lead to outright default (Calvo 1988). If investors have strong confidence in the government's ability to avoid inflationary finance, nominal interest rates will be low (because the currency will be expected to remain stable in value) and the burden of debt servicing will also be low. The budget deficit will therefore be small, and the government will be able to avoid inflationary finance. If, instead, government bondholders believe that inflationary finance will be high, they will require a high nominal interest rate to hold government debt. This, in turn, will lead to a heavy debt-servicing burden and a large budget deficit, so the government will have to resort to inflationary finance. The pessimistic inflationary forecast becomes self-fulfilling, not unlike the contagious flight from currency mentioned earlier.

Credibility and the Costs of Stabilization

There are two important implications of the cases of multiple equilibriums just described. The most direct is that stabilization may fail because of self-reinforcing pessimism about social prospects. The second implication is that the prospects for stabilization tend to be intrinsically uncertain, since rational actors can hold either optimistic or pessimistic assessments. This uncertainty tends to raise the costs of successful stabilization. As macroeconomists have stressed during the past two decades, there is a social premium to be achieved by lowering the uncertainty and raising the credibility of a stabilization program.

The costs of reforms that turn out to be successful but that appeared "incredible" are well described by Calvo (1989). Suppose that the government is trying to end inflation but that government bondholders attach some positive probability to a self-fulfilling panic. Nominal interest rates will be raised in anticipation of expected inflation. Expected inflation will reflect a weighted average of inflation assessments by those who believe a panic will occur and those who do not. Now if the panic does not occur and stabilization is in fact successful, ex post real interest rates will be high because nominal interest rates at the outset of stabilization efforts included a premium for inflation that did not materialize. The resultant high real interest rates can raise the costs of stabilization by leading to bankruptcies, which could spill over into a banking crisis if commercial banks are saddled with bad debts.

Russia's stabilization attempts during 1992–94 show every sign of incredibility. For example, in 1994 nominal monthly interest rates were running 8 to 10 percentage points above monthly inflation, suggesting widespread expectations of subsequent currency depreciation. Since stabilization efforts were on the whole successful during the first half of 1994 in reducing actual inflation, the result was a sustained period of enormously high real interest rates, with attendant risks to enterprises and commercial banks. The rapid buildup of bad debt in mid-1994 seems to have contributed to the subsequent relaxation of monetary policy at the end of 1994. In this sense, lack of credibility appears to have directly undermined the subsequent stabilization effort.

Political Leadership and Credibility

Most of the time, society is not on the knife edge between stability and collapse. In the United States we assign a very low probability to spontaneous flight from the dollar, even though in theory a complete collapse of the dollar might be a self-fulfilling equilibrium. The reason, it seems, as stressed recently by Krugman (1991) and Matsuyama (1991, 1992), is that agents face fixed costs in shifting between "social" and "antisocial" behaviors (such as switching from domestic currency transactions to black market transactions). Because of these costs of adjustment agents take decisions at discrete intervals rather than continuously, and they know that their decisions today will bind them for a discrete period into the future. Moreover, the timing of decisions by individual agents tends to be staggered, so that only a small proportion of the population is shifting between policy regimes at any time. The implication, as Krugman puts it, is that history and expectations together determine whether the good or bad equilibrium emerges over time.

Both Krugman and Matsuyama, using somewhat different approaches, arrive at a key insight. If we let $0 \leq \theta \leq 1$ be a parameter that measures the proportion of the population pursuing the antisocial behavior (flight from the currency, tax evasion), then θ must evolve gradually over time. If θ starts near zero, with most people pursuing the socially desirable strategy, θ will remain close to zero at least for a while, since most people will stick with their earlier behavior at least for a while. As a result, when an individual agent next chooses whether to pursue the social or the antisocial behavior, the historically determined level of θ matters, since it gives an indication of the likely social circumstances in the near future during which the individual's decision will apply.

Consider the case of money demand. If most firms are using rubles (because of past trends in the society), an enterprise making its money-demand decision between rubles and dollars knows that most firms are likely to be using rubles in the near future as well. Thus there is less chance that the equilibrium with complete flight from the currency ($\theta = 1$) will eventually emerge. The firm making its decision now will therefore also have the tendency to demand rubles rather than switch to black market dollars. As a result θ will tend to converge toward zero. But if most firms have already fled from rubles to dollars (θ close to 1), the enterprise will expect the bad steady-state equilibrium in the future ($\theta = 1$) and will flee from rubles as well.

A particularly nice mathematical and substantive result emerges that can apply to any of the versions of the contagion model that we have examined. There are, typically, three intervals for θ that determine the future equilibrium of the society. If recent history has resulted in a low value of θ in the interval $0 \leq \theta < \underline{\theta}$ for some particular threshold level $\underline{\theta}$, each new decisionmaker will choose the socially desirable behavior and θ will eventually evolve to 0. Society will reach the good equilibrium. If history has resulted in a high value of θ in the interval $\bar{\theta} < \theta \leq 1$ for a particular threshold value $\bar{\theta}$, each new decisionmaker will choose the antisocial behavior and society will reach the bad equilibrium. The most interesting case is that in which θ lies in an intermediate interval $\underline{\theta} \leq \theta \leq \bar{\theta}$. In that case, an agent can rationally have either pessimistic expectations (that society will evolve to the bad outcome of $\theta = 1$) or optimistic expectations (that society will eventually evolve to the good outcome of $\theta = 0$).

These three intervals also define three zones of political life. In most industrial countries at most times in recent years, societies operate with θ close to zero. Most people are law abiding, and there are no rational fears of social collapse. There is every reason to believe that even if society is jolted by political or natural disasters, it will evolve again toward the good equilibrium. We might therefore call this first interval the range of "normal politics." In a few disastrous cases, such as Bosnia or Somalia, society has reached a war of all against all. In schematic terms, θ is close to 1. In this circumstance, even if there is a short period of good news, it is rational to be pessimistic: to abjure social behavior on the grounds that all other decisionmakers are likely to do the same. We might call this interval the range of "social collapse."

Russia and other countries in fundamental economic and political transitions find themselves in a third, indeterminate zone, when either a successful or unsuccessful outcome is possible, and rational agents can subscribe to optimistic or pessimistic forecasts. This zone might be called the "interval of political leadership," because political leadership can prove decisive to the outcome.

It is the crucial role of a leader to align society's expectations toward the favorable outcome. It was no mere wordplay when Franklin Roosevelt declared, in the depths of the Great Depression, that the only thing we have to fear is fear itself. Garry Wills has put it perceptively: "[Roosevelt] understood the importance of psychology—that people have to have the courage to keep seeking a cure, no matter what the cure is. America had lost its will to recover, and Roosevelt was certain that regaining it was the first order of business" (1994, p. 76). It is no accident that almost all stabilization programs are identified with particular leaders: Hamilton in the United States (1790), Shacht in Germany (1923), Grabski in Poland (1924), Erhard in Germany (1948), Sanchez de Losada in Bolivia (1985), Balcerowicz in Poland (1990), and so on. This identification is a tribute not only to their technical contributions, but also to the fact that they prodded their compatriots to see the possibility of the "favorable" equilibrium in circumstances clouded by doubt and pessimism.

The Role of External Assistance

The early provision of external aid often is crucial in boosting confidence in a stabilization program. Standard monetary theory gives a clear but limited role to foreign financing during monetary stabilization. Foreign financing allows a government to cover part of the budget deficit without recourse to increases in the money supply, thereby slowing inflation during the period of foreign assistance. In the typical view, which has considerable merit in many historical circumstances, the temporary external help must be accompanied by aggressive budget cutting or else inflation will simply reappear when the external help is withdrawn. Indeed, inflation can come back even more virulently than before the aid, since now the government must cover the repayment of loans as well as the original deficit.

But in a situation of multiple equilibriums, foreign finance can be much more important and its influence more enduring. Not only does the foreign finance give the government breathing room to undertake budget cutting, but it can also shift the whole economy from the bad equilibrium to the good equilibrium by ruling out the possibility of the self-fulfilling contagion. In the examples of social collapse, the possibility of the bad outcome depends implicitly or explicitly on the financial fragility of the government. If the government has financial wealth in reserve—enough to guarantee the stability of the currency, or the provision of public goods, or the enforcement of law, or the punishment of tax-evading regions—only the good equilibrium can occur. In general, this financial reserve can be achieved through fundamental fiscal reform or a line of credit from outside. Reform may be absolutely necessary in the long run but impractical in the short run if the economy is already careering toward the bad equilibrium.[9]

Consider the problem of flight from the currency. Suppose that the government has an international line of credit (a stabilization fund) for sustaining a pegged exchange rate. The government won't actually have to draw on the line of credit to defeat speculation against the currency and rule out the bad equilibrium. The mere availability of the credit line will ensure that it doesn't have to be used. Bruno and Fischer (1990) stress the similar importance of a nominal anchor in ruling out a self-fulfilling collapse of the currency. Obstfeld (1994) considers the case in which a large stock of foreign exchange reserves eliminates the possibility of a self-fulfilling attack on the currency.

In an analysis of comparative disinflation experiences Bruno marshaled the historical evidence of the 1980s and early 1990s in favor of an early exchange rate peg. He stresses the role of the exchange rate peg as a signal of the government's anti-inflationary intentions:

> There are a variety of reasons for targeting the exchange rate rather than a monetary aggregate at the initial stabilization stage—the instability of the demand for money, the frequency of observation of the exchange rate as a proxy for the price index (on a daily basis), and the more widely and intuitively understood signal of the stability of a key price level (in relation to wages, for external competitiveness considerations, etc.)....While monetary targeting with an exchange-rate float has been a plausible policy alternative in stabilization from low or moderate inflations (especially when the safety cushion of exchange reserves does not exist—as in Romania and Bulgaria), this has hardly ever been the case from high or hyperinflations. (1993, p. 270)

It is of course the international community that can determine whether a safety cushion of exchange reserves is in fact available, by providing the country with reserves at the outset of stabilization. Dornbusch recounts powerful historical evidence of stabilization episodes of the mid-1920s in favor of early currency stabilization backed by international reserves. Currency stabilization typically preceded budget balancing:

> Stabilization requires three steps: fixing the exchange rate, balancing the budget, and ensuring the independence of the central bank. Each of these three steps is indispensable. Fixing the exchange rate establishes immediately a stabilizing force and inertia with beneficial effects for expectations, the budget, and politics. Balancing the budget provides the fundamentals that warrant fixing the exchange rate. Finally, the independence of the central bank acts as an insurance against relapse and thus helps improve expectations.
>
> All three conditions might not be achievable at the outset. Specifically, budget balancing may not be immediately possible or convenient, at least not fully. The answer then is for it to be financed not by money but by debt—domestic or external—with a clear limitation on the deficits. Still, exchange rate fixing and the creation of central bank independence can go ahead. (1992, p. 418)

The role of a foreign line of credit in securing confidence in the course of monetary stabilization has been demonstrated repeatedly. A vivid example came at the end of the German hyperinflation in 1923, as described by Hjalmar Schacht (1956) in his memoirs. Schacht became Commissioner for National Currency on November 12, 1923, and eight days later, when the hapless Rudolf Havenstein, President of the Reichsbank, died, Schacht took his place. Schacht quickly engineered a sharp tightening of credit for a few weeks. This early performance commended him warmly to Montagu Norman, Chairman of the Bank of England, who quickly agreed to a crucial £100 million loan to the Reichsbank. A few days later this loan helped Schacht head off a powerful separatist movement in the Rhineland, which was striving to create a separate Rhenish Central Bank with the support of French financial interests. Since Schacht could demonstrate to Chancellor Marx that he had already mobilized £100 million from abroad, and with the promise to raise more, he was given time to carry out his own strategy and to consolidate the stabilization effort. Several months later the Dawes loan of 1924 provided further backing for the new currency.

One can find many other examples of international lines of credit that played a vital role in the early stages of stabilization by bolstering confidence and pointing the public in the direction of the good equilibrium. The stabilizations of high inflation in Central Europe in the interwar period were supported by loans from the League of Nations. Most famously, the mere announcement of the Marshall Plan gave a crucial boost to moderate governments under profound stress from economic crisis. Marshall's speech, remarked U.K. Foreign Minister Bevin, was "like a lifeline to a sinking man. It seemed to bring hope where there was none" (quoted in Isaacson and Thomas 1986, p. 413). More recent cases include a U.S. bridge loan to Mexico in late 1988, which bolstered confidence in the Mexican government after a tumultuous and contested presidential election, and a $1.5 billion stabilization fund for Israel at the start of the 1985 anti-inflation program, which bolstered public confidence and helped the government hold the course in the face of labor and budgetary pressures. The $1 billion Polish stabilization fund, provided by the G-7 countries at the end of 1989, was crucial in convincing the government's own team of the feasibility of quick currency convertibility. Britain's and Sweden's return of prewar gold to Estonia in mid-1992 was critical in backing Estonia's new currency; this early stability gave momentum to more fundamental economic reforms in the summer of 1992.

There are, alas, as many examples of missed opportunities because of lack of confidence, though these are often harder to spot. When a stabilization program collapses, there are always more than enough culprits. Since the pessimistic equilibrium is itself rational, no search party sets out to find the missing ingredient to stabilization. And yet, occasionally, bitter reproaches can be heard. When the Polish currency stabilization collapsed in 1925, leading the way to dictatorship, Vice President Feliks Mlynarksi of the Polish National Bank detailed in a stinging rebuke to the international community how its failure to provide even a small amount of support to tide the country over an unfavorable harvest precipitated the collapse:

> The stabilization of the currency in Poland—strange as it may seem—in July 1925 broke down because of a lack of 15 million dollars. It happened at the time when the question of international cooperation with a view to stabilizing the European currencies was the subject of lively discussion. What were the results of it? Firstly, in order to restore the lost confidence of the public reminiscent of paper money inflation, a considerably greater sum than 15 million dollars was later necessary. (1926, p. 62)

Monetary Conditions in Russia

We are now ready to apply these insights to Russia's struggle for stabilization, using a formal framework to analyze four phases of stabilization since the start of 1992.

A Formal Framework for Monetary Stabilization

A government budget deficit g may be financed in three ways: with domestic bonds b, foreign loans f, or central bank credit to the government cg. Note that b, f, and cg are *flows,* all measured, as is g, as a percentage of GDP. Since $g = b + f + cg$, we can write:

$$cg = g - f - b. \quad (1)$$

In addition to making loans to the government, the Russian central bank extends credits *cb* to commercial banks and credits *cc* to other countries in the Commonwealth of Independent States (CIS). The flow of total credits from the central bank, measured as a percentage of GDP, is given by:

$$c = cg + cb + cc. \tag{2}$$

If central bank interventions in the foreign exchange market are ignored, the change in the monetary base $\dot{M}$ as a percentage of GDP is equal to c, so $\dot{M}/\text{GDP} = cg + cb + cc$. Using equation 1 and defining GDP as equal to price level P multiplied by real GDP Q yields:

$$\dot{M}/PQ = (g - b - f) + cb + cc. \tag{3}$$

We define monetary velocity as:

$$V = PQ/M. \tag{4}$$

Real money balances are $m = M/P$, and inflation is $\pi = \dot{P}/P$; Q is assumed constant.

Using these definitions together with equations 3 and 4 and following some simple calculations, we can write a canonical equation for inflation:

$$\pi = V(g - b - f + cb + cc) + \dot{V}/V. \tag{5}$$

This is our key analytical equation. It is also the underpinning of IMF financial programming exercises. According to equation 5, inflation is the result of several factors:

- *Central bank credit expansion,* which is equal to credit to the government $(g - b - f)$ plus credit to the commercial banks and the other CIS members $(cb + cc)$.
- *Monetary velocity,* V, with higher velocity (caused by prior flight from the currency) causing higher inflation for any given level of central bank credit expansion.
- *Continuing flight from the currency* $(\dot{V}/V)$, which can cause inflation even in the absence of new central bank credits.

The earlier discussion of multiple equilibriums can be rephrased in terms of equation 5. First, the budget deficit $g - b - f$ may itself be a function of optimistic or pessimistic expectations, since an economy may be hit by a contagion of tax evasion, regional separatism, or pessimism of government bond holders (which leads to higher nominal interest rates on government debt service in anticipation of future inflation). Thus, even if the inflation is of a traditional variety—caused by the monetization of a large budget deficit—the size of the deficit can reflect the balance of expectations about the prospects for reform.

Second, the velocity of money is also a function of expectations. Both a high value of V and a rising value of V (that is, $\dot{V}/V > 0$) can result from self-fulfilling fears of future inflation, leading to a flight from the domestic currency. Both a high value of V and a rising value of V provoke a rise in inflation for any given positive level of domestic credit expansion. Indeed, as we shall see, the flight from the ruble ($\dot{V}/V > 0$) seems to have played an important part in Russia's inflation dynamics since 1991.

Third, foreign financing of the budget deficit can directly reduce inflation by reducing the amount of the budget deficit that must be monetized by the central bank. Specifically, a rise in f reduces $g - b - f$ and thereby reduces inflation, assuming that foreign borrowing does not raise expected future inflation (in which case the anti-inflationary effect of the rise in f can be offset by a simultaneous rise in V).

Sources of Russian Inflation, 1992–94

Russia's continued high inflation between 1992 and 1994 has deep structural roots, but it also reflects serious policy misjudgments by the Russian government and the West. Many people believe that the high inflation has been inevitable. Some say that the Russian political situation was too unstable to permit faster and bigger cuts in budgetary spending. Others say that the rigidities of Russian state enterprises, especially the loss-makers, led inexorably to large-scale industrial subsidies as a form of hidden social policy. Still others say that stabilization could not precede privatization and other structural reforms. All of these views overstate the difficulties and costs of stabilization and misconstrue the reasons why stabilization failed during 1992–94.

To clarify the role of the budget deficit in Russia's high inflation and to distinguish it from that of other factors, I compare Russia's case with that of three other countries with high budget deficits but low inflation, Greece, Italy, and Portugal (table 1).[10] Russia stands out in all three dimensions of high inflation: high domes-

Table 1. *Factors in Inflation in Russia and Selected Countries, 1993*

		Domestic credit (percentage of GDP)			*M2 velocity (monthly)*		
Country	*Budget deficit (percentage of GDP)*	*Total*	*Budget*	*Other*	*Rate*	*Percentage change*	*Inflation (monthly)*
Russia	10	11.1	4.6	6.5	1.1	8.0	20.7
Greece	13	–1.6	1.2	–2.8	0.6	0.4	1.0
Italy	9	–1.6	–1.1	–0.5	0.7	1.2	0.4
Portugal	8	1.9	–0.2	2.1	0.4	–0.2	0.5

Note: Velocity is measured as monthly GDP divided by high-powered money (line 14 in the IMF *International Finance Statistics,* or *IFS*) for the corresponding month, averaged for the year. For Greece, Italy, and Portugal monthly GDP is interpolated using annual GDP and monthly prices. Change in velocity is calculated as the monthly proportional change in velocity, averaged for 1993. Credit figures are calculated as the monthly flow of central bank credit divided by nominal GDP, averaged for the year. Inflation is the monthly rate, averaged for 1993. The budget deficit is for the general government. For Greece, credit to the budget is defined as line 12a minus line 12aeb of the *IFS.*

Source: All credit data are from the IMF (line 12 and subcomponents of the *IFS*), except for Russia, which are from *Russian Economic Trends,* various issues. Budget deficits are from *Russian Economic Trends* for Russia and from the OECD for Greece, Italy, and Portugal.

tic credit c $(cg + cb + cc)$, high velocity V, and a rising velocity of V $(\dot{V}/V)$ averaging 8 percent a month. But Russia does not stand out in size of the budget deficit as a percentage of GDP. Russia financed a significant proportion of its budget deficit with central bank credit and arrears,[11] whereas the other three countries have financed most of their deficits by nonmonetary means (domestic and foreign loans). There has been almost no foreign financing of the Russian budget deficit (see appendix).

The IMF has conveyed the impression in the West that Russia's budget deficits were extraordinarily large in 1992 and 1993 and that these deficits lay behind the IMF's reticence to provide large-scale financial assistance. This misunderstanding arose from the IMF's introduction of the concept of an "enlarged deficit," which was calculated as the sum of the actual budget deficit plus imports financed by official Western export credit agencies (U.S. Eximbank, Hermes, and so on). This enlarged deficit was measured at about 20 percent of GDP in 1992, equal to an actual budget deficit of 7 percent of GDP plus import subsidies of 13 percent of GDP.

It is important to understand the flaws in the export credit policy of the West during 1992 and 1993. In essence, Western governments gave credits to Russian enterprises to import goods, and the Russian government assumed the burden of repaying these credits. Thus the enterprises received the imported goods virtually for free, while the Russian government took on the obligation of repaying the loans. This kind of aid led to enormous waste and corruption as enterprises struggled to receive imports from the West, whether they were of use in Russia or not. The credits obviously did not finance the actual budget deficit but were a direct transfer to Russian enterprises (and bureaucrats and local governments) that were able to get their hands on the imports through corruption or sheer luck. While the aid did not directly increase the money supply (the "subsidy" to the enterprise was entirely foreign financed), it will add pressures for monetization as the credits fall due ($3–4 billion worth in 1994).

The great analytical mistake is to believe that the inflationary factors in Russia were inevitable features of the economic scene in 1992–94. Consider the sources of credit expansion in more detail: credit to the budget, credit to commercial banks (mainly for the state enterprises), and credit to other CIS members (table 2). Credit policy during January 1992 to June 1994 falls into four periods. From January to March 1992, in the immediate aftermath of price liberalization, there was no monetization of the deficit. April to December 1992 was a period of highly inflationary policies by the Russian Central Bank, followed in January to September 1993 by progressive tightening of monetary policies. October 1993 to May 1994 was a period of further credit tightening, reflecting stronger government control over macroeconomic policy in the aftermath of President Yeltsin's showdown with the Russian Supreme Soviet in September 1993 and adoption of the Russian Constitution in the referendum of December 1993.[12]

The first source of credit expansion was the budget deficit. No monetization occurred in the first period. In the next three periods credit to the budget amounted to 17 percent, 4 percent, and 7 percent of GDP. Greater domestic and foreign financing of the deficit in place of central bank financing could have diminished this

Table 2. *Domestic Credit Expansion, Money Growth, Velocity, and Inflation, 1992–94*
(percent)

Indicator	*January–March 1992*	*April–December 1992*	*January–September 1993*	*October 1993–May 1994*
Total central bank credit				
(percentage of GDP)	7	42	12	8
Budget	–8	17	4	7
Banks	12	18	6	1
CIS	3	7	6	1
M2 velocity	4.6	4.6	7.2	9.4
Change in M2 velocity	10	–1	8	4
M2 growth (monthly)	13	21	16	11
Inflation (monthly)	34	18	22	13

Note: Credit expansion is the monthly increase in central bank credit, as a percentage of monthly GDP, averaged over the period. The other estimates are monthly values averaged over the period. Inflation is measured with the consumer price index.

Source: Russian Economic Trends.

source of credit expansion. It is also likely that the delay in implementing a real stabilization program exacerbated the budget deficit by encouraging tax evasion, leading to a drop in tax collections.

The second main source of credit expansion during 1992–94 was domestic credit to state enterprises through central bank credits to commercial banks. Credits to commercial banks reached a remarkable 18 percent of GDP during May–December 1992, the period of the most extreme inflationary finance by the central bank. During this period Central Bank Chairman Viktor Geraschenko repeatedly declared the bank's intention to increase the money supply to bolster industrial production. Central bank credits to commercial banks were moderately restricted during January–September 1993 and then severely restricted during October 1993–May 1994.

Most commentators have argued that the large flow of domestic credits to state enterprises reflected a painful tradeoff. Greater credit tightening to reduce inflation, they argued, would have led to a much sharper fall in industrial production and a much faster rise in unemployment. It is alleged, therefore, that continued high inflation was largely a reflection of the underlying structural conditions facing industry.

This argument is much weaker than it appears. It is now well understood that the production decline is structural—enterprises have been producing outputs for which there was no demand in the marketplace—rather than the result of financial policy. The decline in industrial production has occurred throughout the ex-communist region, largely independent of the type of monetary policy being pursued. If anything, it appears that the production decline has been less severe in countries pursuing tough monetary policies, such as Poland. Further, enterprises were losing in inflation much or all of what they received in cheap credits, since the enterprises are the main holders of ruble bank deposits and, therefore, the main bearers of the inflation tax. The net production or employment benefit of the subsidies was minuscule—and even smaller considering that the net credit flows actually financed capital flight of many state enterprises rather than any productive activity.

To a great extent the gross credit expansion to the enterprise sector was actually a consequence of inflation rather than a primary source of inflation. Money-financed budget deficits and transfers to the CIS were fueling inflation, imposing an inflation tax on the enterprise sector, which held the bulk of the bank deposits in Russia. The Russian government and central bank made special subsidized loans to help enterprises replenish their depleted real money holdings. The idea was to insulate the enterprises from the inflation tax, thereby shifting more of the inflation tax to the household sector. If the primary sources of inflation (money financing of the budget deficit and credits to other CIS members) could have been reduced, credits to the enterprise sector could have been reduced as well, since enterprises would have needed less compensation for the losses on their money holdings.[13]

It is difficult to estimate the exogenous flow of credits to enterprises and the "endogenous" flow in response to inflation. Since the net transfer to enterprises—banking credits minus inflation taxation—was perhaps 3 percent of GDP (Sachs 1994c) and may even have been negative (Easterly and Vieira Da Cunha 1994, table 5), I use 3 percent as a rough indicator of the level of net credits that would have been extended in the absence of inflation. Note that a related motivation for the large extension of credits to the enterprises in the summer of 1992 was the development of extensive interenterprise arrears. Rostowski (1993, 1994) and Sachs and Lipton (1993) argue that these arrears should have been addressed through reforms of the payments mechanism and strict market discipline on nonpaying enterprises rather than through an expansion of credit.

The third source of credit expansion was central bank credits to the CIS members, which reached about 7 percent of GDP in the second half of 1992, before falling to 3 percent during January–September 1993 and then to zero during October 1993–June 1994. Again, this credit reflects a basic mistake of monetary policy during 1992–93: the delay in introducing separate national currencies. The Russian Central Bank provided virtually automatic monetary credits to states that remained with the ruble and cut off credits only when those states adopted national currencies. CIS credits finally stopped flowing at the end of 1993, when all the CIS members had adopted their own currencies. (Some interstate credit flows remained, in the form of delayed payments for Russian energy shipments to other former republics, but these credits did not have a direct effect on the money supply.) If the CIS members had adopted separate currencies in the first part of 1992, as strongly urged by Havrylyshyn and Williamson (1991), Sachs and Lipton (1993), and others, it is likely that the credits to the other republics would have been decisively reduced, to perhaps 1 percent of GDP by October–May 1994. Unfortunately, the IMF advised against the early introduction of national currencies.

So while Russian credit expansion was very high during 1992 and 1993, most of the expansion resulted from poor monetary and fiscal policies—especially the lack of national currencies and the absence of nonmonetary financing of the budget deficit—and from inflation itself. Perhaps the pressures for inflationary finance were on the order of 11 to 12 percent of GDP: 8 percent of GDP for the budget, 3 percent in net transfers for enterprises, and 1 percent for the other ex-republics. While this was a large amount of monetary financing, it was not necessarily an explosive amount. It could have been much lower had some or all of the credit needs been covered by international financing rather than domestic credit expansion. Loans of some $10–20 billion during 1992 could have substituted for almost all of the inflationary finance of the budget deficit.[14]

Was Early Stabilization Politically Feasible?

It is also conventional to argue that political conditions in Russia precluded stabilization in 1992 and 1993. The situation was too unstable and complex. Key economic policymakers lacked the necessary authority. Society was too divided. In my view, these characterizations are unconvincing. Instability, complexity, divided authority, and society in turmoil always characterize an economic crisis. Far from stopping stabilization, these conditions often make it possible for a small group of policymakers, backed by international support, to begin stabilization. The question is rather one of sustainability: the chief tactic is to use early successes to bolster later political authority in support of more fundamental reforms.

Did the early political conditions preclude stabilization? Almost surely not. President Yeltsin had enormous political power at the start of the reforms. He was by far the most popular politician in the country, and he was operating under a one-year grant of emergency power that enabled him to govern by decree (*Russian Economic Trends* 1992). The economic reforms, led by Deputy Prime Minister Yegor Gaidar, had considerable institutional reach. Gaidar was simultaneously minister of economy and of finance, though he was to relinquish these positions later in the year to subordinates. He had key reform personnel installed at the top of these and other influential ministries.

Social conditions also were adequate for stabilization. There were no riots or major acts of civil disobedience in the first months of economic reform. There were no general strikes and only sporadic work stoppages of any sort. The public was demoralized, to be sure, but not aggressively in opposition to the reforms and certainly not politically mobilized to stop them.

The major weaknesses came in the conception and execution of reform measures rather than in political or social opposition. No overall stabilization program was put in place, with quantified and monitored macroeconomic targets. There was no strategy for dealing with the Soviet ruble and no strategy for exchange rate management, except to let the ruble float in the new interbank currency markets. There was no strategy of Western assistance, especially to help finance the Russian budget deficit or even to postpone debt payments on old Soviet debts in a clear and consistent manner.

The Costs of Delayed Stabilization

By 1991 the Soviet people had already lost faith in the ruble. Money financing of the budget deficit was enormous (exceeding 10 percent of GDP in 1991). Nominal interest rates on ruble deposits were derisory—less than 10 percent a year when open inflation was accelerating to more than 10 percent a month in the final months of 1991—and repressed inflation (as measured by price movements on the black market) was approaching hyperinflationary rates. Perhaps most startlingly, the authorities displayed a brazen disregard for public confidence in the currency, illustrated by the confiscation of 50- and 100-ruble notes in early 1991, a measure ostensibly taken against "illegal" monetary circulation.

When prices were decontrolled in January 1992, the release of the monetary overhang and the lack of confidence in the currency caused a sharp acceleration in monetary velocity. M2 velocity (monthly GDP divided by M2) rose steadily, doubling from 0.38 in January–March 1992 to 0.79 in October 1993–May 1994.[15] Velocity in terms of high-powered money actually declined between January and August 1992 but rose steadily thereafter. According to equation 5, the rise in velocity has two inflationary effects: the direct effect on prices (through $\dot{V}/V > 0$) for a given level of domestic credit expansion and the indirect effect of translating any given level of credit expansion into inflation (the level effect of V).

Standard models of inflation dynamics beginning with Cagan's 1956 classic analysis treat the level of velocity solely as a function of contemporaneous expectations about the prevailing inflation rate, reflecting the assumption that moneyholders make decisions continuously about the level of money balances that they want to hold. But just as I argued earlier that it is more realistic to assume that decisions over holding money are likely to be made at discrete and staggered intervals by individual enterprises, so too current velocity is likely to reflect not only contemporaneous expectations of inflation but also past expectations about current inflation and current expectations about future inflation (which may partly prove to be self-fulfilling).

These considerations suggest that the rise in velocity in Russia since 1991 is a consequence not only of the reaction of moneyholders to actual inflation but also of shifts in expected future inflation, which may in part have been self-fulfilling. Moreover, the rise in velocity will take time to reverse, even if macroeconomic policies are credible and stabilizing in the future, since it will take time for enterprises and households to reestablish money demand patterns consistent with low inflation. In the summer of 1994, for example, inflation had been reduced to 5 percent a month, and yet monetary velocity was significantly higher than it had been twelve months before.

It is clear that Russia's stabilization program has lacked widespread credibility, even at times when monetary and fiscal policy were relatively restrictive. As of mid-1994, for example, nominal interest rates had fallen much less than inflation, which had dropped sharply. Real interest rates (the nominal interest rate minus the contemporaneous inflation rate) were extremely high throughout the period until October 1994. In the summer months inflation was about 6 percent a month, while nominal interest rates on interbank loans were 15 to 18 percent a month—suggestive of Calvo's incredible stabilization. As the Russian monetary authorities persisted with tight credit during 1994, the high real interest rates led to a rapid and crippling build-up of bad debts in enterprises and banks and of the government debt burden on internal debt. This build-up was one of the factors in the reversal of tight monetary policies in mid-1994.

While lack of confidence in the currency has led to a sharp rise in monetary velocity, the Russian budget has also been plagued by a steady drop in tax revenues as a percentage of GDP, partly as a result of the contagion of criminality and tax evasion discussed earlier. Consolidated tax revenues (central and regional governments) plunged from 33 percent of GDP in 1992 to 20 percent of GDP in the first quarter of 1994 (*Russian Economic Trends* 1994). Tax revenues for 1994 were far below budgetary projections of 29 percent of GDP made at the start of the year. Just as it will take time to reconstruct confidence in the Russian currency, it will take time to reconstruct a system of tax compliance. The weakening of compliance is probably another cost of delayed stabilization during 1992–94.

Some hints of a gradual undermining of fiscal federal arrangements are beginning to emerge. While only a few regions of Russia (Tartarstan, for one) have opted out of the federal tax system altogether and have negotiated separate arrangements, the central government has been pressed by the regions to cede an increasing proportion of tax collections to provincial and local governments. In 1992 the central government kept 63.5 percent of all revenues (leaving 36.5 percent for the regions), while in the first quarter of 1994 it kept just 41.0 percent of the revenues (*Russian Economic Trends* 1994). While this trend is healthy in terms of moving government authority closer to the voters, it has apparently not been matched by a commensurate transfer of expenditure responsibilities. The central government accounted for 61.4 percent of total expenditures in 1992 and 59.6 percent in the first quarter of 1994.

Toward a Credible Stabilization Program

Successful stabilization in Russia will require four actions.

- A clear fiscal program (including fiscal federal arrangements) to keep the budget deficit within reasonable limits.
- Adequate domestic bond financing and foreign financing so that the budget deficit can be financed without excessive reliance on central bank credit.
- Restrictive credit policy toward the enterprises and the CIS members, so that central bank credit expansion is held to a reasonable level.
- Adequate clarity of policy and institutional reform, in order to raise the credibility of stabilization and the confidence in the ruble and to keep monetary velocity low and the change in velocity near zero (to avoid a flight from the currency).

A stabilization strategy directed at these considerations should look something like this. Budgetary policy should be restrictive but realistic. The goal should be to reduce the consolidated budget deficit from around 10 percent of GDP to perhaps 5 percent of GDP in the next three to four years. Improved tax collection through an overhaul of the tax system—aimed at a simplified tax structure with broad-based taxes and low marginal tax rates—is a vital step. Western financing of part of the deficit should be made an explicit medium-term commitment and tightly integrated into Russia's own medium-term financial plans.[16] A reasonable target for foreign financing of the budget would be around 3 percent of GDP ($10 billion in mid-1994), tapering off to just 1 percent of GDP in three years. This foreign financing could be carried out through a combination of IMF and World Bank loans and donor government purchases of Russian government treasury bonds denominated in international currencies.[17]

Domestic bond financing would also be increased to at least 2 percent of GDP and probably to 3 to 4 percent of GDP within a couple of years. Currently, domestic bond financing is hampered by a lack of credibility and the absence of foreign cofinancing. With a consistent medium-term stabilization program, backed as well by foreign inflows, domestic bond borrowing would become considerably easier. To overcome the risks of building self-fulfilling inflationary expectations into nominal interest rates—thereby forcing the government to pursue an inflationary policy to service the high nominal interest rates—the domestic bond borrowing might be undertaken, at least in part, in dollars or indexed bonds.

Credit to enterprises and to the other CIS members has already been tightened in 1994, without disastrous consequence. Of course, as the enterprises lose access to subsidized credits, they must have access to foreign capital and reasonably priced domestic loans. The high cost of borrowing facing enterprises in 1994 is one of the costs of incredible stabilization. Real interest rates would fall if a more credible stabilization strategy were to take hold.

The greatest change in strategy should come in institutional measures to augment credibility. Recent stabilization programs around the world—in Bolivia in 1985, Israel in 1985, Mexico in 1987, Poland in 1990, Argentina in 1991, Estonia in 1992, and Brazil in 1994—have demonstrated that central bank independence and early pegging of the exchange rate are two of the most important methods of building expectations of low inflation and thereby of lowering V and $\dot{V}/V$ in support of the stabilization program. We have seen that a pegged exchange rate can be an important nominal anchor in bolstering the low-inflation equilibrium in an environment with multiple equilibriums.

Conclusion

Russia is in a deep state of crisis that could send the country into a spiral of self-reinforcing destructive behaviors: criminality, regional separatism, tax evasion, and flight from the currency. To overcome these risks, the government should embark on a policy of rapid stabilization, backstopped by substantial Western assistance. This is a feasible course. Sadly, the Western aid effort has fallen far short of real need—in speed, direction, and magnitude.

The concerns raised in this article apply not only to Russia. The current methods of delivering aid are typically too slow for weak states in acute financial crisis and too oblivious of the risks of a "contagion" of state collapse. Exceptions occur, usually when one of the leading nations takes on the effort of support mostly by itself (the U.S. support of Mexican stabilization, for example). More than half the countries of the former Soviet Union were in hyperinflation in 1993; none received the kind of financial support, or even advice, from the international community that was needed under the circumstances. Throughout the world weak, newly democratic states are grappling with an inheritance of high indebtedness and failing public institutions. These countries can overcome their bitter inheritance, but only if the world community responds with urgency and support.

Appendix. International Assistance to Russia, 1993–94

Western aid to Russia has failed to support budget financing or currency stabilization. The bulk of the $23 billion in Western financial aid to Russia during 1992 and 1993 was in the form of export credits, of the wasteful sort discussed in the text (appendix table A.1). Some $2 billion was in the form of grants from other governments, including outlays for technical assistance, and $3 billion was from international financial institutions.

Perhaps $2.5 billion of total assistance can be considered budgetary financing: $1.0 billion from the IMF, $0.5 billion from the World Bank, and about $1.0 billion of grant support. The rest of the IMF money was not available for budgetary support since it was programmed to be held as foreign exchange reserves. Most of the remaining grant money did not provide budgetary financing, since it was paid directly to Western consulting firms or provided in the form of foodstuffs and medicine delivered to various end users without raising counterpart funds for the central government.

The West also provided some measure of debt relief, but in a remarkably desultory and disorganized manner. In November 1991 the G-7 countries insisted that Russia and the other republics adopt a memorandum of understanding committing

Table A.1 *Official Financial Assistance to Russia, 1992–93*
(billions of U.S. dollars)

	1992		*1993*		*1992–93*	
Assistance	*Announced*	*Delivered*	*Announced*	*Delivered*	*Announced*	*Delivered*
IMF	9.0	1.0	13.0	1.5	14.0	2.5
World Bank and EBRD	1.5	0	5.0	0.5	5.0	0.5
Bilateral[a]	13.5	14.0	10.0	6.0	21.0	20.0
Export credits		12.5		5.5		18.0
Grants		1.5		0.5		2.0
Total	24.0	15.0	28.0	8.0	40.0	23.0
Memorandum items						
Aid from international agencies	10.5	1.0	18.0	2.0	19.0	3.0
Budgetary support[b]		0.5		2.0		2.5

a. Includes $2.5 billion of promised relief on interest payments that was not formally granted in 1992.
b. Estimate of aid directly in support of budgetary financing, not counting debt rescheduling (see text).
Source: Based on IMF press release, February 1, 1994, with author's estimates of "budgetary support."

them to two unrealistic and unworkable policies: continued servicing of interest and short-term debt and "joint and several" responsibility for the Soviet Union's foreign debt. The Russian government lacked the reserves to continue debt servicing past January 1992 and fell into default on its foreign debt. Debt rescheduling negotiations dragged on for more than a year in the Paris Club, until agreement was finally reached in June 1993, eighteen months after the onset of default. Negotiations with commercial bank creditors and various suppliers extended into 1994 without resolution. In the interim, Russia was subjected to various harassing lawsuits and continued in legal limbo. The "joint and several" clause also proved to be politically and legally untenable. After a year of internal wrangling, it was replaced by a "zero option," whereby Russia took over all Soviet debts and foreign assets.

The final component of the financial aid package was the long-discussed ruble stabilization fund. The IMF maintained unwaveringly throughout 1992 and 1993 that such a fund should be implemented only after Russia achieved several months of low inflation!

It is sobering to compare the treatment Russia received and the treatment received by Macy's Department Stores, which by coincidence filed for Chapter 11 relief in January 1992, the same month that Russia fell into default on its obligations. By law, Macy's was afforded a complete and automatic standstill on debt servicing on the day of its filing. Two weeks later Macy's obtained a $600 million debtor-in-possession loan to secure working capital for continued operations. It took Russia eighteen months to receive a partial standstill on debt servicing (though Russia was in default during the intervening period) and roughly the same period of time to receive actual disbursements on a $600 million working capital loan from the World Bank.

Notes

1. While this article focuses mainly on stabilization, "shock therapy" has come to mean the combination of rapid stabilization, liberalization, and privatization. In fact, as stressed in Sachs (1990, 1993, 1994a) and Lipton and Sachs (1990), all of these components are mutually reinforcing.

2. On the other hand, the war in Chechnya at the end of 1994 points to grave risks in the nascent democratic institutions.

3. The $50 billion aid package to Mexico in January 1995 was argued for along similar lines.

4. Formally, we treat the production of an individual firm as an increasing function of the level of the public good provided by the state. Production by firm i is given as $q_i = q + ag$ for tax-paying firms and $q_i = q$ for tax-evading firms. We also suppose that the level of public goods g is given by nt, where t is the level of taxation per firm and n is the number of firms paying taxes.

In these circumstances multiple equilibriums can easily arise. We assume that $1 < 1/a < N$. The firm's after-tax income is $q + ag - t$ if the firm pays its taxes and simply q if the firm evades its taxes. The firm's decision is straightforward. It should evade taxes as long as $t > ag = ant$, or as long as $n < 1/a$. If $n = 1$ (all other firms are evading taxes), then the Nth firm should evade taxes as well, since $1 < 1/a$ by assumption. If $n = N$, then the Nth firm should pay its taxes, since $N > 1/a$ by assumption. For related models of tax evasion with multiple equilibriums, see Pyle (1989) and Cowell (1990).

5. As in endnote 4, let g equal the level of the public good and assume that $g = nt$, where n is now the number of federal regions remitting their taxes and t is the (fixed) tax levy per region. Suppose that a noncompliant governor will be punished only if the federal government remains intact until the end of the fiscal year. If the federal president is toppled, then the tax-retaining regional governor escapes punishment. Let P be the probability of survival of the federal government and assume that P is a rising function of the level of the public good g that the Federal government provides:

$$P = ag \quad g < 1/a$$
$$= 1 \quad g > 1/a.$$

Since $g = nt$, we have

$$P = ant \quad n < 1/at$$
$$= 1 \quad n > 1/at$$

Suppose, further, that the regions receive the benefits of g whether they pay taxes or not. That would be the case, for example, for defense spending, federal pension benefits of retirees in the region, or federal unemployment compensation. Let c be the size of the penalty in case the region is in fact punished, with $c > t$. The regional governor's calculation is straightforward. The expected benefit of tax withholding is $t - Pc$. Then, for certain relative values of a, c, and t, it is easy to check that there are two equilibriums: a "good" equilibrium in which every region pays taxes and a "bad" equilibrium in which every region withholds taxes and the federal government collapses.

6. Suppose that there is a sovereign debt burden D that is greater than the current capacity to repay. Formally, $D > q_0$. There are N possible new creditors that can each lend an amount f at interest rate r that can be used for profitable investment in the country. The marginal product of investment is $1 + \mu > 1 + r$. If there are n investors, total new investment is nf, and national income next period is:

$$q = q_0 + (\mu - r)\, nf.$$

Assume that if *all* potential investors invest, there will be enough national income to repay the existing debt:

$$q_0 + (\mu - r)\, Nf > d$$

On the other hand, if there is not enough investment to repay the old debts d, the output gets divided among the old creditors, and the new creditors get nothing.

These ingredients deliver the possibility of an investor panic. If N–1 investors make an investment, the Nth investor can also safely invest. On the other hand, if N–1 investors fail to invest, the Nth investor also will, since the returns on the Nth investment would merely be divided among prior creditors. There must be a sufficiently "big push" among foreign investors to make it possible to overcome an existing overhang of debt. Alternatively, new potential investors must be given priority in repayment, as is standard in bankruptcy cases. See Sachs (1984) for an earlier treatment of creditor panic.

7. Indeed, for almost two years the World Bank resisted the granting of seniority to new oil-sector loans to Russia, to be arranged by the U.S. Eximbank, by refusing to waive the traditional "negative pledge clause" on World Bank loans to the Russian Government.

8. As in the case of Mexico in January 1995.

9. In Mexico in January 1995, international backstopping was needed to prevent a default by the Mexican Government in advance of any long-term policy changes.

10. We must stress that the monetary data for Russia are imprecise and have been revised repeatedly in the past two years. It is possible that they will be revised again when the Russian Central Bank finally undertakes a rigorous and serious overhaul of its statistical operations.

11. The data in table 1 almost surely understate the extent of credit financing of the deficit during 1992–94, since there was probably an especially large amount of financing through arrears at the end of 1993, when the largest part of the year's budget deficit is recorded. *Russian Economic Trends* (vol. 3, no. 1, p. 12) reports that 82 percent of the budgetary shortfall in the first quarter of 1994 was financed by central bank credit. It should be stressed, once again, that the budgetary and monetary data are somewhat murky with regard to timing, cash versus accrual accounting, and so forth, so that it is difficult to be precise about the components of budgetary financing during short intervals of time.

12. Monetary policy was again relaxed in the second half of 1994.

13. Consider a simple illustration. Suppose that velocity is 1 and constant. Suppose that enterprises hold three-fourths of the money supply and households hold one-fourth. Suppose that the budget deficit is 10 percent of GDP and is completely money financed. Initially, inflation is 10 percent a month. Enterprises bear an inflation tax of 7.5 percent of GDP, and households bear an inflation tax of 2.5 percent of GDP. Now suppose that the central bank gives cheap credits to the enterprises to compensate them completely for the inflation tax. Now only the household sector bears the inflation tax. Inflation must rise to 40 percent a month. Enterprises receive a flow of credits worth 30 percent of GDP and pay an inflation tax of 30 percent of GDP, so that they bear no net inflation tax. Households bear an inflation tax of 10 percent of GDP.

14. In the second half of 1992 the dollar value of Russian GDP was approximately $80 billion a year at the prevailing market exchange rate. Monetary financing of 11 to 12 percent of GDP amounted to around $10 billion a year at the prevailing real exchange rate. If Western financial assistance directly to the Russian budget had been more than $10 billion, it would have covered the entire monetary financing at the prevailing real exchange rate. Of course, we should take into account the fact that substantial assistance would have led to a significant real appreciation of the then hugely undervalued currency (the ruble would have stabilized while Russian domestic prices would have continued to rise). Even if GDP measured in dollars had doubled, however, Western assistance to the Russian budget on the order of $15 billion in 1992 would have covered three-fourths of the monetary finance.

15. The most obvious counterpart of increased velocity is holdings of dollar deposits in the Russian banking system. These deposits have risen from $1.5 billion in February 1992 to $12 billion in November 1993, or from 28 percent of ruble deposits in February 1992 to 75 percent in November 1993. These dollar accounts do not carry reserve requirements and so are tantamount to a legal flight from the currency. In addition, there are several billion dollars of U.S. currency circulating in Russia, as well as an estimated $10–30 billion in dollar deposits held illegally in offshore banks.

16. Western donors are also interested in promoting democratization and rule of law. The war in Chechnya jeopardizes both the fiscal and political conditions of aid.

17. There is also considerable scope for important fiscal reforms within these overall deficit parameters. Existing subsidies to industry should be cut by some 4 percent of GDP, with the expenditure savings used to augment spending on social programs. In addition, tax reform should aim to lower marginal tax rates on corporate and personal income and to compensate for lost tax revenues by eliminating exemptions to the value added tax.

References

Alexashenko, S. 1993. "The Collapse of the Soviet Fiscal System: What Should be Done?" In P. Sutela, ed., *The Russian Economy in Crisis and Transition.* Helsinki: Bank of Finland.

Åslund, Anders, ed. 1994. *Economic Transformation in Russia.* London: Pinter Publishing.

Åslund, Anders, and Richard Layard, eds. 1993. *Changing the Economic System in Russia.* London: Pinter Publishers.

Been-Lon Chen, and C. C. Yang. 1994. "Avoidance, Micromotives and Macrobehavior: A Dynamic Model of Crime and Punishment." Institute of Economics, Academia Sinica, Taiwan (China).

Boone, P. Forthcoming. "Why Prices Rose So High: Collapsing Monetary Bubbles in Formerly Socialist Economies." Centre for Economic Performance Discussion Paper. London: London School of Economics.

Boycko, M., A. Shleifer, and R. Vishny. 1993. "Privatizing Russia." *Brookings Papers on Economic Activity* 2. Washington, D.C.: The Brookings Institution.

Bruno, Michael. 1993. *Crisis, Stabilization, and Economic Reform.* Oxford: Clarendon Press.

Bruno, Michael, and Stanley Fischer. 1990. "Seigniorage, Operating Rules, and the High Inflation Trap." *Quarterly Journal of Economics* (May): 353–74.

Calvo, Guillermo. 1988. "Servicing the Public Debt: The Role of Expectations." *American Economic Review* 78 (4): 647–61.

———. 1989. "Incredible Reforms." In Guillermo Calvo, Ronald Findlay, Pentti Kouri, and Jorge Bragade Macedo, eds., *Debt, Stabilization, and Development.* Oxford: Basil Blackwell.

Cowell, Frank. 1990. *Cheating the Government: The Economics of Evasion.* Cambridge, Mass.: MIT Press.

Dornbusch, Rudiger. 1992. "Monetary Problems of Post-Communism: Lessons from the End of the Austro-Hungarian Empire." *Weltwirtschaftliches Archiv* 128 (3): 391–424.

Easterly, William, and Paulo Vieira Da Cunha. 1994. "Financing the Storm: Macroeconomic Crisis in Russia, 1992–93." Policy Research Working Paper 1240. World Bank, Macroeconomics and Growth Division and Europe and Central Asia Country Operations Division II, Washington, D.C.

Fischer, Stanley. 1994. "Prospects for Russian Stabilization in the Summer of 1993." In Anders Åslund and Richard Layard, eds., *Changing the Economic System in Russia.* London: Pinter Publishers.

Havrylyshyn, O., and J. Williamson. 1991. *From Soviet Disunion to Eastern Economic Community.* Policy Analysis in International Economics 35. Washington, D.C.: Institute of International Economics.

IMF (International Monetary Fund). 1994. *International Finance Statistics.* Washington, D.C.

Isaacson, Walter, and Evan Thomas. 1986. *The Wise Men: Six Friends and the World They Made.* Boston: Faber and Faber.

Krugman, Paul. 1991. "History versus Expectations." *Quarterly Journal of Economics* 106: 651–57.

Lipton, David, and Jeffrey Sachs. 1990. "Creating a Market Economy in Eastern Europe: The Case of Poland." *Brookings Papers on Economic Activity* 1. Washington, D.C.: The Brookings Institution.

———. 1992. "Prospects for Russia's Economic Reforms." *Brookings Papers on Economic Activity* 2. Washington, D.C.: The Brookings Institution.

Matsuyama, K. 1991. "Increasing Returns, Industrialization and Indeterminacy of Equilibria." *Quarterly Journal of Economics* 106: 617–50.

———. 1992. "A Simple Model of Sectoral Adjustment." *Review of Economic Studies* 59: 375–88.

Mlynarksi, Feliks. 1926. *The International Significance of the Depreciation of the Zloty in 1925.* Warsaw: The Polish Economist.

Obstfeld, Maurice. 1986. "Rational and Self-Fulfilling Balance of Payments Crises." *American Economic Review* 76 (1): 72–81.

———. 1994. "The Logic of Currency Crises." Working Paper 4640. National Bureau of Economic Research, Cambridge, Mass.

Pleskovic, Boris, and Jeffrey Sachs. 1994. "Political Independence and Economic Reform in Slovenia." In O. Blanchard, K. Froot, and J. Sachs, eds., *The Transition in Eastern Europe.* Vol. 1, *Country Studies.* Chicago: National Bureau of Economic Research and the University of Chicago Press.

Pyle, David. 1989. *Tax Evasion and the Black Economy.* London: MacMillan.

Rostowski, J. 1993. "The Inter-Enterprise Debt Explosion in the Former Soviet Union: Causes, Consequences, and Cures." *Economic Transformation and Communist Economies* 5: 131–56.

———. 1994. "Dilemmas of Monetary and Financial Policy in Post-Stabilization Russia." In Anders Åslund, ed., *Economic Transformation in Russia.* London: Pinter Publishers.

Russian Economic Trends. Volumes 1–3, 1992–94. London: Whurr Publishers.

Sachs, Jeffrey. 1984. "Theoretical Issues in International Borrowing." Princeton Studies in International Finance 54. Princeton University, Princeton, N.J.

———. 1990. "Eastern Europe's Economies—What is to be Done?" *The Economist.* January 13, 1990.

———. 1993. *Poland's Jump to the Market Economy.* Cambridge, Mass: MIT Press.

———. 1994a. "The Case for Shock Therapy." Social Market Foundation, London.

———. 1994b. "Life in the Economic Emergency Room." In John Williamson, ed., *Political Economy of Policy Reform.* Washington, D.C.: Institute for International Economics.

——— 1994c. "Prospects for Monetary Stabilization in Russia." In Anders Åslund, ed., *Economic Transformation in Russia.* London: Pinter Publishers.

Sachs, Jeffrey, and David Lipton. 1993. "Remaining Steps to a Market-Based Monetary System in Russia." In Anders Åslund and Richard Layard, eds., *Changing the Economic System in Russia.* London: Pinter Publishers.

Sah, Raaj K. 1991. "Social Osmosis and Patterns of Crime." *Journal of Political Economy* 99 (6): 1272–95.

Sargent, T., and N. Wallace. 1981. "Some Unpleasant Monetarist Arithmetic." *Federal Reserve Bank of Minneapolis Quarterly Review* 5: 1–17.

Schacht, Hjalmar. 1956. *Confessions of the "Old Wizard."* Cambridge: Houghton Mifflin.

Temin, Peter. 1991. "Soviet and Nazi Planning in the 1930s." *Economic History Review* 44: 573–93.

Wills, Garry. 1994. "What Makes a Good Leader?" *The Atlantic Monthly* (April): 63–80

Comment on "Russia's Struggle with Stabilization: Conceptual Issues and Evidence," by Sachs

John Williamson

In the nearly five years since he achieved fame as the leading economic adviser to governments seeking to make the transition from a command to a market economy, Jeffrey Sachs has become identified with two propositions:

- That stabilization should be pursued with a big bang.
- That stabilization should be supported by extensive aid from the West.

This article provides a far more persuasive rationalization of his position on both issues than any of his previous writing with which I am familiar. I hope that it will advance the debate in a more constructive direction than some of the recent bitter exchanges.

The first innovation is the development of what I think it is fair to term a theory of state collapse. Sachs draws attention to a series of dimensions in which an inability of the state to perform its core functions erodes the normal incentive of private actors to support the state. The system gets locked into a "bad" equilibrium in which the state is unable to finance itself and to provide basic public goods instead of the usual "good" equilibrium. Sachs identifies five cases of this phenomenon:

- In normal times firms pay taxes so as to enjoy the advantages of legality; destroy the ability of the state to provide law and order, and they will join the black economy, further eroding the solvency of the state.
- In normal times potential criminals fear being caught and most therefore refrain from crime; stretch the state's law-enforcement capacity so thinly that the fear vanishes, and the number of criminals escalates, further reducing the chances of detection.
- In normal times subnational units of government pay their tax obligations to the federal government; curb the ability of the center to punish withholding, and revenues will erode, further undermining the feasibility of punishment.
- In normal times governments service their sovereign debts largely by new borrowing; interrupt the flow of new loans, and the ensuing debt-servicing difficulties will persuade creditors that they were right to stop lending.
- In normal times domestic agents hold most of their money balances in domestic assets; make the inflation tax sufficiently high, and agents will economize on

John Williamson is senior fellow at the Institute for International Economics. The comment has not been updated to reflect the update of Sachs's article.

Proceedings of the World Bank Annual Conference on Development Economics 1994

money balances to the point where much faster inflation is needed to yield the same seigniorage.

To this list I would add one further example (or generalization of his last point).

- In normal times domestic agents prefer to hold most of their assets at home; threaten those assets with abnormal risks caused by the financial incapacity of the state, and capital flight will ensue. The capital flight might leave the government with no alternative but to undertake the very expropriation the fear of which motivated agents to transfer their funds abroad.

Once again we have the phenomenon diagnosed by Sachs of the widespread fear that the state is incapable of fulfilling its core functions in a normal way intensifying that inability and thus locking in the state collapse.

Sachs argues that these manifestations of a collapsing state can originate from, as well as perpetuate, extreme disarray in state finances. The origins of Russia's travails are thus to be found in the abandonment of fiscal probity during the Gorbachev years.

Even in advance of the profusion of formal theoretical models and econometric testing that economists will surely be quick to direct at such a suggestive hypothesis, I have to say that I find this theory persuasive. It sheds new light on Sachs's two central policy recommendations of a big bang supported by big bucks from abroad.

Consider for a moment the problem that Sachs has so often confronted of what advice to give a government whose state has collapsed (see also Sachs 1994). One always has to say in such a situation that there is no way of avoiding the need to get the fundamentals right: balance the budget, limit credit, make the real interest rate positive, set a competitive exchange rate, avoid excess demand. Unfortunately, the only theory that gives us much reason to suppose that such measures will lead to a prompt revival of confidence is one that assumes that the public has a full understanding of the situation (rational expectations), which seems a bold assumption in the presence of a collapsing state.

But then we may recall that in many of the spectacularly successful reversals of state collapse—in Schacht's stabilization of Germany in 1923 or Erhard's liberalization in 1948, or Bruno's stabilization of Israel in 1985, or Balcerowicz's reform in Poland in 1990, or Estonia's impressive stabilization in 1992—other things happened as well. Germany in 1923 got a new currency backed by the land of Germany. Monetary reform accompanied Erhard's liberalization as well. Israel got a fixed exchange rate backed by a stabilization fund, Poland got that and convertibility, and Estonia got a currency board. Hence many of us have cast around for some dramatic step that can accompany the act of setting the fundamentals straight, even though we have lacked a theory that told us why that might be a good idea.

I believe that the Sachs's theory of state collapse fills that lacuna. Society has been driven to the bad equilibrium by the inability of the state to fulfill its core functions, and life without public goods turns out to be a Hobbesian jungle rather than a supply-sider's paradise. The public wants to believe that it is possible to return to normality. So if a political leader commits himself to a rule that is simple to understand and to monitor, and is able to show that he can abide by it, he has a good chance of convincing the public that it is in their interest to gamble on the good equilibrium being reestablished. If a sizable portion of the public is convinced, then confidence returns and stabilization is achieved, at least temporarily. The experience of many stabilization programs suggests that this first phase is often remarkably easy. Pegged exchange rates, monetary reforms, Brady deals, currency boards, and even price freezes (the Austral and Cruzado plans) have all enjoyed early success.

That success will, of course, be consolidated only if the fundamentals have indeed been fixed. If it turns out that an inflation tax is still needed, or that corrective or inertial inflation leads to chronic overvaluation of a fixed exchange rate that was supposed to provide a nominal anchor, or that the external debt burden has not been alleviated enough to make the external payments position viable, or that excess demand is allowed to develop when prices are being held down by a freeze, then the program will fail. And experience indicates that next time round it will be more difficult to win initial acceptance of a stabilization.

Hence we have two key questions in deciding whether Russia had or has a sporting chance to stabilize. The first concerns the choice of a transparent and easily monitored commitment that promises a dramatic break with the inflationary past and thus offers the best chance of shocking the economy back from the bad equilibrium to the good equilibrium. The second is how close Russia was and is to fixing the fundamentals.

I believe that in late 1991 the logical candidate for the first role would have been a general price liberalization (such as occurred) complemented by monetary reform designed to eliminate the monetary overhang and so to avoid the need for it to be inflated away by the price explosion of January 1992. This course would have been particularly attractive because the excess money balances could have been funded into vouchers instead of expropriated. It is true that Pavlov's monetary reform of early 1991 had created something of a psychological block, but it would have been better to confront that than to expropriate the public's savings through inflation.

Such monetary reform would have been preferable to fixing the exchange rate for several reasons. One is that the black market rate was at that time so weak that any fixed rate that one could have been confident of holding in the market would have acted as an engine of inflation. Another reason is that fixing the exchange rate depended on the willingness of the G-7 countries to provide a stabilization fund, whereas the main interest of the G-7 in the former Soviet Union at that time seemed to be getting their past loans jointly and severally guaranteed. A third reason is the argument developed in the Balcerowicz and Gelb article (see preceding article in this volume) that an exchange rate peg is useful where the problem is one of open inflation rather than of shortages.

Once the monetary overhang had been inflated away, however, the case for monetary reform vanished. Sachs's solution of a fixed exchange rate then seems sensible for two reasons. The first is his argument that, provided that there is foreign help in endowing a stabilization fund, a fixed exchange rate is something that the government can deliver in the short run and thus start building confidence. The second is that there is evidence that an exchange rate anchor performs better than a monetary anchor—evidence for which Sachs's theory provides a better explanation than was previously available (Bruno 1993; Kiguel and Liviatan 1994). I must add that I am delighted that Sachs now recognizes that using the exchange rate to provide a temporary anchor during the initial stabilization need not preclude a decision to resort to a crawling peg after a few months to safeguard the stabilization against the threat of a growing overvaluation.

The second question is how close Russia was and is to fixing the fundamentals, which in the Russian context means primarily limiting monetary expansion, which in turn requires fixing the budget deficit. Sachs argues that many of us (notably the International Monetary Fund) have been mistaken in taking the published figures at face value. An important part of the monetary emission in 1992 reflected the delay in breaking up the ruble zone. An important part of the measured budget deficit came by including the "import subsidies" on the commodity aid misguidedly provided by Western governments too cowardly to ask their legislatures for honest aid appropriations and seeking instead to salve their consciences while pandering to their export lobbies. And most interesting—this is the second innovation in the article—Sachs argues that most of the credits granted to enterprises have been compensation for the inflation tax rather than an independent source of monetary emission. This is not the first time that it has been argued (with good reason) that under certain institutional arrangements monetary growth was in substantial part endogenous. The implication is that the task of reducing monetary emission is substantially less difficult than appears from the crude figures.

Sachs's proposed program involves financing almost half of the Russian budget deficit of 9 percent of GDP with foreign aid, this being the second of the two ways in which he sees foreign help as being crucial to successful stabilization. The big questions are whether he is right in arguing that a $6 billion stabilization fund plus $14 billion in foreign financing of the budget deficit (provided in real money,[1] not in commodity aid or technical assistance for Western consultants) would enable the government to implement Fedorov's program, and whether successful implementation of that program would cause fiscal revenue to recover promptly as hypothesized by Sachs's theory of state collapse.

I am not prepared to give a dogmatic answer to these questions. I worry, for example, that 9 percent of GDP is an awfully large budget deficit on which to base a stabilization program. I worry that if credits to enterprises were largely a consequence rather than a cause of inflation, one would be unlikely to find inflation lagging three months behind monetary emissions. I worry also that Fedorov does not seem to have great confidence that the government is committed to faithful execution of his program. And I do not think Sachs's justification of Western aid as necessary to induce a jump back to the good equilibrium is consistent with his desire to see aid flows decreasing only gradually over the next five years.

Nevertheless, this article, notably the theory of state collapse that it develops, does make me more inclined to believe that Sachs is right than I was a few months ago, before I had seen the analysis behind his policy recommendations. If we could be transported back to that golden age when the leading reformers were in office, I would be prepared to gamble on his being right. But bygones are bygones, and the reformers have lost influence. Does it make sense to do now what we did not do then? There is an obvious danger that sending a big aid package now will convey the message that the West can be intimidated into generosity: if the loss of Fedorov can produce billions a year in aid plus a stabilization fund, what could be expected by putting Zhirinovsky in office? On the other hand, the benefits of successful stabilization would be so far-reaching that the overwhelming questions are whether the current government is really dedicated to—and capable of—implementing the program that Fedorov set in motion and whether that program was adequate.

Lest readers draw the conclusion that I have lost my critical faculties, let me acknowledge that there are many points on which I disagree with Sachs. I believe he has at times done a disservice to the cause of reform by overshadowing the local reformers with whom he has worked. He got involved in an argument about the size of aid flows when the real complaint concerned the issues of composition and timing he exposes in this article. His attachment to the virtues of big bangs in the abstract sometimes comes at the neglect of the details of the situation in which a country finds itself and the content of the package that is to provide shock therapy. I think he focuses too much on the mistakes made in 1991–92: I agree that they were awful, but bygones are bygones, and those issues should now be set aside until he writes his memoirs. His complaints about the IMF sometimes give aid and comfort to its populist critics.

But one criticism I dissociate myself from: the charge that his advice has been responsible for a catastrophic decline in output. This is not because I doubt the reality of the hardships that have been suffered—the demographic disaster that has afflicted all the economies of Eastern and Central Europe, with the exception of the Czech Republic, leaves no room to doubt that reality (*The Economist,* April 23, 1994). Rather, the evidence is that those countries that have sought a softer path to transition, notably Romania and Ukraine, have suffered an even more catastrophic fall in output. Perhaps we should instead seek common factors between those economies in transition that have not suffered a demographic disaster, namely China and the Czech Republic. Their most obvious common feature is that they did not start the transition in macroeconomic disarray, which suggests that Sachs is correct in his diagnosis of the source of Russia's ills. The policy implication is obvious, though unfortunately it is too late for Russia to profit from it.

Note

1. Sachs suggests that this could be provided by Western governments buying Russian bonds. A variant would be for Western governments to underwrite the issue of Russian bonds.

References

Bruno, Michael. 1993. *Crisis, Stabilization, and Economic Reform.* Oxford: Clarendon Press.

Kiguel, M., and N. Liviatan. 1994. "Exchange Rate–Based Stabilizations in Argentina and Chile: A Fresh Look." Policy Research Working Paper 1318. World Bank, Office of the Vice President, Development Economics, Washington, D.C.

"Living, and Dying, in a Barren Land." 1994. *The Economist.* April 23, p. 54.

Sachs, Jeffrey. 1994. "Life in the Economic Emergency Room." In J. Williamson, ed., *The Political Economy of Policy Reform.* Washington, D.C.: Institute for International Economics.

Comment on "Russia's Struggle with Stabilization: Conceptual Issues and Evidence," by Sachs

Maxim Boycko

I have to start with an explicit disclaimer that the comments here represent my own views and do not represent the views of the Russian government, the State Committee of the Russian Federation on State Property Management, or the Russian Privatization Center.

Jeffrey Sachs has written a stimulating article about stabilization in Russia. The article tries to do four things: it provides a conceptual framework and a formal model of high inflation that is assumed to be relevant to Russia, it gives an overview of monetary conditions in Russia since the late 1980s with particular emphasis on 1992 and 1993, it provides an account of the history of foreign aid to support Russian stabilization, and it outlines a strategy for foreign aid to Russia.

My comments focus mostly on an analysis of the Sachs model and its policy implications, including implications for foreign aid. I find the model to be especially interesting because it helps explain the rationale behind a particular approach to foreign aid to Russia that Sachs has been advocating since 1992 (see, for example, Sachs 1994). I will contrast the Sachs model with an alternative.

The Sachs model starts by assuming that Russia runs a large, but not extremely large, real budget deficit that is financed by money creation. Firms in the economy hold real money balances m and are subject to an inflation tax equal to the rate of inflation π. The deficit is equal to the inflation tax collected, πm.

There is a simple multiple equilibrium story going on in the model. At the macroeconomic level the same amount of real deficit can be sustained in a high-inflation equilibrium when π is high and m is low or in a low-inflation equilibrium when π is low and m is high. At the microeconomic level this story corresponds to rational individual firm behavior: firms prefer to hold high real money balances when inflation is low and low real money balances when inflation is high.

In the Sachs model high inflation is simply a result of bad history and bad expectations that pushed the economy into a bad equilibrium. To stabilize, this economy simply has to move back into a good equilibrium. To achieve this the country does not really need to cut the deficit or change other fundamentals: a change in expecta-

Maxim Boycko is chief executive officer at the Russian Privatization Center, Moscow. The comment has not been updated to reflect the update of Sachs's article.

Proceedings of the World Bank Annual Conference on Development Economics 1994

tions would suffice. And changing expectations requires first and foremost will, leadership, and commitment from the government. Sachs cites numerous historical episodes in which successful stabilizations are attributed to strong political leadership.

In this setting foreign aid turns out to be remarkably effective and efficient. If foreign aid institutions credibly commit to providing sufficient external resources to stabilize the economy, say in the form of direct budget support to the government, nothing else is needed: expectations would change and the economy would indeed stabilize. Moreover, very little money actually needs to be spent over the transition since in the new low-inflation equilibrium the real budget deficit remains unchanged. In the limiting case a mere announcement of an aid package produces stabilization, and not a single dollar needs to be spent! The advice to Western governments is straightforward: come out with enough money, the economy will stabilize, and at the end of the day little of the money will actually be used. (One is tempted to speculate whether the West was indeed trying to test this theory a couple of times in 1992 and 1993 by announcing large aid packages to Russia and delivering very little. Contrary to the theoretical prediction, however, stabilization did not quite happen.)

The Sachs model thus calls for the following strategy to stabilize Russia: the government should attempt to stabilize immediately; it should come out with a plan to cut money growth that should envisage a modest reduction of the real deficit and a rather large inflow of foreign aid to substitute for money creation. Based on this plan the West should come out with the large-scale aid required. This aid is needed on a transitional basis only. Once the economy moves to the good equilibrium, the same amount of deficit financing would be sustainable without external aid. This is essentially the strategy that Sachs has been consistently recommending to the Russian government and the West over the past couple of years.

Although the Sachs model is nice and elegant and undoubtedly tells us an important story about many historical stabilizations, I have strong doubts that this is the right model to have in mind when thinking about stabilization in Russia. I find it difficult to portray today's Russia as a fundamentally sound economy, with a bearable budget deficit, that just happens to be in a bad equilibrium because of a bad history and current widespread pessimism. I believe that there is much more to stabilizing the Russian economy than simply jumping out of a bad equilibrium and landing in a good one.

An alternative model of Russian inflation might start with the more conventional assumption that sustainable stabilization in Russia is not possible without a permanent reduction of the real budget deficit. This reduction, however, is very difficult to achieve or, more precisely, entails very high political costs for the government.

There are a number of structural characteristics of the Russian economy and the political system that make it particularly difficult for the government to cut public spending. Let me provide a few examples.

First, historically, the government has always played a very large redistributive role by allocating subsidies and cheap credits to industries and regions. This redistribution never occurred through a transparent budgetary process but was always a result of bargaining with and lobbying by various industries and regions on a case-by-case basis. The structure of the government makes it extremely susceptible to lobbyists' pressures. It is difficult for government officials to withstand these pressures since many of them are nominees of these lobbying groups or report to such nominees.

I am surprised by Sachs's argument that cutting credits to industry would not be that difficult because real credits net of the inflation tax were low, so that the same net transfers to industry could have been achieved with 3 percent of GDP and zero inflation. The essence of these credits is redistribution by the government. They are by no means equivalent to net transfers. Money is collected from all enterprises and redistributed to the chosen few, and this redistribution cannot be achieved without inflation. Thus it is misleading to assume that cutting inflation while maintaining the same net transfers to industry is a politically painless exercise.

Another reason why cutting the deficit is so difficult in Russia is that the social safety net is underdeveloped and would be unable to cope with the high unemployment that is likely to result from stabilization. Many of the social services (housing, child care, medical care) are provided by enterprises. When credits are tightened, the enterprises cut social expenditures first to strengthen their bargaining position with the government. Thus a reduction in cheap state credits brings about a reduction in social spending, with maximum political costs to the government.

Yet another problem for stabilization is the underdeveloped political system. So far the system seems incapable of concentrating and transforming public frustration with constantly raising prices into a clear stabilization mandate. Public opinion polls taken at the end of 1993 clearly indicated that inflation was perceived as the number one problem by a vast majority of the population. Yet not a single politician ran on an anti-inflation platform.

The alternative model yields very different policy advice to the Russian government. It recognizes that immediate stabilization, even if economically desirable, may not be politically feasible. Russia may first need structural reform in a high (but not hyper) inflationary environment that will significantly lower the political costs to the government of a reduction in the budget deficit before real stabilization is attempted. The fundamental elements of the structural reform would be tax reform, mass privatization to separate enterprises from the state, reallocation of social assets from enterprises to local governments, and overall strengthening of the social safety net, especially unemployment insurance. Equally important is the political reform that would make the government more accountable to a public that is fed up with inflation rather than to special interest groups that are always hungry for subsidies.

In the alternative model foreign aid in the form of a large-scale stabilization package has much more limited power to stabilize the economy. It is quite possible that direct support to the budget may provide only temporary relief and that the slowdown in inflation would not be sustainable without constant new injections of aid money. In fact, there is a real risk that aid money would be wasted.

The alternative model calls for a completely different strategy of foreign aid to Russia. The strategy is to start by supporting structural reform, like mass privatization, development of a social safety net, and tax reform. Only after the critical mass of structural reform is reached and fiscal consolidation becomes politically feasible would large-scale stabilization assistance work.

Finally, the two models offer very different views of how costly delays in stabilization are. The Sachs model argues that when stabilization is delayed the risks of hyperinflation increase significantly because of growing tax evasion and increasing flight from the ruble. The alternative model suggests that when immediate stabilization is not feasible delays are inevitable and warranted provided that structural reform is moving fast enough.

The Sachs model leads one to conclude that 1993 was a lost year for Russia—or even worse—since only limited progress was made in stabilization with inflation staying at about 20 percent a month. The alternative model would acknowledge that Russia made remarkable progress during 1993 with privatization and some other structural reforms, thus laying the groundwork for future stabilization. I believe that the evident deceleration of inflation that occurred in the first half of 1994, with prices growing on average at about 10 percent a month, is more consistent with the latter view.

Reference

Sachs, Jeffrey. 1994. "Prospects for Monetary Stabilization in Russia." In Anders Åslund, ed., *Economic Transformation in Russia*. London: Pinter Publishers.

Floor Discussion of "Russia's Struggle with Stabilization: Conceptual Issues and Evidence," by Sachs

A participant from the World Bank asked if it was not dangerous to focus on budget support at a time when much of that support might be dissipated in inefficient enterprises. Should not some of the support focus on structural reform that cuts off subsidies to state-owned enterprises? Sachs protested that he had said repeatedly that roughly half of foreign aid to Russia should go to the budget and half to structural reform. It is not a question of one thing or the other; these things go hand in hand. Sachs said that he had been an early adviser on structural reform funds. The question now was, how do you get out of a mess? How do you break a vicious cycle and make good things happen? His advice to Russia had always been, move rapidly and radically. You do not postpone stabilization until everything is in place; you do not get better results from structural reform by holding back on stabilization. It is not just a matter of changing expectations, said Sachs: you have to change a process that can get out of control to one that can move toward a healthy, democratic, stable society. Healthy adjustments are made possible by the political integrity of the state and by the marketplace discipline that comes from successful stabilization. Russia is somewhere between the complete collapse in Ukraine and the real success in Poland because it is still somewhere short of being able to make this jump forward. Sachs's advice to Western institutions had been to support stabilization and structural reform as rapidly as possible. Insisting that Russia get everything right, and that stabilization can happen without large-scale budgetary support, will lead only to disappointment. Debating the past is not his point, said Sachs. We have missed opportunities, and we can debate how we missed them, but right now we face new risks and opportunities and that is what we should focus on.

Michael Bruno (chair) asked if Sachs thought stabilization had been possible in Russia at any time through the end of 1993. If so, was lack of foreign finance a key factor in Russia's failure to stabilize in those three years? Or was there another missing link? In Israel, Bruno said, the biggest fear was that foreign financing would come before a program was in place: until then, fixing the exchange rate or receiving foreign financing would not have helped. At least two of the panelists had spo-

This session was chaired by Michael Bruno, chief economist and vice president, Development Economics, at the World Bank.

Proceedings of the World Bank Annual Conference on Development Economics 1994

ken of the need for foreign aid for Russia, said a participant from the University of Pennsylvania, but one hears rumors that the government is not eager for foreign aid, especially aid for safety-net activities. Are these rumors accurate?

Agreeing with Sachs about the self-serving nature of some export credits, another participant asked what Sachs thought about export credits for equipment and supplies in the oil and transport industries, for which there was so much pent-up demand. A former World Bank economist asked if Sachs's model allowed for the world shortage of capital that World Bank President Lewis Preston had referred to earlier in the day. A participant from the IMF asked about the relationship between support and inflation.

To say that Russia does not want foreign aid is demonstrably false, responded Sachs. Prime ministers do not generally invite managing directors of the IMF to dinners in Moscow and to weekends at their hunting lodges simply for pleasant conversation. Someone sitting on top of a government that is collecting 5 percent of GNP in tax revenues wants foreign assistance. The IMF was assiduously courted for $1.5 billion in loans, with the possibility of more later. The IMF's decision to make this loan in the face of so much uncertainty and anxiety was a good one, which opens up an opportunity. To say, wait until Russia's 1995 budget is drafted to take the next step, is to defeat the momentum that has been created. This is the time to do something real, said Sachs, and real does not mean calculating a balance of payments gap and looking around for short-term export credits. It means providing both structural reform and budgetary support to allow the state to function in a noninflationary way. If that is not done, we can rationalize later about why the program did not work. If it is done, we can talk about how we helped to make it work.

A participant from Italy said he saw a link between the role of regional and republic governments and criminality, the underground economy, and tax evasion. One reason the federal government's tax revenues were so low, he said, was that the regional governments collected most taxes directly and the federal government did not have instruments to make them pay—except to delegate spending to the regional governments, but expenditures are not linked to regional tax compliance, so that is unfair. The participant felt that the Russian federal government should clarify relations between central and regional policies, considering how strong regional differences are. He wondered if Western and international organizations should be so liberal in financing the Russian economy before it improved tax compliance. In Italy's experience, he said, once people learn to evade taxes, they will continue to evade them.

Establishing Property Rights

Andrei Shleifer

Establishing secure property rights in transition economies amounts to solving two problems: inefficient structures of control rights over assets and poor contract enforcement. Politicians and bureaucrats still wield excessive control over assets, which results in inefficient underinvestment by entrepreneurs. Corruption is one way of getting around political control, but the drawbacks are considerable, particularly the limited enforceability of corruption contracts. More workable strategies for establishing property rights in transition economies are giving equity to the bureaucrats (and other parties that have control), reforming the civil service, and removing bureaucratic control rights through privatization. Russia's experience shows how privatization, combined with equity incentives for enterprise insiders, transfers control rights from the bureaucrats and stimulates political and economic pressures to protect private property rights.

Poorly defined property rights are blamed for many of the problems of developing countries and transition economies. But just what constitutes "poorly defined property rights" has eluded analysis. The classics of the property rights literature—Demsetz (1967), Alchian and Demsetz (1972), Jensen and Meckling (1976), North and Thomas (1973), North (1981), and Barzel (1989)—offer revealing historical and contemporary examples of the importance of well-defined property rights for efficient resource allocation and economic growth. But they are not very specific in describing poorly defined property rights or in explaining how to establish well-defined property rights.

Poorly defined property rights are usually discussed as a common pool problem: a resource gets overused because too many agents have the right to use it (North 1981; Ostrom 1990; Libecap 1989). In Eastern Europe, however, a major reason for inefficiency in the allocation of resources is that politicians and bureaucrats have excessive control rights over much of the economy, including the private economy. Establishing property rights is therefore to a large extent equivalent to reducing political control. This diagnosis of the problem is not new: many astute observers of

Andrei Shleifer is professor of economics at Harvard University. The author thanks Alberto Ades, Maxim Boycko, Cheryl Gray, Oliver Hart, Jonathan Hay, and Robert W. Vishny for helpful comments.

Proceedings of the World Bank Annual Conference on Development Economics 1994

Eastern Europe, such as Kornai (1992) and Frydman and Rapaczynski (1994), have reached the same conclusion.

Recent work by Grossman and Hart (1986) and Hart and Moore (1990), which associates property rights with residual control rights over assets, provides a framework for analyzing the problem of poorly defined property rights. Inefficient structures of control rights and poor enforcement of contracts are two aspects of the problem. Establishing property rights then means enforcing the contracts through which economic agents try to arrive at more efficient control structures themselves or finding ways to improve the efficiency of control rights directly.

From a Coasian analysis (Coase 1960) of the problem, the obvious strategy for getting around the inefficiencies resulting from political control of assets is corruption. (Coase's theorem asserts that, so long as there are no transaction costs, externalities will not prevent private agents from negotiating to the efficient outcome if physical control rights are protected as legal rights and if contracts are enforced; Cooter 1987.) If private entrepreneurs can bribe politicians, some of the undesirable effects of political control of assets can be undone. But because a corruption contract with a politician who promises not to interfere with the firm in exchange for a bribe is not enforceable, the usefulness of corruption for restoring efficiency is limited. Indeed, the difficulty of enforcing contracts of any kind in many reforming economies suggests that relying on contract enforcement may be a poor strategy for establishing property rights in the first stages of reform.

Three alternative strategies are also explored:

- Giving politicians equity ownership in an asset over which they have control rights, to reduce their incentive to expropriate the asset.
- Reforming the bureaucracy by providing bureaucrats with incentives for maximizing something closer to the public interest or by devaluing the control rights of the bureaucrats, usually through competition among them.
- Eliminating bureaucratic control through the political process, particularly through privatization, which reallocates control from bureaucrats to firm insiders (managers and workers) and outsiders (shareholders), with clear benefits for economic efficiency (Megginson, Nash, and van Randenborgh 1994; Mueller 1989).

Not surprisingly, however, in Eastern Europe and elsewhere privatization and devaluation of the control rights of bureaucrats face enormous opposition from the bureaucracy. Nor is wresting control rights from politicians the end. Getting the benefits of private property rights also means halting the stream of government handouts to firms, which in Eastern Europe is closely related to macroeconomic stabilization. Otherwise, even after control rights are taken away, politicians can direct government resources to subsidize firms and thus continue to get their way with a firm after privatization (Boycko, Shleifer, and Vishny 1994; Shleifer and Vishny 1994a)—witness the many examples in Eastern and Western Europe.

Nor does the transfer of control rights from politicians to shareholders of the firm by itself create secure private control rights. Bureaucrats in many countries, such as Poland and Russia, maintain control rights over corporate assets despite their lack of legal rights. Securing property rights takes strong enforcement of contracts and of private rights as well. Still, contract enforcement is an easier task after control rights have been transferred from politicians than before, because private agents then have an incentive to protect their control rights and to lobby for appropriate regulations.

Russia's experience with privatization gives practical expression to many of the ideas explored here (for an in-depth analysis of Russia's privatization, see Boycko, Shleifer, and Vishny 1993a,b). In particular, Russia's privatization shows how control rights can be removed from politicians through a political process of building coalitions through equity grants to managers and employees and how corporate governance is thereby improved. In focusing on the problem of establishing property rights in transition economies, the analysis ignores problems that arise in other contexts, such as the common pool problem. Much of the discussion is preliminary—considerable theoretical work needs to be done before the issues are fully understood.

What Are Poorly Defined Property Rights?

Property rights, as defined by Grossman and Hart (1986), are residual control rights over assets. Imagine a society in which each person has a collection of control rights over a set of assets. For example, Mrs. A has a right to cultivate a certain field, live in but not sell a certain house, and use a particular road, but she has no rights over her neighbor's house and field. Her neighbor, Mr. B, has a right to cultivate his own field, to live in as well as to sell his own house, and to use the same road as Mrs. A. This list of people, assets, and control rights defines the property rights structure of society.

An Inefficient Control Structure

Grossman and Hart do not focus on the distinction between physical rights and legal rights, a distinction that is crucial to transition economies. A legal right is protected by police and the courts, so recourse is available if legal rights are violated. For example, if Mr. B has the right to cultivate a field and keep its output, he can presumably use the courts or other powers of the state to seek damages from another party that steals his crop. But not all rights are everywhere fully protected by the courts. In many countries, if someone steals Mr. B's crops or dumps garbage on his field, Mr. B does not have legal recourse and has to protect his control rights privately. Even in a market economy, top executives of private corporations often have a physical right to divert some of the resources of the firm to their personal use despite having no legal right to do so. Not surprisingly, making physical rights legal and legal rights physical is part of the work of establishing property rights. The analysis here considers control rights as physical rather than legal rights over assets.

As must be clear by now, the prevailing structure of physical control rights need not be efficient. One reason is the standard externality problem—people overfish a common pool or overuse and fail to fix a road. Most discussions of poorly defined property rights have focused on this problem (Libecap 1989; Ostrom 1990). Alternatively, an inefficient control structure in the Grossman-Hart sense may fail to promote efficient investment even if people are eventually able to negotiate to an efficient outcome. For example, a shopkeeper who does not own the premises might fail to upgrade the store for fear the landlord would then expropriate the higher profits by raising the rent. If the landlord and the shopkeeper do not (or cannot) sign a long-term lease up front, the landlord could later threaten to kick the entrepreneur out and, through this threat, extract higher rents. So, the first sense of poorly defined property rights is inefficient control structures. If the pool or the road were controlled by a single person, or if the shopkeeper controlled the building, the allocation of resources would be efficient.

The Coase theorem, however, argues that even with an externality problem, people renegotiate to the efficient outcome and so (assuming away transaction costs) solve the common pool problem themselves. The fishermen or road users agree on restrictions on the catch or on road use and on mechanisms for keeping up the common pool. Ostrom (1990) shows how farmers in developing countries use and maintain irrigation systems efficiently despite the common pool problems they face.

Unenforceable Contracts

Even in the Grossman-Hart setup, if people can trade control rights ex ante, they will trade to a better control structure before they make any investments. If not all contracts are enforceable, the trading of control rights does not lead to the first-best outcome, but it does lead to the most efficient control structure given the set of allowable contracts. For example, even if the tenant and the landlord cannot sign a long-term lease, the tenant shopkeeper can sometimes buy the building. With enforceable contracts—whether they result from Coasian ex post renegotiation or Grossman-Hart style ex ante renegotiation—people arrive at (constrained) efficient outcomes. Inefficient control structures do not prevent efficient outcomes so long as contracts are enforced.

The trouble is, such Coasian or Grossman-Hart bargaining often relies on contracts that cannot be enforced. Part of the problem is that the underlying physical control rights need not be legal control rights, so public enforcement cannot be counted on. But even if rights are legal, enforcement may be too expensive or otherwise unavailable. If restrictions on fishing cannot be supported by an enforceable contract, or if the sale of the building cannot be upheld in court or through some other enforcement mechanism, Coasian renegotiation is not available to bring about efficiency. Thus the second aspect of poorly defined property rights is the unenforceability of contracts that could lead to more efficient control structures or outcomes.

But contract enforcement is just one of several ways of getting to an efficient control structure and, as shown below, not the best way during the first stage of reform. Other ways, such as reallocating control rights through the political process, may have more to recommend them for transition economies.

Other Aspects of Poorly Defined Property Rights

Other definitions of poorly defined property rights, such as the idea that "rights over some assets just don't exist yet," can be incorporated into the two concepts that I argue are key aspects of poorly defined property rights: inefficient control structures and the unenforceability of contracts. For example, the common pool problem is often described as a case of nonexisting property rights. Hart and Moore (1990) show that it can be thought of as an inefficient control structure called "joint ownership," in which every agent has veto power over the use of the asset. Similarly, it is often said that shareholder rights do not yet exist in Russia—in the sense that there are no rules governing the rights of shareholders to vote, receive dividends, sell their shares, and so on—and therefore that these rights need to be established.

A more fruitful way to think about this problem is to view control rights over corporate assets as belonging to the managers (and perhaps the workers) rather than as not yet existing. With all control rights in managers' hands but cash flow rights dispersed, managers have an incentive to invest in inefficient projects that give them personal benefits, while shareholders have little incentive to invest in monitoring the managers' decisions. Thus this control structure is inefficient. (This result is closely related to the efficiency of the one share–one vote rule analyzed by Grossman and Hart 1988.) Establishing shareholder rights should be viewed as reallocating some control rights from managers to shareholders rather than as introducing new control rights from scratch. In this framework there are no missing rights, just inefficient control structures, and the problem of establishing property rights becomes that of finding ways of moving from inefficient to efficient control structures.

Who Establishes Property Rights?

Whatever the strategy for getting to efficient control structures, it usually has to be implemented by a government. People have argued about what kind of government is likely to establish property rights. One view holds that a strong (but benevolent) dictatorial government is needed to establish property rights. The Republic of Korea and Taiwan (China) are put forth as examples. Even a selfish dictator, the argument goes, is effectively a shareholder in the economy and so has an incentive to establish efficient property rights to maximize the value of his share (North 1981).

But for every dictator who has tried to enforce property rights, several others have destroyed their economies by expropriating assets and eliminating private incentives to invest. Evidence from Africa (Bates 1981; Klitgaard 1990) and from medieval Europe (Veitch 1986; Delong and Shleifer 1993) reveals the economic depredation caused by unlimited dictatorship. Efficient control structures are difficult to sustain over the long term under dictators because dictators always have some control rights over private assets, which they cannot easily be forced to surrender in courts (North and Weingast 1989).

An alternative view argues that constitutional governments, their power limited by courts and other systems of checks and balances, are more successful at establishing property rights since they can more credibly promise not to grab assets for themselves (Brennan and Buchanan 1980; North and Weingast 1989). Evidence from medieval Europe shows that limited governments were associated with faster economic development than autocracies (Delong and Shleifer 1993), but scholars have been unable to establish a strong relationship between democracy and economic growth (Barro 1991). The evidence on the effectiveness of limited government in establishing property rights is far from conclusive. The very limited Russian government of the early 1990s has been completely unable to enforce contracts.

Since the evidence is inconclusive and little useful policy advice is likely to emerge from such a focus, I deal instead with the more prosaic questions of what strategies might work to establish property rights and how to exert pressure on governments to make them more interested in establishing property rights. Effectively, I am assuming that the government in power, for reasons of benevolence or political pressure, has some interest in establishing property rights. The strategies described below work better under a government committed to establishing property rights, but some property rights can be established even under a far from perfect government, as the example of the Russian privatization in 1993 illustrates.

An alternative approach is to consider enforcement mechanisms that do not involve government. Individuals interested in efficient control structures often come up on their own with enforcement mechanisms such as reputation, peer pressure, private arbitration—or violence (Bardhan 1993; Ostrom 1990). These mechanisms are often valuable, but they are too expensive to be the rule, so the police powers of the state are usually needed to protect control rights and enforce contracts.

Political Control: The Leading Example of an Inefficient Control Structure

The literature on poorly defined property rights has focused on the common pool problem, a model relevant to an understanding of economic development but one that sheds little light on property rights in transition economies. It explores how a society moves from a situation in which a forest is common property, to one of reasonably well-defined communal property rights, to one in which the government enforces property rights. The principal insight of this literature is that the community is more likely to move to an efficient control structure when the benefits of having such a structure rise relative to the costs (Demsetz 1967). Several empirical studies support this hypothesis (see, for example, Libecap 1989).

But in Eastern Europe assets are already too valuable to remain common property, and well-defined control structures govern the use of these assets. These control structures give politicians enormous control rights over all assets, including private assets that are politically controlled through regulation (Kornai 1992; Frydman and Rapaczynski 1994; Boycko, Shleifer, and Vishny 1994). In theory, politicians and bureaucrats assume control rights in order to protect public welfare where private control structures are inefficient (for example, if privately owned firms pollute too much). In practice, politicians' control rights seem to be much more extensive than most reasonable calculations of economic efficiency would suggest, and politicians have enormous discretionary control over economic life that is only vaguely related to social welfare. Though some authors distinguish between politicians, who serve the public interest, and bureaucrats, who are selfish (Laffont and Tirole 1993; Banerjee 1994), that distinction appears tenuous: both use their control rights to produce inefficient outcomes that serve their personal goals.

In many countries politicians can shut down a business, kick it off its premises, or refuse to allow it to start up for completely arbitrary reasons tied only loosely to social welfare. Sometimes the politician has a formal excuse (control right) for this behavior, such as violation of a fire or sanitation code, but often that is not necessary. In this situation the structure of control rights is very clear, but it is not efficient. The bureaucrat can take an inefficient action (not issuing a permit because of laziness or ill humor) because someone else bears the cost. And if a complete contract cannot be written in advance between the bureaucrat and the entrepreneur, the bureaucrat can expropriate profits from a business by threatening to shut it down. Anticipating expropriation by bureaucrats, entrepreneurs underinvest in both their human capital and their businesses (Grossman and Hart 1986). Inefficient control structures thus lead to inefficient resource allocation.

De Soto (1989) has revealed with great clarity the tortuous process involved in starting even a simple small business in Peru, which involves securing vast numbers of permits and licenses from bureaucrats. I conjecture that most Eastern European, and surely Russian, entrepreneurs could tell as good a story as De Soto. Examples of the inefficiencies of political control abound on all continents, including Europe (as recent scandals in Italy illustrate), Latin America, and Africa (see the depressing account of Equatorial Guinea in Klitgaard 1990). Rent control, patronage in employment, and abuse of farmers through predatory pricing are just some examples.

Perhaps the most systematic evidence on the inefficiency of control of business by politicians comes from studies of public enterprises (Vernon and Aharoni 1981; Shleifer and Vishny 1994a). The evidence shows compellingly that politicians use their control rights over these firms to force them to overemploy, overpay, locate in areas where it is not efficient to produce, and make products that the market does not want. National airlines such as Olympic and Air France are notorious for their excess employment. Some state companies have built plants that have never produced goods but serve only to put people on the payroll; the mill built by the Italian state-owned steel giant ILVA near Naples is one example (*Economist,* January 22, 1994). The money-losing Concorde was the idea of French politicians, not of private firms (Anastassopoulos 1981). Even in such routine activities as garbage collection, in the United States costs are typically 20 to 50 percent lower for private contractors than for government agencies (National Commission for Employment Policy 1988).

How do political control rights get to be so extensive? Because physical control rights over particular assets are not fully legal in many cases, politicians and bureaucrats appropriate the legal control rights to themselves—and with them the power to receive bribes. For example, tenant rights are rarely complete, and bureaucrats can easily find reasons to threaten to kick tenants out. An art gallery in Moscow used to be closed by the fire brigade every few weeks for fire code violations. The gallery would move a few paintings, pay a bribe, and reopen for business. In other cases politicians try to rewrite laws to take legal control rights away from private parties. When the Russian government approves a law, the draft circulates among the ministries, and each ministry diligently writes in amendments requiring its consent for any private action discussed in the law. Every ministry wants to be involved in giving permission to open a bank or receive an export license. And with the amendments come not only more bribe income but also more staff for the ministries. It is this endless rent-seeking by the bureaucrats that accounts for the extensiveness of political control rights (Tullock 1967; Krueger 1974). In a transition economy the problem of establishing property rights largely comes down to shrinking the range of political control.

Political control is but one example of inefficient control structures in transition economies, though it is the most pervasive, and the analysis developed here can easily be modified to address other inefficient structures. For example, worker control has been blamed for delayed restructuring in many enterprises in Poland. And managerial control that overrides the rights of outside shareholders has often made it difficult to put good managers in Russian companies.

The Limits of Contract Enforcement

In the spirit of Coasian analysis, the problem of poorly defined property rights is often reduced to the problem of contract enforcement: if the government protected physical control rights as legal rights and enforced contracts, private agents would negotiate to efficient outcomes (Cooter 1987).

Under socialism contract enforcement is not very important. Most contracts are between government entities, and the government's direct control over assets ensures that contracts are upheld. Even if contracts are broken, no one gets too upset because the government pays for any losses. If production comes to a halt because an input is not delivered, for example, there are no private shareholders demanding to know why.

But the demand for contract enforcement rises sharply when private parties take over some control of assets or when new, privately controlled assets are created. Private parties govern their relationships through contracts, which need to be enforced. Some governments respond to this demand by providing enforcement mechanisms, but others do not.

The Possibilities and Limits of Corruption

In a pure Coasian world, socialism is as efficient as capitalism: there is no problem with the inefficient allocation of control rights because bribes restore efficiency. Though a bureaucrat can shut down a business or prevent it from opening, bureaucratic control presents no problem because corruption eliminates any inefficiencies resulting from this bad allocation of control rights. If it is efficient for the business to start or to continue, the bureaucrat and the entrepreneur would negotiate to that efficient outcome. Simply put, the entrepreneur bribes the bureaucrat to let him operate or bribes the bureaucrat to refrain from interfering in the future, thereby restoring investment incentives for the entrepreneur.

No normative value is attached to corruption in this analysis. Corruption is no different from any other side payment that restores efficiency. (Leff 1964 and Huntington 1968 have informally presented this argument for corruption as an eliminator of inefficiency in the allocation of control rights; Shleifer and Vishny 1993, 1994a present it more formally.) But corruption is a far from perfect mechanism for restoring efficiency. The most obvious problems are the two famous reasons (the "transaction costs") why the Coase theorem might not apply: asymmetric information (the bureaucrat and the entrepreneur might fail to reach an efficient bargain if they fail to agree on how much the business is worth) and the free-rider problem (if many entrepreneurs must collectively bribe the bureaucrat to rescind some rule that hurts all of them, the expectation of a free ride will keep them from acting together).

A third, deeper problem is that corruption contracts are not enforceable in court: the arbitrary component of bureaucrats' control rights that allows bureaucrats to collect bribes does not constitute a legal right that a court would protect or that bureaucrats can surrender through a contract enforceable in court. In practice that means that the bureaucrat can come back and demand another bribe from the entrepreneur or that a second bureaucrat can come in and demand a bribe. Without enforceable contracts the Coase theorem simply does not work (contrary to the theory the initial allocation of control rights is not irrelevant), and corruption is ineffective in restoring efficiency.

Courts, of course, are not the only mechanism for enforcing contracts. In some East Asian countries, governing parties purportedly maintain a reputation for moderate corruption. If an official demands too large a bribe, the deviation becomes known to the bureaucrat's superiors, and the official is replaced. But in many other countries individual bureaucrats are not in office long enough—nor is the power of reputation strong enough—to sustain corruption contracts on this basis. And if a bribe does not buy control over a business, the entrepreneur will not pay it, so the business will not open. I have little doubt that this is the predicament of many would-be Russian entrepreneurs.

So the problem comes back to government enforcement. On the face of it the idea of the government upholding corruption contracts seems ludicrous, but we must look deeper. Why not respect corruption (meaning enforce it, not just turn a blind eye to it)? It is true that enforcing corruption violates the public image of government. Italy's recent government scandal illustrates clearly that the public does not consider corruption income to be a legitimate reward for public service.

But this explanation also begs the question: why don't voters like corruption if it boosts efficiency? There are two reasons. First, corruption does not boost efficiency when the result of an agreement between a bureaucrat and a businessman is theft of the public assets. Managers of state firms often bribe bureaucrats to allow assets to be diverted to personal use, or to simply steal from the public company. Such corruption can be extremely distortionary and wasteful. Second, enforcing corruption contracts—including the contract that in isolation would raise efficiency—would encourage bureaucrats to generate new control rights for themselves, which would eventually result in stopping all business. Accepting corruption reduces public welfare, and the universal public dislike of corruption reflects the hatred of political control shared by people the world over.

In developing and transition economies many physical control rights are not legal rights, and these physical rights are in danger of being grabbed by bureaucrats. When people do not have full legal rights to occupy a piece of land they are in constant danger of being forced off by bureaucrats. Of course, people might protect their physical rights, making it costly for bureaucrats to try to grab them. Since the willingness of a bureaucrat to engage in such rent-seeking behavior depends on the financial benefits that the rights bring, lack of enforcement of corruption contracts might serve the long-run interest of establishing property rights by reducing the personal benefits of additional control rights.

A good illustration of this principle comes from the Russian State Antimonopoly Committee. Assigned the task of regulating monopolies in Russia, the committee immediately compiled a list of *thousands* of firms in Russia that it classified as monopolies. A few dozen real national monopolies were included, but so were local bakeries, bathhouses, and other small shops. Firms started bribing local antimonopoly officials just to get off the list. If corruption contracts were enforceable, it is not difficult to imagine that every firm in Russia would have become a monopoly under some suitable market definition.

So if corruption contracts are not enforced, bribery cannot eliminate the consequences of the inefficient allocation of control rights when it is politicians who hold these rights. The problem of poorly defined property rights is not solved by transfers that take the form of bribes.

Private Enforcement

What about other cases in which the government is unable or unwilling to enforce contracts? Sometimes private parties create their own arrangements. Arbitration is an example. In Russia in 1991 and 1992 a large volume of internal trade took place through commodity exchanges to facilitate the trade of highly heterogeneous products. On the Russian Goods and Raw Materials Exchange (the largest commodity exchange) buyers and sellers had one minute on the floor to negotiate delivery terms after agreeing on the price. Not surprisingly, more than a quarter of the trades were disputed. The exchange soon set up its own arbitration procedure, which apparently resolved most contract disputes relatively quickly.

Organized crime is another private mechanism for protecting control rights and enforcing contracts. The mafia provides a broad range of services to protect physical control rights (credit, supply assurance, protection from theft), and it enforces contracts through violence. Because Russia has no established bankruptcy procedures, private loan contracts are not viable. Lenders can neither collect on their loans nor seize collateral from their debtors. The mafia steps in to enforce loan contracts through violence: if there are no assets to grab, the loan defaulter is killed. The rise of the mafia in Russia reflects the increase in demand for protection of control rights and enforcement of contracts, which is not being met by the government.

Although private contract enforcement addresses a market need, it is generally less efficient than effective government protection of contracts. When the mafia steps in to replace the government in protecting property rights, it is also capable of expropriating assets from private entrepreneurs. (In this respect, it is similar to government.) Expropriation tends to be excessive since competition between mafias and their short time horizons prevent mafias from becoming effective equity holders in the businesses they protect. Moreover, protection of property rights and enforcement of contracts are increasing-returns-to-scale technologies. A monopoly national force is cheaper than feudal militias, and a monopoly legal system is cheaper than a variety of local systems. Private protection of property and enforcement of contracts are expensive alternatives for a government that fails to provide these services.

Why Contract Enforcement Might Not Be a Top Priority

Many Western observers of the Russian reforms have argued that protection of property rights and enforcement of contracts should be the first priorities of the government. But there are two reasons why a reform government might not move to provide contract enforcement as soon as it gains power. For one, these activities are expensive. Police in Russia are paid very little, so they often prefer to be bribed rather than to protect private property. Civil court justices often refuse to hear commercial cases, arguing that they are paid only to handle divorces. Contract enforcement requires new mechanisms, including courts and other institutions. For another, politicians working to introduce basic reforms do not view property protection and contract enforcement as priorities worthy of a heavy allocation of resources. By and large their primary constituents are not involved in contracts, so this area is not a political priority. Business people, for their part, are not yet a powerful enough political coalition to affect policy, and besides, they often view private enforcement mechanisms as cheaper than public ones.

Initially, then, the government does not even allocate to contract enforcement the resources it could afford to allocate. So there is an impasse: the government does not enforce contracts without political pressure from private business interests, but private business interests cannot accumulate enough resources to lobby the government until contracts are enforced.

According to North (1981) and North and Weingast (1989) progress in establishing property rights occurs when the government is forced by political pressures from the propertied classes to commit itself to protecting property rights. That time generally comes when a weak sovereign wants to tax its subjects who control the assets. In exchange for paying taxes the subjects extract from the sovereign constitutional commitments to protect property rights and not to expropriate property. Throughout history political pressures from business interests have played an important role in prompting government interest in contract enforcement. There is little doubt that in Russia today political pressures emerging from privatization have done more to move the government toward a system of contract enforcement than all the preaching of Western advisers. But these interests emerged after privatization, not before.

What this analysis suggests about the early stages of reform is that contract enforcement, though highly desirable in most cases, is very expensive and not a political priority. It cannot be relied on exclusively as a mechanism for getting to an efficient control structure over assets. Moreover, contract enforcement, especially of bribes, may not be good policy. Contract enforcement thus is not the universal solution to the problem of poorly defined property rights. Alternative strategies for establishing property rights are needed, at least as a first step in reform.

Three Strategies for Improving the Efficiency of Control Structures

Reformers interested in arriving at more efficient allocations of control rights over assets and who choose not to rely (solely) on private bargaining and contract enforcement have several options. One strategy is to turn bureaucrats into shareholders—giving them formal rights to the cash flow from an asset in addition to control rights. Examples of this strategy are the "nomenklatura privatizations" in Eastern Europe and village enterprises in China. A second strategy is to reform the bureaucracy by bringing bureaucrats' objectives in line with public welfare or by devaluing their control rights. This strategy is inspired by East Asia's experience with rapid, government-directed economic growth. A third strategy is to reallocate control rights through the political system—taking control rights from bureaucrats and allocating them to other parties who will presumably use them more efficiently. The leading example of this strategy is privatization.

Turning Bureaucrats into Shareholders

Giving bureaucrats an equity stake (legal cash flow rights) in the businesses over which they have control rights replaces their illegal claim (obtained through a threat of expropriation) to income from the enterprise with a legal claim. The cash flow rights from this stake have to be enforceable, whether through the courts or some other mechanism. A person with both control rights and cash flow rights has an incentive to choose efficient actions (Grossman and Hart 1988), so the selfish interests of a bureaucrat with an equity stake would be more likely to coincide with the decisions of entrepreneurs seeking to reach an efficient outcome for the firm. Threats to shut down the firm or to expropriate its assets diminish as well, because a bureaucrat with a cash flow stake stands to lose his equity by doing so. The bureaucrat has become an entrepreneur.

This approach to more efficient control structures is common in countries with poor contract enforcement. In many developing countries relatives of bureaucrats own businesses expressly because they can get protection from political expropriation. In Eastern Europe, particularly in Russia, local bureaucrats often become equity partners in small privatized businesses, a strategy sometimes referred to as nomenklatura privatization. In a typical transaction a bureaucrat (or a public organization controlled by the bureaucrat) becomes an equity holder in a privatized or newly created small business, such as a vegetable wholesaler. The bureaucrat offers the business protection from expropriation (by other bureaucrats as well as himself) and in return receives dividends in the form of cash or goods. Even when the formal shareholder is a public organization, the bureaucrat ends up with the dividends. A large share of new private enterprises in Russia have such public partners, precisely to solve the problem of bureaucratic expropriation.

Although flawed, these emerging control structures are likely to result in more efficient outcomes than cases in which bureaucrats lack cash flow rights. If equity ownership is transferable, bureaucrats have an incentive to maximize the value of their shares. Even without full transferability, pseudoequity ownership probably reduces the bureaucrat's interest in quick expropriation through bribes. To the extent that nomenklatura privatization lengthens the horizons over which bureaucrats evaluate the cash flow of firms, it is an efficiency-improving adaptation to the problem of excessive bureaucratic control. Relatedly, the longer the bureaucrat's political horizons, the greater the interest in equity ownership over quick expropriation. Nomenklatura privatization has been much more common in regional privatizations in Russia, where the bureaucrats' horizons are relatively long, than in national privatizations, where political turnover is greater.

Another example of effective equity ownership by bureaucrats is the Chinese village enterprise. Some studies have claimed that the success of these firms shows the irrelevance of well-defined property rights (Weitzman and Xu 1993). Recent work by Oi (1994) challenges the claim that property rights in village enterprises are poorly defined. Oi shows that control rights among local party bosses, township party bosses, and the central government are clearly specified. Moreover, detailed agreements govern repatriation of profits to higher levels of government, so local governments and officials who effectively control these firms become residual claimants of their cash flows.

Oi's research suggests that the local party officials who run these firms benefit from a firm's economic success, in the form of bonuses and goods that the enterprise buys for them—a form of nomenklatura privatization, if you will. And in a permutation unique to China, local bureaucrats appear to need the profits from these enterprises to finance local public spending, since they get no money from other sources. So their political survival depends on the enterprises' profitability. Because these personal and political benefits effectively turn local bureaucrats into shareholders, the control structures of village enterprises appear to be reasonably efficient.

Why are these village enterprises different from the enormously inefficient public enterprises in China and elsewhere? Recent evidence shows that state firms in

China are as inefficient as those in Russia (*South China Morning Post,* April 30–May 1, 1994). What keeps local officials from padding the employment rolls of village enterprises with relatives and political supporters? Part of the answer is that local governments simply do not have the money to subsidize inefficient village enterprises. Another is that fierce competition between village enterprises keeps down profits so that firms cannot afford the luxury of excess employment. China's rapid economic growth has contributed as well, making patronage employment less necessary. But if growth were enough, it should have rescued state enterprises too, which it evidently has not.

These answers do not bode well for the future efficiency of China's village enterprises. A recession (perhaps because of a trade shock) could intensify pressures to use village enterprises to create employment, while a turn toward democracy could tempt local bureaucrats to use the enterprises to deliver political patronage. Or the central government might decide to use its power to extract political benefits from village enterprises. These concerns suggest that the efficiency of Chinese village enterprises is fragile. Unless local bureaucrats effectively privatize these firms through full nomenklatura privatization, at some point the village enterprises are likely to suffer the same afflictions as public firms elsewhere in China and the rest of the world.

More generally, the strategy of making bureaucrats shareholders has three serious drawbacks. First, the bureaucrat may not be getting real transferable equity, especially if the equity comes through a shell organization. The less secure the bureaucrat's equity claim, the less efficient the control structure. A bureaucrat fearing dismissal and the loss of an equity claim might threaten expropriation as an income-generating strategy, which would discourage efficient investment by entrepreneurs.

Second, giving bureaucrats equity is obviously unfair, which is presumably why the equity claims are informal in so many countries. Like corruption, this strategy rewards the arbitrary grabbing of control rights and recognizes explicitly that bureaucrats are not acting in the public interest. For this reason, no government has openly engaged in nomenklatura privatization.

Third, entrenching bureaucrats as shareholders improves their incentives but reduces the likelihood that asset control will shift to managers with the appropriate human capital. To the extent that new management is essential for efficient resource allocation, giving equity to bureaucrats can reduce efficiency by entrenching the old human capital.

The general idea of giving equity to bureaucrats can be extended to other parties with control rights over assets, such as enterprise workers and managers. Adding some cash flow rights to control rights strengthens interest in efficient outcomes. Most privatizations in Eastern Europe have awarded large equity stakes to worker and management teams, in part to get their agreement to privatization in the first place.

Reforming Bureaucracy

An alternative strategy for dealing with inefficient political control rights is to reform the bureaucracy to get it to maximize social welfare. That can be achieved either by strengthening bureaucrats' concern with public welfare, so that their interests coincide more with those of shareholders, or by reducing bureaucratic discretion, usually through competition between bureaucrats, who then become powerless to pursue personal goals.

History yields some examples of efficient ("Weberian") bureaucracies, though their public-spiritedness is less clear-cut—the Korean bureaucracy after the 1961 coup, some local (often communist) administrations in Northern Italy and West Bengal, and perhaps some parts of the French civil service. These effective bureaucracies appear under special circumstances. Sometimes they appear in military dictatorships (Republic of Korea and Taiwan, China) or in militaristic organizations (armies, some private companies), where the boss can fire—or even kill—subordinates for ineffectiveness. Effective bureaucracies also sometimes arise where local democracy is well-developed and a free press and strong electorate closely monitor the bureaucrats' behavior (some local governments in the United States). And sometimes they appear when a common purpose or ideology energizes them (communist local governments mentioned above, the New York Turnpike Authority under Robert Moses, perhaps some parts of the French bureaucracy). In some cases, however, the difference between bureaucratic efficiency and the maximization of public welfare may be substantial.

Although creating an effective, public-spirited bureaucracy is theoretically a viable strategy for establishing property rights, by linking the bureaucrats' control rights to a public purpose, I am deeply skeptical that such public-spirited bureaucracies can be created in Eastern Europe or Russia. These countries are not now dictatorships, and the sort of dictatorship that they are at risk of becoming is far from benevolent. Nor are fledgling democratic institutions in these countries ready to provide the close monitoring needed to force public-spiritedness on the bureaucracy. In Russia local political machines are controlled by long-time communists, and the press is often bought off. Finally, in most of these countries government has been publicly discredited, and counting on public-spirited bureaucracies is probably a waste of time. For these reasons, bureaucratic reform strategies in Eastern Europe should probably focus on devaluing political control rights rather than on improving the public-spiritedness of the bureaucracy.

The idea behind the devaluation of political control rights is to make it difficult for bureaucrats to abuse those rights. For example, if a bureaucrat's discretionary behavior gets reported in the press with some regularity and the bureaucrat is penalized as a result, the value of bureaucratic control rights is reduced. Competition, too, can drive the value of bureaucratic control rights down to zero. A bureaucrat in the United States cannot charge a supplement for granting a passport because a citizen will just go to the next window at the passport office. But if there is just one bureaucrat issuing passports and the probability of detection is low, the bureaucrat can credibly threaten not to issue a passport without a side payment and earn some rents from this threat (Rose-Ackerman 1978; Shleifer and Vishny 1993).

Setting up competition between bureaucrats is difficult. More often than not, several bureaucrats end up controlling complementary rights rather than competing over the same right, and control rights expand rather than shrink. For example, if one bureaucracy controls export licenses, another export taxes, a third foreign exchange transactions, a fourth the right to set up a bank account, and so on (roughly the situation in Russia), the bureaucrats are competing with each other but not in prices. The result is a lower volume of trade (Shleifer and Vishny 1993). It is extremely difficult to design bureaucracies with little discretionary control.

As with efforts to establish an efficient bureaucracy or to otherwise reform the bureaucracy, the greatest impediment to the strategy of devaluing political control rights is the dependence on a benevolent dictator or on well-developed democratic institutions that do not exist in Eastern Europe. As a result, it is hard to recommend this approach for increasing the efficiency of control structures in the short run.

Removing Control Rights from Bureaucrats

Another strategy is to use the political process to remove control rights from bureaucrats. Killing incumbent bureaucrats, as often happens in revolutions and coups, is one way. A less horrific strategy is to remove them through peaceful political processes, as Czechoslovakia and Poland, but not Russia, have done. A final strategy is to strip bureaucrats of the legal means of protecting their control rights—something that a reform government might find easier to do than a long-entrenched government—and then to reallocate (or sell) the control rights or allow them to be taken over by agents who can use the rights efficiently. Privatization is the principal form that this reallocation of control rights from bureaucrats to private parties has taken. In Eastern Europe privatization is linked first to the removal of control rights from ministries and then to the reallocation of the rights to enterprise insiders, such as workers and managers, and to outside investors.

Bureaucracies, of course, resist the alienation of their control rights, since they would suffer a large loss of wealth. The essence of every reform, therefore, is to politically reinforce the removal of control rights from bureaucrats, usually by mobilizing the support of those who get the control rights (relatively easy) and the general public. In developed democracies, such as France and the United Kingdom, an electoral mandate to privatize often suffices to remove control rights from bureaucrats. In less-developed democracies, such as Mexico and the Czech and Slovak Republics, a reform government might have considerable power to remove control rights from bureaucrats, but it must also build political coalitions to resist opposition from bureaucrats and their allies, such as unions.

Coalition building in the course of privatization often takes the form of equity awards to political allies. Most countries give enterprise workers preferential equity treatment. In addition, a generalized version of nomenklatura privatization is sometimes combined with the political redistribution of control rights to soften bureaucrats' opposition. When the government is as weak as the Russian government was in 1992–93, the democratic mandate is ineffective, and a lot of coalition building becomes necessary.

When a government is weak, any reform that removes control rights from the bureaucrats must be accompanied by new rules and laws that allow private parties to take over control rights and that forestall efforts by the bureaucracy to prevent change. As Hay (1994) argues, designing such rules is difficult but doable—and essential. The public desire for change, however strong, is not enough. A good example of a dramatic failure of reform despite strong public interest is the attempted reallocation of property rights to land in Russia in 1992–93. Russia has over 40 million very small land plots, used for private farms, garden plots, or building lots. Those who use the land have few control rights: use is restricted, sale is prohibited, and so on. In 1992–93 the government tried several titling procedures to give users fuller property rights. The effort failed miserably, and only a few titles were issued. The reason: the government bureaucracy Roskomzem controlled land surveying prior to the issuance of titles and used its power to collect bribes while issuing few titles. Land users had no recourse to this holdup by the bureaucrats. In late 1993, when President Yeltsin issued a decree allowing land titling without surveys, the bureaucracy moved quickly to control the secondary market for land, demanding the right to issue permits and set prices in all land transactions. Thus despite the enormous political popularity of land reform, it has proved impossible to outwit Roskomzem or to relax its grip on land control rights.

From Transferring Control Rights to Establishing Property Rights

Transferring asset control rights from bureaucrats to firm insiders and shareholders does not, in itself, establish full property rights. The problem of protecting private control rights and enforcing contracts is not solved simply by transferring these rights from politicians: the solution is only delayed. Even after bureaucrats lose control rights, they can use the resources of the treasury to convince, rather than order, firms to pursue political objectives. Firms soon discover that the interests of their shareholders are best served by following the wishes of the politicians and receiving subsidies in return (Boycko, Shleifer, and Vishny 1994; Shleifer and Vishny 1994a). Subsidies render private control rights—even secure private control rights—insufficient for achieving economic efficiency. Also, transferring control rights from politicians to private agents does not ensure the security of those rights. For example, shareholders, despite their legal control rights, might be unable to fire the manager or to sell their shares through an enforceable contract. Or workers might have physical control rights that are greater than their legal rights.

Tightening the Budget Strings

As long as politicians can direct grants and subsidized loans to firms, private control rights do not lead to efficient resource allocation. Thus if politicians are responsive to labor interests and are willing to subsidize employment, even privately controlled firms will not cut employment because profit maximization calls for catering to politicians. So long as subsidies flow freely, privatization will not lead to substantial restructuring.

Analytically, subsidies are similar to bribes (Shleifer and Vishny 1994a). When politicians have control rights, bribes can in principle alleviate the damage from political control and so improve resource allocation. Once control rights are transferred to private agents, subsidies play the reverse role: they allow politicians to counter the benefits of private control by paying shareholders not to be efficient. The unenforceability of bribes limits their effectiveness. Reducing the availability of subsidies should have a similar effect.

Polish enterprises began to restructure in 1991–92 even before control rights were transferred from politicians because a tough monetary policy limited the availability of cheap credit, which was an important mechanism of political control (Pinto, Belka, and Krajewski 1993). In contrast, many Russian enterprises were slow to restructure even after privatization because the government continued to subsidize them. Hard budget constraints are essential for realizing the benefits of private control rights, because they prevent politicians and managers from striking the Coasian bargain (see Boycko, Shleifer, and Vishny 1994 and Shleifer and Vishny 1994a for a more thorough theoretical analysis of these issues).

Improving Corporate Governance

In Eastern Europe when control rights are transferred from politicians, control often goes to insiders: managers and workers rather than outside shareholders gain physical control rights over firms. In practice that means that managers cannot be fired, that workers can delay or prevent restructuring, and in some cases that shares cannot be traded by outside shareholders. While superior to political control, this structure of control rights is far from optimal because the control and cash flow rights of insiders are not perfectly aligned (Grossman and Hart 1988). A more efficient control structure requires transferring effective control rights to outside shareholders and legally protecting their control rights. This process requires the creation of mechanisms of corporate governance (Frydman and Rapaczynski 1994; Phelps and others 1993; Boycko, Shleifer, and Vishny 1993a).

Scholars and practitioners have proposed various mechanisms of external control for improving corporate governance in Eastern Europe: banks and debt finance, boards of directors, stock markets, takeovers, bankruptcy rules, product market competition, core investors, and others. For example, Boycko, Shleifer, and Vishny (1993a) argue that corporate governance mechanisms that rely on debt are unlikely to be effective in Russia any time soon because they rely on bankruptcy or other mechanisms of transferring control to creditors that are not yet in place. Large outside investors are more likely to be the most active agents of corporate governance, but even they require an extensive system of corporate law, corporate voting, independent share registrars, and so on to be able to exercise their control rights.

In fact, critics have argued that much more attention should have been paid to preparing corporate law and other building blocks of a governance system before privatizing enterprises. Specifically, they argue that privatization in Eastern Europe, by focusing on the transfer of control away from politicians, allowed too much control to go to insiders and thus permanently damaged the prospects for effective corporate governance. I believe this argument is wrong, for two reasons.

First, weak reformers require all the support they can get, including the help of enterprise insiders, to wrest control rights from politicians. Managers who feel threatened by privatization would rather strike a bargain with politicians to maintain state ownership and subsidies than venture into privatization. Setting up threatening governance mechanisms before privatization is made effective would only stop privatization.

Second, there simply is no political interest in governance mechanisms before privatization. That interest emerges during privatization, as large outside shareholders are created and come to realize their needs for independent registrars of shares, for laws governing corporate voting, and even for financial markets in liquid assets. Pressure from these new owners can then counter the political influence of enterprise managers and convince the government to adopt regulations that foster corporate governance. Under pressure, the government begins to protect property rights.

The transfer of control rights from politicians to private parties gives the process of establishing property rights a jump-start by creating the political demand for the protection of property rights. As the government begins to respond to this demand, genuine property rights become established.

The Example of the Russian Privatization of 1992–94

The Russian effort in 1992–94 to establish property rights over public enterprises through large-scale privatization shows how two of the strategies outlined above—conferring cash flow rights on those with control rights and using the political process to transfer control rights—were combined. To achieve their goals, the reformers had to build a political coalition strong enough to counter the bureaucratic opposition to loss of control. The transfer started the process of establishing property rights by paving the way for private investors to use their economic and political resources to protect their rights. (This section draws on Boycko and Shleifer 1993 and Boycko, Shleifer, and Vishny 1993a,b, 1994; for additional detail, see Frydman, Rapaczynski, and Earle 1993.)

Following the collapse of communism, the central ministries began to lose control of Russian industrial enterprises to several other "stakeholders." Enterprise managers got substantial control over investment, employment, product development, and many other decisions previously controlled by central ministries. Workers, through their allies in Parliament, had effective veto power over any change in the legal ownership structure of the enterprise, though they had little control over decisions in the firm. Local governments, yet another group of stakeholders, controlled the supply of water, electricity, and other services to firms and wanted enterprises to maintain employment levels and to continue to provide social services for local residents. Finally, the central ministries retained some control over firms in part because they could coordinate supply and distribution much better than the enterprise managers could.

This devolution of control rights from the ministries in the early 1990s followed from the decision of the Gorbachev government not to protect these rights. Thus the rights were not peacefully turned over to new stakeholders but were grabbed by the managers. Throughout this period the bureaucrats attempted to reassert their control rights over firms. Some tried to combine firms into associations, industrial groups, and other cartel arrangements that would be "coordinated" by their former ministries. The Russian gas industry was consolidated into a single state enterprise, bringing the former head of that industry enough political support from the old guard to allow him to become the prime minister.

The control structure that emerged before privatization was not very efficient because ministries and local governments retained enough control over firms to undercut any incentive for managers to restructure. In 1992–93 it looked as though the ministries, arguing the need for Japanese-style *keretsu,* would succeed in merging firms into large associations; the minister of industry ardently advocated that approach. There was also a threat, particularly in 1992, that firms would come under the control of workers collectives, as the Moscow city government had proposed. Finally, the ministries and the central bank continued to subsidize industrial firms in exchange for maintaining employment and output, effectively eliminating most incentives to restructure. Under these circumstances firms were essentially killing time and kept most of their operations intact.

The Russian large-scale privatization program was intended to consolidate the removal of control rights over firms from the central bureaucracy and to allocate those rights to enterprise managers and shareholders. The program demonstrated how a small political mandate could be built up into a successful reform. In the Russian political environment of 1992 a workable privatization program had to combine the reallocation of control rights with the establishment of a new group of stakeholders who would support the program. No consensus on privatization had emerged inside the government, let alone in the much more conservative Parliament. The minister of privatization was a new, and not particularly powerful, political figure. A few reformers in the government would not have been able to carry this program off on their own without stakeholder support.

Control over privatization transactions (but not the rules) was turned over to local privatization offices rather than to the central ministries. That decision allayed the fears of local administrators, since it gave them some power in negotiating the future of social assets controlled by firms and prevented the complete takeover of local firms by "undesirable" outside investors. Removing control over privatization from the ministries effectively stripped them of their control rights over firms, so that in the end the industrial ministries withered away to almost nothing.

The privatization program gave substantial cash flow rights to managers and workers in the privatizing firms. The privatization ministry had proposed offering roughly 30 percent of the shares to workers and managers (option 1), an amount Parliament effectively raised to about 50 percent (option 2). While Parliament's more generous offer did not make the new control structures any more efficient, the larger equity awards may have strengthened the support of managers and workers for privatization, further reducing the viability of bureaucratic control rights.

The privatization also involved all Russian citizens, who were invited to become shareholders through a system of free vouchers distributed to the population at large (Boycko, Shleifer, and Vishny 1993a,b). Vouchers became the sole means of buying shares of privatizing firms, which were sold at auctions. Since the vouchers were tradable, large investors were able to acquire stakes in Russian companies by buying vouchers from the public. Trade in vouchers facilitated the transfer of control rights to outside investors, whose interests are closest to economic efficiency. The popularity of the voucher program, in my opinion, "saved" the Russian privatization by eliminating the threat of quasi-governmental cartels and preventing complete control by insiders.

The program combined the political redistribution of control rights (using managers, the public, and local governments to undermine the power of Moscow bureaucrats) with equity awards to parties that already had control rights (managers and workers). Much of the program's success is attributable to its reliance on a politically viable approach to transferring control rights from politicians. In 1993 alone almost 10,000 industrial enterprises, employing 40 percent of industrial workers, were privatized. By July 1, 1994, when the program was completed, more than 14,000 industrial enterprises, employing almost two-thirds of industrial workers, became private.

But the transfer of control from politicians is only a first step in establishing property rights. Enterprise managers (but probably not the workers) have emerged from the privatizations with enormous control rights. They make most of the corporate decisions, select directors, control shareholder votes, and often control the trading of shares through physical control over share registrars. Through their influence on workers and on the government property funds that still own some shares, many managers almost fully control their firms, even though management teams directly own only about 15 percent of their companies' shares (Boycko, Shleifer, and Vishny 1993a,b; Pistor 1993). Even such nearly complete managerial control is probably better than political control. Though managers are also interested in empire building and preserving their own jobs, their welfare is more closely tied to the profits of the firm than is that of politicians, particularly when managers have an equity stake.

Establishing property rights in these enterprises, however, will require curtailing managerial control and increasing control by outside investors. Progress in this area seems to have begun. Many Russian companies now have core outside investors, Russian and foreign. These investors are interested primarily in profits, and they use whatever control rights they have (votes at shareholders meetings, jawboning the managers) to demand value-maximizing strategies. In a few cases outside shareholders have allied themselves with the workers to replace incompetent managers. Outside investors, including investment funds, have also begun lobbying the government for regulations to protect their control rights (independent share registrars, laws protecting investor rights, secret corporate voting, and so on) and for the creation of a securities and exchange commission to enforce the unrestricted trading of shares. These efforts began to bear fruit toward the end of 1993, as the government adopted regulations protecting shareholder rights. In this way privatization, while not establishing full property rights by itself, has stimulated policies that increase the protection of these rights.

As property rights become established, the restructuring of Russian enterprises should begin. Indeed, once managers had gotten control rights but before they had received cash flow rights, employment in state enterprises began to fall. The share of state employment fell from an estimated 89 percent in 1990 to 74 percent in 1992 (Blanchard, Commander, and Coricelli 1993). Among newly privatized enterprises employment fell again in 1993, by an average of 5 percent (Webster and others 1994). Nevertheless, most firms continue to consider themselves substantially overstaffed. Surveys of Russian enterprises by Webster and others (1994) and the European Expertise Service (1994) show that a substantial number have diversified their product lines, increased exports, and unloaded on municipalities some of the social services they provided. Although these changes are still coming too slowly, they are visible in most firms.

The Russian reform has had much less success in halting enterprise subsidies, the other requirement for making private property rights effective. In 1992–93 the government continued to subsidize private and state firms to maintain employment and output, postponing macroeconomic stabilization (see the article by Jeffrey Sachs in this volume). The continued subsidization preserved political control over firms and substantially delayed restructuring. In 1994, however, subsidies to firms began to fall and restructuring accelerated.

The Russian experience shows how the political transfer of control rights from bureaucrats and the allocation of cash flow rights to parties with control rights can improve the efficiency of the structure of control rights and prepare the way for the establishment of genuine property rights. But that experience also shows how difficult it is to destroy or escape political control. Privatization of shops has worked much less well in Russia than in Eastern Europe because local governments continue to control businesses through leases and regulations. Land reform has been similarly stymied by government agencies with effective control over all land transactions. Even for large-scale privatizations, proposals for consolidating firms into large industrial groups and other quasi-governmental structures continue to resurface even after most firms have been privatized. Moreover, credit policy remains an instrument of political control of privatized firms. It is also plausible to argue that politicians have intentionally delayed protecting private property rights and that, to hold on to their own control rights, have perhaps even condoned crime since fear of the mafia often drives entrepreneurs to seek political protection.

Conclusion

Getting to better defined property rights requires understanding that "poorly defined property rights" means both inefficient structures of control rights over assets and weak contract enforcement. Better contract enforcement, though central to establishing property rights in the long run, may not solve the critical problems in the short run. In particular, better contract enforcement does not solve the problem of inefficient political control of firms; other strategies are needed for that purpose.

In Eastern Europe defining property rights usually means transferring political control rights to private agents through the political process, as well as awarding equity to stakeholders who have control rights over assets. Genuine protection of property rights and enforcement of contracts begin to emerge only after control rights are removed from politicians. Russia's experience with privatization shows how economic analysis of property rights can guide policy in a successful direction even in a politically hostile environment.

References

Alchian, Armen, and Harold Demsetz. 1972. "Production, Information Costs, and Economic Organization." *American Economic Review* 62: 777–95.

Anastassopoulos, Jean Pierre C. 1981. "The French Experience: Conflicts with Government." In Raymond Vernon and Yair Aharoni, eds., *State-Owned Enterprises in Western Economies.* London: Croom Helm.

Banerjee, Abhijit. 1994. "A Theory of Misgovernance." Massachusetts Institute of Technology, Department of Economics, Cambridge, Mass.

Bardhan, Pranab. 1993. "Symposium on Management of Local Commons." *Journal of Economic Perspectives* 7: 87–92.

Barro, Robert J. 1991. "Economic Growth in a Cross-Section of Countries." *Quarterly Journal of Economics* 106: 407–44.

Barzel, Yoram. 1989. *Economic Analysis of Property Rights.* Cambridge, U.K.: University Press.

Bates, Robert. 1981. *Markets and States in Tropical Africa: The Political Basis of Agricultural Policies.* Berkeley: University of California Press.

Blanchard, Olivier, ed. 1993. *Post-Communist Reform: Pain and Progress.* Cambridge, Mass.: MIT Press.

Blanchard, Olivier, Simon Commander, and Fabrizio Coricelli. 1993. "Unemployment and Restructuring in Eastern Europe." World Bank, Transition Economics Division, Washington, D.C. Draft.

Boycko, Maxim, and Andrei Shleifer. 1993. "The Politics of Russian Privatization." In Olivier Blanchard, ed., *Post-Communist Reform: Pain and Progress.* Cambridge, Mass.: MIT Press.

Boycko, Maxim, Andrei Shleifer, and Robert W. Vishny. 1993a. "Privatizing Russia." *Brookings Papers on Economic Activity.* Washington, D.C.: The Brookings Institution.

———. 1993b. "Voucher Privatization." *Journal of Financial Economics* 35 (3): 249–66.

———. 1994. "A Theory of Privatization." Harvard University, Department of Economics, Cambridge, Mass.

Brennan, Geoffrey, and James M. Buchanan. 1980. *The Power to Tax: Analytical Foundations of a Fiscal Constitution.* Cambridge: Cambridge University Press.

Coase, Ronald H. 1960. "The Problem of Social Cost." *Journal of Law and Economics* 3: 1–44.

Cooter, Robert D. 1987. "The Coase Theorem." *The New Palgrave Dictionary of Economics.* London: McMillan.

Delong, James B., and Andrei Shleifer. 1993. "Princes and Merchants: European City Growth before the Industrial Revolution." *Journal of Law and Economic* 36: 671–702.

Demsetz, Harold. 1967. "Towards a Theory of Property Rights." *American Economic Review* 57: 347–59.

De Soto, Hernando. 1989. *The Other Path.* New York: Harper and Row.

European Expertise Service. 1994. "Russian Firms in Transition: Are They Adjusting?" Paris.

Frydman, Roman, and Andrzej Rapaczynski. 1994. *Privatization in Eastern Europe: Is the State Withering Away?* Budapest: Central European University Press, in association with Oxford University Press.

Frydman, Roman, Andrzej Rapaczynski, and John Earle. 1993. *The Privatization Process in Russia, Ukraine, and Baltic States.* Budapest: Central European University Press.

Grossman, Sanford J., and Oliver D. Hart. 1986. "The Costs and Benefits of Ownership: A Theory of Vertical and Lateral Integration." *Journal of Political Economy* 94: 691–719.

———. 1988. "One Share–One Vote and the Market for Corporate Control" *Journal of Financial Economics* 20: 175–202.

Hart, Oliver D., and John Moore. 1990. "Property Rights and the Nature of the Firm." *Journal of Political Economy* 98: 1119–58.

Hay, Jonathan. 1994. "Laws that Work." Harvard University, Department of Economics, Cambridge, Mass.

Huntington, Samuel P. 1968. *Political Order in Changing Societies.* New Haven, Conn.: Yale University Press.

Jensen, Michael C., and William H. Meckling. 1976. "Theory of the Firm: Managerial Behavior, Agency Costs, and the Ownership Structure." *Journal of Financial Economics* 3: 305–60.

Klitgaard, Robert. 1990. *Tropical Gangsters.* New York: Basic Books.

Kornai, János. 1992. "The Post-Socialist Transition and the State: Reflections in the Light of the Hungarian Fiscal Problems." *American Economic Review* 82: 1–21.

Krueger, Anne P. 1974. "The Political Economy of a Rent-Seeking Society." *American Economic Review* 64: 291–303.

Laffont, Jean Jacques, and Jean Tirole. 1993. *A Theory of Incentives in Procurement and Regulation.* Cambridge, Mass.: MIT Press.

Leff, Nathaniel. 1964. "Economic Development Through Bureaucratic Corruption." *American Behavioral Scientist* 8: 8–14.

Libecap, Gary. 1989. *Contracting for Property Rights.* Cambridge: Cambridge University Press.

Megginson, William L., Robert C. Nash, and Mathias van Randenborgh. 1994. "The Financial and Operating Performance of Newly Privatized Firms: An International Empirical Analysis." *Journal of Finance* 49 (2): 403–52.

"Millions Unpaid as State Firms Crumble." *South China Morning Post,* April 30–May 1, 1994.

Mueller, Dennis. 1989. *Public Choice II.* Cambridge, U.K.: University Press.

National Commission for Employment Policy. 1988. *Privatization and Public Employees: The Impact of City and County Contracting Out on Government Workers.* Washington, D.C.

North, Douglass C. 1981. *Structure and Change in Economic History.* New York: Norton.

North, Douglass C., and Robert P. Thomas. 1973. *The Rise of the Western World: A New Economic History.* Cambridge: Cambridge University Press.

North, Douglass C., and Barry Weingast. 1989. "Constitutions and Commitment: The Evolution of Institutions Governing Public Choice in 17th Century England." *Journal of Economic History* 49: 803–32.

Oi, Jean. 1994. "Rural China Takes Off: Incentives for Reform." Harvard University, Department of Economics, Cambridge, Mass.

Ostrom, Elinor. 1990. *Governing the Commons.* Cambridge: Cambridge University Press.

Phelps, Edmund S., Roman Frydman, Andrzej Rapaczynski, and Andrei Shleifer. 1993. "Needed Mechanisms for Corporate Control and Governance in Eastern Europe." *The Economics of Transition* 1: 171–207.

Pinto, Brian, M. Belka, and S. Krajewski. 1993. "Transforming State Enterprises in Poland: Evidence from Adjustment by Manufacturing Firms." *Brookings Papers on Economic Activity.* Washington, D.C.: The Brookings Institution.

Pistor, Katharina. 1993. "Privatization and Corporate Governance in Russia: An Empirical Study." Paper prepared for the Workshop on Economic Reform, Center for International Security and Arms Control, Stanford University, Stanford, Calif.

Rose-Ackerman, Susan. 1978. *Corruption: A Study of Political Economy.* New York: Academic Press.

Shleifer, Andrei, and Robert W. Vishny. 1993. "Corruption." *Quarterly Journal of Economics* 108: 599–618.

———. 1994a. "Politicians and Firms." *Quarterly Journal of Economics* 109 (November): 995–1025.

———. 1994b. "Privatization in Russia: First Steps." In O. Blanchard, K. Froot, and J. Sachs, eds., *The Transition in Eastern Europe,* vol. 2. Chicago: University of Chicago Press.

Tullock, Gordon. 1967. "The Welfare Cost of Tariffs, Monopoly and Theft." *Economic Inquiry* 5: 224–32.

"Two Half Revolutions." 1994. *The Economist,* pp. 55–8, January 22.

Veitch, John M. 1986. "Repudiations and Confiscations by the Medieval State." *Journal of Economic History* 46: 31–36.

Vernon, Raymond, and Yair Aharoni, eds. 1981. *State-Owned Enterprises in Western Economies.* London: Croom Helm.

Webster, Leila, with Juergen Franz, Igor Artemiev, and Harold Wackman. 1994. "Newly Privatized Enterprises: A Survey." In Ira W. Lieberman and John Nellis, ed., *Russia: Creating Private Enterprises and Efficient Markets*. Washington, D.C.: Private Sector Development Department, World Bank.

Weitzman, Martin L., and Chenggang Xu. 1993. "Chinese Township Village Enterprises as Vaguely Defined Cooperatives." Harvard Institute of Economic Research Working Paper 1607. Cambridge, Mass.

Comment on "Establishing Property Rights," by Shleifer

Olivier Jean Blanchard

Early privatization plans (circa 1990) were profoundly naive. They implicitly assumed that state firms belonged to the state and so could be disposed of as the state wished. Had the wisdom of Shleifer's article been absorbed earlier, less time would have been wasted before reality sank in.

Any privatization plan—actually any substantial reform—will do well to follow the steps articulated in Shleifer's article. Assess the initial distribution of control rights. Assess the implications of the reform for the new distribution of rights. And last, but hardly least, assess the political feasibility of the reform to determine how the initial holders of control rights can be induced to accept the redistribution of these rights.

As the example of privatization in Russia shows, there may be more room for politically feasible reform and thus for redistribution than is commonly believed, even in countries with a weak central authority. The reason, emphasized in the article, is precisely why reform is desirable in the first place: the initial structure of control rights might be very inefficient. And the scope for Pareto improvement is exactly what generates the scope for buying off some of the initial stakeholders. To take an example developed by Shleifer, the politician who cannot credibly commit not to expropriate later has control rights that are worth little under the initial structure of rights. He can thus be bought off cheaply.

My comments cover three issues. First, I apply the logic of Shleifer's article to privatization in Poland. Even though the initial structure of control rights is different from that in Russia, Shleifer's approach proves serviceable for Poland as well. Second, I look at control rights within firms, an issue that strikes me as potentially more important in many Eastern European countries than the removal of control rights from politicians. Third, I argue that a frontal assault on politicians, on which the article focuses, is but one of several reforms (not all of them explicitly about control rights) that can achieve a similar goal. As an example I explore the interactions of the safety net, the inflation tax, and control rights in Russia.

Olivier Jean Blanchard is professor of economics at the Massachusetts Institute of Technology.

Proceedings of the World Bank Annual Conference on Development Economics 1994

Control Rights and Privatization in Poland

In Poland ministries and local authorities had few control rights from the start. Those were held by insiders, managers, and especially workers.

While the menu of privatization options is long and complex, it can, with little loss of realism, be reduced to two main options. One is that insiders buy their firms at a discount (known as privatization through liquidation). This method legalizes their control rights, extending their explicit stake further into the future, reducing the inefficiency of the structure of control rights. But insider control also makes it harder to get outside finance and thus limits the scope for restructuring.

Another option is to sell the firm to outsiders, known as privatization. While the insiders get shares at a discount, they in effect give up their control rights to outsiders, who are in a position to get outside finance and thus to restructure.

Four years into the privatization process in Poland, the results are very much what would be predicted from applying the logic of Shleifer's article. A simple formalization may help. Let X be the value of the firm if sold to insiders, and let Y be the value if sold to outsiders; Y is higher than X because outsiders, having access to outside finance and expertise, can more easily restructure. Let B be the benefits of control for insiders. If $Y > X + B$, restructuring is worth enough to insiders to induce them to relinquish control rights in exchange for a share in the success of the firm. If $Y < X + B$, insiders choose the insider privatization route and forgo restructuring.

The evidence in Poland fits this model well. Firms for which restructuring holds the key to better prospects have chosen outsider privatization. But so far only 100 of the 8,000 state firms have chosen this route. Some 1,000 others have chosen insider privatization and are doing little restructuring beyond shedding enough labor to stay in business. The remaining firms have not moved yet; even if many of them move to insider privatization, not much restructuring is likely to result.

On Control Rights within Firms

Shleifer focuses on the removal of control rights from politicians. That may indeed be the major issue in Russia. In the countries of Eastern and Central Europe, a bigger issue is the structure of control rights within firms.

The implications of workers' control and ownership are old topics of economic research. Researchers point out the importance of the transferability of control rights and the problems implied by lack of access to outside capital and by the short horizon of workers. From my perception of the problems of firms in Eastern and Central Europe, whether formally state owned or privatized through insider privatization, I find that this research has largely missed the main issues.

Here again, the focus on physical control rights and on the efficiency of the control rights structure helps considerably. The structure is so complex that, to use Coasian terminology, transaction costs lead to enormous inefficiencies and often to paralysis.

We know that even if a firm is owned by its workers and if transfers between workers are costless, the firm should still choose the efficient level of employment—the level at which the marginal product of labor is equal to the reservation wage. Once this level is chosen, the total product of labor is then distributed between those who keep their jobs and those who do not. When transfers have a cost, however, the outcome will be a larger, inefficient level of employment, possibly to the point where the average product of labor is equal to the reservation wage. In Eastern and Central Europe transfers—think of them as severance payments to those who lose their jobs—are indeed difficult to implement. They have the dimension of present discounted values, and few firms have the cash flow to pay them or the ability to borrow from banks for that purpose. Thus employment is still substantially too high in most firms.

This presentation only scratches the surface, however. The more serious issues involve the time spent building and overthrowing coalitions within firms. Consider a firm that has to close one of its two plants to remain in business. In a Western firm we can simply assume that the manager makes the decision. In a worker-controlled firm the outcome is the result of bargaining between workers in the two plants. Their relative influence depends on their threat points, the damage they can inflict, the side supported by those who control services common to the two plants, and so on. The eventual outcome may turn out to be efficient, but the bargaining takes place in real time, so it is likely to involve delays, changes in decisions, and output losses along the way.

These are far from just theoretical possibilities. We all know of firms with plants that should be shut down, of plants where changing coalitions have led to rapid turnover of managers, of cases where a deal made by the manager with an outside investor is then rejected by another coalition within the firm. Dabrowski and others (1993) present an array of such stories. If we are to make progress in understanding the behavior of firms, whether formally state owned or privatized through insider privatization, and the dynamics of restructuring, these are the issues that we need to think about.

Frontal Attacks

In thinking about how to change control rights, Shleifer considers only frontal attacks—policies explicitly designed to change the structure of control rights. He fails to mention that many macroeconomic and microeconomic policies also can be used. By changing the value of control rights, such measures can change coalitions and achieve many of the same results.

Consider a simple and topical example: the effects of introducing a safety net in Russia. The disclaimer that the assumptions are just short of outrageous and that this is no more than a conceptual toy obviously applies.

Suppose that firms in Russia are composed of managers and workers. For simplicity, assume that they produce nothing and should be closed. By keeping the firms alive, however, managers and workers can extract X in subsidies from the state. Of this, aX goes to managers, who are needed because they know how to extract the subsidies, and the rest, $(1 - a)X$, goes to workers. If a firm is closed, the managers find themselves with zero, and workers receive unemployment benefits B. Both X and B are financed by the inflation tax, levied on the population as a whole.

For given X and B the equilibrium is clear. If $B < (1 - a)X$, workers stay in coalitions with managers to extract the state subsidies. The cost to the budget is X. If $B > (1 - a)X$, workers prefer to receive unemployment benefits and so drop out of the coalitions, and managers are left in the cold. Firms close, which is good. The cost to the budget drops from X to B, which can imply a substantial drop if a was large enough.

Thus, increasing the safety net is good for efficiency (apart from any distributional effect it may have, which is not captured here). In terms of the framework of Shleifer's article, a "divide and conquer" strategy replaces the frontal attack. Workers are bribed to drop out of the coalitions with managers. This policy reduces the cost to the budget and the inflation tax.

The logic of this model, and I believe what it captures of reality, implies that managers should oppose the safety net. Can they? I am not sure how to make the argument tight, but I sense that it might be more difficult for them to launch an all-out attack on the safety net than, say, on the modalities of the privatization program.

This model can be extended in many ways. B, for example, depends on more than unemployment benefits. Prospects for reemployment are also important. Thus, the better are the reemployment and wage prospects in the economy, the easier it may be to destroy coalitions in unproductive firms. Growth in part of the economy makes it easier to reduce subsidies in other parts.

It must be clear that I had fun reading the article. I hope that my comments show how the approach can be extended to analyze the issues of transition.

Reference

Dabrowski, Jr., M. Federowicz, T. Kaminski, and J. Szomburg. 1993. "Privatization of Polish State-Owned Enterprises: Progress, Barriers, Initial Effects." Working Paper 33. Gdansk Institute for Market Economics.

Comment on "Establishing Property Rights," by Shleifer

Roman Frydman

Shleifer's article is an important contribution to the rapidly growing literature reexamining the functions and determinants of property rights in the transition economies. Because his analysis is predicated on the belief that establishing property rights in the postcommunist economies primarily means reducing the detrimental effects of bureaucratic control, it incorporates strategies for reducing the inefficiencies of political control of economic assets.

The first set of reform strategies would leave control rights with bureaucrats and rely on changes in the costs and benefits of political control to reduce the incentives for politicians to allocate resources inefficiently. Institutionalizing corruption, encouraging nomenklatura privatization, reforming the state bureaucracy, and limiting the abuse of political control rights by strengthening democratic institutions are ways of altering incentives. But as Shleifer shows, none of these approaches is likely to be effective in reducing the inefficiency of pervasive political control over assets in transition economies.

Shleifer turns next to the more radical strategy of legally reassigning control rights from state bureaucrats to other parties. Mass privatization programs are the leading example of this strategy. Shleifer recognizes that transferring control rights from politicians to private agents does not fully establish property rights. The transfer is just the first step; it does not ensure the security of those rights. Even after the transfer politicians can use the resources of the state treasury to persuade rather than to order firms to pursue political objectives. Shleifer's article presents only a preliminary analysis of these postprivatization obstacles to establishing private property rights. Here I will briefly discuss two points that require more attention in the analysis of the establishment of property rights.

Shleifer points out that governments in most transition economies are too weak to provide reliable enforcement of contracts and that their political processes do not allocate adequate resources to effective contract enforcement mechanisms. Shleifer further argues that a mass privatization program is likely to create a powerful con-

Roman Frydman is professor of economics at New York University. The author thanks Andrzej Rapaczynski for insightful comments on an earlier version of this piece and for many stimulating discussions in connection with their work on a related set of issues.

stituency among beneficiaries of the program, who will demand that politicians allocate substantially more resources to the protection of their newly acquired property rights. But even with much larger expenditures committed to the task, the protection of property rights by the weak governments in the region may turn out to be more complicated than Shleifer's article suggests.[1]

And complex forms of property, which are ubiquitous in a market economy, require even more complex forms of protection than simple contracts. They require a panoply of complicated corporate and securities laws. And such legal protection is just a beginning. In the market economies important property rights are often further protected by a self-enforcing structure of incentives embedded in the market system. As an illustration consider that the most important aspects of minority ownership, such as the level of dividend income, are only minimally protected by law. Much more effective enforcement comes from the discipline imposed by capital markets and the potential future capital needs of the corporation (Frydman and Rapaczynski 1994). Moreover, even if the legal protection of control rights were sufficient to establish property rights after privatization, politics might stand in the way of a genuine market economy driven by price signals rather than by political decisions about the allocation of resources.

And that leads to my second main comment. Shleifer focuses almost exclusively on preprivatization politics as a key determinant of the political feasibility of privatization. Since reformers are often politically weak, they have to buy support for the program by including preferences for politically powerful groups. This belief has underpinned the Russian mass privatization program, which in effect has transferred control rights to insiders in the majority of Russian enterprises (Boycko, Shleifer, and Vishny 1993; Pistor 1993).

It is too early to tell whether investment by outsiders (individuals not previously employed by the privatized enterprises) will follow under the Russian conditions. As important as preprivatization politics may be, it is clear that the dangers of the continuous politicization of resource allocation decisions and the need for continuous protection of control rights do not necessarily end when a mass privatization program is completed (Frydman and Rapaczynski 1994). Shleifer's article does not really deal with the politics created by the allocation of control rights following privatization. This reallocation modifies the demand for state intervention by the newly enfranchised private actors and therefore leaves open the possibility that the demand for state intervention might not diminish, at least in the short run.

Note

1. Shleifer occasionally suggests that the control rights transferred through a mass privatization program are physical rights. These rights are implicitly considered as less complex than contracts and thus easier to protect. It should be noted, however, that the concept of physical rights is at best applicable to owner-managed firms in which the owners are physically present to exercise their control rights over the assets legally designated as theirs. The notion of physical rights is certainly not sufficient for more complex forms of property, in particular those pertaining to ownership of corporations and other securitized, intangible forms of property that usually result from the privatization of industrial firms in the transition economies.

References

Boycko, Maxim, Andrei Shleifer, and Robert W. Vishny. 1993. "Privatizing Russia." *Brookings Papers on Economic Activity*. Washington, D.C.: The Brookings Institution.

Frydman, Roman, and Andrzej Rapaczynski. 1994. *Privatization in Eastern Europe: Is the State Withering Away?* Prague: Central European University Press, in association with Oxford University Press.

Pistor, Katharina. 1993. "Privatization and Corporate Governance in Russia: An Empirical Study." Paper prepared for the Workshop on Economic Reform, Center for International Security and Arms Control, Stanford University, Stanford, Calif.

Floor Discussion of "Establishing Property Rights," by Shleifer

In an extension of the question Roman Frydman (discussant) posed in his comments, a participant from Harvard University asked why the de jure reassignment of property rights would affect the de facto distribution of control rights in the way Shleifer assumed. Even Western systems with well-defined private property rights still see high levels of bureaucratic intervention, he said. Perhaps the political variables that control bureaucracies are more important than the complete definition of property rights.

Assuming the concrete example of a firm that is under the control of some ministry, Shleifer said that he was talking about mechanisms for depriving the ministry of the opportunity or ability to tell the firm's manager what to do, because that would result in more efficient resource allocation. Does that mean we have arrived at an efficient structure for control rights? Definitely not, Shleifer said. Full managerial control is not ideal, either, and should probably be complemented by the rights of majority and minority shareholders, for example.

In other words, said Shleifer, by refusing to protect the rights of ministries—which is essentially what privatization and corporatization accomplishes in these countries—you begin to reduce political influence on these firms and increase operating efficiency. But laws allowing shareholders and other participants in a market economy to exercise their rights do not come about because Western advisers tell transition governments to write them down. Such laws come about because of internal lobbies and political pressures to create them. The people pushing for securities laws and corporate laws in Russia are the ones who have a financial interest in making sure such laws exist—the new shareholders in privatized companies. The impetus for enforcement mechanisms is created precisely through this reallocation of control rights. So what Olivier Blanchard (discussant) calls the frontal assault is the right first step; enforcement strategies and other mechanisms will follow.

Frydman amplified one point he had only touched on in his comment: yes, one must make compromises at the outset to push a policy through, but it may also be necessary to institute new policies later if the original policies result in inefficient

This session was chaired by S. Shahid Husain, vice president, Management and Personnel Services, at the World Bank.

Proceedings of the World Bank Annual Conference on Development Economics 1994

control structures. One should not assume that once a privatization program is in place it will do only good; examples to the contrary abound. Romania's so-called privatization program, for example, was actually the biggest nationalization program in history: in the end 70 percent of industry was in state hands. A joint project between Bulgaria and the World Bank will basically ensure that bureaucrats control the so-called government-sponsored funds. These were reassignments of control rights, but whether they were efficient is clearly open to question.

A participant from the United Nations asked Shleifer to define the bureaucrat his paper was targeting. Is he talking about the civil service, the ministries, the party cells, or even the workers and managers of state-owned enterprises? It seemed to this participant that Shleifer was saying that property rights originally belonged to the state (or society or the Communist party) but over time accrued, not legally but de facto, to various elements of society, from worker councils up to civil servants or ministerial bureaucrats who had the say over what was sold, at what price, and so on. So the bureaucrat in this view was someone who possessed control rights or negotiated contracts that were not enforceable because the rights were never transferred legally. Which brings us, the participant said, to what Frydman was talking about: how do you make this enforceable when you do transfer the rights in some form? Blanchard had said that the French civil service might be a model, the participant continued, and Shleifer had responded that you cannot reform the bureaucracy, which might well be the case in Russia. But if you cannot reform the bureaucracy, how are you ever going to enforce property rights in law? How are you going to defend those who have residual control rights?

The bureaucrats are certainly not the workers or managers, Shleifer replied. In many of these countries control rights over industrial enterprises tend to lie in the ministries; in smaller enterprises they lie in local governments and administrations. How do you enforce property rights once you transfer them from these bureaucrats? Shleifer said he was still struggling to understand why the point is so controversial, but fundamentally it is difficult to enforce the bureaucrat's rights if the state machine is not supporting the bureaucrats. Once you disengage the bureaucrats from control over an enterprise's assets, it is not nearly as difficult to enforce at least the physical rights of the enterprise managers. And having control rights in the hands of managers instead of bureaucrats leads to more efficient resource allocation because the managers have longer time horizons than the bureaucrats and greater access to owners and to the firms' cash flow. Who will challenge the managers? In some countries, the workers; in others, the shareholders, other managers, or thieves. Some protection is called for, but managers are probably in a better position than bureaucrats to protect control rights from all parties. That is why, Shleifer continued, the first objective of reform should be to eliminate the bureaucrats' control rights.

The second question raised by the U.N. participant—if you cannot reform the bureaucracy, how can you hope to protect property rights?—is the central issue of economic development, said Shleifer. In some ways you need the government to protect property rights, says Shleifer, so why is he arguing against the government so strenuously? The problem in many Eastern European countries and in transition economies is that the governments do precisely the wrong things: they don't enforce contracts and protect property rights and most of their efforts are directed at grabbing additional control rights for themselves. So what is his position on reforming bureaucracy? The East Asian strategy was a bureaucracy-led transformation. Is this a viable alternative for the transition economies? Given what Shleifer knows about Eastern European bureaucracies, that is an insane idea. But the participant is absolutely right, he concluded. At some point civilized government is needed if you want a civilized economy. But reforming the bureaucracy is not the immediate strategy for economic reform.

A participant from the World Bank said that he found Blanchard's explanation of the need for coalitions compelling and that he had never before heard articulated how workers could be involved in the restructuring of firms. But he wondered if there wasn't some inconsistency between trying to create consensus and trying to achieve efficiency. If the problem with workers is that too many decisionmakers create inefficiency, isn't there an inherent contradiction between building coalitions and achieving efficiency? Hasn't the Western experience been that you get efficiency gains only when a minority exercises authority and controls a firm's assets?

You don't want to look at what happens the day after privatization, responded Blanchard; you want to think about what will happen over time. Once a firm has taken the liquidation route to privatization in Poland, for example, there is a period when workers, managers, and ownership are extremely decentralized—when nobody really knows how to play the game. For a while the exact control rights of each worker or plant are not well defined, and you see coalitions coming and going and little positive outcome in terms of restructuring. Over time, however, a gifted leader emerges and puts a coalition together, workers basically give up their control rights in exchange for good decisions, and the result is a governance structure involving a small number of players. It's a strange process, and one that is likely to take a long time and to vary from firm to firm.

A crucial point in Blanchard's model, said a participant from the International Finance Corporation, was comparing unemployment benefits with what workers could extract from the state. Did Shleifer agree or disagree that credible cash constraints might be more important than any assignment of property rights? And does the nature of the firm make a difference? Poland has mainly manufacturing firms, for example, whereas many of the state firms in Russia and Ukraine are involved with oil, gas, and other mineral resources. It may be more difficult to enforce credible cash constraints on the oil and gas firms, and the returns on corruption are much higher in those economies than in economies like Poland.

Shleifer said that he had addressed precisely that question. Obviously, if monetary policy is loose, even if you transfer control rights from the bureaucrats to private agents, bureaucrats could use subsidies and other mechanisms to convince private agents not to restructure, or to pursue policies that the bureaucrats want, which is what's happening in Russia. Monetary stabilization is essential to enterprise restructuring because loose monetary policy can undo all the benefits from transforming property rights. Extending the example of the Polish firm, one might ask if anything really need be done about property rights if you have hard budget constraints. Shleifer is skeptical that such a strategy would be viable in the long run because so long as you retain bureaucratic control over enterprises, either you will have a problem sustaining the hard budget constraint or there will be incessant pressure from within for further subsidies. In the long run you need both hard budget constraints and the efficient allocation of property rights.

Was there a special problem in the oil industry? Shleifer believes that in some ways the oil industry was in the best shape. If you gave management some incentives and cash flow rights, these firms could become profitable in the long run. In terms of property rights it might be easier to establish efficient control structures in these firms than in others. The problem in these firms was theft by managers, even if they owned an equity stake. Eventually, some kind of enforcement must follow the reallocation of control rights.

Property rights are not really enforced by law, said Frydman; they are self-enforced by a decentralized structure of incentives. Even in advanced economies law enforcement works only at the margin. That is why it is important for macropolicy to create a decentralized structure of incentives that support the economic, rather than the political, use of resources. That was the ultimate goal of transition, said Frydman. In a sense macropolicy—including import and other commercial policies—plays two roles: it denies bureaucrats the ability to use subsidies, and it creates incentives by forcing firms to return to the capital market. If a manager knows that he doesn't have to worry about outside investors, the firm is unlikely to attract outside investors.

A participant from the World Bank noted that in an earlier presentation someone had praised the coupon method of privatization, and he wondered if this vehicle was in danger of making ownership even more concentrated than it had been under the communist system. He understood that in the Czech Republic one fund has de facto ownership of 600 industrial units, everything is managed from Prague by absentee landlords, and if, for example, the fund decides to close one textile mill, a unit in Prague is more likely to survive than one elsewhere. Could the method could be modified to bring management closer to the firm's actual location and problems?

Blanchard responded that one problem with Czech privatization had been this concentration of ownership, which is why the commercial banks that adjust management of the funds should not be allowed to purchase shares in them; this policy would disperse ownership of the funds. Whether that policy was politically possible, Blanchard didn't know, but it would certainly make bank ownership weaker and the funds more independent. Shleifer's recollection of the numbers was that the referenced fund, which had tried to concentrate its holdings, had large equity stakes in only 50 enterprises, not 600, and that the funds that had stakes in hundreds of enterprises owned only trivial equity stakes, so things were not so bad as the participant might think. He did not see overconcentration of assets as much of a problem. These funds will develop expertise in providing capital and governance for the enterprises, said Shleifer, and until he saw evidence that they were up to no good, there was no reason to fear them unduly. After all, Fiat controls between 20 and 40 percent of industrial assets in Italy. If the Czech economy were to do as well as Italy... we should all be so lucky.

How Industrial Reform Worked in China: The Role of Innovation, Competition, and Property Rights

Gary H. Jefferson and Thomas G. Rawski

In China early attempts at partial reform unleashed forces that, fifteen years later, have brought China's economy to the brink of a market system. The participation of tens of thousands of enterprises and millions of administrators, managers, and workers over the duration of the reform eventually built a constituency for market-directed change that was far stronger than any official announcement could have produced. Gradual and partial reform shifted the economy toward a market system under a regime of growth, improved productivity, accelerated technical change, and rising exports. Reactions of firms and governments focused increasingly on innovation, cost reduction, and further deregulation, deepening the cumulative impact of reform, rather than on rent-seeking and subsidies. This process of reform is very different from the top-down, centrally planned approach to reform that is widely advocated by international organizations and economic researchers, but it has produced a durable reform constituency that easily rebuffed high-level efforts to roll back reform in the wake of the inflation scare and political repression of 1989.

China's partial and gradual reform has combined rapid economic progress with institutions and policies that deviate widely from standard prescriptions for reform. China's reforms present economists with a puzzle. Why has China "grown so fast when conditions thought to be necessary for growth... were absent?" (Blanchard and Fischer 1993, p. 4). How did China's unorthodox reforms spark an economic surge that has far outpaced results in other ex-socialist economies and in many developing nations?

Many economists view the reform of former socialist economies as a process of replacing old institutions with new structures in an organized top-down fashion

Gary H. Jefferson is associate professor of economics at Brandeis University. Thomas G. Rawski is professor of economics at the University of Pittsburgh. The authors received support for this research from the Henry Luce Foundation, the John S. Guggenheim Foundation, the University of Pittsburgh's University Center for International Studies, Brandeis University's Mazer Fund, and the World Bank's Project on Industrial Reform and Productivity within Chinese Enterprises. The authors are grateful for the research assistance of John Zhiqiang Zhao and for data and comments from E.C. Hwa, Nicholas R. Lardy, Wei Lo, Penelope Prime, Jeffrey Sachs, Inderjit Singh, Wing T. Woo, and Shahid Yusuf.

directed by reformers. The self-interested response of agents within the economy is expected to stimulate profit-seeking behavior and market activity. If progress is inadequate, planners can impose further rounds of reform.

This type of centrally directed reform has undoubtedly played a role in China's economic transition. It was China's central leadership that initiated economic reforms in the late 1970s, expanding the role of prices and market allocation, rolling back long-standing barriers to international trade and investment, transferring authority from central planners to enterprise managers and local governments, creating a system of dual (plan and market) pricing for industrial goods, and so on. But unlike the postcommunist leaders in countries like Poland and the Czech Republic, China's policymakers embarked on a path of reform with no clear vision of what a restructured economy should look like and no consensus about what policy mix or institutional arrangements would best get the economy there (Hua, Luo, and Zhang 1993; Shirk 1993; Naughton 1994).

Not surprisingly, policy announcements from the center were partial and tentative. The center ratified but did not direct the momentous shift from collective to household farming. Central initiatives in industrial reform focused on the incremental relaxation of controls over state-owned enterprises. Even the revolutionary "open door" strategy, reflected in a sequence of central decisions that shattered long-standing barriers to China's participation in the world economy, concentrated on expanding trade and investment activity in a small number of provinces and special zones along China's southeast coast.

From the usual top-down perspective China's recent economic gains seem remarkably large in relation to the central government's modest reform initiatives. In exploring this anomaly, we focus on an analysis of China's reform dynamics that shows how technical innovation, economizing behavior, market-leaning institutional changes, and a multitude of cumulative and mutually reinforcing choices by administrators, managers, and workers reinforced and eventually overshadowed Beijing's partial reform efforts. The focus is on industry, which is both the largest sector of China's economy and the core of its reform problem.

Successive rounds of partial reform have cumulated into significant changes in industrial structure, conduct, and performance affecting every type of firm, including old-line state firms. In this process partial reform initiatives produce unanticipated outcomes in an interplay of action and reaction among changes in economic conditions, ad hoc policy measures by various levels of government, and uncoordinated strategizing by enterprises and individuals. This interaction occurs in an environment of intense competition involving several types of firms, each with its own distinct technical capabilities and institutional constraints. Partial reform expands entry into product markets, and the ensuing intensification of competition erodes enterprise profits and undermines the revenue base at every level of government. These financial strains generate pressures that promote innovation and cost reduction. Government efforts to ease the revenue constraint and enterprise efforts to innovate and reduce costs lead to fresh rounds of market-directed institutional change.

What Needs to Be Explained about China's Industrial Reform

China's recent industrial achievements deviate from the orthodox reform scenarios in the continued dominance of the public sector; its improved performance, despite the absence of any plans for privatization; and the continued presence of important defects in the institutional underpinnings of China's industrial economy.

Rapid growth is amply documented in World Bank reports, which reveal the broad-based nature of industrial expansion. Joint ventures, foreign-owned firms, and private industry contributed only one-sixth of incremental output gains during 1980–92 (table 1). Despite the highly publicized economic boom in China's southern coastal provinces, the region's 36 percent share in aggregate industrial output in 1992 was only modestly above its 30 percent share for 1978—and below the 36.6 percent share in 1952 (Industry 1949–84, p. 145; Survey 1993, p. 72).

The Dominance of Public Enterprise

The output share of state-owned industry (firms "owned by the whole people" and directly or indirectly controlled by agencies of the central government) plunged from three-quarters to less than half between 1980 and 1992 (table 1). This decline reflects dramatic gains by collectives, especially the rural firms known as township and village enterprises (or TVEs). The 1992 output share of public sector industry, however, which includes state firms and urban and rural collectives, exceeds 85 percent. The output share of private domestic firms remains small, at less than 10 percent.[1]

The explosive growth of TVE output has aroused intense interest. TVE firms, although different in many respects from state enterprises, are public enterprises. Calling TVEs "nonstate enterprises" conveys the misleading impression that rural collectives operate independently of officialdom. Some authors have speculated that TVE firms "mimic private enterprises" or operate like "loosely-structured cooperatives" (Singh, Ratha, and Xiao 1993; Weitzman and Xu 1994). TVE operations are closely monitored and often controlled by "local government entrepreneurs" (Zweig 1991, p. 720) who "exhibit characteristics of both de facto owners and senior managers of township corporations" (Whiting 1993, p. 6).[2] The TVE sector is built on the foundation of earlier industrialization efforts undertaken by local governments (Perkins and others 1977). Like their predecessors, the TVE firms of the 1980s and 1990s operate "under close supervision from the township or village industrial departments" (Wong, Heady, and Woo 1993, chap. 9), which contribute start-up funds, appoint managers, and "are intimately involved in major strategic decisions" (Ody 1991, p. iv).[3]

Improved Performance in State Industry

No one disputes the significance of the contributions that TVEs have made to the growth of production, exports, productivity, employment, incomes, and material welfare. Their success shows the insufficiency of assuming that a full and immediate

Table 1. *Overview of Industrial Performance in China, 1980–92*

	Index of real output (1980=100)			*Shares in nominal output (percent)*				*1980–92 (percent)*	
Ownership type	*1985*	*1990*	*1992*	*1980*	*1985*	*1990*	*1992*	*Annual average growth*	*Share of incremental output*
State	148	210	257	76.0	64.9	54.6	48.4	7.8	43.6
Collective	247	554	914					18.4	
Urban				13.7	13.3	10.3	11.8		11.5
Township-village				9.9	18.8	25.3	26.2		28.8
Private[a]	21,752	126,057	241,455	0.0	1.9	5.4	6.8	64.9	7.9
Other[b]	492	3,530	8,736	0.5	1.2	4.4	7.2	37.2	8.3
Total	176	328	480	100.0	100.0	100.0	100.0	13.1	100.0
Total output (¥ billion)				515.4	971.6	2,392.5	3,706.6		

a. Privately owned firms employing fewer than eight workers.
b. Includes private firms employing eight or more workers, joint ventures, foreign-owned firms, and other ownership forms.
Source: Yearbook 1993, pp. 409–13; Rawski forthcoming.

end to official influence over enterprise management, preferably through privatization, is a necessary step in the reform of socialist systems.

But the inconsistency between recent Chinese industrial experience and free-market orthodoxy runs even deeper. China's old-line state enterprises have responded to ongoing partial reform by behaving less like passive bureaucratic followers and more like profit-seeking commercial businesses. Reform has altered the objectives, incentives, and corporate culture of state firms, bringing substantial improvements in performance. With state industry accounting for nearly half of industrial output and absorbing 35 percent of aggregate fixed investment, China's recent economic gains could hardly have occurred had state industry served only as a drag on economic progress.[4]

This article is not the place for a detailed review of evidence supporting these assertions.[5] The discussion here is limited to the following propositions about state industry, each resting on substantial empirical foundations:

- State enterprises, formerly devoted to plan fulfillment, now take profit as their chief objective. Data on state enterprise performance generate increasingly robust statistical relationships of the kind expected from profit-seeking firms operating in a competitive market setting.
- State enterprises have achieved substantial increases in labor productivity and steady, although modest, increases in total factor productivity.[6]
- State enterprises have sharply increased the pace of research and development, new product development, and process innovation (Jefferson, Rawski, and Zheng 1992a,b).
- Exports of state enterprise manufactures, which increased at an estimated annual rate of 18 percent between 1985 and 1992, reflect the impact of greater attention to quality, variety, customer requirements, and cost control.[7]
- State enterprises constitute an important and often crucial source of technology, equipment, funds, information, expertise, and marketing opportunities essential for the successful development of TVEs.

Persistence of Institutional Weaknesses

In looking at China's recent achievements, the challenge is to explain dramatic gains in industrial performance in the absence of comprehensive efforts at the center to promote liberalization and institutional change. The key question concerns the process that has moved public sector firms reared under state planing to place unprecedented emphasis on efficiency, quality, and innovation, with no program or even credible threat of privatization, and to explain how China's industrial advances have occurred without the features that many economists regard as core elements of a market system.

Chinese industry continues to operate in an environment of incomplete specification of property rights. Rules of commerce are neither clearly defined nor consistently enforced. Competing firms in the same industry or locality face widely differing legal, fiscal, and regulatory regimes. Government intervention in business affairs extends well beyond the boundaries observed in even heavily regulated market economies (Japan, Republic of Korea), often with the effect of softening budget constraints. These difficulties restrict innovation and productivity growth, particularly, but not exclusively, in the state sector.[8] They have also enabled insolvent and hopelessly inefficient state enterprises to continue to operate, wasting large amounts of productive resources and requiring subsidies large enough to affect macroeconomic stability (Sachs and Woo 1993; Woo and others 1993). The cost of these institutional shortcomings, although difficult to quantify, appears large.

A Model for Analyzing Induced Industrial Reform

We propose the following model of China's industrial reform, which we see as a cumulative process that begins when partial relaxation of the institutional constraints associated with socialist planning initiates competition in the markets for industrial products. Competition reduces profits, creating financial pressures that induce technical innovations, promote economizing behavior, and stimulate fresh rounds of market-leaning institutional change. This model rests on four key institutional features of China's industrial economy: decentralized supervision, incipient competition, fiscal dependence on industrial profits, and a hierarchy of heterogeneous enterprise types.[9]

Decentralized Supervision

Central control of industrial enterprises was never as tight in China as in Eastern Europe and the Soviet Union (Granick 1990). Decentralization increased during the late 1960s and 1970s as the central government transferred supervision of many firms to provincial and municipal governments. This system of decentralized supervision encouraged provinces and localities to create and pursue their own industrial development strategies. When reform began, decentralized decisionmaking also made it possible to introduce piecemeal reforms and to conduct local policy experiments without disrupting the whole economy. Successful local reforms inspired widespread emulation.

Incipient Competition

The term "incipient competition" well describes the circumstances of domestic Chinese markets for industrial products on the eve of reform. Actual competition was sharply limited by policies that had the effect of creating strong barriers to entry. Removing these barriers, however, quickly revealed multiple competitors in nearly every product line. In China, unlike Russia and other countries of the former Soviet Union and Eastern Europe, deregulation leads to industrial competition, not to monopoly.

Competitive pressures arose from four sources. Rural industry developed widely in the decades prior to reform but was largely confined to fabricating local materials into goods for local buyers (Perkins and others 1977). Entrepreneurial leaders in hundreds of counties and thousands of production brigades were poised to take advantage of deregulation by bursting into markets that they had coveted for years. China's southern regions, excluded from large-scale industrial investment during three decades of central planning, took advantage of the new open door policy to promote industrial growth with the aid of capital, skill, and commercial contacts from overseas Chinese, most of whom trace their ancestry to the southern coastal provinces. Defense conversion brought strong new entrants into a number of civilian industries; by the early 1990s at least two-thirds of output from defense industries consisted of civilian products (Blasko 1994). Finally, China's long-standing policy of building complete sets of state-owned industries in most provinces provided a ready-made source of competition.

Fiscal Dependence on Industrial Profits

Industrial profits and tax payments are a key component of fiscal revenue at every level of government. State enterprises contributed 80 percent or more of adjusted budgetary revenues in every year during 1978–87; in 1988 state industry accounted for 73 percent of profits and profit taxes from all state enterprises (Sicular 1992, table 5 and p. 3).

The fiscal reforms of the 1980s created a system in which each level of government collected taxes from enterprises under its jurisdiction, "turned over a contractually specified amount to the next higher level of government, and could keep the residual." The result was "a shift toward local fiscal power at the expense of the center, as the center's proportion of total government revenue fell" from 50 percent in the 1970s to less than 30 percent in the 1980s (Walder 1994, pp. 17, 19).

Chinese Industry as a Hierarchy of Heterogeneous Enterprise Types

China's industrial sector displays extreme heterogeneity. There is a hierarchy of domestic industrial enterprises ranging from foreign-linked firms to state enterprises, urban and rural (TVE) collectives, and private businesses. These groups of firms exhibit systematic differences in technological capabilities, cost structures, and institutional arrangements. There is an inverse relation between innovative capability and labor costs. Among domestic firms, state enterprises have the greatest technical strength. They also have the highest labor costs and suffer the greatest restriction from institutional constraints. TVEs are least affected by institutional limitations. The interaction of these different enterprise types creates a kind of innovation and competition ladder.

Vernon (1966) and Grossman and Helpman (1991) have developed models of international product cycles and quality ladders that focus on interactions between innovative firms in the "North" and imitators in the "South." Northern firms rely on product innovations to support their high-cost manufacturing operations. Southern firms, with lower production costs, can capture markets from northern rivals by replicating northern products. The North retaliates with fresh rounds of innovation. Rivalry among different types of producers leads to an ongoing evolution of product characteristics, while the locus of manufacturing activity may shift back and forth between firms located in the "industrial" North and those in the "developing" South.

This approach fits nicely with China's recent industrial history once we extend these concepts to encompass the existence of product cycles and quality ladders *within the domestic economy of nations participating in global trade* as well as across high- and low-wage economies. Chinese industrial goods rarely match the quality and characteristics of products manufactured by global leaders. But the most accomplished Chinese firms, on their own or with the cooperation of foreign partners, can produce reasonable substitutes at a low cost. Rapidly growing exports of textiles, garments, footwear, machinery, and consumer durables illustrate China's participation in international quality ladders.

At the top of the international quality ladder are the overseas firms that set the innovative pace in global markets. These firms define technical and quality standards that Chinese firms seek to attain. Chinese industry has its own hierarchy of firms that generates domestic versions of the rivalries, flows, and pressures associated with global product cycles. On the top rung of China's domestic ladder of technological capabilities are foreign-invested firms; below them are state enterprises, urban collectives, TVEs, and privately owned firms. We focus on the three largest categories.

- *Foreign-invested firms.* Close foreign links give these firms better access to foreign capital and technologies than purely domestic competitors. While foreign-linked firms operate under many of the restrictions that apply to state enterprises, they enjoy favorable tax treatment and special autonomy in labor-management relations, wage setting, and foreign trade. China's open door policy has allowed these firms to flourish, with beneficial effects on export growth, technology inflows, and the spread of opportunities for purely domestic firms to explore new approaches to production, management, and sales.
- *State-owned enterprises.* State enterprises were the traditional centerpiece of economic planning. Decades of favorable treatment have endowed them with a legacy of technical capabilities surpassing those of other domestic enterprise types. At the same time, state enterprises bear heavier burdens of social responsibilities and bureaucratic intrusion than any other type of enterprise.
- *Collective enterprises.* Urban and rural collectives are owned by local governments and sometimes by state enterprises. Their operations are generally more labor-intensive than state enterprise production; their products typically cluster at the low end of the price-quality spectrum. Some of these firms have begun to apply modern technologies and sophisticated equipment to produce goods that can compete in national and international markets as well as in local markets.

There is a well-defined hierarchy of domestic technological capabilities extending downward from joint ventures to state enterprises and collectives. Among purely domestic firms state enterprises enjoy superior endowments of equipment, laboratory facilities, and skilled and educated workers, technicians, and managers. This resource differential favoring state firms shows up in the outcomes of quality inspections. In the fourth quarter of 1993, for example, 73.8 percent of goods from a sample of 2,221 firms passed inspection; the success rate was 90 percent for "big state enterprises" but only 62 percent for "township and private manufacturers" (Ma 1994).[10] Managers of urban collectives and TVEs (as well as state enterprises) overwhelmingly identify state firms as the domestic technological leaders in their own industries (Jefferson, Rawski, and Zheng 1992b).

As in the transnational version of the product cycle, technology percolates down China's domestic quality ladder. The example of bar coding illustrates how links with international markets necessitate the mastery of suitable technologies and the achievement of specific quality standards that gradually spread into the domestic economy. Export-oriented firms have learned to use bar codes, which they see as "tickets to foreign supermarkets." Today only a few dozen domestic retail outlets use bar codes. But by the end of 1995 "China aims to have bar codes on all its exported goods and 60 percent of domestic commodities" (Sun 1994, p. 8).

One important and widely overlooked aspect of Chinese quality ladders is the dependence of many TVE producers on funds, equipment, product designs, technical information, management skills, and subcontracting opportunities obtained from state enterprises (Jefferson and Rawski 1994). In southern Jiangsu province (near Shanghai), a center of booming rural enterprise development, "more than two-thirds of township and village enterprises...have established various forms of economic and technical cooperation arrangements with industrial enterprises, research units, and higher educational institutions in larger cities" (Xu, Mao, and Yuan 1993). Officials attempting to develop industry in poor localities are encouraged to pursue "joint operations with scientific research organizations or large- and medium-scale enterprises" (Du, Huang, and Chen 1992).

The domestic quality ladder also resembles its international counterpart in that cost pressures move in the opposite direction from technological capabilities. The manager of a TVE garment firm that had begun with an infusion of cash and used equipment from a much larger state enterprise observed that "in the area of product quality, household producers can't match collectives and collectives can't match state enterprises; but as for costs, state enterprises can't match collectives and the collectives can't match individual households" (interview, June 1993). Wage costs are highest in foreign-invested firms and lowest in TVEs (table 2). The cost advantage of collectives over state firms is a staple topic of discussion in Chinese newspapers and economic journals, which emphasize the extra burden of pensions, taxes, redundant workers, fringe benefits, and welfare responsibilities assigned to state firms, especially compared with TVEs. The extra cost burdens are large and, in some cases, growing rapidly. For example, state enterprises are obliged to pay retirement benefits out of current income. National data (probably excluding the farm populace) show that the ratio of retirees to active workers increased from 1:26 in 1978 to 1:6 in 1990 (Du and Shang 1993). A 1989 sample study showed that enterprises

Table 2. *Average Wages for Different Classes of Enterprise in China's Textile Industry, 1989–91*
(yuan per person-year)

Ownership type	*1989*	*1990*	*1991*
Joint venture	3,663	4,232	5,674
State sector	2,069	2,252	2,377
Urban collective	1,368	1,688	1,862
Township-village	1,132[a]	—	—

— Not available.
a. Average wage for all TVE industries.
Source: Jefferson, Rawski, and Zheng 1994.

paid about 232 yuan per worker for medical costs (Du and Shang 1993); by 1993 a survey of 100 units in Hebei province found average annual medical costs of 1,201 yuan—equivalent to 37 percent of money wages (Li and Qin 1993).[11]

Distinct Technical and Institutional Frontiers

Firms occupying different rungs of the quality ladder face different institutional regimes, which implies that domestic competition may take the form of efforts to remake institutions as well as products. Economists think of innovations as changes in technology (a new product) or managerial systems (just-in-time inventory controls) that expand the production frontiers for individual firms or whole industries, while the firm's objectives, behavior, organization, and surrounding institutional environment remain unchanged. Since the task of economic reform consists precisely of altering these basic circumstances, the assumption of institutional stability within and outside the firm is not tenable in transition economies.

Firms in transition economies face separate technical and institutional frontiers: the technical frontier embraces the standard idea (in its neoclassical or evolutionary form) that firms can draw on alternative blueprints or techniques to transform resources (including knowledge and experience) into products. The institutional frontier delineates the set of resource configurations that is attainable under prevailing custom, law, and regulation. In the context of socialist systems and transition economies, institutional restrictions prevent the exploitation of many options that are technically feasible and block choices that would be made in the absence of institutional change.[12]

Chinese authors routinely comment on the long-standing practice of applying separate laws and regulations to firms operating under different ownership arrangements. We have already mentioned differences in taxation and labor costs. Regulatory regimes affecting labor unions, environmental hazards, workplace safety, and the like are applied more vigorously to joint ventures and state firms than to urban or rural collectives. TVEs benefit from short lines of command. Business decisions are often reached through a single telephone conversation or a meeting of two or three people. State firms, by contrast, often report to multiple supervisory agencies whose overlapping jurisdictions and competing agendas complicate even routine business decisions (Byrd 1992). Shorter lines of command make it easier for TVEs to reach decisions and form business coalitions with domestic or foreign partners. TVEs and joint ventures can dismiss workers more easily than can state enterprises. Jefferson, Lu, and Zhao (1994), using a composite indicator of management authority, find a high degree of decisionmaking autonomy at the enterprise level for nearly two-thirds of 300 TVEs surveyed in 1991 but for less than half of 900 state enterprises. Bankruptcy, long a reality for TVEs, is only now emerging as a possibility for state firms.

The Dynamics of Partial Reform in China's Industry

We see the dynamics of partial reform in China's industry as a succession of responses to imbalance by both enterprises and governments. Our framework is in the tradition of Hirschman's (1958) analysis of unbalanced growth. The dynamic that transforms partial reform into improved performance is simple and direct:

- The government implements partial reform measures that reduce entry barriers and lower the cost of many types of transactions. These initiatives have different impacts on the options available to various groups of firms. Partial reform accelerates the domestic product cycle by facilitating the transmission of cost pressures and technologies up and down the hierarchy of industrial enterprises.
- The differential impact of reform efforts destabilizes the existing division of industrial resources and product markets among different types of firms. Competition in industrial product markets intensifies.
- Stronger competition diminishes the flow of quasi-rents derived from the enforcement of entry barriers and market segmentation. Reduced profitability limits the growth of wages and bonuses for some firms and throws others into a position of financial loss. The erosion of profits also limits the growth of revenues accruing to local and provincial authorities and to the central government.
- Firms react to financial pressures by choosing strategies involving one or more of the following components: restructuring operations, lobbying for further deregulation to facilitate profit-seeking initiatives, and lobbying for government subsidies or official intervention to restore the initial financial position.
- Governments also react to financial pressures that reduce their share of total output and destabilize the distribution of fiscal revenue across regions and administrative levels. Officials face conflicting enterprise lobbying efforts, some demanding further autonomy and deregulation, others seeking protection from the effects of earlier reforms.
- These induced responses of firms and governments further erode entry barriers and reduce transaction costs. Beneficial feedback effects accelerate every dimension of the reform process by intensifying competition, further dimin-

ishing quasi-rents, and motivating enterprises and governments to undertake new reform efforts. These changes set in motion further rounds of technical development, economizing efforts, and incremental reform.

- This entire process affects the attitudes of enterprise personnel and government officials to the direction and outcome of reform. Changing attitudes affect the objectives and strategies of all participants.

Although this mechanism focuses attention on endogenous or bottom-up aspects of the reform process, not every industrial policy initiative undertaken since the beginning of reform represents an endogenous response to the initial partial reform effort. Many policy changes, such as the partial commercialization of bank lending and the reduction of budgetary appropriations for industrial research and development projects, probably represent a combination of endogenous response and exogenous initiative.

Furthermore, there is no guarantee that partial reform will succeed. If governments act to stifle competition, equalize financial outcomes for winners and losers, or alter regulations to restore the prereform status quo in product markets, the endogenous process linking initial reforms with innovation, economizing, and further institutional change may stall.

We see this cumulative process of endogenous response as the key to explaining how China recorded unexpectedly strong achievements in both growth and institutional change despite modest reform initiatives on the part of its central government. Our discussion focuses on seven propositions about Chinese industrial reform corresponding to each element of the model.

Proposition 1: Partial Reform Erodes Market Segmentation, Thereby Lowering Barriers to Technology and Resource Flows

China's reforms of the late 1970s restored household agriculture and reopened rural markets; expanded China's participation in global markets for commodities, capital, and technology; and began to loosen controls in the industrial sector. Each of these policy shifts eroded barriers to competition in industrial factor and product markets.

Agricultural reforms provided a big boost to China's rural industries by increasing the supply of labor and raw materials and, following the quick rise of farm incomes, boosting demand for output. As Sachs and Woo (1994) point out, China's comparatively large rural sector creates possibilities for rapid productivity growth that are not accessible to more urbanized states like the Czech Republic, Poland, and Russia.

The open door policy brought a rapid increase in imports of industrial goods, many of them competing directly with domestic products. Partial liberalization of the external sector sharply reduced the transaction costs associated with international inflows of capital, technology, market information, managerial skills, and equipment. New policies speeded the transfer of capabilities and cost pressures across China's borders and throughout the hierarchy of domestic enterprises. The pace of change was particularly rapid in regions of southern China that benefited from proximity to Hong Kong as well as from accelerated deregulation.

The initial industrial reforms were directed mainly at large-scale, urban-based state enterprises. The objective was to enliven large-scale industry by encouraging firms to shed the passive mentality of plan followers in favor of self-motivated efforts to take full advantage of available resources. Large firms were allowed to retain a portion of their profits. And because discretionary funds cannot stimulate production or innovation unless they can be used to acquire productive inputs, the reforms included measures that diverted industrial resources from planned allocation into market channels.

Although intended to stimulate state enterprises, these measures had their largest impact in the TVE sector. Urban-oriented reform enabled TVEs to obtain inputs formerly reserved for clients of the plan system and to penetrate markets outside their home areas. The relaxation of restrictions on information-sharing, consulting, and technical ties across urban-rural administrative boundaries made it easier for collectives and TVEs to adopt new technologies and to produce substitutes that could compete with state enterprise products. These changes shattered constraints that had previously restricted TVE growth. The result was an unexpected growth explosion in China's rural industries.

These partial and uneven reforms substantially eroded barriers that had long obstructed flows of resources and products across the boundaries separating different types of firms and different administrative and bureaucratic jurisdictions. As old distinctions gradually blurred, resources, products, funds, and information began to circulate in new directions. The new market channels were soon large enough to leave quantitative traces in the form of shrinking divergences in factor returns among different enterprise groups (table 3). The bright growth prospects and high rates of return enjoyed by TVEs at the start of reform attracted a large inflow of funds, which pushed down returns to TVE capital. Naughton (1992) documents a

Table 3. *Profit/Capital Ratios in Different Segments of Chinese Industry, Selected Years, 1980–92*
(percent)

	Before taxes			*After taxes*		
Year	*State enterprises*	*Urban collectives*	*TVEs*	*State enterprises*	*Urban collectives*	*TVEs*
1980	24.8	26.6	32.5	16.0	18.5	26.7
1982	23.4	22.0	28.0	14.4	13.8	20.2
1984	24.2	22.3	24.6	14.9	13.9	15.2
1985	23.8	24.5	23.7	13.2	15.3	14.5
1988	20.6	19.7	17.9	10.4	11.3	9.3
1990	12.4	—	13.0	3.2	—	5.9
1992	9.7	—	14.2	2.7	—	7.2

— Not available.

Note: Rate of return is the ratio of the sum of profit figures (positive or negative) for all firms to the sum of net (of depreciation) value of fixed assets plus average amount of working capital in use.

Source: State enterprises, Yearbook 1991, p. 416; Yearbook 1992, p. 437. Urban collectives, Industry 1984, p. 85; Industry 1986, p. 87; and State Statistical Bureau. TVEs, Yearbook 1991, pp. 377–79; Yearbook 1993, pp. 396–97.

related phenomenon: the convergence of rates of return to capital across different branches of industry. These changes occurred prior to the creation of organized capital markets, which remain embryonic even today.

Access to high-level technical personnel offers another example of declining market segmentation. Comparing data from China's 1985 industrial census with 1989 survey results reveals a big increase in the availability of engineers and technicians outside the state sector. Using the 1989 survey data, Jefferson, Rawski, and Zheng (1992c) find a surprisingly close correspondence between the marginal profitability of upper-level technicians within state enterprises, TVEs, and urban collective firms in three branches of industry.

Proposition 2: Reform Intensifies Competition in Markets for Industrial Products

On the eve of reform China's industry was in a position of incipient competition, with large numbers of potential entrants poised to intensify product-market competition. Partial reform rapidly turned this potential into reality. Booming imports of manufactures, swift expansion of joint ventures and other foreign-linked enterprises, and rapid erosion of the economic and administrative barriers preventing state enterprises from raiding each other's customers all contributed to the upsurge of competition. The greatest impetus to competition came from the growth of TVE production, which leaped from 10 to 25 percent of total industrial output between 1980 and 1990 (see table 1).

Competition expanded most rapidly in markets directly affected by the growth of TVE output, but competitive pressures extended to other markets as well. By the late 1980s more than half of industrial products were being sold through markets, and that share has since risen to more than 80 percent. Less than 10 percent of industrial output is decided through mandatory plans. Concentration ratios are low and declining (Jefferson and Rawski 1994). With competition from manufactured imports on the rise and barriers to domestic trade increasingly porous, it is clear that partial reform has firmly installed rivalrous product markets as a regular feature of everyday operations for most of China's industrial enterprises. Few firms remain immune from competition. The experience of the Luoyang Tractor Works, China's largest manufacturer of wheeled tractors and bulldozers, is illustrative. According to an article in *China Daily,* Luoyang "is trying to improve the quality of its products as well as its marketing and publicity techniques in a bid to offset...sluggish domestic sales.... The Luoyang tractor complex had been forced to sacrifice more than half of its profits in trying discounts, lotteries, and free delivery of goods to boost sales" (Gao 1990).

Proposition 3: Competition Erodes Profits and Curtails the Growth of Fiscal Revenues

Reform has brought a large decline in industrial profits. Rates of return for state enterprises and TVEs in 1990–92 are less than half what they were in 1980–82 (see table 3). Rates of return (including taxes) by industry confirm the impression of declining profits (table 4). Growing opportunities for tax evasion have widened the error margins for reported profit totals. Wang (1992) cites studies suggesting that the hidden profits of state industry in 1990 may have surpassed the amounts reported to the statistical authorities. Some observers (Sicular 1992) argue that the decline in profitability is mild, confined mostly to state enterprises, and may reflect cyclical factors (the retrenchment of 1988–90). Despite these qualifications, the data strongly support the hypothesis of secular decline (see tables 3 and 4), especially since the boom years of 1992 and 1993 brought no revival in rates of return.

Rates of return shown in table 4 also reflect the powerful impact of TVE competition on industrial profitability. In the early years of reform, profits fell fastest in branches with the greatest TVE activity. During 1980–85 falling profitability was concentrated in industries using agricultural raw materials, especially beverages, tobacco, textiles, and apparel. During the second half of the 1980s the downward pressure on profitability extended to branches with little direct TVE competition, including power, chemicals, iron and steel, machinery, and electronics, but profitability eroded even more in branches with strong TVE activity. The 1991 rates of return for branches with extensive TVE participation are less than half the 1980 base; none of the branches with limited TVE participation experienced as steep a drop in

Table 4. *Rates of Return to Capital in Chinese Industry, 1980–93*
(percent)

Sector	*1980*	*1985*	*1991*	*1992*	*1993*
Industry	25.2	23.8	11.9	10.1	10.6
Light industry	49.1	31.8	15.0		
Farm materials	54.7	32.0	15.9		
Nonfarm materials	39.1	31.5	13.0		
Heavy industry	18.5	20.3	10.2		
Sectors with active TVE competition					
Food processing	20.4	17.5	9.7		
Beverage	48.5	28.4	18.6		
Tobacco	326.9	207.4	113.6		
Textile	69.0	26.5	6.6		
Apparel	46.0	26.0	11.7		
Leather, hides	30.3	19.4	5.6		
Handicrafts	43.0	27.4	12.0		
Plastics	31.6	21.2	9.1		
Sectors with limited TVE competition					
Power	20.6	16.0	13.0		
Chemicals	22.0	21.7	14.0		
Ferrous metallurgy	18.3	25.8	15.5		
Machinery	13.0	19.3	7.9		
Electronic	14.0	24.9	8.5		

Note: Rate of return equals taxes plus profits as a percentage of the net (of depreciation) value of fixed assets plus working capital.

Source: Data for 1992 and 1993, Communique 1994. Other data, Industry 1992, pp. 168–78.

profitability. Singh, Ratha, and Xiao (1993), using provincial data for 1984–89, also show that faster growth of nonstate industry (collective, foreign-invested, and private firms) is associated with lower profit rates for state industry.

Profit erosion also affected government revenue, which has declined sharply as a share of total output from about 30 percent in the early 1980s (as reform began) to 20 percent at the end of the decade and to 14 percent in 1992 (Wong, Heady, and Woo 1993). Slow growth of revenues from industry, the chief source of government income, was the principal cause.

Proposition 4: Enterprises React to Market Pressure by Searching for Financial Gain

Enterprises facing competition and declining profit margins have several options for strengthening their financial position. They can improve their performance within existing institutional limits, pressure the government to extend greater autonomy and incentives to the firm, or pursue rent-seeking alternatives (subsidies, soft loans to offset losses, lobbying for restrictions to stifle competition). We examine the firm's opportunities in each of these directions.

Improve performance within existing institutional limits. Chinese state enterprises, particularly firms facing fierce competition and declining profits, have demonstrated a substantial capacity to economize and innovate. As state-owned enterprises came under increasing competitive pressures during the 1980s, total factor productivity improved steadily (Wu 1993). Singh, Ratha, and Xiao (1994) establish an explicit link between competitive pressure and productivity growth by showing that total factor productivity in state industry rose most rapidly in provinces with the largest shares of nonstate production in total industrial output.

We tested this association between competition and state enterprise efficiency using the following regression equation with 1990 enterprise data:

$$(1)\ \ln(Q/L) = \underset{(3.04)}{-1.25} + \underset{(13.94)}{0.63}\ \ln(K/L) + \underset{(2.55)}{0.09}\ \text{COMP} + \underset{(4.72)}{0.65}\ \text{PCOMP} - \underset{(2.54)}{0.11}\ \ln(NK/K)$$

$$R^2 = 0.32,\ \text{obs.} = 496,$$

where Q/L is labor productivity, K/L is the capital-labor ratio, and NK/K is the share of nonindustrial capital held by the enterprise.[13] COMP and PCOMP are measures of competition—COMP is an estimate of the elasticity of demand for the firm's major product and PCOMP reflects the firm's assessment of the overall competitive pressure it faces.[14] Using either panels of provincial data or cross-sectional enterprise data, we consistently find that competitive pressures motivate firms to improve overall efficiency.

The partial reforms of the 1980s also brought a distinct acceleration of innovative activity in state enterprises. One survey of eighty state enterprises found that the value of new products as a share of gross output rose from 13.5 percent in 1980 to 18.7 percent in 1985 and to 24.2 percent in 1989 (Jefferson, Rawski and Zheng 1992b). Similarly, in a 1992 survey of 10 percent of China's large and medium-size industrial enterprises, 91.6 percent of the 954 respondents described efforts at product and process innovation. More than half reported major modification to their main products, 80.7 percent had new products in the marketplace, 60.8 percent were engaged in major process innovation, and 65.5 percent were implementing new production technologies (Ma and Zhao 1993).

A second set of panel data covering 249 enterprises in the textile, electronics, and equipment industries provides information on output of new products (but not on the intensity of competition) that allows us to examine the impact of changes in profitability during 1984–86 on new product innovation during 1986–88. We assume a two-year lag between changes in profitability and shifts in the output share of new products. Product innovation is constrained by two factors: diminishing returns to product innovation, captured by NPS86, the initial 1986 share of new products in total output; and financial capacity, represented by PRO86, the 1986 ratio of profit (including tax) to sales. Our estimation yields the following result:

$$\text{(2)} \quad \begin{aligned} \text{NPS8886} = \underset{(0.617)}{0.005} - \underset{(1.970)}{0.320}\ \text{PRO8684} - \underset{(7.908)}{0.443}\ \text{NPS86} + \underset{(5.921)}{0.371}\ \text{PRO86} \end{aligned}$$

$$R^2 = 0.250, \text{ obs.} = 210.$$

Here NPS8886 is the change in the share of new products in output value during 1986–88 and PRO8684 is the change in the profit-sales ratio during 1984–86.[15] These estimation results confirm that declining profitability creates an incentive to innovate, conditional upon the enterprise's financial capability and the diminishing returns to innovation.

Seek greater autonomy and strengthened incentives. Along with efforts to improve performance within existing institutional limits, financially pressed enterprises seek greater autonomy and a larger share of residual earnings. Through the mid-1980s circumstances and opportunities were widely regarded as more favorable for collective or private firms. Toward the late 1980s published materials and interviews with factory managers began to reveal a gradual shift toward the view that the autonomy associated with collective ownership had come to outweigh the privileges available within the state sector, leaving state enterprises at a competitive disadvantage. State firms complain of administrative interference and cost-inflating obligations that TVE firms and joint ventures often escape. Managers in the state sector have gradually emerged as active agents for reform.

Seek rents in the form of direct subsidies and soft loans. A final avenue of response for financially distressed enterprises is to seek rents in the form of direct subsidies, soft loans, and a competition-stifling resumption of regulation. We assume that whenever such assistance is available, enterprises will pursue it as long as the expected payoff exceeds the cost of lobbying. From this perspective the attitude of governments controls the distribution of enterprise resources between economizing and innovation on the one hand and rent-seeking on the other. The following section considers whether reform has reduced the availability of various types of direct and hidden subsidies for enterprises experiencing financial distress.

Proposition 5: On Balance, Government Policy Increases Industry Autonomy and Market Exposure and Hardens Budget Constraints

The central facts of life for Chinese public finance in the 1980s include a slowdown in revenue growth, a significant hardening of budget constraints for subnational governments (Walder 1994), and repeated episodes of macroeconomic instability attributable to fiscal deficits and excessive monetary expansion.

Subnational governments are generally more able but less willing to subsidize weak firms and industries than their counterparts at the center. The reason is simple: fierce competition among development-conscious subnational jurisdictions. Diverting resources from development spending to subsidies threatens to undercut the ability of provinces, cities, counties, townships, and villages to attract domestic and foreign investment. With local revenues increasingly tied to the growth of profits from local industry, slow growth of investment endangers the revenue prospects of the same bureaus and officials faced with requests for subsidies and protection.

Under these circumstances, how do officials respond to the pleas of firms whose financial interests are damaged by competition? They have two main options: to grant direct or indirect subsidies or to push enterprises toward the market. While subsidies continue, evidence shows that government policy has gradually tilted toward sending enterprises to market.

Subsidies for TVEs are rare. Loss-making firms are closed and their workers are dismissed. At the start of reform, state enterprises typically expected full compensation for losses. By 1986 the ratio of subsidies to losses for state industry had dropped to 0.8 (table 5). Another sharp dropoff in compensation occurred with the retrenchment of 1988 and 1989. Despite some confusion about the exact timing and scope, it is clear that a decade of partial reform has established a declining scale of partial compensation as the general rule for loss-making state industrial firms.

Direct subsidy is not the only avenue of government support for weak enterprises. Public officials can use tax concessions, regulatory protection, and soft bank credits to sustain loss-making firms. Tax concessions are limited by the same constraint as subsidy payments: the high opportunity cost of committing scarce fiscal resources. Regulatory protection runs counter to the general trend of China's domestic and international economic policy. Governments rely on both these tools in specific instances, but large increases in tax concessions or protective trade restrictions are widely viewed as undesirable and unfeasible. In the words of Vice Minister of the State Economic and Trade Commission Chen Qingtai: "In the past enterprises turned to the government when they ran into difficulty because the government could lower taxes and allowed them to retain more profits. This road has now been basically closed" (1994, p. 48).

This leaves the banking system as the primary vehicle for large-scale indirect support of weak firms. China's banks certainly experience strong official pressure to advance funds to weak borrowers. "Policy loans" that are viewed as unrepayable from the start are extended to both large and small industries at the behest of powerful official interests. Finance officials indicate that such loans account for about 30 percent of new lending, with most of the soft credits destined for investment projects (1992 interview).

Policy lending is an important component of Chinese industrial policy, but it is subject to restrictions. Increases in bank lending have the same inflationary potential as government deficits. Furthermore, the banks, which have developed systems of credit ratings as part of their own profit-seeking agenda (Whiting 1993), have already cut the "policy" component of current lending to less than 10 percent (1993 interview). Banks can be expected to defend their business autonomy with increasing tenacity.

Partly for this reason, China's government has begun to implement financial reforms that will create three layers of financial institutions: a central bank, policy banks to support official priorities, and profit-oriented commercial banks. These reforms will shift the locus of conflict without resolving the problems facing loss-makers. The vice governor of the central bank, reaffirming his determination to "exercise stringent control over the money supply," insists that the new policy-lending banks "must be careful not to run in the red." Yao Zhenyan, president of one of the new policy institutions, makes the same point, emphasizing "the importance of investment efficiency" and insisting that "we must ensure the return of principal, although we are not aiming at profits" (Policy Bank 1994). With highly placed bank officials attacking soft credits even at institutions designed to serve this very need, and with ordinary banks eager to "further commercialize their business" (Wu 1994),

Table 5. *Losses and Subsidies for Chinese State Enterprises, 1986–91*
(billions of yuan)

	All public enterprises			*State-owned industries*		
Year	*Loss*	*Subsidy*	*Ratio*[a]	*Loss*	*Subsidy*[b]	*Ratio*[a]
1986	41.71	32.5	0.78	4.71		0.81
1987	48.17	37.5	0.78	5.07		0.72
1988	52.06	44.6	0.86	7.13		0.73
1989	74.96	59.9	0.80	12.80	9.50	0.74 [.53]
1990	93.26	57.9	0.62	27.88	11.80	0.42 [.34]
1991	93.11	50.6	0.54	30.02	14.50	0.48 [.40]

a. Subsidy/loss.

b. Information provided by the World Bank.

Source: All public enterprises: losses, Hwa 1992; subsidies, World Bank 1992, p. 242. State industries: Wong, Heady, and Woo 1993; World Bank estimates.

executives and workers of loss-making firms can expect only limited relief from their financial predicament unless they improve their performance in the marketplace.

The growing reluctance of government to support weak enterprises is reflected in microeconomic data. Survey data analyzed by Morris and Liu (1993) show that, despite an increase in the absolute level of subsidies, there was considerable hardening of budget constraints for state firms during the late 1980s. Other data support the hypothesis that enterprises facing strong competition move (or are pushed) toward the market in the expectation that greater independence will help them resolve their financial problems.

The following regression, based on 1990 data for state enterprises surveyed in late 1991 and early 1992, evaluates the impact of market conditions on the government's grant of decisionmaking autonomy (DMA) to enterprises:

$$\text{(3)}\quad \underset{}{\text{DMA}} = \underset{(19.40)}{1.73} + \underset{(5.02)}{0.12}\ \text{COMP} + \underset{(3.69)}{0.10}\ \text{PCOMP} - \underset{(2.17)}{0.27}\ \text{PROFIT} + \underset{(0.46)}{0.02}\ \text{IND}$$

$$R^2 = 0.10,\ \text{obs.} = 572.$$

In this regression DMA is a composite measure of enterprise control over production and marketing decisions.[16] COMP and PCOMP are the same measures used in equation 1. PROFIT is the ratio of profit (or loss) to the gross value of output in 1990. To control for differences in autonomy that are specific to the light-heavy industry mix, the equation includes IND, a dummy variable in which 0 represents heavy industry and 1 represents light industry. The regression results show that competition (measured by the firm's estimate of the elasticity of demand for its products and the degree of competitive pressure from rivals) is associated with a relatively high degree of managerial autonomy, which we interpret as synonymous with greater exposure to market forces. Low or negative profits also contribute to a greater transfer of production control and marketing rights to enterprise management.

Recent developments in the woolen textile industry illustrate the government's propensity to assist troubled firms with offers of deregulation rather than direct or indirect subsidies. During 1990–91 the requirement that woolen textile exporters sell through foreign trade corporations insulated them from international market changes and led to large inventories and losses. In response to pressures from producers the government allowed woolen textile companies to export directly to overseas customers. Chinese firms soon began to produce semifinished inventories that could be more quickly transformed into final goods that conformed to the specifications and just-in-time production requirements of overseas customers.

Although government intervention continues to cushion some firms, especially state enterprises, against the consequences of weak performance, limited resources, fear of inflation, and changing attitudes have increased the likelihood that firms and their workers will bear the financial consequences of market outcomes. There is a growing gap between financial outcomes for successful and unsuccessful firms. Loss-making industrial enterprises, formerly eligible for full compensation as part of official administrative routine, face growing difficulties under China's steadily deepening reforms. In the rural sector, losses bring a quick exit for enterprises and dismissal for workers. Subsidies continue, but even for urban state enterprises, subsidies have dropped from full coverage of losses to well below half. Workers associated with loss-making enterprises face a growing probability of sanctions such as slow wage growth, deterioration of bonuses, erosion of health benefits and other nonwage income, layoffs with only partial wage payment, delayed wage payments, compulsory transfers and, most recently, dismissal.

Proposition 6: Feedback Mechanisms Amplify and Extend the Reform Process

The consequences of reform are not limited to a linear progression in which new policies intensify competition, reduce profits and fiscal revenues, and create pressures for better industrial performance. At every stage we observe feedback mechanisms that reinforce the momentum of beneficial change. The success of some enterprises in reducing costs or developing new products reverberates up and down the domestic quality ladder, escalating the pressure on rival enterprises to follow suit. Every reform that relaxes institutional constraints on market entry, enterprise autonomy, or technological change shortens the distance separating adjacent rungs along the ladders of technology and cost, increases the probability of competition-enhancing innovation, and raises the risks facing enterprises that are slow to reform. Reductions in fiscal resources caused by falling profits or tax evasion (itself an outcome of reform-induced expansion of enterprise autonomy and financial mechanisms) increase pressures on enterprises by reducing the chances of successful rent-seeking, further widening the gap between "winners" and "losers."

Groves and others (1994) provide a quantitative illustration of feedback mechanisms that shows how state enterprises use grants of autonomy to strengthen work incentives and raise productivity. Their analysis of sample data indicates that enterprise autonomy is associated with large shares of discretionary payments in worker compensation and with high shares of untenured contract workers in the labor force. Their statistical analysis confirms the expected positive link between these incentive changes and productivity growth. Thus incremental grants of enterprise autonomy appear to feed back into faster productivity growth, which in turn intensifies competition, and so on.

Proposition 7: China's Decision to Create a Market-Based Economic System Is an Endogenous Outcome of the Partial Reform Process

China's initial reform efforts sought to improve economic performance; there was no clear picture of what the economy should look like after reform. Partial reform initiated a learning process that expanded the horizons of all participants. Competition among firms organized under heterogeneous institutional arrangements opened the door to a dynamic and interactive reform process in which specific policy initiatives have different effects on the opportunity sets of firms facing different institutional and technological constraints. Enterprises adopted competitive strategies designed to capitalize on the advantages conferred by their institutional as well as technical endowments. Competition forced participants to compare the merits of alternative institutional arrangements in exactly the same way that managers analyze the profit consequences of different product designs, machines, or compensation arrangements. Heterogeneity encouraged a culture of envy in which firms and managers demand access to more attractive institutional possibilities to place them on an equal footing with rivals operating under different institutional arrangements (Liu 1993).

The experience of partial reform created promarket sentiment among former advocates of central planning. Shirk (1993, p. 288; also see Rawski 1994b) shows how managers of large-scale industry changed their views:

> [These leaders] were at first leery of market reforms that threatened to shake them out of their comfortable dependence on the state. But the wrenching experience of the 1980–81 readjustment... gave them a new appreciation of the opportunities offered by the market, and their envy of the benefits of reform enjoyed by smaller enterprises and nonstate enterprises motivated them to demand that these benefits be extended to their own enterprises.... Large state factory managers changed from lazy conservatives coddled by the state to active reformers challenging the state.

Government officials and political leaders experienced a similar change of position.

The rise of promarket sentiments among the political and administrative elite represents the biggest feedback of all in China's partial reform process. In the early 1990s these changes coalesced into a stunning reversal of deep-seated attitudes. Ideas that only ten years earlier stood far beyond the limits of permissible discussion now took center stage as the government announced huge staff cuts, ambitious young bureaucrats began leaving the government to pursue private business careers (K. Chen 1994), and China's Communist party formally announced a national goal of creating a decentralized market economy (Decision 1993).

This remarkable change in values, combined with intense fiscal pressures, has sparked a series of policy innovations aimed at relieving governments of the burden of supporting loss-making enterprises. Although official documents rarely use terms like "ownership reform" or "privatization" to describe these changes, recent initiatives amount to a policy of endogenous or induced privatization. Various ministries, provinces, and localities have begun to lease state-owned industrial firms to private agents (including foreign companies). Some loss-making firms have been forced to merge with stronger enterprises, with substantial loss of jobs;[17] others are simply auctioned off to the highest bidder. The government has also begun to encourage organizational innovations designed to restructure state enterprises as limited-liability entities owned by government, corporate, and private shareholders.

Conclusion

The contrast between the top-down, centrally planned reforms proposed by international organizations (and endorsed by many economists) and the gradual, cumulative reform process described in this article reminds us of earlier controversies between advocates of "balanced" growth (Rosenstein-Rodan 1943; Nurkse 1953) and proponents of "unbalanced" development (Hirschman 1958).

The balanced growth approach portrays economic growth as an event—a big push or great leap—rather than as a process; it downplays the developmental potential of inherited economic structures and ignores international and domestic linkages. These oversights amplified the surprise attending the subsequent export success of economies such as Japan, the Republic of Korea, and Taiwan [Taiwan (China) is the designation used by the World Bank], wrongly identified as "basket cases" on the basis of low initial capability and unfamiliar institutional arrangements.

Although several years of practical experience have muted the all-or-nothing aspect of initial perspectives on socialist reform, there is still a tendency for discussions of reform issues to repeat the mistakes of the balanced growth approach by underestimating the complexity of imposing market systems from above.

James Buchanan insists that "a market is not competitive by assumption or by construction," but "*becomes* competitive, and competitive rules *come to be* established as institutions emerge" to shape behavior (1979, p. 29, our emphasis). Buchanan thinks that economics should focus on this "process of becoming." This orientation seems highly appropriate for the study of socialist reform. China's gradual and partial path of industrial reform was not determined by a few top officials. Industrial reform evolved from sequences of decisions made by tens of thousands of enterprises and millions of administrators, managers, and workers. The large number of participants and the extended duration of the reform process, which gave people ample time to evaluate alternatives and reconsider their initial views, eventually built a constituency for market-directed change that was far stronger than any official announcement could have achieved. This process is very different from Western parliamentary democracy, but it has produced a durable reform constituency that easily rebuffed high-level efforts to roll back reform in the wake of the inflation scare and political repression of 1989.

Before reform, government officials set the agenda for China's industrial firms. Now everyone has an agenda. Enterprises, managers, and workers design strategies for success. The state finds itself reacting to the outcome of decentralized efforts to implement a multitude of uncoordinated agendas. Enterprises and individuals no longer await the government's announcements, but struggle to shape government involvement in ways that suit their own plans. In short, China's industrial economy, despite its subsidies, soft loans, tenured state enterprise workers, and numerous other divergences from the textbook ideal, looks increasingly like a market system.

Notes

1. The share of domestic private enterprise is the sum of shares for individual enterprises employing fewer than eight people (*geti gongye*) and larger private firms. Figures for the latter category are obtained as residuals by subtracting the contribution of joint ventures, overseas Chinese firms, and foreign-owned plants from the output share of "other" (*qita*, or other than state or collective) types of ownership (Industry 1992, p. 7). These figures take no account of private firms masquerading as collectives (Walder 1994); including their output would probably raise the 1992 share of private enterprise to more than 10 percent.

2. Similarly, Chang and Wang (1994, p. 2) emphasize that a TVE is "controlled by the township government...not by its nominal owners, that is, the local citizens."

3. A 1990 survey of 285 TVEs found that only 16 percent had the authority to appoint their own leaders. In 60 percent of cases the supervisory authority (that is, the local government) appointed enterprise leaders without consultation (Jefferson, Lu, and Zhao 1994). An earlier survey found that more than 80 percent of TVE managers attributed their appointments to the local government (Song 1990). Walder (1994, pp.15, 34) observes that "the control of top [local] officials over public firms is greatest" in "the smaller rural jurisdictions" where "the party secretaries or other top officials...play an active role in the management of their valued industrial assets."

4. Data on fixed investment are for 1992 (Yearbook 1993, pp. 145, 150). It is not easy to specify the share of state firms in industrial fixed investment. The 1992 figure for industrial investment of state enterprises occupies an impossibly large 97.5 percent share of the combined total of industrial investment outlays under the three subheads of basic construction, technical renovation, and "other" (a small category that we assign exclusively to industry even though part should be credited to transport and geology).

5. For extended discussion, including numerous references, see Harrold (1992), Rawski (1994b), and Jefferson and Rawski (1994).

6. Wu (1993) summarizes the literature on productive efficiency. Woo and others (1993) employ sample data to show a declining trend for total factor productivity in several branches of industry, but only by assuming a common trend for product and input prices during a period of rising relative prices for industrial materials. Preliminary calculations by Jefferson, Rawski, and Zheng (1994) suggest that the contribution of total factor productivity to output growth may have risen from 25 to 30 percent during 1980–88 to 50 percent during 1988–92.

7. The estimated annual growth rate of state enterprises' manufactured exports was much lower (7.8 percent) for 1988–92 than for 1984–88 (34.4 percent). However, the figure for 1988–92 probably understates actual growth, which may have surpassed 10 percent (Rawski 1994a). Survey data indicate 20 percent annual export growth for a sample of 244 large state enterprises during 1986–89 (Rawski forthcoming). Lardy (1993) points out that state enterprise exports have benefited from direct subsidies (in the 1980s) and special export credits (in the 1990s).

8. China's state firms have a long history of excessive vertical integration. The proliferation of customer-conscious behavior should encourage the spread of efficiency-enhancing specialization. But a major study by Chinese economists finds that high transaction costs arising from inadequate contract enforcement and the consequent prevalence of commercial cheating leads to "an obvious tendency toward nonspecialization outside the state sector" (Jiang and others 1993, p. 35). Whiting's (1993) study of TVE behavior comments on "the unwillingness of the courts to enforce loan contracts" and quotes one frustrated enterprise manager as complaining that "contracts here don't mean anything" because there is no practical means of forcing customers to settle overdue accounts.

9. At the conference the discussants noted that factors outside China's industrial sector, including successful agricultural reform, macroeconomic stability, and complementarities with the adjacent economies of Hong Kong and Taiwan [Taiwan (China) is the designation used by the World Bank] have facilitated the reform of domestic industry. We agree (see Gelb, Jefferson, and Singh 1993), but focus here on initial conditions that are specific to domestic industry.

10. For similar reports, see Chou (1992, p. 5) and *China Daily* (August 28, 1993, p. 1 and August 31, 1993, p. 4). Note that the qualification rate for medium-size and small factories in the survey cited in the text was "only 72.9 percent." This and other evidence points to a scale-related hierarchy of technological capabilities within state industry.

11. Data from Du and Shang (1993) include the employer's share of medical expenses incurred by workers and dependents. The Hebei survey covered the first half of 1993 and found average medical expenses of ¥ 600.69 per worker. In 1991 wages for state sector employees in Hebei amounted to 93.4 percent of the national average (Labor 1992, p. 211). We apply this figure to average 1992 state sector wages of ¥ 2,878 (Survey 1993, p. 44) and assume wage growth of 20 percent for 1992–93.

12. Beijing's Capital Steel Works has developed into a multinational conglomerate on the basis of profits accumulated under a long-term agreement that offered exceptional managerial autonomy in exchange for a promise to deliver a steadily rising flow of funds to the national treasury. The firm's own researchers

attribute more than half of Capital's large profit increments to the simple fact of autonomy: shifts in the output mix with no major changes in main equipment or in annual supplies of raw materials (Shougang 1986). Lacking Capital's political clout, rival firms found themselves stymied by institutional restrictions that prevented them from raising profits by optimizing their output mix.

13. This variable serves as a proxy for the proportion of nonproduction capital and labor in the enterprise that is devoted to the provision of housing and social services. The formulation implies that capital and labor are used in fixed proportions in the provision of housing and social services.

14. COMP and PCOMP are discrete variables, spanning a range of 1 to 3, from inelastic demand or little competition to highly elastic demand or high competition.

15. In this regression NPS is the ratio of new product output to gross output value and PRO is the ratio of profit and taxes to annual sales. NPS8886 = NPS88/NPS86; also PRO8684 = PRO86/PRO84.

16. DMA ranges from 1 (enterprise has no decisionmaking authority), to 2 (limited authority or authority shared between enterprise and supervisory agency), to 3 (enterprise has full control).

17. The summary of an interview with Li Shuguang, deputy director of the Beijing Siyuan Merger and Bankruptcy Consultancy, noted that "the biggest problem with mergers is the job losses involved in merged firms." Li stated that many of the enterprises acquiring loss-making firms "are only interested in obtaining the equipment and extra space in a merger," which creates a "problem of redundancies" (Huang 1994).

References

Blanchard, Olivier Jean, and Stanley Fischer. 1993. *NBER Macroeconomics Annual 1993*. Cambridge, Mass.: MIT Press.

Blasko, Dennis J. 1994. Review of Paul Folta, "From Swords to Plowshares? Defense Industry Reform in the PRC." *Far Eastern Economic Review*, March 3, p. 37.

Buchanan, James M. 1979. *What Should Economists Do?* Indianapolis: Liberty Press.

Byrd, William A., ed. 1992. *Chinese Industrial Firms Under Reform*. New York: Oxford University Press.

Census 1989. *Zhonghua renmin gongheguo 1985—nian gongye pucha ziliao (jianyaoben)* [People's Republic of China 1985 Industrial Census Materials—abbreviated summary volume]. Beijing: Zhongguo tongji chubanshe.

Chang, Chung, and Yijiang Wang. 1994. "The Nature of the Township Enterprise." Carlson School of Management, University of Minnesota.

Chen, Kathy. 1994. "Chinese Bureaucrats Take Hopes Private." *Wall Street Journal*, January 26, p. A10.

Chen, Qingtai. 1994. "Vice Minister on New Enterprise Reforms." U.S. Department of Commerce, Foreign Broadcast Information Service. *Daily Report: China*. January 27, pp. 48–49.

China Daily. Beijing.

Chou, Yi. 1993. "The Practice beyond Property Right Boundaries: Quality Management in Chinese State-Owned Enterprises and Rural Enterprises." Discussion Paper 9302. Taipei: Chung-Hua Institution for Economic Research.

Communique. 1994. "Communique on the National Economy and Social Development in 1993 by the State Statistics Bureau of the PRC." *Renmin ribao* (People's Daily). March 1, pp. 2–3.

Decision. 1993. "China's Central Government Decision on Resolving Several Problems Concerning the Establishment of a Socialist Market Economic System." *Renmin ribao* (People's Daily), November 17, p. 1.

Du Haiyan, and Shang Lie. 1993. "Distribution of Fringe Benefits for Employees of State-owned Enterprises." *Zhongguo gongye jingji yanjiu* (Research on Chinese Industrial Economics). No. 2: 46–52, 30.

Du Miaodeng, Huang Shiqiu, and Chen Xuewen. 1992. "On the Management of 'High Starting Point' Enterprises in Poor Townships and Districts." *Jingji guanli* (Economic Management). No. 12: 55–57.

Gao, Anming. 1990. "Giant Tractor Maker Plagued by Slow Sales." *China Daily*, May 28, p. 4.

Gelb, Alan, Gary H. Jefferson, and Inderjit Singh. 1993. "Can Communist Economies Transform Incrementally?" *NBER Macroeconomics Annual 1993*. Cambridge, Mass.: MIT Press.

Granick, David. 1990. *Chinese State Enterprises: A Regional Property Rights Analysis*. Chicago: University of Chicago Press.

Grossman, Gene M., and Elhanan Helpman. 1991. "Quality Ladders and Product Cycles." *Quarterly Journal of Economics* 106: 557–86.

Groves, Theodore, Yongmiao Hong, John McMillan, and Barry Naughton. 1994. "Autonomy and Incentives in Chinese State Enterprises." *Quarterly Journal of Economics* 109 (1): 183–209.

Harrold, Peter. 1992. "China's Reform Experience to Date." World Bank Discussion Paper 180, Washington, D.C.

Hirschman, Albert O. 1958. *The Strategy of Economic Development.* New Haven, Conn.: Yale University Press.

Hua, Sheng, Xiaopeng Luo, and Xuejun Zhang. 1993. *China: From Revolution to Reform.* Houndsmills, United Kingdom: Macmillan.

Huang, Zhiling. 1994. "Mergers Revive Loss-making Firms." *China Daily,* April 16, p. 4.

Hwa, Erh-cheng. 1992. "Enterprise Reform in China." Background paper. World Bank, Washington, D.C.

Industry. 1949-84. *Zhongguo gongye jingji tongji ziliao 1949–1984* [Statistical Materials on China's Industrial Economy, 1949–1984]. Beijing: Zhongguo tongji chubanshe.

Industry. 1992. *Zhongguo gongye jingji tongji nianjian 1992* [Statistical Yearbook of China's Industrial Economy 1992]. Beijing: Zhongguo tongji chubanshe.

Jefferson, Gary H., and Thomas G. Rawski. 1994. "Enterprise Reform in Chinese Industry." *Journal of Economic Perspectives* 8(2): 47–70.

Jefferson, Gary H., Mai Lu, and John Zhiqiang Zhao. 1994. "The Reform of Property Rights in China's Industrial Enterprises." Brandeis University, Department of Economics, Waltham. Mass.

Jefferson, Gary H., Thomas G. Rawski, and Yuxin Zheng. 1992a. "Growth, Efficiency, and Convergence in China's State and Collective Industry." *Economic Development and Cultural Change* 40 (2): 239–66.

———. 1992b. "Innovation and Reform in Chinese Industry: A Preliminary Analysis of Survey Data (1)." Paper delivered at the annual meeting of the Association for Asian Studies, Washington, D.C., April.

———. 1992c. "Innovation and Reform in Chinese Industry: A Preliminary Analysis of Survey Data (2)." Research Paper Series 30, Socialist Economies Reform Unit, World Bank, Washington, D.C.

———. 1994. "Institutional Change and Industrial Innovation in Transitional Economies." *Journal of Asian Economics* 5 (4): 585–604.

Jiang Xiaojuan, Zhao Ying, Ren Jijun, Liu Hong, and Xiong Yun. 1993. "New Features of China's Industrial Growth and Structural Change." *Zhongguo gongye jingji yanjiu* (Research on Chinese Industrial Economics) 8: 32–40.

Labor 1992. *Zhongguo laodong tongji nianjian 1992* [Statistical Yearbook of Chinese Labor, 1992]. Beijing: Zhongguo laodong chubanshe.

Lardy, Nicholas R. 1993. "China's Foreign Trade Reform in the 1990s." Paper delivered at the annual meeting of the Association for Asian Studies, April. Los Angeles, Calif.

Li Dianjing, and Qin Chengdiao. 1993. "Survey on Conditions of Reimbursement of Employee Medical Expenses." *Zhongguo wujia* (China Price) 11: 33–34.

Liu, Weiling. 1993. "Enterprise Managers Upset by 'Unfair' Regulations." *China Daily,* September 18, p. 2.

Ma, Zhiping. 1994. "Quality of Chinese Products Improves." *China Daily* January 20, p. 3.

Ma Ke and Zhao Yuchuan. 1993. "R&D at China's Large and Medium Industrial Enterprises—Innovative Activity Develops Universally." *Zhongguo tongji* (China's Statistics) 4: 10.

Morris, Derek, and Guy Shaojia Liu. 1993. "The Soft Budget Constraint in Chinese Industrial Enterprises in the 1980s." Oxford University, Oxford.

Naughton, Barry, 1992. "Implications of the State Monopoly Over Industry and its Relaxation." *Modern China* 18 (1): 14–41.

———. 1994. *Growing Out of the Plan: Chinese Economic Reform, 1978–1993.* New York: Cambridge University Press.

Nurkse, Ragnar. 1953. *Problems of Capital Formation in Underdeveloped Countries.* Oxford: Oxford University Press.

Ody, Anthony J. 1991. "China: Rural Enterprise, Rural Industry, 1986–1990." East Asia and the Pacific Country Department II, Country Operations Division, World Bank, Washington, D.C.

Perkins, Dwight H., and others. 1977. *Rural Small-Scale Industry in the People's Republic of China.* Berkeley: University of California Press.

Policy Bank. 1994. "Policy Bank Opens for Key Projects." *China Daily,* April 14, p. 1.

Rawski, Thomas G. 1994a. "Export Performance of China's State Industries." Department of Economics, University of Pittsburgh.

———. 1994b. "Progress without Privatization: The Reform of China's State Industries." In Vedat Milor, ed., *The Political Economy of Privatization and Public Enterprise in Post-Communist and Reforming Communist States.* Boulder, Colo.: Lynne Rienner.

———. Forthcoming. "An Overview of Chinese Industry in the 1980s." In Gary H. Jefferson and Inderjit Singh, eds., *Reform, Ownership, and Performance in Chinese Industry.*

Regulations. 1992. "Text of Regulations on Transforming State Enterprises." U.S. Department of Commerce, Foreign Broadcast Information Service. *Daily Report: China.* July 28, pp. 27–36.

Rosenstein-Rodan, P.N. 1943. "Problems of Industrialization of Eastern and Southeastern Europe." *Economic Journal* (June-Sept). Reprinted in A.N. Agarwala and S.P. Singh, eds., *The Economics of Underdevelopment.* New York: Oxford University Press, 1963.

Sachs, Jeffrey, and Wing Thye Woo. 1994. "Reform in China and Russia." *Economic Policy* (April): 101–45.

Shirk, Susan L. 1993. *The Political Logic of Economic Reform in China.* Berkeley: University of California Press.

Shougang R&D Center. 1986. "How Reform Brought Rapid Efficiency Gains at Capital." In *Shougang Chengbaozhi* [The System of Enterprise Responsibility Contracts at Capital Steelworks]. Beijing: Jingji guanli chubanshe.

Sicular, Terry. 1992. "Public Finance and China's Economic Reforms." Harvard Institute of Economic Research Discussion Paper 1618. Cambridge, Mass.

Singh, Inderjit, Dilip Ratha, and Geng Xiao. 1994. "Non-State Enterprises as an Engine of Growth: An Analysis of Provincial Industrial Growth in Post-Reform China." Research Paper Series 20, World Bank, Socialist Economies Reform Unit, Washington, D.C.

Song, Lina 1990. "Convergence: A Comparison of Township Firms and Local State Enterprises." In William A. Byrd and Qingsong Lin, eds., *China's Rural Industry: Structure, Development, and Reform.* New York: Oxford University Press.

Sun, Hong. 1994. "Public, Merchants Learn to Love Bar Codes." *China Daily Business Weekly,* February 21, p. 8.

Survey 1993. *Zhongguo tongji zhaiyao 1993* [Statistical Survey of China 1993]. Beijing: Zhongguo tongji chubanshe.

Vernon, Raymond. 1966. "International Investment and International Trade in the Product Cycle." *Quarterly Journal of Economics* 80 (2): 190–207.

Walder, Andrew G. 1994. "The Varieties of Public Enterprise in China: An Institutional Analysis." Policy Research Department, World Bank, Washington, D.C.

Wang Haibo. 1992. "Now is the Time to Strengthen the Unity between High Speed Growth and Raising Efficiency." *Zhongguo gongye jingji yanjiu* [Research on Chinese Industrial Economics] 10: 23–28.

Weitzman, Martin L., and Chenggang Xu. 1994. "Chinese Township and Village Enterprises as Vaguely Defined Cooperatives." *Journal of Comparative Economics* 18 (1): 121–45.

Whiting, Susan H. 1993. "Market Discipline and Rural Enterprise in China: A Principal-Agent Approach." Paper prepared for the conference on The Evolution of Market Institutions in Transition Economies, May 8, 1993.

Wong, Christine, Christopher Heady, and Wing Thye Woo. 1993. "Economic Reform and Fiscal Management in China." Asian Development Bank, Manila.

Woo, Wing Thye, Gang Fan, Wen Hai, and Yibiao Jin. 1993. "The Efficiency and Macroeconomic Consequences of Chinese Enterprise Reform." *China Economic Review* 4 (2): 153–68.

World Bank. 1992. *China: Reform and the Role of the Plan in the 1990s.* Washington, D.C.

Wu, Yanrui. 1993. "Productive Efficiency in Chinese Industry." *Asia-Pacific Economic Literature* 7 (2): 58–66.

Wu, Yunhe. 1994. "Central Bank to Cool Fixed Assets." *China Daily,* March 1, p. 1.

Xu Fengxian, Mao Zhichong, and Yuan Juying. 1993. "New Development à la Sunan." *Jingji yanjiu* [Economic Research] 2: 49–55.

Yearbook. Annual. *Zhongguo tongji nianjian* [China Statistical Yearbook, annual beginning 1981, except for 1982]. Beijing: Zhongguo tongji chubanshe.

Zweig, David 1991. "Internationalizing China's Countryside: The Political Economy of Exports from Rural Industry." *China Quarterly* (128): 716–41.

Comment on "How Industrial Reform Worked in China: The Role of Innovation, Competition, and Property Rights," by Jefferson and Rawski

Athar Hussain and Nicholas H. Stern

There are seven propositions in the article by Jefferson and Rawski that embody the authors' description of the process of industrial sector reform in China. Schematically, their contents may be presented as follows:

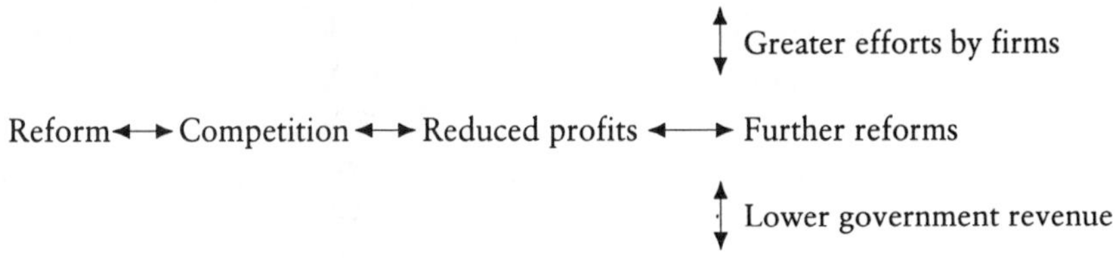

↕ Greater efforts by firms

Reform ↔ Competition ↔ Reduced profits ↔ Further reforms

↕ Lower government revenue

The central driving force is intense competition between state-owned and town and village enterprises (TVEs) which, by eroding the profits of state enterprises, spurs them to innovate or, in the authors' words, to climb the product ladder. Further, since profits constitute a key element of the tax base, reducing profits lowers tax revenue, thereby hardening the government budget constraint. The government responds by reducing subsidies to enterprises, forcing them to maintain the momentum of innovation. Then by drawing lessons from the success of previous reforms, the government embarks on the next round of reform. The article is silent about the fate of enterprises that are unable, or unwilling, to climb. We argue that such enterprises are too numerous to be left out of the discussion.

We agree with much of the argument of the article, but we have doubts about a number of key parts of the story and the treatment of data. First, we question the strength of empirical evidence provided in support of the analysis, particularly concerning profit and innovative activity. We also question some of the underlying descriptions of TVEs and state enterprises and the interactions between them and between firms and government. Finally, we consider the underlying causes of the rapid growth in China, pointing particularly to decentralization and incentives.

Athar Hussain is director of the Development Economics Research Programme at the London School of Economics. Nicholas H. Stern is chief economist at the European Bank for Reconstruction and Development. The authors thank Philippe Aghion for suggestions. These comments draw on the research project on public finance in transition economies supported by the Economic and Social Research Council of the United Kingdom.

Proceedings of the World Bank Annual Conference on Development Economics 1994

Empirical Evidence

We have reservations about taking the falling profit rate as an unambiguous index of competition. Measured profit rates have indeed fallen for all categories of enterprises, but the counterpart has been a sharp rise in the share of value added going to labor. Such a shift seems to be central to the experience of other countries in transition as well. Compared with market economies, the share of wages in value added tended to be low in command economies (Atkinson and Micklewright 1992). The decentralization of wage determination and a relaxation in the rigor of state control seem to have increased the share of labor. Thus, at least part of the fall in profitability is due to rent-sharing rather than competition.

There is also a problem concerning how far the observed trend in profits reflects the actual trend. Compared with firms in a market economy, Chinese enterprises have both greater possibilities and greater incentives to underreport their profits. Independent accounting and auditing are still at a primitive stage, and the underreporting of profits does not carry the same costs for Chinese enterprises as it does for firms in a market economy. For example, Chinese enterprises need not be greatly concerned with the implications of reported profits for stock market valuation or credit rating. Further, a part of the observed decline in profits may be due simply to the hiving off of more profitable activities (and their associated resources) into subsidiary companies, which are private in practice but public in name. This process seems to be widespread and is described by the Chinese as "digging the socialist wall."

The share of new products in total sales, which the authors use as the indicator of product innovation, raises two problems. First, a fall in total sales of old products will be reflected as a rise in product innovation even if such innovation is absent. One would also expect this fall in sales to be accompanied by a fall in profits. Thus the regression results showing a fall in profits apparently driving a rise in innovation may simply indicate a fall in total sales emanating from a fall in sales of old products, which is raising the share of new products and depressing the profit rate. Second, the indicator is susceptible to serious measurement error in the Chinese context. Investment for the production of new goods is treated preferentially in the allocation of investment funds. This preference gives enterprises a strong incentive to repackage, or misrepresent, an old product as new.

Alternative Perspectives on the Process

The story in the article rests on competition between state enterprises and TVEs and innovation on the one hand and the ability or willingness of the government to subsidize loss-making enterprises on the other. While accepting much of what the authors have to say, we question key aspects of their analysis of both parts of the story. The pervasive government intervention in TVEs, which the authors mention, has implications for the interpretation of TVE entry and exit. The local governments that establish TVEs are fired by the goals of developing their area and of extending nonagricultural employment. The authors cite the higher frequency of closure for

TVEs than for state enterprises as evidence of competition and tighter budget constraints. This link between closure and competition may well be part of the story, but the closures may also indicate that many TVEs are established without due regard for financial viability. Moreover, although the TVEs that are closed are loss-makers, many loss-making TVEs continue to operate.

When assessing the role of competition in product markets we should remember that there may well be as many examples of TVEs operating in semiprotected local markets as there are of dynamic TVEs competing with state enterprises. Aside from trade barriers created by a strained transport system, examples of local protection abound; from time to time the central government has to remind local governments that levying duties and putting up barriers to the entry of goods produced in other areas is illegal. Studies of TVEs suggest that they are highly heterogeneous and that their performance and behavior vary across regions (for example, Byrd and Lin 1990). The competitive role Jefferson and Rawski assign to TVEs does hold for a portion of such firms, but not all.

State enterprises are similarly heterogenous. Some of them may innovate and cut costs, but there is no evidence that this is true for all or even most of them. The virtuous circle of competition and innovation sketched in the article is at odds with the mounting concern in China about the insolvency of a large percentage of state enterprises (and also TVEs). A recent System Reform Commission study of state enterprises in Liaoning (a leading industrial center) found that only 12 percent of 1,200 large and medium-size state enterprises in the province are on sound footing. Another 18 percent are operating well with respect to short-term criteria but still may not be able to survive without government assistance. The remaining 70 percent have major problems, and many of them are financially insolvent (Guo 1994). The Chinese economy has a huge number of nonviable enterprises; it has yet to devise an effective way of dealing with the problem.

The regional diversity of China, which is crucial to understanding industrial reforms, does not play a central part in the argument of the article. State enterprises and TVEs are unevenly distributed, and their performance varies widely across regions. The share of state enterprises showing losses is much higher in old, established industrial centers than in provinces with new enterprises (State Statistical Bureau 1993). Dynamic TVEs are often found in areas where state enterprises are thinly concentrated. Competition among enterprises, central to Jefferson's and Rawski's analysis, is often across government boundaries. Local governments have ways of stifling competition or cushioning its impact when their industrial base is threatened. They also differ widely in their attitudes toward industrial reforms. The description of the attitude of subnational governments provided by Jefferson and Rawski is not representative of the whole country.

Thus the characterizations of competition from TVEs as universally intense and of the response of state enterprises as strongly innovative cannot be accepted without substantial qualification. The potential of further piecemeal reform for state enterprises and TVEs alike is now being questioned, and many in China are calling for drastic measures.

We also question the impression given in the article that subsidies to loss-making firms are being rigorously controlled. Only direct subsidies are reported in table 5, and they constitute only the tip of the iceberg. Much larger are the indirect subsidies operating through loss-making state trading agencies. These are essentially price subsidies. A substantial share goes to essential industrial inputs, such as steel and imported capital goods. In 1991, for example, direct subsidies to loss-making industrial enterprises accounted for 28 percent of the total budgetary outlay on subsidies, while budgetary subsidies to trading agencies accounted for 78 percent (Ministry of Finance 1992, p. 938). The authors mention soft loans from the banking system but diminish their importance by categorizing them as "policy loans" destined for investment projects. An investment loan to a nonviable enterprise is still a subsidy. In addition, the web of interenterprise debt (the so-called triangular debt) ultimately has to be underwritten by the government. Finally, a wide range of implicit subsidies are provided through the tax system. Enterprises may be allowed to offset loan principal repayments from their profits tax or even from indirect taxes, as in the electricity industry.

Circumstantial evidence does suggest that both the government (at all levels) and the banking system are taking a harder line on subsidies and loans to loss-making enterprises. Nevertheless, the budget constraints in China are still very soft by the standards of a market economy. Given the government's reluctance to permit bankruptcies, it does not have the option of calling a stop to subsidies to loss-making enterprises even when they are regarded as nonviable.

The fall in fiscal revenue as a share of GNP is real and is cause for serious concern (Hussain and Stern 1992). However, we have to be careful in drawing the conclusion that the budget constraints are sufficiently hard to sustain the process of competition and innovation outlined in the article. The financial capacity of the government to prop up loss-making enterprises, though it appears to have diminished in recent years, is far greater than indicated by its budgetary revenue. The boundaries of the government in a transition economy are far from clear, and the financial constraint it faces cannot be simply deduced from its budget. Nonbudgetary revenue in China has risen from 31 percent of budgetary revenue to 94.5 percent (Ministry of Finance 1992, p. 924). This change is associated with, among other things, commercial pricing policies in public utilities and more entrepreneurial behavior in public institutions.

Factors Other Than Competition in China's Reforms

As economists, we are taught to extol the virtues of competition. But it seems to us that the authors exaggerate the role of competition in explaining recent phenomena in China, to the neglect of incentives and decentralization of decisionmaking in stimulating effort and enterprise. Surely what the Chinese have illustrated is something obvious but fundamental: rewarding effort can elicit a substantial response even in the absence of radical institutional change. Decentralized government also has played a crucial role in the dynamics of China's reforms (Qian and Xu 1993). It has allowed local experimentation, letting some regions race ahead. The proliferation and explosive growth of TVEs owes a great deal to local initiative permitted by decentralization. But decentralization has also delayed reform of the tax system and impeded development of financial regulation and the conduct of macroeconomic policy. These are areas in which centralized decisionmaking has great advantages and can even be essential.

The authors also underplay some other factors that are as important as competition. For example, they attribute to the open door policy a rapid increase in imports of industrial goods, many of which they claim competed directly with domestic goods. In fact, much of China's imports have consisted of capital goods that Chinese industry is unable to produce, such as civilian aircraft, computers, and assembly lines. Imports that "directly compete" with domestically produced goods constitute only a small part of the total. A major contribution of the open door policy has been to upgrade the technology available to Chinese industry. Also, the fact that Chinese economic reforms brought an immediate tangible benefit to a large majority of the population has played a central role in supporting the momentum of piecemeal reforms. Without the popular support that came with these benefits, the process would not easily have been sustained. Notwithstanding the political control of the Communist Party, the Chinese leadership is sensitive to the attitudes of the population.

China and Other Transition Economies

The Chinese example refutes some of the more simplistic versions of the now familiar argument that the best transition is always the fastest. There are, however, important ways in which China's experience and circumstances differ from those in other transition economies. We highlight five.

1. China has been politically and economically stable. Notwithstanding changes in leadership since 1978, the basic approach to reforms has been remarkably consistent.
2. China's prereform economy differed from the command economies of the Soviet Union and Eastern Europe in some major respects. The economy was already highly decentralized in the sense that local governments had a great deal of discretion. This decentralization has made it possible to introduce piecemeal reforms and allow experimentation without disrupting the whole economy. Moreover, since much of industrial output was distributed outside the centralized supply system, the barriers to setting up new enterprises were comparatively low. Inputs for new activities could be obtained relatively easily.
3. An overwhelming percentage of the labor force was, and still is, located in rural areas and organized largely at the household level. Market-oriented reforms are easier to introduce in such an environment than in an economy dominated by large-scale industry and economic organizations. This rural-community-household structure means that market incentives can be introduced without building entirely new institutions. Much activity can be generated merely by lifting the restraints on economic activities. The flexibility of the rural labor market has been crucial in facilitating the growth of TVEs.

4. China began its reform process with none of the major macroeconomic handicaps that afflicted many other postcommunist transition economies. The inflation rate was low, and government finances were in balance. China had no international debt. Notwithstanding the acceleration in inflation since the mid-1980s, the savings propensity of Chinese households continues to be very high, making it much easier to sustain a high growth rate without runaway inflation.
5. Hong Kong has played a crucial role in the rapid expansion of exports and the large inflow of foreign direct investment. It has been the largest source of foreign capital, a major conduit for Chinese exports, and an invaluable source of commercial know-how for exporting to industrial market economies.

In sum, these differences tell us that while China's example debunks some simple slogans masquerading as rigorous analysis, it does not necessarily provide a model for all transition economies.

Finally, we would like to thank the authors for a stimulating article. It provides a challenging perspective on the Chinese experience and raises fruitful issues for discussion and research. The article is surely correct to focus on the relation between TVEs and state enterprises and to emphasize that piecemeal reform can generate a momentum of its own. There is no doubt, to paraphrase Mao, that "letting a hundred enterprises and activities bloom and contend" before destroying the old has served China well.

References

Atkinson, A.B., and J. Micklewright. 1992. *Economic Transformation in Eastern Europe and the Distribution of Income*. Cambridge: Cambridge University Press.

Byrd, William, and Lin Qinsong. 1990. *China's Rural Industry: Structure, Development, and Reform*. New York: Oxford University Press.

Guo Shuqing. 1994. "Some Basic Issues to Be Solved in Deepening State Enterprise Reforms." System Reform Commission, Beijing.

Hussain, Athar, and Nicholas Stern. 1992. "Economic Reforms and Public Finance in China." *Public Finance* (special issue on Public Finance in a World of Transition): 289–317.

Ministry of Finance. 1992. *Zhongguo caizheng nianjian 1992 (Public Finance Yearbook of China 1992)*. Beijing: China Public Finance Publishing House.

Qian Yingyi, and Xu Chenggang. 1993. "Why China's Economic Reforms Differ: The M-Form Hierarchy and Entry/Expansion of the Non-State Sector." *Economics of Transition* 1(2): 135–70.

State Statistical Bureau. 1993. *Industrial Statistics Yearbook of China 1993*. Beijing: China Statistical Publishing House.

Comment on "How Industrial Reform Worked in China: The Role of Innovation, Competition, and Property Rights," by Jefferson and Rawski

Shahid Javed Burki

My view of industrial reform in China is considerably different from the one offered by Gary Jefferson and Thomas Rawski. Before presenting my view of the factors that contributed to the massive increase in industrial output and the dramatic restructuring of the industrial sector in China, I want to provide some basic information about the performance of this sector.

Transformation of China's Industry

The Jefferson and Rawski article offers a great deal of raw statistics to underscore the changes that have taken place in China's industry since the dawn of the reform era. Since the authors chose not to highlight some of the significant changes that have occurred, let me list just a few:

- Between 1980 and 1992 the real output of industry in China increased nearly fivefold—an annual growth rate of 13.1 percent.
- There was a striking change in the pattern of ownership of industrial assets during this period. In terms of output the share of the state-owned enterprises declined from 76 percent to 48 percent, while that of the collectives increased from 24 percent to 30 percent. There was no privately owned industry in 1980; in 1992 private enterprises accounted for 7 percent of industrial output.
- The losses of state-owned industrial enterprises increased sixfold in nominal terms from ¥5 billion in 1986 to ¥30 billion in 1991. The share of the state-owned industrial sector in total losses by state enterprises increased remarkably, from one-ninth to one-third over this period. However, the coverage of these losses by government subsidies declined from 81 percent to 48 percent. The distribution of subsidies to state-owned enterprises shows clearly that the government was not reluctant to expose industrial enterprises to competition. It was more willing to protect nonindustrial state enterprises instead.
- The return on capital invested in industry fell by more than half between 1980 and 1993—from 25.2 percent to 11.9 percent.

Shahid Javed Burki is vice president, Latin America and Caribbean Regional Office, at the World Bank.

Proceedings of the World Bank Annual Conference on Development Economics 1994

Jefferson and Rawski also provide information on wages for different classes of enterprises, changes in the profit-capital ratio, and levels of concentration in different industrial groups.

This is a partial and somewhat idiosyncratic coverage of the data available on the Chinese industrial sector. To get a better picture of the characteristics of the industrial sector and its contribution to the development of the economy, it would have been helpful, for instance, to provide information on the geographic distribution of industrial output and on how it changed following the initiation of reforms. The authors also could have provided information on the geographical distribution of foreign direct investment, the contribution made by different industrial sectors to China's remarkable export performance, or the increase in employment in different industrial categories. Had the authors cast their statistical net over a wider area, they might have reached a different conclusion about the factors that contributed to industrial performance in China.

The Jefferson-Rawski View of Industrial Transformation

It is not always easy to understand the logic that supports the main conclusions Jefferson and Rawski reach on the transformation of the Chinese industrial sector. I have also detected a number of contradictions between the seven propositions presented in the second half of the article and the principal argument laid out in the first half. However, I will not go into these problems. Instead I will focus on the larger picture of China's industrialization.

According to Jefferson and Rawski industrial reform in China was a consequence mostly of endogenous factors: the state gave the industrial sector a big push and then, essentially, sat back and watched internal factors take over and guide the sector's evolution. We are told that enterprises and individuals by and large act on their own, proceeding on the basis of the impulses generated from within the industrial sector. The picture that is offered is that of a benign, laid-back state passively watching—although not in a disinterested way—the evolution of the industrial sector. The disequilibrium that resulted from the actions initially taken by the state has kept the sector out of balance. Impulses move down the vertical ladder—from the state-owned industries at the top of the industrial apex to village enterprises at the bottom—and across the horizontal structure as managers of enterprises at different layers of the system vigorously compete with one another.

For some reason the authors label this process of change "gradualist," contrasting it with the top-down, exogenous, centrally planned reforms they believe were advocated by several international organizations for reforming the industrial sector of the former Soviet Union.

Evolution of Chinese Industry: Another View

I have a number of quarrels with both the hypothesis offered and the "gradualism" label applied to it. Since this is not the place to present my picture of China's industrial reform in detail, I concentrate on one important aspect that is central to the argument advanced by Jefferson and Rawski: the role of the state. I have a fundamental difference with the authors. In my view the state's role was much more continuous and interventionist than the authors suggest. Consider the following six sets of policies adopted and vigorously pursued by the state that encouraged not only a sharp increase in industrial output but also the restructuring of the industrial sector.

The first important decision, taken in the early 1980s, was to permit rural communities to keep the bulk of their incomes as savings and invest them in nonagricultural activities. Thus was born a new class of entrepreneur operating in the countryside. This decision was the logical outcome of the enormous increase in rural incomes that, in turn, was a consequence of the disbanding of communes and the virtual privatization of agricultural assets. The state, by permitting the establishment of industries it could not control, was creating a new force whose full impact it did not then fully appreciate. The result was an enormous expansion in the number of town and village enterprises (TVEs) and a corresponding increase in their output. By the early 1990s the TVEs not only employed the same number of workers as the state-owned sector but also had a considerably higher rate of job creation. The expansion of the TVE sector, therefore, offered some welcome space within which the government could experiment with the restructuring of state-owned industrial enterprises.

Second, having made the decision that led not only to the remarkable growth of the industrial sector but also to its dramatic restructuring, the government, by changing relative prices, altered the environment in which state-owned enterprises had functioned since their founding. The changes in relative prices came gradually, and after a great deal of deliberation and experimentation. By the early 1990s most of the decisions taken at the margin by industrial managers—in both the state and the nonstate sectors—were based on market signals.

Third, Chinese policymakers granted considerable economic autonomy to provincial and municipal governments. The coastal provinces and several large coastal cities were given an extraordinary amount of authority to conduct their economic affairs. But for that, the coastal provinces would not have grown at the rate they did, Chinese exports would not have increased at the rate they did, and joint ventures would not have become one of the most dynamic elements in the Chinese industrial sector.

Fourth, by about the middle of the 1980s the state began to experiment with the restructuring of the industrial enterprises it owned. This experimentation continues today. No satisfactory formula has been found for improving the efficiency of state-owned enterprises, but the state is willing to take time to find the right set of solutions.

Fifth, the slow and deliberate pace of reform of state-owned enterprises is motivated by the leadership's strong desire to maintain social stability. The leadership is unwilling to risk social instability in order to improve enterprise efficiency. It is proceeding on three tracks simultaneously: creating new institutions that will ultimately assume responsibility from state enterprises for providing housing and social security, allowing the nonstate sector to expand rapidly to permit the transfer of workers from the state to the nonstate sector, and continuing in the interim with various experiments to restructure the enterprises.

Sixth, lacking instruments of macroeconomic control for dealing with the frequent boom and bust cycles, the state has applied all manner of administrative and political devices to restore equilibrium in the financial, labor, and product markets and to curb investments in overheated sectors that were attracting speculative capital. The state has also been prepared to use the large external balances it has at its disposal to cool the economy with more imports.

Conclusion

I could go on listing government policies in order to underscore my point: the state in China has been active and interventionist in its approach toward economic reforms, particularly in the industrial sector. It has also been gradualist, but not in the sense implied by Jefferson and Rawski. It moved slowly and continuously after a great deal of experimentation. Its primary concern remains the rapid development of industry that will allow it to restructure state-owned enterprises and accommodate the large number of workers—perhaps as many as 20 to 30 million—that would inevitably be displaced. This, I believe, is a more accurate picture of the transformation of the industrial sector than the one offered by the authors.

Floor Discussion of "How Industrial Reform Worked in China: The Role of Innovation, Competition, and Property Rights," by Jefferson and Rawski

Rawski saw no great disagreement between his and Jefferson's analysis and the discussants' comments; rather, it seemed to him, they were interpreting the same thing in different ways. This was both encouraging, responded Shahid Burki (discussant), and a typical Chinese response to external criticism: to make it endogenous.

A participant asked what role ideas—and ideologies—played in industrial reform in China. Ideas that existed long before 1978, replied Rawski, were important in China's reform; indeed, as far back as 1956 proposals for the second five-year plan involved small-scale industry, decentralized local control, and other elements that surfaced in the reform effort twenty years later. One of the refreshing things about China, added Nicholas Stern (discussant), is that it is one of the most unideological countries imaginable. Pragmatism is much more of a driving force.

Rawski said that he could not agree more with Stern, for example, about the incentive to conceal profits in Chinese industry; he was amazed whenever someone said two-thirds or more of state enterprises lost money, because those loss figures were fiscal data. So he agreed that there was a data problem, but how, then, did Stern explain convergence phenomena?

Stern rephrased the question before responding: why, if the older numbers were made up, would they all converge? He would emphasize another aspect of the data in trying to understand why profits had fallen. In his view, profits had dropped because the labor force had negotiated a larger share of them in response to the firms' greater discretion in the disposal of value added. Then the question is, how far can profits decline? In Stern's view the only constraint on how far you can reduce reported profits is what you can negotiate with local tax authorities. He prefers that interpretation rather than one involving a highly mobile and competitive capital market, which he thinks does not yet exist in China. He would not insist on any interpretation, but he would rather focus on constraints on labor's share than on profits in a mobile capital market. To turn the question of what happened to profits around and ask what happened to labor's share is simply a different way of looking at the same phenomenon. If the profit rate goes down, labor's share goes

This session was chaired by Robert Picciotto, director-general, Operations Evaluation, at the World Bank.

up. But to focus on labor's share does raise different questions, such as how labor's share is determined and what discretion there is. These issues are part of any story about competition and may in fact be more important.

Responding to the repeated mention of labor's increasing share of income in state enterprises, Jefferson observed that labor's share of income had risen from close to 7 percent in 1980 to just under 8 percent in 1990, which as a share of gross output is not that large an increase. A substantial share of compensation for state enterprise workers came from in-kind payments (in the form of housing, health care, schooling, and other social services), but these were unlikely to have represented more than 5 or 6 percent of gross output. Labor's output elasticity in state industry is at least 15 percent, he continued, which suggests that its contribution to industrial output is about 15 percent of total inputs. We would not reject the hypothesis that labor's share of income is consistent with its technical contribution to production, said Jefferson.

We're not referring only to the profit data in the article, rejoined Rawski. Many results based on econometric analyses of sample data from Chinese enterprises—some by Jefferson and Rawski, some by others—are converging on relationships that one would expect to see in a competitive market. If the data are hokey, Rawski asked, where do these results come from?

If the role of the state was so important, Rawski asked Burki, then who pushed the suicide lever that drove the ratio of government revenue to GNP from 35 percent to 14 percent in thirteen to fifteen years? Of course, Rawski acknowledged, the government was active and there were exogenous factors at work; Hong Kong and the open door policy were also important. He and Jefferson were not claiming that everything was endogenous. But despite the strictures of the discussants, Rawski believed an important endogenous process was going on, that competition was important, and that the government was reacting as often as it was leading.

To understand how the Chinese industrial sector has functioned, responded Burki, you have to take a more balanced view. You cannot just factor out the role of the state. And explaining the rapid decline of the state's share in revenues does not demonstrate the correctness of one hypothesis or another. These are outcomes of how the state was proceeding: it would go forward a couple of steps and then retreat one step. The state was at that very moment trying to respond to the problem Rawski had suggested, which is that both enterprises and provinces have benefited greatly from the autonomy the state had allowed them. That is at the crux of the Chinese experience with reform.

Rawski asked Burki if he knew of any document published in China in the early or mid-1980s suggesting that policymakers knew that reform would bring about a big decline in government revenues and yet decided to go forward with it anyway. There would be no such document because this was an unexpected outcome for policymakers, which is why he and Jefferson leaned toward the interpretation that the government, although active and purposeful, was not in charge and was reacting as much as it was acting. Burki was sure Rawski was not surprised that studies of this kind did not exist. Part of the beauty of the Chinese experience, Burki said, was that

China was not only so unideological but also so unplanned. The Chinese take positions without reflecting too much on the long-term consequences, which is why there is constant experimentation, study, adjustment, and so forth. There is very little ex ante work and a great deal of ex post work.

Jefferson said that there may be room for argument on both sides in the debate about a balanced or unbalanced approach to growth. On one side of the debate Rosenstein-Rodan and Nurkse advocated a balanced growth approach to development, and on the other side Hirschman advocated an unbalanced growth approach. Jefferson suspected that in hindsight each might appreciate the other's point of view. Hirschman, besides emphasizing links within the economic—especially the industrial—system, might also acknowledge the importance of coordinated investments by the state. And those on the other side of the debate might appreciate the spontaneous links that exist within the industrial system. Asked to comment, Burki said that China is so complex and unique that it would not further understanding to force China's experience into any particular bottle. He would prefer to reflect on what had happened and try to explain it without bringing in various theories on other situations.

A participant from the University of Massachusetts asked for observations about the training or retraining of China's managerial cadre. Was that approach to training transferable to Eastern Europe? Rawski said that he did not know enough about the training of managers in the 1990s to answer the question usefully. The participant observed that, if managers in China are responding to competitive pressure, surely not all managers are responding equally rapidly or well. Has any work been done to identify the factors that explain differences in managers' ability to respond? Rawski responded that not much is known about managerial labor markets in China and the factors that determine managerial performance.

A participant from the University of Pennsylvania asked for comments on the tremendous investment, technical assistance, and know-how the overseas Chinese had brought to China. Jefferson agreed that their contribution had been very important. The Chinese statistical yearbook, he said, shows an average of 100,000 border crossings a day between China and Guandung Province, and he suspected that most people crossing the border were carrying export orders, technologies, managerial resources, and other factors important to industrial development. This was consistent, he said, with their emphasis on the spontaneous bottom-up nature of reform, even when initiated by the center.

Observing that China's population is far more rural than that of Eastern Europe, a participant from the London School of Economics asked how important that is in terms of providing a spare labor force for industrial activity that was unavailable in Eastern Europe (Eastern Europe's main labor force being trapped in state enterprises). How do they face that problem? Rawski replied that the nonagricultural labor force's low share in China's economy gives China added flexibility, but that a real problem remains: steel enterprises, for example, that need only 50,000 workers employ 150,000. People are being guaranteed pensions when pension funds have not accumulated, people are living in houses that cannot be profitably maintained, and these problems will not go away. Despite a big agricultural sector, China's huge state industrial sector employs 40 million workers, and the problems of reform are immense, painful, and intractable.

Jefferson added that extending the notion of Grossman and Helpman's quality ladder into China's domestic industry was not a mere abstraction; it was based on observation. He and Rawski had recently visited a township and village enterprise (TVE), a garment factory outside Beijing, in which the factory manager told them that she was competing both with state enterprises, which produced higher-quality garments (but at a higher cost), and with households, which produced lower-quality products (but at a lower cost). This suggested to Jefferson and Rawski that product quality and innovations were moving down the ladder and that competition was moving up. Certainly the factory director was aware of the situation.

Burki said that he would place the ladder between Guandung and the rest of the country, because innovation was coming from Guandung and was not restricted to state enterprises. On the contrary, provincial and joint enterprises (in which the state enterprises were not active) had become leaders in innovation and technology.

One participant asked how, in hypothesis testing, the effects of overall changes on a sector or industry were isolated from the effects of TVEs on state enterprises. Jefferson suggested looking at the paper by Inderjit Singh, Dilip Ratha, and Geng Xiao (cited in the Jefferson-Rawski article), who, using provincial panel data, found that the larger was the nonstate share of industrial output, the lower was the profitability—or, the more the nonstate sector grew, the faster profitability fell. They also found that the more the nonstate sector grew, the faster total factor productivity rose.

In fact, said Jefferson, state-owned enterprises are responding to competition. Certainly, many of them are not responding to competition—and they are being left behind. Derek Morris, using another data set, suggests a close relationship between investment and gross profitability, and it does seem that the enterprises that are performing well are those that can capture investment resources and expand production. Those that do not capture resources and cannot expand capacity are not performing well and are falling behind.

A participant from the Congressional Search Division of the Library of Congress observed that with China midstream in the reform process, there was clearly a problem with the distribution of wealth—a cleavage between urban and rural centers and between coastal areas and the hinterlands. So where does the system go? Some economic problems, especially between peasants and factory workers, could become political problems, especially in areas where politics are hanging by a thread.

Income distribution is an important issue in any large country, responded Rawski. At the beginning of the People's Republic, in the early 1950s, there were huge gaps in income distribution between urban and rural citizens and within the rural sector. Chinese policies cut off the tails of the income distribution, but large inequalities remained when reform began. Reform has lessened some inequalities and magnified others. Will distribution be an issue in the future? Of course. But is Chinese politics hanging by a thread? Rawski didn't think so, although he hesitated to comment on such matters.

The Institutions and Governance of Economic Development and Reform

Oliver E. Williamson

Why are the ambitions of economic development practitioners and reformers so often disappointed? One answer is that development policymakers and reformers are congenital optimists. Another answer is that good plans are regularly defeated by those who occupy strategic positions. An intermediate answer is that institutions are important, yet are persistently neglected in the planning process. The article takes a bottom-up, microanalytic approach to economic development and reform. It examines the governance of contract, investment, and private ordering through the lens of transaction-cost economizing. And it assesses the efficacy of the de facto (as against the de jure) institutional environment with respect to credible commitments. In effect, institutional economists are cast in the role of archaeologists of economic reform and development—with the of task unpacking the lessons of the past to inform choices and programs for the future.

The new institutional economics has recently been invited to speak to the issues of development and reform. As it turns out, the new institutional economics offers not one but several (related) perspectives. The main divide is between the institutional environment approach, a more macroanalytic perspective concerned with the political and legal rules of the game, and the institutions of governance, a more microanalytic perspective dealing with firm and market modes of contract and organization. Although many regard the first as the more pertinent for economic development and reform, I work predominantly from the governance perspective, adopting a bottom-up rather than top-down approach to economic organization. Three propositions inform the exercise:

1. Institutions are important, and they are susceptible to analysis.
2. The action resides in the details.
3. Positive analysis (with emphasis on private ordering and de facto organization) as against normative analysis (court ordering and de jure organization) is where the new institutional economics focuses attention.

Oliver E. Williamson is Edgar F. Kaiser Professor of Business Administration and professor of economics and law at the University of California, Berkeley.

Proceedings of the World Bank Annual Conference on Development Economics 1994

Getting the Institutions Right

Figure 1 sketches what I see to be the salient moves that have brought us to the point where institutional economics has been invited to enter the arena. The main divide is between macroanalytic and microanalytic approaches to development and reform. Because institutional economics is concerned mainly with microanalytic matters, that is the strand of principal interest. But there would be much less incentive to turn to the microanalytic side if the macroanalytic approach had been more successful.

Development economics and industrial organization have both undergone similar three-stage progressions.[1] Stage 1 is the aggregative or macroanalytic approach (the Harvard tradition). The neoclassical approach (the Chicago tradition) is conspicuous in stage 2. The new institutional economics does not show up until stage 3. Because it is primitive and still growing, moreover, the new institutional economics is appealed to only as a last resort. The stages are overlapping: the appearance of a new stage does not annihilate its predecessors.

An extreme version of the macroanalytic approach is what Deepak Lal calls the dirigiste dogma. It called for governments to chart and implement "a 'strategy' for rapid and equitable growth which attaches prime importance to *macro-economic* accounting aggregates such as savings, the balance of payments, and the relative balance between broadly defined 'sectors' such as 'industry' and 'agriculture'" (Lal 1985, p. 5; emphasis added). That prescription was disappointing,[2] and the pendulum swung in the opposite direction. Many concluded that "the most important

Figure 1. *From Harvard to Chicago to the New Institutional Economics*

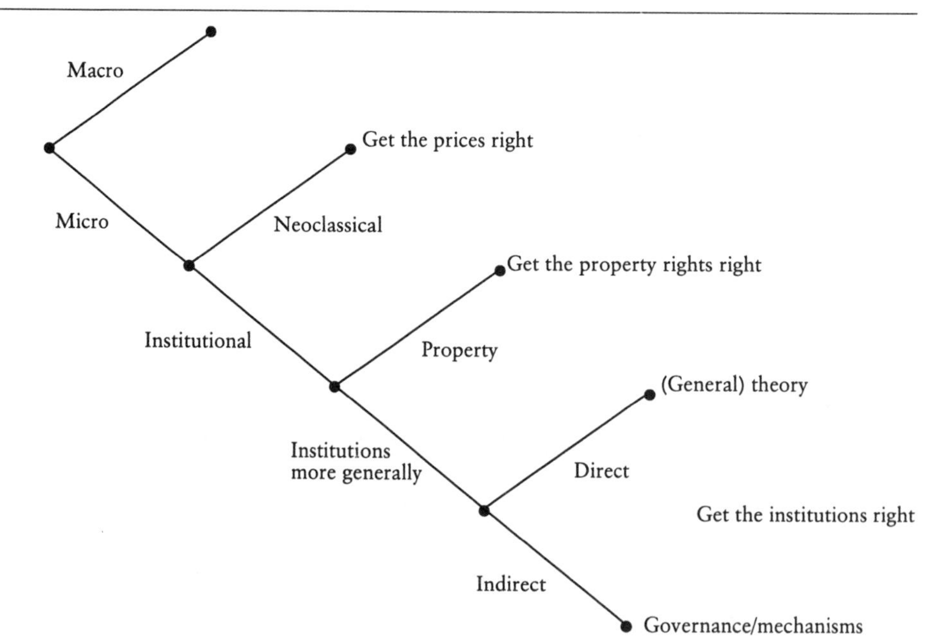

advice that economists can...offer is that of...[the] so-called Price Mechanist: 'Get the prices right'" (Lal 1985, p. 107). Although eliminating tariffs, quotas, and subsidies and making markets work have a lot to recommend them, that prescription too is oversimple and poorly suited to the needs of reforming (as against developing) economies. "Getting the property rights right" seemed to be more responsive to the pressing needs for reform in Eastern Europe and the former Soviet Union.

Privatization thus became the new prescription, but as Roman Frydman and Andrzej Rapacynski (1993) conclude: "the meaning of 'privatization' in Eastern Europe has turned out to be complex and ambiguous. Instead of the clarification of property rights and the introduction of incentives characteristic of a capitalist society, the privatization process has so far often led to a maze of complicated economic and legal relations that may even impede speedy transition to a system in which the rights of capital are clearly delineated and protected" (p. 13). One of the problems is that conflicts developed "between the interests of insiders, intent on retaining authority over their enterprises, and the right of outside investors to acquire control" (p. 13). But the deeper problem is that getting the property rights right is too narrow a conception of what institutional economics is all about. The more general need is to get the institutions right, of which property is only one part.[3] What does this mean?

Both Ronald Coase and Douglass North, in their 1991 and 1993 Nobel Prize lectures, speak frankly to these issues. Coase (1992) observes: "The value of including...institutional factors in the corpus of mainstream economics is made clear by recent events in Eastern Europe. These ex-communist countries are advised to move to a market economy, and their leaders wish to do so, but without the appropriate institutions no market economy of any significance is possible. If we knew more about our own economy, we would be in a better position to advise them" (p. 714). And North (1994) remarks that "polities significantly shape economic performance because they define and enforce the economic rules. Therefore an essential part of development policy is the creation of polities that will create and enforce efficient property rights. However, we know very little about how to create such polities" (p. 366).

As shown in the last node of figure 1, the idea of getting the institutions right can be viewed as an exercise in (general) theory or an exercise in the mechanisms of governance. The first tends to be more ambitious and normative, the second more partial and positive. Gordon Rausser and Leo Simon's (1992) prescription illustrates the first of these, where they aspire to provide:

> a general conceptual framework that provides an overview of the entire transition process, viewing it through a wide-angled lens. An ideal formulation would provide an exhaustive, conceptual classification of the decisions that have to be made, the players that will have to make them, the institutional structures within which decision making will take place and a set of performance criteria against which the process can be evaluated. A particularly important requirement of the ideal formulation is that it be "logically complete," in the sense of specifying an explicit decision-making

process for dealing with "residual contingencies" not dealt with elsewhere in the formulation. (p. 270)

The transaction cost economics approach to economic organization, however, looks to partial mechanisms and works out of variations on a few key, recurring themes. Elster (1994) advises that such a strategy applies more generally: "Explanations in the social sciences should be organized around (partial) *mechanisms* rather than (general) *theories*" (p. 75). The bottom-up approach to the study of development and reform is consonant with this more modest (but more operational) treatment of the issues.

The New Institutional Economics

The new institutional economics has developed in two complementary parts, the first dealing predominantly with background conditions, the second with the mechanisms of governance. The two-part definition proposed by Davis and North (1971) is pertinent:

> The *institutional environment* is the set of fundamental political, social, and legal ground rules that establishes the basis for production, exchange and distribution. Rules governing elections, property rights, and the right of contract are examples....
>
> An *institutional arrangement* is an arrangement between economic units that governs the ways in which these units can cooperate and/or compete. It [can] provide a structure within which its members can cooperate...or [it can] provide a mechanism that can effect a change in laws or property rights. (pp. 5–6; emphasis added)

The second is what I refer to as the institutions of governance and is what transaction cost economics has been predominantly concerned with. This is the bottom-up approach to economic organization.

As it turns out, individuals are also pertinent. The schema set out in figure 2 displays how these three levels—the individual, the governance structures, and the institutional environment—relate to each other.[4] The main effects are shown by the solid arrows. The feedback effects are shown by the dashed arrows.

Institutional Environment

The institutional environment—comprising the rules of the game—is vital to the study of economic organization. But it is easy to assign too much weight to the institutional environment and too little to the institutions of governance. The exaggerated emphasis on court ordering (by the institutions of the state) over private ordering (by the immediate parties and affiliates to a transaction) is one illustration. The propensity to emphasize de jure constitutional arrangements over de facto governance is another.

Governance

Transaction cost economics—and this article—are concerned mainly with governance. By way of overview:

- Transaction cost economics is an interdisciplinary undertaking that joins law, economics, and organization. Law and the judiciary are reflected in the constraints that originate in the institutional environment, which define the rules of the game. Organization theory is implicated through behavioral assumptions (see subsection on individuals below) and by the arrow in the governance box (in figure 2) that turns back on itself. This arrow reflects the proposition that "organizations have a life of their own," which is to say that organizations undergo intertemporal transformations that need to be identified and factored into the analysis. Economics provides the core logic, in that the analysis works out of the "rational spirit" to which Arrow (1974, p. 17) refers. The object is to examine "incomplete contracts in their entirety."
- Transaction cost economics is an exercise in comparative institutional analysis. The efficacy of alternative modes of organization—markets, hybrids, hierarchies, public bureaus—is examined in relation to the attributes of transactions, with which the alternative modes are aligned.
- Adaptation is the central problem of economic organization, of which two kinds are distinguished—autonomous adaptation in the market in response to price signals (Hayek 1945) and cooperative adaptation in the firm with the

Figure 2. *A Layer Schema*

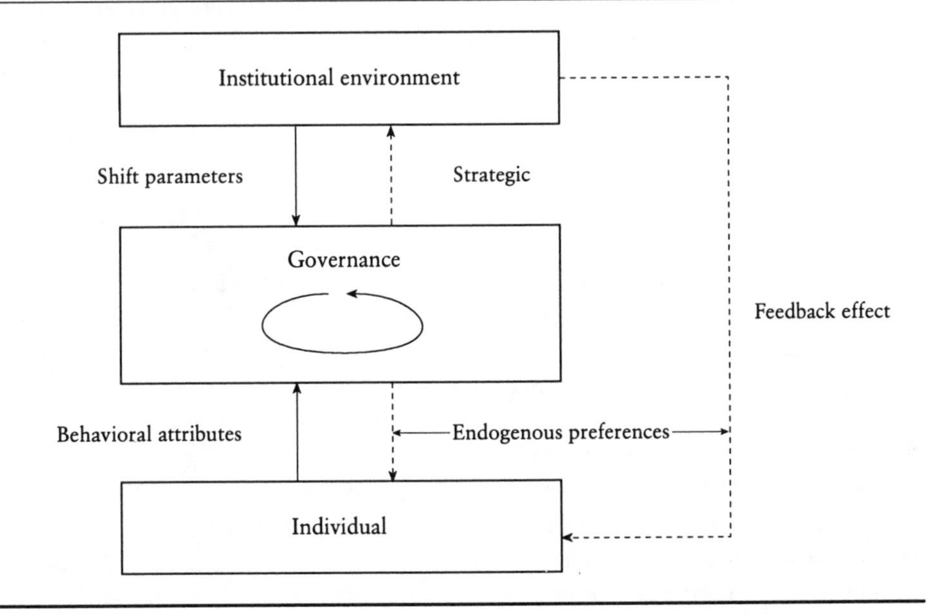

support of fiat (Barnard 1938).[5] A high-performance system will align transactions with governance structures in relation to their adaptive needs (Williamson 1991). Both investment and contracting are implicated.

Individuals

The pressing need is to describe individuals in workably realistic terms. As Herbert Simon (1985) puts it:

> Nothing is more fundamental in setting our research agenda and informing our research methods than our view of the nature of the human beings whose behavior we are studying. It makes a difference, a very large difference, to our research strategy whether we are studying the nearly omniscient *Homo economicus* of rational choice theory or the boundedly rational *Homo psychologicus* of cognitive psychology. It makes a difference to research, but it also makes a difference for the proper design of political institutions. James Madison was well aware of that, and in the pages of the *Federalist Papers* he opted for this view of the human condition (*Federalist*, No. 55): "As there is a degree of depravity in mankind which requires a certain degree of circumspection and distrust, so there are other qualities in human nature which justify a certain portion of esteem and confidence." A balanced and realistic view, we may concede, of bounded human rationality and its accompanying frailties of motive and reason. (p. 303)

Transaction cost economics expressly adopts the proposition that human cognition is subject to bounded rationality—where this is defined as behavior "intendedly rational, but only limitedly so" (Simon 1957, p. xxiv)—but differs from Simon in its interpretation of the "degree of depravity" to which Madison refers. Whereas Simon regards the depravity in question as "frailties of motive and reason," transaction cost economics describes it instead as opportunism—to include self-interest-seeking with guile.

Institutions Matter

The new institutional economics maintains that institutions matter and that institutions are susceptible to analysis (Matthews 1986). The first claim is easy to assert, but convincing demonstrations of the second have been elusive. Partly because of this elusiveness, but also because neoclassical economics appeared to be successful in working out of noninstitutional or preinstitutional setups, economics for a long time proceeded as if institutions could be ignored. That has changed.

Neoclassical economics describes the firm as a production function. Although useful for studying price and output, that approach led to contrived or mistaken interpretations of nonstandard and unfamiliar forms of contracting and organization. Confronted with puzzling irregularities, many economists invoked a monopoly explanation: "If an economist finds something—a business practice of one sort or another—that he does not understand, he looks for a monopoly explanation. And as in this field we are very ignorant, the number of ununderstandable practices tends to be rather large, and the reliance on monopoly explanation, frequent" (Coase 1972, p. 67).

That propensity (and the mistaken public policy ramifications that it led to) was overcome only as an organizational rather than a technological conception of the firm—the firm as governance structure—progressively took shape. As David Kreps (1990) has put it: "The [neoclassical] firm is like individual agents in textbook economics.... Agents have a utility function, firms have a profit motive; agents have consumption sets, firms have production possibility sets. But in transaction cost economics, firms are more like markets—both are arenas in which individuals can transact" (p. 96). Without preexisting market power the presumption is that nonstandard and unfamiliar business and contracting practices have the purpose and effect of economizing on transaction costs.

More than a presumption was needed, however. What is the logic of organization that informs this perspective? What are the refutable implications? Do the data line up? This is the transaction cost economics project as it was successively developed over the past twenty-five years. Without a demonstration that institutions are susceptible to analysis, the proposition that institutions matter would still be ignored.

What transpired in the field of industrial organization has parallels in the fields of comparative economic systems and development. These disciplines, however, have only recently accepted the importance of organization and institutions. Yet Oskar Lange (1938) posed the key issues more than fifty years ago:

> There is also the argument which might be raised against socialism with regard to the efficiency of public officials as compared with private entrepreneurs as managers of production. Strictly speaking, these public officials must be compared with corporate officials under capitalism, and not with private small-scale entrepreneurs. The argument thus loses much of its force. The discussion of this argument belongs to the field of sociology rather than of economic theory and must therefore be dispensed with here. By doing so we do not mean, however, to deny its great importance. It seems to us, indeed, that *the real danger of socialism is that of a bureaucratization of economic life,* and not the impossibility of coping with the problem of allocation of resources. Unfortunately, we do not see how the same, or even greater, danger can be averted under monopolistic capitalism. Officials subject to democratic control seem preferable to private corporation executives who practically are responsible to nobody. (pp. 109–110; emphasis in original)

Considering the study of bureaucracy beyond the reach of economics ("belonging" instead to sociology), Lange was content to dismiss the argument that the burdens of bureaucracy would spell the demise of socialism with an unproved claim that the bureaucratic problems of capitalism were even more severe. The "socialist controversy" thus reverted to an abstract assessment of the allocative efficiency properties of the socialist system, and it was generally agreed that Lange and Abba Lerner had prevailed in their dispute with Friedrich Hayek and Ludwig von Mises on the efficacy of socialism (Schumpeter 1942, pp. 167, 172; Bergson 1948, pp. 424, 435). Indeed, Lerner reportedly went to Mexico to tell Trotsky that "all would be well in a communist state if only it reproduced the result of a competitive system and prices were set equal to marginal cost" (Coase 1988).

Later analysts held that a "preinstitutional" approach to the field of comparative economic systems was a virtue. Tjalling Koopmans (1977), for example, found that he could communicate easily and effectively with his counterparts in the former Soviet Union in the technical language of activity analysis without referring to political, legal, and organizational differences: "Technology and human needs are universal. To start with just these elements has facilitated and intensified professional contacts and interactions between market and socialist countries" (pp. 264–65).

The former Soviet Union was overcome not by failures of activity analysis, however, but by the cumulative burdens of bureaucracy. The propensity within the field of comparative economic systems to eschew institutions and ex post governance in favor of technology and ex ante incentive alignment thus turned out to be fateful. Secondary effects (of a marginal-analysis kind) were emphasized at the expense of primary effects (of a discrete-structural kind). As a consequence, the salient bureaucratic differences between capitalism and socialism were obscured.

The new institutional economics is predominantly an exercise in discrete structural analysis in which alternative modes of organization—markets, hybrids, hierarchies, bureaus—are described as syndromes of related attributes (Williamson 1991; Aoki 1994; and Milgrom and Roberts 1994). The exercise, developed mainly with reference to the traditional concerns of industrial organization, has relevance also to an understanding of the bureaucratic and incentive differences between comparative economic systems.

Institutions Are Susceptible to Analysis

The new institutional economics demonstrates that institutions are susceptible to analysis by focusing on the microanalytics of contract and organization. As Kenneth Arrow (1987) puts it: "the new institutional economics movement...does not consist primarily of giving answers to the traditional questions of economics—resource allocation and the degree of utilization. Rather it consists of answering new questions, why economic institutions have emerged the way they did and not otherwise; it merges with economic history, but brings sharper nanoeconomic... reasoning to bear than has been customary" (p. 734).

Firm and Market Organization

The microanalytics of firm and market organization is developed in three parts: the transaction is the basic unit of analysis and is given dimension, the attributes that describe and distinguish alternative modes of governance are set out, and transactions and governance structures are aligned in relation to a transaction cost–economizing purpose.

Transactions. Transaction cost economics adopts Commons's proposal (1924, 1934) that the transaction be made the basic unit of analysis. That is a critical move because it shifts attention from the orthodox focus on price and output to consider the microanalytic attributes of transactions. But the move is completed only on identifying the critical dimensions in which transactions differ. Transaction cost economics avers that the key dimensions are the frequency with which transactions recur, the uncertainties they are subject to, the degree of asset specificity, and the ease of measurement. As it turns out, asset specificity—the degree to which transactions are supported by durable, nonredeployable assets—is especially important to the governance of contractual relations.

Governance Structures. Transaction cost economics maintains that each generic mode of organization—market, hybrid, public and private bureaus—is defined by a distinctive form of contract law. Each mode also differs with respect to incentives and controls. And each implements the mix of autonomous and cooperative adaptations differently. The upshot is that each generic mode of organization is defined by an internally consistent syndrome of attributes that gives rise to distinctive strengths and weaknesses.

Discriminating Alignment. The ideal organization adapts quickly and efficaciously to disturbances of all kinds, but actual organizations experience tradeoffs. More decentralized forms of organization (markets) support high-powered incentives and display outstanding adaptability to autonomous disturbances, but they are poorly suited to cooperative adaptation. Hierarchy, by contrast, has weaker incentives and is worse at autonomous adaptation but better at cooperative adaptation.

Which mode of organization is used to organize which transactions, and why? Asset specificity (k) is especially important in this. The general argument is that simple transactions require only general-purpose investment (hence $k = 0$, although the amount of capital K may be large) and pose predominantly autonomous adaptation needs. Because the assets can be productively redeployed to alternative uses and users if any contract breaks down and because markets excel at autonomous adaptation, the market-like option is efficacious. (So firms buy rather than make, use spot contracts for labor, use debt rather than equity, eschew regulation, and so on.) Problems with markets arise as bilateral dependencies—and the needs for cooperative adaptation—build up. Markets give way to hybrids, which in turn give way to hierarchies (the organizational form of last resort) as asset specificity increases ($k > 0$) and the needs for cooperative adaptation build up.

Development and Reform

The lessons of firm and market organization carry over to the study of development and reform. Thus in response to the question, how does one describe a high-performance economy, transaction cost economics answers that the nature and level of investment and the characteristics of contracting are crucial. Differences between nation-states in investment and contracting, moreover, are predicted.

Investment. As indicated, asset specificity is the transaction attribute that most determines the mode of economic organization—in intermediate product markets (make or buy), capital markets (debt or equity), labor markets (different governance supports), regulation or deregulation (with ramifications for privatization), and the like. Transactions that pose especially severe contractual hazards, because of bilateral dependency, will either be afforded added safeguards (unified ownership of the two trading stages is one possibility) or be reformed (by shifting from a specific to a more generic technology).

Similar reasoning carries over to the economy, though an added source of investment hazard appears: the state may be the source of investment uncertainty.

Consider the matter of "takings," defined as "constitutional law's expression for any sort of publicly inflicted private injury for which the constitution requires payment of compensation" (Michelman 1967, p. 1165). The question is how this provision, which is not self-enforcing, is to be implemented.

Among the principled ways to implement the constitution is to appeal to political theory, of which John Rawls's treatment of "justice as fairness" is a candidate (Michelman 1967, pp. 1218–24). But that prescription is vague and difficult to operationalize. A second way to approach the issue is from the bottom up. Given the administrative costs of paying compensation and the disincentives that arise (for future investment) if injuries go uncompensated, what attributes of the transaction are responsible for high costs of both kinds?

Transaction cost economics relates easily to this exercise. Not only are the administrative costs of paying compensation a type of transaction cost, but the demoralization costs depend very much on the characteristics of the assets. In addition, the farsighted approach to investment and the idea of "security of expectations" to which Michelman appeals are very much in the spirit of credible commitments.

Michelman (1967) joins these several concepts. He argues that if administrative costs are great, because it is very costly to establish who was adversely affected and to what degree, and if neither those who bear the loss nor interested observers will change the amount (K) or composition (k) of future investments, it would be inefficient to compensate. Administrative costs would be incurred for which there would be little offsetting benefit. But if the failure to pay compensation to losers would "demoralize" investors (both those who bear the losses and interested observers), with the result that future investment is moved to safer but less productive uses, compensation may yield net social gains despite the administrative costs.

Especially critical to an assessment of demoralization is whether the loss is perceived to be strategic rather than adventitious. Investors who perceive themselves to be strategically expropriated will view the government as malevolent. Note, moreover, that assets can be devalued not merely by seizure but also by a variety of control mechanisms—including taxation; input controls; operating requirements;

reporting requirements; rate of return limitations; price, output, and effluent controls; and other bureaucratic and oversight practices.

Investors who realize that they are disadvantaged relative to other, more favored members of society can and will adapt in a variety of ways. Thus more-durable assets will be supplanted by less-durable assets. Nonmobile assets will be supplanted by more-mobile assets. Conspicuous assets will give way to those that can be sequestered. And assets may flee by relocating in more secure jurisdictions. More generally, nonredeployable investments ($k > 0$) that would be made in a secure investment regime will be supplanted by more redeployable assets and by capital flight and asset concealment. Productivity will be lost as a result.

Michelman sets out a series of criteria for assessing how administrative costs net out in relation to demoralization costs (1967, pp. 1217–18, 1223). Perceived opportunism of the government is a recurrent theme. The basic point is this: the quality of a compensation regime is to be inferred not by focusing mainly or exclusively on the de jure constitution (top down) but principally from a de facto, bottom-up examination of the mechanisms.

Contracting. The economywide concept that corresponds with governance is the distribution of transactions. Consider the three-part division of governance as between spot-market trading, long-term contracting, and hierarchy. Both spot-market and hierarchical transactions need little support from the judiciary. Disappointed spot-market traders can easily limit their exposure and can seek relief by terminating and turning to other traders. And internal organization is its own court of ultimate appeal (Williamson 1991). By contrast, transactions in the middle range can be difficult to stabilize.

Parties to such middle-range transactions can provide a variety of private-ordering supports. But when push comes to shove, middle-range transactions will benefit if they can be appealed to a principled authority. Karl Llewellyn's (1931) concept of contract as framework is pertinent here: "the major importance of legal contract is to provide a framework for well-nigh every type of group organization and for well-nigh every type of passing or permanent relation between individuals and groups...a framework highly adjustable, a framework which almost never accurately indicates real working relations, but which affords a rough indication around which such relations vary, an occasional guide in cases of doubt, and a norm of ultimate appeal when the relations cease in fact to work" (pp. 736–37). Unless the ultimate appeal stage works in an informed and uncorrupted manner, transactions in the middle range are in jeopardy.

Such jeopardy will lead to a reorganization of transactions—attended by a change in the degree of asset specificity (Riordan and Williamson 1985)—in which transactions in the middle range will be moved toward one or the other pole.

The upshot is that the quality of a judiciary can be inferred indirectly: a high-performance economy (expressed in governance terms) will support more transactions in the middle range than will an economy with a problematic judiciary. Put differently, in a low-performance economy the distribution of transactions will be more bimodal—with more spot-market and hierarchical transactions and fewer middle-range transactions.

Discriminating Alignment. Discriminating alignments appear for nations as well as transactions. Nations that pose severe investment hazards will support smaller amounts of specialized, durable investment (low k and low K) than will more credible investment regimes; nations with problematic judiciaries will be similarly disadvantaged. That will show up in the technology. Regimes that afford weak supports for investment and contracting will rarely be able to provide strong supports for intellectual property rights. High-technology industries or industries that benefit from specialized, durable investments will thus flee from regimes with great investment and contractual insecurities—for safer havens.[6]

Private Ordering

Compared with neoclassical economics, which presumes that court ordering is efficacious, transaction cost economics places much greater weight on private ordering. Issues of credible commitment and remediableness arise in conjunction with private ordering.

Firm and Market Organization

Private Ordering versus Legal Centralism. The legal centralism tradition presumes that efficacious rules of law regarding contract disputes are in place and are applied by the courts in an informed, sophisticated, and low-cost way.[7] Those assumptions are convenient because they relieve lawyers and economists of the need to examine the variety of ways by which individual parties to an exchange contract out of or away from the governance structures of the state by devising private orderings. Thus arises a division of effort in which economists focus on the economic benefits that accrue to specialization and exchange and legal specialists on the technicalities of contract law.

This tradition maintains that "disputes require 'access' to a forum external to the original social setting of the dispute [and that] remedies will be provided as prescribed in some body of authoritative learning and dispensed by experts who operate under the auspices of the state" (Galanter 1981, p. 1). The facts, however, disclose otherwise. Most disputes—including many that under current rules could be brought to a court—are resolved by avoidance, self-help, and the like (Galanter 1981, p. 2).

The unreality of the assumptions of legal centralism can be defended by reference to the fruitfulness of the pure exchange model. That is not disputed here. Instead, the concern is that the law and economics of private ordering have been pushed into the background. That is unfortunate, since in "many instances the participants can devise more satisfactory solutions to their disputes than can professionals constrained to apply general rules on the basis of limited knowledge of the dispute" (Galanter 1981, p. 4).

Clyde Summers's (1969) distinction between "black letter law" and a more circumstantial approach to law is pertinent. "The epitome of abstraction is the *Restatement,* which illustrates its black-letter rules by transactions suspended in midair, creating the illusion that contract rules can be stated without reference to surrounding circumstances and are therefore generally applicable to all contractual transactions." Such a conception does not and cannot provide a "framework for integrating rules and principles applicable to all contractual transactions" (p. 566).

A broader conception of contract, emphasizing the affirmative purposes of the law and effective governance relations, is needed if that framework is to be realized. Summers conjectured in this connection that "the principles common to the whole range of contractual transactions are relatively few and of such generality and competing character that they should not be stated as legal rules at all" (p. 527). The challenge to economic organization is to identify and explicate the key principles for assessing contracts of all kinds—in intermediate product markets, labor markets, finance, corporate governance, final product markets, and the like. That is what the governance branch of the new institutional economics aspires to do.

Credible Commitments. The concept of credible commitment is especially crucial to private ordering. It is useful in this connection to think of contracts as defined by a triple (p, k, s)—where p denotes price, k denotes contractual hazards (asset specificity), and s denotes safeguards—all three of which are set simultaneously.

The issue of opportunism referred to earlier is usefully examined in this context. Recall that motivational hazards can be described in terms of either opportunism or "frailties of motive." The second is a more benign construction and, for day-to-day affairs, is descriptively more accurate. Frailties of motive do not, however, help to uncover the deep problems of contracting in the same way or in the same degree as does opportunism, which makes provision for self-interest-seeking with guile.

Robert Michel's (1962) concluding remarks about oligarchy are pertinent: "nothing but a serene and frank examination of the oligarchical dangers of democracy will enable us to minimize these dangers" (p. 370). If a serene and frank reference to opportunism alerts us to avoidable dangers that the more benign reference to frailties of motive and reason would not, there are real hazards in adopting the more benevolent construction.

Indeed, although opportunism is a relatively unflattering behavioral assumption, the main lesson of opportunism, for purposes of economic organization, is not the Machiavellian message to breach agreements with impunity because that is what others will do (Machiavelli 1952, pp. 92–93). Instead, farsighted economic agents will ask what they can do to mitigate the hazards of opportunism. Because it is in their mutual interests to avoid ex post opportunism, farsighted parties to a contract will give and receive credible commitments ex ante. Attenuating contractual hazards that would otherwise preclude investments in transaction-specific assets will result in more productive investments and organization.

The simple contractual schema in figure 3 brings these ideas together. The assumption is that a transaction can be produced by either of two technologies and that buyers are asking suppliers to bid on the contract. It will ease comparison to assume that suppliers are competitively organized and are risk-neutral. The prices at which products will be supplied therefore reflect an expected break-even condition. The break-even price associated with Node A is p_1. There being no hazards, $k = 0$. And since safeguards are unneeded, $s = 0$.

Node B is more interesting. The contractual hazard here is $\bar{k}$. If the buyer is unable or unwilling to provide a safeguard, then $s = 0$. The corresponding break-even price is $\bar{p}$.

Node C poses the same contractual hazard: $\bar{k}$. In this case, however, a safeguard in the amount $\hat{s}$ is provided. The break-even price projected under these conditions is $\hat{p}$. It is elementary that $\hat{p} < \bar{p}$.

Bradach and Eccles (1989) contend that "mutual dependence [$k > 0$] between exchange partners...[promotes] trust, [which] contrasts sharply with the argument central to transaction cost economics that...dependence...fosters opportunistic behavior" (p. 111). What transaction cost economics says, however, is that because opportunistic agents will not self-enforce open-ended promises to behave responsibly, efficient exchange will be realized only if dependencies are supported by credible commitments. How is trust implicated if parties to an exchange are farsighted and reflect the relevant hazards in terms of the exchange? A better price ($\hat{p} < \bar{p}$) will be offered if the hazards ($k > 0$) are mitigated by cost-effective contractual safeguards ($\hat{s} > 0$).

Remediableness. The efficiency of a form of organization is customarily evaluated by comparing it with a hypothetical ideal. Although instructive, that can be a

Figure 3. *Simple Contractual Schema*

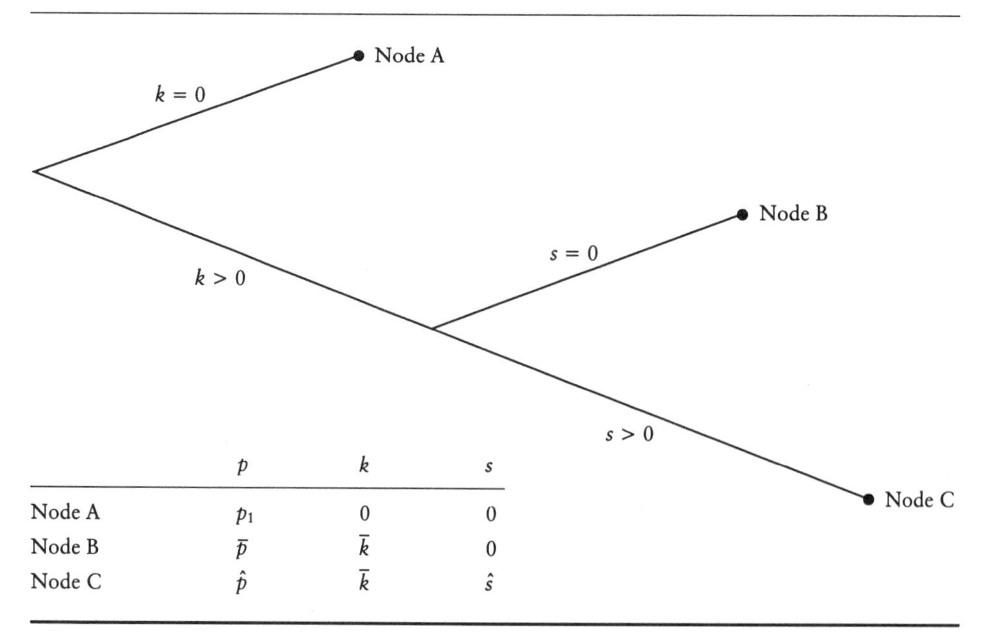

	p	k	s
Node A	p_1	0	0
Node B	$\bar{p}$	$\bar{k}$	0
Node C	$\hat{p}$	$\bar{k}$	$\hat{s}$

misleading or defective test in three respects. First, because all feasible forms of organization are flawed, the relevant comparison is between alternative feasible forms. Second, if one of the alternatives under comparison is in place, allowance needs to be made for incumbency advantages. Thus, even if node A is judged to be inefficient in relation to node B in a simple side-by-side comparison, if node A is in place and node B incurs setup costs, node A may prevail. Third, and related, it may not be possible to implement node B for lack of political support.

Accordingly, the appropriate test of failures of all kinds—markets, bureaucracies, redistribution—is remediableness: *an outcome for which no feasible superior alternative can be described and implemented with net gains is presumed to be efficient.* This comparative institutional test is widely resisted except in application to market failures.

Transaction cost economics is always and everywhere an exercise in comparative institutional analysis, comparing two or more feasible forms of organization. It views all cost differences on a parity, including those due to timing—one mode or technology got there first and does not, therefore, need to incur the start-up costs that a rival but later mode or technology does—provided only that the initial mover does not engage in entry-deterring strategic behavior. So many of the purported "inefficiencies" associated with path dependency (David 1985; Arthur 1989) vanish under the remediableness criterion.

Development and Reform

Much of the transaction cost reasoning developed with the microanalytics of economic organization carries over to the study of development and reform.

De Facto Property Rights. The distinction between legal centralism and private ordering helps to clarify the difference between de jure and de facto property rights. The conceptual hazard in both cases is to assign too much weight to the formal features (court ordering and de jure legal rights) at the expense of the unremarked and more subtle real features (private ordering and de facto economic rights). The issues are nicely posed by the puzzle of Chinese economic reform. As Montignola, Qian, and Weingast (1993) put it:

> The remarkable success of China's economic reforms—fostering economic growth averaging nine percent per year over the past fifteen years—seems to defy conventional wisdom. Consider:
>
> - Economic reform appears to have been successfully pursued without any political reform.
> - The central government seems to retain considerable political discretion, including the ability to reverse suddenly the reform process or to impose onerous exactions on successful enterprises.
> - Finally, there has been little attempt to provide the central feature of private markets, a system of secure private property rights. Nor has an

> attempt been made to develop a commercial law (e.g., property and contract law) or an independent court system for adjudication.
>
> Each of these factors appears to bode ill for economic reform. Without political reform, economic returns remain at the mercy of politics. Political discretion, in turn, implies that there are no impediments to the government reversing the reforms. Leadership turnover, for example, might induce the new government to reverse the reforms, possibly confiscating considerable wealth and punishing those who were successful under the new system. Alternatively, problems may occur during unexpectedly hard times. With severe budget problems and a population clamoring for "solutions, now," the immediate need for revenue produces powerful pressure for a partial or wholesale reversal of the reforms. (pp. 1–2)

Montignola, Qian, and Weingast respond to this puzzle by arguing, in effect, that the hazards are more apparent than real. What China has done is adopt a series of decentralizing reforms, the effect of which has been to introduce de facto federalism into China.

Consider in this connection a two by two matrix in which de jure federalism can be either present or absent and de facto federalism can be either present or absent (figure 4). The usual assumption is that de jure and de facto go together, but Montignola, Qian, and Weingast introduce the possibility that they need not correspond. Cell 2, where de jure federalism is absent but de facto decentralization is extensive, is what Montignola, Qian, and Weingast appeal to in explaining the unusual success of a Chinese economy in which formal legal protection of property rights is lacking. Although they make an interesting case for de facto federalism and

Figure 4. *Forms of Federalism*

De facto federalism		De jure federalism: Present	De jure federalism: Absent
	Present	1 Federalism "ideal"	2 Neglected alternative: "Chinese federalism"
	Absent	3 Bogus federalism	4 Highly centralized, in theory and practice

the effective safeguards accompanying it, two precautions are necessary. First, there is a chronic problem of ex post rationalization in explaining de facto successes.[8] And second, without de jure property rights China is unlikely to be able to support highly specific investments in leading-edge technologies. That inability will pose a challenge to Chinese economic organization in the future.

Credible Commitments. Weingast (1993) addresses the correspondences between political and economic organization: "In important respects, the logic of political institutions parallels that of economic institutions. To borrow Williamson's phrase, the political institutions of society create a 'governance structure' that at once allows the society to deal with on-going problems as they arise and yet provides a degree of durability to economic and political rights. Importantly, these help limit the ability of the state to act opportunistically" (p. 288). A farsighted state will thus recognize that organization matters and that it can take actions that increase confidence in both contracting and investment. But because politics is different, credible commitments may fail to materialize because of ignorance, front-loading, or looting.

The ignorance argument is that long-run-efficiency reasoning does not come easily to politicians more familiar and comfortable with power reasoning. The "invitation" by Mikhail Gorbachev, advising U.S. companies to invest quickly in the Soviet Union rather than wait, is illustrative: "Those [companies] who are with us now have good prospects of participating in our great country...[whereas those who wait] will remain observers for years to come—*we will see to it*" (*International Herald Tribune,* June 5, 1990). That an experienced and sophisticated leader of a huge nation-state in the late twentieth century should choose carrot-and-stick reasoning rather than an offer of credible commitments to encourage investments suggests the counterintuitiveness of credibility.

What Gorbachev evidently failed to understand is that the ready exercise of administrative discretion is the source of contractual hazard. Ready recourse to discretion not only places those who have already invested at greater hazard, but it also drives those who are contemplating investment to think again. The paradox is that fewer degrees of freedom (rules) can have advantages over more (discretion) if they make commitments more credible (Kydland and Prescott 1977). That is not an obvious result.

The front-loading results from the weakness of political property rights: even if parties have the capacity to look ahead and factor future consequences into present policy choices, the political process poses hazards of its own. If current politicians cannot bind their successors, projects that are front-loaded will be preferred, *ceteris paribus* (Moe 1990a,b).

Looting is explained similarly. Thus, although a bigger pie is always better than a smaller pie, *ceteris paribus,* the *cetera* may not be *paria.* If politicians with short horizons can seize assets or otherwise reward favored constituencies now, and if a big (and certain) piece of a small pie is perceived to be better than a smaller (and uncertain) piece of a bigger but deferred pie, credibility may get short shrift.

In consideration of these disabilities, what is to be done? The action resides in the mechanisms of governance: find mechanisms that communicate credible commitments.

Although there is growing agreement that credible commitments are the key (Shepsle 1992; North 1994), the need is to get beyond the agreement stage and engage the specifics. Otherwise, credible commitments will acquire the "well-deserved bad name" that Stanley Fischer (1977, p. 322, n. 5) once ascribed to transaction costs.

The problem with transaction costs in the early 1970s was that the concept was too elastic: anything could be explained by invoking suitable transaction costs after the fact. That tautological status was overcome by moving the analysis of transaction costs from (vague) generalities to the microanalytic particulars of transactions and governance: transactions were given dimension, the fundamental transformation was explicated, the discrete structural attributes of governance were displayed, and so on.

The concept of credible commitments in the 1990s (as employed at the level of the institutional environment, as against the level of governance) is similar: with so many degrees of freedom, any outcome can be rationalized in credible commitment terms after the fact. The parallel prescription for overcoming that tautological status is similarly to engage the relevant microanalytics—in this instance at the level of the mechanisms of the polity. That is an ambitious prescription, but it is beginning to take shape (Soskice, Bates, and Epstein 1992).

Remediableness. It was once customary, and is a continuing hazard, to regard the "government as a benevolent guardian, hampered only by ignorance of proper economic policy as it seeks disinterestedly to maximize a Benthamite social welfare function" (Krueger 1990, p. 172).

One justification for ascribing benevolent properties to the government is analytical convenience. Another is that some people really believe that "the most intractable problems [will] give way before the resolute assault of intelligent, committed people" (Morris 1980, p. 23). Analytical convenience is a poor excuse for bad public policy, however, and so is hubris. Intelligent people need to come to terms with their cognitive limitations, and committed people are rarely disinterested—most have an agenda. If all feasible forms of organization are flawed, references to benign government, costless regulation, omniscient courts, and the like are operationally irrelevant. Comparative institutional economics is always and everywhere beset with tradeoffs.

Lapses into ideal but operationally irrelevant reasoning will be avoided by recognizing that it is impossible to do better than one's best, insisting that all of the finalists in an organization-form competition meet the test of feasibility, symmetrically exposing the weaknesses as well as the strengths of all proposed feasible forms, and describing and costing-out the mechanisms of any proposed reorganization. To this list, moreover, there is a further consideration: making a place for and respecting politics (Stigler 1992). This last has been the most difficult for public policy analysts to concede.

Some Applications

How much support does the literature on economic development and reform provide for a bottom-up institutional economics approach that emphasizes investment, contracting, and the mechanisms of credible commitment? Not much, but that is not surprising. After all, little of this literature was written from an institutional economics perspective. It suffices for my purposes here to establish that there are hints in the literature for which institutional economics provides a useful lens.

The study of Chinese de facto federalism (Montignola, Qian, and Weingast 1993) is one example. The mistaken view of Gorbachev on credible commitments is another. I discuss here two further applications: the World Bank's recent Policy Research Report, *The East Asian Miracle* (World Bank 1993) and its five-nation study of privatization of telecommunications (Levy and Spiller forthcoming).

East Asia

On *The East Asian Miracle,* I begin with three observations. The report is an informative, thoughtful, and cautious treatment of the issues. It relies very little on institutional economics reasoning. Yet institutional economics is pertinent to some of the more interesting phenomena and practices that it reports.

The report interprets East Asian growth through neoclassical, revisionist, and market-friendly lenses (pp. 82–86). The neoclassical view is that growth is best ensured by allocating resources through markets in the context of macroeconomic stability and limited inflation. The revisionist view "sees market failures as pervasive and a justification for governments to lead the market in critical ways" (p. 83). The market-friendly view is that "the appropriate role of government...is to ensure adequate investments in people, provision of a competitive climate for enterprise, openness to international trade, and stable macroeconomic management" (p. 84). It recognizes both market failure and government failure (p. 84).

The institutional approach is closest to the market-friendly view, but it focuses on credible investment and credible contracting. It is also more expressly concerned with the attributes of human and physical assets.

Although readers are told on page 221 that "property rights...[are a] key element of the market-friendly institutional environment discussed in chapter 4," it takes an extraordinarily perceptive eye to ascertain how property rights figure into chapter 4. And while readers are also told that the enforcement of contracts is important (on page 221), that message is almost subliminal. Nowhere in the concluding discussion of the "Foundations of Rapid Growth—Getting the Fundamentals Right" (pp. 347–52) is there mention of either property or contracting. Instead, the "positive lessons" are listed as follows: "keep the macroeconomy stable; focus on early education; do not neglect agriculture; use banks to build a sound financial system; be open to foreign ideas and technology; and let prices reflect economic scarcity" (p. 367). Shift parameters from the institutional environment—culture, politics, and history—receive only limited treatment (p. vii).

Implicit reliance on institutional economics reasoning can nonetheless be inferred from the following:

Investment

- That the report attributes two-thirds of the growth of the eight East Asian economies to high rates of investment in physical and human capital speaks to the importance of credible investment conditions (p. 8).
- The allocation of capital to "high-yielding investments" (p. 8) can be interpreted in asset specificity ($k > 0$) terms.
- The report discusses education mainly with reference to government support for education, especially at primary and secondary levels (pp. 193–203), because of concern with market failures (p. 197). But because it does not address the comparative failures of government symmetrically, it does not address remediableness issues.
- Except for one passing reference (p. 188), the concept of credible commitment goes unremarked in the report. A variety of phenomena could be interpreted as indirect indicators of confidence, however. For example, an economy that infuses confidence will encourage more students to invest in education because they perceive that they will realize future gains. By contrast, secondary school students will bypass education in a predatory regime. Enrollment rates (p. 109) can thus be interpreted in credibility terms. Investments by the government in durable, complementary assets also can signal credibility (pp. 16–17, 221–40, 366–67). Direct foreign investment is also a useful credibility signal, as is the government's sharing information with business (pp. 183–85).
- The hurdle rate for investment is an indirect measure of credibility. Hurdle rates will be lower in countries where political hazards are perceived to be lower—or, put differently, the security of expectations is better (p. 221)—other things being equal.

Contracting

- Repeated reference to support for small and medium-size enterprises (pp. 161, 181, 223, 226) can be interpreted to mean support for contracting—although the report emphasizes credit and related supports rather than contracting. More subcontracting should be observed in regimes where contract laws and their enforcement are perceived to be credible.
- The emphasis on restructuring the labor sector "to suppress radical activity...[and] to ensure political stability" as well as to promote company- or enterprise-based unions (pp. 164–65) can be interpreted as efforts to infuse confidence into labor contracting (Williamson 1985, pp. 255–56). That will encourage greater investments in durable and specific physical assets (K and k).[9]
- The idea that workers should be encouraged to organize cooperatives (p. 165) is followed by the example of organizing taxis (p. 166). There is no mention of the limits of the cooperative form of organization as firms become large and assets more specific (Williamson 1985, pp. 265–68). (Cooperative orga-

nization is limited because contracting for equity capital is problematic if a firm is organized as a cooperative, and debt capital is poorly suited to supporting firm-specific investments [Williamson 1988].) Taxis are highly redeployable assets ($k = 0$) and hence much more easily organized as cooperatives.

Mechanisms

- The report makes numerous references to mechanisms (pp. 168–85). Although many are macroeconomic, others implicate the government and business in more microanalytic ways. These matters need to be described more fully to be adequately interpreted.
- A complicating factor is that linkages sometimes work through "informal networks," as in Indonesia (p. 185).
- Qualified technocrats running the bureaucracy and the suppression of lobbying (pp. 167–79) are important sources of credible commitment. Qualified bureaucrats with job security for whom the effects of reputation work well will have a long-run productivity orientation very different from that of politicians.
- Adaptation goes almost unmentioned, although the adaptability of labor gets a brief remark (p. 266).

Institutional economics can help to interpret what's going on out there. It could be used to even greater advantage if future reports focused on more microanalytic phenomena, emphasizing the institutional supports for contracting and investment.

Telecommunications

The World Bank study *Regulation, Institutions, and Commitment: Comparative Studies of Telecommunications* (Levy and Spiller forthcoming) is a more microanalytic undertaking—and a model of what needs to be done. The study deals with a well-defined purpose (telecommunications) for which governments differ in their perceptions and their abilities to communicate credible commitments. Issues of investment, contracting, and mechanisms are all posed.

The overview chapter by Levy and Spiller and the chapter on British telecommunications by Spiller and Vogelsang (forthcoming) are especially illuminating. The U.K. analysis observes that commitment is more difficult to provide in a parliamentary system than in a division-of-powers democracy. The reason: "The party in power controls both Parliament and the government, and there is no tradition of active judicial oversight of regulatory bodies. Thus governments and regulators cannot easily and credibly commit not to use administrative discretion to tighten the regulatory screws to expropriate a regulated firm's specific assets. Even if the courts rejected a particular regulatory interference, the government could get its way just by introducing new legislation or procedures."[10]

Because the assets in question were durable and nonredeployable, it was vital that the United Kingdom develop mechanisms that infuse investment confidence. In part that entailed creating pricing formulas (of the "price cap" kind) to which both telecommunications companies and regulators could refer with confidence. More important was creating the "regulatory game" in which privatized public utilities were embedded. As Spiller and Vogelsang (forthcoming) put it:

> Built into the regulatory process is a strong commitment, though not unbreakable, to follow the regulatory bargain struck at the time of privatization. The nature of the country's institutions (particularly the courts and informal norms of government decisionmaking) further reduces the likelihood that major regulatory changes will be imposed without the consent of the regulated company. Among the key safeguards:
>
> - To amend the license against the wishes of the company, the government must follow a complex and a precisely specified process. Failure to do so can be contested in courts.
> - Amending the license requires the agreement of several agencies, further reducing the extent of regulatory discretion.
> - Major regulatory powers are delegated to the head of the regulatory agency, limiting power at the ministry level.
> - Use of a price-cap mechanism limits the price-setting powers of the regulator and, because price caps are part of the license, limits the regulator's ability to radically change the price-setting mechanism.

This telecommunications study supports the following: credibility is vital to support the requisite nonredeployable investments; the regulatory regime and the political context jointly determine credibility (or lack of credibility); and the mechanisms of bureaucracy can and, at least in the United Kingdom, do operate in the service of stability and credibility. Without the creation of mechanisms that communicate confidence (if not full credibility), the privatization of telecommunications (and gas, water, electricity, and airports) in the United Kingdom would have been much more problematic. As Newbery (1994) puts it, "The main case for investment in public enterprise is that it is necessary to make up for the lack of private sector confidence in the future rules of the game" (p. 3).

In figure 5, nodes 1 and 2 show why private confidence is lacking. More central to this article are nodes 3 and 4, which work out of a de facto judicial tradition, and node 6, which combines de jure and de facto judicial independence with a strong bureaucracy. Node 6 can be thought of as an ideal, but short of this ideal, privatization can work if it has the requisite supports.

Conclusion

Ronald Coase (1964) once remarked that "we have less to fear from institutionalists who are not theorists than from theorists who are not institutionalists" (p. 196). Not everyone would agree. But the following is (almost) uncontroversial: it is both possible and desirable to combine institutional economics with theory, and the time has come to do precisely that.

Many might nod in agreement, but then return to business as usual. That will not suffice. If the World Bank, OECD, U.S. Agency for International Development, and others are really persuaded that institutions are important, staffing changes are implied. Not only are institutional economists needed to do the archaeology of development and reform, but they should be expressly included in the planning and the oversight. Because this will "mess things up" for those with orthodox predilections, institutional economists will need the support of strong advocates.

Moving the new institutional economics into the study of economic development and reform has so far proved to be difficult.[11] Taking institutions seriously is the first step. Working out the microanalytic logic of economic organization is the second. Explicating the mechanisms comes next. A successful project will feature variations on a few key themes—with adaptation, private ordering, ex post governance, and credible commitments as prominent candidates.

Because development and reform are inordinately complex, the study of these matters will benefit from combining several focused perspectives rather than working entirely out of one. My argument is that the institutional economics approach, especially of a bottom-up kind, helps inform the issues. One useful way to view institutional economists is as the counterpart to archaeologists in Diamond's (1994) recent assessment of the grim state of ecology:

> All over the world, we're launching [projects] that have great potential for doing irreversible *[ecological]* damage.... We can't afford the experiment of

Figure 5. *Interpreting Levy and Spiller*

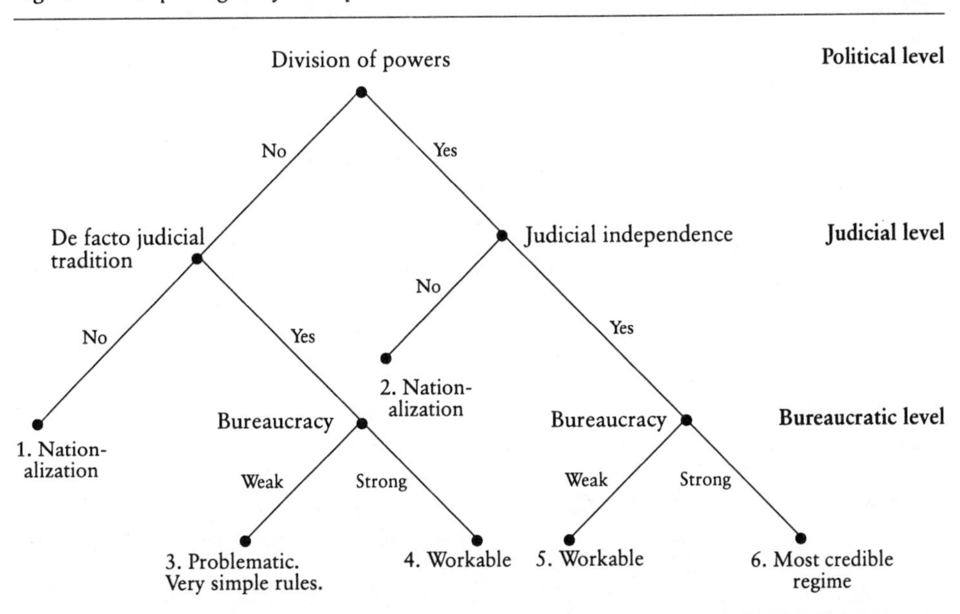

> developing five countries in five different ways and seeing which four countries get ruined. Instead, it will cost us much less in the long run if we hire *archaeologists* to find out what happened the last time. (p. 58; emphasis added)

Substituting "economic and political" for "ecological" and "institutional economists" for "archaeologists," my prescription reads:

> All over the world, we're launching projects that have great potential for doing irreversible *economic and political* damage.... We can't afford the experiment of developing five countries in five different ways and seeing which four countries get ruined. Instead, it will cost us much less in the long run if we hire *institutional economists* to find out what happened the last time.

Notes

1. For a discussion of this progression in antitrust, see Williamson (1985, chapter 14).
2. Disappointments with the Balcerowicz program in Poland—which made "macroeconomic measures such as credit restrictions, wage restraints, and reductions of subsidies" the centerpiece of reform—illustrate the limits of the standard prescription (Rausser 1992, p. 322).
3. Not only is defining property rights sometimes costly—consider the difficult problems of defining intellectual property rights—but court ordering can be a costly way to proceed. Thus, rather than a pure property rights approach, a comparative contractual approach—in which court ordering is often (but selectively) supplanted by private ordering for governing contractual relations (Macneil 1974, 1978; Williamson 1979, 1991)—has much to recommend it.
4. The rest of this subsection is based on Williamson (1985).
5. Although North avers that "we do not know how to create adaptive efficiency in the short run" (1994, p. 367), we know more about governance than we do about the institutional environment. Moreover, the logic and empirical analysis of the governance branch are much more advanced than the logic and empirical analysis of the institutional environment branch (Matthews 1986).
6. As discussed in the subsection below, the de facto property rights that appear to work well in a less-developed economy (such as China) may required additional de jure supports if a move into high technology is to succeed.
7. This subsection is based on Williamson (1985).
8. The obvious remedy is to demonstrate that the *details* of Chinese economic organization line up with the argument, which is what Montignola, Qian, and Weingast (1993) do.
9. For a discussion in the context of Western Europe, see Eichengreen (1994).
10. Quotes from Levy and Spiller (forthcoming) are from a prepublication draft.
11. Relevant institutionally informed work not referred to in the text that deals expressly with development includes Bates 1994; Ostrom, Schroeder, and Wynne 1993; and Nabli and Nugent 1989. North 1990 and Eggertsson 1990 are also pertinent. For an overview, see Furubotn and Richter 1991 (pp. 1–32).

References

Aoki, Masahiko. 1994. "The Japanese Firm as a System of Attributes." In Masahiko Aoki and Ronald Dore, eds., *The Japanese Firm.* Oxford: Oxford University Press.

Arrow, Kenneth J. 1974. *The Limits of Organization.* New York: W.W. Norton.

———. 1987. "Reflections on the Essays." In George Feiwel, ed., *Arrow and the Foundations of the Theory of Economic Policy.* New York: New York University Press.

Arthur, Brian. 1989. "Competing Technologies, Increasing Returns, and Lock-in by Historical Events." *Economic Journal* 99 (March): 116–31.

Barnard, Chester. 1938. *The Functions of the Executive.* Cambridge, Mass.: Harvard University Press.

Bates, Robert. 1994. "Social Dilemmas and Rational Individuals: An Essay on the New Individualism." Harvard University, Cambridge, Mass.

Bergsom, Abram. 1948. "Socialist Economics." In Howard Ellis, ed., *Survey of Contemporary Economics.* Philadelphia: Blakiston.

Bradach, Jeffrey, and Robert Eccles. 1989. "Price, Authority, and Trust." *American Review of Sociology* 15: 97–118.

Coase, Ronald H. 1964. "The Regulated Industries: Discussion." *American Economic Review* 54 (May): 194–97.

———. 1972. "Industrial Organization: A Proposal for Research." In V.R. Fuchs, ed., *Policy Issues and Research Opportunities in Industrial Organization.* New York: National Bureau of Economic Research.

———. 1988. "The Nature of the Firm: Origin." *Journal of Law, Economics, and Organization* 4 (Spring): 3–17.

———. 1992. "The Institutional Structure of Production." *American Economic Review* 82 (September): 713–19.

Commons, John R. 1924. *Legal Foundations of Capitalism.* New York: Macmillan.

———. 1934. *Institutional Economics.* Madison: University of Wisconsin Press.

David, Paul. 1985. "Clio in the Economics of QWERTY." *American Economic Review* 75 (May): 332–37.

Davis, Lance E., and Douglass C. North. 1971. *Institutional Change and American Economic Growth.* Cambridge: Cambridge University Press.

Diamond, Jared. 1994. "Ecological Collapses of Ancient Civilizations: The Golden Age That Never Was." *Bulletin of the American Academy of Arts and Sciences* 47 (February): 37–59.

Eggertsson, Thraine. 1990. *Economic Behavior and Institutions.* New York: Cambridge University Press.

Eichengreen, Barry. 1994. "Institutions and Economic Growth: Europe After World War II." University of California, Berkeley.

Elster, Jon. 1994. "Arguing and Bargaining in Two Constituent Assemblies." Remarks given in January at the Law School, University of California, Berkeley.

Fischer, Stanley. 1977. "Long-Term Contracting, Sticky Prices, and Monetary Policy: Comment." *Journal of Monetary Economics* 3: 317–24.

Frydman, Roman, and Andrzej Rapacynski. 1993. "Privatization in Eastern Europe." *Finance and Development* (June): 10–13.

Furubotn, Eirik, and Rudolf Richter. 1991. "The New Institutional Economics: An Assessment." In Eirik Furubotn and Rudolf Richter, eds., *The New Institutional Economics.* College Station, Tex.: Texas A&M University Press.

Galanter, Marc. 1981. "Justice in Many Rooms: Courts, Private Ordering, and Indigenous Law." *Journal of Legal Pluralism* 19: 1–47.

Hayek, Friedrich. 1945. "The Use of Knowledge in Society." *American Economic Review* 35 (September): 519–30.

International Herald Tribune. 1990. "Soviet Economic Development." June 5, p. 5.

Koopmans, Tjalling. 1977. "Concepts of Optimality and Their Uses." *American Economic Review* 67: 261–74.

Kreps, David M. 1990. "Corporate Culture and Economic Theory." In James Alt and Kenneth Shepsle, eds., *Perspectives on Positive Political Economy.* New York: Cambridge University Press.

Krueger, Anne. 1990. "The Political Economy of Controls: American Sugar." In Maurice Scott and Deepak Lal, eds., *Public Policy and Economic Development.* Oxford: Clarendon Press.

Kydland, Finn, and Edward Prescott. 1977. "Rules Rather than Discretion: The Inconsistency of Optimal Plans." *Journal of Political Economy* 85 (June): 473–91.

Lal, Deepak. 1985. *The Poverty of 'Development Economics'.* Cambridge, Mass.: Harvard University Press.

Lange, Oskar. 1938. "On the Theory of Economic Socialism." In Benjamin Lippincott, ed., *On the Economic Theory of Socialism.* Minneapolis, Minn.: University of Minnesota Press.

Levy, Brian, and Pablo T. Spiller, eds. Forthcoming. *Regulation, Institutions, and Commitment: Comparative Studies of Telecommunications.* New York: Cambridge University Press.

Llewellyn, Karl N. 1931. "What Price Contract? An Essay in Perspective." *Yale Law Journal* 40 (May): 704–51.

Machiavelli, Nicolò. 1952. *The Prince.* New York: New American Library.

Macneil, Ian R. 1974. "The Many Futures of Contracts." *Southern California Law Review* 47 (May): 691–816.

———. 1978. "Contracts: Adjustments of Long-Term Economic Relations Under Classical, Neoclassical, and Relational Contract Law." *Northwestern University Law Review* 72: 854–906.

Matthews, R.C.O. 1986. "The Economics of Institutions and the Sources of Economic Growth." *Economic Journal* 96 (December): 903–18.

Michelman, Frank. 1967. "Property, Utility and Fairness: Comments on the Ethical Foundations of 'Just Compensation' Law." *Harvard Law Review* 80 (April): 1165–1257.

Michels, Robert. 1962. *Political Parties.* New York: Free Press.

Milgrom, Paul, and John Roberts. 1994. "Continuous Adjustment and Fundamental Change in Business Strategy and Organization." Stanford University, Stanford, Calif.

Moe, Terry. 1990a. "Political Institutions: The Neglected Side of the Story." *Journal of Law, Economics, and Organization* 6 (special issue): 213–53.

———. 1990b. "The Politics of Structural Choice: Toward a Theory of Public Bureaucracy." In Oliver Williamson, ed., *Organization Theory.* New York: Oxford University Press.

Montignola, Gabriella, Yingyi Qian, and Barry Weingast. 1993. "Federalism, Chinese Style." Stanford University, Stanford, Calif.

Morris, Charles. 1980. *The Cost of Good Intentions.* New York: W.W. Norton.

Nabli, Mustapha, and Jeffrey Nugent. 1989. *The New Institutional Economics and Development.* New York: North-Holland.

Newbery, David. 1994. "Restructuring and Privatizing Electric Utilities in Eastern Europe." Institute for Policy Research Paper 66, Washington, D.C.

North, Douglass C. 1990. *Institutions, Institutional Change, and Economic Performance.* New York: Cambridge University Press.

———. 1994. "Economic Performance through Time." *American Economic Review* 84 (June): 359–68.

Ostrom, Elinor, Larry Schroeder, and Susan Wynne. 1993. *Institutional Incentives and Sustainable Development.* Boulder, Colo.: Westview Press.

Rausser, Gordon C. 1992. "Lessons for Emerging Market Economies in Eastern Europe." In Christopher Clague and Gordon C. Rausser, eds., *The Emergence of Market Economies in Eastern Europe.* Cambridge, Mass.: Basil Blackwell.

Rausser, Gordon C., and Leo Simon. 1992. "The Political Economy of Transition in Eastern Europe." In Christopher Clague and Gordon C. Rausser, eds., *The Emergence of Market Economies in Eastern Europe.* Cambridge, Mass.: Basil Blackwell.

Riordan, Michael, and Oliver Williamson. 1985. "Asset Specificity and Economic Organization." *International Journal of Industrial Organization* 3: 365–78.

Shepsle, Kenneth. 1992. "Discretion, Institutions, and the Problem of Government Commitment." In Pierre Boudrieu and James Coleman, eds., *Social Theory in a Changing Society.* Boulder, Colo.: Westview Press.

Schumpeter, Joseph. 1942. *Capitalism, Socialism, and Democracy.* New York: Harper and Row.

Simon, Herbert. 1957. *Administrative Behavior.* 2d ed. New York: Macmillan.

———. 1985. "Human Nature in Politics: The Dialogue of Psychology with Political Science." *American Political Science Review* 79: 293–304.

Soskice, David, Robert Bates, and David Epstein. 1992. "Ambition and Constraint: The Stabilizing Role of Institutions." *Journal of Law, Economics, and Organization* 8 (October): 547–60.

Spiller, Pablo, and Ingo Vogelsang. Forthcoming. "Telecommunications Regulation in the United Kingdom." In Brian Levy and Pablo Spiller, eds, *Regulation, Institutions, and Commitment: Comparative Studies of Telecommunications.* New York: Cambridge University Press.

Stigler, George J. 1992. "Law or Economics." *Journal of Law and Economics* 35 (October): 455–68.

Summers, Clyde. 1969. "Collective Agreements and the Law of Contracts." *Yale Law Journal* 78 (March): 537–75.

Weingast, Barry. 1993. "Constitutions as Governance Structures." *Journal of Institutional and Theoretical Economics* 149 (March): 286–311.

Williamson, Oliver E. 1979. "Transaction Cost Economics: The Governance of Contracted Regulations." *Journal of Law and Economics* 22 (October): 233–61.

———. 1985. *The Economic Institutions of Capitalism.* New York: Free Press.

———. 1988. "The Logic of Economic Organization." *Journal of Law, Economics, and Organization* 4 (Spring): 65–93.

———. 1991. "Comparative Economic Organization: The Analysis of Discrete Structural Alternatives." *Administrative Science Quarterly* 36 (June): 269–96.

———. 1993. "Transaction Cost Economics and Organization Theory." *Institutional and Corporate Change* 2 (2): 107–56.

———. 1994. "The Politics and Economics of Redistribution and Inefficiency." University of California, Berkeley.

World Bank. 1993. *The East Asian Miracle.* A World Bank Policy Research Report. New York: Oxford University Press.

Comment on "The Institutions and Governance of Economic Development and Reform," by Williamson

Robert D. Putnam

From the perspective of a political scientist, Williamson's recommendation to "get institutions right" is an important and welcome addition to the catechism for development advisers. The challenge for us all is to spell out what getting institutions right actually means. Williamson parses the new institutional economics into at least two branches: governance (the organizational relations among economic actors) and the institutional environment. The second branch is much less developed, however, and Williamson's relatively few lines on the institutional environment are uncharacteristically opaque, referring generically to the rules of the game, to laws, to politics, and even (citing Weingast) to social consensus.

Differences in the performance of public institutions are obvious, and they have clear effects on the prospects and process of development. But what accounts for those differences? The "new institutionalism" in political science, like its cousin in economics, has emphasized formal rules, such as federalism or the constitutional separation of powers, and Williamson follows this lead. Rules are undoubtedly important, but as a basis for development advice this insight is incomplete for two reasons. First, it is far from clear that any particular set of formal rules is uniquely superior; at least in formal terms, for example, federalism is not closely correlated with superior economic performance. Second, and more important, the de facto institutions of a country often are poorly reflected in its written rules; for example, constitutional provisions for the separation of powers operate very differently in North and South America.

An alternative explanation of institutional performance emerges from a long-term research project that colleagues and I recently completed (for a complete account of the research, see Putnam 1993). To study the environmental determinants of plant development, a botanist might plant genetically identical seeds in different soils and measure their growth. To explore the effects of institutional environment, a political scientist might, by analogy, study the performance of formally identical institutions in different social contexts. Our project exploited a quasi-experiment of this sort.

Robert D. Putnam is Clarence Dillon Professor of International Affairs and director of the Center for International Affairs at Harvard University.

Proceedings of the World Bank Annual Conference on Development Economics 1994

In 1970 twenty constitutionally identical regional governments were implanted in Italy's twenty highly diverse regions—some postindustrial, some preindustrial, some communist, some Catholic, some quasi-feudal. For more than twenty years we closely followed the evolution of these new governments, developing many different measures of their effectiveness—from political stability to administrative efficiency, from legislative innovativeness to citizen satisfaction. Some of the governments turned out to be successful by almost any measure; others were utter failures—inefficient, corrupt, disillusioning to their constituents. What accounted for these sharp differences?

Formal rules were held constant in this experiment, so differences in such rules were not the answer. Nor did wealth or education, urban modernity or party politics, demographic stability or even Williamson's and Weingast's social consensus provide the best explanation. What mattered was what we have come to call "social capital"—norms and networks of civic engagement. With or without elaborate controls for potentially confounding variables, regions with high levels of civic participation and dense networks of civic associations, such as choral societies and football clubs, had distinctly better government performance. (These regions also turned out to have higher rates of economic growth.) Regional differences in civic engagement proved to have deep historical roots, so that administrative efficiency in the 1980s was highly correlated with patterns of civic engagement in the 1880s and even the 1300s. Longitudinal analysis strongly suggested that social capital in this sense explained political and economic development, rather than the reverse.

Analytically, social capital has such powerful consequences because civic networks and norms ease the dilemmas of collective action in several ways. Networks of civic engagement:

- Increase iteration and reduce the attractions of opportunism (in the language of game theory).
- Foster robust norms of generalized reciprocity and social trust, lubricating political and economic transactions.
- Amplify the flow of information and help transmit reputations, further lowering transaction costs.
- Provide templates for future political and economic collaboration.

It is no accident that the institution of impersonal credit (from the Italian *credere*, "to believe") was invented in precisely those communities of north-central Italy that were most endowed with social capital in the twelfth century and remain so today. In a world of multiple social equilibriums and path dependence, societies blessed with high levels of social capital are able to sustain a more productive equilibrium in political, administrative, and even economic terms. Social capital affects economic performance both indirectly, by fostering better government performance, and directly, by reducing transaction costs and facilitating incomplete contracting. In this sense, the social capital approach complements the new institutional economics, as sparked (and here summarized) by Williamson.[1]

Williamson points out that transactions occur not only within spot markets and bureaucratic hierarchies, but also through private ordering. He observes that such middle-range transactions can be highly efficient and suggests that they are ultimately sustained through contract law (with the government stick in the closet). The social capital approach argues that such transactions often are sustained instead by identifiable social networks and by the norms associated with those networks. Social capital, symbolized by the Joy Luck Club (a group of mah-jongg-playing friends that evolved into a joint investment association), is an underappreciated element in East Asia's economic miracles, in industrial districts from northern Italy to Silicon Valley, and even in the Hasidic diamond market.

As the new institutional economics undertakes the important task of explicating the "institutional environment," social capital will, I suspect, play an increasingly important role in the story. High on the agenda of those who study social capital must be to analyze (and empirically confirm) the mechanisms that translate social networks and norms into improved economic and government performance. Equally high on the agenda of those applying this approach to development problems must be to discover ways of accelerating new investment in social capital, avoiding the inadvertent destruction of inherited social capital and exploiting both new and old stocks of social capital more effectively.

Note

1. For citations to the growing literature on social capital and development, contact the author.

Reference

Putnam, Robert D. 1993. *Making Democracy Work: Civic Traditions in Modern Italy.* Princeton: Princeton University Press.

Comment on "The Institutions and Governance of Economic Development and Reform," by Williamson

Peter Murrell

The microeconomics textbook that I used in graduate school some twenty years ago had one reference in the index to *information.* It read "information, perfect." By contrast, the textbook now used by my first-semester undergraduate students contains an entire chapter on the economics of imperfect information, and informational problems are diffused throughout the text (Stiglitz 1993). The revolution in economics over the past twenty years has made informational problems, transaction costs, credible commitments, and the like the daily fare. In all likelihood this revolution will be more significant and enduring than, for example, the Keynesian revolution. The sea change in the spirit of economics is due in no small part to the ideas brought to the fore by Oliver Williamson.

The results of this change in outlook pervade the entire discipline of economics. To use this conference as an example, the notion of credible commitments is a vital element in the articles of Balcerowicz and Gelb, of Shleifer, and of Sachs, and it is the focus of the contribution by Williamson. Obvious questions immediately arise. Is the new institutional economics really a distinctive subdiscipline of economics, or is it simply coterminous with economics? If the first, what is distinctive?

Williamson's description of the origins, insights, and implications for development economics of the new institutional economics shows a distinctive point of view. There is little in that description with which I would strongly disagree. But I might have placed emphases differently—and that is what I do in my comments. I present a view of what constitutes the essence of this new subparadigm of economics, for the most part leaving implicit any differences between my views and those in Williamson's article.

The Perspective of the New Institutional Economics

The new institutional economics begins with an acknowledgement of the importance of bounded rationality, complexity, and costly information, combined with

Peter Murrell is professor of economics at the University of Maryland, College Park. The author would like to acknowledge the support of the IRIS Center at the University of Maryland and to thank Chris Clague, Chas Cadwell, and Mancur Olson for helpful comments.

opportunism. This leads immediately to an emphasis on transaction costs and the insight that a large variety of institutional arrangements can be viewed as mechanisms that reduce transaction costs.

Some strands of the new institutional economics literature display a tendency to moderate the assumption of opportunism. They show an increasing willingness to depict economic actors as having a facility in constructing cooperative solutions to difficult transaction problems or a tendency to adopt norms of behavior that reduce transaction costs. Of course, the behavior implied by such assumptions can be viewed as consistent with opportunism. Nevertheless, the strong emphasis on opportunism might lead to an unnecessary downplaying of other important aspects of the human psyche. For example, it might be just as appropriate to describe human beings as having a propensity to adopt norms as to describe them as having a propensity to barter and trade (see, for example, Sugden 1989).

Writers associated with the new institutional economics, regardless of their assumptions about the human psyche, emphasize the innovativeness of individual and collective attempts to solve transaction cost problems. And they view the resulting arrangements—based on artfully designed incentives or cooperative behavior enforced by social sanctions—as comparatively productive solutions to the difficult problems posed by the economic environment. Examples of such arrangements are provided by Williamson's (1985) analysis of the use of hostages to solve the problem of credible commitments, Ellickson's (1991) observations on ranchers' development of norms on California ranges, and the work of Ostrom (1994) on common-pool resource problems. The picture that emerges of ingenious collective or cooperative problem-solving not only covers private economic relationships but also extends into the political sphere, where cooperative efforts result in new political constructs aimed at solving problems caused by poorly constructed property rights (see, for example, Libecap 1989).

The picture of the economy emanating from the new institutional economics is one of arrangements—or institutions—of enormous variety and complexity that have been developed to solve the difficult problems that arise when economic interactions are other than the simplest kind of spot transactions. This picture does not give us the simplicity and harmony of the Newtonian system that is echoed in general equilibrium economics, but instead has all the complexity of a catalog of the earth's ecology. (It is no coincidence that Williamson uses an analogy from an ecologist to characterize the approach of an economist working in the new institutional economics perspective.) The new institutional economics presents a polymorphic economic landscape, with a deep historical contingency underlying the development and the functionality of each institution. There is thus a need to examine that functionality within a particular historical, social, political, and cultural context. That, of course, is why Williamson emphasizes mechanisms rather than general theories.

Much of the new institutional economics literature is characterized by an undertone of optimism about the results of the individual and cooperative attempts to solve the difficult problems posed by a world with potentially large transaction costs. This undertone appears, for example, in Williamson's emphasis on the importance of private ordering. Some strands of the literature even hint at an implicit underlying premise that competitive markets provide just one example of the invisible hand at work and that there might be many other invisible hand theorems, relevant to worlds other than those of perfect competition and perfect information. But this premise does not imply that the artful construction of institutions allows society to reach the first-best world depicted in general equilibrium theory. Rather, the new institutional economics is firmly rooted in a second-best world, where the relative efficiency of institutional arrangements is the concern. This is the world of Williamson's archaeology of institutions.

Given this optimism, there remains the fundamental question of whether the new institutional economics will eventually spawn some general analysis of efficiency questions that can guide policy. This seems unlikely. Apart from the conceptual difficulty of constructing a general definition of efficiency in a world of high transaction costs, substantial historical, political, and social contingency surrounds the generation of each institution. Thus the world described by the new institutional economics is one fit for relative efficiency analyses for specific institutional arrangements in specific contexts. General statements about policy efficiency and the institutional environment will not be possible.

That is the case unless one takes the perspective of what might be called the neo-Austrian branch of the new institutional economics. This branch emphasizes above all the process by which arrangements are reached, and it views bottom-up processes as superior because they reflect individual actions. While most authors writing from the new institutional economics perspective do not fully subscribe to this process view of efficiency, reflections of the Austrian view can easily be seen in the mainstream of the new institutional economics. Thus, for example, Williamson's disdain for legal centralism echoes Hayek's scorn for constructivism.

This last point leads directly to the simplest summary of the differences between the new institutional economics perspective and that prevailing in the economics profession as a whole. The new institutional economics emphasizes the power of bottom-up processes. It argues that the domain of society's problems amenable to solution by such processes is larger than economists have generally presumed. It thus emphasizes the efficacy of private ordering and the need for a legal system to aid and complement private ordering. The criticism of the legal centralism view of the role of law in society follows. Indeed, there is now a tendency among economists to question the view that government should be regarded as the sole creator of the rules of entitlement within society—a central tenet of the economists' view of law. Social arrangements might be more powerful than the government in establishing the rules that provide the background conditions for economic interactions (Ellickson 1991).

Some Implications

By and large the literature on development and transition reflects the perspective of legal centralism rather than that of the new institutional economics. In the case of transition, for example, the literature views law as imposed on society by government and created by technocrats using abstract principles such as those dictated by efficiency concerns (Murrell 1993). In contrast the new institutional economics would emphasize that the construction of laws is a social process. It would suggest that laws that ignore existing economic arrangements could be counterproductive, since some of these arrangements undoubtedly were driven by efficiency concerns. I would like to draw out two implications of these points for the World Bank's role in development and transition.

Conditionality

The theory of credible commitments shows exactly why policy conditionality can be a productive tool. However, the formulation of conditions pertaining to legal matters is currently based on a model of legal centralism, with the passage (or submission) of laws usually serving as the conditions. But from the perspective of the new institutional economics the passage of abstract laws might be irrelevant at best and possibly counterproductive. That view would lead to the conclusion that economic components of the legal framework should be judged by how well they aid and complement private ordering.

An important question is how to implement this insight. My colleague Christopher Clague has suggested that conditionality could be based on surveys of businesspeople concerning the usefulness and responsiveness of the legal system rather than on the passage of specific legislation. In his World Bank study of transactions in the Brazilian machine tool industry, Stone (1994) uses a survey instrument that could be a model for such conditionality. Indeed, it is no coincidence that Stone bases his study on insights gained from the new institutional economics and that he is able to identify the areas of activity and types of transaction for which a well-functioning legal system is most crucial.

A Modest Proposal: Country Experts

Williamson emphasizes that the structure of an organization should reflect the nature of the transactions that it undertakes. The World Bank undertakes most of its transactions with individual countries that have enormously different histories, politics, cultures, economic structures, and economic problems. Yet the Bank's organizational philosophy gives no emphasis to the notion of a country expert. Indeed, the organizational culture of the Bank denigrates those involved with one country for too long. This culture undoubtedly reflects legitimate concerns about the risks of staff becoming too deeply engaged with a country whose policies they must evaluate dispassionately. But such concerns should dominate only if the analysis embodied in the new institutional economics is rejected. If legal centralism and neoclassical economics are the prevailing philosophies, specialized knowledge of a country is almost irrelevant.

If the new institutional economics view holds sway, however, the world is seen as one in which institutions are deeply embedded in the particulars of time and place.

An understanding of these particulars would be critical to the ability to judge institutional performance and advise on institutional improvements. Acceptance of the new institutional economics and its emphasis on the deep historical and social contingency of economic arrangements also suggests that long-term experience with a country should be a required tool for examining the appropriateness of that country's arrangements. Thus one conclusion that follows directly from an application of the new institutional economics is that the World Bank (and similar organizations) should give the role of the country expert more emphasis.

References

Ellickson, Robert C. 1991. *Order without Law: How Neighbors Settle Disputes.* Cambridge, Mass.: Harvard University Press

Libecap, Gary. 1989. *Contracting for Property Rights.* Cambridge: Cambridge University Press.

Murrell, Peter. 1993. "What is Shock Therapy? What Did It Do in Poland and Russia?" *Post-Soviet Affairs* 9 (2): 111–40.

Ostrom, Elinor. 1994. *Rules, Games, and Common-Pool Resources.* Ann Arbor: University of Michigan Press.

Stone, Andrew. 1994. "Complex Transactions Under Uncertainty: Brazil's Machine Tool Industry." Policy Research Working Paper 1247. World Bank, Private Sector Development Department, Washington, D.C.

Stiglitz, Joseph. 1993. *Economics.* New York: Norton.

Sugden, Robert. 1989. "Spontaneous Coordination." *Journal of Economic Perspectives* 3 (4): 85–98.

Williamson, Oliver. 1985. *The Economic Institutions of Capitalism: Firms, Markets, and Relational Contracting.* New York: Free Press.

Floor Discussion of "The Institutions and Governance of Economic Development and Reform," by Williamson

Williamson agreed with most of the discussants' comments. One dimension of the middle-range activities that Robert Putnam (discussant) emphasized, he said, was the characteristics of assets. If they are very specialized, it becomes difficult to have separated ownership. If they are very generic, it is easy to have spot markets. If there are mixed degrees of specialization, the question is, can we support them? It is a real disability when an economy is relatively unable to support middle-range transactions because it lacks informal organizations or other apparatus; it is an indirect measure of how well-developed that economy is. What Williamson calls "good private ordering" Putnam might call "good social capital," but whatever you call it, the subject needs more work, said Williamson.

Williamson continued that although he considered private ordering an important and relatively neglected area of study, he also considered it important to have good laws and a strong judiciary in the background for purposes of appeal. Not having them limits how far one can push a private ordering regime. He conjectured that a lack of ultimate appeal mechanisms was probably a weakness in China, limiting how far it could push high technology and other activities that involve heavy investment risk, intellectual capital, and the like. He did not pretend to have the answers, but felt we should be alert to what studying these issues from the viewpoint of institutional economics might offer.

Putnam agreed about the importance of private ordering mechanisms but emphasized that not all of them were equally attractive or, for that matter, equally conducive to economic progress. The mafia, for example, is a private ordering mechanism that has not been visibly conducive to economic growth, and it was not clear to him that the private ordering going on in Moscow today was any more so. The question is, what are the conditions under which more productive private ordering mechanisms would work?

A participant from American University found the Italian example interesting but circular. Yes, primitive or traditional societies communicate more readily, he said, but we are trying to move out of informal traditional societies into an institutional

This session was chaired by Johannes F. Linn, vice president, Financial Policy and Risk Management, at the World Bank.

Proceedings of the World Bank Annual Conference on Development Economics 1994

environment that is not informal. Putnam responded that the dichotomy "tradition/modernity" was distinctly different from the dichotomy "high/low social capital." Indeed, areas of Italy that today have the highest level of social capital are also the most modern parts of Italy, although they were not always so.

It is often said that after fifty or even eighty years of communism the countries of the former Soviet Union no longer have a civic culture, said a participant from the University of Delaware, and it takes a very long time—maybe 700 years—to develop one. Must we wait a long time for the postcommunist countries to develop a civic culture or can we advise them on how to get the process under way? Rephrasing the question, Putnam said, even if I am right about the importance of the civil culture, how does one get it? What would the implications be for World Bank operations? This question called for a longer discussion than we have time for, Putnam said, but he answered briefly. First, avoid destroying social capital inadvertently. Much government action has the effect of destroying productive social capital. In the United States, for example, slum clearance had that effect. Second, consider complementarities between investments in physical capital and social capital. As Elinor Ostrom's work shows, much of the physical capital investment in agriculture has been completely unproductive because of inattention to complementarities with social capital. Third, there may be ways in which government action can foster the creation of social capital. Among other things, the county agent system used by the U.S. Department of Agriculture was intended to foster more social capital in rural America, and it did.

A participant from the Foreign Investment Advisory Service understood that China was beginning to attract heavy private investment in infrastructure at a time when China was in a "no" node, with no division of powers and no independent judiciary. This seemed like an apparent contradiction and he wondered if Williamson or anyone else could comment, because the question of credible commitment to private investors was at the heart of how he earned his living. Williamson said that he had visited China twice in the late 1980s and felt that deep knowledge of China was very important for analytical work. He had benefited from the work of Yingyi Qian, who has deep institutional knowledge, combining microanalysis of an organization through the lens of economics with questions of credibility and the breakdown thereof, and who says, let's look at de facto ways of getting around what appears to be government's formal structures. Williamson found that a productive way to go. He was uncomfortable saying that China has been able to put de facto federalism into place by giving the provinces more autonomy and that China has been able to create reasonably strong incentives by letting village enterprises and the like have preemptive claims against net receipts, but he thought that one could go productively in this direction and ask, how far can it go and what can it support?

Williamson said that he had mentioned the importance of development work to a student recently and had suggested the possibility of her working at the Bank. The problem was, the student told Williamson, that she would not be able to work on the country of her origin. On one level this might be a sensible arrangement, said Williamson, but if institutions are really important and deep knowledge of them is vital, there might be a problem. If what she said is true, this is a matter of some importance. A participant from American University complimented Peter Murrell (discussant) on the idea of taking more time on one job and with one country. It would certainly increase accountability and knowledge. Murrell responded that he was simply trying to make the argument that in dealing with a country we need more information about it than we previously thought. But the deficiency he was identifying was relative ignorance. Another deficiency might be classified as opportunism. He could imagine a system of norms, checks, and balances to prevent opportunism far better than he could imagine one to prevent ignorance.

In concluding the session, Johannes Linn (chair) gave an example that linked the discussion of institutions with such words as "opportunism," "mechanisms," "feasibility," and "credibility." At a recent conference in Tokyo organized by the Japanese, heads of state from some hundred countries all sat around a squarish arrangement of tables in a huge room. Initially, one wondered how the conference organizers hoped to keep people from monopolizing the microphone and causing a total breakdown in communications. As it turned out, there were yellow and red lightbulbs in the middle of the tables, visible from all sides. Every head of state had five minutes to speak, and at four minutes the yellow bulb lit up; at five minutes, the red bulb lit up and stayed on. It was extraordinary how this perfectly feasible governance mechanism alleviated the opportunism people normally employ in these settings. People kept their speeches short to avoid embarrassing themselves and the meeting was very efficiently run.

The Impact of Constitutions on Economic Performance

Jon Elster

Constitutions matter for economic performance to the extent that they promote stability, accountability, and credibility. This article considers the nature of political constitutions and their impact on economic efficiency and economic security under three aspects: the basic rights laid down in the constitution, the structure of government, and the stringency of amendment procedures. While emphasizing that constitutions can be useful by serving as precommitment devices, the analysis also emphasizes the dangers of rigidity and the need for flexibility.

The relation between political institutions and economic performance is not well understood. The causal link goes in both directions. Well-designed institutions can improve economic performance, but some institutions may be feasible or effective only at specific levels of economic development. Here I consider only one aspect of the relationship: the impact of institutions on economic performance. However, a full treatment of the subject would consider both aspects, and the following discussion must be read with this important proviso in mind. I further limit myself to the subset of political institutions that are embodied in constitutions.

The study of the impact of constitutions on economic performance is part of what is usually referred to as "constitutional political economy," a field that can be traced back to *The Calculus of Consent,* by Buchanan and Tullock (1962). Buchanan was also the founder of the journal *Constitutional Political Economy.* The public choice approach to constitutions has focused somewhat narrowly on fiscal and monetary "constitutions," although actual constitutions rarely stipulate tax systems or monetary institutions in any detail. The ban on paper money in the U.S. Constitution, for instance, has few analogues in modern constitutions. Moreover, even that document is concerned mostly with other matters, such as the organization of the executive and the legislature, separation of powers, and the relations between the federal government and the states. Constitutional political economy

Jon Elster is Edward L. Ryerson Distinguished Service Professor of Political Science and Philosophy at the University of Chicago. The author thanks José Edagardo Campos, Aanund Hylland, Richard Posner, Susan Stokes, Cass Sunstein, and Jakob Zelinski for their comments on an earlier draft.

Proceedings of the World Bank Annual Conference on Development Economics 1994

must certainly include the study of the economic consequences of noneconomic provisions of the constitution. In fact, because a constitution usually forms a tightly knit whole, even the consequences of economic provisions cannot be identified separately from the political context in which they occur.

To anticipate briefly on the concluding remarks, my claim is that constitutions matter for economic performance to the extent that they promote the values of stability, accountability, and credibility. In more metaphorical language constitutions serve partly as flywheel, partly as feedback mechanism, and partly as precommitment device.

The Structure of Modern Constitutions

The impact of a constitution on economic performance is not simply a matter of the text itself, for three reasons that I shall briefly mention and then largely ignore.

First, constitutions can be written or unwritten. Some countries with a written constitution also have unwritten constitutional conventions. In the United States, for instance, the independence of the central bank (the Federal Reserve Board) is not explicitly stated in the constitution, as it is in some others. Yet the board enjoys considerable de facto autonomy because an unwritten convention ensures that the executive and the legislature would incur costly political sanctions if they tried to interfere. Other countries, notably the United Kingdom, rely exclusively on constitutional conventions (Marshall 1984). I emphasize written constitutions, but I shall also occasionally refer to unwritten conventions.

Second, constitutions can be effective or ineffective. The constitutions of the formerly communist countries played no role in regulating political life—except, paradoxically, as constraints on the transition from communism to democracy. In many countries today the constitution is little more than a piece of paper. Because we do not really understand the conditions under which constitutions make a difference, I shall simply stipulate that they do. To be sure, the respect for the constitution may be an effect of the constitution itself,[1] in which case the choice of the proper regime is further complicated. But I ignore this issue.

Third, in countries with a constitutional tradition the real constitution consists of the thousands of court decisions that have spelled out the abstract and general provisions of the original document and adjusted them to changing circumstances and problems that were unforeseen and unforeseeable at the time the constitutions were formulated (Posner 1987, p. 27). The idea of constitutional design is, therefore, somewhat naive. In much of Eastern Europe today, for instance, constitutions are subject to "continuous creation" by very active constitutional courts. The Hungarian court, for example, has taken on the task of imposing coherence on the patchwork constitutional amendments enacted in 1989–90 (Klingsberg 1992). In the following discussion I ignore the problems that arise when the impact of the constitution on economic performance is underdetermined by the document itself.

In trying to define what counts as a written constitution we may distinguish among three criteria. First, many countries have a set of laws collectively referred to as "the constitution." Second, some laws may be deemed "constitutional" because they regulate matters that are in some sense more fundamental than others. And third, the constitution may be distinguished from ordinary legislation by more stringent amendment procedures. Applying these characterizations does not always yield the same results. Thus New Zealand has a constitution according to the first and second criteria, but not according to the third. Israel has a constitution according to the second and third criteria, but not the first. Some countries have a body of "organic laws" that, although not part of the document referred to as "the constitution," require more than a simple majority for their amendment. Moreover, some aspects of political life that we tend to think of as fundamental, such as electoral laws, are often omitted from the constitution and are not always subject to more stringent amendment procedures. For the purposes of the present article, the third criterion is the most important, because of the centrality of the idea that constitutions serve as precommitment devices.

Modern constitutions contain three main parts: a bill of rights, a set of provisions regulating the machinery of government, and a set of procedures for amending the constitution itself.

The set of constitutional rights can be classified in many ways. For my purposes the most useful typology is a tripartite division of rights into civil and political, social, and economic. In the category of civil and political rights, I emphasize freedom of speech, freedom of association, and the rights that protect the equality of political participation (say, by prohibiting gerrymandering). In the social category I place a number of rights that are, as it were, intermediate between the right to the pursuit of happiness and the right to happiness itself, namely rights that ensure the provision of goods that tend to promote happiness. These include the right to work and to job security, the right to a fair or adequate income, the right to unemployment and pension benefits, and the right to education and health care. In the economic category are provisions that guarantee freedom of property, exchange, and contract.

The machinery of government consists of the relations of state entities to the citizens and to each another. As noted, electoral laws are not always part of the constitution, and even when they are, details (which can be important) are usually left to statute. Relations among government entities are guided by the separation of powers and the system of checks and balances. The separation of powers is partly a form of functional division of labor, partly a protection against corruption and bribery, and partly a protection against time inconsistency (see below). The system of checks and balances also has a number of aspects. Institutions such as bicameralism and executive veto serve functions quite similar to those of delays and supermajorities in constitutional amendments (see below). Mutual guardianship is embodied in judicial review of legislation and in the power to make or to approve appointments to the judiciary. It is worth noting that no constitution, to my knowledge, contains a provision to ensure the independence of state-owned radio or television from the government. Nor do we find provisions ensuring the independence of the central bureau of statistics. In Norway the Ministry of Finance can and does exercise pressure on economists in the statistics bureau to use models that are more likely to yield the prognosis the government wants to see. In the United States the Bureau of Labor Statistics has sometimes been subjected to even stronger pressures.

Transforming such bureaus into a branch of the central bank and giving the bank greater independence could reduce the risk of such interventions (Bruno 1994).

The substance of *constitutions* lies in rights and in the machinery of government. *Constitutionalism* is usually defined as the idea that the components of constitutions are so basic that they cannot be changed through the ordinary legislative process but require a more stringent procedure. Special amendment procedures include supermajorities, waiting periods (amendments have to be proposed during one parliament and adopted during another), confirmation (they have to be passed by two successive parliaments), referendums, and in federal systems, approval by (some portion of) the states as well as the national parliament. Combinations and tradeoffs among these techniques are also observed.

Conceptions of Economic Performance

Debates in modern political philosophy are to a large extent organized around two polar positions. On the one hand there is the view that societies ought to maximize some aggregate of utility (Harsanyi 1955) or wealth (Posner 1992), in the sense of dynamic optimization rather than static allocative efficiency. On the other hand there is the view (usually associated with John Rawls 1971) that societies ought to assure the highest level of well-being for the worst-off members.[2] I refer to the first view as efficiency-oriented and to the second as security-oriented. Although one might first think that efficiency can always be used to subsidize security, a moment's reflection suggests that income transfers to ensure security may undermine efficiency—in part because incentive problems cause the transfer bucket to be leaky (Okun 1975) and in part because those who pass the bucket have to be paid out of it.

Neither the purely efficiency-oriented view nor the purely security-oriented view is satisfactory. Intuition, aided by experimental studies (Yaari and Bar-Hillel 1984), suggests that efficiency-oriented theories accord too little importance to the worst-off and security-oriented theories too much. A more adequate theory would somehow take into account both efficiency and security. Laboratory experiments have shown that the overwhelmingly preferred concept of economic justice is to maximize total wealth, subject to the condition that nobody falls below a certain floor-level of income (Frolich and Oppenheimer 1992). This proposal, however, has two disadvantages. From a philosophical point of view it is unsatisfactory because the floor level is not determined by theoretical arguments from first principles (Rawls 1971, pp. 316–17). From the operational point of view that concerns me here, the proposal suffers from the defect that it does not constitute a unique criterion for assessing performance. It does not, for instance, allow us to compare a society that has a higher GNP per capita with a society that has a higher minimum income. One could try to remedy that defect by stipulating a tradeoff between efficiency and security, rather than qualifying the former as a maxim and the latter as a constraint. However, as Rawls points out (1971, p. 34), that idea is just as subjective as the floor-constraint proposal. Like the optimal security level, the optimal tradeoff between efficiency and security is ultimately determined by intuition entirely unsupported by theory.[3]

In light of these problems, this discussion is divided between assessments of the impact of constitutional provisions on economic efficiency and their impact on security. Certain provisions favorable to one aspect of performance may have a negative impact on the other. Freedom of contract, for instance, can undermine security while enhancing efficiency. Although I cannot, therefore, assess the net effect, it is possible to make unambiguous comparisons among societies regarding their performance on both dimensions. The high-performing Asian economies, for instance, appear to outperform other developing countries in both respects (Campos 1993).

Constitutions and Economic Performance

I have distinguished three major aspects of constitutions pertaining to government, rights, and amendments, and two aspects of economic performance pertaining to efficiency and security. These subdivisions give rise to six different ways in which constitutions affect performance. This division is somewhat artificial since the effects are not separate and additive. For rights to matter there has to be an enforcement mechanism in the machinery of government. Provisions that lay down basic rights and the structure of government matter less if they are easily amended. Conversely, provisions that are difficult to change may not matter much if they regulate only trivial matters like the national flag or anthem. This breakdown therefore has, of necessity, only a rough heuristic value.

Rights and Security

Civil and political rights. Sen (1994; see also Drèze and Sen 1989) has drawn attention to the striking fact that no substantial famine has ever occurred in a country with a democratic form of government and a free press. While fully aware that a free press may not be sufficient to avert catastrophe, he emphasizes the role of the free press in disseminating information about impending disasters and creating an incentive for politicians to alleviate or prevent them. In the United States, for instance, there is no universal health insurance, and the security level is lower than in some developing countries. This fact is well known and well publicized. However, the people who suffer from lack of health insurance are disproportionately unlikely to vote in national elections (U.S. voter turnout is about 50 percent). Politicians who fail to enact health legislation are therefore not necessarily thrown out of office. The culprit here is not lack of political rights but rather the fact that people do not exercise their rights. As many writers have noted (see, for example, Rawls 1971), moreover, rights mean little unless supplemented by a minimum of economic wherewithal. And so the possibility of a vicious circle: for citizens to use their political rights to achieve economic security, they already need to be economically secure.

Social rights. The impact of social rights on economic security might seem more straightforward. If the constitution contains provisions about the right to work, the minimum wage, job security, and the right to free health care and education—provisions that may have been obtained by the exercise of political rights—would not these provisions ensure economic security? We know today that they cannot, because some of these rights are unenforceable; others, if enforced, are self-defeating; and still others ensure one aspect of economic security at the expense of another. Although the formerly communist countries guaranteed the right to work, for example, full employment was achieved only at the cost of huge inefficiencies, which caused remuneration for work to be substantially less than the unemployment benefits offered in many Western societies. It has also been shown that legislation that compels employers to offer tenure to workers who have been employed continuously for x months also causes them to lay off workers after, say, $x - 6$ months, thus decreasing rather than increasing job security. Similarly, minimum wage legislation, while enhancing security for those who have employment, may also increase the number that are unemployed (see the survey cited in Brown 1988). The overall impact on security then depends on the level of unemployment benefits.[4]

The constitutionalization of the right to free or cheap health care raises still more complex issues. If the costs are funded out of payroll taxes, employers will consider them a cost of labor and employ fewer workers, especially full-time employees. Like the right to a minimum wage, these rights support some aspects of economic security but undermine others. But if health care were funded, like public education, out of general tax revenue, this problem would not arise.

Economic rights. There are a number of ways in which untrammeled economic rights can reduce economic security. Unlimited freedom of contract, for instance, can undermine individual welfare by spawning problems ranging from collective action problems through problems of asymmetric information to weakness of will (Trebilcock 1993). In the constitutional context an important application concerns the free alienability of land. The Bulgarian constitution (Article 21.2), for instance, obligates owners of arable land to cultivate it. Although I know little about the motivation behind this clause or its consequences, it appears intended to prevent owner-cultivators from undermining the national interest in agricultural self-sufficiency.

Rights and Efficiency

Civil and political rights. The impact of civil and political rights on economic efficiency raises a new issue: the relation between democracy and constitutional precommitment. Policymakers may want to precommit themselves to a specific course of action for a number of reasons, making themselves unable to deviate from that course of action without considerable political cost. Take Ulysses, who bound himself to the mast and put wax in the ears of his men in order to resist the temptations of the Sirens (Elster 1984), or former cocaine addicts who write self-incriminating letters to be sent off in case of relapse (Schelling 1992). As these examples suggest, precommitment must represent more than a resolute inner stance—the precommitting agent must act through the external environment.

Consider policymakers in a dictatorship who want to precommit themselves to a fixed, long-term policy environment conducive to sustained economic growth. One example is China in the 1980s, when the economy was liberalized and private ownership was allowed to develop. Because economic agents could not know if this state of affairs would last, however, or if they would be allowed to retain their profits, their time horizon was shortened, and many preferred to use their profits for luxury consumption rather than to plow them back into business. While the Chinese leaders may well have wanted to precommit themselves to a hands-off policy, there was no way to do so credibly. Because they had all the power, they were unable to make themselves *unable* to interfere (Elster 1989). The only way a dictatorship could precommit itself would be by making itself vulnerable to the sanctions of international institutions, such as the World Bank or the International Monetary Fund.

By contrast, commitments are of necessity more credible when power is divided among an executive, an independent judiciary, and a democratically elected legislature. This separation of powers is the central theme of North and Weingast's (1989) reconstruction of English political economy in the seventeenth century. After the glorious 1648 revolution, "the credible threat of removal limited the Crown's ability to ignore" (p. 187) Parliament, while at the same time, "the creation of a politically independent judiciary greatly expanded the government's ability to promise to honor its agreements, that is, to bond itself" (p. 819). Finally, "by creating a balance between Parliament and the monarchy—rather than eliminating the latter as occurred after the Civil War—parliamentary interests insured limits on their own tendencies toward arbitrary action" (p. 829).

I suggest that precommitment—to be credible and effective—needs democracy, that is, the possession and exercise of political rights. Although the case of Chile under Pinochet shows that dictatorship and self-limitation are not incompatible (Barros 1993), it is hard to see how an arrangement of that sort could be institutionalized. The promises of an executive are much more credible if there is a well-established procedure for throwing the executive out of office for failing to keep those promises. At the same time executive veto on the legislature may prevent that body from reneging on its promises. In summary, economic efficiency often requires precommitment, which—to be credible—requires that citizens be endowed with effective political rights.

The recent experience of the high-performing Asian economies points in the same direction. Campos (1993) argues that Asia's authoritarian regimes gained the necessary credibility by allowing the formation of proto-democratic institutions (deliberative councils) to provide channels from business, labor, and academics to the seat of power. In creating these institutions,

> the leadership in effect ceded part of its authority over economic policy-making to an independent body consisting of bureaucrats and representatives of the private sector. By doing so, the leaders created confidence among private sector agents that the rug would not be pulled from under them. During the initial stages, this institutional arrangement may not have much credibility. That is, the leadership could just as easily have dissolved the deliberative councils. However, by maintaining the arrangement over time, it becomes more credible. As time passes, the arrangement becomes institutionalized, bearing roots that dig deeper and deeper. Hence, over time, it becomes more and more costly to uproot. (pp. 37–38)

Although this system rests on an unwritten constitutional convention rather than on a formalized constitution, the basic effect is similar. To be effective, power must be divided.

Following Sen (1994), I have argued that civil and political rights can enhance security through the electoral mechanism. Could they also promote efficiency through the same channel? If so, voters would have to care more about efficiency than about security, or security and efficiency would always have to go together. The latter assumption is implausible. The former is certainly not upheld by recent electoral results in Poland and other formerly communist countries. These countries may be atypical, however, because voters are still influenced by the value attached to job security under communism and because current radical reforms have required sharp drops in security levels. Security may therefore loom much larger than efficiency in the eyes of a formerly communist electorate.[5] Even where concern for efficiency dominates, however, citizens vote retroactively, comparing the state of the economy at the beginning and the end of the electoral period rather than by comparing its current state and the state that would have been obtained if an alternative policy had been followed. But while such a comparison is the relevant one for voters, it is also clearly unfeasible. Politicians get rewarded or penalized for what happens on their watch. They will be reelected in upswings and not in downswings regardless of their actual contribution. This tendency does not completely invalidate the argument, but it would seem to weaken it.

Social rights. It is sometimes assumed that social rights are a form of social consumption that takes place at the expense of social investment and efficiency and that developing countries—including countries in transition to a market system—cannot "afford" generous social provisions. While evaluating this statement is well beyond my competence, some elementary observations are in order.

It is obvious that education and health care represent investments in a productive work force.[6] Although they often are slow in coming to fruition, a fact that may induce policymakers to prefer consumption or investments in nonhuman capital that have more immediate results, that very delay may provide a reason for constitutionalizing these rights (see below).

On efficiency grounds unemployment benefits also have obvious value. They prevent the destruction or reduction of workers' productive potential, which would be costly to re-create later. In addition, unemployment benefits contribute to social peace and hence to efficiency. While it is not a proposition easily amenable to empirical demonstration, I believe that these positive effects of unemployment are more important than the negative effect that arises from weakening the incentive to search for jobs.

Economic rights. Economic rights can promote economic efficiency in a number of well-known ways. By ensuring stable property relations, they encourage long-term investment. By allowing freedom of contract and exchange, they encourage Pareto improvements. More subtly, a legal system that underwrites contracts makes promises credible. The right to free entry reduces the likelihood of wasteful monopolistic behavior. Sometimes, though, rights can affect static and dynamic efficiency in opposite ways. Bhalla (1994) finds, for example, with respect to the right to intellectual property that economic efficiency is enhanced by economic freedom, conceptualized as economic openness and measured by the difference between domestic prices and world prices and by the black market premium on foreign currency.

Some Deviations from Conventional Wisdom

To the extent that there is a conventional wisdom regarding the economic effect of constitutionally guaranteed rights, it can be summarized as follows: (1) Social rights promote economic security. (2) Economic rights promote economic efficiency. (3) Social rights undermine economic efficiency. (4) Economic rights undermine economic security. (5) Civil and political rights are to be valued mainly on noninstrumental grounds. While accepting propositions 2 and 4, I have qualified 1 and 3 in several ways, with the most radical departure from conventional wisdom, however, being my emphasis on the instrumental value of civil and political rights for ensuring both security and efficiency.

Government Structure and Security

To the extent that rights matter for security and the structure of government matters for the enforcement of rights, there is an obvious indirect connection between the machinery of government and economic security. In countries without effective judicial review, for instance, the government can violate security-sustaining rights. More directly, constitutions impose checks on government. At the Federal Convention in Philadelphia in 1787, for instance, it was widely thought that the state constitutions had allowed populist elements to enact security-oriented legislation that favored debtors over creditors. A number of provisions in the U.S. Constitution adopted at the convention therefore had their origin in the framers' desire to contain this tendency. On the assumption that the lower house would have dangerously confiscatory tendencies, they introduced a triple check on legislation.

In countries with a large proportion of poor voters the median voter will, if behaving myopically, favor large transfers that the rich will see as confiscatory. In nineteenth-century debates over the extension of suffrage, both radicals and conservatives predicted that universal suffrage would lead to a heavy favoring of security at the expense of efficiency (Przeworski and Limongi 1993). As it turned out, these fears were largely unfounded. Workers have not behaved myopically and have shown little interest in killing the goose that lays the golden eggs (Przeworski and Wallerstein 1982). In any case, the U.S. Constitution, imposed from above by the property-owning elite, successfully prevented any confiscatory claims from being made. The growth of the welfare state may owe as much to the emergence of a robust labor movement as to the extension of suffrage.

I have argued that constitutionalism needs democracy to be stable and credible. The seventeenth-century English example shows, however, that this democracy need not be extensive. At that time limiting the executive political representation of the nobility and gentry was sufficient. Thus ensuring efficiency-oriented constitutionalism may be enough; there may be no need to extend suffrage, creating the conditions for security-oriented redistribution. In the high-performing Asian economies, unlike the English case, the counterweight to the executive is not a legislature but a set of informal consulting arrangements that hardened into a constitutional convention. These arrangements, furthermore, have a strong redistributive component by virtue of which they made a direct contribution to security as well as to efficiency.

Government Structure and Efficiency

Recent discussions of constitutional political economy have emphasized the need for a central bank that is independent of the executive (Cukierman 1992; Canzoneri, Grilli, and Masson 1992). The operation of this bank is usually established by statute rather than by the constitution. One might well ask, therefore, whether independence is really possible in parliamentary systems, since the government controls the legislature. For the purposes of this discussion, I assume that independence is assured by a constitutional convention that makes such two-step interventions—changing the law and then using it to interfere—more difficult. (Alesina and Grilli 1992, p. 71, make the same assumption.)

The argument for an independent central bank is the need to prevent the government from engaging in highly inflationary policies. Because of the desire for reelection, for instance, the time horizon of the government might be excessively short. Even a government that tries to maximize the welfare of society rather than its own political fortune will run into the problem of time inconsistency (Kydland and Prescott 1977). If a policy of no inflation is announced and the public believes it, the government has an incentive to deviate from it. Hence there is a need to remove discretionary control over monetary policy from the government.

Assuming that legislators (or constitution-makers) accept this premise, they might opt for rules rather than discretion and write a specific monetary policy directly into the law (or constitution). But a simple rule, while feasible, would provide too little flexibility for adjusting to unforeseen events, while a rule that tried to specify optimal responses to all contingencies would be impossibly complex.

On the other hand policymakers might entrust fiscal discretion to an independent central bank rather than to the government. Countries have adopted various measures to ensure the real independence of the governor of the bank. The Central Bank of Norway, created in 1816, was located in Trondheim, several hundred miles from the capital and from the seat of government. In countries with a dual executive, the central bank governor may be appointed by the president rather than by the government, on the assumption that the governor would then be more likely to be conservative than activist, that is, to place greater weight on price stability than on employment. The constitution may also explicitly forbid the government from instructing the bank or require that it make its instructions public. Furthermore, price stability may be constitutionalized as the goal of the central bank. In the spirit of Schelling (1960), one may also try to strengthen the bank by taking away some of its powers. To protect the bank from informal pressure from the government, therefore, the bank could be explicitly forbidden from engaging in deficit funding.

While the impact of central bank arrangements on economic efficiency is relatively amenable to analysis, other implications of the separation of powers remain highly conjectural. Economic analysis of bicameralism (Levmore 1992) and of the separation of powers more generally (Silver 1977) have yielded few robust conclusions because the impact on efficiency of any given part of the government machinery cannot be assessed separately, and the assessment of all parts simultaneously is impossibly complex. The effect of choosing presidentialism over parliamentarism, for instance, is heavily influenced by the mode and timing of elections, the mutual veto powers of parliament and president, the role of judicial review as a check on both, the exact allocation of powers between the president and the government, the independence of government from parliament (by devices such as the constructive vote of no confidence), and so on. While one might regress economic growth on these variables to determine their relative importance, this approach would not capture important interdependencies and would suffer from selection bias (Przeworski and Limongi 1993). If we observe that among democratic regimes those with feature X do worse that those without it, for instance, the reason might be either that X is an obstacle to growth or that it undermines democracy.

Constitutionalism and Security

The general role of constitutionalism is to make it more difficult to change constitutional provisions, whether these are valued for their impact on security or on efficiency, or for other reasons. Two main types of hurdles may be imposed on constitutional amendments: supermajorities and delays (waiting periods and confirmation procedures). Supermajorities are required to ensure the stability and predictability of the political system and to protect the rights of minorities. Delays are required to protect the electorate against itself, that is, to reduce the likelihood that a majority will act under the sway of a momentary passion or short-term interest. "Constitutions are chains with which men bind themselves in their sane moments that they may not die by a suicidal hand in the day of their frenzy" (Stockton as cited in Finn 1991, p. 5). Supermajorities can also, of course, perform this function, the limiting case being provisions that are exempt from amendment.

Supermajorities and delays may also differ in mode of adoption. At the founding moment there may well be a consensus on the need for a stable and predictable political system. Suppose that other things being equal group A prefers system X and group B prefers system Y. Nevertheless group A may prefer system Y with stringent amendment procedures over X with less stringent procedures, because the long-term benefits of stability are greater than the immediate benefits from any particular arrangement. Whatever the outcome of the constitutional bargaining (Heckathorn and Maser 1987; Elster 1993), there is a common interest in entrenching it. Similarly, the founders may agree on the need for precommitment to protect themselves (and later generations) against momentary passions and short-term interests.

A very different problem arises, however, when a majority is supposed to precommit itself against acting on a standing passion, such as ethnic or religious fanaticism or deeply held egalitarian beliefs. One may agree that "constitutional provisions should be designed to work against precisely those aspects of a country's culture and tradition that are likely to produce harm through that country's political processes" (Sunstein 1991, p. 385). Yet those provisions are also the least likely to be adopted, precisely because culture and tradition work against them. As Przeworski and Limongi (1993) observed, "advocates of commitment...do not consider the political process by which such commitments are established" (p. 66). And Gunter (1991) notes that one cannot "rely on perfect institutions to rescue imperfect persons" (p. 285). Posner (1987, p. 10) makes a similar point. If the majority among the founders feel passionately about a given topic, it is unrealistic to expect them to pull their punches. An example is provided by the stringent anticlerical clauses of the 1931 Spanish constitution (Bonime-Blanc 1987, pp. 102–3).

There are some ways to get around this difficulty. If the constitution is imposed from the outside—as with the 1946 Japanese constitution (Inoue 1991) or to a lesser extent with the German constitution of 1949 (Merkl 1963)—the external agents may indeed be able to protect the framers against their standing passions. If the constitution is the work of a privileged minority—as at the U.S. Federal Convention of 1787—this minority can use the constitution to protect itself against the future enfranchisement of the majority. In most modern instances of constitution-making, however, the assembly that adopts the constitution is free of external constraints and is representative of the nation as a whole. The body that binds is no other and no wiser than the body that is to be bound. Although one may still try to determine, in the abstract, which constitutional provisions are optimal, there is little reason to think that any specific country would be motivated to adopt them.

It might appear to follow that if constitutional provisions enhance economic security, they will do so better the more difficult it is to amend them. If the rights to freedom of speech, for instance, could be abolished by simple majority, the benefits of that principle would be more fragile than if this right were immune to amendment. However, there are cases—notably in wartime and other extreme emergencies—when freedom of speech and other security-enhancing rights have to yield to more important considerations of security.

A common dictum among constitutional writers then applies: the constitution is not a suicide pact. Should Ulysses bind himself to the mast with no possibility of unbinding himself if he knew that the waters around the island of the Sirens might be so difficult that only he could navigate them? The problem arises not only for security-oriented provisions but also for efficiency-oriented ones.

Is it possible to make it easier to unbind constitutional ties in an emergency without at the same time making it possible to yield to temptation—precisely the case for which self-binding was designed? One might design a tradeoff between delays and supermajorities, as in the constitutions of Bulgaria, Finland, and (with regard to foreign treaties) Norway. When there is an urgent need to do so, it will presumably be possible for these countries to gather a large enough majority to amend the constitution. When a smaller majority is involved, indicating that there is no emergency, delays can be imposed to allow decisionmakers time to cool down. Many constitutions, furthermore, contain provisions for emergency powers and allow the government to suspend (rather than amend) other provisions. As the history of the Weimar Republic shows, however, this solution may generate problems of its own, for the fine-tuning of constitutional powers is particularly difficult in an emergency.

To ensure security, as Sen argues (1982), constitutions must guarantee the exercise of two different rights: free speech to publicize abuses, and political rights to enable people to vote the abusers out of office. If, however, the governing majority in parliament is free to manipulate the mode of election (by instituting proportional voting rather than majority voting in single-member districts), the timing of an election, and the division of the population into electoral districts, it may also be able to deflect the power of popular discontent. By constitutionalizing the electoral process, this particular escape hatch may be blocked. The point is not that there is any particular electoral arrangement that is better suited for expressing "the popular will." In fact, the impossibility theorems of social choice theory suggest that there may not be any such thing as the popular will.[7] Rather, the point is that rigid adherence to one system makes it more likely on the average that officeholders will be voted out of office if they commit abuses.

Constitutionalism and Efficiency

Constitutionalism can enhance economic efficiency by solving the problem of time inconsistency. It has been argued by many writers that individuals tend to discount the future by a nonexponential function that causes them to deviate from their plans (Strotz 1956; Ainslie 1992; Laibson 1993). This is a purely individual phenomenon observable, for instance, in Robinson Crusoe's behavior before the arrival of Friday. There is also the phenomenon, alluded to earlier, that an announced policy is time inconsistent if the policymaker has an incentive to deviate from it because economic agents believe in it. This phenomenon depends on strategic interaction between policymaker and agents and can arise even if there is no discounting of the future.

Both phenomena can influence behavior adversely. Nonexponential discounting is closely related to the phenomenon of weakness of will (Elster 1985), as captured in St. Augustine's prayer: "Give me chastity and continence, only not yet." It may induce me, for instance, to make a dental appointment for February 15 and then to cancel it on February 14, for no other reason than that it is getting closer in time. In strategic interaction, suboptimal behavior may be induced if an announced optimal plan lacks credibility. In both cases precommitment has been advocated as a way to preclude suboptimal behavior. Elster (1984) and Schelling (1985) survey a wide variety of precommitment devices used in individual cases. For the central bank, strategic precommitment to a rigid monetary policy may solve the problem of time inconsistency. More generally, precommitment may be needed to ensure the credibility of rules.

A government, viewed as an individual writ large, may well be subject to this Strotz-like inconsistency when it chooses investment projects with low but immediate yields over projects with higher but delayed yields. Such a government might fully recognize the value of investments in education and health care yet decide to postpone them time after time as the selected date arrives. Constitutionalizing the rights to education and health care, and perhaps entrenching them as unamendable rights, is a way to get around this problem.

Constitutionalizing monetary policy is one precommitment solution to the problem of strategic time inconsistency. More generally, a constitutional commitment to property rights is needed for optimality. In patent policy, for instance, "given that resources have been allocated to inventive activity which resulted in a new product or process, the efficient policy is not to permit patent production" (Kydland and Prescott 1977, p. 477). But such constitutional commitments work only when embedded in a system of checks and balances. A dictator may well announce a constitution with strong and unamendable guarantees for property, but nobody will believe him if there is no mechanism outside his control that can be counted on to sanction violations.

One might ask, however, whether such precommitment might not be a remedy more dangerous than the disease. According to Madison's notes from the Federal Convention in Philadelphia, for instance, George Mason observed that "though he had a mortal hatred to paper money, yet as he could not foresee all emergences, he was unwilling to tie the hands of the Legislature. He observed that the late war could not have been carried on, had such a prohibition existed" (Farrand 1966, vol. I, p. 309). Similarly, when in 1946 the Italian Parliament considered constitutionalizing monetary stability, one objection to that proposal also referred to the need for the government to be free to act in times of war (Spinelli and Masciandora 1993).

The appeal to explicit emergency powers is probably sufficient to prevent the suicide pact from being carried out in wartime. One may imagine, however, sudden shocks to the economy that are not national emergencies in this sense and yet are large enough that rigid adherence to a monetary rule could have a disastrous impact on employment.[8] Society may then be better off by having monetary policy permanently entrusted to the discretion of a central bank governor who—although concerned mainly with price stability—also allows employment some weight (Rogoff 1985). The constitution might constrain the central bank's discretion by emphasizing the goal of price stability, but not to the point of making the bank's governor the mere executor of a preset policy. Again there is a risk that the governor might have unexpectedly rigid principles or be more concerned with his reputation among other central bankers than with the welfare of society. One remedy against this danger might be a constitutional provision allowing a supermajority in the legislature to depose the governor.

Przeworski and Limongi (1993) object to precommitment in general and antidiscretionary precommitment in particular, claiming that "the same forces that push the state to suboptimal discretionary interventions also push the state to a suboptimal commitment" (p. 66). But that cannot be right. Even when policymakers are concerned exclusively with the welfare of society, a state may be "pushed" to suboptimal discretionary interventions. To be sure, such discretionary interventions as subsidies to ailing industries are often the outcome of political pressure. Kydland and Prescott (1977) argue, however, that the lack of a technology for making a credible binding commitment may be sufficient to produce a suboptimal outcome without the addition of political pressure.

Conceived of as a requirement for a supermajority, constitutionalism can promote economic efficiency. For if all laws can be changed by simple majority, lack of stability and predictability will cripple economic activities. Only when economic agents are reasonably confident that expropriation will be undertaken only with full compensation will they engage in activities that enhance the value of their property. Simple majority voting, moreover, has the potential to generate cycling social preferences with all sorts of concomitant social costs. If Caplin and Nalebuff (1988) are right, a 64 percent majority rule can eliminate these costs. Simple majority voting also tends to encourage rent-seeking. "If the vote of a simple majority could change the basic form of government or expropriate the wealth of a minority, enormous resources might be devoted to seeking and resisting such legislation" (Posner 1987, p. 9). Note that this statement suggests or presupposes that there is a systematic and substantial difference in rent-seeking potential between constitutional matters and matters that are subject to ordinary legislation—a claim that to my knowledge has not been tested.

Conclusion

I have discussed a sixfold classification of causal connections between constitutions and economic performance. In concluding, I cover the same ground from a slightly different perspective, by looking at the mechanisms that mediate between the institutional and the economic variables.

- *Accountability.* The constitution must ensure that politicians are held responsible for their actions and that there is a mechanism for voting them out of office. Accountability affects both economic efficiency and security. If the executive is not subject to sanctions, it cannot make credible promises. Also, threats to basic security may not be deflected if those responsible cannot be held accountable.
- *Stability.* The constitution must provide a framework that is relatively stable and immune to strategic manipulation. The provision of basic rights should not be at the mercy of changing majorities. By ensuring stability of the basic framework, the constitution discourages wasteful rent-seeking. Also, stability and nonmanipulability of the political system are needed in order to underwrite accountability.
- *Predictability.* The constitution should facilitate and encourage long-term planning by citizens by protecting them against retroactive legislation and taxation and against expropriation without full compensation. Stability is a necessary but insufficient condition for predictability. The Danish constitution, for instance, is well entrenched but, unlike the Norwegian constitution, has no ban on retroactive legislation—thus, the different procedures for war crime trials in the two countries after World War II.
- *Protection against time inconsistency.* As a form of precommitment, the constitution can solve problems of time inconsistency, both of the individual (Strotz) type and strategic (Kydland-Prescott) type. This function of the

constitution, however, supposes that the precommitting agent is accountable to some other agent or institution.

- *Protection against short-term passions.* The precommitment aspect of the constitution is also evident in the use of delay procedures that allow for cooling down before important changes are made. This can be achieved by building delays into the amendment process. Bicameralism, too, slows the legislative process and thereby reduces the risk of making decisions in the heat of the moment.
- *"Suicide" prevention.* Constitutional precommitment can prevent economic suicide but, if taken literally, can also serve as a suicide pact. A very rigid constitution can occasionally undermine both security and efficiency despite overall good effects. One escape hatch is to constitutionalize exceptions through carefully designed provisions of emergency power. Another is to relax the constitutional rule and to allow room for discretion by an agent insulated from pressure by the executive or the legislature. Finally, stringently constrained appointment or dismissal powers can be instituted to prevent ultraconservative or ultraradical supreme court justices and central bank governors from promoting their ideological views at the expense of society.

Notes

1. Thus de Tocqueville (1990) notes: "I have long thought that, instead of trying to make our forms of government eternal, we should pay attention to making methodical change an easy matter. All things considered, I find that less dangerous than the opposite alternative. I thought one should treat the French people like those lunatics whom one is careful not to bind lest they become infuriated by the constraint" (p. 181).

2. For the present purposes, the distinction between well-being, Rawls's "primary goods," and Sen's "capabilities" (Sen 1982) can safely be ignored. For other purposes, however, it is essential (Cohen 1989). Similarly, the distinction between wealth-maximization and utility-maximization, although crucial for philosophical purposes, is not pertinent here, although utilitarians will admit larger amounts of redistribution than Posnerian wealth-maximizers. Even when redistribution to the poor causes a reduction in aggregate wealth by lowering incentives for profit and increasing the costs of administration, it may nevertheless cause an increase in aggregate utility because of the decreasing marginal utility of money.

3. A brief note on the place of intuition in political philosophy. A theory of distributive justice is to some extent constrained by our intuition about how goods ought to be allocated in particular cases. To reduce the welfare of a large majority by a large amount in order to increase the welfare of the worst-off by a small amount is intuitively felt to be unacceptable. Conversely, a utilitarian prescription to impose large suffering on the few in order to generate a small benefit for the many also runs counter to intuition. But intuition cannot substitute for theory tested against concrete cases.

4. I skirt the problem that security, or level of well-being, is a function of several variables that need not vary together: income, work, health, even education. I am as little able to determine the proper tradeoff among these aspects of security as I am to specify the proper tradeoff between efficiency and overall security.

5. That conclusion, however, does not mean that governments will follow the security-oriented mandate they receive from the electorate. Susan Stokes and Adam Przeworski have drawn my attention (personal communications) to the surprising frequency with which politicians who are elected on a security-oriented platform go on in office to adopt the efficiency-oriented measures that were proposed by their defeated opponents, as illustrated by recent elections in Poland and Hungary.

6. If education and health care were seen exclusively in this perspective, these goods would not be provided as they are in Western societies today. More emphasis would be given to treatment of current and future members of the work force. Smoking might be encouraged rather than discouraged (by dying early, smokers save society a great deal of money). Funding of the humanities and (probably also) the social

sciences would suffer. Whereas existing systems of health care provision can be explained by a combination of security and efficiency considerations, existing systems of education can be explained by a combination of consumption and investment considerations.

7. In this context one should mention an intriguing finding by Caplin and Nalebuff (1988): by imposing relatively weak restrictions on the admissible combinations of individual preferences, they show that a 64 percent majority rule ensures that cyclical preferences will never arise. Although the result eliminates the problem of cycling preferences, it immediately introduces that of incomplete preferences. (I owe this observation to Aanund Hylland.) In the constitutional context, with a well-defined status quo, the problem of incomplete preferences may not be dramatic. But in ordinary legislation, such as the vote on the annual budget, it would be very serious.

8. Posner (1987) points to another tradeoff between stability and flexibility in constitutional design. Parliamentary systems may "be expected to exhibit faster and wider swings of public policy than would [a system of separation of powers], and with destabilizing effects." But, "to the extent that a parliamentary system enables government to turn on a dime, this has its upside (corresponding to our system's downside), illustrated by the swift replacement of Chamberlain by Churchill in 1940 as compared with our inability to replace promptly such *fainéants* as Buchanan, Andrew Johnson, Wilson, Hoover, and Nixon" (p. 30).

References

Ainslie, G. 1992. *Picoeconomics.* Cambridge: Cambridge University Press.

Alesina, A., and V. Grilli. 1992. "The European Central Bank: Reshaping Monetary Politics in Europe." In M. Canzoneri, V. Grilli, and P. R. Masson, eds., *Establishing a Central Bank: Issues in Europe and Lessons from the U.S.* Cambridge: Cambridge University Press.

Barros, R. 1993. "Dictatorship and Legality: Is Autocratic Self-Limitation Possible?" University of Chicago, Department of Political Science.

Bhalla, S. 1994. "Free Societies, Free Markets, and Social Welfare." Paper presented at the Nobel Symposium on Democracy, August, Uppsala, Sweden.

Bonime-Blanc, A. 1987. *Spain's Transition to Democracy: The Politics of Constitution-Making.* Boulder, Colo.: Westview Press.

Brown, C. 1988. "Minimum Wage Laws: Are They Overrated?" *Journal of Economic Perspectives* 2: 133–46.

Bruno, M. 1994. "Political Autonomy of Central Banks: Theory and Practice." Paper prepared for the Conference on the Constitutional Status of Central Banks in Eastern Europe, April 22–23, University of Chicago Law School.

Buchanan, J., and G. Tullock. 1962. *The Calculus of Consent.* Ann Arbor: University of Michigan Press.

Campos, J. E. 1993. "Leadership and the Principle of Shared Growth: Insights into the Asian Miracle." *Asian Journal of Political Science* 1 (2): 1–38.

Canzoneri, M., V. Grilli, and P.R. Masson, eds., 1992. *Establishing a Central Bank: Issues in Europe and Lessons from the U.S.* Cambridge: Cambridge University Press.

Caplin, A., and B. Nalebuff. 1988. "On 64% Majority Rule." *Econometrica* 56: 787–814.

Cohen, G. A. 1989. "On the Currency of Egalitarian Justice." *Ethics* 99: 906–44.

Cukierman, A. 1992. *Central Bank Strategy, Credibility, and Independence: Theory and Evidence.* Cambridge, Mass.: MIT Press.

de Tocqueville, A. 1990. *Recollections: The French Revolution of 1848.* New Brunswick: Transaction Books.

Drèze, J., and A. Sen. 1989. *Hunger and Public Action.* New York: Oxford University Press.

Elster, J. 1984. *Ulysses and the Sirens.* Rev. ed. Cambridge: Cambridge University Press.

———. 1985. "Weakness of Will and the Free-Rider Problem." *Economics and Philosophy* 1: 231–65.

———. 1989. *Solomonic Judgements.* Cambridge: Cambridge University Press.

———. 1993. "Constitution-Making in Eastern Europe." *Public Administration* 71: 169–217.

Farrand, M., ed. 1966. *Records of the Federal Convention.* Vol. 1. New Haven, Conn.: Yale University Press.

Finn, J. E. 1991. *Constitutions in Crisis.* New York: Oxford University Press.

Frolich, N., and J. Oppenheimer. 1992. *Choosing Justice.* Berkeley and Los Angeles: University of California Press.

Gunter, F. 1991. "Thomas Jefferson on The Repudiation of Public Debt." *Constitutional Political Economy* 2: 283–301.

Harsanyi, J. 1955. "Cardinal Welfare, Individualistic Ethics and Interpersonal Comparisons of Utility." *Journal of Political Economy* 63: 309–21.

Heckathorn, D. A., and S. M. Maser. 1987. "Bargaining and Constitutional Contracts." *American Journal of Political Science* 31: 142–68.

Inoue, K. 1991. *MacArthur's Japanese Constitution.* Chicago: University of Chicago Press.

Klingsberg, E. 1992. "Judicial Review and Hungary's Transition from Communism to Democracy." *Brigham Young University Law Review* 41: 41–144.

Kydland, F., and E. Prescott. 1977. "Rules Rather than Discretion: The Inconsistency of Optimal Plans." *Journal of Political Economy* 85: 473–91.

Laibson, D. 1993. "Golden Eggs and Hyperbolic Discounting." Massachusetts Institute of Technology, Department of Economics, Cambridge, Mass.

Levmore, S. 1992. "Bicameralism: When Are Two Decisions Better Than One?" *International Review of Law and Economics* 12: 145–62.

Marshall, G. 1984. *Constitutional Conventions.* New York: Oxford University Press.

Merkl, P. 1963. *The Origin of the West German Republic.* New York: Oxford University Press.

North, D., and B. Weingast. 1989. "Constitutions and Commitment: The Evolution of Institutions Governing Public Choice in Seventeenth-Century England." *Journal of Economic History* 49: 803–32.

Okun, A. 1975. *Equality and Efficiency: The Big Trade-off.* Washington, D.C.: The Brookings Institution.

Posner, R. 1987. "The Constitution as an Economic Document." *George Washington Law Review* 56: 4–49.

———. 1992. *Economic Analysis of Law.* 4th ed. Boston: Little, Brown.

Przeworski, A., and F. Limongi. 1993. "Political Regimes and Economic Growth." *Journal of Economic Perspectives* 7: 51–69.

Przeworski, A., and M. Wallerstein. 1982. "Structural Dependence of the State on Capital." *American Political Science Review* 82: 11–29.

Rawls, J. 1971. *A Theory of Justice.* Cambridge, Mass.: Harvard University Press.

Rogoff, K. 1985. "The Optimal Degree of Commitment to an Intermediate Monetary Target." *Quarterly Journal of Economics* 100: 1169–90.

Schelling, T. C. 1960. *The Strategy of Conflict.* Cambridge, Mass.: Harvard University Press.

———. 1985. *Choice and Consequence.* Cambridge, Mass.: Harvard University Press.

———. 1992. "Self-Control." In G. Loewenstein and J. Elster, eds., *Choice over Time.* New York: Russell Sage.

Sen, A. 1982. "Equality of What?." In A. Sen, ed., *Choice, Welfare, and Measurement.* New York: Oxford University Press.

———. 1994. "Freedoms and Needs." *New Republic* (January 31): 10–17.

Silver, M. 1977. "Economic Theory of the Constitutional Separation of Powers." *Public Choice* 5: 95–107.

Spinelli, F. and D. Masciandaro. 1993. "Towards Monetary Constitutionalism in Italy." *Constitutional Political Economy* 4: 211–22.

Strotz, R. H. 1956. "Myopia and Inconsistency in Dynamic Utility Maximization." *Review of Economic Studies* 23: 165–80.

Sunstein, C. 1991. "Constitutionalism, Prosperity, Democracy." *Constitutional Political Economy* 2: 371–94.

Trebilcock, M. J. 1993. *The Limits of Freedom of Contract.* Cambridge, Mass.: Harvard University Press.

Yaari, M., and M. Bar-Hillel. 1984. "On Dividing Justly." *Social Choice and Welfare* 1: 1–25.

Comment on "The Impact of Constitutions on Economic Performance," by Elster

Adam Przeworski

In the indirect causal chain Elster posits, institutions affect policies and policies affect outcomes. Such arguments risk misspecifying the impact of institutions on policies or that of policies on performance. Take the argument that democracy fosters growth by safeguarding property rights (North and Weingast 1989). The validity of this argument depends on whether democracy in fact protects property rights and whether uncertainty decreases investment, neither of which is obvious.

Formulating theories of constitutional political economy—that is, of effects of institutions on economic outcomes—requires devising economic models. And the validity of such models is not always apparent. Suppose, for instance, that some institutional arrangements constrain tax rates. We will judge the effect of these institutions according to what we think about the effect of taxes on growth. Regarding precommitment, moreover, institutions with a large dose of what Elster calls "constitutionalism" may promote commitment, but not every commitment is to good policies. Elster's objection to the Przeworski and Limongi (1993) argument against precommitment fails to recognize that while it is true that under the Kydland-Prescott assumptions precommitment is optimal, governments exposed to pressures from special interests may precommit themselves to bad policies.

For accidental reasons, I believe, constitutional political economy tends to be associated with anti-statist beliefs that are not always well founded. Hence, even if we knew the impact of institutions on policies, we should remain skeptical about institutional prescriptions. What we sorely need is empirical knowledge about what works and what does not: crude facts. Yet outside the OECD countries we know little about the effects of institutions. And much of the information we do have is systematically flawed.

The reason we know little about the effects of institutions is the most trivial one: money. Consider the institutional features Elster considers important to economic performance: mode of election of the legislature and the executive; provisions regulating the separation of powers as well as checks and balances; political, social, and economic rights; emergency clauses; and amendment procedures. Checks and balances include

Adam Przeworski is Martin A. Ryerson Distinguished Service Professor of Political Science at the University of Chicago.

Proceedings of the World Bank Annual Conference on Development Economics 1994

relations between courts and legislatures, veto powers, bicameralism, and the independence of central banks and other paragovernmental institutions. Amendment procedures include supermajorities, waiting periods, and confirmation methods. The list of rights is equally long. With 139 countries for which comparable economic data are available for the post-1950 period and a rough guess of an average of two constitutions per country, there would be nearly 300 documents to analyze. Moreover, as Elster notes, many of these constitutions are just pieces of paper—Haiti's constitution under Duvalier, for example. Institutions cannot be read from constitutions. We know, for instance, that although the legal independence of central banks is a poor predictor of economic performance, turnover of directors is a good one (Cukierman, Webb, and Neyapti 1992). Hence research is needed to ascertain each country's effective institutional framework, and collecting institutional data is expensive.

Because of selection bias, research on the impact of institutions on economic performance is also systematically flawed. Suppose that we classify political institutions as democratic and authoritarian and discover (as we in fact do) that democracies perform better economically. Running a regression with regime as a dummy independent variable yields a coefficient in favor of democracies. One might, therefore, conclude that democracy is good for economic performance. There are, in fact, more than twenty studies that draw conclusions from such procedures. Yet inferences based on such procedures are fallacious.

The reason is that the regimes we observe are endogenous with regard to their economic performance: the world nurtures successes and eliminates failures. The observed world is thus not a random sample of attempts. Suppose that on average regimes do not affect growth but one of them—democracies—is more likely to die (that is, to become dictatorships) when it declines economically. Because declining democracies will no longer be with us to be observed, comparative studies will observe that democracies are doing better. We cannot, therefore, draw inferences from endogenously generated observations but must correct for their selection. Sampling on the dependent variable only exacerbates the selection bias. And yet this is standard practice in studies of the Asian "miracle" economies, including the latest World Bank (1993) study of their performance.

Political Regimes and Per Capita Income

Instead of commenting directly on Elster's article, I will give some results of statistical analyses derived from a project I am working on with Mike Alvarez (De Paul University), José Antonio Cheibub (University of Chicago), and Fernando Limongi (University of São Paulo). Our data set covers 139 countries between 1950, or independence, and 1990, or the latest year for which data are available. Most analyses are based on 4,055 annual observations. All income figures refer to 1985 purchasing power parity dollars. For lack of space I do not present any details of the economic models but focus exclusively on the impact of institutional variables.

In our study we define democracy as a regime in which some government offices are filled as a result of contested elections. A regime was classified as democratic if the chief executive was directly or indirectly elected, the legislature was elected, there was more than one party, and elections were competitive. Thirty-seven percent of the annual observations were classified as democracies. Regimes that failed to meet these criteria were classified as dictatorships, a term I use interchangeably with "authoritarian regimes."

The average annual rate of growth for the entire sample was 2.09 percent. When the growth rate is averaged by type of regime it appears that democracies grew by 2.44 percent a year and dictatorships by 1.85 percent.

Because democracies are more vulnerable to economic crises than dictatorships, the expected life of a democratic regime that is declining is eighteen years, compared with sixty-eight years for a growing one. The expected life of a declining dictatorship, on the other hand, is forty-one years, while that of a growing one is fifty-three years. Growth rates, in turn, depend on the level of development. Very poor countries do not grow. The effects of poverty and economic stagnation combine, moreover, leaving poor democracies brittle, while wealthy democracies remain immune to economic performance. While the expected life of a very poor democracy (per capita income of less than $1,000 a year) that did not grow during the current year is less than five years, no democracy with per capita annual income of more than $4,335 has ever died, regardless of economic performance.

To examine the effect of regimes on growth, we must therefore correct for the fact that regimes are endogenous. We estimate, therefore, a simultaneous model of selection and performance. Once this is done, the average rates of growth under the two regimes turn out not to be different. Regimes, it seems, do not matter for the growth of per capita income.

The model of growth on which this conclusion is based is purely economic: growth is driven by investment, population growth, catch-up effect, and international demand. Hence regimes are the only political variable considered. We can, however, introduce into the analysis of growth under each regime some institutional and political features that differentiate them. First, there is a burgeoning literature in political science that has its origins in the Condorcet jury theorem, which asserts that on issues about which there is no conflict of interest a larger assembly is more likely to make correct decisions. Second, we have the hypothesis of Olson (1982), according to which old democracies tend to stagnate because of the incrustation of interest groups. Finally, several scholars have argued about the effects of majority-inducing and minority-generating electoral systems on economic performance. The Condorcet hypothesis finds no support in the empirical analysis: the size of legislatures does not matter for economic performance. The Olson hypothesis defends itself: old democracies grow somewhat slower. Democracies in which the largest party controls a larger share of seats in the legislature grow slightly faster. Adding these variables to the economic model does not change, however, the conclusion that the two regimes do not differ in terms of growth.[1]

One conceivable explanation why no difference between regimes is found is that different mechanisms may work at cross purposes (Przeworski and Limongi 1993). The most frequent argument to the effect that democracies inhibit growth is that they process demands for consumption, therefore depressing investment. The argument in favor of democracies focuses on allocative efficiency: dictatorships waste investment either because the rulers extract rents or because they use less information. If both hypotheses are true, the two effects may cancel each other out.

Observed values show a much higher investment share in democracies, at 22.9 percent, than in dictatorships, at 14.9 percent. But this is again an effect of selection bias: investment rises with per capita income and there are few democracies among poor countries. Once we correct for selection bias, the regimes no longer differ in their capacity to mobilize investment. Allocative efficiency, however, is significantly higher in democracies.

According to several recent models, regimes should have an effect on the size of the government, which in turn affects economic growth (Findlay 1990; Olson 1991; Przeworski 1990). We tested these models using alternative specifications of growth equations (Ram 1986; Barro 1990). Once again, the conclusions were negative.[2]

While the question of whether democracy fosters or hinders economic growth is politically important, labeling political institutions as democratic or authoritarian does not capture institutional features that are relevant to economic growth. When selection is considered, no difference in economic growth is observed between authoritarian and democratic regimes.

Democratic Institutions and Per Capita Income

Elster's article demonstrates that all democracies are not the same. Linz (1990a,b) recently drew the attention of political scientists to the differences between parliamentary and presidential regimes. Under parliamentary regimes the legislature can depose the government. Under presidential regimes the government serves independently of its support in the legislature. Of the total sample in our study, 59.4 percent of years were spent under authoritarian regimes, 24.2 under parliamentary democracies, and 12.0 under presidential democracies. (The rest were mixed democratic regimes.)

By distinguishing different types of democratic regimes, it is possible to discern economic differences among them. Observed average annual growth rates are 1.88 percent for authoritarian regimes, 2.85 percent for parliamentary democracies, and 1.45 percent for presidential democracies. After correcting for selection bias, we found using extensive specifications that economic growth is faster in parliamentary than in presidential democracies. We also discovered that democracy lasts much longer under parliamentary than under presidential institutions. Hence our findings support Linz's arguments about the superiority of parliamentarism over presidentialism.

Conclusion

The conclusions derived from our rudimentary data allow for only a crude commentary on Elster's subtle and penetrating article. I have chosen the empirical route, however, to demonstrate how little can actually be tested empirically. Data on institutions are hard to collect. But with arguments about the effect of political institutions on economic performance that are far from obvious, we cannot allow theorizing to outstrip empirical research.

I close with a point that extends beyond the impact of institutions. Policy evaluation research runs two dangers. The first is purely methodological. Learning just from "successes" leads to biased inferences: this is just elementary statistics. Unless we have an understanding of the reasons a particular policy was chosen to begin with, our inferences about the effect of the policy on performance are likely to be biased. If the policy was chosen for reasons that also affect the performance, one cannot expect that it would have had the same effect under different conditions. Second, policy evaluations that are conducted by the same institutions that have advocated these policies in the past tend to be self-justifying: negative findings mean that the institution erred in its policy choice, and this is not an easy admission. As a result, the purported "lessons" appear at times to be no more than restated prejudices.

Notes

1. All the results we report are based on the assumption that the rate of population growth, which is much higher in dictatorships, is endogenous to regimes.

2. Note that we continue to define regimes dichotomously. One reason we may find no difference between democracies and dictatorships is that there are two kinds of authoritarian regimes—in Przeworski and Limongi's (1993) terminology, "autocracies," where the size of the government is too small, and "bureaucracies," where it is too large. We have not yet studied a trichotomous classification.

References

Barro, Robert J. 1990. "Government Spending in a Simple Model of Endogenous Growth." *Journal of Political Economy* 98: S103–25.

Cukierman, Alex, Steven B. Webb, and Bilin Neyapti. 1992. "Measuring the Independence of Central Banks and Its Effects on Policy Outcomes." *World Bank Economic Review* 6: 353–98.

Findlay, Ronald. 1990. "The New Political Economy: Its Explanatory Power for the LDCs." *Economics and Politics* 2: 193–221.

Linz, Juan J. 1990a. "The Perils of Presidentialism." *Journal of Democracy* 1: 51–69.

———. 1990b. "The Virtues of Parliamentarism." *Journal of Democracy* 1: 84–91.

North, Douglass C., and Barry R. Weingast. 1989. "Constitutions and Commitment: The Evolution of Institutions Governing Public Choice in Seventeenth-Century England." *Journal of Economic History* 49: 803–32.

Olson, Mancur Jr. 1982. *The Rise and Decline of Nations.* New Haven, Conn.: Yale University Press.

———. 1991. "Autocracy, Democracy and Prosperity." In Richard J. Zeckhauser, ed., *Strategy and Choice.* Cambridge, Mass.: MIT Press.

Przeworski, Adam. 1990. *Fundamentals of Pure and Applied Economics, vol. 40: The State and the Economy under Capitalism.* Chur, Switzerland: Harwood Academic Publishers.

Przeworski, Adam, and Fernando Limongi. 1993. "Political Regimes and Economic Growth." *Journal of Economic Perspectives* 7: 51–69.

Ram, Rati. 1986. "Government Size and Economic Growth: A New Framework and Some Evidence from Cross-Section and Time-Series Data." *American Economic Review* 76: 191–203.

World Bank. 1993. *The East Asian Miracle: Economic Growth and Public Policy.* New York: Oxford University Press.

Comment on "The Impact of Constitutions on Economic Performance," by Elster

Pranab Bardhan

Elster gives us a clear analysis of the relations among three aspects of constitutional arrangements (basic rights, structure of government, and amendment procedures) and two aspects of economic performance (efficiency and security). Since I agree with much of what Elster has to say, I will concentrate here on one point of serious disagreement and then go on to certain supplementary issues, and I shall give more examples from developing countries, particularly in Asia.

While I agree that constitutional precommitments against political opportunism are important, I have some problems with Elster's discussion of the impact of civil and political rights on economic efficiency through the ability of policymakers to precommit. Elster argues that to be credible and effective, precommitment needs democracy. The promises of an executive are much more credible if there is a well-established procedure for throwing the executive out of office for failure to keep those promises. Power, to be effective, must be divided.

Yet in the recent history of developing countries economic policy pronouncements have been much more credible when coming from a Park Chung Hee or even a Pinochet than from a Rajiv Gandhi. It is the division of powers in a democracy that sometimes makes promises difficult to keep. Promises made by U.S. presidents in international negotiations have sometimes been less credible than those made by their authoritarian counterparts. The U.S. Senate, for example, refused to ratify the second Strategic Arms Limitation Treaty, while Kremlin leaders did not face similar problems. More recently, the U.S. Congress came very close to not ratifying NAFTA, until President Clinton could gain support from congressmen with expensive patronage—a problem President Salinas did not face to nearly the same extent.

The existence of "well-established procedures" for throwing out errant democratic leaders, moreover, does not in practice add much credibility to their precommitments. Take the case of infant industry protection, which has been popular in developing countries, as it was in the early stages of industrialization in today's industrial countries. At the time when such protection is initiated, by the very nature of the argument for temporary protection, it is granted for a short period until the industrial infant can stand on its own. But in most countries infant industry protection

Pranab Bardhan is professor of economics at the University of California at Berkeley.

Proceedings of the World Bank Annual Conference on Development Economics 1994

inevitably runs up against the time-inconsistency problem. When the initial period of protection is about to expire, political pressures for its renewal become inexorable, and in this way the infant industry soon degenerates into a geriatric, protectionist lobby. Given the concentration and visibility of benefits from the perpetuation of this protection and the diffuseness of its costs, there is little organized popular pressure in a democracy against it. No conniving leader faces dismissal on this ground, making constitutional provisions for throwing out the leadership largely irrelevant here.

The most successful cases of infant industry protection in recent history have taken place under some of the authoritarian regimes of East Asia, particularly in the Republic of Korea and Taiwan (China). There have been some remarkable instances in these regimes of the government holding steadfastly to its promise of withdrawing protection from an industry after the lapse of a preannounced duration and of then letting the industry sink or swim in international competition. Clearly, precommitment devices on the part of the government did not have to take any of the rather imaginative forms of self-incapacitation with which Schelling (1980) and Elster have made us familiar. While institutional mechanisms for establishing credibility are important, consistency of past behavior may be enough to establish credibility in a repeated-game situation.

This is not to say that authoritarian regimes are inherently better at establishing economic credibility than democracies. I believe, in fact, that authoritarianism is neither a necessary nor a sufficient condition for credible precommitment or for the autonomy of the state. But I object to Elster's assertion that to be credible precommitment requires a democratic constitution. Nor do I find convincing Elster's explanation that East Asian authoritarian rulers are effectively constrained by "protodemocratic" deliberative councils. The experience of East Asian polities—particularly Korea and Taiwan (China)—in the crucial twenty years from the mid-1960s to the mid-1980s suggests that executive power remained largely untrammelled despite the existence of a dense network of ties between bureaucrats and private business, and the division of power was nowhere near what one normally observes in a democracy. Political sociologist Peter Evans (1995) has described this as "embedded autonomy."

In discussing the impact of the structure of government on efficiency, Elster again stresses the credibility-enhancing effects of separation of powers within government and also the importance of an independent central bank for controlling inflation. Let me first point out that in East Asia (including Japan) central banks have not enjoyed much autonomy, and yet one of the main ingredients of economic success has, until very recently, been the soundness of macroeconomic policy. Even in India, where the central bank does not have much autonomy, the rate of inflation over the past four decades has been relatively moderate (barring brief inflationary spells) and the central bank has generally followed a conservative monetary policy.

Elster also fails to point out that some other aspects of separation of powers can have adverse effects on efficiency. A government structure in which checks and balances are central may involve a multiple veto power system that, to give just one example, may affect endemic corruption in a way not captured by standard assessments in the public choice literature that associate corruption in a simple way with government regulations and rent-seeking. In a system of multiple veto powers the uncertainties inherent in corrupt transactions make corruption more costly than otherwise. I once asked an internationally successful Indian business tycoon who was eloquently describing the evil effects of corruption on India's economic growth how he reacted to stories of rampant corruption in the fast-growing economies of Southeast and East Asia (China, Thailand, Indonesia, the Republic of Korea, and even Japan). Drawing, I suppose, on his own considerable empirical experience, he said that the difference was that in India, unlike in the East Asian economies, you are never sure that the job will get done even *after* the bribe. One reason is the elaborately structured system of multiple veto powers built into the internal organization of the Indian state. The uncertainty of corrupt transactions in a multiple veto system is not unrelated to the inefficiencies of the "independent monopolists" in bribe collection noted by Shleifer and Vishny (1993). They explain the rise of corruption in postcommunist Russia compared with that under the communist regime in terms of the decline of the centralized system of bribe collection.

Two other examples illustrate issues of constitutional political economy that Elster does not discuss. With regard to the effect of social rights on efficiency, for instance, Elster discusses education, health care, and unemployment benefits. Let me instead mention the issue of affirmative action as enshrined in a constitution. As one might expect in an extremely heterogeneous and hierarchical society, the Indian constitution takes affirmative action very seriously and provides for quotas for access to government jobs and to professional schools for historically disadvantaged groups. In recent years populist pressure has caused some state governments, and now the central government, to expand job quotas to cover other so-called backward social groups, so that the constitutionally stipulated ceiling of 50 percent of all government jobs that can be reserved for this purpose will be reached fairly soon. In a country where the government employs two-thirds of all workers in the formal sector, one can imagine the economic implications of this requirement (in terms of splintering the labor market and distorting incentives)—a prime example of how expansion of the political market under a pluralist democracy can constrict an economic market.

Elster also fails to discuss the separation of powers between the federal government and constituent states and other local governments, an important constitutional feature of the structure of government in many large countries. Although this topic is too large to be covered here, I touch on an aspect or two of fiscal federalism and its effects on both economic security and efficiency, with some examples primarily from India and China.

In the theoretical literature on fiscal federalism there has been some discussion of the appropriate level of government for carrying out redistributive programs, taking into account such spillover effects as the interstate migration of taxpayers and transfer recipients. In the United States the idea of "new federalism" favors shifting fiscal responsibility for some redistributive programs from federal to state and local levels. In India the constitution assigns to state governments responsibility for the major part of social and economic expenditures that directly affect the poor (such as for health, education, and rural development). Yet in the allocation of tax bases the most income-elastic revenue sources are left with the federal government, providing a built-in bias toward fiscal deficit at the state level. Without direct power to borrow from the market or to print money, state governments are dependent on transfers from the federal government. With the transfers being substantially cut in recent structural adjustment programs, there has been a serious reduction in state-level social and economic expenditures for the poor and for long-term capital investment and maintenance.

Finally, we should pay attention to the issue of further decentralizing political and economic power below the state level to the local government level. Such decentralization, apart from limiting the influence of special-interest coalitions that normally try to grab rents arising from concentrated power at the center, can tap into local people's large reservoir of information, ingenuity, and initiative, which is bypassed by large-scale technocratic development projects directed from above. Of course, local governments are also prone to "capture," especially since it is easier for the neighborhood mafia to dominate a local institution, whereas at the national level crooks from different regions may neutralize one another to some extent. Land reforms and other measures to reduce inequalities in wealth distribution are therefore important to prepare the ground for effective local political participation.

One reason why the benefits of development may have reached out to most sections of the population more effectively in many parts of East Asia (except the Philippines where, not coincidentally, land reforms have also not been effective) than, say, in India may have to do with the fact that local self-governing institutions (and what Putnam 1993 calls "networks of civic engagement" in Italy) in East Asia have been by and large more vigorous even under authoritarian regimes than they have been in democratic India. The only part of India where local democracy seems to have struck roots is rural West Bengal (with a provincial communist government since 1977). But even there local self-governing institutions have been more effective in carrying out a better and somewhat more equitable distribution of government subsidies flowing from above than in launching autonomous development projects. In this respect the dramatic commercial success of Chinese village and township enterprises in recent years stands out in contrast. A major factor contributing to this success is China's system of fiscal decentralization, which compels local governments to raise their own revenue (a kind of hard budget constraint) and encourages them to do so by making them residual claimants to the revenue they raise. This system has unleashed the entrepreneurial energies of local governments in unprecedented ways. The contrast between the Chinese and Indian fiscal systems is worth a major study in the field of constitutional political economy of development.

References

Evans, Peter. 1995. *Embedded Autonomy.* Princeton, N.J.: Princeton University Press.

Putnam, Robert. 1993. *Making Democracy Work: Civic Traditions in Modern Italy.* Princeton, N.J.: Princeton University Press.

Schelling, Thomas C. 1980. *The Strategy of Conflict.* Cambridge, Mass: Harvard University Press.

Shleifer, Andrei, and Robert Vishny. 1993. "Corruption." *Quarterly Journal of Economics* 108: 599–617.

Floor Discussion of "The Impact of Constitutions on Economic Performance," by Elster

In response to the objection raised by Pranab Bardhan (discussant), Elster said that he claimed only that democratic accountability was a necessary condition for successful precommitment, not that it was sufficient. Some of Bardhan's country examples were examples only against sufficiency, he said. Elster found the Pinochet example fascinating. A student in Chicago is basing his dissertation on unknown empirical material about how the junta implemented self-limitation. The junta was actually a constitutionally governed body with internal separation of power and checks and balances. That fact was not publicly known, so it could not enhance credibility; indeed, Pinochet was seen as an omnipotent dictator, not as part of a self-limiting junta. So their empirical disagreement, said Elster, boiled down to the interpretation of the East Asian economies, about which Elster knew very little. Bardhan, who was an eminent authority, had a different opinion, so Elster had to look for a referee.

Ibrahim Shihata (chair) felt qualified to assume that role. The most powerful argument he'd found in Elster's thought-provoking article was that economic efficiency often requires precommitment which, to be credible, requires that citizens be endowed with effective political rights. And Elster himself had recognized that while this is generally true, there may be alternative mechanisms to ensure the credibility of precommitment, even in the absence of political rights as typically perceived by Western democracies. Consultative bodies serve that function in Asian economies. The World Bank and the IMF impose precommitment when a system would not otherwise generate it. And history reveals great civilizations that have been built without political rights, as now perceived. So historically, Shihata continued, empirical evidence probably does not support the alignment of economic progress with democracy. But political rights do help to empower people by giving them more voice in decisionmaking, thereby making it more likely that governments will ultimately serve the interests of the people.

A participant from one of the Bank's Africa infrastructure divisions observed that it is difficult to get benefits from decentralization without a system of political

This session was chaired by Ibrahim F. I. Shihata, vice president and general counsel, Legal Department, at the World Bank.

Proceedings of the World Bank Annual Conference on Development Economics 1994

representation. Addressing his question to Bardhan, he asked if the very act of decentralization—passing responsibilities on to lower-tier governments, even if those governments are authoritarian—can in the long run promote more popular participation than a system in which authoritarianism is pushed from way, way above. South Africa, he said, may be a good test case. Change there has come about through a process of political accountability. There may be no redistribution. The question is, will the process of political accountability be sufficient without a redistribution of assets to maintain the same level of political participation?

It is no accident, responded Bardhan, that in India communists—in name, but really social democrats—have, by mobilizing people in an agitational mode, essentially demanded and now installed some systems of accountability. In connection with his village service in India, Bardhan was pleasantly surprised by how the landless poor, disenfranchised all these years, would stand up in a public meeting and say, what did you do with that money from the government? That had been unheard of in India for quite some time. It is easy to use agitational politics to demand political accountability, but the crunch comes when the government turns around and demands that communities rather than the center mobilize resources. In East Asia, dating back to the nineteenth century, there has been a continuing tradition of self-governing institutions such as the water users (irrigation) associations resolving conflicts through networks of civic engagement. By and large, these institutions do not exist in other developing countries.

Bardhan had a question for Przeworski, who in discussing election bias seemed to suggest that democracy's longevity is limited across different kinds of economic performance. Przeworski might be right, said Bardhan, but Bardhan's reading of the literature was exactly the opposite: that authoritarian regimes do not survive crises because they lack legitimacy. By his reading, authoritarian regimes are okay when the economy is performing well, but when an economy performs badly for an extended period, democracies sometimes survive just on the grounds of legitimacy, whereas authoritarian regimes do not.

One could say there are two ways to think about the question, responded Przeworski. First, obviously democracy should survive across a broader range of conditions because democracies legitimize themselves not just through economic performance but also through freedom from arbitrary violence and so on, whereas authoritarian regimes typically legitimize themselves only through economic performance and sometimes must be repressive in order to survive. When I talk about an authoritarian regime surviving, I do not mean a particular regime; one military regime may succeed another, but there is a continuous spell of military regimes. If you look at the world this way—that is, 140 countries over forty years or whatever period we have available—you will discover that democracies are much more sensitive to economic performance, especially in poor countries, where authoritarian regimes are almost certain to survive. In countries where annual per capita income is less than $1,000 in 1985 dollars, the expected life of authoritarian regimes is generally 130 years, whether they do badly or not. This is the poverty trap: poverty produces instability, instability produces poverty, and both persist. Poor democracies are quite unstable but extremely sensitive to economic performance. They survive less than five years if they do badly and seventeen or nineteen years (he didn't remember which) if they do well. No democracy with annual per capita income above $4,335 (in 1985 dollars) ever fell. Once democracies are wealthy they seem to be impervious to economic performance.

A participant from Harvard University observed that recent papers on constitutional and political economy have suggested that constitutions, to be effective, must reflect a broad social consensus. What worried the participant was that there did not seem to be any possibilities for social consensus in the Eastern European and post-Soviet systems. If the constitution is a dependent variable, to what extent must it reflect this kind of social consensus to be effective? Elster responded that for a constitution to be respected and have an impact, there probably had to be some kind of consensus, a relatively large majority. There were standout examples of this. At one extreme the Spanish constitution was adopted in 1931 with a bare majority—54 percent, he thought; it was leftist, dogmatic, and anticlerical, and had very divisive consequences. The framers of the 1949 constitution for the Federal Republic of Germany decided that any document that they adopted had to be approved with an 80 percent majority. It was adopted by 81.5 percent of the members of the constituent assembly. Following up on Przeworski's point, Elster did not think that anybody had studied correlations between the majority with which a constitution was adopted (as an independent variable) and durability and effectiveness, and he thought that there would be huge methodological problems in doing so. At least in theory—perhaps in heaven—one could do it.

A participant from the George Washington University, knowing that Elster had written on Marx, was pleased that Elster had taken economic performance as a dependent variable but was surprised that he did not regard institutions, constitutions, and economic performance as dependent variables and technological change as the dynamic independent variable. The participant had heard little about technology at the meeting and wondered where that came into Elster's thinking. Elster said that he had deliberately chosen not to address the question of constitutions as dependent variables as it was a totally separate issue, one he had addressed in a paper for the European Public Choice meeting in Valencia.

Oliver Williamson (speaker from another session) addressed a comment to Przeworski, who had said that more "crude facts" are needed. Which facts? asked Williamson, who did not think that the facts spoke for themselves and thought that we needed a lens for looking at them if we were doing microanalysis. There were too many facts out there; we need something to focus on. We need all the facts we can get, responded Przeworski, especially in foreign countries undergoing adjustment and structural reform, about which we started with no knowledge and no past experience. We have had two, five, seven cases whose histories have rapidly changed the beliefs of everyone who has followed them. If we systematically looked at what we thought not so long ago we would see that, by and large, we have changed our minds. We have no model for the best way of learning from past experience. And lenses allow you to falsify. To be brutal, said Przeworski, once politicians and organizations such as the Bank commit themselves publicly to a particular policy or orientation, they interpret all evidence in their favor. We must avoid that.

Shihata concluded the session. First, as a lawyer, he felt flattered that law's relevance and importance were finally being recognized. When he wrote about law in the 1960s he felt unappreciated by his audience—basically economists—who seemed to feel that he was intruding on their domain. Now there was much greater recognition of law's role in development, whether under the rubric of institutional economics or otherwise. At this conference, however, the concept of law had been confined to written text, whether the subject was basic law (the constitution) or lesser law (legislation, regulation, and what some call soft law). But law is what is applied as law, what the population sees as law. It is a mistake to analyze law only on the basis of the written text; one must also see how it is applied (law enforcement is as important as legislation, if not more so) and how conflict is resolved (in the judicial system). If law were seen as a process encompassing legislation, application, enforcement, and conflict resolution, some comments might have been different, especially in the session on the new institutional economics.

Second, the constitution seemed to have been regarded mainly as providing safeguards against the excesses or arbitrariness of the state, as if the state had a monopoly on either. But a constitution should address all forms of excess or arbitrariness: those of the state, those of the market, and those of the population. The more modern constitutions are drafted in that broader sense and reflect some of the points under discussion.

Urban Concentration: The Role of Increasing Returns and Transport Costs

Paul Krugman

Very large urban centers are a conspicuous feature of many developing economies, yet the subject of the size distribution of cities (as opposed to such issues as rural-urban migration) has been neglected by development economists. This article argues that some important insights into urban concentration, especially the tendency of some developing countries to have very large primate cities, can be derived from recent approaches to economic geography. Three approaches are compared: the well-established neoclassical urban systems theory, which emphasizes the tradeoff between agglomeration economies and diseconomies of city size; the new economic geography, which attempts to derive agglomeration effects from the interactions among market size, transportation costs, and increasing returns at the firm level; and a nihilistic view that cities emerge out of a random process in which there are roughly constant returns to city size. The article suggests that Washington consensus policies of reduced government intervention and trade opening may tend to reduce the size of primate cities or at least slow their relative growth.

Over the past several years there has been a broad revival of interest in issues of regional and urban development. This revival has taken two main directions. The first has focused on theoretical models of urbanization and uneven regional growth, many of them grounded in the approaches to imperfect competition and increasing returns originally developed in the "new trade" and "new growth" theories. The second, a new wave of empirical work, explores urban and regional growth patterns for clues to the nature of external economies, macroeconomic adjustment, and other aspects of the aggregate economy.

Most of this work has focused either on generic issues or on issues raised by the experience of advanced market economies like the United States. Yet arguably the issues raised by the recent work are most salient for smaller, less-wealthy countries like Mexico and Brazil.

Why might the "new economic geography" be more relevant for the developing world than for industrial countries? First, the matter is an urgent one for real-world

Paul Krugman is professor of economics at Stanford University.

Proceedings of the World Bank Annual Conference on Development Economics 1994

policy. Urbanization in developing countries, and particularly the very large agglomerations such as Mexico City and São Paulo, is widely regarded as a problem. Rural-urban migration has, of course, been the subject of a vast literature in development economics, with many papers suggesting that its pace is excessive from a social point of view. Moreover, the sheer size of some cities that such migration now feeds reinforces these concerns. Although nobody can claim to have made a thorough welfare-economic study of the consequences of the emergence of huge cities in developing countries, many observers believe that something has gone wrong, that such giant cities are in some sense parasitic entities that drain vitality from their host economies—Bairoch (1988) has called these metropolises "Romes without empires"—that the environmental and social problems posed by cities with populations in the tens of millions are even greater in poor nations than in the West.

Associated with concern about urbanization and metropolitan growth is related concern about regional inequality. In many developing countries the regions that contain the big cities are also much richer per capita than other regions. The problem of core-periphery patterns within countries is not only economic and social but political as well: it is no accident that a separatist movement has emerged in Brazil's relatively rich south or that armed opposition to the central government surfaced in the bypassed southern regions of Mexico.

On the bright side, urbanization and unequal regional development may be analytically more tractable in developing than in industrial countries. The models developed in recent years, which stress the role of relatively measurable factors like economies of scale and transportation costs in determining urban growth, often seem to miss much of the story in advanced economies. For one thing, in huge economies like the United States or the European Union static economies of scale tend to seem relatively unimportant. For another, in advanced nations that are increasingly in the business of producing information rather than tangible goods, the nature of both the external economies that induce agglomeration and the transaction costs that make distance matter becomes more and more subtle. By contrast, developing countries have much smaller internal markets. For example, although Mexico's population is one-third that of the United States, its dollar purchasing power is about the same as that of metropolitan Los Angeles. Thus conventional scale economies remain relevant. And these countries still devote much more of their labor force and expenditure to tangible products that must be transported by road or rail.

Finally, the radical policy changes that have taken place, or may be about to take place, in some developing countries are likely to have major impacts on urban and regional development, impacts that we want to be able to predict. One need only consider the case of Mexico: the federal district in that country became dominant during a prolonged period of both import-substituting development strategy and extensive government involvement in the economy. As the country has shifted to an export-oriented trade policy, the manufacturing center of gravity has visibly shifted toward the country's northern states. Will the combining of that shift with privatization and deregulation undermine Mexico City's special role, or will other activities maintain its position?

For these reasons, then, it is natural to ask whether, and if so to what extent, the new tools of urban and regional analysis apply to developing countries. The literature on urban and regional issues in development is immense. This article explores a narrow, indeed largely technical issue: what can we learn from looking at urbanization and regional inequality in developing countries through the lens of the specific approach to economic geography that has emerged out of the new trade and growth theories? The article sketches out a minimalist new economic geography model designed to highlight the way a tension between forces of agglomeration and forces of dispersal determines city sizes. The implications of that tension are illustrated by examining a particular issue: how trade policy may affect the tendency of developing countries to have very large, primate cities. Two other factors also are explored that probably have even more important roles in determining urban structure: the centralization of government and the quality and form of transportation infrastructure.

Approaches to Urban Development

Urbanization—and uneven regional development, which is a closely related process—clearly involves a tension between the "centripetal" forces that tend to pull population and production into agglomerations and the "centrifugal" forces that tend to break such agglomerations up. The following tabulation lists the major types of centripetal and centrifugal forces that appear in various models of urban growth:

Centripetal forces

- Natural advantages of particular sites
  - Harbors, rivers, and the like
  - Central locations
- Market-size external economies
  - Access to markets (backward linkages)
  - Access to products (forward linkages)
  - Thick labor markets
- Pure external economies
  - Knowledge spillovers

Centrifugal forces

- Market-mediated forces
  - Commuting costs, urban land rent
  - Pull of dispersed resources, such as farmland
- Nonmarket forces
  - Congestion
  - Pollution

Several key distinctions among these forces are worth pointing out. Among centripetal forces there is a basic distinction between natural factors that favor a site—

such as a good harbor or a central position—and external economies that are acquired and self-reinforcing advantages of a site. Among external economies there is a further key distinction between "pure" external economies, such as spillover of knowledge between nearby firms, and market-size effects, whether in the labor market or in the linkages between upstream and downstream industries.

On the side of centrifugal forces there is a similar distinction between nonmarket diseconomies (such as congestion) and factors such as land prices that are fully mediated through the market. A narrower but sometimes important distinction appears between forces that push business out of a large city, such as urban land prices, and those that pull business away, such as the existence of a dispersed rural market.

Which forces actually explain the pattern of urbanization in developing countries? The answer is, of course, all of them. Nonetheless, to say anything useful we must always rely on simplified models. The typical analytical approach therefore takes "one from column A and one from column B" and thus gets a particular story about the tension between the agglomeration and dispersion that creates an urban system. Several such approaches have achieved wide influence.

Neoclassical Urban Systems Theory

At least within the economics profession the most influential approach to urban development is probably what we might call neoclassical urban systems theory. This approach models the centripetal forces for agglomeration as pure external economies (therefore allowing the modeler to assume perfect competition)[1] and the centrifugal forces as arising from the need to commute to a central business district within each city, a need that leads to a gradient of land rents within each city. In the simplest case the tension between these forces leads to an optimal city size, though there is no guarantee that market forces will actually produce this optimal city.

This neoclassical approach has been extensively developed by Henderson (1974, 1977, 1988) and his followers, who added two important elaborations. First, Henderson pointed out that if cities are the "wrong" size, there are potential profit opportunities for a class of "city developers"; and as an empirical matter, large forward-looking private agents who seem to try to internalize external economies do play a large role in urban development in the United States. Thus Henderson-type models adopt as a working hypothesis the assumption that competition among developers produces cities of optimal size.

Second, according to Henderson, external economies may well be industry-specific (textile plants may convey external benefits to neighboring textile plants; metalworking plants may do the same, but it is hard to see why metalworkers want textile workers nearby). On the other hand, diseconomies of commuting and land rent depend on the overall size of a city, not the size of an individual industry within that city. Thus Henderson-type models predict the emergence of specialized cities, with each city's "export" sector producing a range of industries with mutual spillovers, and with industries that do not benefit from these spillovers seeking other locations. Since cities are specialized, this approach explains the existence of an urban system with many different types of cities; inasmuch as the optimal size of a city depends on the relative strength of external economies and city-size diseconomies, and external economies are presumably stronger in some industries than in others, cities of different types will be of different sizes. Neoclassical urban systems theory therefore offers a framework that explains the existence not only of cities but also of a system of cities of differing sizes.

While the insights gained from this approach are impressive, it has important limitations. First, the external economies that drive agglomeration are treated for the most part as a kind of black box, making it difficult to think about what might influence their strength and thus making it hard even to start to predict how policy or other changes might affect the urban system. Second, the reliance of much of this literature on the assumption of competition between city developers, while a useful clarifying device, strains credibility when applied to huge urban areas: the Irvine Corporation may arguably have played a major role in developing a particular "edge city" within metropolitan Los Angeles, but could any private agent internalize the externalities of São Paulo? Finally, neoclassical urban systems theory is entirely nonspatial: it describes the number and types of cities, but says nothing about their locations. In the past few years an alternative approach has emerged that shares much of the framework of urban systems theory but attempts to deal with these issues.

Monopolistic Competition Theory

In this new literature agglomeration economies are not assumed but are instead derived from the interaction among economies of scale at the plant level, transportation costs, and factor mobility. Economies of scale at the plant level inevitably imply imperfect competition; this imperfection is modeled using the same (unsatisfactory) monopolistic competition approach that has played such a large role in trade and growth theory over the past fifteen years. The "new economic geography" literature, begun in Krugman (1991a,b), bears considerable resemblance to the urban systems approach, but the black-box nature of external economies is gone, there is a spatial dimension, and the models no longer rely on the assumption of city developers who enforce optimal outcomes. In some respects, in fact, the new approach seems closer in spirit to the "cumulative process" description of urban and regional development associated with geographers such as Pred (1966).

The model described below is in this tradition, so it is worth noting the considerable limitations of this approach. Two points stand out. First, multiple-city systems are difficult to model using this approach. Where the urban systems approach easily tells a story of multiple cities of a number of different types, in monopolistically competitive spatial settings (see, for example, Krugman 1993b) multiple-city systems can at this point be modeled only with considerable difficulty, and initial efforts to get some kind of urban hierarchy have encountered surprisingly nasty problems (Fujita and Krugman 1993). Second, going from the black-box external economies of the urban systems model to the derived agglomeration effects of the monopolistic competition model may involve a degree of misplaced concreteness. We will have a seemingly clear story about linkage externalities in the manufacturing sector, but it may be that, say, informational externalities in the service sector are equally important even in developing countries. Attempts to get specific, to open up the black box, always run this risk; nonetheless, it seems greater than usual in this case.

Finally, we should point out one additional risk in both the urban systems and the monopolistic competition approaches to urban modeling: we may be trying to explain too much, engaging in a kind of Rorschach test in which we are trying to find deterministic explanations of essentially random outcomes. While this notion does not exactly constitute a rival theory of urban systems, the idea that they are largely random creations requires at least some discussion.

Random Urban Systems

The general idea suggested by the tabulation above—that city sizes are determined by a tension between centripetal and centrifugal forces—seems to imply the conclusion that there will in any economy be a typical, equilibrium city size. In fact, one sees a whole range of city sizes. The urban systems theory explains that there are different types of cities, each with a characteristic size, and that the size distribution is actually a type distribution. While this argument surely has some validity, it may not be a full explanation. For one thing, urban specialization is increasingly difficult to detect in advanced countries. It is a familiar point that the mix of activities within U.S. metropolitan areas has become increasingly similar since 1950, and the influential study by Glaeser and others (1992) finds, as well, that individual industries seem to grow fastest in more diverse metropolitan areas.

Moreover, the size distribution of cities is suspiciously smooth and regular. City sizes in many countries are startlingly well described by a power law of the form

$$N(S) = AS^{-\alpha} \tag{1}$$

where $N(S)$ is the number of cities that are the same size as or larger than S. Furthermore, the exponent α is generally quite close to 1. In fact, when equation 1 is estimated for U.S. metropolitan areas, α is almost exactly 1, and it has remained close to 1 for at least a century. International evidence is not quite so strong, perhaps because of definitions of city boundaries: Rosen and Resnick (1980) show that when data for metropolitan areas rather than cities proper are used for a number of countries, α almost always moves substantially closer to 1.

Why should this matter? Because while a relationship like equation 1 is difficult to explain with an equilibrium story about determination of city size, it is quite easy to justify with a nihilistic story of the kind analyzed by Herbert Simon (Ijiri and Simon 1977). Suppose that for all practical purposes there is no equilibrium city size—that approximately constant returns to scale appear over some wide range of sizes. And suppose that cities grow through some random process, in which the expected rate of growth is independent of city size. Then as long as the random process generates a widely dispersed distribution of city sizes, that distribution will be well described by a power law like equation 1. (A suggestive explanation of this result is given in the appendix.)

Worse yet, such a nihilistic approach can even explain the tendency of the exponent of the power law to be close to 1. Suppose that there is some minimum viable city size, say S_0, and that the distribution of city sizes above that minimum is well described by equation 1. Then the *average* city size is

$$\bar{S} = S_0 \, (\alpha/\alpha - 1). \tag{2}$$

In other words α close to 1 is equivalent to the statement that the average city size is large relative to the minimum. And it is easy to imagine why this might be the case. Suppose that urban population has grown substantially over a period during which, for whatever reason, few new cities have been founded. Then the existing cities must on average grow much larger than the minimum viable size, and the estimated α will be close to 1.

This nihilistic approach raises real questions about any kind of equilibrium model of an urban system; indeed, if this interpretation is correct, there may be no optimal or equilibrium city size, simply a random process that generates population clusters of many sizes. At some level this interpretation cannot be completely right: surely city size must matter. (This is the same issue that arises in studies of the size distribution of firms, which also seems to obey power laws.) Yet the data may contain less information than we think.

On the other hand, this approach suggests that estimates of relationships like equation 1, together with related measures like "primacy," may be a useful summary indicator of the structure of a country's urban system. Primacy describes the size of the largest city relative either to total population or to some other measure, such as the population of the *n* largest cities. Many have studied city size distributions: Carroll (1982) provides a survey; Rosen and Resnick (1980) is a particularly clear example; Ades and Glaeser (1993) is a recent study inspired by the new economic geography literature. This literature suggests several stylized facts that may help us to think about urbanization in developing countries.

Stylized Facts

While urban experience varies widely across nations, there seem to be four interesting empirical regularities about urban size distributions.

First, per capita income is negatively related to measures of urban concentration, whether one uses α from equation 1 or measures of primacy such as the share of the largest city in the population of the top ten. This observation confirms an impression of giant metropolitan areas in developing countries: to a large extent, of course, the developing world has big cities simply because it has so many people, but even in this light the biggest cities in these countries are disproportionately big.

Second, the concentration of urban population is closely related to the concentration of political power. Countries with federal systems, and thus geographically diffused power, have flatter distributions of city size and, in particular, smaller biggest cities than countries that do not have federal systems. Thus Tokyo, the largest city in centralized Japan, is considerably larger than New York, the biggest city of federal America, even though the United States has twice Japan's population. Australia and Canada, though developed at about the same time, have much less urban concentration than do Argentina or Chile. Dictatorships have more concentrated urban centers than do more pluralistic systems, according to Ades and Glaeser (1993).

Third, the nature of transportation infrastructure has an important effect on urban concentration. Countries in which the capital city has a uniquely central position—something that Rosen and Resnick (1980) proxy by a measure of rail density—tend, not too surprisingly, to have more populous capitals. Obviously, this effect often works in tandem with centralization of political power.

Finally, a less dramatic but still visible relationship is apparent between trade openness and urban structure. More open economies, as measured by the share of exports in gross domestic product, tend to have smaller biggest cities. (This is an other-things-equal proposition. Countries with small populations tend to be open, and also to have a large share of their population in the biggest city—consider Singapore. But countries that are more open than you would expect given their population tend to have smaller biggest cities than you would expect given their population.)[2]

At this point, then, we have described a menu of ways (far from inclusive) to think about urban systems in developing countries and have very briefly set out some stylized facts. The next step is to sketch a particular model as a basis for trying to understand those facts.

A Model of Urban Concentration

This section presents a formal model of urban concentration; the full model is presented in the appendix. As pointed out above, numerous centrifugal and centripetal forces may affect urban concentration. All of them probably play some role in practice, yet the modeler normally chooses only a few to include in any given analysis. In my own work I have generally chosen to include only the centripetal forces that arise from the interaction among economies of scale, market size, and transportation costs, that is, backward and forward linkages. Other external economies are undoubtedly at work in real urban areas, but they are omitted in the interest of keeping the models as simple as possible and of keeping a reasonable distance between assumptions and conclusions.

For similar reasons we can handle only one centrifugal force at a time. It turns out to be useful to move back and forth between two different approaches. One, which is close in spirit to the neoclassical urban systems literature, involves commuting costs and land rent. The other involves the pull of a dispersed rural market. This second approach has already been described in a number of published articles, for example, Krugman (1991a,b, 1993b); thus the formal model described here does not include this effect.

As we will see, attempting to make sense of the stylized facts described above is easiest when keeping both approaches in mind. The role of trade openness in urban concentration is most easily understood by focusing on urban land rent, while one cannot model the effects of political centralization and infrastructure without some kind of backdrop of immobile population and purchasing power.

Imagine, then, a stylized economy consisting of three locations, 0, 1, and 2. Location 0 is the "rest of the world," while 1 and 2 are two domestic locations (say, Mexico City and Monterrey). There is only one factor of production, labor. A fixed domestic supply of labor L is mobile between locations 1 and 2, but there is no international labor mobility.

In this radically oversimplified model the issue of urban concentration reduces to just one question: how equally or unequally will the labor force be distributed between the two locations? It is, of course, a considerable stretch to relate results of this kind to the realities of multicity urban systems, but as always the hope is that despite their oversimplifications simple models yield useful insights.

To generate diseconomies of urban concentration, we assume that in each location production must take place at a single central point. Workers, however, require land to live on. To make matters simple, we make several special assumptions. First, each worker needs a fixed living space, say, one unit of land. Second, the cities are long and narrow, so that workers are effectively spread along a line. This assumption implies that the commuting distance of the last worker in any given location is simply proportional to that location's population (as opposed to depending on the square root of population, as it would in a disk-shaped city).[3]

The diseconomies arising from the need to commute will be reflected both in land rents and in commuting costs. Workers who live in the outskirts of the town will pay no land rent but will have high commuting costs. Workers who live closer to the city center will avoid these costs, but competition will ensure that they pay an offsetting land rent. The wage net of commuting costs will decline as one moves away from the city center, but land rents will always exactly offset the differential. Thus given any wage rate at the center, the wage net of both commuting and land rents will be a decreasing function of city size for all workers.

To explain agglomeration in the face of these diseconomies, we must introduce compensating advantages of concentration. These must arise from economies of scale. Unless economies of scale are purely external to firms, however, they must lead to imperfect competition. So we must introduce scale economies in a way that allows a tractable model of imperfect competition.

Not surprisingly, the easiest way to do this is with the familiar tricks of monopolistic competition modeling. We suppose a large number of symmetric potential products, not all actually produced. Each producer acts as a profit-maximizing monopolist, but free entry drives profits to zero. The result will be that a large concentration of population produces a large variety of differentiated products. (One might think that the average scale of production will also be larger. Unfortunately, in the Dixit-Stiglitz–type model used in the appendix, this plausible effect does not materialize: all scale gains appear in the form of variety rather than production).

Will this advantage make such a location attractive despite high land rent and commuting costs? Only if there are costs of transacting between locations, so that a location with a large population is a good place to have access to products (a forward linkage) and to markets (a backward linkage). Thus we next introduce transportation costs, both between domestic regions and between these regions and the rest of the world. For technical reasons involving the way that monopolistic competition must be modeled, it turns out to be extremely convenient, if silly, to assume that transport costs are incurred in the goods shipped, an assumption sometimes referred to as the iceberg assumption: if one unit of a good shipped between regions is to arrive, $\tau > 1$ units must begin the journey. The same applies to international shipments, except that the transport costs may be different.

We may think of interregional transport costs as "natural" consequences of distance (albeit affected by investments in infrastructure). The costs of transacting with the rest of the world, however, involve not only natural costs but artificial trade barriers. Thus the level of transport costs to and from the outside world can be seen as a policy variable.

And that's it (except for the details laid out in the appendix). The interaction among economies of scale, transport costs, and labor mobility is enough to generate economies of agglomeration; the need to commute generates diseconomies of city size; the tension between centrifugal and centripetal forces provides a framework for thinking about urban structure.

To understand how this model works, consider what would happen in the absence of foreign trade, and within that special case ask only a limited question: Under what conditions is concentration of all population in either location 1 or 2 an equilibrium? Once we have seen this case, it will be easier to understand the results when the model is opened up.

Suppose, then, that the cost of transacting with the outside world is very high, so that we can ignore the role of the rest of the world. Furthermore, consider the determination of relative real wages when almost all domestic labor is in region 1. If the real wage rate of a worker in location 2 is less than that of a worker in region 1 in this case, then concentration of all labor in region 1 is an equilibrium; otherwise it is not.

We first note that the nominal wage paid at the center of city 2 (w_2) must be less than that at the center of city 1 (w_1). The reason is that almost all output from a firm in 2 must be sold in 1 and must therefore incur transport costs. At the same time the zero-profit output for firms is the same in each location. So goods produced at location 2 must have sufficiently lower f.o.b. prices to sell as much in 1's market as goods produced at location 1. It can then be shown that

$$w_2/w_1 = \tau^{(1-\sigma)/\sigma} < 1 \tag{3}$$

where σ is the elasticity of substitution among differentiated products.

This wage premium at location 1, which results from its dominant role as a market, essentially represents the backward linkages associated with the concentration of demand there.

Next we notice that if almost all labor is in location 1, almost all goods consumed in 2 must be imported, implying a higher price of these goods:

$$T_2/T_1 = \tau \quad (4)$$

where T_i is the price index for goods (excluding land rent) at location i.

If the wage rate is higher in 1 and the price of consumer goods lower, must not real wages be higher in 1? No—because land rent or commuting costs (or both) are higher. With almost all of the labor force L concentrated in 1, the most remote workers in 1 must commute a distance $L/2$, and all workers who live closer to the center must pay a land rent that absorbs any saving in commuting costs. Meanwhile, the small number of workers in 2 pay almost no land rent and have essentially no commuting distance. So the real wage difference turns out to be

$$w_1/w_2 = \tau^{(2\sigma - 1)/\sigma}(1 - \gamma L). \quad (5)$$

In this expression the first term represents the centripetal forces—the backward and forward linkages described in equations 3 and 4, which arise from the concentration of suppliers and purchasing power at location 1; the second term represents the centrifugal forces of commuting cost and land rent.[4]

Our next step is to examine the relation between trade openness and urban concentration.

Trade Openness and Urban Concentration

The previous section demonstrates how a concentration of labor in one location may be sustainable, despite the commuting and land rent diseconomies of urban size, through forward and backward linkages. Now suppose that the economy is open to international trade, albeit with some natural and perhaps artificial barriers. How does this change the story? It should be obvious that the effect is to weaken the centripetal forces while leaving the centrifugal forces as strong as before.

Consider a hypothetical primate city, a Mexico City or São Paulo, in a country with a strongly protectionist trade policy. Firms will be willing to pay a wage premium in order to locate at that center precisely because so many other firms, and thus the bulk of their market, are concentrated there. They also may be attracted by the presence of other firms producing intermediate inputs—something not explicitly represented in the model in the appendix, but similar in its effect. On the other side workers will face high land rents or commuting costs, but these will be at least partly offset by better access to the goods and services produced in the metropolis.

But now throw this economy open to international trade. The typical firm will now sell much of its output to the world market (and perhaps get many of its intermediate inputs from that market as well). To the extent that production is for world markets rather than for the domestic market, access to the main domestic market becomes less crucial—and thus the wage premium that firms are willing to pay for a metropolitan location falls. At the same time, workers will consume more imported goods; they will therefore be less willing to accept high commuting and land costs in order to be close to the metropolitan suppliers. The result can be to make a previously sustainable metropolitan concentration unsustainable.

The easiest way to confirm this intuition is through numerical examples. Figures 1 and 2 show, for one set of parameters, how the qualitative behavior of our two-location model changes as the economy becomes more open (that is, as the cost of shipping goods to and from the world falls). Each figure shows how equilibrium real wage rates in the two locations vary as the share of the labor force in location 1 changes. If we assume that workers move toward whichever location offers the higher real wage rate, these figures show a picture of the economy's dynamic behavior. When the real wage differential is positive, labor moves toward location 1; when it is negative, labor moves toward location 2.

When the costs of transacting with the outside world are fairly high, so that the economy is not very open, there is an equilibrium, though unstable, in which labor is equally divided between the two locations (figure 1). If slightly more than half the labor is in location 1, that location will offer higher wages, inducing more labor to move there. This will strengthen the forward and backward linkages and induce still more labor to move there, and so on. Thus in this closed-economy case a cumulative process leads to a concentration of population in a single metropolis. (Obviously this result does not fully obtain in practice, but perhaps it suggests how a very large primate city is established.)

If the economy is more open, we get a result like that in figure 2.[5] Now the equilibrium in which the population is equally divided between the two locations

Figure 1. *Response of Labor Force to Relative Wages under High Costs of Transacting with Outside World*

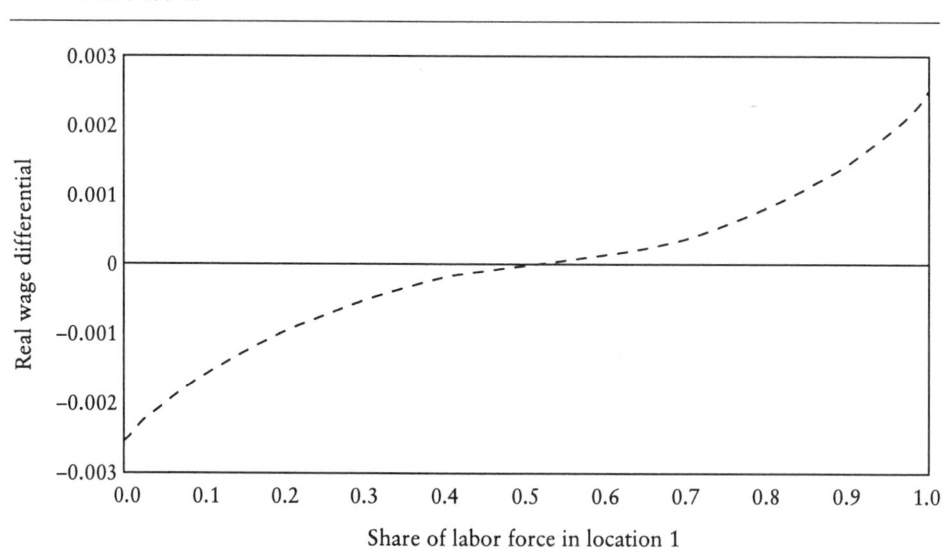

is stable, and a concentration of population in only one location is unsustainable. Thus in this situation we tend to have two equal-size cities rather than one very large metropolis.

It is, of course, obvious that Mexican industry has been shifting its center of gravity away from Mexico City as the country has shifted toward exports. In that case, however, the explanation lies at least partly in the role of access to the U.S. border, as well as in the role of the *maquiladora* program in fostering export industry in the country's north. Our analysis suggests, however, a more generic reason why inward-looking policies may encourage the growth of primate cities, and outward-looking policies may discourage that growth; the empirical evidence described above offers at least modest support for the belief that such a generic tendency exists.

Political Centralization and Regional Inequality

While the theoretical and empirical relationship between trade policy and urban structure is a surprising, and thus gratifying, insight, it is surely not the most important reason why developing-country cities grow so large, or why regional inequality is so marked in developing countries. Almost surely the most important reason is the role of political centralization.

Political centralization has effects at several levels. The most obvious is that the business of government is itself a substantial source of employment: employment in Paris is larger than it is in Frankfurt in part simply because there are so many more people working for the government, or supplying nontraded services to those who work for the government.

Figure 2. *Response of Labor Force to Changes in Relative Wages under Relatively Low Costs of Transacting with Outside World*

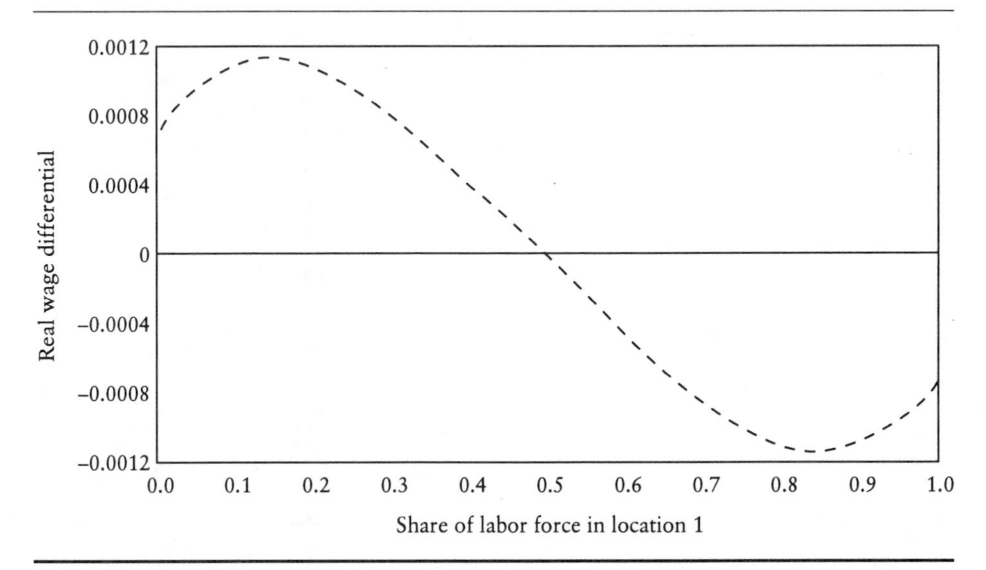

A more subtle source of urban concentration is the importance of access to the government, especially in highly interventionist states. In its simplest form this is simply a result of the concentration of lobbyists. More subtly, if government policies tend to be more responsive to those close at hand (if, say, subsidies or protection to prevent strikes are more forthcoming in the capital than in the provinces), this exerts a hard-to-measure but doubtless important attraction of the capital area for business.

Economic modeling per se cannot contribute much to our understanding of these political concerns. It can, however, help us understand a further consequence of political centralization: the multiplier effects on regional concentration that can result from asymmetric government spending.

Consider a variant on the approach described in the last two sections. Put the commuting and land-rent diseconomies to the side and suppose instead that there is an immobile rural population divided between two regions. Manufacturing will be drawn to concentrate in one region by the forward and backward linkages we have already seen in action, but against this force will be the pull of the market provided by the rural population. A model along exactly these lines is worked out in Krugman (1991b). I show there that the outcome depends on the parameters. For some parameters one gets the type of result shown by the dashed curve in figure 3: the stable equilibrium is one in which manufacturing is equally divided between the two regions.

But now suppose that a government collects taxes from the rural population in both regions but spends it all in one region. Obviously the latter region becomes the larger market, thus attracting more manufacturers. However, the forward and backward linkages that are generated attract still more manufacturing to that region, fos-

Figure 3. *Response of Manufacturing to Relative Wages*

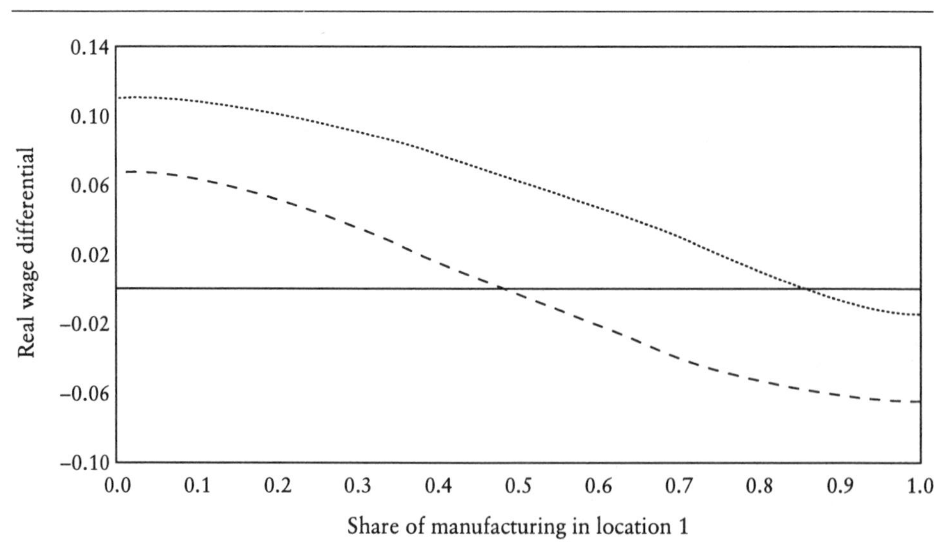

tering a cumulative process of concentration. In figure 3 we start with an economy in which the natural state of affairs has 50 percent of manufacturing in each region. In this example a tax equal to 20 percent of rural income was collected in both regions, but spent only in region 1. The result is shown by the upward shift in the schedule relating the real wage differential to the allocation of manufacturing between the regions (the dotted curve). In this case the multiplier effects cause a concentration of approximately 85 percent of manufacturing in the favored region. The direct transfer of resources from the periphery to the core is only 8 percent of GDP, but the end result is to raise the favored region's share of GDP (before taxes) from 50 to 74 percent.

Although it is not explicitly modeled here, there ought to be an interaction between the strength of multiplier effects producing regional concentration and the degree of openness of the economy. Locating manufacturing near the capital in order to take advantage of the market that the government and its employees provide will be much less attractive in a very open than in a very closed economy.

Transportation Infrastructure

The extent and form of a country's investments in transportation infrastructure can affect the tendency to form large urban centers in at least two ways.

First, the higher transport costs are within a country, the stronger the advantages in terms of backward and forward linkages of locating production near an established metropolitan concentration. This effect may be seen directly in equation 5, which asks whether the linkages are strong enough to sustain an established concentration in the face of the diseconomies of urban scale. In this expression the higher are the transport costs, the more likely is the condition for sustainability to be satisfied.

The implication is that the tendency to concentrate economic activity in a single large city may be reinforced if the government neglects the transportation network. This makes intuitive sense, and corresponds to workaday perceptions about the contrast between location decisions in advanced and developing economies. In advanced economies good transportation to markets (and good communications) is available virtually everywhere, whereas in developing countries roads and telecommunications often peter out quickly as one moves away from the capital.

A more subtle issue involves the form of the transport system. A system that is centered on the primate city is more likely to promote concentration than one that does not favor movement of goods and services in any particular direction.

This point also seems intuitively obvious, but it may be worth sketching out how it works in formal models. Imagine, as in Krugman (1993a), a country with not two but three regions. And suppose that instead of being equal in all directions, transport costs between location 1 and both other locations are lower than those between 2 and 3, so that 1 is in effect the hub of the transport system. Then it is straightforward to show that even if all three regions offer the same size market, region 1 will be a preferred location for goods produced subject to scale economies: it offers better access to the national market than does either of the other locations. Of course, such an advantage will not usually stand alone. Typically, concentration of population and centralization of the transport system reinforce one another: transport links point toward the primate city because that is where the markets and suppliers are, and business concentration is all the greater because of the role of that city as a transport hub.

One might speculate that the apparent tendency of developing countries to have more concentrated distributions of urban size is due to an important extent to the way that their relative poverty leads to a limited transport system. In advanced countries the volume of traffic is sufficient to ensure that good roads link even minor centers; railway lines will often provide direct connections that bypass the biggest cities.[6] In developing countries traffic is sufficient to support good roads pointing only toward the capital, if any at all. Here, too, there is probably a political linkage—a system that centralizes political power in the capital is likely to concentrate investment in infrastructure either near it or on projects that serve it.

Policy Implications

One wants to be very careful about drawing policy implications from any discussion of urbanization and regional growth. By its nature this is a subject that deals extensively with external economies and diseconomies; while neoclassical urban systems theory may suggest that competition among city developers yields optimal results, the newer literature does not contain any such suggestion. Yet the extent and even the direction of the deviations from optimality may be sensitive to the particular form of the external effects. One could in principle argue that since the growth of cities necessarily involves positive external economies, the biggest cities tend to be too small. Or one could argue that the diseconomies of congestion and pollution—or the inability of markets to internalize the benefits of creating new cities—mean that primate cities are too big. Most people have an instinctive feeling that the biggest cities are too big. I share that prejudice, but it must be said that it is only a prejudice at this point.

That said, the general moral of the models described here seems to be that a desire for cities in developing countries to be not quite so big may be fulfilled indirectly by the kinds of liberal economic policies currently favored by most international institutions for other reasons. Liberal trade policy appears likely to discourage primate city growth; so does a reduction in state intervention and a decentralization of power. Investment in better transportation infrastructure—a traditional role of government—also seems to work in the same direction.

The tentative conclusion, then, is that neoliberal policies seem likely to have the unexpected side benefit of partly alleviating any problems created by the growth of very large cities. The definite conclusion is that whatever the changes made in economic policies, their implications for urban and regional development within countries are an important, neglected issue.

Appendix

In this appendix I present the formal structure of the model of the determinants of urban concentration sketched out in the second section of the article and illustrated in the third. For a full description of how the model is solved, and an exploration of its properties, see Krugman and Livas Elizondo (1992).

A Formal Model of Urban Concentration

We consider an economy with three locations: 0, 1, and 2. Labor is mobile between 1 and 2, but not from the rest of world.

Each location is a linear city, populated by workers who must work in a central business district but require one unit of land to live on. Thus if a location has a labor force L_i, the distance the last worker must commute is

(A.1) $$d_j = L_j/2.$$

We assume that commuting costs are incurred in labor: a worker is endowed with one unit of labor, but if he must commute a distance *d*, he arrives with a net amount of labor to sell of only

(A.2) $$S = 1 - 2\gamma d.$$

These assumptions immediately allow us to describe the determination of land rent given the labor force at a location. Let w_j be the wage rate paid at the city center per unit of labor. Workers who live at the outskirts of the town will pay no land rent, but will receive a net wage of only $(1 - \gamma L_j)\, w_j$ because of the time spent in commuting. Workers who live closer to the city center will receive more money, but must pay an offsetting land rent. The wage net of commuting costs declines as one moves away from the city center, but land rents always exactly offset the differential. Thus the wage net of both commuting and land rents is $(1 - \gamma L_j)\, w_j$ for all workers.

The total labor input of a location, net of commuting costs, is

(A.3) $$Z_j = L_j\,(1 - 0.5\gamma L_j)$$

and the location's total income—*including* the income of landowners—is

(A.4) $$Y_j = w_j Z_j.$$

Next, we assume that everyone in the economy shares the constant elasticity of substitution utility function

(A.5) $$U = \left(\Sigma_i C_i^{\frac{\sigma-1}{\sigma}} \right)^{\frac{\sigma}{\sigma-1}}.$$

To produce any good i at location j involves a fixed as well as a variable cost:

(A.6) $$Z_{ij} = \alpha + \beta Q_{ij}.$$

The properties of monopolistic competition models like this are by now very familiar. As long as many goods are produced, and as long as we make appropriate assumptions on transportation costs (see below), each producer faces an elasticity of demand equal to the elasticity of substitution, and will therefore charge a price that is a constant markup over marginal cost:

(A.7) $$P_j = (\sigma/\sigma - 1)\ \beta w_j.$$

Given this pricing rule and the assumption that free entry will drive profits to zero, there is a unique zero-profit output of each product:

(A.8) $$Q = (\alpha/\beta)\ (\sigma - 1).$$

And the constancy of output of each product implies that the number of goods produced at each location is simply proportional to its net labor input after commuting:

(A.9) $$n_j = (Z_j/\alpha\sigma).$$

It will save notation to make two useful choices of units. First, units are chosen to make the f.o.b. price of goods produced at any given location equal to the wage rate at the region's city center. Thus:

(A.10) $$P_j = w_j.$$

Second, there is no need to count goods one at a time. They can be equally well counted in batches, say, of a dozen each. To save notation, the batch size is such that

(A.11) $$n_j = Z_j.$$

To preserve the constant elasticity of demand facing firms, the costs of transacting between locations must take Samuelson's "iceberg" form, in which transport costs are incurred in the goods shipped. Thus we assume that when a unit of any good is shipped between location 1 and location 2, only $1/\tau$ units actually arrive; thus the c.i.f. price of a good shipped from either domestic location to the other is τ times its f.o.b. price. Only a fraction $1/\rho$ of a good imported from location 0 is assumed to arrive in either location 1 or 2. For simplicity, exports are assumed to take place with zero transport costs.[7]

We take τ to represent "natural" transport costs between locations. The parameter ρ, however, is meant to be interpreted as combining natural transport costs with artificial trade barriers. It would be straightforward (and would yield similar results)

in this model to introduce an explicit ad valorem tariff whose proceeds are redistributed, but here we simply imagine that any potential revenue is somehow dissipated in waste of real resources.

Given these transport costs and the utility function, we may define true consumer price indexes for manufactured goods in each location. First, let us define the shares of the three locations in the total number of products produced, which are equal to their shares of net labor input:

$$\lambda_j = \frac{n_j}{\sum_k n_k} = \frac{Z_j}{\sum_k Z_k}. \tag{A.12}$$

Let the wage rate in location 0 be the numeraire; then the true price indices are

$$T_0 = K\left(\lambda_0 + \lambda_1 w_1^{1-\sigma} + \lambda_2 w_2^{1-\sigma}\right)^{\frac{1}{1-\sigma}} \tag{A.13}$$

$$T_1 = K\left[\lambda_0 \rho^{1-\sigma} + \lambda_1 w_1^{1-\sigma} + \lambda_2 \left(w_2 \tau\right)^{1-\sigma}\right]^{\frac{1}{1-\sigma}} \tag{A.14}$$

$$T_2 = K\left[\lambda_0 \rho^{1-\sigma} + \lambda_1 \left(w_1 \tau\right)^{1-\sigma} + \lambda_2 w_2^{1-\sigma}\right]^{\frac{1}{1-\sigma}} \tag{A.15}$$

where

$$K = \left(n_0 + n_1 + n_2\right)^{\frac{1}{1-\sigma}}. \tag{A.16}$$

We will take Z_0 as given. Suppose we know the allocation of labor between locations 1 and 2. Then we can determine Z_1 and Z_2. As we will see, we can then solve the model for equilibrium wage rates w_j. Labor is, however, mobile, and we will have a full equilibrium only if all domestic workers receive the same net real wage. This net real wage in location j can be defined as

$$\omega_j = w_j (1 - \gamma L_j)/T_j. \tag{A.17}$$

A situation in which real wages are equal in the two domestic locations is an equilibrium. Such an equilibrium may, however, be unstable under any plausible adjustment story. To get some rudimentary dynamics, we impose a simple Marshallian adjustment mechanism,

$$dL_1/dt = -dL_2/dt = \delta\,(\omega_1 - \omega_2). \tag{A.18}$$

We have now laid out a complete formal model. It is not a model with a closed-form analytical solution. However, if one is willing to rely on numerical examples, it is straightforward to solve the equations on the computer for any given parameters and see how the wage differential depends on the allocation of labor between the two locations, thereby deriving diagrams like figures 1 to 3. As explained in the text, such pictures allow us to see how the patterns of urban or regional concentration change as the parameters change.

City Growth and Power Laws

As mentioned in the text, the size distribution of cities is startlingly well described by a power law of the form

$$N(S) = AS^{-\alpha} \tag{A.19}$$

where $N(S)$ is the number of cities with populations larger than S, and the exponent is very close to –1. (As an illustration, figure A.1 plots the log of metropolitan area rank against the log of city population for the United States in 1991.)

If the distribution of cities were continuous and there were no maximum city size, equation A.19 would be equivalent to saying that the density of cities of size S is

$$n(S) = \alpha AS^{-\alpha-1}. \tag{A.20}$$

Now imagine that cities come only in discrete sizes, with units of, say, 10,000 people. Let k be the number of units in the population, and $n(i,k)$ be the number of cities with i units; then equation A.19 with an exponent of –1 becomes the statement that

$$n(i,k) \approx B(k)i^{-2}. \tag{A.21}$$

Figure A.1 *Relation of U.S. City Rank and City Size*

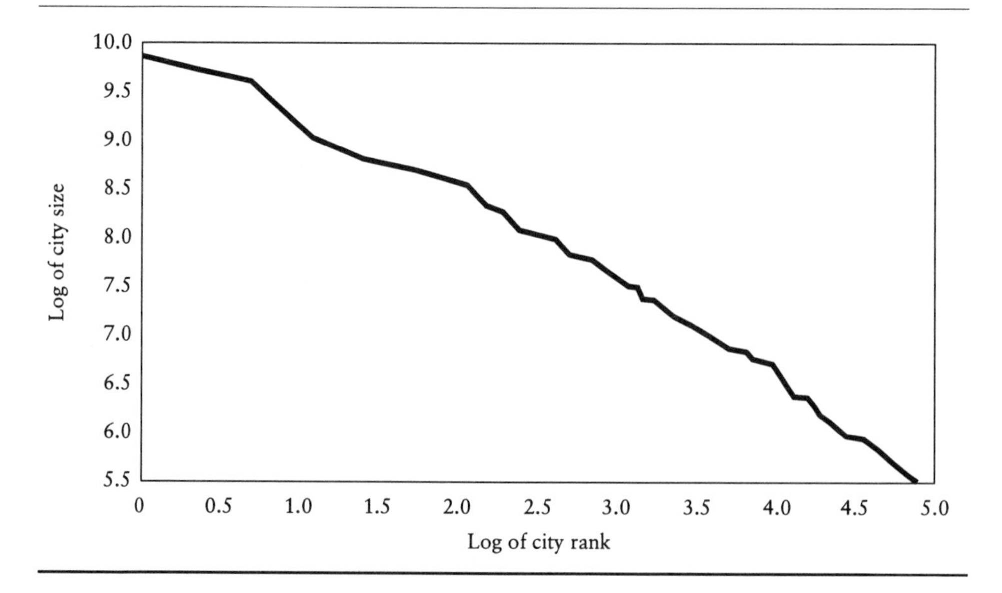

Why should something like equation A.21 be true? In 1955 Herbert Simon offered an ingenious explanation, which is a bit short of a formal proof. I offer here a heuristic version of Simon's argument, which is in turn less than rigorous, so it should be viewed only as a suggestive justification.

Imagine that urban growth proceeds according to the following process: new units arrive in the economy successively over time; each new unit is attached to an existing city with a probability that is proportional to the number of units already there. (In Simon's original formulation, some units form the nuclei of new cities; I return to that issue below.) Thus a city of size i has a probability i/k of getting the next unit.

What is the expected change in the number of cities of size i when a new unit is added? That number can change in two ways. First, a city of size $i - 1$ can acquire the new unit, in which case it becomes a city of size i, adding 1 to the total. Second, a city of size i can acquire the unit, in which case it becomes a city of size $i + 1$, reducing the number of i cities. It therefore follows that

$$E[\Delta n(i,k)] = \frac{(i-1)n(i-1,k)}{k} - \frac{in(i,k)}{k}. \tag{A.22}$$

Now comes the crucial ad hoc step. Simon asks us to imagine that the frequency distribution of city sizes approaches a steady state. This cannot be quite right, since the largest city keeps on getting bigger. But suppose that it is approximately true. Then the number of cities of size i must grow at the same rate as the population, implying

$$E[\Delta n(i,k)] = \frac{n(i,k)}{k}. \tag{A.23}$$

From equations A.22 and A.23 it follows that

$$\frac{n(i,k)}{n(i-1,k)} = \frac{i-1}{i+1} \tag{A.24}$$

and thus that

$$n(i,k) = \frac{i-1}{i+1}\frac{i-2}{i}\cdots\frac{1}{3}n(1,k) \tag{A.25}$$

or

$$n(i,k) = \frac{2}{i(i+1)}n(1,k) \approx 2n(1,k)i^{-2} \tag{A.26}$$

for large i.

That is, in the upper tail of the size distribution, equation A.21 should be approximately true!

This derivation is a bit slippery. It can be bolstered, however, by simulation results; these show that a wide variety of stochastic growth models will produce upper tails for which equation A.21 is very close to true. For example, in Krugman

Figure A.2 *Relation of Simulated City Rank and Size, Top 100 Cities*

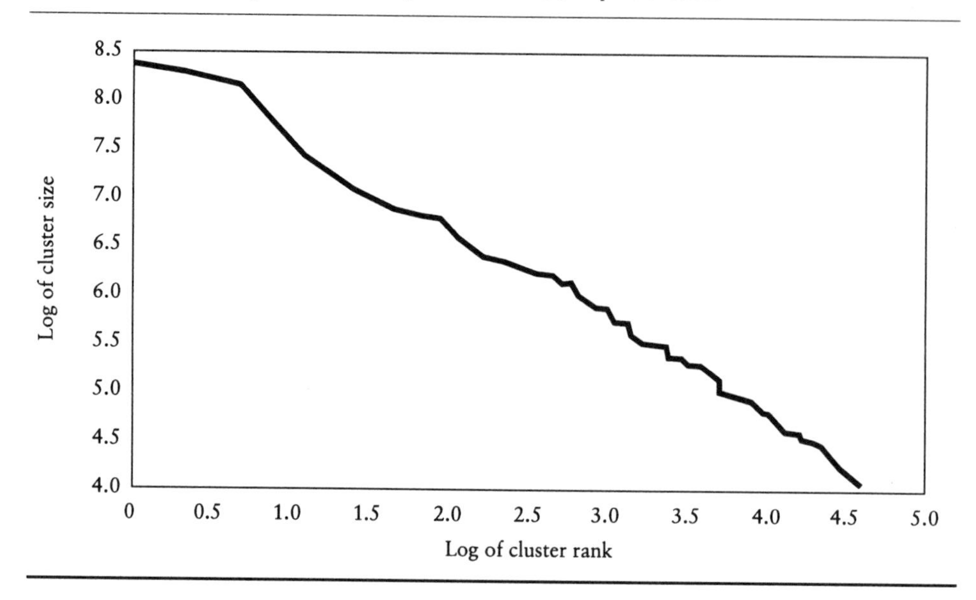

(forthcoming) I consider a model of the following form. A city is begun by an entrepreneur who starts a business. She has two foremen, each of whom with probability p leaves to set up a new factory in the same town. Each foreman has two foremen. Suppose that the probability of defection is close to 0.5, as it must be if towns are to grow very large. Then the results are startling. In figure A.2, I started with 1,000 original businesses, and set $p = 0.49$; the figure shows the relationship between rank and size for the top 100 "cities."

There is a close affinity between Simon's work and the trendy current work on "self-organized criticality," which attempts to explain such observed power-law relationships as the Gutenberg-Richter law relating the sizes and frequencies of earthquakes (Bak 1991).

Notes

1. It is possible, without any real change in the structure, to derive external economies from a monopolistically competitive sector that produces nontraded inputs. See Abdel-Rahman (1988) and Rivera-Batiz (1988).

2. Before the Rosen and Resnick study (1980) most writing on primacy assumed that export orientation would tend to *increase* primacy. The ruling image was of a primary exporting country in which the primate city would be the country's main port; the implicit argument was that the economies of scale involved in building infrastructure for exporting were larger than those involved in selling to the domestic market. One can hardly deny that this effect has existed in some times and places; the evidence that the effect runs the opposite way is not overwhelming. This kind of ambiguity arises in any attempt to summarize the richness of cross-national variation with a short list of explanatory variables.

3. In what are commuting costs incurred? It is easiest to assume that they are incurred only in workers' time, and that time spent commuting is time not spent working. In this case, as shown in the appendix, the net wage rate of the most remote worker in a city of population L takes the form $w\,(1 - \gamma L)$, where w is the wage at the center.

4. In this story all workers end up concentrated in one location, earning the same wage. It thus appears to be a model of urban concentration but not of regional inequality. Suppose, however, that not all workers are mobile. Then it is apparent that a core-periphery pattern could emerge in which mobile workers agglomerate in one region, leaving behind an impoverished rump of those workers who for whatever reason cannot or will not move. Stories along the same lines can surely also be relevant to the extreme regional inequality one sees in some developing countries.

5. Krugman and Livas Elizondo (1992) show that there may be a range of parameters in which both dispersed and concentrated stable equilibriums exist. Numerical examples suggest, however, that this range is quite narrow.

6. Cronon (1990) shows that the rapid growth of Chicago in the nineteenth century came to an end largely because the growing density of the U.S. rail network made its traditional position as a rail hub increasingly unimportant.

7. Even though we make exports costless, an increase in ρ, which reduces imports, must necessarily decrease exports as well. The mechanism through which this happens is a rise in the prices of domestic relative to foreign output—in effect, a real overvaluation that prices domestic goods out of world markets.

References

Abdel-Rahman, H. 1988. "Product Differentiation, Monopolistic Competition, and City Size." *Regional Science and Urban Economics* 18: 69–86.

Ades, A., and E. Glaeser. 1993. "Trade and Circuses: Explaining Urban Giants." Department of Economics, Harvard University, Cambridge, Mass.

Bairoch, P. 1988. *Cities in Economic Development.* Chicago: University of Chicago Press.

Bak, Per. 1991. "Self-Organizing Criticality." *Scientific American* 264 (January): 46–53.

Carroll, G. 1982. "City-Size Distributions: What Do We Know After 67 Years of Research?" *Progress in Human Geography* 6: 1–43.

Cronon, W. 1990. *Nature's Metropolis: Chicago and the Great West.* New York: Norton.

Fujita, M., and P. Krugman. 1993. "Monopolistic Competition and Systems of Cities." Department of Regional Sciences, University of Pennsylvania.

Glaeser, E., H. D. Kallal, J. Scheinkman, and A. Shleifer. 1992. "Growth in Cities." *Journal of Political Economy* 100: 1126–52.

Henderson, J. V. 1974. "The Sizes and Types of Cities." *American Economic Review* 64: 640–56.

———. 1977. *Economic Theory and the Cities.* Oxford: Oxford University Press.

———. 1988. *Urban Development.* Oxford: Oxford University Press.

Ijiri, Y., and Simon, H. 1977. *Skew Distributions and the Sizes of Business Firms.* Amsterdam: North-Holland.

Krugman, P. 1991a. *Geography and Trade.* Cambridge, Mass.: MIT Press.

———. 1991b. "Increasing Returns and Economic Geography." *Journal of Political Economy* 99: 483–99.

———. 1993a. "The Hub Effect: Or, Threeness in Interregional Trade." In W. Ethier, E. Helpman, and J.P. Neary, eds., *Theory, Policy, and Dynamics in International Trade.* Cambridge: Cambridge University Press.

———. 1993b. "On the Number and Location of Cities." *European Economic Review* 37 (March): 293–98.

———. Forthcoming. *The Self-Organizing Economy.* London: Basil Blackwell.

Krugman, P. and R. Livas Elizondo. 1992. "Trade Policy and The Third World Metropolis." Working paper 4238. National Bureau of Economic Research, Cambridge, Mass.

Pred, A. 1966. *The Spatial Dynamics of U.S. Urban-Industrial Growth, 1800–1914.* Cambridge, Mass.: MIT Press.

Rivera-Batiz, F. 1988. "Increasing Returns, Monopolistic Competition, and Agglomeration Economies in Consumption and Production." *Regional Science and Urban Economics* 18: 125–53.

Rosen, K., and M. Resnick. 1980. "The Size Distribution of Cities: An Examination of the Pareto Law and Primacy." *Journal of Urban Economics* 8: 165–86.

Simon, Herbert. 1955. "On a Class of Skew Distribution Functions." *Biometrika* 52: 425–40.

Comment on "Urban Concentration: The Role of Increasing Returns and Transport Costs," by Krugman

Andrew M. Isserman

Paul Krugman does many important things extremely well. Whether his research has created the basis for a new regional economics or economic geography remains to be seen, but his research and proclamations already have infused the field with new enthusiasm, energy, and hope. He demonstrates that its messy problems can be studied with today's formal mathematical models and argues that the field will grow in prestige and importance. Yet some charge Krugman with ignoring prior work and, worse yet, with presenting no new insights. To use his own words, "I am having a terrible time with my current work on economic geography; referees tell me that it's obvious, it's wrong, and anyway they said it years ago" (quoted in Gans and Shepherd 1994, p. 178). How valid are these criticisms with respect to this article?

Is the Model So Simple That It Yields Misleading Conclusions?

Krugman argues that people concentrate in cities because of the greater variety of goods available. Firms concentrate there because cities offer larger markets for their goods. In perhaps a spatial wrinkle on Say's law, firms create their own markets by concentrating their locations. Wages are lower in the countryside because firms must absorb the costs of reaching the city market; prices are higher because of the cost of transporting goods there from the city. The lower wages and higher goods prices in the countryside do not stimulate everyone to move to the city because higher rent and commuting costs in the city balance its higher wages and lower prices.

Krugman predicts that free trade can reduce the pressures on large cities by opening up alternative markets to the firms concentrated in the cities. Firms no longer need to seek out locations that maximize their access to the national market. Likewise, having access to goods from around the world, consumers need not locate in the city and pay high commuting and land costs.

Central to evaluating the model and its predictions is how the model defines its key components—primate cities, countryside (or smaller cities), traded goods, transportation infrastructure, and migration. The main advantage of modeling is simpli-

Andrew M. Isserman is director, Regional Research Institute, and professor of economics and geography at West Virginia University.

Proceedings of the World Bank Annual Conference on Development Economics 1994

fication. Its focus on selected attributes can yield new insights. The main danger of modeling is that those insights might be wrong because of ill-chosen simplification or gross mischaracterization.

Primate cities in the model are production points that can offer wage premiums because they are the market centers and incur low transport costs to reach that market. Commuting costs increase and rents decrease with distance from the center. Primate cities have more people than other places. That's about it for the primate city. The countryside must offer lower wages to absorb the costs of transporting goods to the city market. That's about it for the countryside. As Krugman says, the model is simple.

Now, is there mischaracterization and oversimplification? First, the primate city is not only a manufacturing center. Typically, it is the center of just about everything. Thus, even if a greater proportion of its production is sold to foreign markets as a result of free trade, only one part of its economic base is freed from dependence on the primate population concentration. Its other functions, particularly finance, government, trade, and communication, might expand and reinforce its dominant position. Krugman acknowledges some of these roles; his formal model does not. Consequently, the model may yield erroneous conclusions regarding the overall effects of free trade on population concentration.

The posited manufacturing trade effect might not occur at all. Its basis is the substitution of foreign markets and goods for primate city markets and goods. For that substitution to occur, primate city manufacturers must be able to produce for the international market, and city residents must be able to afford the goods produced by the international market. To the extent that these assumptions do not hold, the posited trade effect will be weaker. To the extent that local producers will be eliminated by foreign competitors or by competitors newly located at now optimal points that serve both the world and primate markets, the trade effect will be stronger. In the model's theoretical extreme the primate city will cease to exist if all manufacturing moves to the third point, that is, out of the country to the rest of the world. We cannot know the nature or size of the trade effect on population concentration until we know more about the trade, goods, income levels, and distribution systems of the particular country.

Meanwhile, what is going on in the countryside? Presumably, some small cities and rural places will grow because of their production for world markets. Rural areas, however, produce food, natural resources, and other goods and services that are tied to place-specific attributes, many of which cities cannot produce. That these goods are missing from the model becomes a problem when drawing conclusions about the effects of trade on urbanization. Trade liberalization may have very big effects on agriculture, for example. Unlike manufactured goods, agricultural goods might be perfect substitutes for goods now consumed in the world market. Agricultural trade may evolve precisely as Krugman postulates for the primate city's manufactured goods.

If so, trade liberalization might have serious repercussions for primate cities, but opposite to those Krugman posits. Imports might destroy domestic agriculture, as is feared in France, Japan, the Republic of Korea, and many other countries. The plausible outcome in developing-country settings is more, not less, migration from the countryside to the primate city. Alternately, trade liberalization might enable the country to expand its exports, quite plausibly, by making agriculture more capital intensive in order to increase output for world markets. This change also might destroy the current agricultural system and cause additional rural unemployment and migration to the primate city.

The nature of transportation infrastructure in the model is important, too. What is assumed in the model and what is implicit in the trade liberalization predictions appear to be inconsistent. Crucial to Krugman's predicted trade effect is the ability to produce outside the primate city for world markets. Yet, according to the model, production is concentrated in the city largely because high transportation costs to the city from elsewhere in the country push people to the city as consumers and push firms there as producers.

Enter trade liberalization, and the transportation system seems suddenly different. Now it suffices to serve more points. For Krugman's Mexican border case that argument is easy: the transportation system that matters is outside the country once the border or port is reached. For other cases the story becomes a bit mysterious. We must now assume an adequate transportation infrastructure from a place to the world market, but before we assumed no system existed from there to the primate city that could take away the latter's locational advantage. Somehow, for the predicted trade effect to occur, we must change the world of the model or at least the country's transportation infrastructure. Creating additional markets through trade liberalization will weaken the domination of the primate city only if those markets can be reached at reasonable cost from several points within the country. Again, the actual outcome will depend on the particulars of each national case.

Finally, migration is implicit in the model. People move to the primate city until increases in land rents and commuting costs bring the urban system into equilibrium. But in reality people also move abroad. Trade liberalization that fosters greater production at home might reduce emigration—as NAFTA supporters argued—and thus might spur migration within the country, particularly to places where output and employment demand increase. Those places might well include the primate city, again confounding Krugman's posited trade effect.

I would be delighted to learn that the messy issues raised here can be readily resolved within the model. I fear, however, that the model is too simple and the predicted effects of trade on population concentration might not hold.

Although a look through Krugman's "new lens" may not give us an accurate view of the world, it does help reveal obstacles that block our view. Those obstacles deal with the nature of cities, countryside, production, infrastructure, and migration in individual countries—all standard elements of the old economic geography. By concluding that the knowledge of the old economic geographers, the area specialists, can teach us a lot about the effects of trade liberalization on urban concentration, I may be committing heresy for one trained in economics. My response to Krugman's model and his "what can we learn" question is, however, a call not for a return to the old economic geography but for recognition of the virtues of both old and new. Perhaps the main implication of Krugman's article is that understanding the relationship between trade and urbanization in developing countries calls for still richer models that are rooted in critical "ground truth" on key parameters and variables.

Does Krugman's Model Teach Us New Things?

Are Krugman's policy conclusions regarding trade, centralization, taxes, and infrastructure surprising insights into our world? Do they flow directly from the model, or are they actually the product of "older," less-formal reasoning? What have we learned through that new lens? Krugman concludes that the desire that cities in developing countries not be quite so big may be served indirectly by liberal trade policy, a reduction in state intervention and a decentralization of power, and investment in better transportation infrastructure. He sprinkles these conclusions with qualifiers—"may be served," "appears likely," and "seems to work"—perhaps to express a wise author's recognition that this is the best his models can do at this point.

That changes in trade policy can create production advantages for certain regions is conventional knowledge, not just of economists (Ruane 1983; Williamson 1986), geographers (Sheppard 1982; Warf and Cox 1993), and sociologists (Portes 1989), but also of French farmers and other folk. That trade liberalization will discourage the growth of primate cities can be predicted simply by pointing to opportunities being created elsewhere in the country, but neither such common sense reasoning nor Krugman's formal model means that the prediction will be correct. Too many factors, absent from both, will determine what will happen in a particular country.

Krugman argues that political centralization is "almost surely the most important reason" that cities in developing countries grow so large. Yet it does not appear explicitly in the model. Centralization can be linked to the model, as Krugman does by pointing out that government is itself a major employer. He also asserts that if the government is more interventionist, access to government is more important, so more lobbyists will be contributing to the economic base and size of the city. Thus decentralized government and less-interventionist government will mean fewer people in the primate city. That argument may well be true, but it does not qualify as a new insight *provided by the model.* Furthermore, trade liberalization need not be accompanied by decentralized and less interventionist government despite being part of the same Washington consensus.

Krugman's political section contains an interesting formal modeling exercise. It shows that if the government taxes rural income and spends the revenues in the city, further concentration in the city will result. That illustration, a nifty by-product of the model, is also not a new insight. Agricultural economists and others have argued for a long time that overtaxation of the countryside through low food prices has subsidized cities and stimulated urban and industrial growth. It was a key concept of Soviet economic planning, it underlies the Chinese economic system, not to mention feudal economies, and it is a shibboleth of the urban bias literature.

Finally, there is Krugman's argument for investment in infrastructure to discourage primate city growth. This recommendation comes from the model and is a direct reflection of the role played by transportation costs. Yet it is also an old point in regional and development economics (Hansen 1965; Hirshman 1958; Williamson 1965). Poor transportation linkages within the country and transportation systems focused on the primate city reinforce the city's dominant role. As Krugman notes, these points seem intuitively obvious, as does the related policy recommendation.

Conclusion

Perhaps the most important argument of the article, even if it is not based on the model, is that a whole constellation of popular policies can contribute to urban deconcentration. That the Washington consensus policies can lead to population decentralization is a striking, intriguing observation. Does it matter that it does not follow directly from the model? Does it matter that each piece of that conclusion can be found in earlier work? Does it matter, in short, whether Krugman is guilty of his referees' charges: "it's obvious" and "someone else already said it?" No! To require that a model teach us new things is to set a very demanding standard. Most models do not meet it. Usually, we are content if our modeling exercises reproduce known things or focus our attention on important parameters. Even if some of Krugman's conclusions are wrong, others obvious, and none virginal, the article focuses our inquiry, raises stimulating questions, and makes us appreciate the limits of our modeling capabilities and our knowledge.

Yes, Krugman is right. His style—"maybe by claiming more originality than I really have"—not to mention his many achievements, invites referees and commentators to apply unusual standards to evaluate his work. I propose another unusual challenge. At the 1992 conference, Bank President Lewis Preston stressed that research into why development takes place in some settings, and why poverty persists in others, is central to the Bank's mission (Preston 1993). Krugman's article has refocused our attention on markets, transportation costs, and government centralization to explain why development occurs in some places and not in others. He has not yet focused his remarkable skills and talents on why poverty persists. I encourage the World Bank to invite him to speak at this conference again, but this time on spatial aspects of poverty. Poverty economics, too, will benefit immensely from being stirred up by his ideas.

Paul Krugman's work and his models are worthy and exciting additions to the classic location theory of von Thunen, Weber, Losch, and Christaller. I agree wholeheartedly with his "definite conclusion...that whatever the changes made in economic policies, their implications for urban and regional development within countries are an important, neglected issue."

Note that this time Krugman offers no qualifiers. This conclusion is "definite." Although we in regional economics and economic geography have not neglected these issues, to our chagrin others in academia and public agencies have ignored them. The stimulating work of Paul Krugman will make it more difficult for them to continue to do so.

References

Gans, Joshua S., and George B. Shepherd. 1994. "How Are the Mighty Fallen: Rejected Classic Articles by Leading Economists." *Journal of Economic Perspectives* 8 (1): 165–79.

Hansen, Niles M. 1965. "Unbalanced Growth and Regional Development." *Western Economic Journal* 9 (1): 3–14.

Hirshman, Albert O. 1958. *The Strategy of Economic Development.* New Haven, Conn.: Yale University Press.

Portes, Alejandro. 1989. "Latin American Urbanization During the Years of Crisis." *Latin American Research Review* 24 (3): 7–44.

Preston, Lewis T. 1993. "Opening Remarks." *Proceedings of the World Bank Annual Conference on Development Economics* 1992: 7–8.

Ruane, Frances R. 1983. "Trade Policies and the Spatial Distribution of Development: A Two-Sector Analysis." *International Regional Science Review* 8 (1): 47–58.

Sheppard, Eric. 1982. "City Size Distributions and Spatial Economic Changes." *International Regional Science Review* 7 (2): 127–51.

Warf, Barney, and Joseph Cox. 1993. "The U.S.-Canada Free Trade Agreement and Commodity Transportation Services among U.S. States." *Growth and Change: Journal of Urban and Regional Policy* 24 (3): 341–64.

Williamson, Jeffrey G. 1965. "Regional Inequality and the Process of National Development: A Description of the Patterns." *Economic Development and Cultural Change* 13 (4/2): 3–45.

———. 1986. "Regional Economic-Demographic Modeling: Progress and Prospects." In Andrew M. Isserman, ed., *Population Change and the Economy: Social Science Theories and Models.* Boston, Mass.: Kluwer-Nijhoff Publishing.

COMMENT ON "URBAN CONCENTRATION: THE ROLE OF INCREASING RETURNS AND TRANSPORT COSTS," BY KRUGMAN

J. Vernon Henderson

Paul Krugman provides an interesting and useful overview of what the new economic geography has to say about urban development. Given the breadth of the article, I limit my comments to four items.

Key Modeling Differences between the Neoclassical Urban Systems and the New Economic Geography

Krugman suggests that a critical difference between the urban systems approach and the new economic geography is in the specification of imperfect versus perfect competition. In fact, the urban systems models consider imperfect competition among producers within cities (Abdel-Rahman 1988), across cities (Henderson and Abdel-Rahman 1992), and as among land developers (Henderson 1977, 1988). Rather, the differences are in the specification of the nature of agglomeration benefits, in the treatment of space, and in the potential role of large agents in land markets.

The urban systems models assume that agglomeration benefits arise from localized, external economies of scale. Microeconomic foundations for these scale economies include Dixit-Stiglitz diversity of nontraded intermediate inputs going into production of a city's export good (Abdel-Rahman 1988); search and matching in local labor markets (Helsley and Strange 1990); information spillovers (Fujita and Ogawa 1980, 1982); and Becker-Murphy intraindustry specialization. Information spillovers can involve a market where information products are bought and sold, but information is subject to spatial decay. In contrast, the new economic geography assumes that agglomeration benefits arise solely from savings on transport costs from concentrating producers and trade at a point. There is a reality issue here of what is important in modern metropolitan areas, as well as the welfare implications of choices of assumption.

The second difference is that the new economic geography tries explicitly to model space between cities and intercity transport costs. The urban systems models do not introduce national space explicitly, which is clearly a loss. However, partic-

J. Vernon Henderson is Eastman Professor of Political Economy at Brown University.

ularly in empirical applications, they do consider the impact on prices received or paid for products in cities with better access to national and international markets.

Finally, while the urban systems models are solved with both atomistic and large agents in land markets, that approach tends to focus on large agents, whereas the new economic geography ignores them. By institutional facts, local governments are large agents in land markets since half of urban land is in the public domain and the other half is controlled by planning and zoning. In addition, new cities, such as edge cities in the United States, tend to be the product of individual private developers, who engineer massive reagglomerations of employment and population.

Although the explicit introduction of national space is highly desirable, it is hard to do so and still retain the essential features of systems of cities. By introducing space the new economic geography has been unable to model a system or hierarchy of cities in which cities are of different sizes and specialize in the production of different bundles of goods. This inability limits sharply the application of the model to questions of urban concentration, as we will see. And so far the introduction of national space has been at a very elementary level.

Urban Concentration Issues in the New Economic Geography

Krugman considers an example of how to analyze the impact of the opening of trade on national space and urban concentration. He starts in autarky with two sites, call them A and B, where because of agglomeration benefits production is concentrated at one site. Let's say the two sites are on the coast, equidistant from international markets, as in Krugman. With the opening of trade, if the pull of international markets is strong enough, we end up with two cities of equal size focused on international exports.

I have three comments on this treatment. First, in Krugman's model or in variants of it that he has developed, we could have started in a different region of parameter space, where in autarky there are two (stable) equal-size cities, in which case trade would have no impact on urban concentration. Second, if we start with population concentrated all at one site, trade need not induce a shift of some population to the other. Population can remain concentrated. Third, the results depend on the two sites being equidistant from international markets.

Suppose, instead, that we start with a coastal periphery site and an interior central site. If in autarky all production is at the coast, the introduction of trade has no impact on urban concentration. If, however, in autarky all production is in the interior, trade also will not affect urban concentration: either all production will remain in the interior or it will all shift to the coast.

These examples show that the impact of trade on national space is situation-specific, depending on the precise geography of the country. The analysis of urban concentration here also is limited to a country of just two cities. Countries, even small ones, with a few city-state exceptions, have dozens if not hundreds of cities. There, urban concentration concerns only the portion of the population living in relatively big cities. In thinking about urban concentration, we may want a more generic or general framework.

Urban Concentration in Urban Systems Models

Urban systems models are full general-equilibrium models in which there are agglomerations of population and investment in cities (Henderson 1988). The models are designed to capture the essentials of what we see in large, urbanized economies. Cities endogenously specialize in production of different export goods or groups of goods. Because they produce different sets of export goods, there are different types of cities. The size of any city type depends on the extent of localized external economies of scale in its specific production. The greater are the scale economies, the larger is the city size for that type. The grouping of products into a city type involves a tradeoff between the benefits of greater specialization at the detailed industry digit level and the benefits of diversity, such as the exchange of information and products with related industries. The numbers of each type of city depend on its equilibrium size and the national demand for its product. The greater the demand, the more cities of that type.

Now to the issue of urban concentration. Consider a simple hierarchy of four types of cities differentiated by the products in which they specialize:

City size	*Goods produced*
Villages and small towns	Agriculture
	Traditional manufacturing
	Traditional textiles
	Food processing
	Simple metal working
	Nonmetallic minerals (clay, glass)
Medium-size cities	Modern manufacturing
	Primary metals
	Machinery
	Transport equipment
Metropolitan areas	High-tech development and modern services
	Instruments
	Electronics
	Finance
	Publishing
	Arts
	Instruments

In autarky we start with a composition of city types and numbers, based on the economy's stage of development, technology, and national demand. That could involve low urban concentration, with many villages and small towns and just a few medium-size cities, or metropolitan areas producing modern manufacturing and services, or the other way around.

The introduction of trade will alter the composition of national output, which will alter the number of required cities of each type. A shift to more modern manufacturing or services involves a reduction in the relative number of villages and small towns and an increase over time in the absolute and relative number of medium-size cities and metropolitan areas, thereby increasing urban concentration. That's the standard urbanization of a country. In a growing economy, this is accomplished through stagnation or declines in the population of most villages and small towns, with some former small towns growing into new medium-size cities and some former medium-size cities growing into new metropolitan areas. Typically, the original one or two metropolitan areas will also grow as the composition of their internal production changes.

Of course, the shift in urban concentration can go the other way, as a country specializes in more traditional manufacturing, such as production of labor-intensive parts and components. With liberalization of international trade some countries, such as Mexico, seem to be following that path. Regardless, this type of analysis is a natural way to get at a change in urban concentration, even before we introduce specific effects due to the spatial dimensions of the geography of the country in question.

With this same model we can address the impact on urban concentration of government policies, such as protectionist trade policies or minimum wage laws affecting the national composition of output. But perhaps more critically in the long term, we can examine the impact of institutions on urban concentration. For example, empirical evidence suggests that central, as opposed to federal, systems of government bias investments in infrastructure toward large metropolitan areas such as the national capital. Decentralization of decisionmaking about investments in local public infrastructure may mean decreased urban concentration as smaller and medium-size cities compete more effectively in the national allocation of public investment.

But the effects may be more subtle. State-owned heavy industry may choose to locate in basically silly places, such as the national capital (far from raw material supplies), drawing other private producers there. Or the central government may restrict the location of foreign producers to a few key metropolitan areas. Consider the impact on urban centralization in Brazil, where protectionist policies favoring heavy industry in the postwar period were combined with the location of the government portion of the iron and steel industry in São Paulo or on the São Paulo–Rio axis and the restrictions on the locations of foreign automobile plants. That's like forcing iron and steel and auto plants to locate in New York City, rather than in the midwest. We don't even need to discuss São Paulo's air quality as a function of locating the heaviest polluters next to the greatest number of victims. Note that the suggestion here is that greater São Paulo has the wrong industrial composition, not that it is necessarily too large.

Even more subtle institutional examples exist. Take the lending policies of banks in a system dominated by state-owned banks, such as Indonesia. Often there is an effective spatial hierarchy, in which local banks in smaller towns are limited in the sizes and types of business loans that they can make. Such restrictions create a spatial bias in capital markets, affecting firms' location decisions and encouraging urban centralization and concentration. More generally, access to a centralized bureaucracy in countries where the central government directly or indirectly is a major player in industrial markets forces centralization of firms.

The Rank Size Rule

My final comment is a more technical one. Krugman cites the rank size rule for an economy under which the power relationship Rank = C_0 (Urban Population)$^{-\alpha}$, has $\alpha = 1$. Rank is the rank of a city in the economy by its population size. We know from standard urban economics texts (for example, O'Sullivan 1992) that when the power law in Krugman's equation 1 is estimated for *all* U.S. metropolitan areas, α in fact is not 1.0, as Krugman suggests; it is 0.9. In a power relationship that is a big, rather than trivial, difference. Now rather than Rank times Population being a constant, Rank times Population declines exponentially against Rank, or Rank times Population = C_1 (Rank)$^{-.11}$. That's an 11 percent rate of decline!

Nonetheless, a general power law provides an excellent fit for the data. This power law may be derived from a variety of models, as examples, including the urban systems models. But most people feel it is a common statistical artifact, with no special meaning, suggesting neither random processes nor some fundamental law of nature.

References

Abdel-Rahman, H. 1988. "Product Differentiation, Monopolistic Competition, and City Size." *Regional Science and Urban Economics* 18: 69–86.

Fujita, M., and H. Ogawa. 1980. "Equilibrium Land Use Patterns in a Non-Monocentric City." *Journal of Regional Science* 20: 455–75.

———. 1982. "Multiple Equilibrium and Structural Transition of Non-Monocentric Urban Configurations." *Regional Science and Urban Economics* 12: 161–96.

Helsley, R., and W. Strange. 1990. "Matching and Agglomeration in a System of Cities." *Regional Science and Urban Economics* 20: 189–212.

Henderson, J. V. 1977. *Economic Theory and the Cities.* New York: Academic Press.

———. 1988. *Urban Development: Theory, Fact, and Illusion.* New York: Oxford University Press.

Henderson, J. V., and H. Abdel-Rahman. 1992. "Urban Diversity and Fiscal Decentralization." *Regional Science and Urban Economics* 22: 103–22.

O'Sullivan, A. 1993. *Urban Economics.* Homewood, Ill: Irwin.

Floor Discussion of "Urban Concentration: The Role of Increasing Returns and Transport costs," by Krugman

A participant from the World Bank emphasized the importance of government structure to the size and distribution of cities. One side effect of U.S. federalism is cities proportionately much smaller than in Latin America (where governments tend to be centralized). A third of Chile's population lives in Santiago, and a third of Argentina's lives in Buenos Aires. If New York City held a comparable proportion of the U.S. population, its population would be about 85 million.

Without question, said Krugman, in the cross-sectional work federalism is the single most clear-cut factor affecting the degree of urban concentration. Politics is more important—or at least more transparently important—than any strictly economic issues. To the question of whether it is the inherent concentration or the urban hierarchy that drives the political system, rather than the opposite, he responded that at some level it is all endogenous. Repeating a quotation from the Penguin Atlas of Ancient History—"As history is a branch of the biological sciences, its ultimate expression must be mathematical"—he said that at some level it is all quantum mechanics. And yet, while it is true that the political systems of Canada and the United States are endogenous, it is also true that they were set at a time when the countries were agricultural. So yes, the existence of multiple political centers in the United States led to the federal, decentralized U.S. system, but it was also predetermined. Those multiple centers were New England shipping and fishing versus Virginia tobacco exports, not Atlanta versus Boston.

A participant from the Bank asked Krugman how the opening of trade between cities would affect the size distribution of cities. It is a question not only of space between cities but one of space within cities as well. In South Africa, for example, there are true cities with economic nodes (such as Johannesburg), and there are dormitory towns further away (such as Soweto). As trade opens between those cities, does Krugman predict that Johannesburg will get a shock? Will Soweto emerge as a new metropolitan setting? Krugman responded with a "factoid," which, he said, was as far as one could go with such limited data: modern metropolitan areas—which are based largely upon automobile rather than rail systems, and in which fax machines and similar technologies are available—do seem to want to be polycentric.

This session was chaired by Jessica P. Einhorn, vice president and treasurer at the World Bank.

Los Angeles, of course, has sixteen or so of what pass for downtowns, or edge cities, and developing countries' cities seem to be evolving in a similar direction. Mexico City has no single center; it looks more like Los Angeles than like Chicago in 1950. In that sense, one might expect greater interpenetration in the big picture—a big Johannesburg-Soweto sprawl in which races and types of activities are intermingled—together with intense segregation at the micro-level.

Krugman had discussed how political structures and issues influence the development of urban systems. A participant from the Bank wondered if a stronger argument might be made for the federal structure being the result of a preexisting urban system. Economic activity normally precedes political organization, said the participant; the United States has a federal structure because there were several economic centers, none willing to seek political dominance over the other. You have the same thing in Canada and elsewhere, including India. In a way the movement toward opening up in Mexico may have come from the realization that this was a way to solve problems of the urban system, rather than the reverse. Or look at the relations between European countries: the United Kingdom, which has a highly centralized political structure, is unwilling to cede power to another power center.

In empirical work, responded Krugman, researchers have tried to control for other factors in fairly large cross-sections of countries by dividing the sample into federal, decentralized systems and those that are more centralized. At the margin this is to some extent an arbitrary division, but the nature of the system itself does seem to contribute to deconcentration, over and above other factors that are controlled for. The capital market has a strong spatial bias toward concentration, said Krugman, offering as an example the built-in hierarchy in lending policies in Indonesia's banking system, which is dominated by state-owned banks: there are sharp limits on the size and class of loans to businesses in smaller cities, fewer limits on loans to businesses in medium-size cities, and very few limits on loans to businesses in larger cities. If you look at the data—especially before and after liberalization and similar changes—you will see that institutional behavior influences firms' decisions about location in a way that favors concentration and centralization.

Krugman said that common sense dictated that a truly unified European economy ought to have a "top dog" city larger than any of the national top dog cities in Europe. Following Zipf's law, Europe's primate city ought to contain 25 million or 30 million people. The interesting question is, what would happen if that city turned out not to be Paris? The geographic consequences of European integration involve important issues of city size, city roles, and regional roles. Europe is a vastly more polycentric economy than the United States. If post-1992 Europe is eventually going to look like the United States, some fairly interesting problems of political economy are going to arise in the course of adjustment.

A participant from the Stockholm School of Economics asked Krugman if the nihilistic and non-nihilistic models were not perhaps complementary in the sense that they address different things: one deals with binary choices and the other, in a sense, with the law of large numbers. Other models don't have an explicit growth process or dynamics attached to them, said the participant. If you get growth rates distributed close to normal, you always get something that looks like a law of normal distribution, so these would be complementary rather than conflicting. Krugman wished it were as simple as the nihilistic and non-nihilistic views being different magnifications of the same phenomenon. The nihilistic story occurs wherever you have random city growth, where the expected rate of growth does not really depend on city size, provided growth goes far enough. The problem, he said, is that everything we have to say about economics suggests that there ought to be a maximum city size and that therefore expected city growth ought to depend on city size. In Henderson-like models, there ought to be a set of typical sizes for cities. It was unclear to Krugman whether there is some fix-up, whether lurking in the hidden logic of such models there is a way to create the optical illusion that markets don't care how big cities are. At the moment it appeared to him to be a paradox.

A participant from Oxford University was curious about Krugman's thinking on increasing returns and the relative shift that appears to occur between internal and external economies of scale. Krugman responded that plant-size economies are a decreasingly important factor in advanced countries, partly because manufacturing is now less important there and partly because the markets are now so much bigger relative to plant size than they used to be. The forces of agglomeration, he surmised, are increasingly external in form. The disturbing fact that the average size of enterprises is smallest in the largest cities would strongly suggest an external-economy explanation for what goes on.

That raises a substantial question about the kind of model described here, and, said Krugman, evokes the inevitable image of reinventing the wheel. But even if you don't like a particular model, there is something to be said for simply putting the spotlight on how important spatial issues are in daily life and economics. It seemed to him an obvious empirical fact that there are agglomeration economies in regional and spatial economics. A proliferation of different research approaches is beneficial because we are not competing for resources but collectively drawing the attention of economists and others to a field that has been stunningly neglected. Before the conference he had looked at two of the principle economics textbooks; he had found no reference to cities in one text and only one reference to cities in the other (a brief allusion to the Harris-Todaro model). He is bewildered about why regional science has not had a greater impact. Perhaps what is needed, he said, is buttoned-up, tied-down, neat demonstration models that offer a bridge to mainstream economics. A great deal of intelligent work is being done in regional science but it does not deliver the kind of neatly tied models that economists prefer.

Interaction between Regional and Industrial Policies: Evidence from Four Countries

Ann Markusen

After World War II, policies to promote industrialization—both to substitute for manufactured imports and to encourage exports based on unskilled labor—often successfully complemented regional polices to better distribute economic activity. The recent shift toward high technology, however, has strongly favored major urban areas, undermining efforts at regional decentralization and stabilization. Furthermore, countries are increasingly abandoning top-down regional policy and passing on responsibility for development to provincial and local levels, setting off vigorous interregional competition for economic activity and often favoring a few, relatively well-endowed regions. Evidence from Brazil, Japan, the Republic of Korea, and the United States shows how the recent emphasis on high-tech exports and decentralized regional policy may reinforce polarization and slow progress toward eliminating regional growth and income differentials.

Since the end of World War II most industrial and developing countries have devoted considerable resources to industrial and regional policies. The goal of industrial policy is to create capacity in key industries, to develop domestic markets, and to reduce imports and build export capacity. Regional policies are designed to moderate regional growth rate differentials, ameliorate regional differences in per capita income, integrate stalled regions into the national economy, and spread urbanization from a single metropolis to multiple sites. The sometimes conflicting goals of long-term growth, efficiency, equity, and political peace motivate both sets of policies.

This article explores the compatibility and tension between industrial and regional policies in four countries since World War II. Industrial policy can influence the location of economic activity, either directly through government siting or indirectly

Ann Markusen is director of the Project on Regional and Industrial Economics at Rutgers University. The research summarized in this article was partially funded by a grant from the National Science Foundation, Program in Geography and Regional Science, for a four-country research project on new industrial districts. The author thanks Sam Ock Park, Clelio Campolina Diniz, Masayuki Sasaki, Masatomi Funaba, Candace Howes, Mohamad Razavi, Mia Gray, Elyse Golob, Yung-Sook Lee, Marlen Llanes, and Barbara Brunialti for their insights and help. Comments on earlier drafts from Michael Storper and Peter Hall, as well as World Bank staff members, also are appreciated.

through incentives to the private sector. Governments can use industrial investment to promote development of laggard regions or to favor a more decentralized pattern of capacity distribution in the sector. On the other hand regional policy priorities can hamper the effectiveness of industrial policy design. Agglomeration economies may be lost by placing new industrial activity away from major industrial cities, while opting for more rather than fewer new centers risks missing out on economies of scale.

Policymakers acknowledge short- and medium-term efficiency losses to their regional policies, but argue that increased equity compensates. In the long term well-executed regional policies may also enhance growth and efficiency. With sufficient early aid, industrial complexes anchored far from existing centers of activity can become new growth poles, with their own internal dynamism. Furthermore, a flatter urban hierarchy with more medium-size cities may protect the national economy against diseconomies in its dominant city by offering lower-cost sites for cost-sensitive firms. Finally, dispersed growth centers can improve income distribution and fuel growth through both savings and demand effects.

Postwar Industrial and Regional Policies

Economists believe that both economies of scale (increasing returns to size of plant) and agglomeration economies (cost savings from the co-location of complementary economic activity) are positively associated with city size over a sustained period of development, although they may ultimately be reversed. These economies discourage government efforts to redirect industrial and economic activity away from congested, high-income regions. Industries subject to increasing returns to scale, which also benefit from the neighboring presence of complementary industries or shared labor, resource, and information pools, are particularly poor targets, since they are generally drawn into a process of "cumulative causation" biased toward the more prosperous regions (Myrdal 1957; Kaldor 1970; Krugman 1992).

Recent increases in international trade and new export-oriented policies affect regional development in contradictory ways. A location central to a regional or national market may lose advantage to peripheral or coastal locations.[1] But international markets permit larger-scale industries, whose reliance on agglomeration economies may solidify their commitment to existing metropolitan centers while displacing smaller, regionally oriented units. As high-tech industries expand, investments are drawn to nationally dominant cities where skilled labor, information, and business services are more available. The increased importance of legal and political issues such as trade barriers, technology transfer, market access, and intellectual property rights favor national capital cities.

Working in the opposite direction, diseconomies of scale from hyperurbanization encourage regional decentralization of capacity (Richardson 1980). Congestion and high input costs encourage firms to accept government directives or incentives to relocate. Economists and geographers studying industrial culture also suggest that large and powerful oligopolistic industries, especially in mature or declining sectors, discourage entrepreneurship and restrict the supply of land, labor, and capital to other industries within the region (Chinitz 1960; Markusen 1985). Such sectors will not act as seedbeds of innovation as Friedmann (1972) envisioned but may instead repel newer industries, which then take root in underdeveloped regions (Markusen and McCurdy 1988; Hall and Preston 1988).

This article argues that the compatibility of industrial and regional policy depends on the sectors targeted and their requirements for scale and agglomeration economies. The greater the economies of scale and agglomeration for targeted sectors in a centralized location, the less likely that industrial policy will further regional policy goals and the more costly imposed regional priorities may be to industrial goals.

Industries vary both in factors such as capital intensity and minimum efficient scale of production and in agglomeration potential depending on their market orientation (domestic or export) and their degree of maturation. For domestic-oriented industries replacing manufactured imports, regional goals may be achievable when industries are linked to adequate infrastructure for domestic distribution. Export-oriented industries with standardized mass production processes can also locate away from major urban centers—particularly coastal areas—without much disadvantage. Innovative industries that demand skilled labor, business services, and access to information will be less successful in remote locations. Even when inputs and information can be procured over distance, the uncertainty and risk introduced by rapid change in product and technology keeps these industries rooted in major urban centers.

Many industrial countries have begun to shift their industrial policies from sectors such as textiles, apparel, chemicals, machinery, and consumer electronics to high-tech, innovative sectors such as computers, aircraft, producer electronics, communications equipment, and pharmaceuticals. As standardized manufacturing capacity moves to lower-cost countries, industrial countries focus on sectors requiring innovation and human capital investment. But despite the "technopolises" created to house new technology, industrial development, and government research and development, regional goals may be sacrificed.

Regional policy approaches also are changing. Regional policies used to be common, often centrally planned and implemented through agencies devoted to regional matters. But political difficulties in implementation of regional policy and mixed results have encouraged a decentralized approach to economic development in the past decade.[2] The power of agglomerative forces, central government fiscal pressures, and political conflict over the regional deployment of resources have contributed to disillusionment with regional policy. A federal model in which provincial and local governments wield greater discretion over infrastructure provision and economic development incentives is currently in vogue. This shift may decentralize economic activity, but it may do so in an uneven and costly manner without achieving regional policy goals.

The relations among changing growth, industrial policies, and regional policies are complex. Comparative studies that identify contributing and contextual factors lend insight. The remainder of this article analyzes the industrial and regional strategies of four countries—the Republic of Korea, Brazil, Japan, and the United States—since World War II. These countries vary by size, development experience, political structure, and natural resource endowment. Results are gauged for sectoral efficiency and interregional equity and stability.

Republic of Korea: Regional Industrial Enclaves

Over the past four decades Korea has vigorously pursued industrial policy by selecting key sectors and working with and developing the dominant *chaebol,* or large-firm conglomerates (Song 1990; Amsden 1989). Tax incentives, import controls, access to finance, training subsidies, and export-promotion policies were used to build capacity in industries deemed to have export potential. Three eras can be identified: labor-intensive industries such as textiles and apparel in the 1960s and early 1970s; chemicals and heavy industries including automobiles, shipbuilding, petrochemical, machinery, and consumer electronics in the 1970s (Park 1990; Y. S. Lee 1988); and high-tech industries such as semiconductors since the 1980s.

Simultaneously, the Korean government addressed lopsided regional development patterns by exercising its command powers over the private sector. Early industrial policy disregarded spatial array, and thus activity concentrated in Seoul, creating congestion and pollution. Beginning in the late 1960s the government encouraged industries to locate outside of Seoul. Political concerns also favored decentralization since Seoul lies close to the northern border. In the 1970s the government aggressively seeded new industrial complexes outside the Seoul region, building each of them around one or more key industries. With the rise of high-tech activity in the 1980s the Korean Institute of Technology and other government research institutes were built near Taejon. In theory this strategy blended regional with industrial policies in a complementary way (Park 1990).

The Korean government used powerful instruments not unlike the command structures that built new industrial cities in China and the Soviet Union. The Local Industrial Development Law of 1970, the Free Export Zone Establishment Law of 1970, and the Industrial Distribution Law of 1977 all promoted industrial dispersion. Some firms were issued relocation orders—a number of small, polluting industries were forcibly ejected from Seoul to an industrial park in Ansan expressly for polluters (Choe and Song 1984). In other cases the government built the necessary infrastructure for new complexes and invited the chaebol to participate. In the early 1970s the chaebol were ordered by the military government to manufacture machinery for military purposes in Changwon (Markusen and Park 1993).

The strategy successfully created new industrial enclaves and slowed the growth of employment in Seoul. The traditional Korean industrial cities—Seoul, Pusan, and Taegu—remain the largest in the 1990s, but by the early 1980s their employment growth rates were below the national average, most conspicuously in Seoul (Republic of Korea 1981, 1984, 1986, 1987). Inchon, the satellite port of Seoul, continued to grow rapidly, but six other industrial cities experienced faster than average job growth over the past two decades (Markusen 1994b). Each has a specialization: Ulsan, chemicals and automobiles; Pohang, steel; Changwon, military and defense; Kumi, electronics and textiles; Ansan, polluting industries such as chemicals, soaps, dyes, and metal finishing; and Taejon, traditional manufacturing and high-tech, research-oriented activity.

Although locational directives and incentives successfully dispersed heavy industries like steel, automobiles, and chemicals from Seoul, they have been less successful with high technology (Park 1991). Because Seoul has better schools and more corporate headquarters, business services, and government offices and institutes, firms outside the region are handicapped. Strong agglomeration economies anchor leading-edge activities to the Seoul area. The current emphasis on high-tech industry and government research and development is likely to enhance centripetal tendencies.

The industrial enclaves may not continue to grow. Their location separates them from major service and supplier functions in Seoul (although no city is more than five hours by car). Each consists of a collection of branch plants of major Korean and multinational corporations, and indigenous entrepreneurship and interindustry linkages are often lacking (Park and Markusen forthcoming). Most plants are linked with external parent firms, suppliers, and export markets but not with other units in the complex. Taejon may be best positioned because of its proximity to Seoul and its role as host of Taeduk Science Park and the Korea Institute of Technology. The auto-based complex at Ulsan also shows promise with good linkage potential and growth prospects since it serves both export and domestic markets. But Changwon and Kumi are specialized, landlocked districts. In Changwon military machinery plants were constructed far from Seoul's electronics and optical industries, which provide important inputs, and the automobile assembly industry around Ulsan, a growing market for Changwon. Some critics believe that Korea could more efficiently purchase its defense equipment abroad (Jee 1991). Korean textiles must move upscale to gain an edge over lower-cost Asian countries, but textile production in Kumi is separated from the design and fashion center in Seoul.

Nor do these new industrial cities represent an unqualified regional policy victory. One, Ansan, is close to Seoul; another, Taejon is in the middle of the country; and the other four are concentrated in the southeast. The southeast region was favored because it was the home of President Park and military leaders of the 1970s. The southwest, the poorest region in the country and the base of political opposition to the military government, received no industrial investment until after the military regime was displaced by the restoration of democracy in the late 1980s.

Growth and income differentials among regions are still large. Regional policy slowed the growth of industrial employment in the Seoul region after 1975, but only modestly (Republic of Korea 1963, 1975, 1984; M.W. Lee 1991). The Young Nam region increased its share of employment, but two other major regions—Choongchung and Honam—lost shares. By 1984 the Seoul region still accounted for 47 percent of the nation's manufacturing employment, down only 1 percent over the previous decade. The new industrial cities had little effect on regional employment shares—Young Nam, host of Pohang, Kumi, and Changwon, increased its employment share by only 3 percent over forty years.

The Korean government now plans two new sets of initiatives: the transfer of responsibility for economic development to the provinces and new investment in the southwest. Although local autonomy measures to be implemented in 1995 will increase local power and revenue, this power will still be less than that of the central government. Provincial governments will borrow to build infrastructure to attract firms to high-tech industrial parks. Of course, the provinces will lack the agglomeration economies of Seoul.

The Korean government also plans to construct three large industrial complexes on the southwest coast, two to manufacture and export automobiles to China (only a short distance by sea) and one heavy-industry complex. The government is also building a high-tech industrial park and a government institute of technology in Kwangju, the largest city in the southwest. Regional policy concerns impel these commitments, although the automobile complexes complement export-oriented industrial policy. The viability of a Kwangju high-tech complex is not clear, and its remoteness from Seoul may mean it will remain a disadvantaged enclave.

In Korea regional and industrial policies appear to have worked in concert during the early era of emphasis on heavy industries, but this was less the case once policy shifted to high-tech industries. The transfer of authority and revenue for economic development to the provincial level will disperse new infrastructure investments but may cause inefficient use of resources and high rates of failure without achieving the goals of regional policy.

Brazil: The Relative Failure of Regional Policy

Brazil spans much of South America and many climate zones, making economic integration difficult. Mineral extraction and cultivation of sugar in the colonial period left skewed patterns of land ownership and resource depletion that generated ongoing poverty and inequality. Poverty increased in areas such as the northeast, but robust growth and industrialization occurred in the triangle formed by the three largest cities of São Paulo, Rio de Janeiro, and Belo Horizonte.

Brazilian development policy after the 1930s shifted from an emphasis on primary exports to encouraging industry to substitute for imported goods. The business structure of Brazil at the time was more complex than that of Korea in a later period. While some key industries were publicly owned (especially minerals, metals, petrochemicals, and utilities), Brazilian development depended on the activities of private firms—both national and international. The government encouraged industrial development with far less force than in Korea. It provided infrastructure and subsidies and operated state-owned enterprises.

Through the early 1970s import-substitution policies favored the São Paulo area (Cano 1977). Entrepreneurs in coffee-related industries moved upstream into the production of machinery and downstream into processing. The state of São Paulo increased its share of the nation's industrial production from 16 percent in 1907 to 58 percent in 1970, at the expense of other regions (Diniz 1994). Not until later in the 1970s did marked differentials in costs and congestion begin to slow the growth of São Paulo (Diniz 1994; Cano 1985).

In the 1970s the Brazilian government invested heavily in resource-based and capital goods industries and simultaneously adopted regional initiatives to decentralize economic activity. Since the largest investments took place in state-run enterprises—steel, oil, petrochemicals, chlorochemicals, coal, mining, and paper—and because these industries were noxious and land-extensive, the state located these activities in outlying regions. It proved more difficult to entice private firms to outlying regions. A government effort to regulate decentralization failed in the mid-

1970s because of bureaucratic bungling, insufficient resources, and political pressures from interest groups in São Paulo. Turning to less intrusive methods, the government offered tax incentives through special agencies set up to encourage projects in the northeast, the north, and the city of Manaus. The government also invested in infrastructure to integrate the national economy and to lower business costs in peripheral regions (Diniz 1994).

Despite these efforts—one study estimates that 60 percent of gross capital formation in Brazil in the 1960s and 1970s was accounted for by investment in state companies and public infrastructure (Baer 1978)—regional decentralization of economic activity has been modest at best. Regions rich in natural resources fared best from direct government investment. For example, Espiritu Santu, a coastal state near the mineral-rich Minas Gerais, benefited from investments in iron ore and steel for export, and Manaus grew explosively with the development of Amazonia.

But incentives to attract industry to resource-poor regions have been disappointing (Cavalcanti 1981; Guimaraes-Neto 1986). The northeast, a highly visible target area, increased its share of industrial production from 5.7 percent to 8.7 percent between 1970 and 1989; most of the growth occurred in Bahia, around the publicly built petrochemical pole of Camacari. Incentives available within the more prosperous states, such as São Paulo, counteracted national subsidies.

While investments in communications and highway infrastructure integrated the national economy, they had perverse effects. Companies in and around São Paulo achieved greater economies of scale by reaching distant markets. Some plants formerly serving isolated regional markets closed because they could no longer compete with national firms in São Paulo (Diniz and Razavi 1993).

São Paulo metropolitan and state shares of population and industrial output have declined since 1970. Some people have welcomed this decline as evidence of rising costs in São Paulo and the efficacy of regional policy (Townroe and Keen 1984; Richardson 1980). But Azzoni (1986), Storper (1991), and Diniz (1994) point to robust growth in metropolitan centers within a São Paulo "agglomerative field" of 150 kilometers. Areas outside of the São Paulo metropolitan area but within the state increased their share of national production from 14 percent to 20 percent since 1970. Diniz (1994) demonstrates that most new economic activity has located within a polygon defined by Belo Horizonte, Uberlandia, Londrina-Maringa, Porto Alegre, Florianopolis, and São Jose dos Campos, all arrayed around São Paulo. This region increased its share of national industrial production from 32 percent to 45 percent between 1970 and 1990, more than compensating for São Paulo's loss of share. Diniz argues that state government resources for infrastructure and incentives furthered this growth and that national market integration and concentration of purchasing power around São Paulo anchored industry within the polygon.

Other municipalities also posted higher than average growth rates over the past twenty years, exceeding those of São Paulo and Rio de Janeiro (Diniz 1994). Resource-related industries (metals, fertilizer, cement, agroindustry), which still account for more than one-third of industrial production in Brazil and have been targeted by government programs over the postwar period, explain growth in some of these municipalities. Some (Salvador, Manaus) owe their prosperity to government investments and incentive programs, and others (Porto Alegre, Caxias, Blumenau) to a tradition of diversified agriculture, crafts, and industry (Diniz 1994).

Diniz and Razavi (1993) and Storper (1991) argue that diseconomies associated with higher land, labor, and congestion costs have created pressure for decentralization, but that unless agglomeration economies are achievable elsewhere, decentralization will not occur. In their view, the government—at both national and state levels—has been essential in creating minimal conditions for new growth poles. The cities of Campinas and São Jose dos Campos, for instance, experienced employment growth of 127 and 187 percent between 1970 and 1985. Each received major public investment. Campinas received UNICAMP, the top research university in Brazil; the research and development facility of the national telecommunications company, Telebras; and the Central Foundation for Information Technology. São Jose dos Campos hosts the Aeronautical Technical Center and its five research and teaching institutes, the Institute for Space Research, and EMBRAER, Brazil's public-private joint venture in aircraft. Spinoff businesses generated new growth, and accumulated labor pools and infrastructure proved attractive to foreign and national capital. Although these agglomerations are close enough to enjoy many of the benefits of São Paulo, they are criticized for being overly specialized, vulnerable to downturns, and prone to rather rigid strategies with respect to technological and market potential (Diniz and Razavi 1993; Granovetter 1985).

Industrial policy in Brazil from the 1930s through the 1970s concentrated economic activity in the São Paulo area. Beginning in the 1970s investments in heavy, high-tech, and resource-related industry decentralized activity somewhat. However, four factors diminished the effectiveness of regional policy. First, subsidies and incentives proved to be relatively weak tools. Second, infrastructure investments to integrate the national economy allowed core-area plants to expand their markets and outcompete smaller regional plants. Third, prosperous states such as São Paulo counteracted national commitments to decentralization. Finally, public investments in education, research institutes, and high-tech industries continued in the state of São Paulo, ensuring a concentration of leading-edge economic activity in the dominant region.

Regional decentralization in the 1990s may be slowing as agglomeration economies increase. National industrial policy is increasingly export-oriented, with an emphasis on high-tech sectors like aeronautics, electronics, and information technology. Although knowledge-intensive industries create what Storper (1991) calls "windows of locational opportunity," their requirements for skilled labor and specialized business services often tie them to large urban centers. Government investment in universities, research institutes, and industries such as aerospace and telecommunications have overwhelmingly favored core metropolitan areas (Haddad 1989). In addition, slow growth, budget shortfalls, and the debt crisis that began in the 1980s have cut deeply into private sector investment and public funds for infrastructure, incentives, and state investments. These may be reversed under the new administration. Finally, a reliance on foreign capital for new investment has favored better-known cities and regions (Schoenberger 1985).

Democratization has also weakened central government resolve in regional policy. The influence of elites from São Paulo has grown, making the dispersion of new industrial complexes less likely. The system of municipal taxation currently under discussion would shift power even more decisively to the states. Leaders of São Paulo state in particular argue for retention of a greater share of the taxes their citizens pay.

Brazil's integration into the Latin American and world economies will also affect the future compatibility of industrial and regional policy. The Mercosul proposal for an integrated market in the southern cone favors the neighboring São Paulo polygon. Export-oriented growth favors resource-rich regions, port cities, and urban concentrations with comparative advantages in key industries. If income distribution does not improve, the market advantages of locating in the polygon will persist. Furthermore, under current liberalization policies, protected markets will face stiffer competition and some will fail. To the extent that weak firms are located in outlying regions, their demise will increase concentration.

Japan: Dominance of Industrial over Regional Policy

Industrial policy in Japan since World War II has pursued export strength in automobiles, electronics, and other high-income-elasticity commodities (Howes and Markusen 1994). As in Korea the central government worked with large corporations and mobilized considerable financial resources to provide incentives, import protection, and public infrastructure to encourage exports. Also like Korea, Japan is poor in natural resources and found a comparative advantage in industry beginning with textiles, apparel, and toys, later moving into steel, chemicals, and automobiles, and then into consumer electronics, semiconductors, and other sophisticated equipment.[3]

After the war Japan reconstructed industry at prewar sites: Tokyo, Yokohama, Nagoya, Osaka, Kobe, and Hiroshima. In the 1950s steel, oil, and petrochemical plants were added on the outskirts of these regions. Industrial policy sought economies of scale in plant size and start-up costs. Industries concentrated in the axis between Tokyo and Osaka drew immigrants from surrounding regions (Kitayama 1993; Friedman 1988). By the end of the 1950s political, financial, educational, cultural, administrative, and industrial functions were centered in Tokyo.

This centripetal pattern continued. The population of the three largest metropolitan areas—Tokyo, Osaka, and Nagoya—increased by more than 11 million during the 1960s, while the total population in the other nine regions of the country fell. Net migration slowed in the 1970s, but by 1985 more than half the nation's population lived in these agglomerations. The Tokyo area accounted for most of this growth, adding 17 million people in just thirty-five years (Tsuya and Kuroda 1989). The greater Tokyo region still grows disproportionately even in manufacturing, and regional income disparities worsened in the 1980s (Takeuchi 1991; Abe and Alden 1988).

Criticism has come from outlying regions. The National Income Doubling Plan of 1960 targeted sites within the corridor between Osaka, Nagoya, and Tokyo for new and relocated plants. The Liberal Democratic Party, with representation from rural advocates and local governments, protested. The subsequent National Development Plan of 1962 addressed regional imbalances. Fifteen new industrial cities, built around heavy industry, were designed to become growth poles. Revenue sharing with local governments and the public provision of infrastructure encouraged firms to locate in these cities (Kitayama 1993).

Tokyo remained dominant, but per capita income differentials diminished. In 1955 twenty-five prefectures (or districts) had average per capita incomes of less than one-half that of Tokyo; by 1975 only four districts did (Igarashi 1991, cited in Kitayama 1993). But the peripheral industrial complexes depended on imported oil and raw materials and were hit by the oil crisis of the early 1970s. Asian competition in everything from textiles to shipbuilding challenged the mature industries in these complexes. New research- and design-intensive industries developed around Tokyo. By 1980 the number of prefectures with per capita income lagging Tokyo by more than 50 percent had again risen to twelve.

In the early 1980s, to counteract this widening gap, the Ministry of International Trade and Industry planned technopolises in dispersed locations (Tatsuno 1986; Morris-Suzuki 1991). Like Silicon Valley and Research Triangle Park in the United States, these growth centers of high-tech activities in production and research were to take pressure off of Tokyo, where land prices and congestion costs were soaring. Planners hoped to improve local human capital and to transfer technology to indigenous firms. In a process reminiscent of the new industrial cities effort twenty years earlier, politics expanded the number of cities designated by the ministry from the one or two first envisioned to a dozen and then to twenty-six. The central government ultimately awarded a technopolis designation to virtually every city with a population of more than 150,000 (Glasmeier 1988).

Unlike the earlier effort, responsibility for the development of these cities rested with local governments (Stohr 1985). The central government contributed principally with tax incentives to attract firms to the technopolises. Some analysts believe that the ministry intentionally leveraged local public sector resources by creating competition among prefectures, similar to that between U.S. states and localities (Glasmeier 1988). Many prefectural governments responded to the challenge by creating full-scale economic development organizations and borrowing heavily to provide infrastructure and develop land.

Results to date are disappointing (Markusen, Sasaki, and Funaba 1995; Sasaki 1991; Morris-Suzuki 1991). Some technopolises have barely gotten off the ground. Others are drawing economic activity from city centers to suburbs (Higashi-Hiroshima). Some attracted branch plants of large corporations, but largely in routine production rather than leading-edge research with growth potential (Markusen and Sasaki 1995). A few have built new industrial concentrations with indigenous businesses and entrepreneurship (Masser 1990; Tatsuno 1986). But cities not awarded technopolis status have restructured based on small- and medium-size businesses (Sasaki 1989; Kitayama 1993).

Some companies that might have left Japan altogether, however, did not. Companies that considered offshore sites for the manufacture of integrated circuits in the 1980s found in the technopolises—temporarily at least—alternatives to the high-cost Tokyo region (Fujita 1991; Sasaki 1991). The policy also spread the burden of infrastructure creation from central to local government (Glasmeier 1988). And because technopolises are located principally in suburbs, the strategy furthers national goals to expand domestic demand by increasing housing and automobile consumption (Markusen, Sasaki, and Funaba 1995).

Still, Tokyo dominates. Through the 1980s the greater Tokyo region generated a disproportionate share of new employment. Japan's fastest-growing industrial cities are concentrated in the corridor from Osaka to Tokyo (Funaba 1993). And new plants in the technopolises closest to Tokyo have grown faster than those farther away (Stohr and Ponighaus 1992).

Several causes explain the weak impact of Japanese regional policies. First, resources have been insufficient. Unlike Korea, Japan has not built and operated dispersed industrial complexes nor forced companies to locate in them (Glickman 1979; Samuels 1983). Second, both major efforts were diminished because politics spread resources thinly over too many areas. Third, the government sent mixed messages to the private sector. The construction of Tsukuba Science City close to Tokyo eliminated the possibility of a stand-alone research growth pole like the U.S. Silicon Valley (Takeuchi 1991). By the end of the 1980s Tsukuba hosted forty-six national research organizations (32 percent of the national total), accounted for 45 percent of the national research budget, and had attracted a sizable share of corporate research and development labs (Sasaki 1991). Thus public, quasi-public, and private research and development organizations remain concentrated in the greater Tokyo region (Toda 1987).

Furthermore, the Japanese government also sought to establish Tokyo as a cosmopolitan city in the 1980s, with investments and regulations centering financial, cultural, and political functions in Tokyo. This showcasing of Tokyo hampered other cities from competing for international business and financial services (Kamo 1991).

Finally, the efficiency concerns of industrial policy have dominated public investment allocation. The current commitment to high technology, emphasizing innovation and human capital, is hardly compatible with decentralization. The lack of resources for regional development may reflect a government belief that dispersal would reduce the efficiency and performance of Japanese industry, and Japanese companies appear to agree based on their decisions to locate. Mera (1986) found central government investment to be geographically correlated with private sector investment, with only a slight bias toward spatial redistribution over much of the postwar period.

Despite these centripetal forces economic activity in Japan may disperse somewhat over the next few decades. Congestion and costs have increased in Tokyo, and communications technologies may reduce the need for face-to-face business and eliminate the handicap of firms in the provinces. Whether this will encourage the growth of suburbs around urban areas, as in the past two decades, or spur growth by more distant Japanese cities remains to be seen.

The United States: Informal Industrial Policy as Regional Policy

The United States has had little formal industrial or regional policy and might at first glance be considered a test case of the distribution resulting from private forces. In the United States diseconomies of scale appear to have reversed centripetal forces. Over the past several decades economic activity has shifted away from the major industrial regions—the bipolar manufacturing belt stretched around New York and Chicago—toward the south and west. Los Angeles has overtaken Chicago as the nation's "second city," and by 1990 metropolitan employment in Los Angeles exceeded that of New York (Markusen and Gwiasda 1994). Large cities lost ground to medium-size cities. Of the thirty-six metropolitan areas that added manufacturing employment at rates of 50 percent or more between 1970 and 1990, only two were in the old industrial belt. Since the late nineteenth century, moreover, regional per capita income differentials have diminished dramatically as southern incomes have risen and midwestern incomes have fallen toward the national norm (Markusen 1987).

But the United States has practiced both regional and industrial policy under different names, and these policies have affected the spatial distribution of economic activity, helping to create the fluid, multipolar system that now exists. Formal regional policy has promoted industry in underdeveloped but populated regions with exhausted mining or agricultural resources. The New Deal of the 1930s developed river basins, such as the Tennessee River Authority experiment, combining resource management (flood control and soil conservation) with power development to create conditions for industrialization. In the 1960s area redevelopment programs, such as the Appalachian Regional Commission effort, invested in infrastructure and human resources to create urban growth poles. Recent evaluations found the efforts of both the 1930s and the 1960s to be successful (Isserman and Rephann 1993; Gray and Johnson 1991).

More important, informal regional policy embedded in the U.S. federal structure has helped to disperse national development resources (Markusen 1990, 1994a; Friedmann and Bloch 1990). First, Congress allocates resources for infrastructure and other public investments, and representation is strongly territorialized. Regional caucuses work together for their states and regions, regardless of party distinction. Some have spun off research institutes such as the Northeast-Midwest Institute. Congressional committees distribute funds for highways, education, public works, urban and rural development, and defense installations and contracts, preempting the functions of a central regional planning bureaucracy.

Second, state and local governments have the responsibility and tax power to be active agents for economic development. Local groups with a stake in the regional economy levy demands on the national government through congressional representatives and mobilize local resources for infrastructure, business incentives, and human capital development. As cities and regions compete for business, increased resources are devoted to these efforts, redistributing resources from local taxpayers to business investment and income, potentially resulting in excess capacity.

The urban hierarchy remains flatter in the United States than in other countries because major urban functions are not concentrated in a single primate city but are distributed among several of the largest cities. New York is the financial capital of the country; Washington, D.C., the political capital; Chicago, the industrial capital; Boston, the educational capital; Los Angeles, the military industrial capital; and San Jose, the high-tech capital. New York is thus not a global city in the same sense that Tokyo or London is (Markusen and Gwiasda 1994). The decentralization of major urban functions in this national system of cities has contributed significantly to amelioration of regional income differentials, but it may also be inefficient in an increasingly integrated world economy.

Competition among urban areas also offers would-be entrepreneurs and youthful industries a choice among locations. When large monopolies or oligopolies encumber the resource markets of urban agglomerations, other sites are available. Pittsburgh and Detroit declined because their steel and auto companies dominated regional business culture, wages, labor practices, land-use patterns, and the supply of capital for small business. This repelled new, diversified business activity (Chinitz 1960; Markusen 1985).

The informal regional policy in the United States may have enhanced efficiency, offered extraordinarily good channels for democratic participation, and shifted economic activity to peripheral regions. It has not, however, facilitated long-term regional planning or interregional equity (Markusen 1994a).

Informal industrial policy has been a more powerful regional developer in the postwar United States. Since World War II the U.S. government has devoted 5 to 7 percent of gross national product (GNP) to military preparedness. The cold war shifted priorities toward a set of capabilities—airborne, nuclear, automated, remote control—that nurtured the aircraft, communications, computing, and electronics industries (Markusen 1991b). Preparedness policy, organized in the Pentagon, encompassed every aspect of industrial policy as practiced in Japan and Europe: research and development commitments, long-term procurement contracts, investment guarantees, and bailouts for failing corporations (Markusen 1986).

Although the policy was undoubtedly inefficient, it created top-performing export industries. Sectors like computers and semiconductors depended on federal dollars for research and development support through the late 1950s, and government sales made up more than 70 percent of their revenues, though commercial sales later dwarfed military sales. Others, such as aircraft and communications equipment, depend on the public sector for more than half their sales, as well for the lion's share of their research and development funds (Markusen and Yudken 1992).

For complex reasons, these high peacetime military commitments encouraged a dramatic spatial restructuring of U.S. industry. First, the military-industrial capacity initiated during World War II expanded with aircraft and missile production during the cold war. Fears of vulnerability to long-range bombers brought military production to interior cities like Wichita, St. Louis, Dallas, and Fort Collins both during the war and through the 1950s. Second, military officers responsible for siting military installations and awarding contracts had discretionary power to favor cities and regions. The Air Force, for example, has favored the west. Third, local business groups, especially from California and other parts of the west, lobbied successfully to obtain a disproportionate share of military plants, bases, and contracts. The mature manufacturing belt—the nation's military outfitter for tanks, trucks, guns, ordinance, and ammunition—lost share. The outstanding exception is New England, whose decline in traditional industries began in the 1950s. New England successfully reoriented existing capacity to serve the cold war (Markusen 1991a; Markusen and others 1991).

The "gunbelt" rose, to some extent, because the business culture in the industrial heartland was dedicated to commercial markets and antagonistic to government oversight, repelling cold war–related military industrial activity. Furthermore, when military contracts shifted toward the gunbelt in the 1950s after the Korean war, industrial belt firms enjoyed vigorous demand both from pent-up consumers savings and from Japan and Europe for industrial goods to be used in reconstruction (Markusen and others 1991).

The informal industrial policy practiced by the Pentagon thus acted as a powerful regional policy, revitalizing New England and shifting population and manufacturing activity toward the south and west. Social goals showed mixed results. First, regional differentials in per capita income narrowed as high-wage employment came to enclaves in the south and southwest, and incomes in the industrial belt fell. However, the west, the mountain states, and New England continued to enjoy per capita incomes about 20 percent above the national average (Markusen and others 1991). Furthermore, prosperity from military-industrial activity in the south and southwest concentrated in enclaves (Huntsville, Titusville-Melbourne, Colorado Springs, and Albuquerque), doing little for the vast regions of rural poverty in those states (Glickman and Glasmeier 1989).

Second, military industrial expenditures helped to seed new government-oriented industrial complexes removed from the heartland region, where business cultures and practices had been shaped by oligopolistic Fordism. As a result, places like Los Angeles, Colorado Springs, Orange County, Seattle, and Silicon Valley remain highly dependent on defense spending, although Seattle and Silicon Valley have sprouted commercial businesses from military industries that are higher-tech, more flexible, and better positioned on the international market. What would have happened in the absence of cold war spending is unclear, but at least two caveats apply. High-tech industries in European countries did not require spatial separation from older industries for success. And the spatial separation of high-tech industries from older commercial sectors leaves both regions more vulnerable to political and business cycles.

Third, the buildup of the gunbelt created an internal brain drain from industrial states with better educational systems to outlying areas (Ellis, Barff, and Markusen 1993; Campbell 1993). The regions of exit, like Chicago, Boston, and New York, suffered the loss of technical labor and innovative capacity (Markusen and McCurdy 1988). Moreover, the separation of scientists and engineers in military centers from their business counterparts reduced cross-fertilization (Markusen and Yudken 1992).

For the nation as a whole, scarce resources were used on infrastructure in new centers, while infrastructure in some older industrial cities was underutilized.

Other public investments forgone because of military spending could have enhanced private sector productivity. Furthermore, the regional bias in defense expenditures created constituencies determined to maintain military-industrial complexes and high levels of expenditure even though the cold war is over (Markusen and others 1991).

Conclusion

Industrial policy has shown compatibility with regional policy in the four countries under review, though this is less the case for innovation-intensive export sectors. In the 1960s and 1970s Brazil, Korea, and Japan invested in smaller cities and underdeveloped regions when possible. Most successful were industries based on resources and traditional manufactured goods for either the domestic or export market. In the United States military strategy replaced formal industrial and regional policy, encouraging the development of high-tech enclaves remote from existing industrial regions.

Regional policy achievements of the 1960s and 1970s were modest in all countries but the United States. The dominant national cities of São Paulo, Seoul, and Tokyo essentially maintained their shares of employment and industrial output. In each country, however, a number of smaller industrial cities—typically beneficiaries of industrial and regional policy efforts—have grown faster than the dominant national cities. But many of these smaller cities are close to the dominant city. And in each country many outlying regions remain well below national standards of per capita income, though the gaps diminished in all four countries and regional growth rate differentials lessened. Urban hierarchies flattened somewhat, offering more options to firms searching for locations.

Over the past fifteen years, tensions have increased between industrial and regional policy efforts in all four countries. World markets have integrated, world economic growth has slowed, and government resources have diminished. Trade integration has both heightened the tendency toward larger within-nation growth differentials and prompted increased specialization (Markusen, Noponen, and Driessen 1991; Howes and Markusen 1994). All four nations have turned to high-tech industrial policies. Because high-tech industries are youthful, reliant on external services, and subject to rapid rates of innovation, they tend to locate in the major centers of innovation and diversified economic activity where agglomeration economies can be realized (Markusen, Hall, and Glasmeier 1986). Government investments are reinforcing this tendency, and per capita income gaps between regions are widening.

As the tension between industrial and regional policies grows, governments have favored industrial policy and have increasingly left responsibility for development with local and provincial governments. This is the case in all four countries. Although some localities and regions will succeed and economic activity will disperse, the more well-endowed regions and those closer to national core regions are likely to be the most successful.

Decentralized regional policy may be more efficient in determining industrial location. It is not easy for central governments to gauge scale and agglomeration economies or diseconomies as they try to balance regional and industrial policies.[4] Letting provincial and local governments deploy infrastructure and incentives creates a quasi market, but the efficiency gains may be only short term. Central government commitment to building detached complexes—taking into account optimal complex size, interindustry economies, and public infrastructure utilization rates—is a more far-sighted policy. Substituting decentralization for centrally designed regional policy is apt to neglect equity goals as uneven development occurs.

Continued reliance on high-tech industrial policy and decentralized regional economic development appears inevitable, however, as long as slower growth, fiscal constraints, and pressure for public sector austerity restrict available resources. Brazil is the only country poised for a resurgence of growth. Nonetheless, for political and economic reasons regional policy remains a legitimate sphere of action for central government in all four countries. Politically strong democratic institutions demand regional inclusiveness. Equity and long-term efficiency considerations argue for a dispersed and robust system of cities. Policies that stabilize communities are also important. Bolton (1988) finds welfare and efficiency gains from respecting a "sense of place," which he argues is an economic asset. Yet as world market integration proceeds, all cities and regions must specialize and trade to maintain employment and grow (Howes and Markusen 1993). Major shake-ups in national urban systems and regional fortunes may generate new pressures for centrally designed regional policies.

Improving regional equity while minimizing costs to industrial policies will be the challenge for regional policy. Success will require more research on agglomeration economies disaggregated by sector. Empirical attempts to determine optimal city size have failed by operating on too aggregate a scale. Good policy requires knowledge of the number of national automobile (or computer or aircraft) plants the world market can support. Planners should take into account the degree to which capacity can be decentralized in each industry without sacrificing efficiency.

Notes

1. An empirical test of this proposition failed to confirm that coastal cities in the United States benefited disproportionately from heightened international trade activity (Noponen, Driessen, and Markusen 1995).

2. This is also true in the European case, not discussed in this article. See Bachtler and Michie (1993); Peschel (1992); and Vanhove and Klassen (1987).

3. For the debate on the efficacy of Japanese industrial policy, see Friedman (1988), Johnson (1982), and Samuels (1987).

4. A number of scholars have argued that large cities are efficient (Alonso 1991; Mera 1977), but few sector-specific studies have been done to assess the significance of agglomeration economies.

References

Abe, H., and J. D. Alden. 1988. "Regional Development Planning in Japan." *Regional Studies* 22 (5): 429–38.

Albrechts, L., F. Moulert, P. Roberts, and E. Swyngedouw, eds. 1989. *Regional Policy at the Crossroads: European Perspectives.* London: Jessica Kingsley Publishers.

Alonso, William. 1991. "Europe's Urban System and Its Peripheries." *Journal of the American Planning Association* 57 (1): 6–13.

Amsden, Alice. 1989. *Asia's Next Giant: South Korea and Late Industrialization.* New York: Oxford University Press.

Azzoni, Carlos Robert. 1986. *Industria e Reversao da Polarizacao no Brasil.* São Paulo: IPE-USP.

Bachtler, John, and Rona Michie. 1993. "The Restructuring of Regional Policy in the European Community." *Regional Studies* 27 (8): 719–25.

Baer, Werner. 1978. *Dimensoes do Desenvolvimento Brasileiro.* Rio de Janeiro: Campus.

Bolton, Roger. 1988. "An Economic Interpretation of a 'Sense of Place.'" Working paper. Williams College, Department of Economics, Williamstown, Mass.

Campbell, Scott. 1993. "Interregional Migration of Defense Scientists and Engineers to the Gunbelt during the 1980s." *Economic Geography* 69 (2): 204–23.

Cano, Wilson. 1977. *Raizes da Concentracao Industrial em São Paulo.* São Paulo: Difel.

———. 1985. *Disequilibrios Regionais e Concentracao Industrial no Brasil.* São Paulo: Global.

Cavalcanti, Clovis. 1981. *Nordeste do Brasil: Um Desenvolvimento Conturbado.* Recife, Brazil: FJN/Massangana.

Chinitz, Benjamin. 1960. "Contrasts in Agglomeration: New York and Pittsburgh." American Economic Association, *Papers and Proceedings* 40: 279–89.

Choe, S. C., and B. N. Song. 1984. "An Evaluation of Urban Decentralization in Seoul Region." *Journal of Environmental Studies* 4: 73–116. (Seoul).

Diniz, Clelio Campolina. 1994. "Polygonized Development in Brazil: Neither Decentralization nor Continued Polarization." *International Journal of Urban and Regional Research* 18: 293–314.

Diniz, Clelio Campolina, and Mohamad Razavi. 1993. "Emergence of New Industrial Districts in Brazil: São Jose dos Campos and Campinas Cases." Working paper. Universidad Federal de Minas Gerais, CEDEPLAR, Belo Horizonte, Brazil.

Ellis, Mark, Richard Barff, and Ann Markusen. 1993. "Defense Spending and Interregional Labor Migration." *Economic Geography* 29 (2): 1–22.

Friedman, David. 1988. *Misunderstood Miracle: Industrial Development and Political Change in Japan.* Ithaca, N.Y.: Cornell University Press.

Friedmann, John. 1972. "A General Theory of Polarized Development." In Niles Hansen, ed., *Growth Centers in Regional Economic Development.* New York: Free Press.

Friedmann, John, and Robin Bloch. 1990. "American Exceptionalism in Regional Planning, 1933–2000." *International Journal of Urban and Regional Research* 14 (4): 576–601.

Fujita, Kuniko. 1991. "The Technopolis: High Technology and Regional Development in Japan." *International Journal of Urban and Regional Research* 15: 566–94.

Funaba, Masatomi. 1993. "The Changing Face of Regional Economic Structure and the Formation of New Industrial Regions in Japan." Working paper. Kobe University of Commerce.

Glasmeier, Amy. 1988. "The Japanese Technopolis Programme: High-Tech Development Strategy or Industrial Policy in Disguise?" *International Journal of Urban and Regional Research* 12 (2): 268–84.

Glickman, Norman. 1979. *The Growth and Management of the Japanese Urban System.* Baltimore, Md.: Johns Hopkins University Press.

Glickman, Norman, and Amy Glasmeier. 1989. "The International Economy and the American South." In Lloyd Rodwin and Hidehiko Sazanami, eds., *Deindustrialization and Regional Economic Transformation: The Experience of the United States.* Boston: Unwin Hyman.

Granovetter, Mark. 1985. "Economic Action and Social Structure: The Problem of Embeddedness." *American Journal of Sociology* 91: 481–510.

Gray, Aelred, and David Johnson. 1991. "TVA's Regional Development Planning: The First Twenty Years." Paper presented at the American Collegiate Schools of Planning and Associated European Schools of Planning International Congress, July, Oxford, England.

Guimaraes-Neto, Leonard. 1986. *Nordeste: Da Articulacao Comercial a Integracao Economica.* Campinas, Brazil: UNICAMP.

Haddad, Paulo. 1989. "Os Padroes Locacionais das Atividades de Alta Tecnologia: A Questao dos Desequilibrios Regionais de Desenvolvimento Reexaminada." Paper presented at the Seminario Revolución Tecnólogica y Reestruturación Productiva: Impactos e Desafíos Territoriales. Santiago, Chile.

Hall, Peter, and Paschal Preston. 1988. *The Carrier Wave: New Information Technology and the Geography of Innovation, 1846-2003*. London: Unwin Hyman.

Howes, Candace, and Ann Markusen. 1993. "Trade, Industry and Economic Development." In Helzi Noponen, Julie Graham, and Ann Markusen, eds., *Trading Industries, Trading Regions.* New York: Guilford Press.

———. 1994. "Industrial Strategy and Economic Growth: What the U.S. Can Learn From Japan." Working paper. Rutgers University, Project on Regional and Industrial Economics, New Brunswick, N.J.

Igarashi, Tomiei. 1991. *Chiiki kasseika no hasso* (Visions for Revitalizing Regional Development). Tokyo: Gakuyo Shobo.

Isserman, Andrew, and Terance Rephann. 1993. "The Economic Effects of the Appalachian Regional Commission: An Emphemeral Assessment of 27 Years of Regional Development Policy." Research paper 9328. University of West Virginia, Regional Research Institute, Morgantown.

Jee, Man Won. 1991. *Whither the Korean Military?* Seoul: K. Y. Son.

Johnson, Chalmers. 1982. *MITI and the Japanese Miracle: The Growth of Industrial Policy, 1925–75.* Palo Alto, Calif.: Stanford University Press.

Kaldor, Nicholas. 1970. "The Case for Regional Policies." *Scottish Journal of Political Economy* 17: 337–48.

Kamo, Toshio. 1991. "The Tokyo Problem as a 'Japan Problem.'" Paper prepared for the conference on New York, Tokyo, and Paris: Nodes in the Global System of Cities, 1950–2020,October 14–15, Tokyo.

Kitayama, Toshiya. 1993. "Local Governments and Small and Medium-Sized Enterprises." EDI Working Paper 93-38. World Bank, Economic Development Institute, Washington, D.C.

Krugman, Paul. 1993. "Toward a Counter-Counterrevolution in Development Theory." In Lawrence Summers and Shekhar Shah, eds., *Proceedings of the World Bank Annual Conference on Development Economics 1992.* Washington, D.C.

Lee, M.W., ed. 1991. *Regional Economy of Korea.* Seoul: Korea Institute for Industrial Economics and Trade.

Lee, Y. S. 1988. "The Role of Government in Trade and Industrialization of Korea." Working paper. Korea Institute for Economics and Technology, Seoul.

Markusen, Ann. 1985. *Profit Cycles, Oligopoly and Regional Development.* Cambridge, Mass.: MIT Press.

———. 1986. "Defense Spending: A Successful Industrial Policy?" *International Journal of Urban and Regional Research* 10 (1): 105–22.

———. 1987. *Regions: The Economics and Politics of Territory.* Totowa, N.J.: Rowman and Allenheld.

———. 1990. "Regional Planning and Policy: An Essay on the American Exception." In Edward Bergman and Uwe Schubert, eds., *Comparative Regional Research: Setting the Post-1992 Agenda.* Hannover, Germany: FRG Urbinno.

———. 1991a. "Government as Market: Industrial Location in the U.S. Defense Industry." In Henry Herzog and Allan Schlottman, eds., *Industry Location and Public Policy.* Knoxville: University of Tennessee Press.

———. 1991b. "The Military Industrial Divide: Cold War Transformation of the Economy and the Rise of New Industrial Complexes." *Space and Society* 9 (4): 391–416.

———. 1994a. "American Federalism and Regional Policy: An Essay on Political Structure and Economic Performance." *International Regional Science Review* 16 (1): 3–15.

———. 1994b. "The Interaction of Regional and Industrial Policies: Evidence from Four Countries (Korea, Brazil, Japan and the United States)." Working paper 66. Rutgers University, Center for Urban Policy Research, New Brunswick, N.J.

Markusen, Ann, and Vickie Gwiasda. 1994. "Multi-Polarity and the Layering of Functions in World Cities: New York City's Struggle to Stay on Top." *The International Journal of Urban and Regional Research* 18 (2): 167–93.

Markusen, Ann, and Karen McCurdy. 1988. "Chicago's Defense-Based High Technology: A Case Study of the 'Seedbeds of Innovation' Hypothesis." *Economic Development Quarterly* 3 (1): 15–31.

Markusen, Ann, and Sam Ock Park. 1993. "The State as Industrial Locator and District Builder: The Case of Changwon, South Korea." *Economic Geography* 69 (2): 157–81.

Markusen, Ann, and Masayuki Sasaki. 1995. "Satellite New Industrial Districts: A Comparative Study of United States and Japanese Cases." Working paper. Rutgers University, Project on Regional and Industrial Economics, New Brunswick, N.J.

Markusen, Ann, and Joel Yudken. 1992. *Dismantling the Cold War Economy.* New York: Basic Books.

Markusen, Ann, Helzi Noponen, and Karl Driessen. 1991. "International Trade, Productivity and Regional Growth." *International Regional Science Review* 14 (1): 15–40.

Markusen, Ann, Masayuki Sasaki, and Masatomi Funaba. 1995. "Japanese Technology Policy: A Reinterpretation." Working paper. Rutgers University, Project on Regional and Industrial Economics, New Brunswick, N.J.

Markusen, Ann, Peter Hall, Sabina Deitrick, and Scott Campbell. 1991. *The Rise of the Gunbelt.* New York: Oxford University Press.

Masser, Ian. 1990. "Technology and Regional Development Policy: A Review of Japan's Technopolis Programme." *Regional Studies* 24 (1): 41–53.

Mera, Koichi. 1977. "The Changing Pattern of Population Distribution in Japan and Its Implications for Developing Countries." *Habitat International* 2: 455–79.

———. 1986. "Population Stabilization and National Spatial Policy of Public Investment: The Japanese Experience." *International Regional Science Review* 10 (1): 47–65.

Morris-Suzuki, T. 1991. "The MFP and the Japanese Development Model." In G. McCormack, ed., *Bonsai Australia Banzai: Multifunctionpolis and the Making of a Special Relationship with Japan.* Leichhardt, NSW, Australia: Pluto Press.

Myrdal, Gunnar. 1957. *Economic Theory and Underdeveloped Regions.* London: Duckworth.

Noponen, Helzi, Karl Driessen, and Ann Markusen. 1995. "Trade and American Cities: Who Has the Comparative Advantage?" Working paper. Rutgers University, Project on Regional and Industrial Economics, New Brunswick, N.J.

Park, Sam Ock. 1990. "Government Management of Industrial Change in the Republic of Korea." in D. C. Rich and G. J. R. Linge, eds., *The State and Management of Industrial Change.* London: Routledge.

———. 1991. "High-Technology Industries in Korea: Spatial Linkages and Policy Implications." *Geoform* 22 (4): 421–31.

Park, Sam Ock, and Ann Markusen. Forthcoming. "Generalizing New Industrial Districts: A Theoretical Agenda and an Application from a Non-Western Economy." *Environment and Planning.*

Peschel, Karin. 1992. "European Integration and Regional Development in Northern Europe." *Regional Studies* 26 (4): 387–97.

Republic of Korea, National Bureau of Statistics, Economic Planning Board. 1981 and 1986. "Establishment Census." Seoul.

———. 1984 and 1987. "Employment Structure Survey." Seoul.

———. 1963, 1975, and 1984. "Statistical Report of Manufacturing and Mining Industry." Seoul.

Richardson, Harry. 1980. "Polarization Reversal in Developing Countries." *Papers of the Regional Science Association* 45: 67–85.

Samuels, Richard. 1983. *The Politics of Regional Policy in Japan.* Princeton University Press.

———. 1987. *The Business of the Japanese State.* Ithaca, N.Y.: Cornell University Press.

Sasaki, Masayuki. 1989. "Endogenous Development of the Urban Economy in Kanazawa City." Paper presented at Asia Areas Exchange International Symposium, October 14–15, Kanazawa, Japan.

———. 1991. "Japan, Australia and the Multifunctionpolis." In McCormack G., ed., B*onsai Australia Banzai: Multifunctionpolis and the Making of a Special Relationship with Japan.* Leichhardt, NSW, Australia: Pluto Press.

Schoenberger, Erica. 1985. "Foreign Manufacturing Investment in the United States: Competitive Strategies and International Location." *Economic Geography* 61 (3): 241–59.

Song, B. N. 1990. *The Rise of the Korean Economy.* New York: Oxford University Press.

Stohr, Walter. 1985. "Regional Technological and Institutional Innovation: The Case of the Japanese Technopolis Policy." Discussion Paper 26. Interdisziplinäres Institut für Raumordnung Stadt- und Regionalentwicklung Wirtschaftsuniversität, Wien, Austria.

Stohr, Walter, and Richard Ponighaus. 1992. "Towards a Data-Based Evaluation of the Japanese Technopolis Policy: The Effect of New Technological and Organizational Infrastructure on Urban and Regional Development." *Regional Studies* 26 (7): 605–18.

Storper, Michael. 1991. *Industrialization, Economic Development and the Regional Question in the Third World: From Import Substitution to Flexible Production.* London: Pion.

Takeuchi, Atsuhiko, 1991. "Spatial Conflicts Arising from the Restructuring of Japanese Industry." In G. J. R. Linge and D. C. Rich, eds., *The State and the Spatial Management of Industrial Change.* London and New York: Routledge.

Tatsuno S. 1986. *The Technopolis Strategy: Japan, High Technology and the Control of the Twenty-First Century.* New York: Prentice Hall.

Toda, T. 1987. "The Location of High-Technology Industry and the Technopolis Plan in Japan." In J. F. Brotchie, P. Hall, and P. W. Newton, eds., *The Spatial Impact of Technological Change.* London: Croom Helm.

Townroe, Peter, and David Keen. 1984. "Polarization Reversal in the State of São Paulo, Brazil." *Regional Studies* 18 (1): 45–54.

Tsuya, Norikio and Toshio Kuroda. 1989. "Japan: the Slowing of Urbanization and Metropolitan Concentration." In A. G. Champion, ed., *Counterurbanization: The Changing Pace and Nature of Population Deconcentration.* London: Edward Arnold.

Vanhove, Norbert, and Leo Klaassen. 1987. *Regional Policy: A European Approach.* 2nd ed. Aldershot: Avebury.

Comment on "Interaction between Regional and Industrial Policies: Evidence from Four Countries," by Markusen

William Alonso

Markusen's analysis of regional policy and its tension with industrial policy in four countries is dense with information and reasonable in its judgments. Along with the tensions between the vertical industrial and horizontal regional policies, Markusen takes up two classic themes of regional planning at the national level: urban size and income disparity among regions. These two issues are often linked but present distinct policy problems. I will focus the first part of my comments on the issue of city size.

Primate cities (often capital cities) are viewed in equivocal and contradictory ways. Because they are big, congested, and polluted they are seen as wasteful, inefficient, and parasitic. And because of positive externalities and agglomeration economies, they are viewed as too rich and as obstacles to interregional equity.

Nobody knows how big is too big or how small is too small. Indeed, it is not clear how city size should be measured, although population and, more rarely, gross domestic product are used. Discussions of urban size often compare static instances. But urban size is a dynamic, historical process; it evolves with technology, national and international developments, and many other variables. Moreover, if a right size could be determined, for whom would the size be right? Under certain conditions the optimal size for the inhabitants of the city would be too small for the nation as a whole (Alonso 1971). Stockholm provides an example. When the European Community was taking shape, Stockholm seemed too big (the actual size and perception may be little related), and plans were made to control its growth. But Sweden abandoned these plans when it considered the competitive position of Stockholm in the face of the increasingly integrated constellation of major cities in Europe.

Concerns about excessive size may be unfounded, yet it is useful to consider the effectiveness of policies aimed at stopping or reversing growth. Sometimes growth-pole and cognate policies can induce growth elsewhere, but relative to the size of the primate city the diversion is trivial. From Moscow to London and Paris and from Lagos to Jakarta, policies to stop growth have proved ineffective. In short, half a century of experience shows the modest ability of policy to control primacy.

William Alonso is Saltonstall Professor of Population Policy, Department of Sociology, Harvard University.

Markusen discusses the formation of an economically dynamic polygon formed by cities a few hundred miles from São Paulo, Brazil's primate city. Such an adaptation to the problems of size is not uncommon, and variants of it are evident in Korea and Japan in Markusen's examples, as well as in Indonesia and Mexico. Primate cities in those countries have adapted to the diseconomics of urban size by extending their urban fields to include subcenters, thus sustaining economies of scale, agglomeration, and urbanization, while reducing congestion, pollution, and land rents. New York and Los Angeles also have adapted this way. In all these cases, varying mixes of market forces and policy interventions have encouraged this "polynucleation." Because large cities can usually adapt this way, it is important to keep issues of primacy and issues of interregional equity separate. Policies to address regional equity disparities would be more effective if they would focus on the problems and opportunities of the target regions rather than on the question of city size.

An interesting demographic issue that Markusen does not address is the low or falling fertility rates in the four countries examined. The fertility rate in Japan is among the world's lowest—only two-thirds of generational replacement; in the United States the fertility rate is 20 percent below replacement, with some regions even lower. Fertility rates in Korea have fallen rapidly with economic development, and Brazil also has experienced a rapid fall in fertility, especially in urban areas. Brazil may find that some of its concerns about the geographic concentration of population will be overtaken by demographic realities.

These new demographics complicate the issue of primacy, especially perceptions based on population. The picture is also complicated greatly by international migrations from poor to rich countries—European countries and the United States are gravely concerned about the social, political, and economic effects of legal and illegal migrants and of a growing number of refugees. Japan, which has long anticipated labor shortages, has moved vigorously to automate industry and encourages foreign investment for exporting capital and technology. Even so, this most racially homogeneous of countries now countenances some half-million illegal immigrants and is hesitantly considering importing temporary labor. The great urban concentrations of Europe, the United States, and Japan will be the first to experience population decline stemming from low fertility; they will also receive the bulk of the international migratory flows. Recent outbreaks of xenophobia suggest that social and political problems of ethnic diversity may add an unfortunate dimension to future discussions of primacy.

Markusen does address the tendency away from centralized regional planning and toward responsibility by provinces or states. Such devolution is an implicit regional policy. It may be merely a way for the central government to save money and wash regional problems off its hands. But it can also reduce the centripetal tendencies of central planning that arise from attempts to reduce transaction costs (see Krugman in this volume). It will also increase the geographic pull of provincial capitals. The consequences of devolution should be examined alongside policies of privatization and unbundling of public services such as infrastructure.

Markusen notes that regional policies are often implicit; that they may be undertaken for reasons of industrial development, foreign trade, or defense, but they influence regional development. She highlights the policy shift from traditional, materials-based industries to high-tech, information-based industries. Older, materials-based production now migrates to emerging economies, while new high-tech industries (many in the service sector) develop in industrial countries.

Markusen observes, as have others, that one of the most common regional policy strategies is to encourage the dispersal of mature industries to less-developed regions, accelerating market tendencies for mature industries to trade agglomeration economies—particularly useful in the early stages of their development—for lower costs at other locations.

With trade and production becoming internationalized, however, transitional industries may move to other countries. At the same time, new, information-based industries appear to be attracted to urbanization and agglomeration economies. Thus internationalization and the shift to information-based economies threaten regional policy based on innovation-diffusion strategies. The analysis is plausible, but more research is needed. Markusen deserves credit for advancing the research agenda.

There is an asymmetry in our understanding of the pattern of location of both types of industry. For materials-based industry we have some theories and many detailed case and industry studies. For information-based industries we have only anecdotes and unsubstantiated claims that these industries are sensitive to urbanization and agglomeration economies. We do not even have, in these rapidly evolving sectors, good categories in the standard industrial classification system or measures of productivity or value added—much less an input-output framework for the analysis of forward and backward links. Examples that expose our ignorance are not hard to find. How can we confirm the repeated references (not just in Markusen's article) to the geographic concentration needs of high-tech industries when the largest and most successful software company, Microsoft, is in Redmond, Washington, or when U.S. companies contract programmers in India and keyboard operators in the Philippines? As information technology grows, the tyranny of distance and the friction of space disappear. Yet we continue to see the agglomerative forces of information-based activities as overwhelming.

We currently know little about who does what, with what, in information-based industries. Selecting a location as an act of choosing may be less relevant for information-based industries than for materials-based industries. The growth and development of information-based industries may depend far more on innovation and entrepreneurship—so that industry is not so much located as it is grown in place. If our theories of location for such industries are poor, our theories of innovation and entrepreneurship are more so.

Finally, Markusen rightly stresses the tension between regional and industrial policies. Macroeconomic policies create additional tension. I agree with Markusen that regional policies often lose to competing policies. I have thought a great deal about why that happens, and I think that the velocities and rhythms of the various policies are part of the reason. Macroeconomic policy moves fast, often with daily and even hourly rhythms. It demands constant attention. The rhythm of industrial policy may be quarterly, with some slower rhythms (capital investment) of a year or more. But the rhythms of regional change are much slower—measured in decades or more. Urban size and income disparities change slowly; it takes generations to develop a frontier region; national highway or regional water systems can take years just to design. Even when those in power are concerned with these three policy realms, the wheel that squeaks gets the grease. It is extremely difficult for the political process to remain focused on slow-moving issues, and that is one reason that regional policies are generally ineffective.

Regional policy also has been ineffective because it has so often been bad. Its concepts have often been vague, romantic, and metaphorical, based on fuzzy notions of balanced growth, anti-urban (or pro-urban) bias, utopian cities, and unrealistic attitudes toward the environment (whether exploitative or pantheistic). Too often policy has been shallowly voluntaristic, seeming to assume that the spatial distribution of economic activity was akin to rearranging the living room furniture—a matter of taste and display.

Regional policy should be understood as the territorial dimension of overall policy—the projection on the map of a multidimensional socioeconomic system. This territorial dimension matters, both for itself and for the functioning of the other dimensions of the system. This is the obverse of Markusen's observations on implicit regional policies: regional policies, if they are more than words and colored maps, have consequences for the other dimensions of the system. Regional planning will move from ineffectiveness and triviality only when it is formulated in light of this multidimensionality.

Reference

Alonso, William. 1971. "The Economics of Urban Size." *Papers of the Regional Science Association* 26: 67–83.

Comment on "Interaction between Regional and Industrial Policies: Evidence from Four Countries," by Markusen

Michael E. Porter

From different directions and traditions, there is a growing interest in the effect of location on competition and economic geography. From my work at the level of the firm and industry, I find in Markusen's article an opportunity to engage the literature on regional development. Especially since beginning research for my book *The Competitive Advantage of Nations,* I have been interested in how location affects competitive advantage and how firms choose headquarters locations from a strategic perspective.

This article is just one piece of a remarkable body of work by Markusen, and I agree with much of her work. Here I comment on six areas in which I believe her analysis could be sharpened and the literature as a whole extended.

The Scope of Agglomeration Economies

Markusen focuses on generalized urban agglomeration economies in areas such as infrastructure, communications, input access, and available market. I agree that such economies can be significant in developing countries with poor infrastructure, centralized institutions, and a heavy role for the central government. Many of these economies, however, are induced by government policy, not by the underlying economics. With development they should decline in importance. Moreover, as the costs of communications and of moving goods decline and access to distant markets becomes easier, the importance of generalized urban economies diminishes.

My research suggests that agglomeration economies at the cluster level influence competition more profoundly. A cluster is a group of industries connected by specialized buyer-supplier relationships or related by technologies or skills (Porter 1990). The cluster, not the individual industry, is the appropriate unit of analysis on empirical grounds and because externalities may be powerful among related industries.

Regionally concentrated clusters occur in both industrial and developing countries even though many countries, through regional policies, have worked against cluster formation. (Note that I use the word "region" as does Markusen to refer to

Michael E. Porter is C. Roland Christensen Professor of Business Administration at Harvard Business School.

Proceedings of the World Bank Annual Conference on Development Economics 1994

subunits of nations.) Detailed research, for example, has documented widespread regional clustering within Germany, India, Italy, Portugal, Spain, and the United States (Porter 1990; Porter, Ghemawat, and Rangan 1994; Monitor Company and Porter 1994; Monitor Company 1990).

Contrary to the implication in Markusen's article, clusters may not be associated with large cities. In Massachusetts, for example, a plastics cluster lies in the western part of the state, jewelry on the Rhode Island border (and across it), fiber optics around Sturbridge, and textiles and apparel near New Bedford and Fall River (Porter and Monitor Company 1991). In Germany, Italy, Portugal, and Spain clusters also are often located in small and medium-size towns. The phenomenon of regional clustering is highly developed in the United States, perhaps because it is a large economic area with few trade and investment restrictions and considerable homogeneity of language, culture, and laws.

The existence of regional clusters is well documented in case studies, but systematic empirical research is scarce (Enright 1990, Krugman 1991, and Henderson 1994 are the notable exceptions). Empirical research on the geographic distribution of industries and the prevalence of clustering within national economies is complicated by the existence of purely local industries (for example, real estate, retailing, utilities) and by the difficulty of distinguishing between "home bases"—the strategy and development centers for business units or product lines—and branch plants, sales offices, and distribution centers. The standard industrial classification system also confounds research because categories are overly broad, and industries in the same cluster may be assigned to different two-digit sectors. Moreover, data on corporate location patterns are limited and tend to include either all establishments or only the corporate headquarters, with almost nothing in between. Research is needed to distinguish between urban agglomeration economies and cluster agglomeration economies and to explore how both evolve with country development and government policy.

The Nature of Agglomeration Economies

The concept of agglomeration economies in Markusen's article and much of the literature is focused narrowly on static efficiencies such as economies of scale and access to inputs and markets. Following Hirschman (1958), the notion of backward and forward linkages is usually defined in terms of derived or induced demand.

Such agglomeration advantages are of diminishing importance in modern national and international competition. Access to distant markets has become less costly, so that many companies export early in their development, and sales outside the home state or province constitute the majority of many companies' sales. Sourcing inputs from disparate locations is now the rule. Indeed, since inputs can be efficiently provided from a distance, their availability at home no longer offers much competitive advantage. Input costs and other static efficiencies influence the location of branch plants and other activities sensitive to factor cost, but they influence the location of home bases for product lines and entire businesses much less. Home bases, as used here, consist of general management, core product and process development, and a critical mass of sophisticated production or service provision.

The most important agglomeration economies are dynamic rather than static efficiencies and revolve around the rate of learning and the capacity for innovation. Regional clusters grow because of concentrations of highly specialized knowledge, inputs, and institutions; the motivational benefits of local competition; and often the presence of sophisticated local demand for a product or service (Porter 1990). Geographic, cultural, and institutional proximity, which may not necessarily coincide with political boundaries, is integral to the rapid flow of highly applied knowledge and the motivational benefits of clusters.

Home bases for product lines tend to emerge and grow in the most favorable cluster locations. Firms gravitate to favorable cluster locations even if corporate ownership is based elsewhere. This preference for locations where there are already established clusters of firms in the same field helps explain why, for example, most world-class pharmaceutical companies have a major presence in the United States, especially around Philadelphia and New Jersey. It may be time to shed the term "agglomeration economies," because it obscures distinctions that are crucial for economic modeling and public policy.

The Extent of Agglomeration or Cluster Economies

Markusen argues that agglomeration effects (and growth potential) are largest for industries that are high-tech, knowledge-intensive, innovative, and young. She implies that developing countries need these industries because they support a higher standard of living.

Research on industrial and developing economies suggests that this perspective may be misleading. The productivity of an industry is what matters for standard of living. It is not what industries a nation or region competes in that most affects standard of living, but how it competes in them. Italy supports high wages in shoes and textiles, for example, whereas Holland and Denmark create high levels of wealth in agriculture. Most industries today can employ high technology and achieve high levels of knowledge intensity. These characteristics have less to do with industry or maturity than with the competitive environment.

Regional clusters often are a mixture of mature and emerging industries. In the Pittsburgh metropolitan area, for example, the large cluster in metal and materials processing includes not only steel companies but also companies producing process automation software and advanced process equipment. Young industries do not necessarily gravitate to big cities, as the examples of Austin, Texas; Salt Lake City, Utah; and Boulder, Colorado, indicate. Studies of developing countries with highly interventionist government policies may bias Markusen's view.

The Effectiveness of Targeting or Industry-Specific Intervention

Markusen seems to accept the notion that government targeting of particular industries is appropriate and effective. Given the fallacy of distinguishing types of industries, I believe that the whole premise of targeting industries is flawed. Instead, governments should upgrade all industries. Moreover, our research suggests that efforts to upgrade industry are most successful when they start from an established base of firms instead of with attempts to stimulate new businesses in fields where local expertise is lacking.

For our forthcoming book on Japan, Hirotaka Takeuchi and I gathered evidence on the role of government targeting in industry competitiveness (the Japanese case is important since arguments for targeting typically cite Japan). We titled the book *The Two Japans* because we verify the simultaneous presence of a highly competitive and a highly uncompetitive Japanese economy. We found similar practices, including targeting organizations into legalized cartels (*keiretsu*) and lifetime employment, in both the competitive and the uncompetitive Japans. Targeting was actually more prevalent in the uncompetitive Japan, while a large proportion of the competitive industries had no government targeting. The inescapable conclusion is that targeting and other commonly accepted reasons for Japan's competitiveness do not discriminate between successful industries and failures.

The Conduct of Regional Policy

Markusen, in finding that regional policy has been largely ineffective, tacitly accepts a traditional formulation of regional policy that includes broad incentives for firms to locate in less-developed regions. In my view this conception of regional policy is flawed and doomed to failure. Regional policy should promote specialization, upgrading, and trade among regions. Cluster formation can be encouraged by locating specialized infrastructure and institutions in areas where factor endowments, past industrial activity, or even historical accidents have resulted in concentrations of economic activity.

Many governments, in the name of regional policy, impede cluster formation and development. They induce firms to locate in areas where they lack supporting infrastructure and face competitive disadvantages. Not surprisingly, these efforts exact a high cost in terms of subsidies.

Economic Policy Decentralization

It is easy to take away from Markusen's article the message that regional policy efforts should cease, but in my view there are powerful arguments for greater decentralization of economic policy to subnational regions. The relevant economic area is smaller than most large and medium-size countries. Pushing many economic policy choices down to the regional level aligns policy with competitive reality. Levers for enhancing the competitive environment—specialized training and infrastructure, information services regulation that promotes innovation, and support for research centers—are often best pulled at the state or regional level based on the local cluster mix. Decentralization of policy choices also fosters accountability to citizens and creates competition among governments. Effectiveness and efficiency can thus improve relative to a monopolistic national government.

The view that "smokestack chasing" by state governments is destructive competition is based on an inappropriate conception of regional or state policy. When states use tax incentives and subsidies to bid against each other for every new plant, the competition is indeed zero-sum. But by investing in specialized training, building cluster-specific infrastructure, and improving the business climate with streamlined regulations, states can attract investment and upgrade the national economy.[1]

Contemporary literature increasingly favors supranational institutions and markets as the relevant unit of economic analysis. Developments in competition necessitate international policy coordination in such areas as trade, financial markets, and the environment. Such coordination is often easier to achieve in regional trade blocs, such as Europe or Latin America. Nonetheless, national and local differences still matter for competitive advantage—perhaps even more. In smaller nations the relevant economic area and national borders may coincide. In larger nations relevant economic areas are often smaller than the nation and larger than states; yet national governments are needed to manage macroeconomic policy, provide information, and make rules. Roles and responsibilities at various levels of government must be re-sorted but not necessarily eliminated.

Note

1. Smaller countries, such as Austria, Chile, Denmark, Hong Kong, and Singapore, and large countries where much policy is made at the state level, such as Germany and the United States, seem to share economic advantages over other large countries. An interesting research question would be to find out why.

References

Enright, Michael J. 1990. "Geographic Concentration and Industrial Organization." Ph.D. diss., Harvard University, Department of Economics and the Graduate School of Business Administration, Cambridge, Mass.

Henderson, Vernon. 1994. "Externalities and Industrial Development." Paper prepared for The Prince Bertil Symposium, June 12–14, Stockholm.

Hirschman, Albert O. 1958. *The Strategy of Economic Development*. New Haven, Conn.: Yale University Press.

Krugman, Paul. 1991. *Geography and Trade*. Cambridge, Mass.: MIT Press.

Monitor Company. 1990. "Building the Competitiveness of Euskadi." London.

Monitor Company and Michael E. Porter. 1994. *Construir as Vantagens Competitivas de Portugal*. Lisbon: Cedintec.

Porter, Michael E. 1990. *The Competitive Advantage of Nations*. New York: The Free Press.

Porter, Michael E., and Hirotaka Takeuchi. 1994. "The Two Japans." Harvard Business School, Cambridge, Mass.

Porter, Michael E., and Monitor Company. 1991. "The Competitive Advantage of Massachusetts." Office of the Secretary of State, Boston.

Porter, Michael E., Pankaj Ghemawat, and U. Srinivasa Rangan. 1994. "Developing Competitive Advantage in India." Harvard Business School, Cambridge, Mass.

Floor Discussion of "Interaction between Regional and Industrial Policies: Evidence from Four Countries," by Markusen

A participant from the European Investment Bank asked if regional policies ever conflict not just with industrial policies but with labor and other policies. If the wage rate is fixed at the same level in both less-developed and more-developed regions of a country, for example, but productivity is higher in the more-developed regions, isn't there a disincentive for private firms to invest in the less-developed regions, as has happened in Italy and might well be happening in Germany?

After pointing out that she was not a labor expert, Markusen observed that in the United States one of the main factors in regional distribution, especially of older manufacturing industries, was the southern tradition of low-wage labor (a function of slavery, sharecropping, right-to-work laws, and so on). This was very different from Europe, where nationwide labor unions kept wage rates similar across regions. One could argue that things were better in the United States because economic activity was able to move to the south, said Markusen, but, first, it moved south for twenty years and then it moved somewhere else; and second, many people in the older inner cities from which firms exited suffered unemployment and poverty as a result. These issues have to be dealt with. Markusen suspected that the availability of lower-wage labor in the United States meant less pressure to be technologically innovative; that firms in congested, higher-cost regions in Europe were under more pressure to be innovative about processes and technology.

A participant asked whether political economy might not be part of the reason for decentralized clusters: that one reason high-tech industrial districts can get the specialized public goods, infrastructure, training, and research facilities that they need is that high-tech industries produce a big enough share of regional value added to have political clout. Is this not a counterbalancing factor to the forces of conurbation Markusen talked about in her article? Markusen agreed about high-tech decentralization, and shared both discussants' belief that information technologies would result in greater decentralization of all industries as people overcame their resistance to them. She and Andrew Isserman (discussant in another session) now have a very efficient e-mail relationship, for example; they used to talk more on the telephone,

This session was chaired by Armeane M. Chokski, vice president, Human Resources Development and Operations Policy, at the World Bank.

Proceedings of the World Bank Annual Conference on Development Economics 1994

but she thinks that they now say more important things faster through e-mail, which she at first resisted. Business people she has interviewed report increasing reliance on technological rather than face-to-face communications; this will permit decentralization, although she still thinks some specialized businesses will locate in cities.

Markusen questioned the concept of "specialized public goods" as being somewhat tautological. Don't you need specialized goods for specialized sectors? She would argue, however, that government choices about where to locate resources and how to allocate infrastructure do influence development. The Japanese government's decision to put Tsukuba in the greater Tokyo region, for example, has irrevocably anchored high-tech development in that region. And in the United States the Pentagon, by investing in research and development in New England, Silicon Valley, and Los Angeles, essentially underwrote (and was also the single most important market for) the development of computing, aircraft, aerospace, electronics, and similar industries in those regions. But those two examples, Japan and the United States, show that government support does not necessarily mean that an industry will be either inside or outside the primate city region.

Michael Porter (discussant) was fascinated by an apparent paradox: that the United States—the country where there is the most fluidity of movement (of goods, people, information), so little cultural difference, such legal homogeneity, and so on—is so strikingly specialized geographically. It was not at all clear to him that technologies that allow easy, frequent communication and information flow would cause decentralization, although he found that an interesting issue. It might be that they would allow more specialization, which is a different kind of point; we would have just a few centers for each specialty rather than the same industries spread widely. In Porter's view the new technologies and new ways of moving goods and information nullify certain traditional reasons for locating firms but may at the same time emphasize the importance of other factors that are even more location-sensitive.

A participant from one of the World Bank's Africa infrastructure divisions asked Porter whether there is so much uncertainty about what allows agglomerations to grow (whether cluster agglomerations or the traditional type) that central governments are better off not trying to disperse economic units across regions or countries. Porter agreed with the spirit of the comment, that with so much uncertainty about what sectors can develop where, it was a big mistake for any central government to get into the business of saying this industry will be here and that industry will be there. Judging from historical case studies and his own experience, Porter felt that central governments should help disperse universities and research-related institutions in geographically diverse locations and allow them to specialize, depending on their own sense of how they could build on local strengths. Rather than see themselves as a central brain reallocating things from place to place, central governments should get out of the way and allow provinces, regions, and states to build up their strengths as they perceive them.

Whether generalized agglomeration economies or sector-specific economies matter is an empirical question, said Markusen. She had been studying rapidly growing cities in six different countries, and one of the most remarkable studies had been that of Seattle. She went there expecting to find tremendous clustering, very strong networks, and so on. What she found, instead, was four or five major industries—aircraft, software, biotechnology, port-related activity, resource-related activity—with very little connection to each other and very little networking between large and small firms, except for contractual relationships between Boeing and its suppliers. But she found a robust pervasiveness of agglomeration economies of the traditional type, having to do with skilled labor market, business services, and so on. As an empirical question, she found this worth pursuing.

A participant from the World Bank asked whether and to what extent private groups (such as chambers of commerce or industry associations), rather than regional or local governments, should be charged with strengthening clusters. Markusen said that although she did not fully share Porter's vision of regionally specialized clusters, a lot of research was being done about what private booster groups were doing in regional development. There are competing business groups at the local level. Traditional chamber of commerce groups, which she would call "local fixed capital," have a stake in regional growth per se because of real estate, utility, or other investments. Their agenda is to lower the cost of doing business—wages, taxes, worker compensation systems, and so on—and generally be just like everybody else. New sector-specific groups have a difficult time challenging this traditional coalition to secure public investment and build new networks. Still, Analee Saxenian, in her work on Silicon Valley, has called for more private groupings of this sort, and some regional governments have played a major leadership role in regional development.

William Alonso (discussant) reported his delight with the discussion. Fifteen or twenty years ago, he said, there might have been a discussion about the location of an industry, but the existence of industry was a given. In the past fifteen or so years—through new research that may have overstressed job formation by small and new enterprises and through the ideology of the Reagan-Thatcher years—the style has gone much more to "grow your own" rather than raid each other in a zero-sum game. The new style probably makes sense, but romanticism about the creative energy of the small entrepreneur has in some cases led to mistaken and, at the very least, wasteful policies.

This discussion was really the beginning of a much longer conversation, said Markusen. Mostly, everyone seemed to agree about locally grown clusters that build on local comparative advantages. But she still thought that the nation had a role to play and wanted to address comments made by the discussants. First, she thought what Alonso said about political structure was important, which was why she had taken some issue with the Krugman article. The issue was not whether the government was centralized or not; there were important nuances about political structure. The Republic of Korea, a strong, centralized, illiberal government, had been quite effective in decentralizing economic activity. And why? For strategic reasons. Strategy had a lot to do with the successful postwar decentralization of economic activity in countries like Israel, the United States, the Soviet Union, and Korea.

Second, experience in Brazil and Korea shows that if elites from regions of the country outside the capital region control the central government, it is quite possible that regional policy, infrastructure, and so on will be deployed in ways that do not reinforce the center. That is why it is important to build such institutional considerations into our model, Markusen said. Apropos of Alonso's comment about regional policy being the loser, while she appreciated the cleverness of the idea about slow versus fast, she had an alternative interpretation of why certain policies mattered. In her view, the reason financial or macroeconomic policy dominates regional policy is that finance capital is more powerful in nation-states and has become more so as the world has integrated in recent years. Finance capital is more powerful than industrial capital, which in turn is more powerful than regional elites.

While we could at least theoretically argue that world integration is precipitating greater specialization—at least that's what comparative advantage models would suggest—Markusen was not so sure that it was empirically true. It would be interesting to go back in history to see just how specialized cities and regions had been in earlier periods. Specialization has always been a hallmark of places. It would also be interesting to look at the relative openness or nonopenness of cities and to test some of the propositions in Krugman's article, Alonso's work, Porter's work, and her work.

Markusen concluded by making two points about the virtues and vices of competition between regional and local governments. First, she was concerned about wholesale acceptance of the notion that competition between state and local governments was an efficient way of deploying public resources. Charles Tiebout had celebrated the existence of separate suburban jurisdictions as a way for voters to vote with their feet, she said, but she felt that urban political structure in the United States had been profoundly responsible for the huge problems U.S. cities are having today. Similarly, cities and localities could also lose from such competition between them. Whether you are talking about Brazil, Japan, Korea, or the United States, many cities and localities are better positioned than others precisely because governments provided them with large increments of infrastructure in the past. Certainly this was true of cities in California. So in a way it was unfair to say at this point, "Now we are going to let you sink or swim on your own; you have to organize your own resources, and soon."

Second, there is a serious possibility that we will see overinvestment in local infrastructure. That is what is happening in Japan today: the technopolis program set up an artificial competition among prefectures, and many prefectures went deeply into debt, floating public bonds, to build infrastructure that would supposedly attract high-tech activity. Many of the prefectural technoparks are empty and underutilized, and there are going to be defaults. Defaults may be quietly covered up with redistribution from the center, but quite possibly competition among localities (encouraged by tax incentives and so on) has resulted in the overbuilding of infrastructure and the diversion of taxpayer resources away from other public goods and services, toward a lower cost of doing business for certain business sectors.

European Migration: Push and Pull

Klaus F. Zimmermann

In recent decades Europe has experienced periods of push and pull migration. Whereas pull migration has been seen as economically beneficial, there is concern that push migration will accelerate the employment crisis. This article qualifies this view by arguing that migration may erode institutional constraints. The theoretical framework behind this idea accounts for heterogeneous labor, monopoly union behavior, and unemployment with regulated migration. A review of empirical studies for Europe concludes that migration was largely beneficial in the past. New econometric investigations suggest that immigration from countries that are targeted for recruitment was strongly driven by business cycle effects (demand-pull) and chain migration (supply-push), but that the processes changed with the halt in recruitment in 1973. Contrary to general expectations, flows of asylum seekers and refugees (supply-push) are also affected by relative economic conditions in the receiving countries.

The interest that European migration has recently attracted is due to increased public tensions about foreigners in several countries of the European Union (EU). Following years of experience with immigration since World War II, these current tensions have more to do with large inflows of asylum seekers and persistently high and increasing unemployment rates all over Europe than with migration as such. During some decades, especially the 1960s, demand-pull migration was seen as beneficial to the economy. In the 1970s immigration policies became more restrictive. The unemployment crisis in Europe in the past fifteen years has stirred fears of a jobless society, with current and expected migration induced by conditions in sending countries adding to mass unemployment. Both optimistic and pessimistic views on migration have an accepted place in standard economic reasoning. This article elaborates and qualifies these views. It defines push and pull from the economic perspective of the receiving country.

Migration can be defined in various ways. In the public debate, "immigration" often refers to permanent labor in-migration, and "immigration policy" is often

Klaus F. Zimmermann is professor of economics at the University of Munich and co-director of the Human Resources Programme of the Centre for Economic Policy Research in London.

Proceedings of the World Bank Annual Conference on Development Economics 1994

used synonymously with active labor recruitment. European governments traditionally deny following such a policy even if they apply measures to control the inflow of nonnatives. This article does not distinguish between permanent and temporary migration or between migration for economic and noneconomic reasons. Where necessary, the context is explained more deeply.

Examination of ethnic and structural patterns of migration shows that the numbers of migrants and their ethnic composition differ considerably among countries. Migration policies also differ. And several European countries that once actively recruited labor migrants turned to restrictive policies in the 1970s. Policy instruments successfully organized pull migration but largely failed to avoid push migration or to enforce out-migration.

This article develops a simple theoretical framework to study the implications of immigration with heterogeneous labor in the face of unemployment caused by institutional constraints like trade unions. If migrants form a competitive fringe to labor markets and if skilled and unskilled workers in the economy are complements, native unemployment may decline. A review of the empirical literature suggests that in Europe's experience migration was not harmful.

New econometric evidence is presented on two aspects of pull and push migration. A review of the cyclical sensitivity of migration to Germany from the key recruitment countries before and after the halt in recruiting shows that, contrary to expectations, cyclical variability did not decline for countries with the tightest restrictions on mobility. New data show that relative economic conditions in the receiving countries have affected the flow of asylum seekers and refugees in Europe.

Defining Push and Pull Migration

Each of the member countries of the European Union regulates migration. An inflow of workers is possible only in accordance with the policy goals of the governments. I will define demand-pull migration and supply-push migration in terms of classic textbook analysis of aggregate supply and demand in the receiving economy. Assume a standard price-output diagram like figure 1, panel A, with an upward-sloping supply curve, such as characterized the 1950s and 1960s. If aggregate demand increases, output and prices rise. Rising wages make it beneficial to allow for immigration to curb inflation and to obtain a further increase in output. Hence the supply curve shifts downward, and AB in panel A represents the effects of pull migration—immigration drawn in by a strong economy and sometimes by active governmental encouragement. Conversely, an inflow of migrants without a change in demand shifts the supply curve downward and prices fall while output rises. Hence AC in panel A represents the effects of push migration—migration spurred by conditions in the home, or sending, country. In short, push-supply migration affects the aggregate supply curve alone while pull-demand migration deals with migration (and hence a shift of the supply curve) that responds to a shift in the demand curve. All internal factors affecting aggregate demand that cause migration are considered to be pull migration, while all internal or external factors that affect the aggregate supply and that are associated with migration are defined as push migration. This definition of push and pull stresses the economic context of the inflow of workers.

The framework has changed somewhat since the 1970s. The aggregate supply curve of the economy is considered to be vertical, since the supply and demand curves of labor are now affected only by real wages (figure 1, panel B). If the trade unions (or other institutional constraints) fix real wages above the equilibrium level, say, at A_1 (panel C), unemployment of about A_1A_2 results. Immigration (or push migration) shifts the labor supply curve and increases unemployment and thus government deficits through payments of unemployment compensation. This development affects demand and increases prices while leaving output constant. Hence push migration causes stagflation.

In practice various factors may impel push migration. Among them are better economic conditions in the receiving than in the sending countries as measured by unemployment, wages, working conditions, social security benefits, the structure of the economy, and the like; demographic characteristics of the labor force; the wishes of the families of migrants to reunite; and conditions that foster the migration of asylum seekers and refugees. Family migration may also be affected by family reunification policies in destination countries. Though in a certain sense this is pull migration, I consider it push-supply migration because it affects the supply curve of the receiving economy alone.

How useful are these definitions in an empirical context? First, as always, definitions help to organize thinking even if their empirical implementation is difficult. Here I agree with Paul Krugman: "Those who can, do, and those who can't, worry about definitions." Aggregate supply and demand in macroeconomics is an example. For instance, taxes affect both the supply and demand side of the economy, with

Figure 1. *Push and Pull Migration and the Economy*

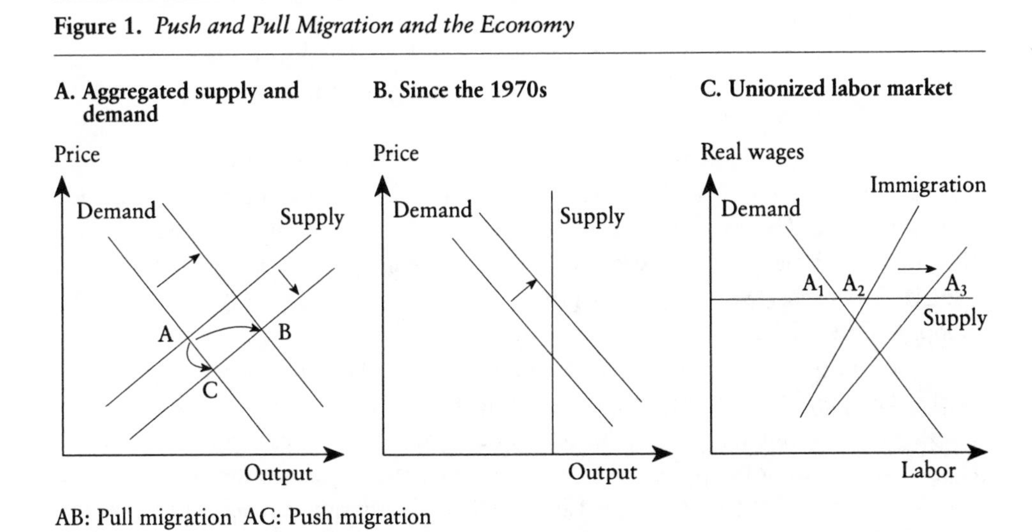

AB: Pull migration AC: Push migration

implications that are often ignored (Zimmermann 1987). Or, if technical progress is endogenous (as the new growth literature suggests and as was well known from the industrial organization literature long ago), any supply-side policy is a demand-side policy by affecting output, and vice versa. Second, implementation problems can arise. In an empirical context one may need further a priori assumptions to allow identification of push or pull migration, a need that will become clear when the concept is applied later.

Push and Pull Migration after World War II

Migration across Europe after World War II was complex, and no accepted and detailed statistics document it. Furthermore, in most countries the only criterion for differentiating between migrants and natives is citizenship (in the United States the crucial variable is whether a person is foreign born or native born). The problem is compounded in countries that have received many naturalized migrants like France and the United Kingdom, or that, like Germany, have taken many people with the same ethnic origin, who have the right to become citizens immediately. I therefore concentrate on general trends instead of detailed analysis. Further evidence is given in Maillat (1987), Salt (1989), Heisbourg (1991), Fassmann and Münz (1992), and Tapinos (1993).

I distinguish four periods: war adjustment and decolonization (1945–early 1960s), labor migration (1955–73), restrained migration (1974–88), and the dissolution of socialism and its aftermath (from 1988 on). Heisbourg (1991) estimates that 20 million people displaced by the war migrated. According to Schmidt and Zimmermann (1992) 12 million Germans had left Eastern Europe by 1950, and about 8 million went to the Federal Republic of Germany. Between 1950 and the construction of the Berlin Wall in 1961, some 2.6 million Germans moved from East to West Germany. Belgium, France, the Netherlands, and the United Kingdom were affected by return migration of their colonists and by inflows of native workers from their former overseas territories. More than 1 million French residents of Algeria resettled in France during and after the Algerian war of independence, 1954–62 (Fassmann and Münz 1992).

Labor migration characterized the second period, 1955–1973. In the 1950s labor shortages in some countries had already induced openness to labor immigration and even active recruitment. For instance, Germany established a "guest worker" system through recruitment treaties with Italy (1955), Spain and Greece (1960), Turkey (1961), Morocco (1963), Portugal (1964), Tunisia (1965), and Yugoslavia (1968). About 400 recruitment offices of the German Federal Labor Office operated in these countries on behalf of German firms. Similarly, Italians from the south moved to Switzerland, and Portuguese and Spaniards to France. On balance, 5 million people migrated to the north from the Mediterranean countries. France received most of the African migration, while the transoceanic migration from India, Pakistan, and the West Indies went to the United Kingdom. The Netherlands received immigrants from Indonesia, Latin America, Morocco, and Turkey. Especially in the cases of France and Germany, immigration was procyclical.

The period of restrained migration, which lasted until 1988, began throughout most of Western Europe at the end of 1973, when labor recruiting halted abruptly in the face of increasing social tensions and fear of recession following the first oil price shock. Inducing return migration turned out to be difficult. To the contrary, the foreign population increased because of higher fertility rates, continued immigration of family members, and the admission of refugees and asylum seekers. The number of illegal immigrants is also believed to have risen significantly. After a drop in 1974–75, particularly in France and Germany, immigration began rising again in 1976. Family immigration and political immigration dominated this period.

The period of dissolution of socialism and its aftermath (from 1988 on) was dominated by east-west migration and a heavy inflow of asylum seekers and refugees. According to the United Nations High Commissioner for Refugees the number of asylum seekers and refugees in Europe soared from 189,550 in 1987 to 700,850 in 1992. The other large part of the east-west migrants were ethnic Germans moving directly to Germany, particularly in 1989, the year the Berlin Wall fell. In 1992 Germany received 1.49 million new immigrants; net immigration was 0.79 million and the number of new asylum seekers and refugees was 0.44 million. The dimension of the inflow is most visible in terms of its relation to population. In 1950–61 immigration per year into Germany represented 1.09 percent of its beginning-of-period population. This figure rose to 1.42 percent for 1962–73, fell to 0.93 percent for 1974–88, and jumped to 2.47 percent for 1989 and after. By comparison the number for the United States in 1901–10, when immigration into that country was at its heaviest, was 1.16 percent. (Note that the numbers for Germany count ethnic Germans as immigrants, which is not the standard approach in official statistics.)

An interesting issue is the extent to which the European Union and its predecessors fostered internal migration—and continue to do so. Since World War II the European nations have forged increasingly strong economic ties. By 1995, when Austria, Finland, and Sweden will join, the European Union will have fifteen members. Yet, as Straubhaar (1988) has pointed out, the formation of the Common Market did not significantly stimulate labor migration among its member countries.

As this analysis suggests, European migration after World War II was largely controlled migration, with a major switch in policy in 1973. This change can be explained in terms of the push-pull concept. The periods of war adjustment and decolonization, restrained migration, and the dissolution of socialism and since are periods of predominantly push migration. Only the period of labor migration was a time of pull migration. Nevertheless, push migration did not harm receiving countries despite high unemployment rates. What permits immigration to be beneficial under such conditions? This issue is taken up in the section on labor migration and the economy. The next section studies the ethnic, geographical, and sectoral distribution of foreigners today and draws conclusions for future migration flows.

Ethnic Patterns and Migration Potentials

Six demographic challenges face the world in the coming decades if current trends prevail. First, 80 million to 100 million people are predicted to migrate from less-developed regions. Second, the potential for east-west migration is estimated at between 5 million and 50 million people in the next decade. Third, Western European populations will decline, including a 2 percent drop for the countries of the European Union by 2025, following growth of 17.4 percent between 1960 and 1990. Fourth, excluding migration, the total European population is predicted to grow by about 3 percent by 2025, led by a 19 percent increase in Eastern Europe (Poland will increase by 17 percent, the Commonwealth of Independent States by 22 percent, and Albania by 56 percent). Fifth, the countries in the south are expected to grow even faster: Morocco and Turkey by about 60 percent, and Algeria by about 100 percent. Finally, the Western European labor force will age considerably. In the EU labor force the twenty- to thirty-nine-year-old age group was 25 percent larger than the forty- to fifty-nine-year-old group in 1990; by 2020, the younger group will be 17 percent smaller.

This picture suggests that demographics will be a driving force in the coming era of push migration, reinforcing underdevelopment, political instability, and the rising number of asylum seekers and refugees. If push migration is unavoidable, to which countries are migrants likely to be attracted? Because the answer lies largely in ethnic networks, I provide a breakdown of migrants in European countries according to nationality and compare the sectoral participation of foreign workers in Germany and Switzerland with that in the United States.

Only 3 percent of the total EU population in 1991 came from outside the union (table 1). Countries in the European Union harbored about 5 million people from other member states, 3.2 million from "other Europe," and 2.7 million from Africa. Most migrants from within the European Union are in France, Germany, or the United Kingdom. People from other European areas go mainly to Germany. Africans concentrate in France, Germany attracts Turks and people from the former Yugoslavia, and the United Kingdom harbors mainly migrants from EU member states. This picture would likely be different if migrants were defined as "foreign-born"; the United Kingdom, which has a large number of naturalizations, would then have the most Asians. Among the other states, the Benelux countries also have a pronounced ethnic structure of foreigners.

Germany has by far the largest number of foreign workers—almost as many as France and the United Kingdom combined (table 2). Leaving Luxembourg aside, Belgium, France, and Germany have the largest shares of foreign workers in the total labor force. The number for Germany is much smaller than it was for the Federal Republic of Germany before unification because the People's Democratic Republic of Germany had virtually no foreign workers. There are specific established networks. Most immigrants in Germany are from Turkey or the former Yugoslavia. French immigrants came mainly from the south of the European Union (Greece, Italy, Portugal, and Spain) and from developing countries. Most U.K. workers are from developing countries and from Ireland. The ratio of foreigners to foreign workers shows the extent to which foreigners do not work (table 2). Italy places first with 13.7 foreigners for each foreign worker, and Luxembourg last with 1.5. De facto labor immigration countries like France, Germany, and the United Kingdom have low numbers—about three foreigners for each foreign worker—possibly the result of guest worker programs, of regulations for family migrants, or of the smaller families of the ethnic groups these countries receive. Nevertheless, one can conjecture that there is relatively less labor migration in Greece, Italy, and Spain than elsewhere.

In which industries do foreigners work? In 1982 the share of foreign labor was about 25 percent in Switzerland and 9 percent in the Federal Republic of Germany, while in the United States the share was about 8 percent (table 3). The statistics for Germany and Switzerland do not count naturalizations, which is especially a prob-

Table 1. *Residents in Countries of the European Union by Region of Origin, January 1, 1991* (percent except as noted)

Host country	*Total population (thousands)*	*Natives*	*Other EU*	*Other EEA*[a]	*Central and Eastern Europe*	*Other Europe*[b]	*Africa*	*Asia*
European Union	343,881.1	97.0	n.a.	0.1	0.2	0.9	0.8	0.5
Belgium	9,987.0	90.9	5.5	0.1	0.1	1.0	1.9	0.2
			(11.1)	(1.5)	(1.1)	(2.9)	(6.8)	(1.5)
Denmark	5,146.5	96.9	0.5	0.5	0.1	0.8	0.1	0.8
			(0.6)	(7.0)	(1.1)	(1.3)	(0.3)	(2.5)
France	56,652.1	93.7	2.3	0.0	0.1	0.5	3.0	0.4
			(26.5)	(3.5)	(10.2)	(8.7)	(60.5)	(14.9)
Germany	79,753.2	93.1	1.8	0.3	0.5	3.2	0.3	0.7
			(27.0)	(63.0)	(65.9)	(75.6)	(7.3)	(33.7)
Greece	10,120.0	97.7	0.5	0.1	0.3	0.1	0.2	0.4
			(1.1)	(1.7)	(4.2)	(0.3)	(0.7)	(2.4)
Ireland	3,524.0	97.6	1.9	0.0	0.0	—	—	—
			(1.3)	(0.1)	(0.0)			
Italy	57,746.2	98.6	0.3	0.0	0.1	0.1	0.4	0.2
			(3.0)	(4.5)	(6.6)	(1.9)	(8.8)	(9.2)
Luxembourg	384.4	70.1	26.6	0.4	0.2	0.8	0.5)	0.4
			(2.1)	(0.4)	(0.1)	(0.1)	(0.1)	(0.1)
Netherlands	15,010.4	95.4	1.1	0.0	0.1	1.5	1.3	0.4
			(3.4)	(2.1)	(1.3)	(6.9)	(6.9)	(3.5)
Portugal	9,858.5	98.9	0.3	0.0	0.0	0.0	0.5	0.0
			(0.6	(0.4)	(0.1)	(0.0)	(1.7)	(0.3)
Spain	38,993.8	98.8	0.7	0.1	0.0	0.0	0.1	0.1
			(5.5)	(6.2)	(0.5)	(0.3)	(1.5)	(2.4)
United Kingdom	56,705.0	95.7	1.4	0.1	0.1	0.1	0.3	0.8
			(15.8)	(9.5)	(8.9)	(2.0)	(5.5)	(29.7)
Total foreigners (thousands)	n.a.	n.a.	4,957	337	619	3,169	2,699	1,525

— Not available.
n.a. Not applicable.
Note: Figures in parentheses are shares (percent) of nationalities across the European Union.
a. European Economic Area. Includes Austria, Finland, Iceland, Liechtenstein, Norway, and Sweden.
b. Includes Switzerland, Turkey, and Yugoslavia.
Source: Eurostat, Schnellberichte 1993/6.

lem for the German data since, according to German law, immigrating ethnic Germans are immediately eligible for a German passport.

In the United States the sectoral distributions of foreign-born and native workers were similar. In Switzerland and Germany foreigners were heavily represented in construction and manufacturing and lightly represented in trade and other services. Some of the differences between the European countries and the United States may reflect the more temporary nature of immigration in Europe and its concentration in industries with less attractive jobs. Institutional factors were probably at work too, since immigration to Switzerland and Germany was partially selective according to labor market needs.

The future of European migration is difficult to assess. It depends largely on long-term economic developments and on political stability in potential sending regions and migration policies in potential receiving countries. Although the basic demographic framework I have outlined suggests that the more important immigration scenario in the next decades will be south to north migration, most speculations are about east to west migration. Here the migration potential is estimated in the range of 5 million to 50 million, mostly over a period of ten to fifteen years. Layard and others (1992) suggest a potential flow of 3 percent of the current size of the population in Eastern Europe for the next fifteen years, implying a migration inflow of about 3 million ethnic Germans and 10 million others. Is this a problem? Not really, if considered in isolation and in terms of pure quantities. The average annual inflow would represent 0.4 percent of the current EU population, which is very low compared with Germany's postwar experience. If all 3.7 million ethnic Germans in Eastern Europe moved to Germany in ten years, the relative inflow would be less than 0.5 percent per

Table 2. *Foreign Workers in Countries of the European Union by Sending Region or Country* (percentage of foreign workers in receiving countries except as noted)

Host country/year[a]	*Total foreign workers (thousands)*	*North EU*[b]	*South EU*[c]	*Yugoslavia*
Belgium (1989)	196.4	29.7	42.0	1.0
Denmark (1990)	46.8	23.9	3.4	7.7
France (1988)	1,172.5	3.5	46.7	2.6
Germany (1991)	1,898.5	6.5	20.2	17.1
Greece (1990)	23.2	32.8	6.0	0.9
Ireland (1988)	19.9	77.4	3.5	0.0
Italy (1983)	57.0	15.8	8.8	—
Luxembourg (1990)	78.4	55.4	39.0	1.3
Netherlands (1990)	200.0	35.5	11.0	3.0
Portugal (1985)	30.5	13.8	8.5	0.0
Spain (1983)	57.0	35.1	3.5	—
United Kingdom (1985)	820.9	38.7	9.8	0.4

— Not available.

a. Data are the latest available.

b. Belgium, Denmark, France, Germany, Ireland, Luxembourg, the Netherlands, and the United Kingdom.

c. Greece, Italy, Portugal, and Spain.

year. Even if all 13 million predicted above moved, the proportion would be only 1.6 percent, though, of course, the ethnic composition and language proficiency would be substantially different and adjustment costs would be larger.

Migration Policies in Western Europe

This section surveys experience with migration policies in Europe. Evidence is examined for the European Union and for countries covering different models of immigration policy: the rotation principle (Germany, Switzerland) and the policy of permanent residence (France, the United Kingdom). (Useful literature references are Hammar 1985, Kubat 1993, OECD 1992, and Zimmermann 1994a.)

EU Policy on Mobility

The European Union has no explicit collective immigration policy. However, the elementary relationship between migration and welfare was part of the motivation for the Common Market. The Treaty of Rome of 1957, which established the European Economic Community, provides for the free movement of labor. It stipulates that "freedom of movement for workers" entails the "abolition of any discrimination based on nationality between workers of the member states with respect to employment, remuneration, and other conditions of work and employment." As amended by the Single European Market Act, the treaty requires that after January 1, 1993, the "four freedoms"—the free movement of people, capital, goods, and services—be observed. This requirement implies the abolition of any restrictions on

Turkey	*Morocco*	*Others*	*Foreign workers as a percentage of labor force*	*Ratio of foreign population (1991) to foreign workers*
5.8	10.7	10.7	5.3	4.6
14.3	1.3	49.4	1.8	3.4
2.0	11.2	33.9	5.5	3.1
33.3	1.0	21.8	5.1	2.9
4.7	0.0	55.6	0.6	9.9
0.0	—	19.1	1.8	4.3
0.0	1.8	73.7	0.3	13.7
0.1	0.1	4.1	45.6	1.5
20.5	13.5	16.5	3.1	3.5
0.0	0.0	77.7	0.7	3.5
—	—	61.4	0.5	8.5
0.8	0.4	49.8	3.3	3.0

Source: Statistisches Bundesamt, Vierteljahreshefte zur Auslandsstatistik 4/1992. Labor force data: *ILO Yearbook of Labor Statistics* 1992. Population data: Statistisches Bundesamt, Statistisches Jahrbuch für das Ausland, various issues, and OECD 1992. Eurostat, Schnellberichte 1993/6.

Table 3. *Distribution of Foreign and Native Employees by Sector, Switzerland, Federal Republic of Germany, and the United States, 1982* (percent)

Sector	Switzerland			United States			Federal Republic of Germany		
	Foreigners[a]	Natives	Share of foreign workers (percent)	Foreigners[a]	Natives	Share of foreign workers (percent)	Foreigners[a]	Natives	Share of foreign workers (percent)
Agriculture	1.0	8.8	3.1	3.6	3.4	8.4	1.0	1.1	7.9
Mining	0.4	1.1	8.0	0.7	1.0	5.7	2.0	2.4	7.3
Construction	11.5	5.0	38.2	4.7	6.0	6.4	9.9	7.6	11.3
Manufacturing	45.9	27.3	31.3	25.3	19.2	10.2	56.1	38.4	12.4
Transportation and public utilities	2.9	7.1	10.0	4.2	7.2	4.8	3.9	5.0	7.0
Trade	9.7	14.8	15.1	20.4	20.7	15.2	6.5	14.6	8.7
Wholesale	—	—	—	3.9	4.4	7.1	3.3	5.8	5.2
Retail	—	—	—	16.5	16.3	8.1	3.2	8.8	3.5
Finance, insurance, real estate	2.8	5.6	11.8	6.6	6.2	8.4	0.7	4.1	1.7
Other services	15.3	14.0	20.3	32.3	31.5	19.5	17.4	19.9	11.8
Private household	1.4	—	—	1.8	1.2	11.5	0.7	1.9	3.6
Miscellaneous	13.9	—	—	30.5	30.3	8.0	16.7	18.0	8.2
Public administration	10.6[b]	16.3[b]	17.1[b]	2.4	4.9	4.1	2.6	7.0	3.4

— Not available.

a. United States: foreign born. Germany and Switzerland: foreigners.

b. Includes education and health services.

Source: Sehgal 1985; Statistisches Bundesamt, Statistisches Jahrbuch 1990. Statistisches Bundesamt der Schweiz, Statistisches Jahrbuch der Schweiz 1984 and 1993, Bundesamt für Ausländerfragen in "Die Volkswirtschaft," 1983 and 5/1992.

internal labor mobility, including border controls. It attempts to overcome obstacles to movement like language differences, disparate education systems, insufficient recognition of academic degrees and other qualifications, and cultural differences.

However, the Single European Market also requires more consistent and probably stricter control mechanisms at outside borders. Another important issue is whether free movement inside the European Union applies to foreigners who have been allowed to enter one EU country. Economic logic suggests allowing free movement for all residents, but doing so requires a common visa policy, which does not exist. So far, most common measures aim at better control mechanisms and broader harmonization of asylum laws. Immigration policies tend to be left to the national governments.

The Schengen Accords of 1985 (Schengen I) and 1990 (Schengen II) were directed at eliminating internal border checks, establishing consistent and tighter external border controls, developing a more unified visa policy, and coordinating asylum policies. The Schengen initiative is not a community activity, however, since Denmark, Ireland, and the United Kingdom refused to participate. The initiative will be put into effect on March 26, 1995 between most member states of the accords. Under the terms of the accords foreigners from outside the European Union are allowed to work only in the country that they enter, and they have only three months in which they can visit other EU countries. Even workers from an EU country must leave their EU host country within three months of losing their job.

In the Dublin Convention of 1990 all twelve member states agreed on a joint procedure for asylum seekers. It basically confirms asylum policies of the Schengen Accords and addresses the difficult issue of multiple asylum claims. The Maastricht Treaty of 1992 gives the European Commission co-initiative power with the EU member states on immigration policy. A working group preparing the Maastricht Treaty had defined more-active common policy elements, including labor immigration, the harmonization of visa policies, and common measures against illegals. Other internal EU committee proposals include more detailed suggestions about a quota system and stepwise labor immigration, first on a temporary basis. However, there is by no means any clear indication that the European Union officially considered an immigration law.

Specific Country Policies and Effects in Europe

Immigration policies of individual European countries are of two main types, rotational and permanent residence.

Germany. The German government does not accept the view that Germany attracts immigrants for permanent or temporary settlement. It is true that there was never any intention after World War II to attract non-Germans permanently. Nevertheless, there was always a migration policy whose basic elements were ethnicity, rejection of permanent non-German immigration, integration into the European Union, and adjustment of migration measures to labor market conditions.

The policy was expressed by giving ethnic Germans priority in citizenship as required by the German Basic Law, actively recruiting foreign workers in the 1950s and 1960s but not after the early 1970s, and then attempting to stimulate return migration.

Most immigrants to the Federal Republic of Germany since the end of World War II were ethnic Germans—*Übersiedler* from the German Democratic Republic and *Aussiedler* from the countries in Eastern Europe. Because ethnic Germans immediately receive a German passport, this stream of permanent immigrants is easy to overlook. They accounted for 12 million immigrants before 1950 and 4.8 million between 1950 and 1988 (3.2 million *Übersiedler* and 1.6 million *Aussiedler*). In 1989–90, 774,000 more came. Altogether, about 26 million ethnic Germans and other migrants moved to the Federal Republic of Germany between 1950 and 1989.

Responding to excess demand for labor in the 1950s and especially in the 1960s, Germany signed recruitment treaties with Greece, Italy, Morocco, Portugal, Spain, Tunisia, Turkey, and Yugoslavia. Under state recruitment German firms filed offers for contracts with the labor authorities, who forwarded the offers to recruitment officers in the individual countries. These officers then selected workers on the basis of qualifications, health, and employment records. By law offers had to be identical to those for equally qualified Germans.

The elements of immigration control are visas, residence permits, and work permits. EU nationals can move freely; other labor migration is at the administrative discretion of the authorities. After the recruitment policy ended with the economic crisis in 1973, family migration became more and more important. Policies were liberalized in several steps, and the government concentrated more on active integration programs.

At the same time attention turned to whether return migration should be fostered by financial measures. Such a program was not promulgated until 1983, however, after a new conservative government came into power. Foreigners from countries with which Germany had a recruitment treaty were eligible if they were unemployed or performed short-term work. Financial support was 10,500 deutsch marks plus 1,500 deutsch marks for each child leaving the country with the worker. Interested individuals had to apply within eight months of the program's introduction. About 17,000 applications were received (19,000 were expected), and about 14,000 were accepted, most of them from Turkish guest workers. Though the government considered the program successful, it was not continued.

The Foreigners Act of 1991 eased the requirements for naturalization, especially for people born or raised in Germany, and provided for the return to Germany of those who had grown up in Germany but had gone back to their country of origin. In the face of exploding numbers of asylum seekers and low acceptance rates, the law was changed in 1993 so that unfounded applications would be easier to reject. Readmission treaties like those signed with Poland and other Central European countries are expected to further help control abuse of the asylum right. There are also new employment treaties with countries in Central and Eastern Europe that allow German firms to subcontract with firms in those countries and to employ a certain number of their workers, mostly in construction. In 1992 employment of this type had reached about 116,000.

Switzerland. Switzerland has a clear preference for temporary and selective labor immigration according to the rotation principle. Regulation and control of immigration derive from the Federal Law of Abode and Settlement of Foreigners of 1931 and later (slight) amendments. The government decided on annual entry quotas based only on national interests. The law requires that these decisions take into account Swiss cultural and economic interests, especially labor market conditions and the degree of foreign infiltration.

The law recognizes three categories of foreigners: seasonal workers, people with a permit of abode and a yearly work and residence permit, and permanent residents. In practice commuters form another category—people who live close to the Swiss border and receive a work permit but no residence permit; they must renew their permits every year. The dual nature of the permit of abode is a distinguishing characteristic of the Swiss system. For the first five years the permit must be renewed every year; thereafter it is good for two years at a time. Family members can follow after fifteen months. Permanent residence can be obtained after five to ten years, depending on the source country. Seasonal workers may remain for no more than nine months. A special police force supervises the foreign population and has great discretionary powers.

As these provisions suggest, Switzerland resists permanent immigration. Since 1970 the government has set quotas for yearly and seasonal work permits. In 1989–90 the quotas were 10,000 abode permits and 156,725 seasonal visas. Decisions are based on whether a Swiss native could take the job. Foreigners must be paid according to local labor market conditions. Migrants are accepted only from the European Union, the European Free Trade Area, and the former Yugoslavia. The government was prepared to join the European Economic Area, which would have required substantial changes in its migration policy, but the population voted against participation in 1992. The Swiss migration policy is generally considered effective and successful. Since the rotation principle has worked well, fostering return migration has not been an issue.

France. Though it has a long tradition of permanent immigration, France has become more restrictive recently. Traditionally, policy aimed at the assimilation of permanent migrants and their families, who often had roots in the former French colonies. Naturalization was easy. Yet France is neither prepared nor willing to become a multicultural society. In the 1950s an active immigration policy sought to meet the needs of the labor market. In the 1960s and early 1970s the government followed a laissez-faire policy. In 1974 immigration was halted, and in 1977 measures were introduced to induce return migration. Family migration was restricted, and measures were taken to protect the national labor market. In the 1980s special attempts, including stricter border controls, were made to stop illegal immigration and work in the shadow economy. On the other hand, family migration was liberalized again, and efforts were made to integrate and assimilate migrants.

Two programs were introduced to induce return migration. The first, in 1977, offered all unemployed migrants who were eligible for unemployment compensation 10,000 francs (F) if they agreed to return home, F 5,000 to the spouse if he or she was also unemployed (F 10,000 if employed), and F 5,000 for each dependent child who had a work permit. The program was largely a failure. In the first three months only about 10 percent of the potential returnees took advantage of the program, and in total about 100,000 migrants, 60 percent of them workers, returned. In 1991 a voluntary repatriation scheme for unsuccessful asylum seekers was launched on an experimental basis. People were offered travel expenses and F 1,000 per adult and F 300 per child, but response was low. A similar program for foreigners required to leave the country was created in late 1991. In 1993 the new conservative French government announced a restrictive program to halt immigration.

United Kingdom. The United Kingdom has traditionally been a country of emigration. In recent decades, however, significant immigration has taken place, mostly from the British Commonwealth and Ireland. The Nationality Act of 1948 allowed anyone from the New Commonwealth to move to the United Kingdom. The Commonwealth Immigration Acts of 1962 and 1968 and the Immigration Act and Nationality Act of 1971 were enacted to control the ethnic inflow. Concerned with keeping strict control over its population, the United Kingdom aims its policy at controlling immigration, not attracting it.

The Immigration Act of 1971 gives patrials—people with close connections to the United Kingdom by birth, descent, or marriage—free entry with an unrestricted work permit. Others (except those from other EU countries) have to apply for a permit, which is approved, initially for one year, on the basis of skill level, age, and language proficiency. After four years permit holders can apply to have the time limit lifted. Applicants for work permits in high-skill occupations are investigated more speedily than others. Labor migration has been increasing steadily in recent years, with work permits now totaling 34,627; more than half are long-term permits, about 80 percent of them held by professional and managerial workers.

Common Results

Immigrants contributed significantly to economic growth after World War II, and immigration policy largely reflected economic motives. Many Western European countries had active labor recruitment policies, which came to a halt everywhere in 1973, the time of the first oil crisis, a development that can be explained in push-pull terminology. Assimilation policies either were not followed or achieved little success. (See Tapinos 1993 and Zimmermann 1994a for elaborations.) A policy of temporary migration seems to work only when it is based on a strict rotation system, as in Switzerland. Germany, with its guest worker system, actually ended up with permanent migrants. Even the French model, with its planned settlements, ignored the dynamic of migration. Family (chain) migration has counteracted policy objectives. Measures to induce return migration were not successful or achieved only limited success because they were not rigorously pursued.

Labor Migration and the Economy

Economic theory suggests that the market will eliminate regional disparities in prosperity over time if they are other than "compensating differentials." Compensating differentials are differences in industrial structure, public goods, the environment, individual preferences, and so on. For instance, if a region is a relatively unattractive place to work but an attractive place to live, it must pay higher wages and will exhibit higher unemployment rates in equilibrium. People who prefer living there are less mobile and less willing to accept jobs. If unemployment is increasing, wages will tend to decline. On the one hand, this decline will stimulate labor demand; on the other, it will spur some workers to move to other regions or to quit and become voluntarily unemployed. Unemployment and wages may then rise. To summarize: it is not necessary for differences in economic conditions to disappear in the long run to rule out migration. Regions with above-average wages may also have above-average unemployment rates.

Of further importance is how quickly labor markets adjust. Some European studies demonstrate that this process is typically slow within countries (see Pissarides and McMaster 1990, for instance, for the United Kingdom). Despite large economic differences among countries, migration within the European Union has never been large, even after barriers have been lowered. It is often concluded that a regional policy could considerably reduce adjustment costs. It can also be argued that migration from non-EU countries can help speed up adjustment and avoid adjustment costs for natives.

In general the higher the substitutability of foreign for domestic workers, the more likely it is that increased immigration will depress the wages of the domestic labor force or, if wages are inflexible, that unemployment will rise. However, immigrants are often complements to native workers, in which case rising immigration would be expected to lead to higher native productivity (and wages). Furthermore, immigration creates demand for the goods and services natives produce and therefore has a multiplier effect. (Most empirical studies suggest that immigration is not too harmful or is even beneficial to the labor markets of receiving countries. Greenwood and McDowell 1986, Simon 1989, Borjas 1990, and Straubhaar and Zimmermann 1994a review the empirical literature. Stark 1991 provides the best and most up-to-date theoretical treatment.)

Most of these studies are for the United States, however, and their findings are not necessarily transferable to Europe. Europe differs from the United States and Canada in at least three distinct ways (Zimmermann 1994b). The European labor market is less flexible and adjusts slowly to economic differences; labor inflows can compensate for these characteristics. Unemployment and labor market imperfections are more persistent in Europe, which makes the effects of immigration less predictable. And views on cultural variety and social networks in Europe stress cultural assimilation much more than in the United States. The analysis here concentrates on the theoretical framework of push and pull migration and on a review of central empirical findings in the European context. It neglects demand for public goods by migrants. Since evidence suggests that migrants benefit the public coffer (Simon 1989), this does not alter the basic conclusions.

Theoretical Framework

If labor is homogeneous, the standard competition framework predicts that immigrants will increase total welfare at the expense of labor because the wage rate will decline. However, wages may not be downwardly flexible, perhaps because of unions (Schmidt, Stilz, and Zimmermann 1994). If union behavior remains unaffected by immigration, unemployment may rise, perhaps substantially. On the other hand, unions may be swayed in their choice between maintaining wages and employment by the pressures of rising unemployment or by the possibility of giving more weight to the interests of one group of workers over another.

If labor is heterogeneous, the key issue in evaluating the wage effects of immigrant labor is whether foreigners are substitutes for or complements to native workers. To simplify the analysis, assume that there are only two types of labor, qualified or educated workers (the skilled) and less-qualified or less-educated workers (the unskilled). One reasonable simplification is that skilled and unskilled workers are complements and that immigrants tend to be substitutes for unskilled natives and complements to skilled natives. In that case increases in immigration may depress wages and (possibly) increase the unemployment of unskilled workers and may induce the opposite effects for skilled workers. Based on a theoretical model outlined in the appendix, the immigration of both skilled and unskilled workers can be shown to be beneficial even in the face of unemployment.

While a formal treatment is left to the appendix, I will briefly outline the framework and provide the intuition. The model assumes that the economy produces a single output according to a constant-returns-to-scale production function with capital, skilled labor, and unskilled labor. Output prices are predetermined, and both types of labor are q-complements (the standard case). Natives supply input factors at fixed levels. Immigrants are perfect substitutes for unskilled natives, they bring no capital with them, and they have no effect on the demand side of the economy. The level of immigration is fixed by governmental rules. A monopoly union sets the wage w^L on the market for unskilled labor, and employers then choose the level of employment in this market. Though the wage of skilled labor is determined by competitive forces, the union cares about these wages as well, which are affected by the employment level in the market of unskilled workers.

The consequences of skilled and unskilled labor immigration in such a model are shown in figure 2. The monopoly union sets wages above the equilibrium for unskilled labor (B_0 in panel B). This action causes unemployment at level $\bar{L}$–L for unskilled labor. Because the union is concerned about the earnings of both skilled and unskilled workers, it accepts a lower wage for unskilled workers (B_1) following immigration by unskilled workers (see the shift of the labor supply curve in panel B) because the increase in the employment of the unskilled (L_1) shifts the demand curve for skilled workers upward (panel A). Since the two types of labor are complements, the wage rate of skilled workers increases (from A_0 to A_1 in panel A). As a further result, the union wage for unskilled labor falls and drives the economy toward the equilibrium point of a competitive labor market. Native unemployment may rise or fall. It may fall if the degree of complementarity or the weight assigned to skilled workers in the union's objective function is sufficiently strong (B_1 in panel B, for example).

The case of immigration of skilled labor is even more obvious. As the supply of skilled labor increases, the equilibrium point shifts down from C_0 to C_1 (panel C).

Figure 2. *Immigration and the Labor Market*

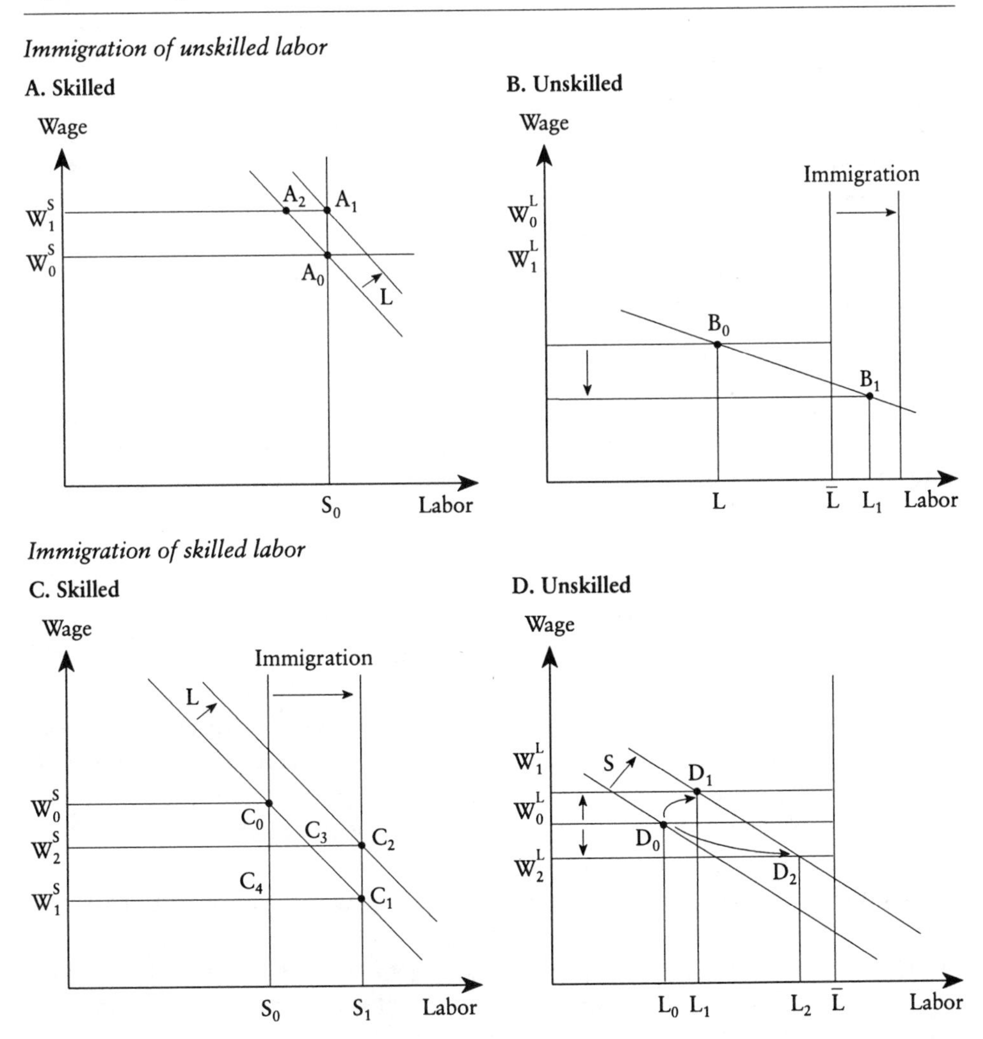

The demand for unskilled labor increases because of complementarity (the shift in the demand curve in panel D) and more unskilled workers will be employed whether the union decreases the unskilled wage (D_2) or increases it (D_1). The increase in the level of unskilled employment again shifts the demand curve for skilled labor upward (C_2 in panel C). Hence immigration of skilled workers may or may not cause an increase in the wages of the unskilled. The larger the weight of the skilled wage and the smaller the weight of native unemployment in the union's objective function, the more likely a decrease. Native unemployment falls no matter what happens to the unskilled wage.

The conclusion from this analysis is that high unemployment is not in itself an argument against immigration. Migration may even be beneficial in such a situation. In practice this is an empirical matter, crucially dependent on whether skilled and unskilled labor are q-complements. The rest of this section will address empirical issues in a European context.

Empirical Evidence

The dominant microeconomic topics on the integration of foreign labor are how do the migrants assimilate, how do they perform, and what are the consequences for native labor? Studies on earnings assimilation of permanent migrants in Australia, Canada, and the United States have shown that an initial earnings gap between immigrants and native labor narrows considerably over time, indicating the willingness of foreign labor to invest in human capital (see Greenwood and McDowell 1986 for a review of the evidence). Dustmann's studies (1993) of the earnings adjustments of guest workers in Germany did not confirm this selectivity. His empirical results indicated that foreign workers in the German labor market receive lower wages than natives throughout their work career, even after adjusting for individual differences. The reason, he concluded, is the temporary nature of migration to Germany.

This finding was contradicted by Schmidt (1992b). Using the same data set, he found that after about seventeen years of residence the average immigrant to Germany achieves earnings parity with the equivalent native. Pischke (1992) confirms that finding. The solution to this puzzling difference in findings seems to be that Germany tends to attract immigrants with relatively low skills, who are and stay blue-collar workers. Whether immigrants are found to adjust is therefore a consequence of the choice of the group to study. Since Dustmann (1993) included all natives in the analysis, whether blue- or white-collar workers, his nonconvergence result is understandable. However, the sample contains few recent immigrants, so it is difficult to study earnings dynamics. Pischke (1992) and Schmidt (1992a) also studied the relation of country of origin to convergence of native and immigrant earnings. One conclusion of these studies was that ethnic groups with the largest initial earnings disadvantage realized the highest wage growth. Dustmann (1994), who also investigated the issue of language, showed that proficiency, especially in writing, considerably improves the earnings of migrants.

There are also studies about the performance of wages of immigrants for other European countries. Kee (1993) studied the relative income performance of immigrants in the Dutch labor market (see also Hartog and Vriend 1990). Niesing, van Praag, and Veenman (1994) found severe unemployment for ethnic minorities in the Netherlands compared with native Dutch, which they trace to employer discrimination. In their investigation for Sweden, Aguilar and Gustafsson (1991) found that earnings converge for the 1969 cohort of immigrants but not for the 1974 cohort. Chiswick (1980) found little difference in the earnings of native-born and foreign-born white men in the United Kingdom. Granier and Marciano (1975) studied wages for immigrants in France, Grossman (1984) studied the occupational attainment of immigrant women in Sweden, and Moulaert and Deryckere (1984) have investigated the employment of migrants in West Germany and Belgium.

Winkelmann and Zimmermann (1993) studied the frequency of direct job changes and of unemployment spells for natives and foreigners in the Federal Republic of Germany during 1974–84 using a count data estimation technique. The empirical evidence shows that foreign workers change jobs more readily on average and are also more frequently unemployed, especially later in life. Robust Poisson estimates indicate that there is a U-shaped relationship between age and frequency of unemployment for both German and foreign workers but that foreigners face lower unemployment risks than natives in early career stages and higher risks in later stages. Natives change jobs less frequently as they grow older, and foreigners less frequently the longer they are in Germany. The share of foreign labor affects the frequency of unemployment significantly but has no effect on job mobility. Hence the larger is the share of foreign workers the greater is native unemployment. Simulations with the predicted age structures for Germany and the European Union from 1995 to 2020 show that job changes and unemployment will first decrease and then increase, while general development in the European Union is less marked.

The unemployment effects of immigration were also small or statistically insignificant in other European studies. Using a micro-data set of unemployment histories in the 1980s for a German panel and controlling for various individual and industrial characteristics and unobserved heterogeneity using a simulated estimation probit technique, Mühleisen and Zimmermann (1994) found no evidence that foreign labor induces unemployment, perhaps because wages were adjusting flexibly in this period (De New and Zimmermann 1994a,b). Hunt (1992) found that the impact of the 900,000 repatriates to France from Algeria in 1962 on the 1968 unemployment rate of nonrepatriates was at most 0.3 percentage point. Her cross-section regression controlled for education, age, and industrial and regional differences.

Are natives and foreigners substitutes or complements in production? Gang and Rivera-Batiz (1994) found the results from the U.S. literature to be inconclusive. Using European data to estimate a translog production function, they found that education is complementary with unskilled labor and experienced labor in production. A 1 percent increase in the endowment of unskilled labor would raise the returns to education by close to 0.75 percent and the returns to experience by 2.5 percent. Similarly, a 1 percent increase in the endowment of education augments the returns to unskilled labor by 0.62 percent and raises the rate of return on experience by approximately 1.8 percent. Finally, an increase in the supply of experienced labor raises the remuneration of unskilled labor by about 0.31 percent and that of education by 0.25 percent. Drawing useful conclusions from these findings, however, requires evaluating the net impact of immigrants, which depends on the quality structure of the immigrant and native work force as well as the size of immigration, which is difficult to simulate.

Using German micro-data, De New and Zimmermann (1994a,b) studied the impact of the share of foreign labor on wages for native blue- and white-collar workers. A higher share should affect wages positively if foreigners are complements and negatively if they are substitutes. The econometric evidence implies that an increase of 1 percentage point in the overall share of foreign labor results in a 4.1 percent reduction in the average hourly wage of all workers. The wages of blue-collar workers decline by about 5.9 percent, but those of white-collar workers increase by about 3.5 percent. Since most immigrant workers are blue-collar workers, this is evidence of complementarity between white-collar and blue-collar workers. The findings of Hunt (1992) for the impact of the 1962 repatriates to France from Algeria are also modest. She estimates that their arrival lowered average annual salaries in 1967 by at most 1.3 percent.

Immigration and the Business Cycle: The German Case

Earlier sections have reviewed the history of postwar labor migration in Western Europe: the heavy migration in 1955–73, the restrained migration of 1974–88, and the effective policy measures that attracted migrants in the first period and the perhaps less successful attempts to control or even prevent labor immigration in the second. According to our analysis so far, Germany was a country of substantial immigration in which pull migration should have dominated until 1973 and push migration thereafter. This suggests an exploration of the cyclical sensitivity of immigration from the recruitment countries. Of countries that had recruitment treaties with Germany until 1973, Greece, Italy, Portugal, Spain, Turkey, and Yugoslavia offer reliable time-series data beginning around 1960. All but Turkey and Yugoslavia are members of the European Union today, but workers from countries that joined the European Union at a later stage (Greece in 1981 and Portugal and Spain in 1986) were not allowed free mobility for seven years. Therefore, only Italians belonged to a common international labor market with Germany throughout the period under study. The analysis concentrates on net immigration from all sources. The time series display a strong correspondence with the business cycle in Germany (proxied by real GNP growth rates) until 1973 (figure 3). After 1973 the cyclical variability continues for most countries, but at different levels and with different lags. In Italy and Spain the cycles seem to converge.

From the previous analysis immigration seems driven largely by policy measures that reflect the economic motives of the receiving country. In such a framework migration flows should be determined by labor demand and not by labor supply factors. Determinants of individual migration decisions, like relative wages and relative unemployment rates, should not matter. Since goods demand is the dominant factor of labor demand and labor migration was basically a response to recruitment until 1973, the analysis is simple. Net immigration is assumed to be a linear function of the business cycle, with a regime switch around 1973 to allow for the drastic change in migration policy. The business cycle is proxied by real growth. Since labor is recruited, suggesting that labor is planned, migration is expected to respond simultaneously to demand. Real growth, however, can also be affected by supply factors in the receiving economy such as productivity. It is assumed here that productivity change is exogenous and may potentially change with the regime switch in 1973. This will consequently be captured by a constant under both regimes.

Figure 3. *Net Immigration from Recruitment Countries to Federal Republic of Germany and German Business Cycle*

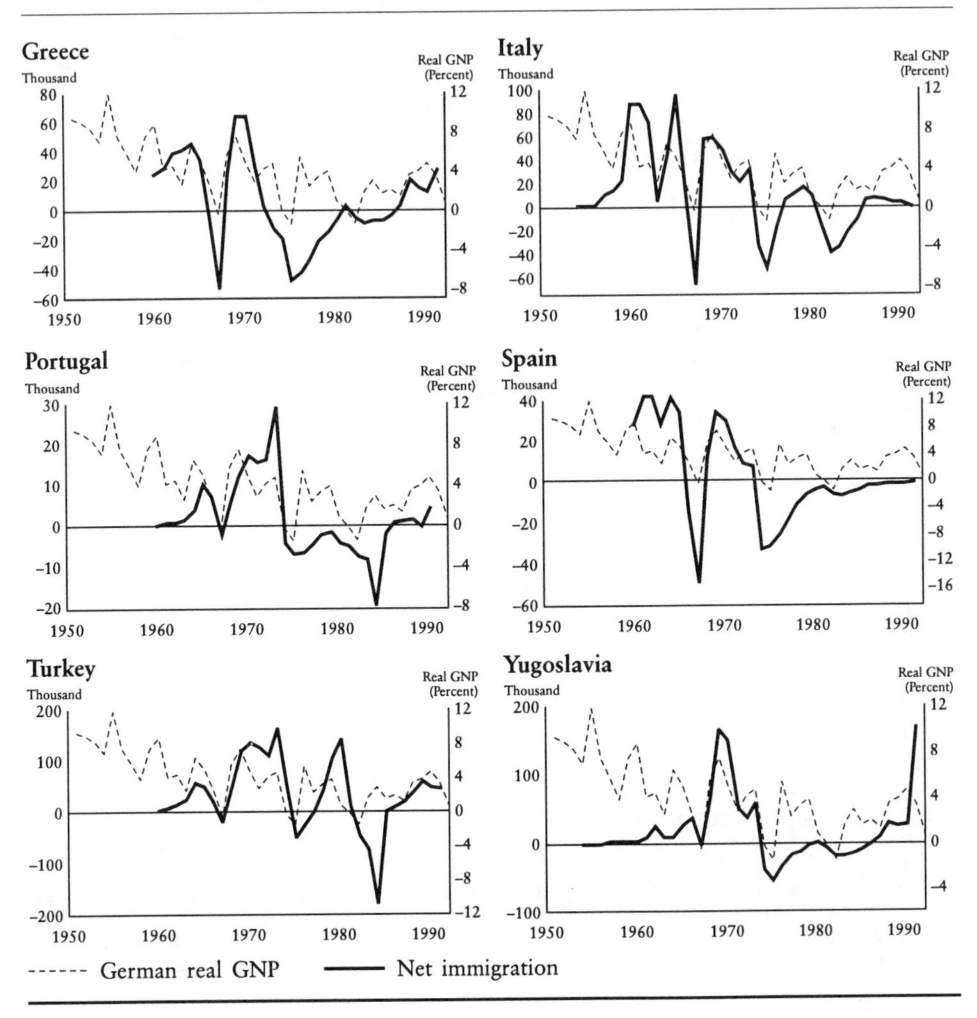

I explored the relationship between 1960 and 1991 using an ordinary least squares regression of immigration from each recruitment-targeted country (table 4). Real growth is assumed to capture the pull factors; lagged net immigration (a measure of persistence and network migration) and the time trend (as a proxy of unobserved variables operating in the sending and receiving countries) are assumed to capture the push factors. (Remember that lagged immigration is not seen as pull migration since it is not caused directly by the economic conditions in the receiving country.) Since regression results are likely to change with the switch in policy regime in 1973, the approach chosen allows for different parameters before and after that year. All time series were examined for stationarity using the augmented Dickey-Fuller test for both subperiods in all countries (not reported here). It was not possible to reject a unit root in all cases, although the respective coefficients were

Table 4. *Migration from Major Recruitment-Targeted Countries*

Variable[a]	*Italy (1960–91)*	*Greece (1961–91)*	*Spain (1961–91)*	*Portugal (1961–88)*	*Yugoslavia (1960–90)*	*Turkey (1961–91)*
Constant	–44,624	–25,586	–19,168	–8,905.3	–56,716	–42,179
	(–3.0)	(–2.1)	(–2.1)	(–2.3)	(–2.6)	(–1.1)
Real GNP growth	16,013	12,319	10,227	2,305.4	10,849	14,071
	(6.4)	(6.2)	(7.4)	(3.2)	(3.4)	(1.9)
Growth * D74	–9,098.8	–11,644	–10,259	–1,962.8	–7,657.8	–1,940.2
	(–2.6)	(–3.8)	(–5.3)	(–2.0)	(–1.6)	(–0.2)
Lagged migration[b]	0.274	0.447	0.371	1.159	0.467	0.876
	(2.1)	(3.6)	(3.4)	(5.5)	(2.8)	(3.2)
Lagged migration[b] * D74	0.205	0.040	–0.278	–1.054	–0.278	–0.336
	(0.8)	(0.1)	(–1.0)	(–4.3)	(–0.9)	(–1.1)
D74[c]	22,917	–23,969	–26,652	4,114.9	–29,478	16,360
	(1.4)	(–0.7)	(–1.5)	(1.0)	(–0.8)	(0.4)
Trend		–2,025.4	–1,855.7		4,352.3	
		(–2.0)	(–2.5)		(2.1)	
Trend * D74		3,951.7	3,431.7		–1,203.1	
		(2.3)	(3.6)		(–0.5)	
$\bar{R}^2$	0.77	0.80	0.84	0.76	0.72	0.51
DW	2.26	1.71	1.21	1.97	1.19	2.03
Godfrey LM[d]	1.0	0.9	6.7	0.0	6.9	0.0
Box-Pierce[d]	0.7	0.6	4.3	0.0	4.2	0.0
Box-Ljung[d]	0.8	0.7	4.7	0.0	4.6	0.0
SC-LRT[e]	9.6	22.6	28.2	22.0	11.5	1.5

Note: Numbers in parentheses are t-statistics.

a. The dependent variable is net immigration.

b. Lag of net immigration.

c. Dummy variable: 1 after 1973, 0 otherwise.

d. χ^2-distributed test statistic with 1 degree of freedom. The critical 5 percent value is 3.84 and the 1 percent value is 6.63.

e. Structural change-likelihood ratio test. χ^2-distributed test statistic with critical 5 percent value of $\chi^2_3 = 7.81$ and $\chi^2_4 = 9.49$ and 1 percent value of $\chi^2_3 = 11.34$ and $\chi^2_4 = 13.28$.

Source: Statistisches Bundesamt, *Statistisches Jahrbuch*, various issues; Sachverständigenratsgutachten 1992/93.

about –1. Since this is probably the consequence of the small sample sizes, I proceeded using the migration flow variable.

In most cases the estimates indicate that behavior changed significantly after 1973. This conclusion is confirmed by the structural change-likelihood ratio test (SC-LRT). It strongly rejects constancy in behavior for Greece, Portugal, and Spain (the countries that joined the European Union in the 1980s but had not yet reached the status of free labor mobility). The rejection is less strong but nevertheless significant at the standard 5 percent level for Italy and Yugoslavia, but insignificant for Turkey. Despite the fact that Italians were unrestricted, their behavior seems to have changed, whereas Turks, to whom such mobility restrictions largely applied, obviously did not change their behavior. These results suggest the need for a more detailed breakdown and explanation of the underlying factors.

According to the respective coefficients, immigration from Italy responds strongest to the business cycle followed by immigration from Turkey, Greece, Yugoslavia, Spain, and Portugal. The response coefficients are significantly lower after 1973 for Greece, Italy, Portugal, and Spain, but not for Turkey and Yugoslavia. The persistence coefficients (of lagged migration) are large for Portugal and Turkey and small for Italy and Spain. With the exception of Portugal, for which the parameter changes to zero, the coefficients remained stable after 1973. The constant did not change after 1973 for any country, indicating that the switch in the policy regime was either neutralized by other factors or operated only through changes in the other coefficients. Time trends played a role only in Greece, Spain, and Yugoslavia, and the trend factor remained unchanged in the case of Yugoslavia. For Greece and Spain the time trend affected immigration negatively until 1973, but switched soon afterward.

An analysis of residuals with various χ^2-distributed test statistics (DW, Godfrey LM, Box-Pierce, Box-Ljung) suggests that only the residuals for Spain and Yugoslavia depart from white noise. (Table 4 reports only tests with one lag. Tests with higher lags gave no different results.) Residual analysis of explicit estimates for the two subperiods clearly demonstrates that the process in Spain and Yugoslavia is quite different after 1973 and that the departure from white noise originates in this period. Results of maximum-likelihood estimates for the second period, which explicitly model the autoregressive residual process, reveal no effects on the qualitative findings for the variables in the equations. Similarly, I investigated whether the large estimate for lagged migration in Portugal in the first period is causing econometric problems. The equation was reestimated for 1961–73 in first differences for the endogenous variable with no relevant changes for the parameter estimates of the remaining variables.

As should be expected, there are elements of push and pull migration in both subperiods. Nevertheless, the distinction between the two is confirmed through this investigation by the fact that the cyclical variability of immigration largely decreased after 1973 in most countries. It is practically zero in Greece, Portugal, and Spain and (though still positive) substantially lower in Italy, despite the Italians' free mobility. This is not the case in Turkey and Yugoslavia, where the persistence coefficients dominate the immigration process; in Yugoslavia, moreover, a deterministic time trend operates. For Turkey the statistical significance of the coefficient of the real growth variable is low anyway. One may conclude that push migration was always more important for these countries. An explanation for the drop in cyclical variability for Italy is the abandonment of the active recruitment policy, which implied a substantial increase in mobility costs.

EU Asylum Seekers and Refugees

The large inflows of asylum seekers and refugees are at the heart of the public debate about migration in Europe and are the major reason for serious political tensions. In France only 25 percent of asylum seekers are currently accepted; the rate in Germany is only 6 percent. How many of these immigrants act from economic motives? It is sometimes argued that many asylum seekers are actually labor migrants who have no other way to enter the European Union legally. Moreover, even true asylum seekers and refugees might choose a country within the European Union for economic reasons. A main difference between a true asylum seeker or refugee and a labor migrant is that only the labor migrant will care about economic factors in the country of origin. In this section I will assume that economic conditions in the country of origin do not matter and that the political migrant is attracted by countries in the European Union that are performing relatively well. Ethnic networks should also matter, since they reduce information and adjustment costs.

The inflow of asylum seekers and refugees can be considered the standard case of push migration: someone will decide to migrate solely to escape politically motivated persecution or war. Even here economic motives may enter; a migrant may choose a country whose economic performance is best among possible destinations. This section explores whether asylum seekers and refugees to the European Union exhibit such economic motives. The statistical significance of such determinants does not, however, contradict that asylum seekers and refugees are push migrants, as long as they react only to economic differences in the equilibrium levels between potential host countries and not to changes in aggregate demand in the country of choice.

Using recent unpublished data from the United Nations High Commissioner for Refugees on asylum seekers and refugees and newly published Eurostat data on the stock of migrants in Europe, I compare the explanatory power of network migration with that of pure economic determinants. This data base allows substantial additional insights. The data on asylum seekers differentiate between sending and receiving regions and identify the ethnic networks. The total number of asylum seekers in Europe was 159,000 in 1980, 170,000 in 1985, and 701,000 in 1992. Throughout this period Germany attracted by far the largest share of these migrants: the low was 29 percent in 1983, and the high was 69 percent in 1980. France, Sweden, and Switzerland had the next highest shares, but in any given year these never approached half of Germany's share.

The empirical analysis is restricted to the ten EU countries and the period (1983–92) for which data on asylum seekers and refugees were available (Ireland and Luxembourg are excluded). A further split was made according to the ethnic networks or regions of origin—Eastern European, African (excluding North Africa), Arabic (the Middle East, primarily North Africa), and Asia. Regions of origin with only marginal flows were excluded. The potential sample size was 400; missing data restricted the sample used to 355. The data were analyzed in logged form to capture nonlinear relationships. Among the regressors are economic variables and measures of ethnic networks (as listed and defined in table 5). The dependent variable (number of asylum seekers and refugees varying with receiving and sending countries) varies over time, country, and ethnic group, whereas relative unemployment, real relative wages, and the relative size of the labor market are identical across ethnic groups since they reflect the conditions in the receiving countries. The only reliable data on the number of ethnic residents (based on passports) are from Eurostat for 1991, but these data vary across ethnic groups and countries.

Table 5. *Analysis of the Log of Asylum Seekers, 1983–92*

	Pooled ordinary least squares			*Random-effects panel model*		
Variable	*Ia*	*IIa*	*IIIa*	*Ib*	*IIb*	*IIIb*
Constant	6.66	6.54	7.06	7.19	6.65	7.27
	(18.2)	(18.2)	(17.3)	(11.4)	(16.8)	(15.9)
Relative unemployment[a]	−0.89	−0.81	−0.82	−0.99	−0.77	−0.79
	(−4.2)	(−4.0)	(−4.1)	(−3.8)	(−3.3)	(−3.3)
Real relative wages[b]	1.53	1.55	1.57	1.08	1.43	1.39
	(4.9)	(5.2)	(5.3)	(4.6)	(4.8)	(4.7)
Relative size of the	0.38	0.37	0.29	0.83	0.48	0.42
labor market[c]	(4.4)	(4.4)	(3.2)	(2.9)	(4.6)	(3.7)
Ethnic network[d]	0.26	0.19	0.38	−0.05	0.11	0.28
	(4.1)	(2.8)	(3.8)	(−0.9)	(1.5)	(2.8)
European ethnic network[e]		0.19	−0.07		0.18	−0.10
		(4.0)	(−0.6)		(3.8)	(−0.9)
African ethnic network[e]		0.15	0.18		0.15	0.18
		(2.8)	(3.3)		(2.8)	(3.3)
Arabic ethnic network[e]		−0.06	−0.32		−0.06	−0.34
		(−1.2)	(−2.8)		(−1.2)	(−3.0)
Distance[f]			−1.25			−1.33
			(−2.6)			(−2.7)
$\bar{R}^2$	0.27	0.33	0.34	0.19	0.34	0.35

Note: The sample size is 355; t-statistics in parentheses. The dependent variable is the log of the number of asylum seekers and refugees of the respective receiving and sending countries. The Asian ethnic network is the reference group in columns II and III.

a. The unemployment rate (as a percentage of total labor force) for a country divided by the unemployment rate of OECD-Europe.

b. The log of real hourly earnings for a country minus the log of real hourly earnings for OECD-Europe; real hourly earnings are hourly earnings in manufacturing corrected by purchasing power parity.

c. The number of employees divided by the average number of employees in European countries (employees in manufacturing).

d. The log of size of ethnic group.

e. Ethnic network times a dummy variable for the sending region.

f. One if the sending region is Asia or Africa; zero otherwise.

Source: OECD, *Main Economic Indicators*, various issues; ILO, *Yearbook of Labor Statistics* 1992; UNHCR 1993; Eurostat 1993.

An individual asylum seeker or refugee should be more likely to move to an EU country with a healthy economic environment and with a rich ethnic network that reduces adjustment costs. Hence real relative wages, the relative size of the labor market, and the ethnic network should exhibit a positive effect, whereas relative unemployment and distance (which measures transportation costs) should have a negative effect. The regression analysis tests for these implications. Two methods—ordinary least squares and random-effects panel models with country-specific random effects—and three behavioral specifications (I, II, III) were employed. Though the estimates of the economic variables do not differ substantially between the two methods, the Breusch-Pagan Lagrange multiplier test statistics all reject the ordinary least squares estimates; I therefore rely on the random-effects panel models.

All results are consistent with expectations and have the following interpretation: the larger is the unemployment problem in a potential EU host country, the less likely it is that it will receive asylum seekers and refugees. The larger is the size of the labor market and the real relative wages, the larger will be the migration inflow. Distance has a negative impact on immigration. The ethnic network variable is less stable and indicates that the coefficient differs between ethnic groups. Model IIIb suggests that the African network effect is stronger than the European and Asian effects (note that the Asian network is the reference group), whereas there is no Arabic network effect. Since ethnicity is measured here on a highly aggregated level, one must interpret cautiously. A much finer breakdown of the data or the use of micro-data would be necessary to have more confidence in these results. One can conclude from the results presented here that asylum seekers and refugees are highly sensitive to differences in the economic conditions of potential host countries in the European Union. This does not, however, make them (illegal) economic migrants. It merely suggests that economic considerations play an important role in their choices.

Conclusion

This article has surveyed major trends in migrations in postwar Europe and in immigration policies. With the exception of the 1960s most labor migration periods were dominated by push migration. The statistical analysis has revealed the importance of ethnic migration networks, whether made up of families or chains. These migration dynamics can counteract policy measures to induce return migration. A general concern now is that a substantial increase in push migration will aggravate the unemployment problem. A review of empirical studies reveals that experiences with labor migration in Europe were beneficial, or at worst not harmful. From a theoretical point of view immigration can break up institutional constraints and reduce unemployment.

New econometric evidence was presented that explored the inflow of migrants to the Federal Republic of Germany, a major receiving country in Europe in the 1960s, 1970s, and 1980s, and the inflow of asylum seekers and migrants to the European Union in the 1980s. For most sending countries immigration to Germany responded substantially less to the business cycle after 1973, and this development was supported by economic policy measures. Hence pull migration lost its importance and was replaced largely by push migration. Immigration from Turkey and Yugoslavia, however, continued to be dominated by elements of network migration and was affected hardly at all by economically motivated immigration policy.

The inflow of asylum seekers and refugees is often considered to be entirely push migration. This view does not imply that economic factors are unimportant in general. My study reveals that such flows to the countries of the European Union are affected largely by economic differences among receiving regions. According to the push-pull concept presented here, these flows remain push migration for the receiving country as long as immigration is not fostered by increases in demand for goods.

Appendix

This analysis develops a model suggested by Schmidt, Stilz, and Zimmermann (1994). The economy is assumed to produce a single output according to a constant-returns-to-scale production function with capital, skilled labor S, and unskilled labor L. Output prices are considered to be predetermined, and both types of labor are q-complements (the standard case). Natives supply input factors at fixed levels. Immigrants M, which are fixed by government rules, are perfect substitutes for unskilled natives N, do not carry any capital, and have no effect on the demand side of the economy. A monopoly union sets the wage w^L on the market for unskilled labor, and employers then choose the level of employment in this market; the wage of skilled labor is determined by competitive forces.

Employed unskilled natives are $N = \alpha L$, where $\alpha = \bar{N}/(\bar{N} = \bar{M})$, $\bar{N}$ being the fixed level of unskilled natives and $\bar{M}$ being the fixed level of immigrants. The union's objective is considered to be

$$\text{(A.1)} \qquad \max_{w^L} \Omega = \delta w^S \bar{S} + (w^L - \eta)\, \alpha L + \eta \bar{N} - {}^{\phi}\!/_{2}\, (\bar{N} - \alpha L)^2$$

where $\bar{S}$ is the fixed level of skilled natives, $NU = \bar{N} - \alpha L$ is native unemployment, η is fixed unemployment insurance benefits, and δ and ϕ are weights for the income of skilled workers and unskilled unemployed workers. The union cares about both skilled and unskilled native workers.

Profit maximization of the firm implies that wages are equal to marginal productivity. In linearized form, one obtains

$$\text{(A.2)} \qquad \bar{w}^L = a^L - b^L L + c\bar{S}$$

$$\text{(A.3)} \qquad w^S = a^S - b^S \bar{S} + cL$$

where a^S, a^L, b^S, b^L, $c > 0$, and $\bar{w}^L$ are predetermined by the union. Hence, from the first-order condition it follows that

$$\text{(A.4)} \qquad \frac{\delta c}{\alpha b^L} \bar{S} = L - \frac{1}{b^L}[w^L - \eta + \phi(\bar{N} - \alpha L)].$$

Additional immigration of unskilled workers affects the union's choice of w^L. For simplicity, the effect of α is investigated instead of $\bar{M}$ since both effects have the opposite sign: sign $dw^L/d\bar{M}$ = –sign $dw^L/d\alpha$. Of further interest is the resulting native unemployment *NU*. Straightforward calculations imply:

(A.5)
$$\frac{dw^L}{d\alpha} = \frac{\frac{\delta}{\alpha} c\bar{S} + \phi L}{2 + \phi \frac{1}{b^L}} > 0$$

(A.6)
$$\frac{dNU}{d\alpha} = \frac{\delta c\bar{S} - 2Lb^L}{2b^L} \begin{matrix} > \\ = \\ < \end{matrix} 0.$$

Result 1: Immigration of unskilled workers reduces the union wage w^L and drives the economy in the direction of the competitive labor market model. Native unemployment may rise or fall. If the degree of complementarity c or the weight δ is sufficiently strong, native unemployment may even fall.

Immigration of skilled workers (*SM*), which are substitutes for skilled natives (*S*), implies:

(A.7)
$$\frac{dw^L}{d\overline{SM}} = \frac{c\left(\alpha + \phi \frac{\alpha^2}{b^L} - \delta\right)}{2\alpha + \frac{d}{b^L}} \begin{matrix} > \\ = \\ < \end{matrix} 0$$

(A.8)
$$\frac{dNU}{d\overline{SM}} = -\frac{\alpha c}{b^L}\left[\alpha + \frac{\phi}{b^L}(1 - \alpha^2) + \delta\right] < 0.$$

Result 2: Immigration of skilled workers may or may not cause a drop in the wages of unskilled labor. A drop is more likely the larger is the weight of skilled income and the smaller is the weight of native unemployment in the union's objective function. Native unemployment falls no matter what happens to the unskilled wage.

Note

The author thanks Thomas Bauer, Veronika Klusak, Ralph Rotte, and Michael Vogler for able research assistance, and Ira Gang and anonymous referees for many helpful comments on earlier drafts.

References

Aguilar, Renato, and Bjorn Gustafsson. 1991. "The Earnings Assimilation of Immigrants." *Labour* 5(2): 37–58.

Borjas, George J. 1990. *Friends or Strangers: The Impact of Immigrants on the U. S. Economy.* New York: Basic Books.

Chiswick, Barry R. 1980. "The Earnings of White and Coloured Male Immigrants in Britain." *Economica* 47(1): 81–87.

De New, John P., and Klaus F. Zimmermann. 1994a. "Blue-Collar Labor Vulnerability: Wage Impacts of Migration." In Gunter Steinmann and Rolf Ulrich, eds., *Economic Consequences of Immigration to Germany*. Heidelberg: Physica-Verlag.

———. 1994b. "Native Wage Impacts of Foreign Labor: A Random Effects Panel Analysis." *Journal of Population Economics* 7(2): 177–92.

Dustmann, Christian. 1993. "Earnings Adjustment of Temporary Migrants." *Journal of Population Economics* 6(2): 153–86.

———. 1994. "Speaking Fluency, Writing Fluency, and Earnings of Migrants." *Journal of Population Economics* 7(2): 133–56.

Fassmann, Heinz, and Rainer Münz. 1992. "Patterns and Trends of International Migration in Western Europe." *Population and Development Review* 18(3): 457–80.

Gang, Ira N., and Francisco L. Rivera-Batiz. 1994. "Labor Market Effects of Immigration in the United States and Europe: Substitution vs. Complementarity." *Journal of Population Economics* 7(2): 157–75.

Granier, R., and J. P. Marciano. 1975. "The Earnings of Immigrant Workers in France." *International Labour Review* 111(2): 143–65.

Greenwood, Michael J., and John M. McDowell. 1986. "The Factor Market Consequences of U.S. Immigration." *Journal of Economic Literature* 24(4): 1738–72.

Grossman, Jean B. 1984. "The Occupational Attainment of Immigrant Women in Sweden." *Scandinavian Journal of Economics* 86(3): 337–51.

Hammar, Tomas, ed., 1985. *European Immigration Policy: A Comparative Study*. Cambridge: Cambridge University Press.

Hartog, Joop, and Nick Vriend. 1990. "Young Mediterraneans in the Dutch Labour Market: A Comparative Analysis of Allocation and Earnings." *Oxford Economic Papers* 42(2): 379–401.

Heisbourg, François. 1991. "Population Movements in Post-Cold War Europe." *Survival* 33(1): 31–43.

Hunt, Jennifer. 1992. "The Impact of the 1962 Repatriates from Algeria on the French Labor Market." *Industrial and Labor Relations Review* 45(3): 556–72.

Kee, Peter. 1993. "Immigrant Wages in the Netherlands: The Valuation of Pre- and Post-immigration Human Capital." *The Economist* 141(1): 96–111.

Kubat, Daniel, ed., 1993. *The Politics of Migration Policies*. New York: Center for Migration Studies.

Layard, Richard, Oliver Blanchard, Rudiger Dornbusch, and Paul Krugman. 1992. *East–West Migration: The Alternatives*. Cambridge, Mass.: MIT Press.

Maillat, Denis. 1987. "Long-Term Aspects of International Migration Flows: The Experience of European Receiving Countries." In *The Future of Migration*. Paris: Organization for Economic Cooperation and Development.

Moulaert, Frank, and Philippe Deryckere. 1984. "The Employment of Migrant Workers in West Germany and Belgium: A Comparative Illustration of the Life-Cycle of Economic Migration (1960–80)." *International Migration* 22(3): 178–98.

Mühleisen, Martin, and Klaus F. Zimmermann. 1994. "A Panel Analysis of Job Changes and Unemployment." *European Economic Review* 38(3/4): 793–801.

Niesing, Willem, Bernard M. S. van Praag, and Justus Veenmann. 1994. "The Unemployment of Ethnic Minority Groups in the Netherlands." *Journal of Econometrics* 61(1): 173–96.

OECD (Organization for Economic Cooperation and Development). 1992. *SOPEMI—Trends in International Migration*. Paris.

Pischke, Jörn-Steffen. 1992. "Assimilation and the Earnings of Guestworkers in Germany." Mannheim. Zentrum für Europäische Wirtschaftsforschung Discussion Paper 92–17.

Pissarides, Christopher A., and Ian McMaster. 1990. "Regional Migration, Wages and Unemployment: Empirical Evidence and Implications for Policy." *Oxford Economic Papers* 42(4): 812–31.

Salt, John. 1989. "A Comparative Overview of International Trends and Types, 1950–80." *International Migration Review* 23(3): 431–56.

Schmidt, Christoph M. 1992a. "Country-of-Origin Differences in the Earnings of German Immigrants." Universität München Discussion Paper 92–29. Munich.

———. 1992b. "The Earnings Dynamics of Immigrant Labor." Universität München Discussion Paper 92–28. Munich.

Schmidt, Christoph. M., and Klaus F. Zimmermann. 1992. "Migration Pressure in Germany: Past and Future." In Klaus F. Zimmermann, ed., *Migration and Economic Development.* Berlin: Springer-Verlag.

Schmidt, Christoph. M., Anette Stilz, and Klaus F. Zimmermann. 1994. "Mass Migration, Unions, and Government Intervention." *Journal of Public Economics* 55(2): 185-201.

Sehgal, E. 1985. "Foreign Born in the U.S. Labor Market: The Result of a Special Survey." *Monthly Labor Review* 108(7): 18–24.

Simon, Julian L. 1989. *The Economic Consequences of Immigration.* Cambridge: Basil Blackwell.

Stark, Oded. 1991. *The Migration of Labor.* Cambridge: Basil Blackwell.

Straubhaar, Thomas. 1988. "International Labour Migration within a Common Market: Some Aspects of EC Experience." *Journal of Common Market Studies* 27(1): 45–62.

Straubhaar, Thomas, and Klaus F. Zimmermann. 1993. "Towards a European Migration Policy." *Population Research and Policy Review* 12(3): 225–41.

Tapinos, Georges. 1993. "The Dynamics of International Migration in Post-War Europe." In Giacomo Luciani, ed., *Migration Policies in Europe and the United States.* Dordrecht: Kluwer Academic Publishers.

Winkelmann, Rainer, and Klaus F. Zimmermann. 1993. "Ageing, Migration and Labour Mobility." In Paul Johnson and Klaus F. Zimmermann, eds., *Labour Markets in an Ageing Europe.* Cambridge: Cambridge University Press.

Zimmermann, Klaus F. 1987. "Transfers, Perfect Foresight and the Efficacy of Demand Policy." *Journal of Institutional and Theoretical Economics* 143(4): 652–57.

———. 1994a. "Immigration Policies in Europe: An Overview." In Horst Siebert, ed., *Migration—A Challenge for Europe.* Tübingen: J.C.B. Mohr.

———. 1994b. "Some General Lessons for Europe's Migration Problem." In Herbert Giersch, ed., *Economic Aspects of International Migration.* Heidelberg: Springer-Verlag.

Comment on "European Migration: Push and Pull," by Zimmermann

Julian L. Simon

I enjoyed reading Professor Zimmermann's article and preparing this comment. The article contains much valuable material, and its conclusions and implications seem sound and important.

Effects in the Labor Market

These are the main findings I find in the article, all of which apply to the labor market.

Difference in Occupational Patterns

There is a considerable difference between the nature of immigration into Western Europe and into North America, as shown very nicely by the distribution of occupations by industrial sector in Zimmermann's table 3. Unlike in Canada and the United States immigrants in Europe work in various branches of the economy in rather different proportions than do natives. This useful observation is novel, so far as I know.

There are several economic implications of this fact:

- A negative implication is that there are more effects (in both the up and down directions) on the wages and labor earnings of natives than if the immigrant and native occupational distributions were similar. Natives in occupations where few immigrants enter—such as trade, services, and probably (as in the United States) the law—can expect increased earnings, whereas those in occupations where there are relatively many immigrants—such as manufacturing and probably (as in the United States) medicine—can expect decreased earnings. On balance, natives will suffer only a trifling decrease in labor income, which is more than made up by a slightly larger increase in income from capital; both of these aggregate effects are so small that they can be disregarded. Unfortunately, the resulting public expressions in press and politics are not likely to balance out. The losers scream while the gainers are not likely to even be aware of their gain, let alone make noise about it.

Julian L. Simon is professor of business administration at the University of Maryland, College Park.

Proceedings of the World Bank Annual Conference on Development Economics 1994

- A positive implication is that the difference in occupational patterns implies more complementarity between natives and immigrants, and hence more benefits to natives, than when immigrants are distributed similarly to natives. This benefit from complementarity is of particular interest because I believe that I have shown theoretically that when the pattern of the occupational inflow is like the existing occupational pattern, there are no Ricardo-trade-like benefits to natives from the immigration, but rather the migrants get all the gains. (Here I must note that this theory—briefly sketched in my 1989 book—runs counter to common belief among economists, and is rejected by almost all who hear or read it. Many, including one Nobel Prize–winner, say that they will provide counter examples; but none has yet provided one, so my confidence in this theory is increased.)
- There also is an important implication of the difference in occupational patterns that Zimmermann shows for our interpretation of research results. It implies the unpalatable proposition that empirical research done in North America is not immediately applicable to Europe. This is unfortunate because the body of such research increased by leaps and bounds in recent years but is mostly concentrated on North America and Australia.

Effect on Unemployment

Zimmermann reports that his review of work by others and himself finds no evidence of increased unemployment of native workers caused by immigrants. This result—which I repeat on Zimmermann's authority though I have not examined the studies he cites—is important because it is so counterintuitive for noneconomists. The finding agrees with the evidence from the United States which may be regarded as strongly reinforcing the European studies because the similarity in occupational structures in the United States between immigrants and natives makes an unemployment effect *more* likely rather than less likely.

There is the solid body of careful econometric studies, using a variety of data sources and methods, that shows that immigrants into the United States do not raise the rate of native unemployment:

- Muller (1984) of the Urban Institute compared labor market conditions in Los Angeles County to those in the rest of the United States. "To what extent did the influx of immigrants entering Southern California in the 1970s reduce the jobs available to nonimmigrant workers? ...little if at all."
- Muller and Espenshade (1985) of Princeton studied black unemployment across hundreds of metropolitan-areas in the United States, concentrating on fifty-one metropolitan areas in Arizona, California, and New Mexico with many people of Mexican origin. "Black unemployment rates are not increased—if anything they are lowered—by a rise in the proportion of Mexican immigrants."
- McCarthy and Burciaga Valdez (1986) of the Rand Corporation compared unemployment in California with that in the rest of the United States using

Census Bureau and Department of Labor data. Immigrants' "negative labor market effects have been minor and concentrated among the native-born Latino populations."

- DeFreitas (1986) of Columbia University used 1980 census data to investigate the effect of Hispanic immigrants, many of them illegal, on native Anglos, blacks, and Hispanics. "For no racial-ethnic group, male or female, is there a discernible negative effect of illegal immigration on unemployment. In fact, most of the [effects] are positive."
- Card (1990) of Princeton found that blacks and women did not suffer displacement from jobs in Miami, despite the huge influx of Cuban immigrants there.
- Altonji of Northwestern and Card (1991) studied the effects of immigrants on less-skilled natives in 1970 and 1980 data on cities. "We find little evidence that inflows of immigrants are associated with large or systematic effects on the employment or unemployment rates of less-skilled natives."
- Simon, Moore, and Sullivan (1993) studied the relationship between the rates of immigration and the unemployment rates across cities in the United States during all the years for which data exist: 1960–77. The effect was at most insignificant; it is likely that there was no effect at all.

Sensitivity to Economic Conditions

Zimmermann's graphs are more than sufficient to convince one that in Europe, as in the United States in the past, migration flows are sensitive to economic conditions in the receiving countries. This is important because many of the immigrants are considered refugees, a fact that might call into question whether their economic characteristics are similar to those of other immigrants. But the evidence shows that, whatever their motivations, more immigrants come when demand for them is high than when it is low, so that they make an optimum contribution to the receiving country across business cycles (figures 1 and 2).

The single aspect of Zimmermann's article that I question is the push-pull distinction mentioned in his title. This criticism is unimportant for policy purposes, so I'll make it only briefly.

The push-pull concept has usually been used in *explanation* of immigrant flows, rather than for *analysis* of types of flows or effects; the concept does not seem to work well in characterizing flows or their effects, in my view. It has several shortcomings. The relevant universe is not just the closed world of two countries that the push-pull analysis presupposes; rather, many countries are involved. The geometric demonstration Zimmermann offers is much too simple in the factors it includes. Further, that geometry implicitly embodies the assumption of a fixed number of jobs; it does not reflect the benefits conferred by an additional immigrant who finds employment and does not displace a native, no matter whether it is push or pull immigration. And finally, if there were a big push-pull difference, the charts in Zimmermann's figure 3 would not fit so well in the latter period as they seem to.

The notion Zimmermann is trying to express with the push-pull distinction is this, I think: immigration flows are a function of differences in conditions, and a change at either end can alter the differential. But the results in the receiving country may differ depending on whether the change is a worsening of conditions in the sending country or an improvement in conditions in the receiving country. In an upturn an additional immigrant faces more empty slots, and hence mobility is more beneficial than is true in static conditions or in a downturn. Zimmermann's push-pull theory does not say all this.

The Welfare Payments Issue

Zimmermann's article focuses on the labor market effects of immigrants, which is one of two main concerns of the public and of government policy. But there is a second major concern: the worry that immigrants will exploit the welfare systems at the expense of natives.

Mention immigration and a Western European replies with an anecdote about a family from Turkey or East Germany that arrived with half a dozen children and

Figure 1. *Net Immigration from Recruitment Countries to Federal Republic of Germany and German Business Cycle—with Italy*

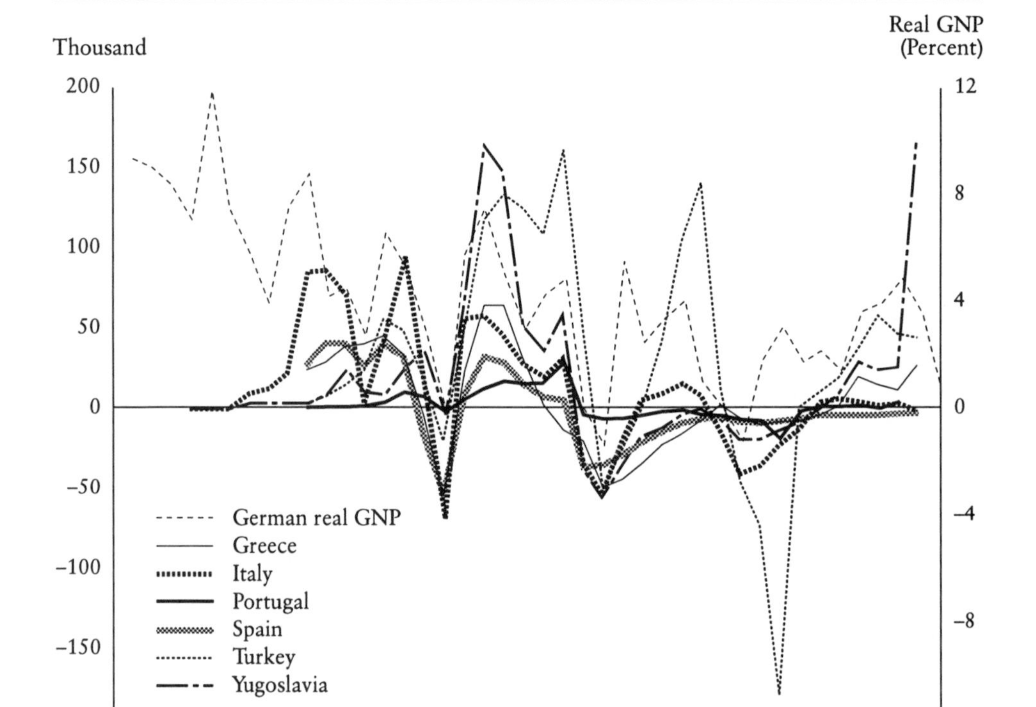

proceeded to batten off the public coffers. Supposed welfare abuse has long been a major objection to immigration in the United States, too.

But when data were gathered for the United States (reviewed in Simon 1989) and Canada (Akbari 1989, 1991), the results showed no welfare exploitation by immigrants. In fact, for many years after arrival the average immigrant family pays more in taxes and receives less in government benefits than does the average native family. The net balance is about $2,500 each year in current dollars. This positive flow occurs because the immigrants tend to be young people just starting their labor force years, rather than old people, whose support is the main drain on the welfare system. The young are the most flexible and have the fewest roots, whereas old people and the handicapped lose pensions and support systems if they leave.

The cumulative flows from each immigrant family enable one native breadwinner to retire two years earlier than otherwise because of the lighter tax burden during the native's lifetime. Indeed, because it increases taxes, the existence of the welfare state makes immigration even more beneficial to natives inasmuch as immigrants typically contribute more to the public coffers in taxes than they use in government services.

Figure 2. *Net Immigration from Recruitment Countries to Federal Republic of Germany and German Business Cycle—without Italy*

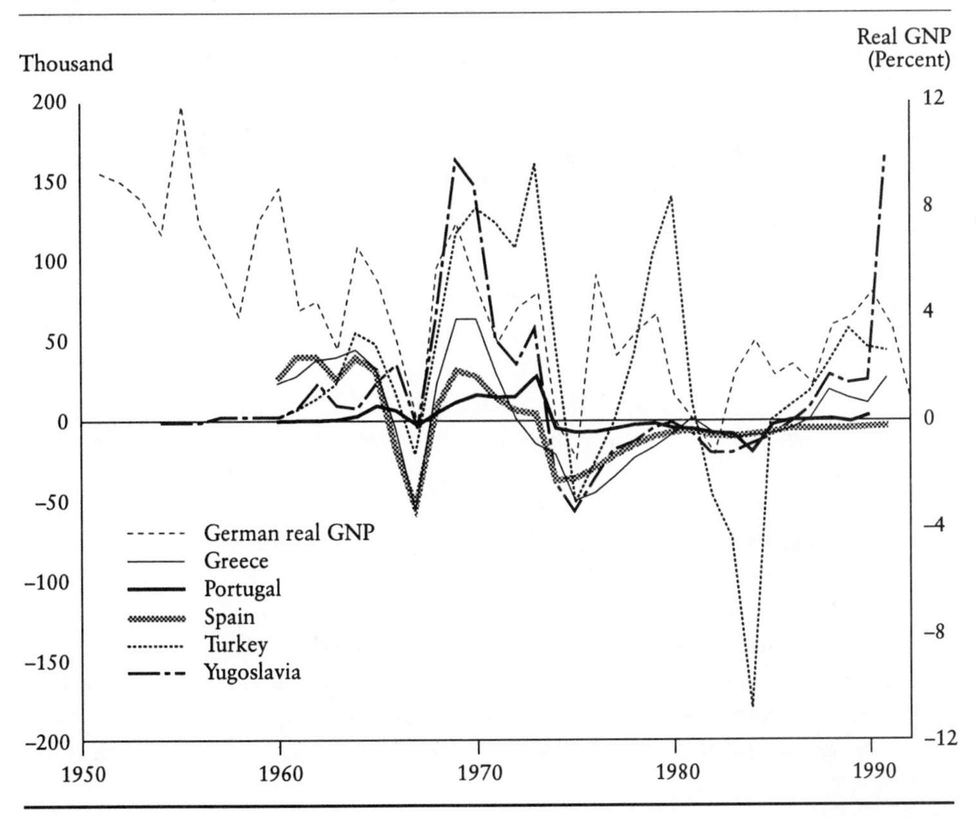

"But conditions are different in Europe," the European invariably replies, "because we give expensive family benefits that you do not provide in the United States." Indeed, Germany and some other countries give parents $50 or more monthly for the first child, and most Western European countries give somewhere around $100 monthly for the second and subsequent children. Moreover, some provide grants for maternity leave, income tax rebates connected with children, and public health programs. The United States offers none of these.

These family programs do not reverse the positive contribution immigrants make to fiscal balance in the United States, however. Even in the United States there is (on average) less than one child of dependent age in immigrant families at any time after arrival, and Eastern European families are considerably smaller. So even if European-style benefits were given in the United States, they would not absorb even half the surplus of the net contribution immigrants make to the public coffers in the United States.

Furthermore, the overall level of taxes paid in Europe—40 percent of total income in Italy and the United Kingdom, 44 percent in Germany, 47 percent in France, and as high as 59 percent in Denmark—is much higher than the 31.5 percent of income paid in the United States. Hence immigrants pay more in taxes in Europe than in the United States.

Some research on the subject has now been done for Europe:

- Gustafsson (1990) analyzed Swedish data and found that "the net difference between income taxes paid and public sector transfers received was...somewhat larger for most groups of immigrants compared to the natives, indicating that natives, through this channel, benefit from immigration."
- Preliminary results of a study of a Swiss governmental labor market survey by Simon and Dhima (1992) show that for each entry cohort of immigrant families (except the oldest)—that is, for each set of families defined by migrating to Switzerland within specified years—the tax contributions are much larger than are the transfer payments. Even more important, the excess of taxes over transfers is greater for each of the immigrant family cohorts than for native families (except the oldest immigrant cohort, whose members are the least numerous).
- Steinmann and Ulrich (1992) studied a 1984 German government socioeconomic survey. The results show a much greater positive difference between taxes and transfers for all immigrant cohorts than for native families. For all immigrants taken together, this difference is more than double that for natives, and the excess is more than two-thirds of the total tax payments—a large contribution to the public coffers by any standard.
- Simon and Akbari (1994) analyzed the 1989 German microcensus and found a somewhat different pattern than the other data showed. For the *most recent* immigrant cohorts, the differences between taxes paid and services used are *not* systematically larger than for natives. The reason is the lower mean incomes of immigrants (despite a higher labor force participation rate due

mainly to their heavy concentration in the working ages and their small numbers of retired persons). And the lower mean incomes are the result of relatively low average education in these newest cohorts. On the other hand, there is no evidence here that these newest immigrants are relatively heavy users of welfare services, including education. The cohorts who arrived *before 1980,* in contrast, have as much or more education than the natives and correspondingly high incomes and tax payments. Taken altogether, we can safely conclude that even less-schooled immigrants make net contributions to the public coffers.

Conclusion

Though none of the above sets of data is conclusive by itself, the general conclusion seems solid: the popular belief that immigrants get fat off the public coffers has no basis. Rather, immigrants put in more than they take out.

The positive effect through the public coffers flows from the most important characteristic of immigration: immigrants arrive when they are young, strong, and healthy—a stage of life when people work and produce, and many years before they collect pensions and expensive public medical care.

The situation differs somewhat according to when the immigrants arrived, but immigrants who pay less taxes also tend to receive less benefits. Still, each cohort on balance is likely to be a net contributor if these European data, together with the United States experience, are a sound guide.

Back-of-the-envelope approximations show why immigrants in Europe, just as in North America, put more money into the public coffers, and take out less in public services, than do natives. Assume that income in Europe is 80 percent of that in the United States and that immigrants finance only half as much of the defense burden and other "public goods" in Europe as they do in the United States. The costs of all government services for average immigrant and native families are approximately 50 percent higher in Europe than they would be if U.S. benefit practices were followed. And taxes paid by immigrants are some 40 percent higher in Europe.

The results of these calculations suggest that immigrants in Europe from Eastern Europe make a net contribution to the public coffers at least 75 percent as large as do immigrants in the United States, as a proportion of income. In other words immigrants are likely to transfer to natives perhaps 7.5 percent of their income each year. And they might well contribute even more to the public coffers in Europe than in North America. Whichever is the case, net contribution is quite the opposite of the net burden that public opinion expects.

If European public and government opinion were to accept the central point of Zimmermann's article—that immigrants do not have ill effects on the labor market—then the welfare payments situation might improve, at least in Germany. Refugees would be allowed to work immediately upon arrival instead of being forcibly kept on the dole for a year, thereby largely reducing those welfare payments.

References

Akbari, Ather H. 1989. "The Benefits of Immigrants to Canada: Evidence on Tax and Public Services." *Canadian Public Policy* 15(4): 424–35.

———. 1991. "The Public Finance Impact of Immigrant Population on Host Nations: Some Canadian Evidence." *Social Science Quarterly* 72(2): 334–46.

Altonji, Joseph G., and David Card. 1991. "The Effects of Immigration on the Labor Market Outcomes of Less-Skilled Natives." In John M. Abowd and Richard B. Freeman, eds., *Immigration, Trade, and the Labor Market.* Chicago: University of Chicago Press.

Bloom, David E., and Richard B. Freeman. 1986. "The Youth Problem: Age or Generational Crowding?" *Employment Outlook.*

Card, David. 1990. "The Impact of the Mariel Boatlift on the Miami Labor Market." *Industrial and Labor Relations Review* 45: 245–57.

DeFreitas, Gregory. 1986. "The Impact of Immigration on Low-Wage Workers." Columbia University, New York, N.Y.

DeFreitas, Gregory, and Adriana Marshall. 1983. "Immigration and Wage Growth in U.S. Manufacturing in the 1970s." *Industrial and Labor Relations Review 36th Annual Proceedings.*

Gustafsson, B. 1990. "Public Sector Transfers and Income Taxes among Immigrants and Natives in Sweden." *International Migration* 28(2): 181–99.

McCarthy, Kevin F., and R. Burciaga Valdez. 1986. *Current and Future Effects of Mexican Immigration in California.* Santa Monica, Calif.: The Rand Corporation.

Muller, Thomas. 1984. *The Fourth Wave: California's Newest Immigrants. A Summary.* Washington, D.C.: The Urban Institute.

Muller, Thomas, and Thomas Espenshade. 1985. *The Fourth Wave: California's Newest Immigrants.* Washington, D.C.: The Urban Institute.

Simon, Julian L. 1989. *The Economic Consequences of Immigration.* Oxford: Basil Blackwell.

Simon, Julian L., and Ather H. Akbari. 1994. "The Effects on Immigrants on the German Public Purse." University of Maryland, College Park.

Simon, Julian L., and Georgio Dhima. 1992. "The Tax-and-Transfer Effects of Immigrants into Switzerland." University of Maryland, College Park.

Simon, Julian L., Stephen Moore, and Richard Sullivan. 1993. "The Effect of Immigration upon Aggregate Native Unemployment: An Across Estimate." *Journal of Labor Research* 4 (Summer): 299–316.

Steinmann, Gunter, and Ralf Ulrich. 1992. "The Impact of Immigrants on Economic Welfare of Natives: Theory and Recent Experiences of Germany." Paper presented at the IASSA Conference on Mass Migration in Europe, Vienna.

Topel, Robert H., and Robert J. LaLonde. 1989. "Labor Market Adjustments to Increased Immigration." In R. Freeman, ed., *Immigration, Trade, and the Labor Market.* Chicago: University of Chicago Press for the National Bureau of Economic Research.

Comment on "European Migration: Push and Pull," by Zimmermann

Xavier Sala-i-Martin

This is an interesting analysis of the type of migration that occurred in Europe after World War II and its consequences. In this comment I highlight three main messages from among the many interesting results presented by Zimmermann. The first is that we can successfully decompose migration into supply-push and demand-pull flows. The second is that empirically even push migration seems to respond to the economic conditions of the host country. The third is that exogenous migration may not be bad, even when there is unemployment in the host country.

The Distinction between Supply-Push and Demand-Pull Migration

One of the main points of the article is that the distinction between demand-pull and supply-push immigration is useful. I think Zimmermann's theoretical and empirical definitions are inconsistent. At the theoretical level Zimmermann defines demand-pull migration as migration that responds to a shift in the demand curve for aggregate goods and supply-push migration as migration that affects the aggregate supply curve only. Because both types of migration represent increases in aggregate labor, they both affect the aggregate supply curve.

When the idea is implemented empirically, however, Zimmermann defines demand-pull migration as responding to economic growth or to the level of income and the unemployment rate in the host country. Supply-push migration, on the other hand, responds to previous migration, which is supposed to capture the existence of ethnic networks in the country and variables operating in the sending country. In other words, instead of relying on the theoretical definitions in terms of aggregate demand or aggregate supply, he now considers demand-pull migration as the one that responds to the economic conditions of the host nation and supply-push as the one that does not.

Let me give some examples that show the inconsistency of Zimmermann's theoretical and empirical definitions. First, imagine that country A experiences an increase in productivity. In the aggregate supply and demand model Zimmermann has in mind (see his figure 1), the supply curve would shift to the right, but at the

Xavier Sala-i-Martin is professor of economics at Yale University.

Proceedings of the World Bank Annual Conference on Development Economics 1994

same time workers' wages would increase with the rise in productivity. This development would clearly attract migrants from other countries and induce a further shift in the supply curve. The aggregate demand curve would remain unchanged. According to the theoretical definition this would be an example of supply-push migration (only the supply curve moves). The empirical definition, however, would consider this demand-pull migration because it would be accompanied by improvements in the economic conditions in the host country in the form of a positive growth rate. The two definitions yield different answers.

A second example: the decision to migrate is a forward-looking one. Expectations about future wages and future economic conditions are important. Consider an expected improvement in country A's economic conditions. This alone will trigger (pull) migration, regardless of what happens to today's supply or demand. On top of this the aggregate demand curve may move as people smooth consumption and firms anticipate future profits with high current investment. The theoretical definition would call this push migration because migrants would be reacting not to any shift in aggregate demand but to expected higher future wages. The empirical definition, however, would view the migration as pull migration because it comes along with growth in the host country.

A third example is even more striking. Consider an exogenous increase in migrants. The theoretical definition says that this increase is supply-push migration. Since the movement affects the economic conditions of the economy, we would observe a simultaneous improvement in output and migration. The empirical definition, therefore, says that it is demand-pull.

The conclusion is that the theoretical and empirical definitions are often contradictory. My impression is that the correct distinction between demand-pull and supply-push migration should be related to the supply and demand of migrants (as opposed to aggregate supply and demand). The market for migrants has a supply and a demand, just as any other market does. The equilibrium amount of migration can increase in response to shifts in the supply or demand functions, both of which depend on economic conditions in the host country (as reflected in wage rates, unemployment, income per capita, and so on). When an improvement in the economic conditions in the host country shifted the demand for migrants we would say that migration is demand-pull. Whether these improvements are the consequence of aggregate demand factors (like higher government spending) or aggregate supply factors (like improvements in productivity) should not matter much. The important fact is that labor market conditions pull people from other countries. In this framework, we would define supply-push migration as exogenous increases in the supply of migrants. Following Milton Friedman's famous monetary analogy, supply-push is a "helicopter drop of people."

The problem is that if we take this definition seriously, it is almost certainly true that we will never see pure supply-push migration, even at the theoretical level. As Zimmermann correctly points out at the end of the article, people may be pushed away from Spain, Turkey, or Yugoslavia, but nobody pushes them into Germany. In other words, once people know that they want to (or have to) leave their country of origin, they still have to choose where to go. There is an almost unlimited array of potential host countries. People may choose to go to Australia, Germany, or Switzerland, but they may also choose Greece, Mexico, or Somalia. Why do most choose the first set of countries? It may have to do with political or sociological reasons. It may even have to do with the distance from the country of origin. But to a large extent, it has to do with the good economic conditions in these host countries. In other words, given an exogenous increase in the worldwide supply of migrants, the economic conditions of each country will determine the exact distribution of these migrants across host countries. Hence, in an international framework we will probably never observe pure supply-push migration. In fact, this is one of Zimmermann's empirical findings, but note that it questions the validity of the whole theoretical concept of push and pull.

The Empirical Evidence

Zimmermann's second message is that, empirically, even push migration responds to economic conditions in host countries. Here we confront an identification problem: economic conditions affect migration and migration affects economic conditions. I think that there is little hope of distinguishing supply-push from demand-pull migration using the type of single ordinary least squares (OLS) time-series regressions presented in table 1. There are usually two ways of solving identification problems. First, we can search for good instruments that allow us to identify the effects of pure exogenous shifts in the supply of migrants. My guess is that such instruments will be difficult to come by. The second alternative, which has been used in the labor literature, is natural experiments. Hunt (1992) conducted one for migration in the case of Algerian immigrants to France. Zimmermann also conducts one for the case of asylum seekers (see table 5).

In table 4 Zimmermann uses six time-series regressions of the flows of net migrants (as the independent variable) on the contemporaneous growth rate of aggregate output, lagged migration, and a time trend. He allows for all the coefficients to take different values before and after 1973. If the real growth variable is significant, migration is considered to be demand-pull; significant coefficient values for the time trend and lagged migration are seen as identifying push factors. The main result is that the coefficient on the contemporaneous growth rate is positive before 1973 and decreases after 1973. The conclusion is that demand-pull migration was important during the first period and less so during the second.

Several aspects of these regressions trouble me. The first is the use of the contemporaneous growth rate. Taken literally, this means that when Germany grows 1 percent above trend between January 1 and December 31 of year t, 12,319 Greeks, 16,013 Italians, and 14,071 Turks arrive in the country (on net) within the same year. This is very surprising because, among other problems, the growth data are probably not available immediately. Furthermore, once a family has made the decision to migrate, it needs some time to make arrangements before actually moving. It is really surprising that migrants react so quickly to current market conditions.

How else can we interpret the estimates of table 4? If we think of migration as a permanent decision based on the present values of income differentials, the estimates of table 4 can be interpreted as migration demand equations only if the contemporaneous growth rate conveys information about future economic performance. But does it? If so, is it the best instrument we have for forecasting future income differentials? I think that some discussion of these issues would be useful. This reasoning, however, suggests that the lag structure of the equations estimated in table 4 is not quite correct.

But let me give an alternative interpretation. The simple neoclassical model of Solow (1956) and Swan (1956) suggests that the growth rate of per capita output is a positive function of the exogenous saving rate and a negative function of the initial level of income, the rate of population growth, and the depreciation rate:

$$\Delta\log (Y/L)_t = \beta_0 - \beta_1 \log (Y/L)_t - \beta_2 n + \text{other} \tag{1}$$

where Y is aggregate output, L is the stock of population, and n is the rate of growth of population. The dependent variable, $\Delta\log (Y/L)_t$ (the log difference of Y/L between t and $t + 1$), is the growth rate of per capita output. "Other" includes the saving rate, the rate of depreciation, and some disturbances. This equation can be reorganized as

$$\Delta\log L_t = \alpha_0 + \alpha_1 \Delta\log Y_t + \alpha_2 \log (Y/L)_t + \text{other} \tag{2}$$

where $\Delta\log L_t$ is the growth rate of population, n, which in this case would be similar to the rate of migration. Note that this equation is similar to the one estimated by Zimmermann:

$$\Delta\log L_t = a_0 + a_1 \Delta\log Y_t + a_2\text{time} + \text{other}, \tag{3}$$

where a time dummy has been substituted for the log of per capita output. Under this interpretation table 4 is just an estimation of the growth equation as characterized by the familiar Solow-Swan model. But if this is correct, one could ask why the coefficient α_1 is lower after 1973. One possible reason is that the true regression involves the level of income as an explanatory variable, while the estimated equation involves a time trend. Hence temporary deviations of log of output per capita from a linear trend (that is, temporary business cycles) are embodied in the error term. When Germany's growth rate is more or less smooth (pre-1973), an approximation of log Y_t by a time trend is not so bad. But in the presence of big cycles (post-1973), the error term is negatively correlated with the explanatory variable $\Delta\log Y_t$, so the estimate of α_1 is biased toward zero.

Is this the correct interpretation? I don't know. But this example illustrates the simultaneity problems that plague the results in table 4. And the fact that migration reacts so fast to contemporaneous growth rates makes alternative interpretations look more attractive.

But let's take Zimmermann's interpretation seriously. Note that the countries for which the growth rate becomes insignificant after 1974 are those for which the net flow of migrants becomes negative: Greece, Portugal, and Spain (see Zimmermann's figure 3); that is, these are the countries for which return migration is important after 1974. Should return migration be affected by economic conditions in the host country? I don't know, but if we could analyze immigration into Germany entirely omitting the economic conditions of the sending country, I guess we could do the same thing now: return migration should depend on economic conditions in the country of origin, independent of Germany's variables. Hence the result in table 4. Now is this evidence of a reduction in the importance of pull migration? I don't think so. It is evidence of the existence of return migration after 1973.

Finally, I have some specification questions in the elaboration of table 4. For example, why were level variables omitted? (Note that in table 5, the explanatory variables that will proxy for the economic conditions of the host country will be the wage and unemployment rates, not the growth rates.) Why were the economic conditions of the sending country omitted? Why was the dependent variable the number of migrants rather than the growth rate? Why was the measure of the business cycle the contemporaneous growth rate of aggregate output rather than of output per capita? Why was it the growth rate rather than some deviation from trend (a measure business cycle theorists much prefer)? None of these questions can be answered because we do not have a model that tells us the exact specification to be estimated.

The results in table 5 are more interesting. Using panel data, Zimmermann studies the reaction in the number of asylum seekers to wage differentials, unemployment differentials, and some variables called "ethnic networks." As I said, looking for natural experiments is a way to solve the identification problem. If we think of the people in the sample as being true supply-push migrants, then this is a natural experiment that identifies supply-push migrants (although the problem of country selection is still valid here). In this sense I interpret table 5 as follows: every year there is a helicopter drop of migrants in the EU countries. These migrants can choose their country of destination. Inasmuch as these are supposed to be people who are forced out of their country of origin, it is natural to substitute the relative conditions of the potential host countries for the home country economic conditions (which is what Zimmermann does). Table 5 provides evidence that the asylum seekers tend to go to the country with the best economic conditions, as measured by low unemployment rates and high levels of income. In terms of push and pull migration this table shows that even push migration reacts to economic conditions.

To make the table more complete, one could compute a dummy variable that assigns a value to the political or legal impediments to migration. Countries in trouble might be tempted to reduce the number of migrants through regulation. Hence the level of economic activity could be partly proxying for these legal effects, which then biases the coefficients on wages and unemployment toward zero (and against Zimmermann).

Is Migration Bad?

A third point of the article is that migration may not be bad, even if it is driven exogenously and even in the presence of unemployment in the host country. In fact, some people argue that one of the disadvantages Europe faces today relative to the United States is the lack of population movements, a consequence of language barriers, cultural barriers, and so on. These people think that migration is good in some sense. In a neoclassical equilibrium world with no externalities or public goods migration is beneficial. But Zimmermann goes further and (correctly) argues that even unemployment is not an argument against migration. The desirability of migration depends on the relative elasticities of substitution across types of workers.

As economists we have to be puzzled by the behavior of all the governments surveyed in the article: if migration is good, why do they oppose it? The answer could be that the governments don't understand anything, so we need to explain things to them more carefully. The Virginia view of the world would say that governments (or politicians) do understand, but that they do not seek the country's welfare. Finally, the Chicago view of the world would say that governments do understand so our analysis must be missing something important. (Of course, migration may be politically unattractive for other reasons, such as racism or bigotry.) Let me take the Chicago view and try to propose two alternative reasons for not liking migration.

Imagine that output in country A can be produced with three inputs: private capital, labor, and a public good. The public good, in turn, is subject to congestion. We can think of highways, the legal system, or public hospitals; we could also think of natural resources such as land or water. The greater the number of people using this good, the less useful it is. For example, suppose that output Y for firm i in a particular country is given by

$$Y_i = A\,(K_i^{\alpha} L_i^{1-\alpha})\,(G/L)^{\eta} \qquad (4)$$

where K_i and L_i are capital and labor used in firm i, G is the supply of this public good or natural resource, and L is the total number of people in the economy. Note that this production function exhibits constant returns to scale (a proportional increase in all inputs, including G and L, leads to a proportional increase in output). Note also that, holding population constant, the higher is the stock of public goods, the higher is the output and the higher are the private marginal products of capital and labor. Finally, note that while holding the public good G constant, an increase in total population reduces the productivity of the public good and all private inputs; that is, population congests the public good.

In terms of the labor market pictures proposed in the article, a direct effect of an inflow of people is to shift the labor supply curve to the right. An indirect effect is that these people congest the public good, they reduce the marginal product of labor for all levels of employment, and the demand curve shifts inward. If the initial number of people is small relative to the public good or natural resource (as in the United States in the twentieth century), the first effect will tend to dominate, so labor demand shifts to the right. As the aggregate number of people per unit of public good increases, the congestion effect will tend to dominate and, as a result, migration will become undesirable (this could be the case in Europe after 1973).

How important are these public goods? I don't know. Public goods obviously exist, and public spending is more than 30 percent of the economy in virtually all of the countries under consideration. And one could easily argue that all public goods are subject to congestion (even national defense or pensions).

Another argument against certain types of migration is related to human capital externalities derived from human interaction. This idea has been popularized by Lucas (1988) in his now famous model of endogenous growth. Suppose, as Lucas does, that there is an externality from the average stock of human capital. And suppose that different individuals enjoy different levels of human capital. If we increase the number of highly skilled people, then the average human capital increases and everybody's productivity goes up. However, an increase in the number of low-skilled people lowers the average stock of human capital and, as a result, reduces the productivity of all workers. Migration of low-skilled people would reduce the average wage and income per capita of the economy and therefore would be damaging for locals.

Note that the arguments proposed here are similar: migration may lower everybody's income. The main difference is that in the case of public goods, all migrants are bad, while in the second case, only low-skilled migrants are bad. The problem with these stories is that they are not arguments against migration. They are arguments against free migration. In other words, to solve the problem of migration we should not forbid population movements, we should simply charge people for entering the country. In the first case the optimal migration policy would be to charge migrants a user fee for using the public goods of the host economy. In the second case migrants should be charged for the exact amount of the externality. These solutions would be better than simply prohibiting migration.

References

Hunt, J. 1992. "The Impact of the 1962 Repatriates from Algeria on the French Labor Market." *Industrial and Labor Relations Review* 45(3).

Lucas, R. 1988. "On the Mechanics of Economic Development." *Journal of Monetary Economics* 22: 3–22.

Solow, R. 1956. "A Contribution to the Theory of Economic Growth." *Quarterly Journal of Economics* 70: 65–94.

Swan, T. 1956. "Economic Growth and Capital Accumulation." *Economic Record* 32: 344–61.

Floor Discussion of "European Migration: Push and Pull," by Zimmermann

Julian Simon (discussant) believes migration is generally good, said Ismail Serageldin (chair), in opening the discussion, and Xavier Sala-i-Martin (discussant) believes that there is an explanation for why it can be seen as bad, so there is plenty of ground for divergence.

On the simultaneity problem, Maurice Schiff from the World Bank agreed that, theoretically, there is a problem with the distinction between demand-pull and supply-push. Whether there is a problem empirically depends on how important migration is in terms of changes in the labor market. If the distinction is important empirically, maybe there is a big problem. Zimmermann appreciated the concern. There is always a question of definitions, he said—are they useful, or are they not?—and whether we can identify supply and demand by regressions is a big issue. He did not worry about it too much in this case because he did not believe that the growth rate variable is much affected by migration itself. Migration has some effect on growth, but that effect takes years to work. And regressions are not meant to supply much information; in a sense they are only descriptive.

More important, felt Schiff, was the point Sala-i-Martin had made about how something could be bad even though its badness wasn't evident. In Germany, for example, if it is true that when the share of migrants in the labor market goes up 1 percent, the share of blue-collar workers drops 3.94 percent, he could see why German workers would complain. Maybe the economy as a whole did not suffer: blue-collar residents lost, white-collar residents gained, so on average unemployment did not change. Obviously, the white-collar residents who gained would not complain. But one could see why the blue-collar workers would. Yet one has to think beyond that. What if the immigrants are blue-collar, earn blue-collar wages, and pay taxes that are lower than white-collar taxes? Assume that the distribution of services is uniform across all people, or that the lower-income workers get more services because they go to public schools, have more children, and so on. In such a case—even though nothing is happening with average wages—net gainers and losers may change because revenues change and so does the use of public services.

This session was chaired by Ismail Serageldin, vice president, Environmentally Sustainable Development, at the World Bank.

Empirical study is needed to confirm such a trend. To amplify on a point made earlier about congested public goods, Schiff referred to what he called "social capital"—that residents of a place feel they share values, culture, history, and so on. Schiff, who authored two papers on social capital and migration, suggested that people do not feel threatened by a few immigrants but may feel threatened when a population with a very different culture and background becomes large.

There was yet another explanation for why people often misstate the effects of immigrants, said Simon. To understand an economic phenomenon, you have to understand the indirect effects (spread over time and space) as well as the direct effects, and laymen (noneconomists) focus only on the direct effects. We have some empirical evidence for that, he said. In surveys, for example, if you ask Americans, "Are you in favor of having more immigrants? Are immigrants good for us?" they will answer, "No, they are not." But if you ask them, "What about the immigrants you know personally? Are they good?" they will answer, "Oh yes, they are great folks." What they know with their own eyes they can talk about with reliability, but they cannot talk with reliability about this issue because they do not understand economics. This is one of many things the public systematically misunderstands, said Simon. They also believe we are running out of resources. They believe that resources are becoming more scarce, when all the data show they are becoming more available. They believe our air and water are becoming dirtier, when in fact our air and water are becoming cleaner.

Addressing Simon, Andrew Isserman (discussant from another session) said that the data in table 3 seemed to be data on occupation distribution, not data on employment distribution, and he thought occupation data would look quite different for the United States, especially by place. Low-skilled immigrants tend to settle in a place like California, for example, which has a high concentration of high-skilled labor, whereas Appalachia gets more than its share of engineers, doctors, and professors. And complementarities of work by occupation can be hidden in employment data: a Honda executive, a skilled craftsman in the automobile industry, and a textile worker in Los Angeles are all in manufacturing, but occupation data for them would be quite different. Simon responded that he was not suggesting that the distribution of immigrants and natives in the United States was identical; only that it would seem to be more different in Europe than in the United States.

To wrap things up, Serageldin said, we can say that on balance, Zimmermann favored controlled immigration and felt that immigration had been beneficial, partly by adding flexibility to the labor market; he did not foresee immigration being replaced by the movement of capital and goods. Among the powerful statements Simon had made, Serageldin was particularly struck by his emphasis on how research in the United States was not necessarily transferable or applicable to Europe. As for why there was so much resistance to immigration, Serageldin was struck by the observation about social capital and felt that the resentment people feel about the "browning of the West"—changes in the makeup of the people you see around you—may explain some of the unease people feel, regardless of statistics. If, as had been stated, definitions of push-pull had little relevance for policy purposes, and if there was no evidence of immigrants exploiting welfare, Serageldin wondered why a group that believed in markets and in bringing people into economic activity would not favor letting immigrants work immediately. Sala-i-Martin had stated that people who consider immigration bad are concerned mainly with excess consumption of public goods.

Radical change—involving labor, international capital movements, global financial markets, transport technology, and so on—is changing the way things work, said Serageldin. In this context labor—especially in places like Europe—is not clearly defining its role anymore. Is its purpose to expand employment or to protect the benefits of those already employed in the face of high unemployment? Labor must rethink its raison d'être, because its role in society is being questioned. The share of labor that is unionized is declining, especially in places like the United States. And the concepts on which labor unions are philosophically based are going to be severely challenged by observable economic trends, whether in Europe or in the United States. The assumption behind collective bargaining is to guarantee some form of equality, but that will have to be redefined. We are moving away from equality toward much greater inequality because we are moving toward a knowledge-based society, in which inequality is inherent. At the same time, boundaries and relationships between different sectors are changing, and so are relations between firms. Are Toyota and General Motors competitors or partners? They are partners in some things and competitors in others, often in the same market but not always in the same market niche. And so we should think about immigration in the context of a rapidly changing labor market.

Frontier Issues in International Migration

Oded Stark

Drawing on the general assumption that information is imperfect, this article addresses three main issues: First, why do some migrants return even though the intercountry wage differential does not reverse? And who returns? Second, why do migrants who stay tend to share their higher earnings with others at origin, even in the absence of altruism or of a need to establish an exchange relationship? And can the size of these transfers be predicted? Third, what explains the earnings of migrants? Why do they often dominate the earnings of equivalent native-born workers even if differences in human capital are fully controlled for?

The article suggests these answers: First, when informational symmetry is reestablished, the low-skill workers, who are no longer pooled with the high-skill workers, return. Second, migrants' remittances are conceived as side-payments, made under asymmetric information, by high-skill migrant workers to low-skill workers, who, if they were to migrate, would erode the wages of the high-skill workers. And third, the edge migrants have over native-born workers arises from the lower recognition costs of partners to trade whose type is unknown.

This article delineates a number of frontier issues in international labor migration. Why do migrants return even though the wage differential does not reverse? Who returns? Why do migrants who remain and enjoy higher wages share their earnings with others at home, even in the absence of altruism or of a need to establish an exchange relationship? And why do the earnings of migrants often dominate those of native-born workers even when differences in human capital are controlled for? By the very nature of these issues, the analysis is preliminary and suggestive, the link with empirics is partial and often indirect, and the policy repercussions are tentative. Should these issues prove responsive to concrete policies, answers to these questions could serve real-world concerns. The analysis delineates a number of concrete, testable implications and several distinct policies.

Oded Stark is professor of development economics at the University of Oslo. The first section of this article is based on Stark (1995b); the second and third sections are based, respectively, on chapters 4 and 5 of Stark (1995a).

Migration is significant in almost every country, whether as an inflow or an outflow. The questions of how migrants perform in the marketplace and what explains their performance, which to a considerable extent involve efficiency and equity concerns, are basic to research on migration.

Moreover, remittances are not a pittance. In 1980 workers' remittances accounted for as much foreign exchange as exports did for Pakistan and Upper Volta, more than 60 percent of exports for Egypt, Portugal, and Turkey, and about 40 percent for Bangladesh and Yugoslavia (World Bank 1984).

Despite difficulties in assessing return migration, there are reasons to believe that the numbers are often large, even in countries ordinarily viewed as countries of destination such as the United States and Germany. Data for 1908–57, when the United States collected information on the arrival and departure of migrants, show that of the 15.7 million migrants admitted, 4.8 million—nearly one-third—departed (LaLonde and Topel 1993). Moreover, the foreign population in the Federal Republic of Germany was no larger in 1988 than it was in 1983 (OECD 1990); during these six years the outflow of the foreign population was 2,378,000. Of course, this outflow includes asylum seekers whose requests were refused. The number of asylum seekers received by Germany during the period was 389,000. Abstracting from the lags and subtracting *all* the asylum seekers, the outflow totals 2 million, which all indications suggest consists largely of returns. Because no administrative barriers hamper migration between Puerto Rico and the United States, issues of asylum and work permits do not arise, making estimates of return migrants much simpler. In 1980 about 1 million people born in Puerto Rico were residing in the United States, but 283,000 returned to Puerto Rico from the United States, where they had resided between 1970 and 1980 (U.S. Department of Commerce 1983, 1984).

A recent survey of young Irish labor market participants provides additional helpful evidence. Of 1,299 Irish school leavers in 1981–82, 378 migrated at least once between leaving school and 1988; of these, 117 returned by 1988. The returnees were significantly less educated than the migrants who remained. Controlling for labor market conditions at destination, return migration is more likely from European Union countries—other than the United Kingdom—in which employers are said to "fail to recognize Irish qualifications" (Reilly 1994).

I have addressed the questions posed in this article before, in *The Migration of Labor* (Stark 1991). This article steps beyond that work. Whereas the book highlights the importance for migration outcomes of the relationship between migrants and their families at home, this article emphasizes the relationship between migrants and their employers and among migrants themselves. Moreover, this article assumes that information is imperfect and examines the repercussions of this assumption for migration outcomes. Agents that meet to conduct a transaction usually do not fully know the characteristics of fellow agents that impinge on the transaction's outcome. In the context of an employment relationship this applies to the skill level of (new) employees (the first and second sections). In the context of marketplace trades this applies to the type of partner (the third section). This article demonstrates the considerable explanatory and predictive powers of analyses based on the assumption of imperfect information.

In the first section, Dynamics and Return, the theory of labor migration under asymmetric information is used to generate an integrated set of predictions. The key results are the prevalence of return migration and a characterization of the migrant workers who return. In particular, in the discrete case with only two skill levels, low-skill workers return while high-skill workers stay. The wage of the high-skill workers increases over time, but not as a result of skill enhancement. When individual skill levels of migrant workers are unknown to employers, the workers receive a wage based on the average product of the group. This averaging invites low-skill workers to move along with high-skill workers. Once informational symmetry is restored through monitoring and observation and wages are adjusted accordingly, low-skill workers return. The high-skill workers stay, and their wages rise. Now a yet higher-quality subset of workers migrates, and the process is replicated. By migrating, workers constituting the first subset block the migration of workers constituting higher-quality subsets. But by subsequently exposing themselves to identification, these workers pave the way for the migration of higher-quality workers. Thus migration proceeds in waves, with each wave breaking into workers who stay and workers who return; within waves the returning migrants are the low-skill workers.

The second section of the article, Remittances as Side-Payments, supplements the model developed in the first section with a structure to incorporate the possibility of transfers by migrants. The key results are the identification of a new motive for remittances and the determination of their size as a function of model parameters. The idea here is that since high-skill workers benefit if low-skill workers do not migrate, they should be willing to remit to induce them to stay put. The conditions under which such transfers are made are detailed, and their magnitude is determined. Migrants remit to nonmigrants not out of altruism, but out of self-interest: remittances protect the wages of high-skill workers from the contaminating presence of low-skill workers in the same pool.

The basic premise of the first two sections is that incentives to migrate, return, and remit arise from wage differentials conditional on informational regimes. The issue of incentives lies at the heart of migration research, and it has also recently been incorporated into the analysis of the absolute and relative performance of migrants in the marketplace at destination: if migrants differ from nonmigrants in that they face an exogenous probability of return migration and the receipt of lower wages, they have an incentive to work harder and save more than nonmigrants (Stark 1991, chap. 27 and 28).

But the key to migrants' performance may be found on yet another ring: a group attribute. The third section, Recognition Costs and Performance, considers a population consisting of two groups, migrants and indigenous people. Each group consists of agents who trade cooperatively, *C*, and agents who trade noncooperatively, *NC*. Assume that members of each group trade only with members of their own group (this assumption can be relaxed). Agents do not know the type of the agents with whom they trade (again, information is imperfect), but they can obtain such information at a cost. The idea is that the cost that migrants incur in assessing whether a fellow migrant is a type *C* or a type *NC* is lower than the analogous cost incurred by nonmigrants. In this situation the equilibrium share of C-type agents in the migrant group is higher than that in the nonmigrant group. And since, by construction, the payoff matrices of each of the groups are the same, the per capita payoff of migrants is higher than that of nonmigrants: the migrants outperform the nonmigrants. If the cost-of-information advantage is not present, however, migrants do not fare better than nonmigrants. The key results here are thus the ability to explain the differential performance of migrants without recourse to individual human capital attributes, and a prediction that when there are different groups of migrants, all else equal, the groups with low recognition costs will outperform the groups with high recognition costs.

The theoretical literature on labor migration is remarkably silent on return migration. Yet the number of migrant workers in any country is as dependent on departures as on arrivals and, as already demonstrated, evidence suggests that migration is often shorter than the duration of life or of working life. With conventional theory attributing migration to a positive wage differential, a conventional explanation of return migration is, not surprisingly, a negative wage differential (Dustmann 1993). While this explanation might be correct, considerable return migration appears to take place even in the absence of a reversal of the relative wages of the sending and receiving countries.

The typical explanations are that migrants return because of failure or because of success: if reality does not tally with expectations or if the draw from a mixture of good draws and bad draws (random shocks) is bad, migrants may return. Alternatively, migrants whose returns on human or financial capital are higher at home than abroad may find it optimal to return (Borjas and Bratsberg 1992).

There are other reasons for return migration, however. One is that a family member may migrate to diversify the ways in which the family earns its income. If income earned abroad and income earned at home do not covary fully and there is a post-migration pooling and sharing of income, the family's risk is lowered. Just as bearing one risk makes agents less willing to bear another risk, *not* bearing that one risk makes agents more willing to bear another risk (Pratt and Zeckhauser 1987; Kimball 1993). People at home are then free to experiment with a relatively high-risk, high-return option, for example, a high-yield seed variety. If the experiment is successful, the need for migration-provided insurance ceases. Thus the reason for return migration is not that the migrant accumulated capital with an expected high return at home but rather that his or her migration facilitated a high-return investment at home by others (Stark 1991).

Return migration may also occur because of the higher purchasing power of savings (generated from work abroad) at home than abroad. Researchers have incorporated the possibility that consumption at home is preferable to consumption abroad into carefully argued models (Hill 1987; Djajic and Milbourne 1988). In research in progress Stark, Helmenstein, and Yegorov (1994) attempt to identify what underlies such a consumption preference, if it exists, and to account for return migration even if that preference is absent. Specifically, we investigate the role of purchasing power of given amounts of savings in facilitating different levels of consumption at home and abroad. While earlier work considered the effect of the probability of return migration on migrants' optimal savings (Stark 1991, chap. 27), this work develops the opposite line of inquiry: how migrants' savings determine the optimal timing of return. Among other things, this work points to a negative relationship between the optimal duration of migration and the purchasing power differential. Further, in some cases it shows a negative relationship between the optimal duration of migration and the wage abroad.

Yet return migration may be caused by reasons beyond the disposition of savings or the elimination of risks. And little is known "about whether it is high- or low-skilled workers who choose to return home" (LaLonde and Topel 1993).

Research on migrants' performance has essentially assumed that the key to the relation of migrants' income to that of the native-born population lies in their ability, skills, and productivity. This assumption has channeled considerable research energy into measuring, estimating, and testing migrant characteristics (Borjas 1985; Chiswick 1986a and 1986b; LaLonde and Topel 1993). Recent work has considered the possibility that the performance of migrants could be attributed directly to their incentives to exert effort and to save, thereby shifting the focus of analysis from the vector of characteristics to the structure of incentives (Stark 1991, chap. 27 and 28).

Yet groups too, not only individuals, have characteristics, and incentives contingent on an exogenous probability of return migration are nullified when the probability of return approaches zero.

Research on remittances has tended to attribute motivations to remit to altruism—concern for the well-being of family members who stay behind—or to self-interest arising from the intention to return, aspirations to inherit, maintenance of investments at home, or a need for insurance against unfavorable income realizations at destination, such as spells of unemployment (Stark 1991). But these considerations do not exhaust the set of motives, and in particular situations none of them may apply.

Dynamics and Return

This section presents an implementation of the theory of labor migration under asymmetric information wherein return migration is an integral, structural part of the migration process. The addition of an explicit intertemporal dimension to the static model of labor migration under asymmetric information (Stark 1991) amplifies the model and makes it possible to differentiate and characterize workers who never migrate, workers who migrate and stay at their destination, and workers who migrate and subsequently return home.

Suppose, first, that in a given occupation workers fall into two groups according to their skills—low-skill and high-skill. The theory offers the following predictions: migration is ex post fully positively selective even though ex ante it is not; it breaks into workers who stay and workers who return; and the returning migrants are low-skill workers. The judgment concerning the selective nature of migration is thus sensitive to the time at which the judgment is made. Whereas the end result of migration is not sensitive to the information regime (symmetric or asymmetric), the migration path is: it is single phased under symmetric information, but multiphased under asymmetric information. With the introduction of some auxiliary structure, the theory identifies a procedure that allows the receiving country to skim off the high-quality workers without engaging in costly screening.

Suppose next that workers in the profession constitute four skill levels. A plausible implementation of the theory of labor migration under asymmetric information generates the following predictions: migration is sequential or phased; not all workers who end up as migrants move at the same point in time. Each wave of migration breaks into workers who stay and workers who return. The century-old "law of migration" that "each main current of migration produces a compensating counter-current" (Ravenstein 1885) turns out to be a derivative of a variant of the asymmetric-information approach to migration. Within waves (cohorts) the returning migrants are the low-quality workers; thus migration is ex post positively selective within cohorts. When the migration process is fully completed, migration is mildly positively selective—the average quality of migrants is superior to the average quality of workers found at origin—but not all migrants are of higher quality than all workers at origin. (Only in the case of two types of workers does migration turn out to be ex post fully positively selective.) The average quality of migrants rises with each cohort.

We next present the basic model of labor migration under asymmetric information, and follow it with migration patterns arising from an example with two skill levels. We then examine a case with four skill levels and derive the resulting migratory patterns. Finally, we place the approach utilized in this section of the article in the context of related research on labor migration.

Labor Migration under Asymmetric Information: The Basic Model

Assume a world consisting of two countries: a rich country, *R*, and a poor country, *P*. We can likewise assume a country consisting of a rich urban area and a poor rural area. In a given occupation let the net wages for a worker with skill level θ be $W_R(\theta)$ in the rich country and $W_P(\theta)$ in the poor country, such that $\partial W_P(\theta) / \partial\theta > 0$ and $\partial W_R(\theta) / \partial\theta > 0$.[1] (Thus workers' productivities in the sending and receiving countries are ranked identically.) To reflect the fact that *R* is rich and *P* is poor, $W_R(\theta) > W_P(\theta)$ for all θ.[2] Also, without loss of generality, let θ be defined upon the closed interval [0,1] and let the density function of *P* workers on θ be $F(\theta)$.

In addition, given that *P* workers are likely to have a preference for a *P* lifestyle because of cultural factors, social relationships, and so on, it is assumed that they apply a discount factor to *R* wages when comparing them to *P* wages. Thus when making the migration decision, they compare $kW_R(\theta)$ with $W_P(\theta)$, where $0 < k < 1$. A *P* worker will therefore migrate from *P* to *R* if

$$kW_R(\theta) > W_P(\theta). \qquad (1)$$

Clearly, without further restrictions on $W_R(\theta)$ and $W_P(\theta)$ there may be several values of θ for which $kW_R(\theta) - W_P(\theta) = 0$. Hence there may be several distinct skill groups along the skill axis (figure 1).

Thus the workers in skill intervals $[0,\theta_1]$, $[\theta_2,\theta_3]$, and $[\theta_4,1]$ migrate, whereas those in the complementary intervals do not. The case in which there are at least

Figure 1. *Disjoint Skill Intervals of Migration under Symmetric Information*

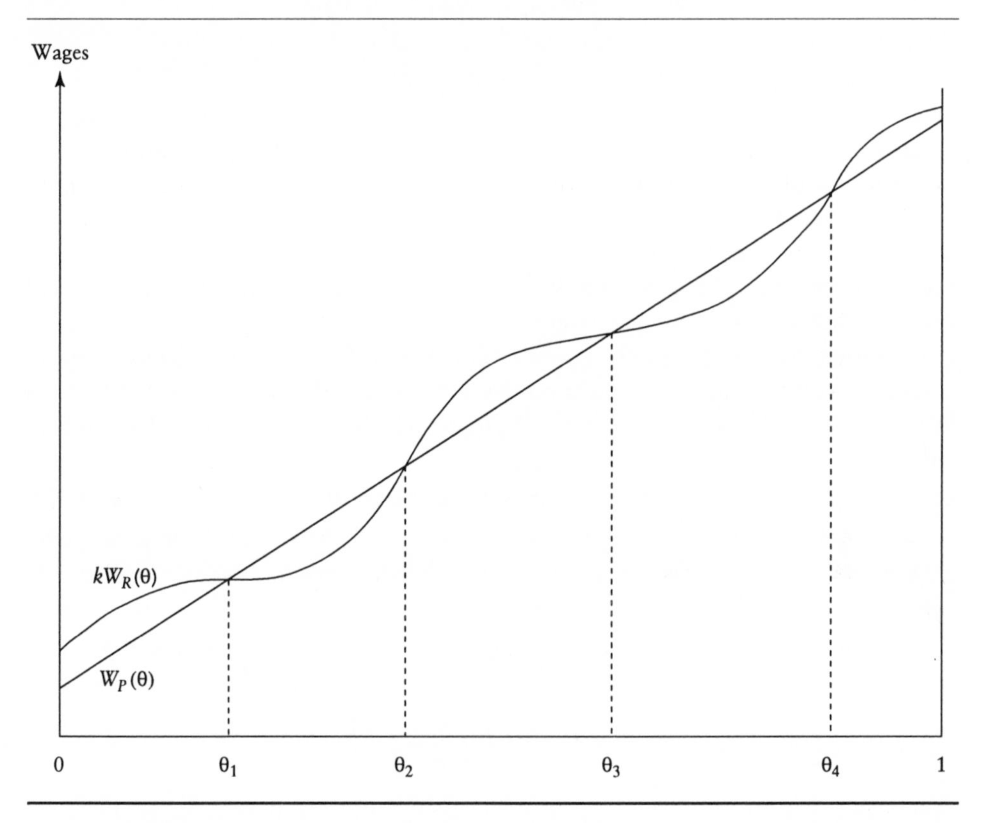

three distinct groups (for example, along the θ axis, migrating, nonmigrating, and migrating)—a situation that can occur only if at least one of the $W_P(\theta)$ and $W_R(\theta)$ functions is nonlinear in θ—will be referred to as the nonconvex case. Similarly, the case in which there are two or fewer distinct groups will be referred to as the convex case.

Let us now assume that the skill of each potential migrant is known in *P*, where he or she has been observed for a while, but is unknown in *R*. When markets are isolated in the sense that information does not flow across them (or does not flow costlessly and freely), employers in one market may possess information on worker productivity—for example, as a byproduct of monitoring and coordinating activities—but the information is employer- or market-specific. Also, for the moment, let us exclude the possibility that true skill is revealed in *R* over time.

Facing a group of workers whose individual productivity is unknown (only the distribution of earnings abilities is known), the employer will offer the same wage to all, and it will be related to the average product of the group. Let us assume that the actual individual wage offered is equal to the average product of the group and that wage offers are known to all workers.[3]

Hence denoting by $\overline{W}_R$ the wage payable in the rich country to a migrant of unknown skill level and assuming n distinct migrating groups, $\overline{W}_R$ is given by

(2)
$$\overline{W}_R = \sum_{i=1}^{n} \int_{\underline{\theta}^i}^{\overline{\theta}^i} W_R(\theta) F(\theta) d\theta \bigg/ \sum_{i=1}^{n} \int_{\underline{\theta}^i}^{\overline{\theta}^i} F(\theta) d\theta$$

where $\underline{\theta}^i$ is the lowest skill level and $\overline{\theta}^i$ is the highest skill level among the migrants in group i, where i is one of the continuous groups migrating, and where the skill level increases with i. (Note that $0 < \underline{\theta}^1 < \overline{\theta}^n < 1$ for nonempty migrating sets.) It follows immediately that $\overline{W}_R < W_R(\overline{\theta}^n)$. The following result (lemma) can now be established.

Under asymmetric information, if the top skill level migrating is $\overline{\theta}^n$ then any skill level $\tilde{\theta}$, where $\tilde{\theta} < \overline{\theta}^n$, will also migrate.

To prove this result consider any $\tilde{\theta}$, such that $\tilde{\theta} < \overline{\theta}^n$. Now, since by assumption a worker with $\overline{\theta}^n$ migrates, it must be that $k\overline{W}_R > W_P(\overline{\theta}^n)$. Also, since $\tilde{\theta} < \overline{\theta}^n$ then $W_P(\tilde{\theta}) < W_P(\overline{\theta}^n)$ and hence $k\overline{W}_R > W_P(\tilde{\theta})$ so that a worker of skill level $\tilde{\theta}$ also migrates.

The implication of this result is that under asymmetric information everyone with a skill level less than or equal to $\overline{\theta}^n$ migrates, so that all workers in the interval $[0, \overline{\theta}^n]$ migrate. Note the contrast with the case of full information, as shown in figure 1, where the migration pattern could be nonconvex.

Thus under asymmetric information the wage payable to all migrating workers in R is

(3)
$$\overline{W}_R = \int_0^{\theta^*} W_R(\theta) F(\theta) d\theta \bigg/ \int_0^{\theta^*} F(\theta) d\theta$$

where θ^* is the top skill level migrating. Thus $\overline{W}_R$ can be written as $\overline{W}_R(\theta^*)$.

Under asymmetric information, then, workers of skill level θ for which

(4)
$$k\overline{W}_R(\theta^*) > W_P(\theta)$$

will migrate from P to R.[4]

Given this characterization of the migration pattern under asymmetric information, we can now proceed, first, to an example of a convex (two-group) case and then to an example of a nonconvex case.

A Convex Case

Assume there are just two types of workers: low-skill workers, whose skill level is θ_1, and high-skill workers, whose skill level is θ_2, with skill-related wage rates $W_i(\theta_1)$ and $W_i(\theta_2)$; in the poor country $i = P$ and in the rich country $i = R$. Assume that low-skill workers constitute α percent and high-skill workers $1 - \alpha$ percent of workers in the profession. Suppose that no costs are associated with migration except those embodied in k, and that k is such that $kW_R(\theta_1) < W_P(\theta_1)$ yet $kW_R(\theta_2) > W_P(\theta_2)$. This assumption is introduced to capture the differing migration incentives of the symmetric and asymmetric information states. It implies that under symmetric information only the relatively high-skill workers will migrate. However, if we assume that

$$\alpha k W_R(\theta_1) + (1-\alpha)\, k W_R(\theta_2) > W_P(\theta_2) \tag{5}$$

then, under asymmetric information, the θ_2 workers will again migrate but this time the θ_1 workers will migrate as well (a result that follows immediately from the above lemma). If employers in R correctly identify the skill levels of individual workers and adjust pay accordingly at the end of the first employment period, the low-skill workers will return to P and the high-skill workers will stay in R. Since θ_1 workers are not pooled with θ_2 workers, θ_2 workers' R wage can only be higher, that is

$$kW_R(\theta_2) = \alpha k W_R(\theta_2) + (1-\alpha)\, k W_R(\theta_2) > \alpha k W_R(\theta_1) + (1-\alpha)\, k W_R(\theta_2). \tag{6}$$

By assumption, the right-hand side of the inequality is larger than the alternative poor country wage, $W_P(\theta_2)$.

This outcome has three implications. First, considering the entire migration experience, we see that migration is positively selective. Even though no selectivity is observed initially—both low-skill workers and high-skill workers leave—with the passage of time and the removal of informational asymmetry, the return of the low-skill migrants to their home country produces a feature of positive selectivity. Whereas initially migration is not selective in skills, ex post it is.

Second, the judgment concerning the selective nature of migration is sensitive to the time (phase) at which the judgment is being made. (At first, migration appears not to be selective; at last, it is fully positively selective.) Empirical findings concerning the selective nature of migration are thus phase dependent.

Third, even though the end result of migration is not path dependent, the symmetric information single-phase path (with only workers of skill level θ_2 migrating) is different from the asymmetric information multiphase path (with group θ_2 found in R only when migratory moves halt altogether).

What if the rich country wishes to have only high-skill migrant workers from the start, that is, it is unwilling to await return migration by the low-skill migrant workers? Suppose that screening individual migrants (would-be or actual) is costly or unreliable. The asymmetric information approach identifies an instrument that facilitates skill differentiation. Return migration and this instrument are thus mutually exclusive.

The rich country can announce an entry tax (visa fee) of $\bar{T}$ units. This tax must be large enough that low-skill workers find migrating not worthwhile under asymmetric information but not so large as to swamp the high-skill workers' discounted wage differential. To secure these dual requirements, it is necessary to find the minimal tax that solves

$$k\left[\alpha W_R(\theta_1) + (1-\alpha) W_R(\theta_2) - \bar{T}\right] < W_P(\theta_1). \tag{7}$$

That is, the tax $\bar{T}$ should solve

$$(7') \qquad k\left[\alpha W_R(\theta_1)+(1-\alpha)W_R(\theta_2)-(\bar{T}-\varepsilon)\right]=W_P(\theta_1)$$

where $\varepsilon > 0$ is a sufficiently small constant, while maintaining

$$(8) \qquad k\left[W_R(\theta_2)-\bar{T}\right]>W_P(\theta_2).$$

From equations 7 and 8 we obtain

$$(9) \qquad k\alpha W_R(\theta_1)+k(1-\alpha)W_R(\theta_2)-W_P(\theta_1)<k\bar{T}<kW_R(\theta_2)-W_P(\theta_2).$$

Existence then requires that

$$(10) \qquad W_P(\theta_2)-W_P(\theta_1)<\alpha k\left[W_R(\theta_2)-W_R(\theta_1)\right].$$

Existence is thus more likely the steeper the wage profile is by skill in the rich country relative to that in the poor country. If the share of low-skill workers in the occupation under review, α, is relatively large, and if the rate-of-location discount is not high, the entry tax that solves equation 7′ will also fulfill equation 8.

A numerical example illustrates the convex case. Suppose $W_P(\theta_1) = 7$, $W_P(\theta_2) = 9$, $W_R(\theta_1) = 10$, $W_R(\theta_2) = 20$; $F(\theta)$ is such that $\alpha = 1 - \alpha = 1/2$; and $k = 2/3$. Thus under symmetric information only θ_2 migrate as $kW_R(\theta_2) = 2/3 \times 20 > 9$ but $kW_R(\theta_1) = 2/3 \times 10 < 7$; under asymmetric information both skill levels migrate as $k\alpha W_R(\theta_1) + k(1 - \alpha)W_R(\theta_2) = 2/3 \times 1/2 \times 10 + 2/3 \times 1/2 \times 20 = 10 > [W_P(\theta_1) = 7;\ W_P(\theta_2) = 9]$. As for the tax scenario, equation 7′ gives a tax $\bar{T} = 4.5 + \varepsilon$. With this tax in place it can be seen that low-skill workers will be worse off regardless of whether they migrate with the high-skill workers or alone: in the first case, their prediscounted wage will be $10.5 - \varepsilon$ units, which is worth less to them than the alternative home-country wage ($2/3\,(10.5 - \varepsilon) < 7$); in the second case, their prediscounted rich-country wage will be $5.5 - \varepsilon$, which is below their home-country wage. Not so for the high-skill workers, whose post-tax, discounted rich-country wage is still superior to the home-country wage ($2/3\,(15.5 - \varepsilon) > 9$).

A Nonconvex Case

Assume that there are four types of workers with skill levels θ_i increasing in i ($i = 1, \ldots, 4$) with corresponding wage rates of $W_P(\theta_i)$ in the poor country and $W_R(\theta_i)$ in the rich country. Suppose that $F(\theta)$ is given, that is, the proportion of skill type i in the profession is α_i. Once again it is assumed that no costs are associated with migration except those embodied in k. Suppose that even though $W_R(\theta_i) > W_P(\theta_i)$ for all $i = 1, \ldots, 4$, the skill-specific wage rates are such that $kW_R(\theta_2) > W_P(\theta_2)$ and $kW_R(\theta_4)$

$> W_P(\theta_4)$, whereas $kW_R(\theta_1) < W_P(\theta_1)$ and $kW_R(\theta_3) < W_P(\theta_3)$; thus it is efficient for the most able and third most able groups to migrate, but not for the other two. It follows at once that under symmetric information only θ_2 and θ_4 migrate. Once informational asymmetry is introduced, the possibilities become quite rich. We limit the discussion to one interesting case, where

$$k\left(\sum_{i=1}^{2}\alpha_i\right)^{-1}\sum_{i=1}^{2}\alpha_i W_R(\theta_i) > W_P(\theta_2)$$

and

$$k\left(\sum_{i=3}^{4}\alpha_i\right)^{-1}\sum_{i=3}^{4}\alpha_i W_R(\theta_i) > W_P(\theta_4)$$

while

$$k\left(\sum_{i=1}^{3}\alpha_i\right)^{-1}\sum_{i=1}^{3}\alpha_i W_R(\theta_i) < W_P(\theta_3)$$

and

$$k\sum_{i=1}^{4}\alpha_i W_R(\theta_i) < W_P(\theta_4).$$

Ruling out strategic considerations (but see the discussion at the end of this subsection), this configuration means that under asymmetric information workers of skill levels θ_1 and θ_2 will migrate whereas workers of skill levels θ_3 and θ_4 will not migrate, even though the latter would have found it advantageous to migrate if they could do so alone—which by the lemma proved earlier we know that they cannot.

If, as a byproduct of the employment and production processes, information is completely revealed at the end of the first employment period, workers of skill level θ_1 return to *P* while workers of skill level θ_2 stay in *R*. Both these groups are fully removed from the pool of workers subject to asymmetric information.[5] Now types θ_3 and θ_4 find it attractive to migrate. Thus at this time, group θ_1 is found in *P* whereas groups θ_2, θ_3, and θ_4 are in *R*. However, if once again information about individual skill levels is complete after one employment period, workers of skill level θ_3 return to origin whereas workers of skill level θ_4 stay in *R*. There now emerges a pattern of migration in which workers of skill levels θ_2 and θ_4 are found in *R*, whereas workers of skill levels θ_1 and θ_3 are in *P*. Once again it turns out that even though the end result of migration is not path-dependent, the symmetric-information single-phase path (with workers of skill levels θ_2 and θ_4 migrating right from the start) is very different from the asymmetric information multiphase path (with groups θ_2 and θ_4 found in *R* only when migration halts altogether).

When there are more than two skill levels, the asymmetric-information approach to labor migration can produce several regularities: migration is sequential, each wave of migration produces a counterflow of return migration,[6] and migration is positively selective but not strongly so. This result implies that migration is ex post fully selective within cohorts but only partially selective across cohorts. When migration halts altogether, types θ_1 and θ_3 are found in the poor country and types θ_2 and θ_4 in the rich country. Since type θ_3 workers are more highly skilled than type θ_2 workers, not all migrants have a higher skill level than all nonmigrants. Put differently, there is a migrant group at destination (θ_2) that is dominated by return migrant workers at origin (θ_3). It is therefore incorrect to argue that only low-quality workers return (θ_2 do not, while θ_3 do) even though this claim is true within cohorts. Moreover, as in the case of two skill levels, a judgment concerning the selective nature of migration is highly sensitive to the phase at which the judgment is made. At first glance migration appears to be overall negatively selective (θ_1 and θ_2 leave, while θ_3 and θ_4 stay); subsequently, as type θ_1 return, migration is moderately negatively selective (type θ_2 are migrants, types θ_3, θ_4, and θ_1 are not), and so on. Since the completed or final outcome of migration is revealed only over time, consideration of migration patterns in isolation from past and anticipated dynamics produces an inaccurate account.

Migration is perpetual in the sense that one wave breaches the dike blocking a subsequent wave. A widespread belief in the literature holds that the perpetual, phased structure of migration arises as early waves provide employment and job-related information to subsequent waves (Stark 1991). The asymmetric-information approach suggests a new explanation of the externality that a given wave confers on subsequent waves: highly-skilled waves (say, types θ_3 and θ_4) migrate only because, as a cloud of informational asymmetry dissipates, the lower-skilled workers (types θ_1 and θ_2) are eliminated from the pool of workers who are lumped together. Types θ_1 and θ_2 initially block the migration of types θ_3 and θ_4 but, having been identified, these lower-skilled workers pave the way for the migration of higher-quality workers. Information does play a role, but it is a very different role from the one conventionally assumed. This approach predicts that the average quality of migrants rises in the order of their cohort.[7]

Finally, we need to address the possibility that workers time their migration strategically. Consider the earning sequence of the θ_4 workers. In period 1 they earn $W_P(\theta_4)$, in period 2 they earn $(\alpha_3 + \alpha_4)^{-1} [\alpha_3 W_R(\theta_3) + \alpha_4 W_R(\theta_4)]$, and in period 3 they earn $W_R(\theta_4)$. The reason for this earning profile is that the period in which the θ_4 workers earn a wage in R based on their skill level alone must be preceded by a period in R in which their wage is based on an averaging of skill levels. Why not then bring forward (from 3 to 2) the period at which $W_R(\theta_4)$ is earned by bringing forward (from 2 to 1) the employment-with-averaging period? Instead of earning $W_P(\theta_4)$ at period 1, θ_4 workers could earn $(\alpha_1 + \alpha_2 + \alpha_4)^{-1} [\alpha_1 W_R(\theta_1) + \alpha_2 W_R(\theta_2) + \alpha_4 W_R(\theta_4)]$—if θ_4 workers join θ_1 and θ_2, the latter groups will find it advantageous to migrate a fortiori—and thereafter earn $W_R(\theta_4)$ per period. We know, however, that

$$k \sum_{i=1}^{4} \alpha_i W_R(\theta_i) < W_P(\theta_4)$$

and it is unlikely that

$$(\alpha_1 + \alpha_2 + \alpha_4)^{-1}\left[\alpha_1 W_R(\theta_1) + \alpha_2 W_R(\theta_2) + \alpha_4 W_R(\theta_4)\right]$$
$$< \sum_{i=1}^{4} \alpha_i W_R(\theta_i) = \left(\sum_{i=1}^{4} \alpha_i\right)^{-1} \sum_{i=1}^{4} \alpha_i W_R(\theta_i).$$

The reason for this inequality is that the weights of the low wages $W_R(\theta_1)$ and $W_R(\theta_2)$ on the left-hand side are relatively higher than those on the right-hand side, while the high wage $W_R(\theta_3)$ is deleted altogether (two lowering effects), even though the highest wage $W_R(\theta_4)$ is weighted more (one increasing effect). But by transitivity, $k\,[\alpha_1 W_R(\theta_1) + \alpha_2 W_R(\theta_2) + \alpha_4 W_R(\theta_4)] < W_P(\theta_4)$. Therefore, if we impose the additional conditions that capital markets (and other institutions) preclude borrowing against future returns to human capital investments (especially migration), and that in themselves $W_P(\theta_i)$ are too low to permit consumption smoothing—or if, alternatively, we assume a strong time preference, a strategic migratory move will not take place. To close the argument note that θ_3 cannot possibly move along with θ_4 since if they were to do so, the rich-country average wage for θ_4 (as multiplied by *k*), $k\,\Sigma_{i=1}^{4}\alpha_i W_R(\theta_i)$, would clearly be less than their poor-country wage, $W_P(\theta_4)$, a shortfall that, as a result of any of the above restrictions, implies that θ_4 will not migrate.

A numerical example serves to illustrate. Suppose the wage rates in the poor country are $W_P(\theta_i) = 6, 8, 21, 21\frac{1}{2}$, and in the rich country are $W_R(\theta_i) = 10, 30, 40, 48$; workers are uniformly distributed across the four skill categories, that is $F(\theta)$ is uniform; and $k = \frac{1}{2}$. Thus whereas under informational symmetry only θ_2 and θ_4 migrate (as $kW_R(\theta_2) = \frac{1}{2} \times 30 > W_P(\theta_2) = 8$ and $kW_R(\theta_4) = \frac{1}{2} \times 48 > W_P(\theta_4) = 21\frac{1}{2}$, but $kW_R(\theta_1) = \frac{1}{2} \times 10 < W_P(\theta_1) = 6$ and $kW_R(\theta_3) = \frac{1}{2} \times 40 < W_P(\theta_3) = 21$), under informational asymmetry only θ_1 and θ_2 migrate. Clearly, θ_3 and θ_4 are better off staying in *P* since $k\overline{W}_R(\theta^*)\,|_{\theta^*=\theta_3} = \frac{1}{2} \times \frac{80}{3} < W_P(\theta_3) = 21$ or $k\overline{W}_R(\theta^*)\,|_{\theta^*=\theta_4} = \frac{1}{2} \times \frac{128}{4} < W_P(\theta_4) = 21\frac{1}{2}$. Verification that $\theta_1 + \theta_2$ will migrate is also straightforward as $k\overline{W}(\theta^*)\,|_{\theta^*=\theta_2} = \frac{1}{2} \times \frac{40}{2} > [W_P(\theta_1) = 6;\ W_P(\theta_2) = 8]$.

Once information is revealed completely, workers of skill level θ_1 return to *P* and workers of skill level θ_2 stay in *R*. Types θ_3 and θ_4 now migrate as $k\overline{W}_R(\theta^*)\,|_{\theta^*=\theta_4} = \frac{1}{2} \times \frac{88}{2} > [W_P(\theta_3) = 21;\ W_P(\theta_4) = 21\frac{1}{2}]$. Once again, the revelation of full information splits the migrants into returnees and stayers: workers of skill level θ_3 return to *P*, since $kW_R(\theta_3) = \frac{1}{2} \times 40 < W_P(\theta_3) = 21$, while workers of skill level θ_4 stay in *R* because, for them, $kW_R(\theta_4) = \frac{1}{2} \times 48 > W_P(\theta_4) = 21\frac{1}{2}$. Since the (location discounted) earning profile of the θ_4 workers is $21\frac{1}{2}$, 22, and 24, advancing their migration results in an earning sequence of $14\frac{2}{3}$, 24, and 24 that under any of the restrictions postulated above cannot be sustained.

Complementary Remarks

This setup—all workers know what wages will await them; in response, they stay put, migrate and stay at destination, or migrate and return; and stayers, movers, and those who return are fully characterized—is new. In many professions (for example, science and engineering) in which employers know little about new workers' abilities and in which workers' abilities correlate strongly with productivity, the improvement in information as time passes rests with the employers, not with the migrant workers.

The sequential, relative, and return attributes of migration as derived in this section of the article do not arise, then, from imperfect information about wage rates at destination. If they did, even if the migrants had precise information on their *expected* wage at destination, the reality of wage variance would induce some migrants to return and others to stay. But if we recognize that worker attributes differ, the attributes must be systematically correlated with realized wage rates. It is not enough merely to argue that return migration is a decreasing function of premigration information (McCall and McCall 1987) or that "migration back to an original location occurs because expectations were not fulfilled" (Polachek and Horvath 1977).

Dynamics in general, and return migration in particular, could be generated by changes in information in a more subtle way. Suppose that workers have information on wages in location *i*, where they are currently located, and on wages in a series of other locations *j*, *k*, *l*, and so on. Suppose further that workers always have more information on the location they are actually in than on other locations. Finally, suppose that the value of this information relates inversely to its quantity. Suppose now that workers move from *i* to *j*. Then, not only does information on *j* become less valuable than it was before the move, it could also become less valuable than information on *i*, *k*, *l*, and so on. Since the only way to convert information on a wage elsewhere—that is, now, on wages in *i*, *k*, or *l*, and so on—to an actual wage is to move, one move may well lay the ground for subsequent moves. Clearly, one such move is back to *i*. Here, too, changes in information could play a role—motivating migration, including return migration—but the changes take place in the information the migrant workers have, not the employers, and a systematic link with workers' attributes is missing.

A simple cobweb model could generate some dynamics if we assume, again, that realized wages differ from anticipated wages. An initial wave of migrants lowers the wage at destination, an outcome not foreseen by the migrants. Consequently, some migrants return. As a result the wage at destination rises somewhat and thus pulls in some migrants. And so on. Once again, this approach assumes homogeneity of workers' attributes, that the workers drawn in and the workers pushed out are always randomly selected, and that workers are unable to assess accurately their destination wages.

Finally, sequential migration could arise because the technology of production exhibits economies of scale to the application of skill. Consider the following example. For each skill level θ, workers in economy R are paid more than workers in economy P, with the wage differential increasing in θ. Skills can be acquired, albeit at a cost, and migration from P to R can take place at a cost c. Initially, the system is in full equilibrium with no migration. Suppose that as a consequence of an exogenous shock, c falls so that now $W_R(\theta^n) - c > W_P(\theta^n)$, where θ^n is the top skill level. As θ^n-type workers migrate, they confer both positive and negative externalities: the productivity of skilled workers in R rises because of the enlargement of the pool of skilled workers and the operation of scale economies. $W_R(\theta^n)$ rises as a consequence. Workers in P with skill levels below θ^n who previously had no incentive to invest in acquiring additional skills now find that the joint return to such investment and migration is greater than the sum of the returns arising from each of these investments undertaken separately. They also witness a decline in their wage earnings due to the absence of the θ^n workers. They therefore invest in acquiring skills and then migrate, spurring a second wave of migrants. The process repeats until the cost of migration exactly offsets the increase in the wage differential induced by the (two-ended) scale economies, or until all skilled workers leave P for R. Notice that if the reason for the initial distribution of skills is ability (see Miyagiwa 1991), the quality of migrants, as measured by their ability, will decline in the order of their cohort.

Remittances as Side-Payments

Several reasons besides the large magnitude of remittances encourage modeling of remittance behavior. First, predictions of the response of remittances to perturbations in the incomes of both remitters and recipients are sensitive to the motive for remitting. Policy is likewise sensitive. Consider altruism and exchange as motives. According to the altruism hypothesis, remittances received and recipients' pretransfer income will be inversely related: altruistic migrants will remit more when recipients' income falls short. But if transfers are motivated by self-interest and exchange considerations, recipients' income and remittances can be positively related. For example, if transfers pay for care of cattle left behind, an increase in the recipients' market wages will drive up the price of the services they provide. If remittances are viewed as an informal mechanism to increase welfare and equalize income, governments may refrain from hindering them or may, indeed, support policies favoring them. The policy choice should be contingent on the underlying motive.

Second, remittances are a unique form of transfer. Although transfers between family members who coreside are difficult to measure, remittances between migrants and their families who stay behind are measured more easily. And observed transfers between family members can unravel hidden underlying intrafamily relationships.

Third, interest in nonmarket exchange, intrafamily transfers, and intergenerational linkages is growing. The study of remittances constitutes part of this inquiry and could advance it considerably.

In this section we study a strategic motive for remittances that has not been explored in the literature. The basic idea is that when employers at destination lack information on the skills of individual migrants, they will pay all migrants a wage based on the average product of the group. High-skill workers should be willing, then, to make a transfer to low-skill workers to dissuade them from migrating. Thus migrants remit to nonmigrants motivated not by altruism but by pure self-interest.

Motivating Remittances

Consider the basic model and the two-group example of the first section, but suppose now that workers can form cohesive groups and act jointly. Since the high-skill workers wish to protect their wages from contamination by the presence of the low-skill workers in the same pool, they should be willing to make a transfer to the low-skill workers to induce them to stay put. This will free the high-skill workers from being pooled with the low-skill workers *right from the start.* Of course, the transfer (a cost) must be smaller than the associated benefit conferred by the difference between the R country wage of the high-skill workers if they were to migrate alone and their R country wage if the low-skill workers were to migrate with them. Put differently, the transfer must be smaller than the high-skill workers' symmetric information–asymmetric information wage differential. Formally, the transfer $\tilde{T}$ has to fulfill the condition

(11) $$\tilde{T} < W_R(\theta_2) - \left[\alpha W_R(\theta_1) + (1-\alpha) W_R(\theta_2)\right]$$

where

(12) $$\tilde{T} = k\alpha W_R(\theta_1) + k(1-\alpha) W_R(\theta_2) - W_P(\theta_1) + \varepsilon$$

where $\varepsilon > 0$ is a sufficiently small constant. From equations 11 and 12 we obtain

(13) $$k\alpha W_R(\theta_1) + k(1-\alpha) W_R(\theta_2) - W_P(\theta_1) < \tilde{T} < W_R(\theta_2) - \left[\alpha W_R(\theta_1) + (1-\alpha) W_R(\theta_2)\right] = \alpha\left[W_R(\theta_2) - W_R(\theta_1)\right].$$

Considering the last expression in equation 13 we see the importance for existence of a steep wage profile by skill in the rich country.

For $\tilde{T}$ that fulfills equation 13 we thus obtain the following: by offering the low-skill workers $\tilde{T}$, the high-skill workers succeed in having the former stay put. Notice that the low-skill workers cannot extract a transfer larger than $\tilde{T}$ by threatening to migrate as this threat would not be credible: if they were to migrate, these workers would receive a payment valued at $k\overline{W}_R = k\alpha W_R(\theta_1) + k(1-\alpha) W_R(\theta_2)$. But if they stay put they receive $W_P(\theta_1) + \tilde{T}$, which is larger than $k\overline{W}_R$ by ε. And, of course, the high-skill workers are still better off in the wake of such a transfer because they are left with $W_R(\theta_2) - \tilde{T}$ which is worth $k[W_R(\theta_2) - \tilde{T}]$ to them, and this, by construction, is better than a payment worth $k\overline{W}_R$.

Subject to the existence condition for $\tilde{T}$ holding, six predictions and implications emerge. First, if workers can act jointly, they will form action groups by type, and migration will be selective right from the start; only the high-skill workers will migrate. Testable implications then are that selectivity and remittances are positively related and that return migration and remittances are negatively related.

Second, migrants remit to nonmigrants to buy them off—to prevent them from migrating and contaminating wages at destination. Remittances will thus be targeted to those at home who *have* earning power since there would be no need to remit to those who would not credibly threaten to migrate. Migrants who remit to nonmigrant members of their own households, or even to their community at large (as, for example, Turkish migrant workers in Germany are reported to do), may do so in part to enhance the welfare of the stayers, but also to improve their own well-being.[8] Quite often, migrants from a given area in P work together in the same site in R, so remitting to a well-defined target set of potential migrants effectively preserves the migrants' wage. This small-scale effect also helps prevent free riding by an individual migrant who might be tempted to avoid remitting while enjoying the benefits of other migrants' contributions.

Third, the role of remittances is cast in a new light. Remittances enhance allocative efficiency by countering the effect of informational asymmetry, thus enabling *all* agents to locate on the utility frontier as implied by the first-best allocation rule of equation 1.

Fourth, in addition to explaining why remittances are initiated and predicting their precise magnitude, the strategic motive explains why they come to a halt. Once high-quality workers are identified, their wage is immune to erosion from migration of low-quality workers. The need to buy off the low-quality workers evaporates, and remittances cease.

Fifth, group formation may involve some organizational cost. The asymmetric-information approach to labor migration predicts that the formation of groups is more likely when the rich-country wages of the high-skill workers and the low-skill workers differ greatly and when skill levels of individuals become known only slowly.

Sixth, suppose an entry tax $\bar{T}$ is in place that is large enough to dissuade low-skill workers from migrating under asymmetric information but not so large as to swamp the high-skill workers' own discounted wage differential. (A formal derivation of the entry tax was provided in the first section.) Even if workers could form groups by type, low-skill workers would be unable to extract a transfer because they lack a credible threat of migration. Thus taxing migrants and transferring remittances to nonmigrants are mutually exclusive. Consistent with our third point, the entry tax *enhances* efficiency.

Take a numerical example. Suppose $W_P(\theta_1) = 7$, $W_P(\theta_2) = 9$, $W_R(\theta_1) = 10$, $W_R(\theta_2) = 20$, $F(\theta)$ is such that $\alpha = 1 - \alpha = 1/2$, and $k = 2/3$. If the high-skill workers offer to transfer $\tilde{T} = 3 + \varepsilon$, given by equation 12, the low-skill workers will stay put. Any threat to migrate to extract a larger transfer would not be credible: if they were to migrate these workers would receive 15 (which is worth only 10 to them). But if they stay put they receive an assured $7 + 3 + \varepsilon > 10$. And of course, the high-skill workers are still better off in the wake of such a transfer because they are left with $17 - \varepsilon$, which is worth $11\frac{1}{3} - \varepsilon$ to them, and this is better than a payment worth 10.

This example helps elucidate an additional point about incentives and coordination. Suppose θ_1 and θ_2 are a pair of brothers, and suppose that there are two such pairs. If all four migrate and the brothers share their wage evenly, each will receive 15, the value of which is 10. Now suppose that a high-skill brother attempts to induce his low-skill brother, z, to stay put. This scheme will not work. In the absence of migration by z, the remaining migrants will receive $1/3\,(10 + 20 + 20)$, the value of which is $11^1/_9$. This is better than 10 and therefore desirable, but there is only $(1^1/_9 - \varepsilon)\ ^3/_2 = 1^2/_3 - \varepsilon$ to be transferred by z's brother to z, and since $7 + 1^2/_3 - \varepsilon < 10$, the unwarranted migration cannot be blocked. If, however, z's brother persuades the other migrant workers to join him in remitting to z, the scheme will work. Say each needs to remit $1 + \varepsilon$, which means that z will receive $10 + \varepsilon$, while each migrant will be left with $^{50}/_3 - 1 - \varepsilon$ and this is worth $^2/_3\ (^{47}/_3 - \varepsilon) = 10^4/_9 - \varepsilon$, which is better than 10. Of course, a still better outcome would be secured if the two high-skill workers banded together to "screen out" their two low-skill brothers; numerically though, the result would be identical to the one involving equal shares of each type of worker alluded to in the preceding paragraph. What is especially interesting about this example is not only that coordination can secure a Pareto improvement that individual action cannot, but also that some migrants may remit to nonmigrant workers for whom they have no altruistic feelings. Moreover, by illustrating the dependence of strategic remittances on coordination and monitoring, the example implicitly suggests that remittances per migrant will decline as the group of migrants expands. The free-riding problem associated with buying off the low-skill workers who, from the point of view of the high-skill workers, are public "bads," is more likely to arise the larger and less cohesive is the group of high-skill workers.

Complementary Remarks

Earlier research sought to model and test the idea that migration is a strategy to secure remittances for the migrant's family (Stark 1991). The motives were taken to be concern for those staying behind or the need to pay them for past, ongoing, or future services. This article steps outside this framework. It argues that migrants may remit to nonfamily members to protect their wages from contamination by fellow migrants in a pool whose members receive a wage based on the average product of the group rather than on individual product. If this motive operates, screening migrants at the point of entry will adversely affect remittance flows. This consideration connects with, and should thus impinge on, the political economy of migration legislation, especially procedures aimed at sorting workers.

Empirical inquiries concerning the relationship between transfers and the characteristics of recipients have produced conflicting results. Some studies conclude that remittances are motivated by altruism; others point to exchange or insurance as motives. And still others see remittance behavior as governed by a combination of motives.[9] The conflicting results may have to do with a possible misspecification of the empirical remittance functions that stems from ignoring the strategic motive for migrant transfers. Suppose that the donor is the dominant player in the remittance arrangement, so that transfers from migrant to nonmigrant are given according to equation 12. This equation contains three variables: the migrant's actual earnings, the recipient's actual earnings, and the recipient's potential earnings in country R. The equation predicts that the coefficient for actual recipient earnings is –1. Suppose an empirical remittance equation is estimated that contains the actual earnings of migrant and recipient but not the recipient's potential earnings. The coefficient for recipient earnings in such an equation would be affected by omitted-variable bias. The direction of the bias is upward because the recipient's potential earnings have the effect of raising remittances, and the recipient's actual earnings and potential earnings in *R* are likely to be positively correlated. As a consequence of the omission, the positive effect of potential earnings in *R* is attributed to actual earnings, resulting in an algebraically higher coefficient. The possible omitted-variable bias might explain why empirical remittance functions produce conflicting sign patterns for the impact of recipient income on transfers, as the values of the omitted-variable-bias terms are likely to vary from one instance to another.[10]

Our analysis also forges a link between remittances and the ease with which employers can make judgments about individual skill levels. Consider the effect of occupational licensure on remittances. If migrants possess some certification that is recognized fairly quickly by employers in *R*, the informational asymmetry problem becomes less severe and might well disappear. If so, migrants working in occupations that are commonly licensed would have a diminished incentive to remit. Similarly, if a migrant is self-employed, informational asymmetries will not affect his or her earnings much, and again, incentives to remit will diminish. Thus the strategic model predicts that remittance flows will be sensitive to the occupational structure of the migrant group. In particular, we expect that occupational status would be significant in empirical remittance equations even after controlling for the preremittance incomes of donors and recipients. Further, if we were to broaden our analysis to include occupational choice, we might expect that informational asymmetry would give migrants an added incentive to become self-employed. Indeed, a testable implication is that the higher the dispersion of skill levels at origin (and, therefore, the greater the potential wage erosion), the more likely that high-skill migrants (who seek to avoid both pooling and remitting) will self-select into self-employment.

Recognition Costs and Performance

This section of the article seeks to account for the empirical finding that migrants often outperform the native population. The underlying idea is that how migrants fare, absolutely and relative to the indigenous population, depends on group attributes rather than on individual abilities and skills. It is postulated that characteristics of the market environment and trade technology, rather than returns to traditional characteristics of human capital, help explain this outcome.

Trade as a Game with Recognition Costs

A population consists of two groups: migrants and the native born. Each group consists of agents who trade cooperatively, *C*, and agents who trade noncooperatively, *NC*. In the model members of each group trade only with other members of their own group (see the appendix for a relaxation of this assumption). Agents do not know whether those with whom they trade are *C* or *NC* (again, information is imperfect), but they can obtain such information at a cost. The idea is that the cost to migrants of information about fellow migrants is lower than the analogous cost to nonmigrants. In this situation the equilibrium share of *C*-type agents in the migrant population is higher than the equilibrium share of *C*-type agents in the nonmigrant population. And since, by construction, the payoff matrices of each subpopulation are the same, the per capita payoff of migrants is higher than that of nonmigrants—the migrants outperform the nonmigrants.[11] If their cost of information is not lower, however, migrants will fare no better than nonmigrants.

We proceed as follows. Let a prisoner's dilemma type of table represent the payoffs from cooperation and noncooperation for two agents, *E* and *F*, matched at random:

		Agent *F*	
		C	NC
Agent *E*	C	(*T*, *T*)	(*R*, *U*)
	NC	(*U*, *R*)	(*S*, *S*)

In this payoff matrix $U > T > S > R > 0$ (and $2T > U + R$; total payoffs are maximized when both agents cooperate). The share of type-*C* agents in a given group is P_C and the cost of finding out the type of another agent is $K \geq 0$. In this environment there is no memory—every trade is conducted as if it were the first—and *C*-type agents act first. If all *C*-type agents engage in trade without determining the type of the trading partner, the payoff to a given *C*-type agent is $\Pi_C = P_C T + (1 - P_C) R$. If, however, a type-determining cost *K* is incurred, the payoff will be $\tilde{\Pi}_C = T - K$.[12] The cost will be incurred if $\tilde{\Pi}_C > \Pi_C$, that is, if $K < (T - R)(1 - P_C) = K^*$. Thus for values of $K < K^*$, a *C* agent will have a payoff of $T - K$ while an *NC* agent will have a payoff of *S*. Assuming for the rest of this article that

$$T - K > S \tag{14}$$

(that is, the cost is never so large as to swamp the difference between the payoff from joint cooperation and the payoff from joint noncooperation), the *C* agents will have an edge, and their share of the population will rise.[13] If, however, $\tilde{\Pi}_C < \Pi_C$, that is, if $K > K^*$, the *C* agents will trade randomly. In this case, though, the payoff to an *NC* agent will be $\Pi_{NC} = P_C U + (1 - P_C) S$. The *NC* agent will have an edge if $\Pi_{NC} > \Pi_C$, that is, if $P_C U + (1 - P_C) S > P_C T + (1 - P_C) R$, which indeed holds since $U > T$ and $S > R$.[14] Then, the share of the *NC*-type agents in the population will rise. We see that equilibrium obtains when $K = K^*$; that is, when

$$P_C = 1 - \frac{K}{T - R}. \tag{15}$$

Two comments are in order. First, the equilibrium is stable since if the share of agents of a given type happens to be larger than the equilibrium share, their payoff will be lower than that of agents of the other type (and their share in the population will shrink), and vice versa. For example, if P_C happens to be lower than its equilibrium level, K^* must maintain $K^* > K$ since $\partial K^*/\partial P_C < 0$. Hence the inequality $\tilde{\Pi}_C > \Pi_C$ will hold, that is, the payoff of the *C*-type agents will be larger than the payoff of the *NC*-type agents and the population share of the *C*-type agents will increase.

Second, since $K \geq 0$, $T > R$ and $K < T - S < T - R$ (the first inequality is due to equation 14, the second to the payoff matrix), $K/(T - R)$ is a fraction between 0 and 1. Therefore, P_C must maintain $0 \leq P_C \leq 1$. This means that except for the two boundary cases, in equilibrium the population is a mixture of *C*-type agents and *NC*-type agents (such an equilibrium is called polymorphic). The two polar cases are as follows: If K happens to be as large as $T - R$ (that is, as large as the difference for a cooperating agent between the payoffs from trading with a cooperator and with a noncooperator) there will be no cooperators; P_C will be zero. (If they incur the recognition cost, the *C*-type agents will have a payoff R; because R is less than Π_{NC} for all values of P_C, however, the *C*-type agents will be driven out.) On the other hand, if K is as low as zero, $P_C = 1$; the noncooperators, who will always have a payoff of only S ($< T$), will be driven out.

Equation 15 entails the following first result: the equilibrium share of the *C*-type agents in a population is inversely related to the cost of establishing the type of a party to trade. The proof is $\partial P_C/\partial K = -1/(T - R) < 0$.

What are the payoffs to *C*-type and *NC*-type agents at the equilibrium point? For a *C*-type the payoff is $T - K$, and for an *NC*-type it is S. Therefore, the per capita payoff is $y = P_C (T - K) + (1 - P_C) S$. This entails the following second result: the larger the share of the *C*-type agents in the population, the higher the per capita income. The proof is $\partial y/\partial P_C = T - K - S > 0$ where the inequality sign is due to equation 14.[15]

Complementary Remarks

The cost of establishing the type of a partner to trade helps account for the performance of migrants compared with that of the indigenous population. Typically, migrants originate in a closely linked group, constitute a more homogeneous and cohesive group than nonmigrants do, live in closer proximity to each other, and constitute a minority share of the population they join. These attributes render it cheaper for a migrant to trace the type of a fellow migrant. This cost advantage results in a larger equilibrium share of cooperating agents, which in turn leads to a higher per capita payoff.[16] The findings of Chiswick (1986a and 1986b) and Bloom and Gunderson (1991)—that migrants who have been in the destination country for some time often have a higher mean income than the indigenous population—are explicable in this light.[17] The higher incomes are not the result of superior skills and human capital or unobserved abilities and innately higher productivity, but of a trade and exchange environment that induces more cooperation.

An interesting implication is that various "anti-clustering" processes aimed at assimilating migrants may, by raising the cost of establishing the type of a partner to trade, lower rather than enhance the well-being of migrants. Conversely, processes that reinforce cohesion among migrants tend to improve their economic performance.

Conclusion

Under asymmetric information pertaining to skill levels, a mixed-skill group of migrant workers will split into low-skill workers, who return, and high-skill workers, who stay. Migration will not be selective to begin with, but will be positively selective thereafter. The wages of the migrant workers who stay will rise. This rise occurs not because of an increase in the human capital of individual migrants, but as a consequence of the increase in the average level of human capital (skill level) of the group of migrants. Recalling the example of skill levels θ_1 through θ_4, the possibility that the skill composition of migrants will be first (θ_1, θ_2) then (θ_2), then (θ_2, θ_3, θ_4) and, finally (θ_2, θ_4) implies that empirical tests of the selectivity of migration could produce conflicting results merely because a given dynamic migration process is observed at different points on its path.[18] If high-skill migrants bind together to buy off low-skill workers, remittances will be made to low-skill workers at origin and migration will be positively selective from the start. Remittances and selectivity will thus be positively related. Furthermore, remittances will be related to the occupational structure of the migrants: the higher the share of self-employment in total employment, the lower remittances will be. Under imperfect information about agent types, the per capita income of migrants belonging to a cohesive group or to a closely knit ethnic group will be higher than the per capita income of native-born workers or, for that matter, than the per capita income of migrants who belong to less-cohesive groups. Ethnic or group cohesion positively affects measured market performance beyond individual attributes and incentives. Once again, it is not human capital (conventionally defined) that drives a migration outcome.

The policy implications of the analysis can also be briefly summarized. Time—an implicit policy tool—will result in the departure of low-skill workers who, under initial asymmetric information, migrated along with high-skill workers. If the country of destination is impatient, however, a precisely defined entry tax can be imposed to screen out the low-skill workers. If remittances as side-payments are feasible, the imposition of the tax means that the country of destination will reap a revenue that substitutes for remittances to the country of origin. There is considerable social and public policy interest in the assimilation and absorption of migrants. Economics literature tends to measure assimilation by migrants' relative earnings (LaLonde and Topel 1993). Thus measured, assimilation is served by policies aimed at enhancing the cohesion of a group of migrants at destination rather than by policies aimed at inducing their dispersion.

Whereas the literature tends to attribute migration-related phenomena to human capital and to changes in human capital, assuming that information is symmetric and perfect, the current article has followed a reverse track: migratory outcomes have been attributed to states of information and to changes in them, while levels of human capital were held either unchanged or undifferentiated. In real-world migratory processes, information and human capital change over time, with the variance in migration outcomes attributable to variations in both. Indeed, how optimal investment by migrants in human capital—including devices and means that affect the cost and lag of skill discovery—responds to informational states lies on the frontier of research on international labor migration.

Appendix

Suppose that trade between migrants and nonmigrants can take place, that an agent can costlessly identify the type of group a trading partner belongs to but not the partner's *C*- or *NC*-type, and that a *C*-type agent can find out a partner's trait but at a cost. This cost, however, is larger than the cost pertaining to within-group detection. It is easy to show that a *C*-type migrant will not trade with a nonmigrant. If he were to do so, incurring a cost $K' > K$ where K' is the across-group cost and K is the within-group cost, his payoff would have been $T - K'$, which is lower than $T - K$. If, however, he were to trade randomly, his payoff would have been

$$\Pi'_C = \left[\alpha P_C^M + (1-\alpha) P_C^{NM}\right] T + \left[\alpha (1 - P_C^M) + (1-\alpha)(1 - P_C^{NM})\right]$$

where α $(1 - \alpha)$ is the share of the migrant (nonmigrant) group in the combined population and P_C^M (P_C^{NM}) is the proportion of *C*-type agents in the migrant (nonmigrant) group. This payoff is lower than the payoff arising from a random within-group trade. The proof is

$$\begin{aligned}\Pi_C = P_C^M T + (1 - P_C^M) R &= \left[\alpha P_C^M + (1-\alpha) P_C^M\right] T \\ &+ \left[\alpha (1 - P_C^M) + (1-\alpha)(1 - P_C^M)\right] R > \left[\alpha P_C^M + (1-\alpha) P_C^{NM}\right] T \\ &+ \left[\alpha (1 - P_C^M) + (1-\alpha)(1 - P_C^{NM})\right] R = \Pi'_C\end{aligned}$$

since (because of the detection-cost advantage) $P_C^M > P_C^{NM}$. Thus a random trade with nonmigrants will not take place. Since migrants reject trade with nonmigrants, nonmigrants who may have attempted to engage a migrant in trade will be quickly turned away: language, accent, color of skin, and other similar traits are recognized costlessly, correctly, and immediately. We conclude then that the possibility of intergroup trade need not result in such a trade and hence that the migrants' edge is immune to this possibility.

This last case assumes that agents are "hard-wired" as *C* or *NC*. But what if agents who are *C* within their own group turn out to be *NC* when trading with outsiders? The answer is that the foregoing conclusion that trade will not take place holds a fortiori: now the possible appeal that migrants may have to pursue trade with nonmigrants is even weaker since the actual P_C^{NM} migrants would encounter upon trade would be lower.

What if a reverse switch is allowed? In particular, consider the possibility that in order to facilitate trade with migrants, the *NC*-type nonmigrants will, upon trading with migrants, behave as if they were *C*-type. This switch cannot erode the migrants' edge either. To see why note that the migrants will now face a group of nonmigrants, all of whom are of *C*-type. By assuming an *NC*-type, the *C* migrants will derive *U* from a trade with a nonmigrant whose payoff will therefore be *R*. This is clearly worse than what the nonmigrants can obtain by trading with members of their own group. Hence such a scheme will not work.

Notes

1. To make the analyses tractable we assume throughout that the wages in both *R* and *P* are dependent only upon a worker's skill level and not upon the excess supply of or demand for labor. In this we follow the similar assumption made in the optimal tax literature. Thus for example, $W_R(\theta)$ and $W_P(\theta)$ may be linear in θ such that $W_R(\theta) = r_0 + r\theta$, $r_0 > 0$, $r > 0$ and $W_P(\theta) = p_0 + p\theta$, $p_0 > 0$, $p > 0$. It can be shown that these equations are reduced equilibrium forms, where in each equation the left-hand side is the equilibrium wage and the right-hand side is the productivity of a worker with skill level θ (Stark 1991, chap. 12).

2. This may, for example, result from a higher capital-to-labor ratio in *R*, from superior technology in *R*, or from externalities arising from a higher average level of human capital per worker in *R*.

3. If employers are risk neutral and production functions are linear in skills, the employer does not suffer from his or her ignorance of the true skill level of each worker, so paying the average product per worker is the competitive outcome. These are the commonly accepted assumptions in the screening literature (see, for example, Stiglitz 1975).

4. Equation 4 provides a cut-off condition that results from individual rationality. The arising equilibrium is compatible with, indeed ensues from, the other side of the market, namely, the behavior of firms in the destination *R* (Stark 1991, chap. 12).

5. Since θ_1 and θ_2 are removed from the averaging process, we can normalize θ_3 and θ_4 to constitute the [0,1] interval, and therefore $\overline{W}_R(\theta^*)$ is fully defined as per equation 3.

6. This is Ravenstein's (1885) well-known law of migration. Indeed, the analytically derived sequential pattern of migration is also in line with Ravenstein's observation that migration streams have a built-in tendency to increase over time.

7. Borjas (1987) provides evidence that the quality of migrant cohorts from Western Europe to the United States increased over 1955–79. However, his measures of quality are different from the one used in this article.

8. The article's two-skill-level implementation of the asymmetric-information theory predicts that the nonmigrant household members will be low-skill workers.

9. For example, some studies find an inverse relationship between recipient income and remittance amounts (Kaufmann and Lindauer 1986, El Salvador; Kaufmann 1982, the Philippines; and Ravallion and Dearden 1988, rural households in Java). This finding is consistent with altruism; the poorer receive more transfers. But other studies find a positive relationship between recipient income and remittance amounts (Lucas and Stark 1985, Botswana; Ravallion and Dearden 1988, urban households in Java; and Cox and Jimenez 1991, urban households in Peru). This finding is inconsistent with purely altruistic motives for remittances.

10. For example, the correlation between potential and actual wages is likely to be lower if low-skill workers in country *P* are subject to binding minimum wages.

11. Migration enables agents to utilize a production technology specific to the country of destination that is superior to that for the country of origin (Galor and Stark 1991). Hence the benefits to agents from migration are not conditional on migrants trading with nonmigrants.

12. By incurring cost *K*, the *C*-type agent attains a trade with a *C*-type agent with probability 1. To see why, suppose the *C*-type agent announces his intention to undertake the type-determining action. Since this action determines a type perfectly, no *NC*-type agent will approach a *C*-type agent, knowing that such a meeting will not result in a trade. The *C*-type knows that the *NC*-type knows this, which could tempt the *C*-type not to incur the cost after all. However, what works against such a temptation is the

realization that any failure to pursue type-determining could result in the *NC*-type approaching the *C*-type, which in turn will result in a trade that was considered undesirable when the decision to incur *K*, rather than trade randomly, was taken.

13. For an explicit evolutionary exposition see Bergstrom and Stark (1993).

14. Suppose that by incurring some cost $\tilde{K}$ the *NC* agents can identify the *C* agents in an attempt to trade with them rather than to trade randomly. But then the *C* agents will be reluctant to trade randomly as this confers a payoff of *R* which is worse than Π_C; the *C* agents will fare better by incurring *K* (and will receive a payoff $\tilde{\Pi}_C$). Thus invoking the assumption that the *C* agents "move" first, the possibility of *NC* agents incurring $\tilde{K}$ is negated.

15. The assumption that the payoff matrices of each of the subpopulations are the same can be relaxed without affecting this result. Even if the payoffs to migrants from trade with fellow migrants are systematically lower than the analogous payoffs for nonmigrants, the recognition-cost edge could result in the per capita income of migrants dominating that of nonmigrants.

16. Ethnic minorities that concentrate in ethnic enclaves and fare well may succeed not in spite of their concentration but because of it.

17. Interestingly, the studies reporting that migrants outperform the indigenous population point out that they do so only some time after arrival. Perhaps a time-consuming process of convergence to an equilibrium P_C accounts for this result.

18. We referred to ongoing research that attributes return migration to maximization of lifetime consumption which, in turn, leads to disposition at home of savings accumulated abroad. And we developed the argument that return migration of low-skill workers arises from the reinstatement of symmetric information. These two explanations may be complementary. Presumably, revelation of information is quicker than accumulation of savings. Hence in a return process that takes a long time to unravel, there will be an initial bout of information-induced return, followed by return induced by consumption maximization. LaLonde and Topel (1993) report that in the United States much of the total return migration occurs shortly after arrival, with the rest spread over as much as several decades (that is, until about one-third of the migrants return).

References

Bergstrom, Theodore C., and Oded Stark. 1993. "How Altruism Can Prevail in an Evolutionary Environment." *American Economic Review* 83 (May): 149–55.

Bloom, David E., and Morley Gunderson. 1991. "An Analysis of the Earnings of Canadian Immigrants." In John M. Abowd and Richard B. Freeman, eds., *Immigration, Trade, and the Labor Market.* Chicago: University of Chicago Press.

Borjas, George J. 1985. "Assimilation, Changes in Cohort Quality and the Earnings of Immigrants." *Journal of Labor Economics* 3 (October): 463–89.

———. 1987. "Self-Selection and the Earnings of Immigrants." *American Economic Review* 77 (September): 531–53.

Borjas, George J., and Bernt Bratsberg. 1992. "Who Leaves? The Outmigration of the Foreign Born." University of California, San Diego.

Chiswick, Barry R. 1986a. "Human Capital and the Labor Market Adjustment of Immigrants: Testing Alternative Hypotheses." In Oded Stark, ed., *Migration, Human Capital and Development.* Greenwich, Conn.: JAI Press.

———. 1986b. "Is the New Immigration Less Skilled than the Old?" *Journal of Labor Economics* 4 (April): 168–92.

Cox, Donald, and Emmanuel Jimenez. 1991. "Motives for Private Income Transfers Over the Life-Cycle: An Analytical Framework and Evidence for Peru." Boston College, Boston, Mass.

Djajic, Slobodan, and Ross Milbourne. 1988. "A General Equilibrium Model of Guest-Worker Migration: A Source-Country Perspective." *Journal of International Economics* 25 (November): 335–51.

Dustmann, Christian. 1993. "Return Intentions of Temporary Migrants." Paper presented at the Seventh Annual Meeting of the European Society for Population Economics, Budapest.

Elbadawi, Ibrahim A., and Roberto de Rezende Rocha. 1992. "Determinants of Expatriate Workers' Remittances in North Africa and Europe." Policy Research Working Paper 1038. World Bank, Transition and Macro-Adjustment Division, Washington, D.C.

Galor, Oded, and Oded Stark. 1991. "The Impact of Differences in the Level of Technology on International Labor Migration." *Journal of Population Economics* 4: 1–12.

Hill, John K. 1987. "Immigrant Decisions Concerning Duration of Stay and Migration Frequency." *Journal of Development Economics* 25: 221–34.

Kaufmann, Daniel. 1982. "Social Interaction as a Strategy for Survival Among the Urban Poor: A Theory and Evidence." Ph.D. dissertation, Harvard University, Department of Economics, Cambridge, Mass.

Kaufmann, Daniel, and David L. Lindauer. 1986. "A Model of Income Transfers for the Urban Poor." *Journal of Development Economics* 22 (July/August): 337–50.

Kimball, Miles S. 1993. "Standard Risk Aversion." *Econometrica* 61 (May): 589–611.

LaLonde, Robert J., and Robert H. Topel. 1993. "Economic Impact of International Migration: A Survey of Empirical Findings." University of Chicago, Department of Economics, Chicago, Ill.

Lucas, Robert E.B., and Oded Stark. 1985. "Motivations to Remit: Evidence from Botswana." *Journal of Political Economy* 93 (October): 901–18.

McCall, B.P., and J.J. McCall. 1987. "A Sequential Study of Migration and Job Search." *Journal of Labor Economics* 5 (October): 452–76.

Miyagiwa, Kaz. 1991. "Scale Economies in Education and the Brain Drain Problem." *International Economic Review* 32 (August): 743–59.

OECD (Organization For Economic Cooperation and Development). 1990. *Continuous Reporting System on Migration* (SOPEMI). Paris: OECD, Directorate for Social Affairs, Manpower and Education.

Polachek, Solomon W., and Francis W. Horvath. 1977. "A Life Cycle Approach to Migration: Analysis of the Perspicacious Peregrinator." In Ronald G. Ehrenberg, ed., *Research in Labor Economics,* vol. 1. Greenwich, Conn.: JAI Press.

Pratt, John W., and Richard J. Zeckhauser. 1987. "Proper Risk Aversion." *Econometrica* 55 (January): 143–54.

Ravallion, Martin, and Lorraine Dearden. 1988. "Social Security in a 'Moral Economy': An Empirical Analysis for Java." *Review of Economics and Statistics* 70 (February): 36–44.

Ravenstein, Ernest George. 1885. "The Laws of Migration." *Journal of the Royal Statistical Society* 48 (June): 167–227.

Reilly, Barry. 1994. "What Determines Migration and Return? An Individual Level Analysis Using Data for Ireland." University of Sussex, Sussex, U.K.

Stark, Oded. 1991. *The Migration of Labor.* Oxford and Cambridge, Mass.: Basil Blackwell.

———. 1995a. *Altruism and Beyond: An Economic Analysis of Transfers and Exchanges Within Families and Groups.* The Oscar Morganstern Memorial Lectures. Cambridge: Cambridge University Press.

———. 1995b. "The Path of Labor Migration When Workers Differ in their Skills and Information Is Asymmetric." *Scandinavian Journal of Economics.* Forthcoming.

Stark, Oded, Christian Helmenstein, and Yury Yegorov. 1994. "Migrants' Savings, Purchasing Power Parity, and the Optimal Duration of Migration." Institute for Advanced Studies, Vienna.

Stiglitz, Joseph E. 1975. "The Theory of 'Screening,' Education, and the Distribution of Income." *American Economic Review* 65 (June): 283–300.

U.S. Department of Commerce, Bureau of the Census. 1983. *General Social and Economic Characteristics, United States, 1980 Census of Population.* Washington, D.C.: Government Printing Office.

———. 1984. *General Social and Economic Characteristics, Puerto Rico, 1980 Census of Population.* Washington, D.C.: Government Printing Office.

World Bank. 1984. *World Development Report 1984.* New York: Oxford University Press.

Comment on "Frontier Issues in International Migration," by Stark

Michael J. Greenwood

Few parts of the world are untouched by contemporary international migration. The United States, Canada, Europe, and Australia are most frequently written about, but many other parts of the world are affected by migration. Yet we have not seen any hard data on worldwide international migration.

Determinants of International Migration

The determinants of migration are those factors that influence migration decisions, including the magnitude of the various influences. In the context of international migration, the term refers to factors that influence decisions to cross international boundaries and to settle in the receiving country. However, the concept of an international migrant is fuzzy. For no two countries is international migration defined and measured in the same way. Moreover, the distinction between permanent and temporary migration is not clear, so what is regarded as temporary in one country may be permanent in another.

In econometric studies these types of problems necessitate a focus on individual countries to keep definition and measurement problems under control. The best studies deal with the source countries of immigrants or the destination countries of emigrants, but for many countries emigrants are not tracked. A major problem with many studies of the determinants of immigration and emigration is that institutional constraints are not taken into account. These constraints may be entry or exit barriers that inhibit the international flow of labor and that blunt the influences of economic incentives, creating differential economic advantages.

Despite such problems, differential economic advantage repeatedly shows up as a key determinant of international migration. This conclusion holds in cross-sectional studies, in temporal studies, and in studies that pool cross-sectional and temporal data. It holds in historical and contemporary studies, and it holds in studies that use aggregate data and in those that combine aggregate data and microdata. However, two aspects of differential economic advantage have been ignored almost completely.

Michael J. Greenwood is professor of economics at the University of Colorado.

Proceedings of the World Bank Annual Conference on Development Economics 1994

The first is social programs in source and destination countries. Unemployment insurance, family allowances, sickness and maternity benefits, and old age, survivors, and disability benefits are not universally available. Moreover, among countries that have such programs, benefit levels differ widely. So do eligibility and portability. Since such programs entail income redistributions between various groups in source countries, they may influence not only the number of migrants between various countries, but also who migrates.

To place the potential importance of social programs in perspective, consider that in 1980, 8.0 percent of male and 9.2 percent of female U.S. immigrants were 50 years of age or older. By 1988 the respective percentages were 12.1 percent and 15.2 percent. Then consider source countries. In 1972, 1.5 percent of male and 1.5 percent of female immigrants from India into the United States were 50 or older. In 1988 the respective percentages were 20.3 percent and 23.8 percent. The corresponding percentages for Korean immigrants in 1972 were 3.8 percent for men and 3.9 percent for women; by 1988 the respective percentages were 13.4 percent and 16.6 percent. The family reunification provisions of U.S. immigration law facilitate such migration. If we think that employment or wage opportunities for these migrants lie at the heart of their migration decisions, I believe we are wrong.

Second, in spite of the importance of the topic, little theoretical or formal empirical work has ever been done regarding the demographic composition of either international or internal migration. Oded Stark is one of the few to study the issue of skill composition. Sociologists have done some empirical work on gender composition, but in general the influence of differential economic advantage and the costs of migrating on gender, age, and skill composition have been neglected.

The gender, age, and skills of immigrants have implications for destination countries. These factors influence the degree and the ways in which immigrants directly compete in the labor market with the native-born and earlier immigrants. They also have a potentially important bearing on immigrants' use of social programs in receiving countries and on precisely which social programs they use. In the United States, for example, the gender, age, and skill composition of immigrants influences both contributions to and withdrawals from the Social Security Trust Fund.

Consequences of International Migration

Rather than focusing on the effects of immigration in general, the contemporary U.S. literature is orientated toward the effects of unskilled immigration on the U.S. economy. This orientation is due at least partly to a significant downward shift in the skill composition of legal U.S. immigration during the early 1970s and to the presumably high and continued in-migration of illegal aliens with few skills and little education. Twenty years ago the literature emphasized the consequences of migration of the highly educated and skilled for countries of origin—the brain drain. One of the most hotly debated issues now concerns the effects of immigration on U.S. workers. Do immigrants depress domestic wages and displace domestic workers?

Empirical conclusions regarding the effects of immigration on U.S. workers have frequently been based on circumstantial rather than direct evidence. Several authors conclude, for example, that, at least in the short run, the least-skilled domestic workers suffer reductions in wages and employment opportunities because of the immigration of less-skilled individuals, but they also generally conclude that these effects are not sizable. Such results are frequently based on simulations of the effects of immigration in which estimates of the relevant elasticities underlying the simulations refer to prime-age males or to economywide averages rather than to the specific labor markets in which the immigrants compete.

More research is required to identify the markets in which immigrants compete, as well as to measure the relevant elasticities of demand and domestic labor supply in these markets. One observation seems clear, however. The more narrowly defined the industrial sector or the region, the more likely are investigators to find adverse effects of immigrants on natives and earlier immigrants. Both wages and employment opportunities may suffer severely. One example is citrus pickers in Ventura County, California. Offsets to such negative consequences operate, but since they are often spread among other workers, employers, consumers, and regions, they are difficult to identify and, especially, to quantify.

Several studies conclude that more highly skilled domestic workers are positively affected, or perhaps are unaffected, by immigration, again at least in the short run. In general, however, the literature lacks studies that identify precisely why. Such short-run benefits could result from factor complementarity, from the demand effects of the immigrants, from capital accumulation directly related to immigration, or from other causes. Almost nothing is known about the specific demand effects of immigration, and little is known about its effect on capital accumulation. Immigration is also likely to cause intersectoral and interregional shifts of capital, but such shifts have not been documented empirically. In fact, with respect to contemporary U.S. immigrants, many potentially important channels through which immigrants might influence others have been almost completely ignored. Among these channels are demand for fixed capital (for example, housing) and land, technological change, regional and national net exports, remittances, and externalities.

A long-run effect of immigration concerns subsequent generations of immigrants. Because the 1980 and 1990 Censuses failed to identify second-generation immigrants, investigators have little idea about the performance of the U.S.-born children of more- and of less-recent immigrants. Moreover, almost nothing has been done to address the impacts that such individuals have on other residents.

Measuring the economic consequences of U.S. immigration is not easy. Most studies show little effect of immigrants on native-born workers, but a somewhat greater negative effect on earlier immigrants. Three possible reasons may underlie the difficulty in measuring significant impacts on native workers. First, immigration makes a relatively small contribution to labor force growth. Second, immigration involves offsetting shifts of labor demand and labor supply relationships. Finally, any effects of immigration quickly spread across the country. Let us consider each of these possibilities.

The first possibility suggests that the effects are simply not great because although immigration is large, its contribution to labor force growth has been relatively small, especially during a period when the labor force grew sharply (as the baby boom matured and as labor force participation rates of women rose). Since all of the baby boom is now of labor force age and since dramatic increases in women's labor force participation rates have ceased, the measured impacts of immigration could conceivably be somewhat greater during the 1990s than during earlier periods.

Even if immigration contributed relatively modestly to labor force growth at the national level, its contribution in certain regions was far greater. Why have various regional studies also failed to uncover significant impacts of immigrants on native workers? That question brings us to a second possibility—that offsetting forces are at work. Whereas immigrants may be substitutes in production for various groups of native workers, they also positively influence demand for labor in the areas in which they reside. For example, they bring with them various forms of wealth, and their contributions to wealth have a positive effect on local consumption, including housing services.

A third possible reason for the failure to find much influence of immigrants on native workers in areas with relatively heavy concentrations of immigrants is that in an economy with efficient markets, the effects of immigrants are quickly arbitraged or spread across the country through migration (because of lower wages and higher rents) and interregional (and international) trade. In this case, there are effects, but they are so widely spread geographically that they are not easily detected. The problem with this explanation is that immigration continues to focus on a few areas, such as southern California. Unless the adjustments are almost instantaneous, investigators ought to be able to find some effects in such areas.

The large influx of low-skilled immigrants in recent years has spurred concern that immigrants may constitute a burden on transfer programs. While transfer payments apparently are higher on average to immigrant families than to native families, this differential reflects differences in characteristics between the two groups, according to recent research. With the exception of recent refugees, immigrant families are no more likely, and are perhaps even less likely, to rely on welfare than are native families with similar characteristics. Since factors such as age, education, and English language ability significantly affect the probability of receiving transfer payments, policymakers should be aware that changes in the composition of the immigrant group may also affect its relative use of the transfer-payment system. Moreover, these studies generally do not provide any direct link between use of transfer programs and contributions made (such as in the form of tax payments), and thus they do not furnish a complete analysis of the fiscal effects.

Recent research also indicates considerable differences in use of transfer programs by immigrants according to where they came from and when. The reasons that use differs for immigrants from different countries are not well understood. Our knowledge in this area will no doubt progress in tandem with our general knowledge about the performance of specific immigrant groups in the U.S. economy—in terms of, say, wages and general assimilation.

Changes over time in the use of transfer programs by more broadly defined immigrant groups or by immigrants in general appear to be attributable largely to the shift in the mix of national origins. Research in this area is not totally settled, however. Certain methodological matters, such as the reliance on unverified assumptions and the use of data more recent than the 1980 Census, must be addressed. Moreover, we need to quantify immigration's indirect influence on transfers through induced changes in the wages and employment of the native population. Because such changes appear to be small, these indirect effects on transfers may also be small, though some authors have speculated that they may be large.

While at the national level little evidence indicates that immigrants impose net costs on other residents, an overall assessment at the state and local level is less certain. There is considerable speculation that, since the costs associated with immigration fall disproportionately at those levels, immigration may have a net adverse fiscal impact on state and local governments. For certain areas (for example, Los Angeles county), some evidence appears to support this contention. Such findings are not easily generalized, however. For instance, even disregarding methodological issues, such findings may result from targeting a study on an area where the probability of a negative impact is high. Of course, this explanation does not alleviate the problems faced by local units where negative impacts may be found. However, no study illustrates that state and local governments in general or in the aggregate suffer such an impact.

During the past several years an important body of literature has focused on adjustments of immigrants' skills. Several studies show that as immigrants are assimilated into the U.S. economy, the earnings gap between them and comparable indigenous workers closes and, for certain immigrant groups, perhaps even reverses. Such conclusions have generally been based on cross-sectional evidence. Recently, certain investigators have speculated that time-series data would yield different results. Using quasi-panel data—that is, charting the earnings growth of immigrant cohorts between cross-sections of data from various censuses—considerable research effort has been devoted to declines in the quality of immigrants' skills. While a number of important influences on immigrant earnings (such as age at migration) have been revealed, the evidence does not generally support any decline in quality within immigrant groups. Empirical evidence has not resolved this matter, however, primarily because appropriate time-series data have not yet been generated or identified. Moreover, evidence suggests that overall quality has declined, since the mix of immigrants by country of origin has changed over time.

The earnings differentials among groups from different countries are not well understood. According to various studies, country-of-origin characteristics are important determinants of these differentials, suggesting a selection process in immigration that is associated with those characteristics. A related issue concerns the factors that help determine who stays and progresses in the U.S. economy and who returns to the country of origin. Does some threshold level of human capital, including English language skills, help determine these dynamics? The size and composition of immigrant cohorts seem potentially important for the earnings of immigrants, but are only recently attracting attention. If, as certain authors conclude, current immigrants tend to compete with past immigrants, then the size and composition of future cohorts could affect the economic progress of any given cohort. Issues such as these underscore the importance of generating appropriate time-series data on immigration. To date, census data relating to year of arrival have been used, but they suffer from selectivity and other problems.

Comment on "Frontier Issues in International Migration," by Stark

Mark R. Rosenzweig

This article is one of many that Oded Stark has authored or coauthored that bring new insights into migration phenomena. Stark has fruitfully brought to bear on the study of migration family processes, risk considerations, game-theoretic behaviors, and concern for relative incomes, among other aspects of human behavior. These studies have shown that much can be learned about the dimensions of migration beyond the simple, but not unuseful, proposition that migrants respond to spatial wage differentials or employment probabilities, and in some cases he has shown that even this proposition is not true.

The current article highlights information constraints and strategic behavior. They are used to explain three important aspects of migration: the selectivity of migration and return migration, the selectivity and dynamics of remittances, and the relationship between migrant-native wage differentials and group cohesion.

Information economics is developed in the first parts of the article, which are well-integrated, and I will mainly discuss them. Two years ago at this same conference, I presented a paper written with Andrew Foster that examined the implications of information constraints in labor markets generally (Foster and Rosenzweig 1992). We examined theoretically and empirically a number of labor market phenomena. While we discussed some aspects of migration in an information-theoretic framework, we did not examine the interesting issue of the selectivity of return migration or consider the strategic issues in Stark's article.

The basic features of information economics in the labor market are that workers are heterogeneous in skills and employers pay wages according to the information they have, which is incomplete. Information held by employers is least complete about workers with less exposure to employers, whether newly arrived migrants, older women working for the first time, or teenagers. Wages are paid according to the characteristics observed or known by the employer that are thought to be relevant to worker productivity (in the absence of the expression of employer preferences). Over time, as increased exposure permits employers to discern true skills, wages conform more closely to the true productivity of the workers. Then, among workers who looked identical when hired, higher-skill workers experience a

Mark R. Rosenzweig is professor of economics at the University of Pennsylvania.

Proceedings of the World Bank Annual Conference on Development Economics 1994

wage increase and lower-skill workers experience a decline. Employer ignorance thus translates into a tax on high-skill workers and rents for lower-skill workers.

Note that the increase in the dispersion in wage profiles over time and the lowering of some workers' wages do not require that there be asymmetric information: *both* employers and migrants may not know initially who is more or less productive. Symmetric ignorance still leads to widening disparities in wages with exposure, given true heterogeneity in worker skills or abilities. And the possibility that the postrevelation wage in the labor market of destination may decline for some migrants so that it becomes lower than the wage in the origin area—the particular aspect Stark emphasizes—also does not require asymmetric information. Thus neither return migration nor the negative selectivity of return migration, the focus of the first part of Stark's article, requires information asymmetries. Employer ignorance is sufficient.

The notion that workers know their skills before migrating and employers do not, as in Stark's article, creates scope for opportunistic behavior, policy interventions, and additional testable implications concerning who migrates and the nature of remittances. Indeed, Stark does not go far enough in the first section of the article, in my view; he ignores the absence of empirical verification in drawing out the implications of imperfect or asymmetric information for migration phenomena. Let me indicate a few.

First, Stark shows that a fixed cost of migration—a tax in his model—will deter the self-aware workers with low skills more than those with high skills, leading to positive selectivity of immigration. But one important determinant of migration, which acts as a fixed cost, is distance or moving cost. The model thus implies that migrants from nearby areas will be less positively self-selected and will be characterized by higher propensities to return, which is negatively selective. Thus migration from Mexico and Canada to the United States will be less positively selective than migration from, say, India to the United States. Consistent with the fixed cost idea, distance is a powerful determinant of the skill characteristics of immigrants to the United States (Jasso and Rosenzweig 1990). It would be nice to have data on return migrants from the United States, who make up 20 to 40 percent of U.S. immigrants, to verify the relevance of distance to the selectivity of this group.

Second, an important feature of imperfect information in the labor market is the increase in wage disparities with exposure. In Foster and Rosenzweig (1992 and 1994) we showed, using data on rural migrants in Pakistan, that the wage variance of cohorts of migrant workers defined by date of entry increased the longer each cohort had been in the village. In this particular labor market there is little human capital investment, so exposure or experience in the local market did not increase average wages, only wage dispersion. We also found in data from rural India that the wages of women became more closely matched to their actual work performance the longer they had been in the labor market, a finding consistent with skill revelation and information constraints.

Finally, the essence of the information-theoretic models is statistical discrimination. In the absence of full information on an individual worker's skills, employers use relationships based on group characteristics they can see. Because what often distinguishes international from internal migration is in part how visible the foreign-born are, the issue of statistical discrimination and its implications for who migrates and who returns might be explored more thoroughly.

I believe that a fair amount of evidence supports the notion that there is imperfect information in labor markets, with learning by employers, and thus that the exploration of information issues is an appealing research agenda, which the first part of Stark's article advances somewhat. With respect to the second part of the article, my initial reaction was less favorable. The hypothesis here is that self-aware, high-skilled migrants use remittances to deter potential migrants known to them to have low skills but who would appear identical to destination-area employers. This is done to maintain a higher level of initial wages for migrants, which reflects group averages. I find the logic of this idea impeccable but the importance of this phenomenon implausible, given coordination problems and the likelihood that the payoff will be small if employers can identify individual skills relatively quickly. However, it is not the plausibility of an idea that matters, but whether it can better predict actual phenomena. Thus I examined some data sets containing information on remittances to test the migration-deterrence hypothesis.

The particular implication from Stark's model of remittance behavior that can be tested with the data I have assembled is that remittances are negatively selective with respect to the characteristics of the recipients; remittances are provided to individuals in the area of origin who would look productive but in fact are not relative to the average worker in the observationally identical group. Note that these remittances are precisely the rents earned by the low-skill workers in an environment in which employers cannot discern (at least initially) who is productive. Thus, for example, among individuals with the same level of schooling (a plausibly visible characteristic) those with lower origin-area wages would be more likely to receive a remittance. Similarly, among workers in the origin area earning the same wages, those with higher levels of schooling would also be more likely to receive a "bribe" not to migrate, in the form of a remittance; they are the truly less able among their education group. So if we run a regression of remittances received on workers' wages and schooling attainment we should observe a negative coefficient for the wage variable and a positive one for the schooling variable, that is, negative selectivity for remittances.

To test the negative selectivity of remittances, I examined two data sets with the requisite information: the third round of the 1976–77 Malaysia Family Life Survey and the 1970–71 Additional Rural Incomes Survey of the National Council of Applied Economic Research in India (Vashishtha 1988). These data sets have information on worker wages, on schooling, and on remittances received for a national probability sample of Malaysian households with an ever-married woman and all rural Indian households, respectively.

Maximum-likelihood probit estimates of the determinants of the probability that a husband of the sample respondent in Malaysia received a financial transfer in the year before the survey are shown in table 1. In addition to the natural log of earnings and schooling attainment of the husband, the specification includes his age and its square and the household's total wealth. In this sample 14 percent of the husbands received a remittance from a donor located at least 40 miles from the household or in a foreign country, so this income source is not rare and is worth understanding. The estimates reported in the first column accord with the Stark model: remittances are negatively related to the wage and positively related to schooling, with the coefficients in both cases statistically significant using conventional standards of statistical significance. The point estimates imply that among men with the same schooling, those whose wage was twice the average would have a 24 percent lower probability of receiving a remittance; those with the same wage but with schooling approximately double the average (an increase of six years) would be 18 percent more likely to receive a remittance.

The results appear to be consistent with the model of preemptive bribes to potential migrants with poorer skills. However, if deterrence of migration is really the motive, the relationships predicted should be most salient for those most likely to migrate. And we know from almost all studies of migration that these are predominantly the young. The negative-selectivity results should therefore be stronger for the younger men in the sample than for the older men. To check this proposition, I split the sample at age 35. Contrary to expectations, the results reported in the second and third columns of table 1 do not support the hypothesis for the younger group, which poses the migration threat, but only for the older men, who are far less likely to migrate. Thus it does not appear that the selectivity of remittances in Malaysia is a migration phenomenon, as the Stark model of asymmetric information suggests.

Table 1. *Test of Negative Selectivity of Remittances in Malaysian Sample: Maximum-Likelihood Probit Estimates of Probability of Receiving a Remittance*

		Age	
Variable	*Total sample*	*Under 35*	*Over 35*
ln wage	−1.51	0.250	−0.185
	(2.30)	(1.48)	(2.55)
Years of schooling	0.0358	0.0205	0.0268
	(2.06)	(0.499)	(1.40)
Land owned	0.000208	0.00278	0.0103
	(1.29)	(5.49)	(1.03)
Age	0.0113	−0.0544	0.0115
	(3.35)	(1.50)	(1.97)
Age squared ($\times 10^{-3}$)	−0.835	8.23	−0.867
	(2.72)	(1.58)	(1.81)
Constant	−3.70	5.43	−0.347
	(4.11)	(0.89)	(1.98)
Number	825	279	546

Note: Sample consists of husbands of sample respondents in the third round of the 1977 Malaysian Family Life Survey. Numbers in parentheses are absolute values of robust t-ratios.

Source: Author's calculations.

The results for the Indian sample are similar (table 2). Here the sample consists of men earning agricultural or nonagricultural wages, 5 percent of whom received remittances in the year before the survey. In the first column the sign patterns for the coefficients on wages and schooling conform to the negative-selectivity model, and these coefficients are jointly statistically significant. However, as in the Malaysian sample, when the sample is split by age the relevant coefficients are only statistically significant for the older group, which does not constitute a migration threat. In India, too, no evidence suggests that remittances are used to deter potential migrants.

Stark's article is truly on the frontier—the models are not fully worked out, but they do suggest useful areas of inquiry. While not all of the specific hypotheses are likely to have high payoffs, information economics is an interesting area of relevance to migration. What the article does not make clear is the particular relevance of the models to international migration. The case is made that information constraints, return migration, remittances, and issues of group cohesion are at least potentially applicable to migration phenomena in general. But a distinguishing feature of international migration is the attempt by governments to regulate it. Thus the salient questions not covered in the article include whether international migration should be restricted and, if so, in what ways? How do the criteria now used affect the composition of international migration flows, and what are the consequences for origin and destination economies? Most important from the perspective of the World Bank, what is the relation between international migration and economic development? We are a long way from having answers to these questions.

Table 2. *Test of Negative Selectivity of Remittances in Indian Sample: Maximum-Likelihood Probit Estimates of Probability of Receiving a Remittance*

		Age	
Variable	*Total sample*	*Under 35*	*Over 35*
ln wage	−2.10	−0.0705	−0.354
	(1.21)	(0.25)	(1.25)
Primary schooling	0.304	0.504	0.0913
	(1.43)	(1.75)	(−0.32)
Land owned	−0.0266	−0.0203	−0.0316
	(2.78)	(1.87)	(2.06)
Age	−0.000121	0.0614	0.0649
	(0.04)	(0.43)	(0.55)
Age squared (x10^{-3})	0.0266	−1.30	−0.557
	(0.07)	(0.42)	(0.50)
Constant	−1.37	−2.20	2.91
	(2.61)	(1.41)	(0.97)
Number	1,981	1,023	958

Note: Sample consists of men earning agricultural or nonagricultural wages in 1970–71 in the Additional Rural Incomes Survey, National Council of Applied Economic Research. Numbers in parentheses are absolute values of robust t-ratios.

Source: Author's calculations.

References

Foster, Andrew D., and Mark R. Rosenzweig. 1992. "Information Flows and Discrimination in Labor Markets in Rural Areas in Developing Countries." *Proceedings of the World Bank Annual Conference on Development Economics* 1992: 173–203.

———. 1994. "Information, Learning, and Wage Rates in Low-Income Rural Areas." *Journal of Human Resources* 28(4): 759–90.

Jasso, Guillermina, and Mark R. Rosenzweig. 1990. *The New Chosen People: Immigrants in the United States.* New York: Russell Sage.

Vashishtha, Prem. 1988. "Changes in the Structure of Investments in Rural Households, 1970–71 – 1981–82." *Journal of Income and Wealth* 10: 111–26.

Floor Discussion of "Frontier Issues in International Migration," by Stark

Surprised by the motive to remit presented in Stark's article, a participant from the World Bank asked why a highly skilled immigrant would send remittances to a specific low-skilled person he does not even know. The intuitive assumption would be that remittances are sent to the family left behind in an endogenous form of decisionmaking: we will send you over there, and maybe it won't be much fun, but you will make more money for a while and will send some back to us. Stark had spoken of highly skilled immigrants sending remittances to low-skilled workers to discourage them from migrating. I might be willing to send money to keep another Moroccan in Morocco, said the participant, but what do I do about the Tunisians, Egyptians, Turks, and so on? The participant was more convinced by the argument about asymmetric versus imperfect information. If the information is asymmetric—I know that I am not so good, but the others don't—then I know that they will discover I am not so good over time, and this could be incorporated into the model of my decision to migrate, along with the cost of migration. Of course, if the cost of migration is zero, I don't care: I go and I come back. But if the costs of migration are significant, the probability of my lack of skill being discovered over time should be incorporated into my decision. Whether I migrate will depend on how far I am from average, how long it takes, the cost of migrating, and so on.

In his book *The Migration of Labor,* Stark responded, he devotes four chapters to motives behind remittances, and several pages to the issue of free riding and coordination, but a point made in the current article addressed this concern: "Quite often, migrants from a given area in *P* work together in the same site in *R,* so remitting to a well-defined target set of potential migrants effectively preserves the migrants' wage. This small-scale effect also helps prevent free riding by an individual migrant who might be tempted to avoid remitting while enjoying the benefits of other migrants' contributions." Stark fully agreed that without this small-scale effect the whole argument falls apart. *The Migration of Labor,* he explained, addresses a spectrum of motives ranging from self-interest to altruism, with many submotives in between. This article's particular motivation is outside that spectrum and additional to it.

This session was chaired by Marcelo Selowsky, chief economist, Europe and Central Asia Regional Office, at the World Bank.

A participant from one of the World Bank's Africa infrastructure divisions was also curious about the motivation behind sending remittances to keep someone at home, but from another point of view. In 1972–74, when the oil shock hit, Bangladesh started sending workers to the Middle East. If you walked through the airports in Jedda and Riyadh, you would find Bangladeshis cleaning floors, Filipinos managing stores, and Moroccans managing the airport. It seemed to this participant that the Bangladeshi worker got stamped "Made in Bangladesh" and made a certain (low) wage. The reaction of the Bangladeshi government at that time—to prevent skilled migrants from migrating—might have been the wrong policy. Perhaps they should have expanded the supply of skilled workers so that the "Made in Bangladesh" stamp indicated higher quality, increasing the amount of remittances sent home. This participant congratulated Stark on his style of presentation, on being bold enough to put numbers and formulas out there so that people could use them as a language, and for explaining so clearly how to use that language.

A participant from the International Finance Corporation was surprised not to hear more about the family unit's role in a model of labor flows, which would seem to him as important as interest rates in a model of capital flows. It seemed to him that most remigration decisions must depend on considerations about your future family, that if home-country wages were indeed repressed you might remain abroad if your children would do better as a result. It might be an old-fashioned theory, but it would help explain the empirical observation about the increasing age of migrants from India, for example. For him, it was a clear family decision that those who made it are now getting their parents into the country. These decisions are not made on the basis of wages or short-term considerations; they are long-term family decisions.

Nor had there been a discussion of how one's stage in the life cycle affected such decisions, added Marcelo Selowsky (chair). As you get older, your price deflator is different. When you retire, elder care becomes much more important and its relative cost is generally lower in the country of origin. This is so obvious that it might not do much good to add it to the model, Selowsky continued, but there must be clear data on the people who retire to their country of origin. Stark responded that his original effort (a work still in progress) had been to write a very different article, one that would model return migration. The idea of that effort was that many of the returns to migration accrue from return migration, with a key reason being that you want to dispose of your life-cycle savings in the place where they will support the highest consumption.

A participant from the OECD was more interested in the distinction between contract workers (who are recruited for specific periods of time but must then go home, and who can sometimes but not always return again) and what you might call settlement migration, which is what Australia, Canada, and the United States encourage. It seemed to him that developing countries are probably more interested in contract workers, and there was some evidence that contract workers remit proportionately more of their income home than do settlers, who have more interest in taking everything with them. He wondered if Stark had included this factor in his model, or whether Stark thought it made a difference what legal restrictions migration was subject to.

If you have an underlying heterogeneity of workers, Stark replied, you might want to devise a tax—a "visa fee," one might call it—or administer an examination. Every bricklayer who wanted to enter the United States, for example, would go to the local U.S. consulate, pay $20, and take a bricklaying test. If you passed the test, you would get a certificate saying that you are a bricklayer of quality A, B, or C. The problem is, what do you do about occupations (such as engineering) where screening would be either costly or ineffective? Such examinations might not be practical or perfect; you probably have to live with some information imperfection.

A participant from the World Bank said that in the early literature on human capital, migration was considered a form of human capital, and immigrants might arrive with additional human capital independent of the migration itself. But if migration is itself a form of human capital, one would expect migrants to have higher earnings when they return. Is there any evidence that this happens? Stark responded that the skill level (θ) was kept constant in his article. When migrants move, their θ does not depreciate. In other words, θ is not, as is often the case, country-specific—migrants do not lose their θ when they move. Nor does the move result in an increase in θ. But as he pointed out in the last paragraph of the article, the merging of information considerations with human capital considerations is probably at the edge of the migration research frontier, for several reasons.

Think about the case where a migrant has a low θ and wants to earn more. He or she can increase his or her θ, but, said Stark, my article implies that there is another option available, which involves acquiring means and devices that do not increase θ but rather make it costlier and more time-consuming for employers to decipher the true θ. And vice versa: when a migrant's θ is high, he or she may not necessarily want to have more θ, but instead may want to invest in means that decipher θ, to ensure that the lag of discovery is brief. And probably in real life what we have is some sort of meshing of investment in θ and investment in devices that conceal or reveal θ.

Michael Greenwood (discussant), Stark said, gave me a challenge yesterday when he asked how I explain situations where people move from *A* to *C*, and others where they move from *A* to *B*, and then from *B* to *C*. The answer could lie here. If migrants move from *A* to *B* they have one period in which they are averaged with others. If they then move to *C*, they have another period in which they are averaged. If they go directly from *A* to *C* they have one period over which they are averaged and a second period over which they are not averaged. Lower-quality workers will benefit by being averaged twice rather than once. So the entire pattern of international migration or, if you like, of migration in general can be conceived as an attempt to reap returns conditional on θ and the information pertaining to θ. So, Stark concluded, the story will really be completely told when you merge human capital with information considerations in the way he suggested.

Selowsky asked participants to suggest further questions for research, particularly of a normative nature. Perhaps something about migration's effect on the ones left behind, the effect of the brain drain, for example? A visiting scholar from the Massachusetts Institute of Technology said that this was precisely the kind of question she had been discussing with colleagues at the World Bank for several months in seeking to understand the relation between development and migration, especially focusing on factors, stages, and elements in development that affect population movements. The expectation is that the relation will change over time: there may be some loosening of patterns early in development so that migration increases, but over the long term migration will decline. We do not know much about that relationship, said the scholar. Phil Martin called it "the hump," an inelegant term that comes from work done for the U.S. Commission on International Migration and Cooperative Economic Development. It is a subject that we need to explore. International migration infuses itself into many aspects of what the World Bank does, including labor market issues. In Malaysia and the Republic of Korea, for example, what should be done about the current reliance on illegal migration? From a strictly neoclassical point of view maybe the Bank need not bother doing anything about it, but from a normative point of view there is an issue, she asserted. What is Bank policy on this sort of thing going to be? In Viet Nam, for example, we see a tremendous amount of inward and outward migration. Viet Nam recently announced that it intends to become the major labor exporter for southeast Asia, undercutting the Philippines. What implications will that have for regional development, for patterns of investment in the Philippines, and so forth?

Selowsky asked, are migration processes generating distortions that call for government intervention? You have the sign reversed, a participant responded. International migration already attracts more government intervention than any other labor process. Is the government intervening too much? asked Selowsky. No, said the participant. The question is to understand and optimize what is going on—not whether there should be intervention, but what is the intervention doing?

We know that there will be migration laws and government intervention, said another participant, and we know that they will affect some countries more than others. Perhaps what we should do is suggest options that will serve as the destination countries' objectives or convince them that their objectives are wrong, but somehow arrive at solutions that have the least negative effects. Should they liberalize trade, for example? Should they do something about foreign direct investment? Should they enforce migration laws more strongly? And so on.

From what I have heard, responded Selowsky, nothing has changed the classical view that the freer is migration, the better. The examples we have heard suggest that we should lift as many restrictions as possible. That's not true, said a participant. The brain drain is a problem, for example.

Migration is so heavily controlled, said a participant, that from the developing countries' viewpoint not much migration is going on. The average annual increase in the labor force in most developing countries is extremely small, and you can count the exceptions on one hand: Mexico, the Philippines, countries in the Caribbean, and a few others. Much of that is contract migration to the Middle East. And there is an increasing flow into a few East Asian countries that are now labor-scarce. Many of the old arguments about guest workers in Germany are now being rehashed. With such pressures on migration in the OECD countries, countries still open to migration will go for more selectivity in terms of skill. Countries may decide that what they really want is highly skilled people who make a difference in terms of ideas and innovation. A new brain-drain issue might have consequences for development if that idea got going.

Stark closed the discussion by responding to the comments made by Mark Rosenzweig (discussant) on the likely scope of strategic remittances. Rosenzweig, Stark said, seemed to miss the point about asymmetric information. Whereas the skill levels of *individual* workers are accurately known to each and every worker, certain employers, namely those *at destination,* know only the *distribution* of skills of the group of migrant workers. Given the wage determination rule, workers can thus time migration so that, as noted in the article, not all workers migrate simultaneously. If the workers too were ignorant about their true skills, this pattern of sequential migration would not occur.

With regard to strategic remittances, Stark continued, Rosenzweig applies an inappropriate test. The argument in the article is that *if* migration takes place under conditions of asymmetric information, then, subject to several additional conditions as offered, we should observe *strategic* remittances. Conversely, if *strategic* remittances are not observed, migration may not have taken place under informational asymmetry in the first place. Obviously not all migratory flows are "informationally asymmetric" and not all remittances are strategically motivated. To properly test the theory we need to consider the group of workers whose members, although heterogeneous in skills (for example, due to different work experience), appear equivalent to destination employers (for example, all have the same number of years of schooling). If high-skill workers migrate and remit in order to persuade low-skill workers to stay home, Stark said, remittances will be negatively correlated with the skill level of would-be migrants. The key condition is that *the migrants* appear to be identical to *the nonmigrants.* Rosenzweig's examples, which are devoid of information about the relevant attributes of *the migrants,* are thus inappropriate tests of the theory.

Whether one type of migration is different from another type in kind or in degree is not always clear-cut. Stark believes that informational issues arise naturally, particularly in the context of international migration, because information that is readily available and easily deciphered by employers within a country is hard to come by and interpret across countries. And contrary to Rosenzweig, the relevance of the model as developed in the article for government policy is transparent: governments have an interest in the skill composition of the migrants they admit and want to know how to influence the skill mix of new arrivals. They need to be aware that under informational asymmetry a particular policy tool, such as an entry tax, will have a crowding-out effect on strategic remittances. This *is* a consequence of international migration policy for the origin economy. Moreover, Stark continued, since remittances are usually conducive to economic development at origin, there is a distinct link between migration policy at destination and economic development at origin.

Labor Market Responses to a Change in Economic System

Robert J. Flanagan

The economic transitions in Eastern Europe have produced a contraction in the aggregate labor supply and the beginnings of a reallocation of labor from investment goods and heavy industry to consumer goods and services. The expansion of the private sector has reversed—if not eliminated—many of the labor market distortions created under central planning. Thus the first years of economic transition recorded increasing returns to human capital. There is some evidence that growth in the private sector has led to more rational wage structures. Labor unions and minimum wage legislation have done little to inhibit labor market adjustments. Rather, labor market programs and incomes policies—with their emphasis on passive measures and wage subsidies—have retarded the adjustment of wage structures and the restructuring of labor in state enterprises. But, the article observes, changing to active labor policies would probably not reverse the decline in employment. Unemployment in the transition economies is largely a matter of insufficient demand, and labor market policy is unlikely to have much impact until the mismatch between vocational training systems and modern production methods is solved.

The collapse of central planning systems has been closely tied to a collapse of total factor productivity. In the early postwar decades labor force participation rates and capital resources increased in socialist countries, and their economic growth rates compared favorably with those of capitalist countries. But with the exhaustion of possibilities for extensive growth, these economies needed to use their resources more efficiently to achieve intensive growth, and failing this, their economic growth faltered. In command economies the increases in total factor productivity growth needed to overcome slowing labor force and capital growth were not forthcoming. This sluggish total factor productivity growth, moreover, confirmed market-oriented economists' warning that central planning processes would produce both allocative and X-inefficiency.

Robert Flanagan is Konosuke Matsushita Professor of International Labor Economics and Policy Analysis, Graduate School of Business, at Stanford University. The author wishes to thank John Earle for comments on earlier drafts.

Proceedings of the World Bank Annual Conference on Development Economics 1994

Today, however, the experience of economies in transition has turned this economic prediction on its head. Despite the strong presumption among Western economists that transition from central planning to more market-oriented economies will eliminate the inefficiencies associated with central planning and produce higher growth, there is no clear vision of the processes through which this fundamental economic goal might be achieved. Gains in efficiency, moreover, might be offset initially by drastic declines in labor force participation.

Macroeconomic stabilization has largely dominated the labor market research agenda during the early stages of Eastern Europe's transition. The importance of macroeconomic stability notwithstanding, there is a real danger that policies adopted for short-run purposes will conflict with fundamental long-run objectives. The damage such conflicts can do, moreover, is potentially greater for transition than for operating market economies.

This article focuses on the extent to which labor market policies, institutions, and behavior at the microeconomic level facilitate or impede economic restructuring. Any effort to tell a general story risks glossing over important differences among countries. It is equally risky to generalize from the experience of one country about developments throughout a region. One must decide which variations really matter, or else there will be no story to tell. The standard warning about data quality and availability also applies—particularly with regard to the private sector. Until better raw material is available, many issues of labor market adjustment easily explored in OECD countries must remain largely conjectural when speaking of former command economies.

Aggregate Labor Market Adjustments

The early phases of economic transition in Eastern Europe brought sharp declines in state sector output and real wages to virtually all the countries of the region.

Table 1. *Change in Labor Force Status of Working Age Population, 1989–92*
(percent distribution)

	Bulgaria			*Czech Republic*			*Hungary*		
	1989	*1992*	*Difference*	*1989*	*1992*	*Difference*	*1989*	*1992*	*Difference*
Men									
Employment	88.3	69.0	−19.3	81.2	75.5	−5.7	85.5	70.9	−14.6
Unemployment	0.0	9.5	9.5	0.0	1.8	1.8	0.4	10.4	10.0
Inactive	11.7	21.5	9.8	18.8	22.7	3.9	14.1	18.7	4.6
Women									
Employment	85.1	62.1	−23.0	75.2	65.3	−9.9	78.1	64.3	−13.8
Unemployment	0.0	11.8	11.8	0.0	2.6	2.6	0.4	7.9	7.5
Inactive	14.9	26.1	11.2	24.8	32.1	7.3	21.6	27.8	6.2

Note: Figures are annual averages, except for the Czech Republic, where data are for the end of the year, and the Slovak Republic, where employment data are for the end of the year.

Declines in state sector employment ranged from about 33 percent in Hungary to about 20 percent in Bulgaria, the Czech and Slovak Republics, and Poland (Blanchard, Commander, and Coricelli 1993). In Romania employment in state enterprises dropped by about 23 percent, but that figure was closer to 40 percent when employment in cooperatives was included (Earle and Oprescu 1993).

These large net declines in employment reflect the private sector's failure to expand its activity at a pace that absorbed the labor shed from the state sector. The different patterns of net employment change shown in table 1 reflect how much offsetting employment growth the private sector was able to generate. Among countries with intermediate declines in the state sector, the Czech Republic had the strongest private sector development and Bulgaria, Hungary, and the Slovak Republic the weakest.

The allocation of net employment declines between unemployment (appearing for the first time since the onset of central planning) and departure from the labor force is determined in part by differences in incentives for market and nonmarket activity, influenced in part by labor market policy. Policy effects aside, however, the real wage declines in Eastern Europe should produce both substitution and income effects on aggregate labor supply. The substitution effect is visible in withdrawals from the labor force in response to deteriorating market rewards. The income effect is visible in the increased participation of individuals attempting to maintain family income as other family members lose their jobs. In virtually all OECD economies the substitution effect dominates, and labor supply elasticities are highest for women and for both sexes at the extremes of the age distribution (OECD 1983).

Absent unusually large income effects on the labor supply in Eastern European countries, one would have expected the aggregate labor supply to contract during the early phases of economic transition. Labor force participation rates did indeed decline in four of the countries surveyed. Consistent with Western experience, net withdrawals from the labor force were higher for women than for men in these four

	Poland			*Romania*			*Slovak Republic*		
	1989	*1992*	*Difference*	*1989*	*1992*	*Difference*	*1989*	*1992*	*Difference*
Men									
Employment	82.6	71.9	–10.7	87.5	81.0	–6.5	87.1	72.8	–14.3
Unemployment	0.0	9.4	9.4	0.0	5.3	5.3	0.0	8.8	8.8
Inactive	17.4	18.7	1.3	12.5	13.6	1.1	12.9	18.5	5.6
Women									
Employment	68.6	58.3	–10.3	80.7	80.9	0.2	78.9	58.8	–20.1
Unemployment	0.0	10.6	10.6	0.0	9.3	9.3	0.0	9.7	9.7
Inactive	31.4	31.1	–0.3	19.3	9.8	–9.5	21.1	31.5	10.4

Source: Commission of the European Communities, 1993, p. 15. For Hungary, Poland, and the Czech and Slovak Republics the data are based on establishment surveys and administrative records, except the 1992 data for Hungary are from a labor force survey. Bulgarian and Romanian data are from administrative records (including labor office registrations for unemployment) and estimates of private employment.

countries. But in Poland labor force participation was close to a wash (with some increase for women), and in Romania it actually increased, mainly because of the large influx of women into the labor force. The labor force response of women in these countries is contrary to postwar experience in most market economies and recent experience in other Eastern European countries. It is, however, reminiscent of the old "additional worker effect" said to have influenced female labor force participation during the Great Depression. Relatively strong income effects are plausible in Eastern European labor markets, even in the absence of labor market policy influences, given low asset levels and the rapid elimination of monetary overhang by early transition price shocks.

The allocation of net employment declines between unemployment and nonparticipation was not uniform throughout the region. The comparative importance of increased nonparticipation stands out in the Czech Republic and—to a lesser extent—in Bulgaria and the Slovak Republic, while in Hungary, Poland, and Romania increased unemployment was more important. While policy-induced incentives appear to have affected each country's experience, the history is too short to establish the connection rigorously. Overall, unemployment insurance systems in transition economies are less generous than those in OECD countries (Scarpetta, Boeri, and Reutersward 1993).[1] The Czech and Slovak Republics, although their eligibility requirements and replacement ratios are in the middle of the range, offer the briefest duration of benefits and (along with Bulgaria) impose the lowest maximum benefit payments, thereby discouraging long periods of joblessness. Preliminary evidence indicates that the generosity of the unemployment insurance schemes affects the allocation of net employment reductions between unemployment and labor force withdrawal in predictable ways.

Unemployment

Unemployment is influenced by labor market policies and institutions. North-American-style unemployment consists of relatively high inflows to and high outflows from joblessness, with most spells of unemployment being comparatively brief. A scenario in which workers released from state enterprises queued for jobs for a brief period before moving into private sector jobs would produce such an unemployment pattern. In contrast, however, European-style joblessness is marked by low exit rates from unemployment—either because employers are reluctant to hire or workers are reluctant to accept jobs—and long durations of unemployment. Long unemployment itself, moreover, reduces the odds of getting a job.

There is now considerable evidence that Eastern European countries have developed *super* European-style unemployment (Blanchard, Commander, and Coricelli 1993; Boeri 1993). Inflow rates are lower than in most Western European countries—in part reflecting the widespread use of early retirement incentives. But as the importance of this adjustment necessarily declines, future inflow rates should increase. While the majority of the newly unemployed in formerly command economies are workers released from state enterprises, there are also important inflows from outside the labor force (particularly among inexperienced workers who have completed their schooling and cannot find a job) and from the private sector. Outflow rates have been even lower than in Western Europe, and many spells of unemployment do not end with a job. While the low outflow rates reflect general demand problems indicated by extremely low ratios of job vacancies to unemployment, there also appear to be important structural influences.

In addition to the influence of unemployment compensation arrangements on the willingness to accept jobs, at least two structural policies can make employers in transition economies reluctant to hire. The former Czechoslovakia, Hungary, and Poland all have regulations governing collective dismissals that require consultation with employee representatives, advance notice of dismissals, and severance pay ranging from one to six months (Scarpetta, Boeri, and Reutersward 1993). While these costs may slow flows into unemployment, they also make employers reluctant to hire and thereby slow the movement from unemployment to employment. Incomes policies that limit growth of the wage bill also discourage hiring. Since these regulations apply only to state enterprises, however, their damage to restructuring may be slight.

Labor Market Programs

When unemployment is on the rise, a common recommendation is for greater spending on labor market programs. Eastern Europe is no exception, and the absence of rudimentary job-matching and safety-net institutions at the beginning of the economic transition added urgency to the recommendations. Some advocates of labor market programs suggest that such programs will substantially reduce unemployment in transition economies. Experience in the West, however, suggests that that is likely to be true only under special circumstances. The key questions, then, are whether current policies are likely to facilitate restructuring and whether labor market programs in general can reduce unemployment.

By fiscal 1992–93 most transition economies had higher unemployment rates than most OECD countries yet spent less (as a percentage of GDP) on labor market policies that might improve the skill levels and the matching prospects of the unemployed. Moreover, public expenditure on labor market policy has concentrated on such passive measures as unemployment compensation and early retirement, measures that may, in fact, extend joblessness and facilitate withdrawal from the labor force. Active measures, on the other hand, contribute directly to employment or the efficiency of future labor inputs (OECD 1993a).

Active labor market policies in transition economies have not focused on skill development. Expenditure is disproportionately weighted toward wage subsidies and public employment by comparison with such spending in Western economies. Although most wage subsidy expenditures in European countries do not go to state firms that should be shedding labor (OECD 1993a), much of the expenditure appears to support employees who would have been hired anyway. A case can be made for targeting wage subsidies to support new entrants into the labor force (to provide work experience and on-the-job training) and those unemployed a long time (to prevent skill depreciation), but for reasons developed below, the case is not secure. Overall, however, current labor market policies throughout Eastern Europe do not appear to facilitate either restructuring or unemployment reduction.

Nor would changing the mix of labor market policies be likely to alter substantially the region's unemployment experience. One difficulty is that active policies cannot solve the problem of insufficient demand. Training and related measures do not create vacancies but only help to fill them, and in Eastern European labor markets the difficulty is not in filling vacancies but rather in their general absence. With limited demand, active labor market policies can change the order of workers in the job-seeking queue but not the length of the queue itself. Analysis of the effects of active labor market policies, moreover, rarely considers the extent to which the gains of targeted groups are obtained by displacing nontargeted groups (OECD 1993a). Policy measures, therefore, can seek to attain only such limited social gains as can be realized from changing the order in the unemployment queue.

A second problem is that wage subsidies do not always deliver on their promise. In a full-information world wage subsidies should theoretically provide more jobs, yet the experience of some Western countries indicates that targeted policies can produce outcomes quite contrary to expectations. When information is unevenly distributed—as when employers are imperfectly informed about workers' productive potential, for instance—workers with superior abilities will need to signal their superiority in a credible manner, that is, in a way that less-qualified workers cannot imitate. Remaining outside labor market programs could be just such a signal. In the United States, for example, employer participation in targeted wage-subsidy programs has been low. There is also evidence that employers prefer to hire unsubsidized workers, suggesting that they associate public labor market programs with lower-quality workers. High-quality members of a targeted group have therefore effectively signaled their quality by remaining outside wage-subsidy programs—an option that is not available to low-quality workers, whose poor productivity would subject them to dismissal. Policies providing employers with general wage subsidies may mitigate this problem, but even when subsidies are paid to employers, targeting would raise the signaling issue.

In Eastern Europe such ideas are far from theoretical. The private sector hires almost exclusively from state firms rather than from among the unemployed (Beleva, Jackman, and Nenova-Amar 1993; Commander and others 1993; Vecernik 1993) and avoids using the new labor offices. While the signaling stigma appears to be less severe for training and other labor market programs designed to increase productivity, some taint may still apply.

In summary, the labor force in Eastern European countries has contracted. Workers unemployed for long periods may become virtually unemployable, also reducing the effective future labor supply. New cohorts of school-leavers lack employment opportunities, a particularly troublesome characteristic because the newest cohorts, who have the strongest incentive to make the major human capital investments required by change, are needed to accomplish major economic restructuring.

At this point unemployment in Eastern Europe is largely a demand problem. The exact nature of the structural problems that labor market policy might address will not become clear until there is a closer balance between job vacancies and unemployment. Yet the pattern of labor market programs in the region does not seem to be facilitating restructuring, and the emphasis on passive measures may even retard it.

Sectoral Employment and Wage Adjustments

Following the communist takeovers in Eastern Europe in the late 1940s, central planners sought to develop and expand investment goods and heavy industry at the expense of consumer goods and services. With some exceptions, job matching was left to workers and employers, while central planners developed national wage structures to encourage workers to follow planning preferences. National tariff wages were established for job categories under a national job evaluation that gave weight both to considerations familiar to Adam Smith, such as the qualifications required and onerousness of work, and to planning objectives, such as the social importance of the industry. Before long, industry wage structures throughout Eastern Europe had adapted to the tariff wage structure, with large increases in relative wages in industry and construction and decreases in trade and services (Adam 1984). Tariff wage policies reduced both returns to human capital and interregional wage differentials and weakened the link between managerial performance and pay.

Overall wage levels were kept low to permit high investment levels. Low wages produced high quit rates, but the range of labor mobility was severely circumscribed by housing shortages. To counter management efforts to attract and retain workers, furthermore, central planners imposed tax penalties for excessive increases in enterprise wage bills—an early form of tax-based incomes policy.

Labor unions in centrally planned economies had no bargaining role. Their main role was to challenge dismissals. Whether labor's weakness under central planning helped or hindered efficiency depends on whether "monopoly" or "voice" theories of union behavior were more applicable in Eastern Europe. Limitations on labor exit and voice opportunities, however, demonstrably reduced job satisfaction to well below Western levels (Blanchflower and Freeman 1993).

To some degree, all Eastern European labor markets have moved away from the outcomes influenced by central planners. Since 1989 employment has shifted from industry and agriculture toward services. Within the service sector, employment has grown especially in trade, health, and education—sectors generally neglected under central planning.

Private sector employment has grown in all countries (albeit at very different rates), but the private sector offers heterogeneous job opportunities that range from small service organizations with one or two employees to large manufacturing operations. In most countries large-scale privatization has proceeded slowly, and state enterprises remain the main source of employment. The private sector's share of total employment is largest in Poland (45 percent) and Hungary (35 percent), both of which had significant private economic activity before the late 1980s, but throughout the rest of Eastern Europe it remains at less than 20 percent.

To what extent, then, has private sector expansion helped to reverse the labor markets' vestiges of planners' preferences? To address this question, we must examine private sector wage policies and the nature of labor market competition between the state and private sectors.

Public-Private Pay Differentials

The analysis of labor market competition between private and state firms in Eastern Europe is hampered by limited documentation of the private sector. The following discussion, therefore, considers three levels of information in an effort to ascertain the role of wages in competition between the state and private sectors: official data (uncontrolled for human capital and other compositional influences) on average wages in each sector, household surveys of individuals (with statistical controls for some influences on wages), and recent World Bank surveys of private firms in the region.[2]

For Bulgaria there is only survey evidence to show that private firms tend to pay higher wages but lower benefits and bonuses (Beleva, Jackman, and Nenova-Amar 1993), and no reliable information has been reported for Romania (Earle and Oprescu 1993).

Two studies of Czech data find substantial differentials. An analysis of a June 1991 government survey of wages in the Czech Republic found that men working in the private sector earned more than one and one-half times what men of the same education and age range earned in the state sector. The differential was smaller for men over forty-five years of age and negligible for women on the basis of average monthly wages (Flanagan 1993a). (At this early stage of Czech privatization, however, the sample contained few private sector observations.) A year later, in June 1992, Vecernik's (1993) analysis of the Survey of Economic Expectations and Attitudes found—after controlling for age, education, and broad occupational and industrial categories—that employees in private firms were earning about 13 percent more than employees in state enterprises and about 19 percent more than employees in cooperative organizations.

In Hungary wage differentials between private and state firms emerged before the fall of communism, yet the Hungarian Household Panel data suggest that wage differences are somewhat smaller there than in the Czech Republic. After controlling for age, schooling, occupation, and broad industrial category, Commander and others (1993) found that employees in the partly private sector had monthly incomes (wages and earnings, including all cash payments) that were about 9 percent higher than those offered in the state sector—and 6 percent higher for the fully private sector. The results are much weaker for hourly earnings, possibly reflecting the greater use of profit-sharing and other bonus arrangements in the private sector. Respondents to the World Bank survey of private manufacturing indicated that they tried to pay higher salaries than the state sector (Webster 1993a).

Official Polish statistics indicate that average private sector wages exceed average state wages in construction and transportation, but that state wages (which do not distinguish between the old cooperatives and the new private sector) are higher in industry and trade. There is some evidence that private sector wages tend to be higher for high-wage jobs and lower for low-wage jobs (Coricelli, Hagemejer, and Rybinski 1993). But for labor market behavior the key comparison is for jobs in which the private sector competes with the state sector. According to a World Bank survey of private manufacturing firms in Hungary and the Czech Republic, entrepreneurs reported that they typically paid unskilled workers 10 percent more than they could have made in state enterprises and skilled workers what they could afford, which could be up to twice what state enterprises were paying (Webster 1993a; Webster and Swanson 1993).

To some extent, however, higher wages in the private sector are offset by higher nonwage benefits paid by the state. It is widely believed—if not precisely documented—that fringe benefits and services are greater in the state sector. The difference appears to be greatest for the largest state firms. The World Bank survey of private manufacturing in Hungary found that fringe benefits were indeed lower than in the public sector but not by enough to offset wage differences. Nonwage benefits within the private sector are no doubt smallest in the smaller service firms, which are not well covered by current statistical systems. Bank surveys also indicate that private sector employers are likely to use dismissals as disciplinary and motivational tools. Although there is some turnover among private firms, recent large-scale employment losses in state firms have sharply reduced differences in job security between the sectors.

In summary, where private sector firms compete directly with state firms for particular skills, private firms appear to pay higher average wages, although the margin and composition of the overall compensation package vary across sectors and countries. Since the private sector appears to offer fewer nonwage benefits, some of the smaller wage differences may reflect compensating differentials. The larger wage differentials indicate two aspects of the labor reallocation process in transition economies.

First, the prevalence of a private sector wage premium in most transition economies implies that new firms favor the relative wage mechanism over the job vacancy mechanism as a strategy for attracting workers from state enterprises. Given current conditions in Eastern European labor markets, the existence of job vacancies in private firms should be sufficient attraction to the unemployed even in the absence of a wage differential. Throughout Eastern Europe, however, private sector employers are filling most vacancies by hiring employees directly from state jobs rather than from the pool of unemployed (Beleva, Jackman, and Nenova-Amar 1993; Commander and others 1993; Vecernik 1993). A large proportion of workers who lose state jobs and leave the unemployment rolls return to jobs in the state sector. Indeed in Hungary the private sector is a net contributor to unemployment.

The composition of the private sector pay package is also consistent with a strategy for selecting out of the state sector workers who are generally younger and more motivated to acquire extra rewards for extra effort rather than to seek social benefits. The preliminary impression is therefore that private firms are using wage policy to attract relatively qualified workers away from the state sector and that unemployment is seen by employers as a signal of lower qualifications.

Human Capital Returns

Compared with rates of return in market economies, returns to schooling and experience under central planning were positive but low. Average returns to schooling in 1988 for men in the Czech Republic were lower than in any of a comparison group of market economies (table 2).[3] Returns for Hungarian men, which were about 1 percentage point higher, were well within the range of estimates for market economies with centralized bargaining systems (German Federal Republic, Norway, Sweden), which often share the socialist economic objective of narrowing the structure of earnings across occupations. Rutkowski (1994) reports similar pretransition returns in Poland. Differences in returns are particularly notable at the university level. Relative to a high school education, a university degree provided a wage premium of 65 percent (in 1987) for U.S. males, 32 percent (in 1990) for Polish males, and 16 percent (in 1988) for Czech males (Goldin and Margo 1992; OECD 1993b; Flanagan 1993a). Pretransition wage structures also showed comparatively low returns on experience potential.

The pretransition pattern of returns to education reflects the type of human capital development encouraged under central planning. Central planners tended to value physical over mental work and production over service sectors. Young men were oriented toward vocational schools and apprenticeships, and—except for the *nomenklatura*—university-level education was devalued. In the late 1980s roughly 8 to 10 percent of the labor force in centrally planned economies had a university education, compared with 10 to 20 percent in most advanced market economies. Eastern European enrollment rates in secondary and higher education were also

Table 2. *Returns to Schooling, 1980s*
(percent)

Country, year	*Men*	*Women*
Czech Republic, 1988	3.8	5.4
Hungary, 1988	4.7	6.1
Australia, 1986	4.5	4.1
Federal Republic of Germany, 1985–88	4.9	5.4
Norway, 1982	4.5	3.8
Sweden, 1980	4.3	4.3
Switzerland, 1987	5.5	7.4
United Kingdom, 1985–88	7.0	9.3
United States, 1985–88	7.0	8.1

Note: All estimates are from a basic human capital earnings function specification in which the natural logarithm of the wage is a function of schooling. Potential experience is specified as a quadratic. All estimates are significant at .01 level.

Source: Flanagan 1993b; unpublished regression results provided by Francine Blau and Larry Kahn.

lower than in industrial countries. Most enrollments in secondary education in Eastern Europe were in vocational programs, compared with 35 to 40 percent in continental European market economies and about 10 percent in the United Kingdom (Boeri and Keese 1992). This appears to be the major distortion in human capital formation under central planning.

Central planning appears to have produced overinvestments in vocational and apprenticeship education and underinvestments in university education. To the extent that markets correct distortions associated with planner preferences, returns to university education should increase while those to vocational training should decrease during economic transition.

In fact, when the tariff wage system was abandoned, overall wage variation increased and returns to schooling began to rise. By mid-1991—just eighteen months into the transition—the average rate of return to schooling for men in the Czech Republic had increased by 0.6 percentage point, reflecting rapidly declining returns to vocational education and rising returns to university education (Flanagan 1993a). (Returns for women were unchanged.) Returns in Hungary rose from 4.7 percent in 1988 to 7.5 percent in March 1992 (Commander and others 1993). In several countries, vocationally trained workers not only saw their wages fall relative to those of university graduates but also experienced relatively high rates of unemployment. In contrast, in Romania, where there has been little private sector development, the wage structure for different schooling levels barely changed in the early transition years. In 1992 a Romanian university degree provided only a 30 percent wage premium over high school completion. Contrary to the pattern in other transition economies, post-transition movements in industrial relative wages in Romania appeared to reinforce the traditional preferences of central planners (Earle and Oprescu 1993). With the exception of Romania, then, the first years of economic transition have reversed the main pretransition distortions in human capital formation brought about by central planning.

What mechanisms produced these changes? In a well-functioning market, changes in the structure of wages in the state sector would mirror pay developments in the private sector, as state firms attempted to retain employees. For most countries in Eastern Europe except the Czech Republic, however, there is too little data on the private sector to test this hypothesis. In the Czech Republic the emerging private sector appears to be competing primarily for middle-level educated workers rather than university-educated workers. Rising returns to schooling appear to be an artifact of the pattern of structural changes in the state sector rather than of increased demand in private business. Public enterprise restructuring has increased the relative importance of industries that have always provided the highest returns to university education. Higher returns to education are available in the market, but not in most sectors.

Institutional Influences

From the perspective of labor in transition economies, the key questions are whether labor market institutions inhibit transfers to the private sector and the development of more rational pay structures. In the case of unions there is also the concern over their potential for generating wage pressures.

Labor Unions

Eastern Europe has only recently introduced collective bargaining over wages and working conditions. The extent of union representation, moreover, is difficult to assess given that membership figures are provided by the unions—a dubious source even in Western countries. Early estimates place union densities across Eastern Europe in the range of 35 to 70 percent (Freeman 1992). In no country of the region is the domain of unions as broad as in the most unionized Western countries (such as Scandinavia) and in no country is it as limited as in the least unionized Western countries (France and the United States).

Throughout Eastern Europe unionization is essentially limited to the state sector and is far from complete even there. Most private firms are nonunion and have little expectation of becoming unionized. World Bank surveys of firms in the region found little evidence of unionization. In the former Czechoslovakia none of the surveyed firms had unions, although about 10 percent of firms had workers councils that mostly abided by earlier contracts made under state ownership (Webster and Swanson 1993). None of the firms in the Bulgarian survey were unionized (Beleva, Jackman, and Nenova-Amar 1993), nor were the few firms in Romania's private sector (Earle and Oprescu 1993). In Hungary employers were amused that interviewers asked whether their workers bargained through a union or council (Webster 1993a; Lado 1993 reports similar findings). In Poland neither unions nor workers councils represented workers in any of the establishments surveyed, and employers claimed that their workers did not see the need for unions (Webster 1993b).[4] No respondent in any of the firms surveyed listed unions as a constraint on the firm's progress. It appears that private employers can set pay levels, pay structures, and employment conditions unilaterally, subject only to state regulations.

Given the distribution of union representation in Eastern Europe, differences between state and private wages provide tolerable estimates of union-nonunion wage differentials, since unions only have a life in the public sector. The evidence therefore indicates that the union wage "premium" in Eastern Europe is largely negative—a result that is either rare or nonexistent in Western countries. That wages in the declining (public) sector are lower than in the expanding (private) sector is good news for the allocational objectives of the economic transition and should challenge the widespread presumption that incomes policies are needed to restrain union power in the state sector. The absence of unions in the private sector, moreover, has enabled employers to lay off workers as a response to performance and discipline problems.

Union power is notoriously difficult to measure for a single country, and cross-country comparisons are particularly hazardous where unions have such different objectives as wage levels, security of employment, and income equality. Even within a single country, moreover, reports from the field are often conflicting. Many observers, for instance, stress the potential power of the Polish workers councils, which have had a highly variable effect according to enterprise surveys. Managers in Poland's state enterprises cite incomes policy regulations and not pressure from workers organizations as the major barrier to restructuring (Pinto, Belka, and Krajewski 1993). Similarly, Romanian unions cannot mobilize their members for widespread collective action even though they represent about 60 percent of workers and, according to one survey, have negotiated agreements covering about 90 percent of employment (Earle and Oprescu 1993). Unions in Hungary and the Czech Republic have been particularly quiescent.

Because of the confounding effect of incomes policy regulations in Eastern Europe, the effect of unions on the wage structure is difficult to assess. Nevertheless, the decentralization of some bargaining structures, such as those in Bulgaria and Romania, has contributed to pay dispersion among enterprises. In state enterprises unions continue to inhibit the use of dismissals for poor performance or disciplinary reasons. They may also be able to impose conditions on restructuring when large state enterprises are privatized. Although potentially significant, these union restrictions on operation are poorly documented. Unions cannot, however, thwart transfers to the private sector because workers can quit state enterprises with impunity.

Minimum Wage Policies

Throughout Eastern Europe minimum wage policies have been instituted to assist the least productive workers, with little consideration for any potentially adverse effects on employment. At this stage of massive state employment reductions in Eastern Europe, however, it is impossible to isolate the effects of minimum wage policies on employment. Attention has therefore focused on their effects on the wage structure. Relatively high minimum wages produce (or maintain) compressed wage structures, which could inhibit the reallocation of labor from less productive to more productive tasks.

Some Western countries index the minimum wage to consumer prices, which was also the initial intention in several Eastern European countries. But where other wages were not indexed (or were indexed less generously), some unions (notably in Czechoslovakia) negotiated tripartite agreements with explicit real wage reductions. In addition to affecting the wage structure, minimum wage policies also have direct implications for government budgets, since many social benefits (pensions, family allowances, unemployment benefits) are linked to the level of the minimum wage (UNECE 1992).

Faced with these considerations Eastern European governments have moderated and even abandoned explicit indexation procedures, and minimum wages declined as a proportion of the average wage to levels well below those typical of industrial market economies (table 3). Thus far, there is little evidence that minimum wage policy has seriously interfered with wage structure adjustment during transition.

To summarize, two distinct wage determination mechanisms have emerged during the economic transition in Eastern Europe. In the growing private sector, one mech-

Table 3. *Minimum Wage Relative to Average Gross Wage, Selected Countries, 1989–93* (percent)

Year	*Bulgaria*	*Czech Republic*	*Hungary*	*Poland*	*Romania*	*Slovak Republic*
1989	51.1	—	35.0	11.6	63.7	—
1990	44.6	—	42.0	21.4	73.0	—
1991	58.4	53.0	39.0	34.7	60.3	52.0
1992	35.9	45.9	36.0	37.0	45.7	47.5
1993						
First quarter	—	41.1	39.0	41.1	—	46.4
Second quarter	—	36.6	35.0	39.3	—	42.5

— Not available.
Source: Commission of the European Communities 1993.

anism resembles the nonunion wage determination found in some advanced market economies. Because employers are subject to hard budget constraints, performance must ultimately support pay levels. Unions are absent, and—subject to market conditions and incentive consideration—employers appear to have considerable discretion in wage-setting. In the large (but diminishing) state sector, enterprises are still subject to soft budget constraints. In many state enterprises unions or workers councils exist and have initiated collective bargaining, although at this point neither union activity nor government minimum wage legislation has substantially influenced relative wage structures in the state sector. Unions may, however, have slowed the downsizing of the state sector.

Organizational Efficiency during Transition

The discussion so far has focused on improved allocation of labor as a source of productivity gain in transition economies. In a world of long job tenures and "career" relationships, productivity gains also depend on incentives in firms' internal labor markets. Training systems, performance evaluations, and payment systems that link pay to performance all contribute to internal efficiency, and all these mechanisms were generally absent from public enterprises under central planning. The problem of determining appropriate managerial pay mechanisms, therefore, is particularly acute in transition economies.

Information on the role of the emerging private sector in introducing more sophisticated internal wage payment incentives and human resource management systems is regrettably scarce. The practices of foreign firms and joint ventures (which link wages to performance through merit systems, profit sharing, and other performance-related bonuses) contrast sharply with past practice in the state enterprises, where the large nonpecuniary component of compensation was unrelated to performance.

It is not yet known to what extent market incentive practices have been adopted by state enterprises and the indigenous private sector in Eastern Europe. Sharper competition between the two sectors would hasten such transference, but private and state firms rarely compete directly in product markets. Where competition does occur, incomes policies tend to impede the efforts of state enterprises to emulate the incentive systems of private firms (Pinto, Belka, and Krajewski 1993).

Evidence is limited to Hungary, Poland, and the Czech Republic. Private manufacturers responding to World Bank surveys noted that vocational schools and the organization of work in state enterprises had produced overspecialized workers who lacked the flexibility to adjust to new technologies (Webster and Swanson 1993; Webster 1993a,b). Many respondents also reported poor motivation among employees who had worked for years in settings where there was little connection between productivity and profitability. Only in Hungary—where workers no longer looked to the state sector for employment security—did entrepreneurs comment favorably on worker motivation. When faced with nonproductive employees, most Hungarian employers were quick to lay off workers and establish acceptable norms (Webster 1993a). A World Bank survey of private manufacturers in Poland found that several employers had instituted profit-sharing schemes and escalating production incentives (Webster 1993b).

From the limited evidence it appears that the changing wage signals observed in the aggregate data do not necessarily describe changes within organizations. This disjunction is mainly an issue for state organizations. Training systems developed under central planning, moreover, are inadequate for modern jobs and work organization.

Macroeconomic Policy and Microeconomic Objectives

While the government's role in pay determination has diminished throughout Eastern Europe, all countries in the region adopted incomes policies as part of their transitional macroeconomic policy packages. Such policies present an inherent tension between macroeconomic and microeconomic objectives in any economy, since the policy rules advanced to contain upward wage pressure may distort wage structures. This tension is particularly acute in Eastern Europe, where wage structures are much further from equilibrium than in the West. Incomes policies that thwart the development of incentive structures in labor markets can therefore inhibit labor reallocation and restructuring.

The Case for Incomes Policy

Two motivations underlie most applications of incomes policies in Western countries. The first is a belief that market power, particularly that of labor unions, is a significant source of upward wage pressure and that postwar economic developments were favorable to union bargaining power. A second motivation is to reduce inflationary expectations. Incomes policies have thus been used in efforts to prevent the emergence of inflation and to wind down existing inflation. Eastern European governments face a third consideration. As the residual claimants on the incomes of state enterprises, Eastern European governments have a distinct budgetary interest in moderating wages in the state sector. Because government tax revenue depends on the difference between sales revenues and the wage bill of state enterprises, wage increases in the state sector implicitly lower tax revenues.

The standard arguments for incomes policies appear weak in Eastern Europe. The bargaining power of most unions in Eastern Europe is limited. Policies to restrain inflationary expectations would cover the entire economy, not just the state sector. Nor can resort to incomes policies rest on the demonstrable achievements of these policies or on careful analyses of compliance incentives and responses at the microeconomic level. In the West, policies based on explicit guidelines for wage and price increases or social contracts (or multilateral negotiations among labor, management, government, and other economic interest groups) regarding the growth of incomes have foundered because of unresolved distributional conflicts and weak to nonexistent compliance incentives. Such policies have never achieved durable success, with the possible exception of Austria (Ulman and Flanagan 1971; Flanagan, Soskice, and Ulman 1983). Tax-based incomes policies, which have been more talked about than used in the West, would give firms and workers tax incentives to moderate wage and price increases, thereby providing incentives for compliance and scope for allocational flexibility, since firms could exceed the guidelines and rationally incur the tax if economic circumstances warranted.

The inexperience of and lack of incentive for Eastern European managers in the state sector to bargain hard provides a stronger basis for concern about wage pressure. Soft budget constraints have permitted state-owned enterprises to be sloppy about costs and weak in resisting wage demands. Managers who expect to revert to employee status as their enterprises are privatized, furthermore, have even less incentive to resist union wage demands. Weak bargaining effectively reduces government revenues from state enterprises. Through incomes policy governments in the region effectively avoid ceding authority for tax reductions to enterprise managers. The case for such policies in Eastern Europe thus rests more on the weakness of management than on the strength of workers organizations. It remains to be seen whether incomes policies actually stem inflation.

Policy Effects

Eastern Europe has adopted tax-based incomes policies—the policies advocated in the West—because they seem to offer greater allocational flexibility than other policy designs. Yet the mechanism of these policies seems flawed when applied to the state enterprises of the region. Incomes policies are supposed to increase management's bargaining resistance by threatening the loss of a firm's marginal profits as the penalty for noncompliance. These policies are best suited for managers who are accustomed to seeking profits. Such policies should follow rather than precede the development of property rights and hard budget constraints, since management must face financial incentives in order to take the consequences of noncompliance seriously. Policies motivated by managerial weakness under soft budget constraints, therefore, cannot depend for their effectiveness on managerial responses to (nonexistent) hard budget constraints. The willingness of many Eastern European managers to grant "excess" wage payments despite punitive taxes underscores this flaw, and governments are often unable to collect such taxes (Jackman and Pages 1993; Earle and Oprescu 1993).

Even where successful, tax-based incomes policy designs in Eastern Europe do not allow the allocational flexibility permitted in policy formulations in the West. Tax-based incomes policies have a longer history in centrally planned economies than in the West because they were used by central planners to restrain the growth of enterprise wage bills to limit consumption demand. Such policies included punitive tax rates for wage increases in excess of the target—a feature that has been incorporated in the current incomes policies of transition economies. Thus Eastern European incomes policies have great potential to interfere with government efforts to achieve greater allocational efficiency through systemic reform.

A policy that targets the average wage, for instance, can penalize companies that downsize to shed their least-efficient workers or those that expand and hire workers who are more highly skilled. In each case changes in work force composition could raise the average wage sufficiently to incur a penalty tax. Average wage targets also create incentives to freeze or further compress the internal wage structures of organizations—the opposite of what is desired, in most cases, to provide incentives for training and additional effort. Policies that target the enterprise wage bill, by contrast, do not penalize the downsizing of the work force. Indeed, the downsizing can be accompanied by an increased average wage to attract and retain superior workers. However, a wage bill target taxes employment growth, making firms reluctant to hire, slowing outflows from unemployment, and creating incentives for further skill compression.

Evidence from Eastern European labor markets increasingly indicates that these concerns are far from theoretical. Both wage bill and average wage targets have been applied to Polish enterprises, for instance, at different times. Under the average wage target, managers of state-owned enterprises complained of restraints on downsizing and restructuring. They clearly preferred wage bill targets. They also reported that wage targets had induced pay compression and that policy discrimination between state and private employers inhibited public enterprise managers from transforming their enterprises and emulating the behavior of private managers (Pinto, Belka, and Krajewski 1993).

Wage structure developments at the sectoral level in Bulgaria, the Czech Republic, and Hungary are consistent with these reports. Without violating the incomes policy wage rules and incurring penalty taxes, state enterprises in Bulgaria were unable to alter the compressed wage structure inherited from central planning (Beleva, Jackman, and Nenova-Amar 1993). In the Czech Republic, although the overall return on schooling—especially the return to university education in the state sector—increased rapidly during the first eighteen months following the "velvet revolution," the relative wage of university graduates *fell* in virtually all industrial sectors. The general increase, therefore, was an artifact of structural change (Flanagan 1993b). Similarly, in Hungary, although the relative wage of professional workers rose by 8 percent between 1989 and 1992 in industry as a whole, there was little change in the relative wages of professional workers or manual workers within sectors. Nor was much change in pay differentials for skill discernable among branches of Hungarian industry (Jackman and Pages 1993).

When wage policy is applied to sectors with a large nonwage component, it encourages the substitution of nonwage (and untaxed) benefits for wages, diluting the incentive effects of the compensation system. There is evidence that tax-based incomes policies in the USSR "merely induced enterprises to shift further still to the use of bonuses and direct payments in the form of goods and services, often acquired on a barter basis from other enterprises.... At the macroeconomic level the ratio of nonwage to wage forms of remuneration rose steadily from the 1950s onward, at least until the advent of perestroika" (Standing 1991/92, p. 244).

If incomes policy has not had a beneficial effect on wage structures in Eastern Europe, its use to achieve macroeconomic stability has had equally questionable results. In several of the countries where it was tried, wages were actually below incomes policy norms in the early months of the transition. The fear of a wage push from workers was strongest in Poland. Yet recent analyses have concluded that wage policy was not effective in Poland—liquidity constraints at the beginning of 1990 made such policy redundant (Coricelli, Hagemejer, and Rybinski 1993). Other countries also stressed the role of liquidity constraints and concerns for job security as more important reasons for wage setting (Jackman and Pages 1993). No analysis of Eastern European labor markets in the World Bank country studies has claimed evidence of a substantial macroeconomic effect of the policies.

In summary, incomes policies seem rather poorly suited for the transition environment. Such policies always present a tradeoff between macroeconomic and microeconomic objectives, but the tradeoff seems particularly acute in transition economies. To the extent that incomes policies are effective in their macroeconomic objectives, their potential for inhibiting the allocative functioning of wage structures is great. While this potential may be acceptable in market economies with strong allocational signals, in Eastern Europe today such policies impose delays on adjustment and restructuring that run counter to systemic reform. Even if incomes policies were instrumental in stabilizing the macroeconomy (which has yet to be shown), the lack of change in wage structures in the region would be troublesome.

Conclusion

With few exceptions the aggregate supply of labor in Eastern Europe has contracted and threatens to contract still further if the long duration of unemployment (implied by current flows in and out of unemployment) continues. The principal problem is insufficient demand. Until the demand problem is solved, moreover, labor market policy alone is unlikely to have much impact on unemployment. When job vacancies and unemployment are more closely aligned, a reorientation of labor market policies away from passive measures and wage subsidies toward training programs seems desirable. There is ample testimony from the emerging private sector regarding the limitations of traditional Eastern European vocational training for producing workers skilled in modern production methods. And the problem can only worsen as the private sector expands.

With respect to the allocation of labor the evidence is mixed. New private firms appear to have little trouble expanding (subject to the training problems noted above), but they take few risks in hiring the unemployed. Within the state sector there is evidence that some of the distortions in labor market signals under central planning have been reversed, if not eliminated, at the market level. Limited evidence indicates, however, that the private sector has not yet become the force driving these changes. Rather, the changes have resulted from the downsizing of state enterprises.

In virtually all the transition economies in the region the major institutional barrier to adjustments of pay structures and to employment restructuring within the state sector has been incomes policy regulations. These policies seem poorly designed for the transition environment, and their use rests more on tradition than any demonstrated effectiveness. A better option might be to alter management bargaining incentives by altering management compensation schemes, which would give managers a personal stake in resisting demands for pay increases. Broader use of arrangements that link pay to enterprise surpluses could also provide incentives to resist general pay demands and create stronger internal performance incentives. Each country, furthermore, could fix its exchange rate to a basket of Western currencies—much like the hard currency policy adopted by Austria for many years. While this solution does not directly address the problem of managerial bargaining incentives, it would underscore the fact that excessive wage increases could lead to job loss and would therefore strengthen managers' bargaining hand.

Notes

1. Atkinson and Micklewright (1991) warn that the broad descriptive parameters of unemployment insurance systems may be a poor guide to the incentives actually at work. To discover their true effects on job acceptance, detailed research into the implementation of these systems will be necessary.

2. Three surveys covered the manufacturing sector and included interviews at 121 firms in the former Czechoslovakia in January 1992, 106 Hungarian firms in September 1991, and 93 Polish firms in May 1991. In each country firms were drawn randomly from the population of registered, majority privately and domestically owned manufacturing firms with seven or more employees. See Webster (1993a,b) and Webster and Swanson (1993) for details. A fourth survey of 200 firms in the two largest cities in Bulgaria included respondents from industry, trade, construction, business services, and publishing (Beleva, Jackman, and Nenova-Amar 1993).

3. These conclusions would not be altered by comparing returns to schooling in centrally planned economies with returns in countries whose level of economic development is lower than that of advanced market economies, for returns to schooling tend to be inversely related to stage of development. A survey of the international literature on educational returns reports ballpark returns to schooling (derived from the specifications used here): Africa, 13 percent; Asia, 11 percent; Latin America, 14 percent; countries with an intermediate level of economic development, 8 percent; and advanced industrial countries, 9 percent (Psacharopoulos 1985, table 3).

4. The firms surveyed, like most private firms in Eastern Europe at this time, were relatively small, "with 60 percent having fewer than twenty workers and almost 75 percent of firms reporting monthly sales of less than US$50,000." Most firms in the survey were limited-liability companies owned by groups of three to six people. Ninety percent had originated as private firms, mainly since 1988. The rest originated in the state or cooperative sectors (Webster 1993b, pp. 2–3).

References

Adam, Jan. 1984. *Employment and Wage Policies in Poland, Czechoslovakia, and Hungary Since 1950.* New York: St. Martin's Press.

Atkinson, Anthony B., and John Micklewright. 1991. "Unemployment Compensation and Labor Market Transitions: A Critical Review." *Journal of Economic Literature* 29(4): 1679–27.

Beleva, Iskra, Richard Jackman, and Mariela Nenova-Amar. 1993. "The Labour Market in Bulgaria." Paper prepared for World Bank Conference on Unemployment, Restructuring, and the Labor Market in Eastern Europe and Russia, October 7–8, Washington, D.C.

Blanchard, Olivier, Simon Commander, and Fabrizio Coricelli. 1993. "Unemployment and Restructuring in Eastern Europe." Paper prepared for World Bank Conference on Unemployment, Restructuring, and the Labor Market in Eastern Europe and Russia, October 7–8, Washington, D.C.

Blanchflower, David, and Richard B. Freeman. 1993. "The Legacy of Communist Labor Relations." Discussion Paper 180. Centre for Economic Policy Research, London.

Boeri, Tito. 1993. "Labour Market Flows and the Persistence of Unemployment in Central and Eastern Europe." Paper prepared for Workshop on the Persistence of Unemployment in Central and Eastern Europe, OECD, Center for Cooperation with Economies in Transition, September 30–October 2, Paris.

Boeri, Tito, and Mark Keese. 1992. "Labour Markets and the Transition in Central and Eastern Europe." *OECD Economic Studies* 18: 133–63.

Commander, Simon, Janos Kollo, Cecilia Ugaz, and Balazs Vilagi. 1993. "Hungary." Paper prepared for World Bank Conference on Unemployment, Restructuring, and the Labor Market in Eastern Europe and Russia, October 7–8, Washington, D.C.

Commission of the European Communities. 1993. *Employment Observatory: Central and Eastern Europe.* Brussels.

Coricelli, Fabrizio, Krzysztof Hagemejer, and Krzysztof Rybinski. 1993. "Poland." Paper presented at World Bank Conference on Unemployment, Restructuring, and the Labor Market in Eastern Europe and Russia, October 7–8, Washington, D.C.

Earle, John S., and Gheorghe Oprescu. 1993. "Aggregate Labor Market Behavior in the Restructuring of the Romanian Economy." Paper presented at World Bank Conference on Unemployment, Restructuring, and the Labor Market in Eastern Europe and Russia, October 7–8, Washington, D.C.

Flanagan, Robert J. 1993a. "Labor Market Policy, Information, and Hiring Behavior." Paper presented at Conference on Institutional Frameworks and Labor Market Performance, November 27–28, Nuremberg, Germany.

———. 1993b. "Were Communists Good Human Capitalists? The Case of the Czech Republic." Working paper. Stanford University, Graduate School of Business.

Flanagan, Robert J., David Soskice, and Lloyd Ulman. 1983. *Unionism, Economic Stabilization, and Incomes Policies: European Experience.* Washington, D.C.: Brookings Institution.

Freeman, Richard B. 1992. "What Direction for Labor Market Institutions in Eastern and Central Europe?" NBER Working Paper 4209. National Bureau of Economic Research, Cambridge, Mass.

Goldin, Claudia, and Robert A. Margo. 1992. "The Great Compression: The Wage Structure in the United States at Mid-Century." *Quarterly Journal of Economics* 107 (February): 1–34.

Jackman, Richard, and Carmen Pages. 1993. "Wage Policy and Inflation in Eastern Europe." Paper prepared for World Bank Conference on Unemployment, Restructuring, and the Labor Market in Eastern Europe and Russia, October 7–8, Washington, D.C.

Lado, Maria. 1993. "Wages, Incomes Policy, and Industrial Relations." In G. Fischer and G. Standing, eds., *Structural Change in Central and Eastern Europe: Labour Market and Social Policy Implications.* Paris: OECD.

OECD (Organization for Economic Cooperation and Development). 1993a. *Employment Outlook.* Paris.

———. 1993b. *Structural Change in Central and Eastern Europe: Labour Market and Social Policy Implications.* Paris.

Pinto, B., M. Belka, and S. Krajewski. 1993. "Transforming State Enterprises in Poland: Evidence on Adjustment by Manufacturing Firms." *Brookings Papers on Economic Activity* 1.

Psacharopoulos, George. 1985. "Returns to Education: A Further International Update and Implications." *Journal of Human Resources* 20: 583–604.

Rutkowski, Jan. 1994. "Changes in Wage Structure and in Returns to Education during Economic Transition: The Case of Poland." Center for International Studies, Woodrow Wilson School, Princeton University.

Scarpetta, Stefano, Tito Boeri, and Anders Reutersward. 1993. "Unemployment Benefit Systems and Active Labour Market Policies in Central and Eastern Europe: An Overview." Paper presented at Technical Workshop on the Persistence of Unemployment in Central and Eastern Europe, OECD, Center for Cooperation with Economies in Transition, September 30–October 2, Paris.

Standing, Guy. 1991/92. "Wages and Work Motivation in the Soviet Labour Market: Why a BIP and Not a TIP Is Required." *International Labour Review* 130: 237–53.

Ulman, Lloyd, and Robert J. Flanagan. 1971. *Wage Restraint.* Berkeley: University of California Press.

UNECE (United Nations Economic Commission for Europe). 1992. *Economic Survey of Europe in 1991–92.* New York.

Vecernik, Jiri. 1993. "Poverty, Welfare Policy and Work Incentives in the Czech and Slovak Republic." Institute of Sociology, Academy of Sciences of the Czech Republic, Prague.

Webster, Leila M. 1993a. *The Emergence of Private Sector Manufacturing in Hungary: A Survey of Firms.* World Bank Technical Paper 229. Washington, D.C.

———1993b. *The Emergence of Private Sector Manufacturing in Poland: A Survey of Firms.* World Bank Technical Paper 237. Washington, D.C.

Webster, Leila M., and Dan Swanson. 1993. *The Emergence of Private Sector Manufacturing in the Former Czech and Slovak Federal Republic: A Survey of Firms.* World Bank Technical Paper 230. Washington, D.C.

Comment on "Labor Market Responses to a Change in Economic System," by Flanagan

Richard Layard

While I agree with much of Robert Flanagan's interesting and wide-ranging article, I focus here on the issue of active labor market policy and my disagreement with Flanagan's argument that insufficient demand is the principal problem in Eastern European labor markets. Labor market policy, he claims, is unlikely to have much impact on unemployment until the demand problem is solved; later, when job vacancies and unemployment are more closely aligned, labor market policies ought to be reoriented away from passive measures and wage subsidies toward training programs suited to modern production methods.

I disagree for several reasons. To begin, I do not think insufficient demand is Eastern Europe's principal labor market problem. And even if it were, supply-side improvements would always help. Wage subsidies would then be especially useful in a downturn because they could help prevent the loss of future employability that results from long-term unemployment. Training would also be vital, but in business and service sector skills rather than in production methods.

Not a Case of Deficient Demand

In most of Eastern Europe unemployment has risen from zero to alarmingly high levels (table 1). Except for the Czech Republic unemployment levels in most countries are now similar to those in Western Europe. How far can we expect these levels to fall when the recovery of output begins?

It does not seem realistic to expect massive falls. Inflation has been fairly stable in most of these countries since 1992, so it seems that these countries are not hugely above their current NAIRU (nonaccelerating inflation rate of unemployment), as determined by supply-side considerations such as labor market policy, union behavior, and mismatch. As in Western Europe the main problem is massive, long-term unemployment, which remains high even in periods of recovery.

It is true that in Eastern Europe vacancies registered at employment exchanges are very low, but this is because so little of the flow of hiring goes through the labor exchanges. There is, in fact, a substantial flow of hiring in these economies.[1] While

Richard Layard is professor of economics at the London School of Economics.

it is less than in Western Europe, that is because the flow of unemployed is also lower than in Western Europe (Blanchard, Commander, and Coricelli 1993). In Poland and Hungary in 1992, state firms hired new workers equal to 10 percent of their total employment—similar to Italian hiring rates and exactly what one would expect given a high level of employment protection.

This view of Eastern European unemployment is quite different from one that stresses the role of restructuring. While the rapid restructuring going on in Eastern Europe adds to the amount of labor market mismatch, in my view unemployment has risen from zero to Western European levels primarily because in a free society there is no way to contain inflation except with adequate unemployment. The actual level required will depend on the supply-side features of the labor market.

Improve the Supply Side

There is ample evidence of the Phillips curve in Eastern Europe.[2] The key policy problem is how to shift its location closer to the origin. Once this is done, unemployment will be lower for any given inflation target. It is just as important to be able to reduce unemployment when inflation is expected to fall as when it is expected to rise. The aim, therefore, is to increase the supply capacity of the economy for any particular inflation rate.

Wage Subsidies and the Substitution-Displacement Issue

In this strategy there is a key role for active labor market policy. If people are permitted to drift into long-term unemployment, they became unattractive to employers and thus exert no deflationary effect (Layard, Nickell, and Jackman 1991). As in much of Western Europe the NAIRU becomes very high. Within, say, a year of losing their jobs, all unemployed people should get some offer of training or temporary work. Training is especially important when a whole population has to be re-educated for market-oriented activity. But not everybody will benefit from training, and something must be done to keep workers within the labor market.

The Czech and Slovak Republics both established programs for socially purposeful jobs to provide subsidies for new jobs. Since mid-1992 the number of subsidized

Table 1. *Unemployment Rates, Second Quarter of 1993*

	Less than one year	*More than one year*	*Total*
Bulgaria (1992)	6.0	6.1	12.1
Czech Republic	1.8	0.4	2.2
Hungary	7.3	3.5	10.8
Poland	8.9	6.7	15.6
Slovak Republic	8.4	4.1	12.5
European Union	5.4	5.0	10.4

Source: Boeri 1993; OECD 1994.

jobs has averaged 3 percent of the labor force in the Czech Republic and 4 percent in the Slovak Republic (Ham, Svejnar, and Terrell 1993). Adequate time-series data are not yet available to explain fully the different unemployment rates in Eastern Europe, but no other country in the region has used wage subsidies on the scale of these two republics. We know that Slovakia was hit exceptionally hard by the end of the Cold War, and it appears at least initially that wage subsidies have played an important part in the Czech Republic's low unemployment rate.

Against this picture Flanagan brings to bear the perennial argument about substitution and displacement effects which he says are "rarely considered." In my experience (at least in the United Kingdom) these arguments are invariably considered and normally given such credence as to kill off any positive proposal. Where does the problem of substitution and displacement come from? Flanagan is explicit—it comes from insufficient demand. But why should the level of real demand be taken as given? Even if nominal demand is fixed, any policy that reduces the NAIRU reduces inflation and increases employment. If the inflation target remains fixed, a fall in the NAIRU will lead to an equal increase in employment (through the necessary expansion of nominal demand).

So how far will the NAIRU fall if a given group of unemployed are made more employable? Suppose, for example, that the number of long-term unemployed is cut by x thousand by improving their attractiveness to employers. By how much will short-term unemployment increase because long-term unemployed people now receive positive discrimination in employment? Obviously there is a short-term effect on the job chances of other people. But if those others were originally employable they will eventually find other jobs, because the number of jobs responds to the number of employable people. If long-term unemployed people are made more employable, the number of jobs will increase. The adjustment process is so diffuse that it is difficult to observe. But the line of reasoning is consistent with all standard labor market experience (see appendix). There is in essence no difference between asserting that labor market measures do not increase jobs and asserting that immigration does not increase jobs. Both fallacies stem from the same lump-of-labor fallacy.

Flanagan, however, proposes a second argument based on screening. He argues that people may not like to be helped because accepting help reveals weakness. But the other evidence he quotes (that private sector firms do not hire the unemployed or use labor offices) seems to reinforce the importance of giving the unemployed some extra leverage. There are many ways in which wage subsidies can be organized. The Czechs subsidize new jobs. Russia is keeping open unemployment low through the widespread use of unpaid leave (typically for a month or so) among workers, although in some cases all workers are sent on unpaid leave together.[3] In 1993, while GDP in Russia fell by 12 percent and employment fell by 1.4 percent, hours worked fell by 4 percent. In addition, wages have been exceptionally flexible. In industries where employment has fallen by λ percent (in excess of the average), relative wages have fallen an average 6λ percent. This method also keeps unemployment mainly within the firm and has been encouraged by official policy. The

Russian Employment Service is allowed to pay workers on unpaid leave a stipend equal to the (very low) minimum wage.

What do we think of this? I suggest that long-term unemployment is an absurdity, and it is a tragedy that Eastern Europe has followed Western Europe in letting some 5 percent of its work force drift into this position. Active labor market policy is essential. It is probably more efficient for short-term unemployment to be open rather than hidden within firms, though the latter approach is not the end of the world if it is more politically acceptable. Workers in such a situation do search for other jobs, and the provision of the subsidy in Russia, meant to be conditional on the provision of adequate retraining programs, may prevent long-term unemployment of adults. The biggest problem will be young people, who get no help of this kind.

Training

Training is also exceptionally important. Under communism the bulk of vocational education and training was based on the physical sciences. Yet in a market economy most workers are engaged in activities based on the social sciences—especially business-related studies. In this I include not only management of large and small business but sales (wholesale and retail), accounting, financial services, law, and much of clerical work. Thus a massive retraining effort is required throughout Eastern Europe for the unemployed plus a complete reform of youth training. In such a radical reform process, returns to the retraining of unemployed people to develop commercial skills are surely high, even if they do not immediately secure employment.

Yet in Eastern Europe the scale of the training for the unemployed has been dismally low because of a lack of trained teachers and of the right kind of teaching materials in the right language. Fortunately, this is an area where there are massive economies of scale. Too much foreign aid has gone into particular projects in particular institutions with limited spillover. But now some good things are happening that may yield real scale economies. In my own area of acquaintance in Russia, the U.K. Know-How Fund has embarked on a major program of translation and teacher training for business skills. The World Bank, too, has some excellent proposals in this area, although given the urgency of the issue the slowness with which Bank projects evolve is frustrating.

Incomes Policy

There is much in what Flanagan says about the other key labor market policy issue, incomes policy. But in Russia, where the politics were too difficult, the government decided against it. In early 1992 there were extensive discussions within government, and the March 1992 Memorandum of Economic Policy signed with the IMF included—with Russian reservations—a much-simplified Polish-style incomes policy. But the political situation was far too difficult to operate any policy that limited the growth, rather than the level, of wages.

Thus Russia had only one nominal anchor—credit. Firms lacking a bulwark against wage increases pressed for more credit. And since the central bank had no nonmonetary inflation controls, it could concede to the pressure with no loss of consistency. This experience makes me believe that Poland succeeded in controlling inflation, where many believed it could not, partly through its incomes policy. But each country must decide how important that objective is compared with greater flexibility of relative wages.

Appendix. Equilibrium Unemployment with Positive Discrimination for Long-Term Unemployment

In equilibrium, unemployment is determined so that inflation is stable. Inflationary pressure in turn is determined by employers' difficulties in finding workers (measured by the duration of vacancies) and unemployed workers' ease in finding jobs. To see how equilibrium unemployment changes when the long-term unemployed are offered positive discrimination, assume that hirings per week are given by $H = V^{\alpha}(cU^{1-\alpha})$, with $0 < \alpha < 1$, where H is hirings per week, V is vacancies, c is average effectiveness of unemployed people as fillers of vacancies, and U is the unemployed.[4] The difficulty of filling vacancies is V/H, and the ease of finding work for unemployed people with 100 percent effectiveness is H/cU.

Then $V/H = (V/cU)^{1-\alpha}$ and $H/cU = (V/cU)^{\alpha}$.

Since inflationary pressure depends on V/H and H/cU, stable inflation requires a given value of $(V/cU)^{\alpha}$. Call this ϕ. Hence, in equilibrium, $H/cU = \phi$. Since the outflow of unemployment (H) has to equal the inflow, cU is fixed.

Suppose now that there are only two types of unemployed (short-term S and long-term L). Then, from the preceding argument: $c_S U_S + c_L U_L$ = constant. If the long-term unemployed are helped, c_L rises. What happens to U_S and U_L?

The outflow rate per week from short-term unemployment remains ϕ times c_S. If the inflow to unemployment is constant, the stock of the short-term unemployed (U_S) therefore remains constant, and U_L falls in inverse proportion to the rise in c_L. There is no displacement or substitution. In equilibrium the stock of long-term unemployed falls so that, although their chances of getting a job rise, the number of hirings accounted for by the long-term unemployed does not change.

Notes

1. In this context it may be significant that the private sector generally pays at least as much as the public sector—which would be unlikely if the demand deficiency were massive.
2. On Poland, see Jackman, Layard, and Scott (1992); on Hungary, see Commander and others (1993); on Russia, see *Russian Economic Trends* (1993, p. 65). These studies use at least two observations on wages and unemployment (or sales) at the two-digit industry level.
3. For further details see Layard and Richter (1994).
4. The argument would go through with any constant returns to scale hiring function.

References

Blanchard, O., S. Commander, and F. Coricelli. 1993. "Unemployment and Restructuring in Eastern Europe." Paper prepared for the World Bank Conference on Unemployment, Restructuring, and the Labor Market in Eastern Europe and Russia. October 7–8, Washington, D.C.

Boeri, T. 1993. "Unemployment Dynamics and Labor Market Policies." Paper prepared for the World Bank Conference on Unemployment, Restructuring, and the Labor Market in Eastern Europe and Russia. October 7–8, Washington, D.C.

Commander, S., J. Kollo, C. Ugaz, and B. Vilagi. 1993. "Hungary." Paper prepared for the World Bank Conference on Unemployment, Restructuring, and the Labor Market in Eastern Europe and Russia, October 7–8, Washington, D.C.

Ham, J., J. Svejnar, and K. Terrell. 1993. "The Czech and Slovak Labor Markets During the Transition." Paper prepared for the World Bank Conference on Unemployment, Restructuring, and the Labor Market in Eastern Europe and Russia, October 7–8. Washington, D.C.

Jackman, R., R. Layard, and A. Scott. 1992. "Unemployment in Eastern Europe." Working Paper 175, Centre for Economic Performance, London School of Economics.

Layard, R., S. Nickell, and R. Jackman. 1991. *Unemployment: Macroeconomic Performance and the Labour Market.* London: Oxford University Press.

Layard, R., and A. Richter. 1994. "Labour Market Adjustment in Russia." In *Russian Economic Trends,* vol. 3, no. 2. London: Whurr Publishers.

OECD (Organization for Economic Cooperation and Development). 1994. *Economic Outlook.* Paris.

Russian Economic Trends. 1993. Vol. 2, no. 2. London: Whurr Publishers.

———. 1994. Vol. 3, no. 2. London: Whurr Publishers.

Comment on "Labor Market Responses to a Change in Economic System," by Flanagan

John Pencavel

Flanagan's article is a useful description of certain prominent features of the labor markets in Eastern European economies. I agree with much of what he writes. However, following the customary role of discussant, my comments concentrate on issues on which we differ and on those I would tend to emphasize more.

Wage Subsidies

Flanagan doubts the value of wage subsidy schemes in Eastern Europe. He claims that evidence from the United States suggests "employers prefer to hire unsubsidized workers." If the evidence refers to the 1980–81 wage voucher experiment in Dayton, Ohio, however, then this places too much weight on an idiosyncratic and poorly designed program.

With respect to their operation in Eastern Europe, Flanagan writes that much of the expenditures on wage subsidies appear to support employees who would have been hired anyway. I do not know the source for that judgment. My understanding is that, in the Czech and Slovak Republics, in order to receive subsidies firms must sign agreements to create jobs for people who would otherwise be unemployed. Similarly, in Hungary and Poland wage subsidies operate only when employers hire the long-term unemployed (Scarpetta and Reutersward 1994). Perhaps these people would have been hired anyway by these firms, as Flanagan maintains, but it is difficult to determine this.

As a permanent labor market policy, wage subsidies have much to commend them. I am envisaging here not discretionary policies targeted to particular firms or to workers who have been unemployed for a certain length of time, but a program that reaches every firm and worker meeting simple eligibility criteria. The idea is simply to structure the payroll tax system such that, below a specified wage rate, payroll taxes actually become negative. Such negative payroll taxes on low-wage labor increase firms' incentives to hire such labor, and as a welfare program for workers, such a program has fewer work disincentive effects than many other benefit programs. Insofar as labor markets are competitive, it is immaterial whether

John Pencavel is professor of economics at Stanford University.

these negative payroll taxes are paid to firms or to workers. There are certainly issues of evasion and fraud that need to be addressed with such a system, as there are in all benefit and welfare programs, but the attraction of using a price mechanism to increase the probability of hiring the unemployed (most of whom are low-wage workers) has much to commend it. (To make it at least partly self-financed, payroll taxes on high-wage labor may be increased.)

Pensions

An omission in Flanagan's article concerns pensions and their impact on labor markets. Since the late 1980s Eastern European governments' expenditures on pensions have increased dramatically: in Poland pension expenditures represented almost 12 percent of GDP and 25 percent of government spending in 1992. Yet in many Eastern European countries older people constitute a smaller fraction of the population than in Western European countries. Here the legacy of the old regimes is truly a millstone: under communism people were promised pensions at an earlier age and often on more generous terms than in the West. Unless these pensions can be reduced by making them less generous or by inducing the pensioners to rejoin the labor force (thereby mitigating the falls in labor force participation rates of older people), the productive sector of the economy will be encumbered by an enormous burden.

Regional Issues

Flanagan also fails to discuss regional disparities in labor market performance which, in some instances, are quite sharp. Some areas are experiencing virtual boom conditions, and others are in deep recession. An economywide description risks missing these contrasts.

This illustrates an issue that pervades all discussions of the economics of transformation, namely, that the development and performance of one class of markets is not independent of that of other classes. In this case I am reminded of how the performance of labor markets is often critically dependent on features of housing markets. The shortage of housing in East European economies and the reliance on nonprice methods of rationing available stocks tend to inhibit the movement of labor across regions to exploit differences in economic opportunities. In other words, reforms in housing markets would yield returns in terms of the operation of labor markets.

A Model

While Flanagan provides a helpful description of major features of East European labor markets, missing from his article is a simple model that might serve as a useful characterization of the labor market problems of the area. The model I have in mind is fully consistent with the description that Flanagan provides.

There are two sectors, private and state. The labor markets in the private sector are largely unregulated. They operate primarily in the services and trade sectors. Average firm size is small, and decisions with respect to wages are mostly unencumbered by regulations. It is true that there are minimum wage regulations and that decisions about layoffs may be circumscribed by various rules about severance pay and notification requirements. But these regulations may not be binding or may simply be ignored. Labor unions are almost nonexistent. The private sector employs a minority of the economy's labor force, but it is a growing minority. A textbook model of competitive labor markets would serve as an appropriate characterization of this sector.

Second, there is the sector that is more closely tied to the state. It may consist of enterprises that are owned by the state or simply those whose buying and selling activities are so closely monitored by state bureaucracies that they are effectively under the state's regulations. The average size of these firms is much larger than those in the private sector, and they dominate the manufacturing, construction, and utilities sectors. Labor market activities are more closely regulated by the state. Labor unions are more common. This sector employs a larger share of the economy's work force, but it is a declining share. The essential features of these enterprises is that they are involved in some sort of bargaining relationship with the state bureaucracies, so a model of bargaining must be used to characterize this sector.

Because the property rights in these state enterprises are not well-defined, their objectives are murky. In some sense, of course, they are pursuing the interests of the people employed in them, but there are different groups of people in these organizations—for instance, managers and rank-and-file workers—and they may place different weights on their wage rates, their hours of work, and their employment. For instance, when subject to a budgetary shock, some of these organizations will be willing to adjust work hours and maintain employment, while others will maintain real wages and lay off marginal workers. In other words, a tough market environment will produce different responses from different organizations.

However, what characterizes many of these state and quasi-state enterprises is the fact that often they are not presented with a hard budget constraint that forces such awkward choices on them. Their soft budgets give them the impression that they may raise wages without suffering any loss of employment.

What distinguishes the bargaining environment of these enterprises is that unemployment affects them in a different way from its effect in mature market economies, where budget constraints are harder and the state sector is smaller. When a state organization bargains with the government in such economies, a high level of unemployment tends to weaken the enterprise's bargaining position because workers find themselves confronted with tough choices of layoffs, work sharing, or wage reductions. By contrast, in an environment of soft budget constraints, a high level of unemployment may increase the bargaining power of state enterprises: when threatened with a loss of subsidies, these enterprises may conjure up a picture of mass layoffs that will add to the already heavy unemployment; it may seem to the state that, when choosing between subsidies to organizations that keep people employed and payment of unemployment benefits, it might be better to maintain subsidies to state organizations. The consequence, of course, is inflation fed by subsidies to inefficient organizations and subsidies that are difficult to curb in a market characterized by already high unemployment. In other words, in Western economies unemployment tends to act as a discipline on state enterprises in bargaining over resources, whereas in Eastern European economies unemployment may augment the bargaining power of state enterprises.

Government is in an awkward position in these circumstances: a tough stand risks heavy unemployment that may have political repercussions, compromising the march toward reform, while maintaining subsidies to the enterprises only delays the growth of the private sector. A judicious compromise may involve the government stating a fixed and planned annual reduction in subsidies to state enterprises. Unlike an abrupt and sweeping elimination of state subsidies, a strict schedule to reduce the level of subsidies in a series of steps will not present the private sector with a huge and precipitous increase of unemployment to absorb. Rather, the steady and systematic contraction of the state sector may be accompanied by continuous private sector growth.

Even as the state sector shrinks, there will remain the important question of how wages are to be determined in state-owned and -regulated enterprises. The state will be the largest single employer in Eastern European economies (as it is in virtually all Western economies) for years to come even with a vigorous privatization program. The question of setting the pay of government workers is also, of course, a perennial question for Western governments that operate some mix of mechanisms including pay comparability studies and arbitration schemes. Flanagan's article discusses the macroeconomic problems of pay setting for government workers in Eastern Europe and the role played by incomes policies in this process.

There are also the microeconomic questions of determining an appropriate wage structure within the state sector and the wages of government compared with private sector workers. Procedures need to be developed for the determination of wages of state sector workers that do not make these pay settlements the norm to which workers in the private sector aspire.

Reference

Scarpetta, Stefano, and Anders Reutersward. 1994. "Unemployment Benefit Systems and Active Labour Market Policies in Central and Eastern Europe: An Overview." In *Unemployment in Transition Countries: Transient or Persistent?* Paris: Center for Cooperation with the Economies in Transition.

Floor Discussion of "Labor Market Responses to a Change in Economic System," by Flanagan

A participant from the World Bank asked John Pencavel (discussant) if job sharing would be a good idea in Eastern Europe, where the argument against job sharing—that fewer people are then competing for jobs outside, so there is more inflationary pressure—would not apply. Pencavel responded that job sharing, which he calls "work sharing," would be fine if firms wanted to take the hit in that form. It was up to the organization to decide.

The Bank participant then asked Richard Layard (discussant) why unemployment is so high in Central and Eastern Europe and so much lower in countries of the former Soviet Union, where wages seem to have taken the brunt of adjustment. Do reasons on the demand side explain the difference in these two patterns? Layard responded that wage flexibility exists in countries of the former Soviet Union because the workers' position relative to management is weak, which has led to much more job rotation (as he would call it) than in other countries. If workers would rather stay with an enterprise on unpaid leave, rotating on some kind of short-term unemployment system rather than sever their connection, that is quite acceptable. It is a system of promoting short-term unemployment within the firm rather than long-term unemployment outside of it. It is not as if they were sitting on their backsides being paid nothing; they might be looking for work as effectively as if they were long-term unemployed. But Layard would not subsidize that system. If he were giving subsidies, he would subsidize the hiring of unemployed people into new jobs. Flanagan agreed with the discussants' comments on job sharing.

Another participant from the Bank wanted to hear more about the efficacy of training. In his view the belief that training works is a hope or a prejudice. In developed market economies the evidence is at best mixed or slightly positive. In the absence of thorough evaluations, why are so many people persuaded that training will work? Pencavel shared the participant's skepticism about training programs and considered his description of the evidence generous. We have little evidence that training works, said Pencavel, and he, unlike some others, would not make training an essential component of an active labor market program. Layard disagreed. It is absolutely critical, Layard said, to realize that skills training in a society where for

This session was chaired by Lyn Squire, director, Policy Research Department, at the World Bank.

all practical purposes those skills were unavailable would have a quite different rate of return than training in a society where the skills already exist. Like Pencavel and the questioner, Flanagan was skeptical about training, believing it to be, like incomes policies, based more on hope than on a proven record of performance, but he agreed with Layard that its efficacy depended on the level from which the country was starting.

The World Bank participant asked why people thought job training would work better than such alternatives as subsidies—which could simply be investment tax credits—so taxes could be lower and job creation higher? In Slovenia, where the unemployment rate is 15 percent, about 10 percent of labor force participants are receiving subsidies, he said. A participant from the United Nations described the panel as divided on the issue of wage subsidies—two for, one against—and the one against was against them because of adverse signaling. The participant asked what kind of wage subsidies would be appropriate in Eastern Europe. His reading of the Czech situation was that those who receive wage subsidies do not become employable, particularly outside of big cities. In his home country, Belgium, workers are given subsidies for a year but are not then hired—they go back to the pool of those out of school and get subsidies for another year. In other words, enterprises cream off rents from the state. A participant from the IMF agreed, adding the example of ABM, the system in Germany: once people are off the wage subsidies, they are fired. They are hired as temporary employment, and as soon as the subsidy ends their employment ends. Have these cases been studied?

Layard said that some rational employers would fill jobs on a temporary basis. That is called cycling, and to Layard's way of thinking that is perfectly okay. It is a way to keep workers in the habit of completing an activity, of having a work record, of staying in touch, and of having some money to go to the pub. The employer cannot keep them on in that role, but studies show that their chances of being employed three or four months later are greater if they have had some kind of temporary work. They would find employers willing to accept subsidized temporary workers through employment services.

Pencavel said that his vision of a wage subsidy was different from the one that had been implemented to date. In his vision a wage subsidy scheme would be like a negative payroll tax. Currently, when workers are employed, either the employer or the worker (depending on the country's system) pays a tax immediately, no matter what wage is paid. In Pencavel's scheme a negative income tax would be geared not to workers' incomes but to their hourly wage rate. At a certain wage rate—$6 an hour, for example—you would pay no payroll tax and receive no wage subsidy. At $7 an hour you would start paying positive payroll taxes. At $5 an hour you would get a subsidy from the state. Unlike the temporary subsidy described for Germany, this negative payroll tax would be permanent. The question then becomes, does it matter whether the subsidy was paid to the employer or directly to the employee? If labor markets were completely competitive, it would not matter; it would be irrelevant who actually paid the tax. If you thought that there were signaling problems, you would pay the subsidy to the employer, who would pass it on to the workers according to the slopes of the supply and demand curves. If you believed labor markets were not competitive, then it might well matter to whom you paid the subsidy.

On the issue of wage subsidies Flanagan said that he thought that the discussants had implied more of a difference between them than actually existed. Layard, for example, had mentioned a wage subsidy for downsizing—that is, to limit cyclical unemployment. In that situation, he said, it was hard to imagine what kind of signaling would be involved. The person has been employed with the firm for a while, you know the quality of his or her work, and the subsidy would just prevent a layoff, if a layoff were the way you were going. Based on U.S. experience with subsidies targeted to particular groups of workers, Flanagan was not convinced that paying the subsidy to the employer gets around the problem, because for some problems the employers choose not to use the subsidy. But that may be associated with targeting. Flanagan said he realized that it was an item of faith in the active labor market community that targeting increases efficiency, but there is at least some evidence from U.S. targeted wage subsidy programs that targeting may facilitate adverse signaling.

Lyn Squire (chair) said it was difficult to summarize the discussion when there had been no real consensus, at least on active labor market policies. Squire said that he would have liked to have heard a bit more about passive labor market policies such as unemployment benefits because he thought that the discussants would probably agree about shifting from passive to active labor market policies, even if they could not agree on the composition of those policies.

ROUNDTABLE DISCUSSION

Employment and Development

The panelists for this roundtable discussion were Nancy Birdsall, executive vice president, Inter-American Development Bank; Paul Collier, professor of economics at the Centre for the Study of African Economies, Oxford University; Richard B. Freeman, professor of economics at Harvard University and associated with the National Bureau of Economic Research and the Centre for Economic Performance at the London School of Economics; and Christopher A. Pissarides, professor of economics at the London School of Economics and Political Science. The moderator was Michael Bruno, chief economist and vice president, Development Economics, at the World Bank.

Nancy Birdsall on Growth, Inequality, and the Labor Market

Labor economics is at the heart of development because it is where the economics of growth and the politics of inequality meet. I hope that *World Development Report 1995* on labor will advance the way we think about the relationship between growth and inequality. With this in mind, I want to state and explain three prejudices of mine about public policy and labor market institutions in developing countries. I wish I could call them propositions, or at least testable hypotheses, but they are based largely on crude generalizations. They are meant to provoke thinking and help shape new research questions—especially about the political economy of labor markets and inequality in developing countries. Perhaps new work, including the *World Development Report,* will vindicate them in some form.

Prejudice 1: In the medium run (five years or more) labor market institutions are largely irrelevant to the welfare of the working class. What matters is nonlabor policies; what matters is the pattern of growth.

Labor did well in East Asia between 1960 and 1990. Wages increased as fast or faster than GDP, nearly doubling or more in absolute terms during the 1980s (Fields 1993), while unemployment declined and the mix of jobs improved. This improvement occurred in Hong Kong, where unions were tolerated but remained weak; in Japan, where unions were strong and recognized by government; and in Singapore, where the government deliberately and successfully repressed labor and wages in the

1970s but abandoned wage repression in the 1980s as labor shortages emerged. Wages grew rapidly in the Republic of Korea, too, where the labor movement was repressed throughout most of the 1980s (for political not economic reasons) but not wages—wages rose largely in line with productivity and GDP growth.

What was common across East Asia was not the approach to labor institutions (which, of course, are not confined to unions but include minimum wages, tripartite mechanisms, severance arrangements, unemployment insurance, and the like) but the approach to growth itself and to the idea of "shared growth" (World Bank 1993). Beyond macroeconomic stability, a necessary condition for growth was an emphasis on nonlabor policies and programs for ensuring that the working class, the nonelite, would benefit from growth. East Asian governments used many different mechanisms to encourage the sharing of growth: land reform in Korea and Taiwan (China), generous subsidies for housing in Hong Kong and Singapore, credit targeted to small business and massive investment in rural infrastructure in Indonesia, Malaysia, and Thailand.

But two policies can be singled out as favoring labor: the emphasis on exports, which ensured high demand for labor and drove up employment and wages, and heavy public investment in universal basic education, which supported increasing labor productivity of the initially unskilled and, thus, productivity-based wage growth that was broadly based and fully shared. Widespread basic education also encouraged employer-financed training by reducing the costs and raising the returns to such training. In one of many of the virtuous circles of growth, reduced inequality, faster accumulation of human capital, and productivity-based wage growth fed back to demand for education, ensuring the future supply of more educated and trainable workers and thus continuing gains in labor productivity and wages (Birdsall and Sabot 1994).

These three fundamentals—macroeconomic stability, exports, education—matter much more for labor's welfare than unions or their repression, minimum wages or their absence, or the degree of nonwage costs. The converse also seems to be painfully true: labor institutions cannot insulate workers from wage declines when the fundamentals are all wrong. Declines in real wages in Africa and Latin America, even in countries where labor institutions have been relatively strong, illustrate this vulnerability.

Prejudice 2: Labor market policies and institutions are a perverse vehicle for progressive social policy, especially in developing countries and most especially in developing countries (like most in Latin America) with unequal distributions of income, political power, and privilege.

In Latin America and elsewhere there has been a conflation of labor policy with social policy. The political left, in a tradition rooted in European conditions described by Marx, has defined social justice as fundamentally an issue of workers' rights or entitlements. This tradition is alive and well in much of Latin America. An example: the social rights section of Brazil's 1988 Constitution devotes one four-line paragraph to education, health, and social security, and four pages with thirty-four numbered items to such (constitutionally guaranteed) entitlements as protection against layoffs without just cause (which becomes a matter for the courts), the right to severance pay, the right to a maximum forty-four-hour work week and eight-hour day, and the right to job security in the face of automation. An entirely different and equally detailed article specifies the rights to union representation—also in the section entitled social rights.

Ideas do make a difference. The idea that social justice can be attained by guaranteeing certain entitlements to the wage worker seems to be a bad one, and one worth challenging. The resulting labor institutions have probably had efficiency costs in many Latin American economies. Cox-Edwards (1993) points out several such costs—for example, the chilling effect on the entry and growth of high-technology industry of severance pay obligations that increase with the tenure and experience profile of a firm's labor force. The efficiency costs have probably been higher in the public sector since these entitlements cannot be effectively enforced in the private sector. In some countries job security entitlements in the public sector make civil service downsizing legally impossible and have created costly resistance to the privatization of public enterprises.

But worse than any efficiency costs are the probable costs in reinforcing and exacerbating inequality in Latin America's societies. There are two main reasons for this. First, the truly underprivileged are outside the formal sector—women working as domestics, women and children self-employed in low-productivity street businesses, and the landless and otherwise disenfranchised in rural areas. Higher labor costs in the protected sector reduce these workers' chances of obtaining higher-productivity jobs. Second, emphasis on worker entitlements has distracted government and the well-meaning left from giving attention to the fundamentals of growth—including a labor-demanding growth strategy—that are key to overcoming poverty and inequality.

Happily, these ideas are changing. In Chile and Mexico, for example, market-oriented governments are trying to reshape labor institutions to be market enhancing while developing complementary social policies that do not rely on labor institutions alone to address the structural problems of poverty and inequality.

Prejudice 3: A laissez-faire, let-the-market-work approach is not good public policy.

Why should government get involved at all? One reason is that societies may want to collectively agree on enforcing certain standards, such as prohibiting child labor and ensuring minimum safety in the workplace. This is true even though there is a tradeoff between mandated standards and the efficient working of incentives. Laws in some Latin American countries that guarantee a thirty-day vacation seem to me to reflect the wrong tradeoff, but so does the absence of any minimal safety standards. As the NAFTA debate in the United States showed, the issue of standards is now central to international trade, as well as to domestic labor policy.

Another reason for government involvement is that ensuring a competitive market, in labor as in other areas, often requires some government intervention. The East Asians were not laissez-faire in their approach; they managed the labor market to minimize monopoly rents and to ensure that the market was competitive. In Latin America government is not reducing monopoly rents but rather is an instrument of such rents. Government institutions are also often the victim of strong public sector labor unions—as in Venezuela, where 80 percent of unionized workers are in the public sector.

A third, and most important, reason for government to get involved is that healthy labor institutions, including democratic unions, can ease the difficult process of structural adjustment and the often necessary sharing of the costs of adjustment. The costs of adjustment have not been shared in Latin America—the elite has too often managed to insulate itself.

This brings me full circle to the politics and economics of inequality—where I hope new work on labor will start. Chile's recent reforms of labor institutions provide an interesting model, combining a tripartite discussion on the guidelines for wage increases in an agreed framework that says the minimum wage should be increased in line with economywide productivity gains and projected inflation. The government refuses, however, to engage itself in any bilateral collective bargaining. This kind of limited government intervention, which enhances rather than undermines the labor market, seems to be the right direction to take. I look forward to continued discussion and experimentation at the country level to further our understanding in this important area.

Paul Collier on African Labor Markets

African economic performance is problematic. Indeed, on plausible scenarios, Africa has more person-years of future poverty than any other region. To what extent might failures in the labor market account for this? Posed more bluntly: if Africa had East Asian–style labor markets, with an emphasis on education and flexibility, would its performance start to converge with that of East Asia?

I first discuss two models. One analyzes African labor market failure, the other is ostensibly orthogonal but, I suggest, potentially more pertinent. I then turn to the political economy of African labor markets, arguing that an underlying feature is aversion to the high risks currently endemic in African economies.

The Harris-Todaro Model

Only one really well-known model has come out of the analysis of Africa, and it happens to be about labor market failure. The Harris-Todaro (1970) model postulates that wages were institutionally rigid at a high level and that this rigidity induced high unemployment through a jobs lottery. This model has proved to be a false start. Wages are not institutionally rigid, and labor markets are not job lotteries.

Time-series data on real wages in Africa have shown an astonishing degree of downward real wage flexibility as inflation has eroded real wages (Jamal and Weeks 1993). The exception is the franc zone, where price stability impeded labor market adjustment, something that the recent devaluation will correct. But even in the franc zone real wages have been flexible. One test of wage flexibility is the cross-section relation between local wages and local unemployment rates. In North America this relation is negative: high unemployment depresses wages. The Harris-Todaro model predicts that this relation should be positive in Africa: high wages attract job seekers. In fact, the relation is negative—even more negative than in North America (Hoddinott 1993). African labor markets are highly flexible; unfortunately, they have needed to be so.

Nor are African labor markets a lottery. The context that inspired the Harris-Todaro model was Nairobi in the late 1960s, where unemployment was indeed high. But this labor market should be subjected to closer scrutiny. Unemployment was concentrated among secondary school leavers, a pattern reflecting the abrupt change in secondary education policy from famine to feast at the time of independence. The stock of secondary school–educated labor was expanding by 20 percent a year. Wage adjustments could not fully equilibrate this massive supply shock, and firms became more selective, discriminating in terms of such characteristics as examination results. In 1968, for example, the group that had failed the examination had the highest unemployment rate. But they learned: four years later those who had failed the examination had the lowest unemployment rate because their expectations had adjusted to the new reality (Collier and Lal 1986). Note that firm screening in terms of examination performance and school subjects does not induce an inefficient signaling response: students simply try harder and study more useful subjects. This result can be contrasted with the bumping model (Fields 1974), in which firms screen only by years of education, which induces a socially costly and explosive growth in average years of schooling. In Kenya the urban unemployment rate dropped to less than 6 percent, typical of rates elsewhere in Africa with a few exceptions.

To summarize, whatever might be the problems of African labor markets, high unemployment is not among them: markets are equilibrated by both wages and selection criteria. Yet this flexibility does not seem to have alleviated the problem of poor economic performance.

Employment in a High-Risk Environment

I now turn to a model that is neither inspired by an African context nor is about the labor market, but that I think has more to offer. The model (Dixit 1989) concerns the relation between fixed investment and risk. It shows why even agents who are not risk averse have an incentive to defer investment in a high-risk environment. By retaining liquidity, asset holders gain by keeping their options open. This model is directly pertinent to why Africa has failed to attract investment despite reform of incentive structures. Risk is an important deterrent to investment in Africa not only because there is a high incidence of policy shocks and trade shocks, but also because these shocks occur against a background of slow growth. Large shocks and slow growth imply that investments can easily get beached, whereas in high-growth economies investments hit by negative shocks are soon likely to be bailed out by generalized expansion. Over the past decade foreign direct investment to developing countries has tripled, yet Africa's share has fallen to negligible levels. This neglect has not been offset by domestic investment. The investment failure is in part accounted for by the high-risk environment.

This relation has a direct corollary for African labor markets, because labor is the predominant mechanism for resource mobility. When macroeconomic reform changes relative prices and newly profitable firms are reluctant to invest, changing employment becomes the only way to achieve an output response.

However, I think that the main importance of the investment-under-risk model for African labor markets may be in the form of a simple extension. Many employment decisions have an investment component, and so a high-risk environment discourages such employment just as it discourages fixed capital formation. I offer three examples of the investment content of employment. First, there is evidence for industrial countries that hiring and firing decisions are lumpy because they have fixed costs (Caballero and Engel 1993). These fixed costs represent an investment. Second, a standard result of labor economics is that firms must finance the accumulation of firm-specific skills. Third, in agriculture the long lags between employment and output and the high risks in that output give labor hiring the risk-taking characteristics of investment.

If indeed the high-risk, slow-growth environment discourages investment-intensive employment, this relation affects the character of labor processes. In the formal labor market it induces slow growth of employment. This conclusion is consistent with African evidence: formal employment accounts for a small and diminishing share of the labor force: 12 percent in 1980 and 9 percent in 1990 (Mazumdar 1994). Within the formal sector the discouragement of investment-intensive employment induces a greater reliance on casual employment and a slow pace of skill accumulation. Evidence from Zimbabwe shows firms employing a relatively small core of long-term workers in whom they invest and a large group of casual workers (Velenchik 1994). There is evidence that rates of return to education are falling despite the fact that the African labor force has little education. This may be happening because the casualization of the labor force does not provide a context in which education can be well harnessed. Enrollment rates in schools are dropping in many parts of Africa, probably due to falling returns.

In agriculture the problem manifests itself as too little labor hiring (Collier 1989). In most of eastern and southern Africa less than 10 percent of the labor force on smallholdings is hired. Yet land-labor endowment ratios on holdings are diverging. Land has ceased to be abundant and is overwhelmingly acquired through inheritance rather than purchase or tenancy. Labor transactions are insufficient to equalize factor returns across African farms of different sizes. Hence, within rural Africa the same analytic question arises as in the debate on globalization and wages: to what extent can specialization in the goods market substitute for a labor market?

Not only does the high-risk agricultural environment reduce labor hiring, but there is also a feedback from the resulting thinness of the rural labor market to increased risk. Agricultural households facing adversity do not have reliable access to wage labor as a safety net. Nor does the other obvious rural risk-reducing strategy, diversification, appear to work very well. In rural Asia there is a clear negative relation between income and diversification: households choose to buy security at the price of income. Yet in Africa, where exposure to risk is probably greater, there is a positive relation between income and diversification (Krishnan 1994). Poor households are least able to diversify because there are entry barriers to nontraditional activities in the form of capital and information (Bevan, Collier, and Gunning 1989).

The Political Economy of a Risk-Averse Society

I now want to suggest that this high-risk environment with limited coping strategies may help account for two political-economy phenomena that are of major importance in African formal labor markets. The common theme is that we would expect households to be highly risk averse.

First, risk aversion might help account for the intense popular pressure to provide public sector employment. The share of the public sector in wage employment became markedly larger during the 1970s and 1980s in Africa than in other continents. Under the pressure of this employment expansion, public sector wage rates collapsed. The public sector is no longer lucrative: indeed, it is usually not possible to live on a public sector salary. Yet such employment is safe. In effect, the public sector labor market has become the domain of social security policy, offering a low but secure income supplement to many households. A by-product is that the public sector, despite being very large, is in a poor position to deliver services: the public sector is both too large and too small.

Second, risk aversion may help account for at least part of the opposition of the formal sector labor force to macroeconomic reform. The centerpiece of such reform has been devaluation. It is conventional wisdom that labor loses from devaluation. Real wages need to fall as part of the reduction in expenditures involved in balance of payments improvement, and this drop is achieved by a failure of nominal wages to keep up with the inflation that devaluation triggers. This conventional wisdom is correct for a devaluation such as that of the CFA franc, an unusual case in the African context. More commonly, African governments have already contained their payments deficits through trade restrictions by the time they devalue, so that the devaluation is trade liberalizing. Relative prices change, but there need be no reduction in real expenditure. Real wages need not fall during trade liberalization; the losers are those who received quota rents and capital owners in the import-substitution sector.

Yet the opposition to reform is typically more widespread, including more or less the whole of the formal wage labor force—a potent force. Part of the reason is that beneficiaries of reform are typically not in the labor market but in the smallholder export sector, which is politically weak in Africa (Bates 1981). But the active opposition of the formal labor force goes beyond this.

The import-substituting manufacturing sector naturally tends to lose from trade liberalization. This loss is exacerbated if the reform is accompanied by foreign assistance, since the aid will appreciate the exchange rate (Collier and Gunning 1992). If there was a fully integrated national labor market, workers would not mind this effect: the Stolper-Samuelson mechanism would ensure that all workers gained and that capital owners bore the losses. However, studies of trade policy lobbying in industrial countries have found that workers and firms tend to take the same side:

rents are sufficiently shared that interests are common. In Africa this seems to be less the case. For example, in the Zimbabwean trade liberalization, manufacturing firms were instrumental in lobbying for the liberalization, but employee organizations were vocal opponents.

The manufacturing sector in Zimbabwe is largely import substituting, but some firms anticipate becoming substantial exporters. In the labor market this pattern implies both net labor shedding and a reallocation of workers as import-competing firms contract and exporting firms expand. Freeman (1993b) has modeled gainers and losers in such a process, but in his model there is no risk aversion: at the announcement stage all workers support reform because positive income changes are expected. More commonly there is acute opposition at the announcement stage because workers correctly anticipate a greater risk of job loss. The hope is that as the reform proceeds workers in the expanding export sector constitute a lobby of gainers to counter this perception of enhanced risk.

Whether this group of reform promoters emerges depends on whether workers in the firms that become more profitable share in the benefits. Recent results for Ghanaian manufacturing (Jones 1994) show that, as in industrial country labor markets, wages are higher in firms that are more profitable: there is rent-sharing. This relation is true only in the upper echelons of the labor market. For production workers there is no relation between profitability and earnings. Production workers in export manufacturing have no reason to counter the opposition to reform that will come from production workers in the import-substituting sectors. The conjunction of an efficient labor market for production workers within the manufacturing sector and a failure of the labor market to encompass the bulk of the labor force produces a bias toward opposition to liberalization. Manufacturing workers either lose or are indifferent, whereas the major export sector of most African economies has few formal wage employees.

The other major group of workers opposing reform is in the public sector. Ordinary public employees are unlikely to lose directly from a trade-liberalizing devaluation, since they are not usually the beneficiaries of quota rents. However, public sector retrenchment is generally included as part of the adjustment package. A political by-product of this packaging may be that groups that lose from logically distinct policy changes can find common cause in opposition. Public sector retrenchment is a classic example of a reform in which the gains are so diffused that nobody realizes that they have benefited, whereas the risk of job loss creates a well-defined group of losers.

The high degree of opposition that reforms have encountered in Africa has in turn provided a feedback into the high-risk environment. The public does not agree on the reforms, and so there is a significant risk of policy reversal.

Conclusion

I started with a question of whether Africa, if it had more flexible labor markets and a more educated labor force, would start to perform more like East Asia. I have suggested that neither rigidities of the labor market nor shortages of educated labor are central to African problems. African labor markets are remarkably flexible. But a high-risk, low-growth environment is not conducive to high returns to human capital. Rather, it is conducive to the politics of risk aversion: large, badly paid public sectors and opposition to reform.

Africa cannot become East Asia by directly emulating its labor markets. Rather, its labor markets will start to look like East Asia's only when African societies succeed in producing a convincing consensus committed to the maintenance of reform.

Richard B. Freeman on the Global Labor Market

The following developments are, arguably, bringing labor markets closer together, leading to a global labor market with consequences for workers in industrial and developing countries:

- The rapid growth of employment in industry and manufacturing in developing countries—from 136 million workers or 43 percent of the world total in 1970 to 219 million workers or 53 percent of the world total in 1990.
- Increased education in many developing countries that in part underlies the growth of employment in industry and that makes an increasing share of the world's work force able to do similar tasks. Mean years of schooling in developing countries rose from 3.4 years in 1970 to 5.3 years in 1990. With 75 percent of the world labor force in developing countries, the increase in mean schooling implies millions more workers with relatively high levels of education.
- The growth of trade in manufacturing between developing and industrial countries. Through trade, manufacturing workers in many industries in developing countries have become substitutes for manufacturing workers in industrial countries. Perhaps the most striking indicator of this change is the rising share of manufactures in developing country exports to industrial countries, from 16 percent in 1970 to 53 percent in 1989 (Wood 1994).
- The growth of promarket and protrade institutions in many developing economies. The successes of Hong Kong, the Republic of Korea, Singapore, Taiwan (China), and, more recently, Chile and the collapse of communist autarkic regimes have shown that the path to sustainable development rests on market institutions and membership in the world trading community.
- Increased immigration from developing countries or economies in transition (whose GDPs per capita would put them in the developing countries category) to industrial countries. Between 1970 and 1990 the immigrant share of the U.S. population nearly doubled, with the bulk of new immigrants coming from developing countries. The immigrant share of the population also rose in Australia, Canada, and Western Europe.
- The transmission of modern technology through the expanded operations of multinational firms around the world and the education in industrial countries of high-level students from developing countries.

These changes are related in various ways that are susceptible to detailed analysis. Here I simply note them as indicators of the growing interconnection of labor in the emerging global labor market.

If the globalization of the labor market is important, we would expect to see it show up in changes in the economic well-being of workers among countries. Do have we evidence of such changes?

There are two facts that some regard as evidence of the growth of a global labor market. The first is the decline in labor demand for less-skilled workers in industrial countries—a decline that shows up in falling real wages in the United States and falling employment and high unemployment in Western Europe. The second fact is the increased demand for modern sector workers in developing countries that have joined the world economy—an increase that shows up in growing modern sector employment and higher real wages. These developments have the flavor of a world in which factor price equalization has begun to operate in a substantive way. If workers around the world are in the same labor market, workers with similar skills will ultimately be paid comparable wages.

Wood (1994) has argued that these two facts are linked not only conceptually but also empirically: falling demand for less-skilled workers in the West is the flip side of the improved position of comparable workers in newly industrializing countries. My reading of Wood's empirical evidence and that of others (Freeman 1993a; Sachs and Schatz 1994) does not, however, support such a sweeping generalization, appealing though it is as a unicausal explanation of ongoing changes.

It is no easy task to quantify the effects of labor market globalization on workers in industrial or developing countries, but evidence suggests that the magnitude of the effects of trade with developing countries does not come close to explaining the deteriorated position of less-skilled workers in industrial countries. At the same time the evidence does not support the view that trade and immigration have had no effect on wages around the world. Just as trade has benefited workers in some developing countries, it has created problems for some workers in the West, though it is far from the main cause of their economic problems. Most important, perhaps, as modern technology spreads and more developing countries with huge populations (such as China, India, and Indonesia) join the world economy as major exporters of manufactured items, it is hard to imagine that this will not have even greater effects on labor markets than globalization did in the 1980s. To dismiss the potential effects of globalization on the job markets in diverse countries may be to miss the change in the world economy that will most affect those who earn their living from work in the next several decades.

Globalization of the labor market gives rise to several policy issues. The first and currently most visible issue relates to the demands by some industrial countries for higher labor standards in developing countries. How will governments and the international trading community respond to the demand for labor standards—minimal modes of treatment of workers—that arise when countries purchase products from countries with different levels of output per capita and labor codes?

In industrial countries the demand for global labor standards has two sources. One is the desire of consumers that the products they consume be made under decent conditions (this section summarizes Freeman 1994). For goods sold at the same price most consumers, when given a choice between goods produced under decent conditions and those made under slavery, by prison labor, or by ill-treated workers, would choose the products produced under decent conditions. Many would even be willing to pay more for those products, up to a point. This yields a demand curve for standards: the extra money consumers will pay for goods they know are produced under better working conditions. The ideal free market way to meet this demand is through information—labeling products with the labor conditions under which they are produced. If a labeling strategy is impractical or unreliable (say, because producers or retailers will stick "Made under good conditions" labels on products made by forced labor in prison camps), other methods for regulating the market on behalf of consumers may be needed, ranging from government pressures to muck-raking campaigns and organized boycotts.

The net effect of a consumer-driven demand for standards should be a rise in labor standards, paid for by consumers willing to pay for an "extended product" that includes better conditions for those who make the good. Legislation in China in 1994 on child labor, motivated by concern over the attitudes of Western consumers, provides a good example of the development of consumer-driven standards. While economists have trouble arguing against demands based on consumer preferences, it would be remiss to ignore the danger that consumers in industrial countries may demand standards that are too high for developing countries to afford, with consequences that run counter to the underlying desire of consumers. For instance, an unwillingness to buy any products made by child labor could push child labor from the formal sector into the streets, rather than into schooling or other desirable activities. Information about what is economically plausible as well as about the conditions of work in developing countries is needed for the push for standards to be a boon rather than a detriment to the economic well-being of workers.

The second reason behind the demand for global labor standards is protection of existing workers or firms. Many trade specialists believe that the demand for global labor standards is just old-fashioned protectionism disguised as altruism. That some groups that argue for labor standards in international settings—labor unions in industrial countries in sectors that potentially compete with workers in developing countries—have a clear self-interest in limiting competition from lower-paid competitors suggests reason for such concern. In the debate over NAFTA in the United States, it was the AFL-CIO labor union, historically a supporter of free trade, that opposed NAFTA on the grounds that increased integration of the Mexican and U.S. economies would harm low-skill U.S. labor, while the manufacturing community, proponents of tariffs in decades past, supported the agreement, in part because it gave greater surety to investments in Mexico. In this case a higher social safety net in the economically less advanced country might be the appropriate means of defusing protectionist sentiments and enhancing the move toward an open economy.

Globalization makes workers in developing countries potential beneficiaries of protectionist sentiments in industrial countries.

The second policy issue is how quickly the wages of workers in developing countries that enter the world trading system approach wages in industrial countries. If we are entering an era of increased pressure toward factor price equalization, what we want are huge increases in wages and working conditions in developing countries, not huge decreases in wages and working conditions or long-term unemployment in industrial countries.

In the newly industrialized economies of Asia that are widely heralded as development successes, wages have in fact increased at historically unprecedented rates. Wages in manufacturing have zoomed upward in Hong Kong, Korea, Singapore, and Taiwan (China) in the past twenty years, from about 5 percent of U.S. wages to roughly 30 percent in 1993 (at current exchange rates). The living standards of workers in these economies are even closer to those in the United States and other countries—on the order of 60 percent of U.S. living standards. These differences are potentially largely skill-related, considering the lower education of workers. Korea has not yet reached the standing of a high-income economy according to World Bank classifications, but Hong Kong and Singapore have—and Taiwan (China) would be close if it were included in the Bank's data. If other developing economies that enter the world economy in a big way experience equally rapid increases in real wages, increased pressure toward factor price equalization will take the form largely of improved earnings for traditionally low-paid developing-country labor, rather than of a threat to the jobs of less-skilled workers in industrial countries. The best outcome for workers in a global economy is a rapid increase in the pay of labor in developing countries.

What policies and institutions might best bring the wages of workers in developing countries toward the levels in industrial countries? In the West improvements in labor conditions were accompanied by the rise of trade unions and various labor market regulations. For the most part the newly industrializing Asian economies have not followed this route, at least not until recently. But unions, once suppressed in Korea, have struggled toward a legitimate place in society. Korea and Taiwan (China) have enacted social legislation protecting labor. There appears to be a natural pattern in which economies "buy" greater labor standards and protection for workers as they develop and in which unionization and other forms of collective activity by workers similarly grow with democratization and economic advancement.

Some economists regard these patterns as inimical to economic advancement. I do not. They are part and parcel of successful market economies. The danger is not that economically successful countries will choose too much regulation and interference with markets (though some may do that) but that those that have not (yet) succeeded may try to "buy" a social product that they cannot afford. Uruguay is often cited in this respect as having a social security system that exceeds its productive capacity. Many of the transition economies in Eastern and Central Europe have similar problems. Just as consumers want to know that the products they buy are produced under decent conditions, the citizenry in all countries wants certain regulations of job market outcomes and processes. But the demand for these "goods" must be conditioned on what the economy can afford, not on best practices in more advanced economies.

The third policy issue is the extent to which many developing countries can follow the same path of development in a global economy at the same time, or whether some countries will be forced to the wayside in the new international division of labor. Will China's increased movement into the world economy mean that the Philippines will lose its opportunity to advance through exporting, say, children's toys? Will Colombia, Korea, and Malaysia be able to move up to the next rung in development? Will the transmission of advanced technologies reduce demand for certain types of labor in developing countries, as has occurred in industrial countries? Or will some countries simply fail to develop the institutional infrastructure needed to compete in a global economy?

One surprising result emerging from studies of tariffs and quotas in developing countries is that some countries have protected products made with low-skill labor, such as textiles or footwear, where these countries would be expected to have a comparative advantage relative to industrial countries. In Mexico the reduction of tariffs and quotas appears to have harmed less-skilled labor because trade barriers were highest in unskilled, labor-intensive industries (Feliciano 1994). Whether such trade policies reflected fears of competition from even lower-wage countries or from higher-wage but technologically more advanced countries is an interesting question. Globalization does not necessarily mean shifts in demand toward the products of any particular country, regardless of its wage level.

In sum, the ongoing globalization of the world's labor force is a major development that has the potential of affecting workers throughout the world. We may never reach the point where what happens in the labor market in Calcutta determines wages in Amsterdam, Manila, or New York. But what happens in Calcutta (or Shanghai or Dacca) has the potential for increasingly affecting wages throughout the world. Indeed, I can envisage a map of the world based on the skills of workers and their place in the global labor market—a map based not on political boundaries but on economic competency. Some segments of developing countries would be in the global market and other segments would not, just as some groups in industrial countries would be part of the market and others not. In the ideal global labor market education and skills will ultimately matter more than residence in a particular political entity.

Christopher A. Pissarides on Lessons of European and U.S. Labor Markets

I structure my discussion around a comparison of the experience of the United States with that of the major European countries and then draw some lessons about the role of labor market policy for developing country labor markets. In making this comparison I do not argue that one labor market is better than the other. One cannot point to a model to emulate but only to some lessons of experience and, occasionally, to solutions. The views expressed by the leaders of the G-7 nations at the jobs summit in Detroit in March 1994 are instructive. Each leader went to the summit hoping to learn from the experience of the others, with the Europeans envying the U.S. job creation record and the Americans envying the Europeans' earnings record. I concentrate here on unemployment and earnings.

Since the 1960s unemployment in the United States has fluctuated within a 5 to 10 percent band. There have been cycles, but since the 1973 oil crisis unemployment has been on a flat trend. By contrast, unemployment in the European Union (EU) has been on an upward trend. Again, there have been cycles, but each new trough has been higher than the previous one. As a result unemployment, which was only about 2.5 percent in the early 1970s, has fluctuated between 8 and 10 percent in the 1990s.

Higher unemployment is associated with a longer duration of unemployment in all countries, though the relation is closer in countries where the cause of higher unemployment is lack of job creation (rather than more job destruction). In the United States in 1990, of the 5.5 percent unemployed, 5.6 percent were unemployed for more than one year. In the European Union the incidence of long-term unemployment is much higher. In Germany, 46.3 percent of the 4.9 percent unemployed had been unemployed for more than a year; in the United Kingdom it was 36.1 percent of 5.9 percent. In the European Union as a whole long-term unemployment averaged 51 percent of an 8 percent unemployment rate (OECD 1993).

Every economy needs some unemployment to function properly. Just how much is a matter of debate. What is certain, however, is that long-term unemployment is wasteful in terms of the loss of skill and the disenfranchisement it entails from labor market institutions and processes. There is evidence that long-term unemployment ceases to act as an inflation deterrent on unions and that the long-term unemployed are less likely to be offered jobs by employers, other things equal. They are also more likely to be discouraged (Layard, Nickell, and Jackman 1991; Blanchard and Diamond 1994).

The high incidence of long-term unemployment must be regarded as a failure of European labor markets. An associated failure is the rising trend of unemployment. Even if there is disagreement about the right level of unemployment, it is difficult to find factors to justify an increase in the European equilibrium unemployment rate from 2.5 percent in 1973 to more than 8 percent in 1993.

The unemployment experience of Europe and the United States contrasts with their earnings experience. Real average earnings in the European Union have been on a steep upward trend since the 1960s. In the United States they have increased hardly at all. More striking is the behavior of earnings at the low end of the earnings distribution. Unskilled earnings in the United States have been on a declining trend for several years, decreasing by 10 percent since 1972 (at the top end, real earnings increased by 4.4 percent over the same period). European workers in the bottom 10 percent of the wage distribution earn 44 percent more in real terms than their U.S. counterparts, despite the higher average standard of living in the United States.

Europeans often envy the U.S. record on job creation. A comparison of unemployment records seems to justify that envy. But closer examination shows that looking only at the number of jobs created is misleading.

In the long run job creation is driven largely by the supply of labor. The supply of labor has risen faster in the United States than in Europe, which accounts for much of the higher job creation in the United States. In the short run job creation is also driven by job destruction. A country that destroys a lot of jobs is also likely to create more, because those that lose their jobs will be looking for new ones. Job destruction rates are on the whole higher in the United States than in Europe. Finally, the quality of the new jobs is also relevant. A lot of the jobs created in the United States require low skills, are of short duration, and are mainly in services; although they keep young and untrained workers off the unemployment books, they are dead-end jobs that are not likely to facilitate the transition to more permanent employment.

Why the disparity in the unemployment and earnings experience of Europe and the United States? To find the answer we have to look at the low end of the labor market, since unemployment in Europe affects mainly the unskilled. It is clear from the record that in the past twenty years the industrialized world has experienced a negative shock at the unskilled end of the labor market. The task that confronted the labor markets of the industrialized world was how to shift employment from low-skill manufactures to other sectors. In this regard the U.S. labor market has been more successful than have European markets, but at the cost of a large class of "working poor." Although a higher mobility of labor in the United States than in Europe has something to do with this record, the main reason, I believe, has to do with labor market policy.

Labor Market Policy

At the risk of oversimplification, I can put the main lesson of the diversity of experience just described as follows: in the face of negative shocks a welfare policy that does not pay attention to labor market incentives can be much more costly, in terms of forgone output and financial cost, than a policy that does. The absence of a labor market policy encourages the creation of many unstable, low-income jobs that do not offer productive training opportunities, while a passive labor market policy that protects low incomes gives rise to inflexibility, especially at the low end of the market, and to long-duration unemployment.

Labor market policy is of two general kinds: policy that regulates the employment relationship without money transfers (restrictions on the dismissal of employees, legally enforced consultation with workers) and policy that transfers money from one part of the labor market to another.

Regulation is a form of tax on employers and the less there is, the more job creation there is likely to be. Although some basic worker rights need to be protected by law (for example, the granting of rest periods), restrictions on the firm's ability to quickly recruit and dismiss workers tend to reduce flexibility at small obvious benefit to workers. There is a clear relation between the degree of employment-protection legislation and job turnover (Nickell 1982) and, consequently, between employment-protection legislation and long-term unemployment. Countries that impose more restrictions on the dismissal of labor tend to have longer durations of unemployment (figure 1), presumably because the restrictions discourage both job destruction and job creation.

Transfers from the government to the private sector take the form of spending on "passive" policy measures and spending on "active" measures. Passive labor market measures usually include income support for the unemployed and other low-income groups without preconditions, and active measures mean programs that encourage faster transition from unemployment to employment. Passive measures are good for reducing poverty and for achieving a more equitable distribution of income, but they reduce the incentives for work at the low end of the market.

Passive measures are much more common in European countries than in the United States, one reason for the difference in behavior of their labor markets. Generous income support in Europe acts as a floor on wages and so discourages low-income job creation. As a result, unemployment tends to be of longer duration. When income support is absent, as in the United States, unemployment turnover is higher and job creation and destruction are more frequent.

Experience in the OECD shows that the most important policy influence on the duration of unemployment is not the level of income support but its duration (Jackman, Pissarides, and Savouri 1990). Most unemployed workers leave unemployment quickly. Even generous unemployment benefits, provided they do not last long, have little effect on the rate at which people leave unemployment. But when benefits are available for long periods of time, more of the unemployed enter long-term unemployment and stay there (figure 2).

With the rise in European unemployment, and the impressive unemployment record of Sweden and the other Scandinavian countries that pursued active labor market policies, most European countries started devoting more attention to active policy measures in the 1980s. These have taken the form of spending on public employment services and administration, labor market training, measures to help young workers and members of disadvantaged groups find regular employment, and subsidies paid directly to firms for job creation. In the early 1990s OECD countries spent half as much on active policy measures as on passive (Jackman, Pissarides, and Savouri 1990; OECD 1993). Although the administration of such measures is more costly than the administration of passive measures, they have proved popular, mainly because of their success in reducing long-term unemployment.

The proportion of long-term unemployment is plotted against spending on active measures per unemployed worker (as a percentage of GDP) in figure 3. Sweden does not appear in the chart because its high spending on active measures places it too far out on the horizontal axis and distorts the picture (Sweden's place on the horizontal axis is 119). Its long-term unemployment rate is one of the lowest in Europe, at 4.8 percent in 1990. Germany is also missing from the chart because during 1990–92 its spending on active measures was distorted by unification. The chart reveals a negative correlation between spending on active measures and long-term

Figure 1. *Employment Protection Legislation and Long-Term Unemployment, 1990*

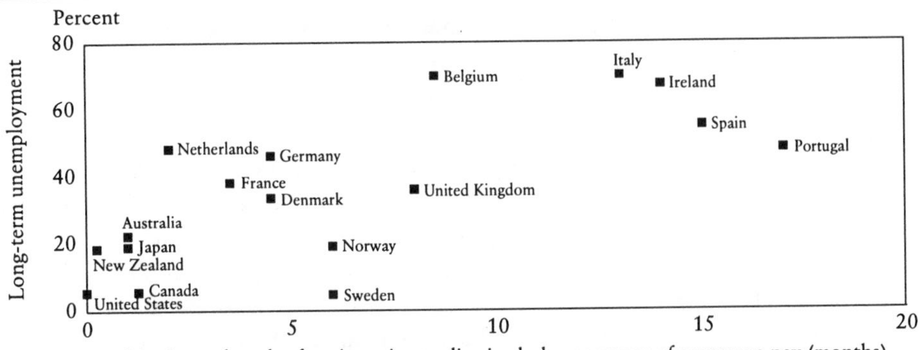

Figure 2. *Passive Policy Measures and Long-Term Unemployment, 1990*

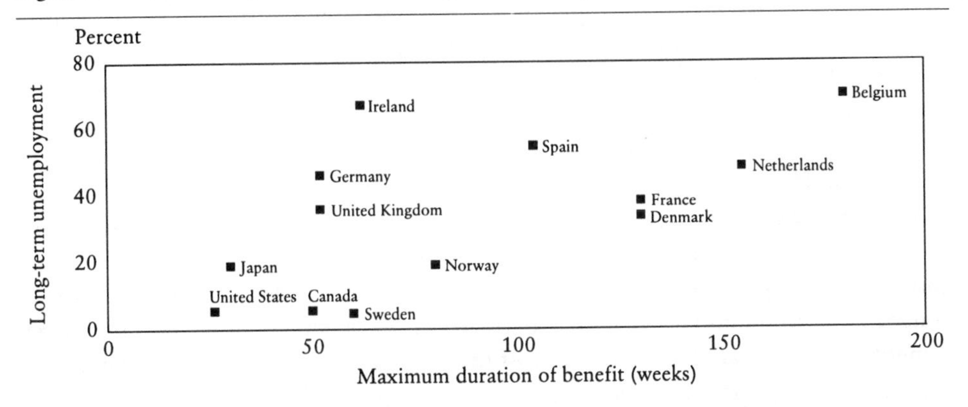

Figure 3. *Active Policy Measures and Long-Term Unemployment, 1990*

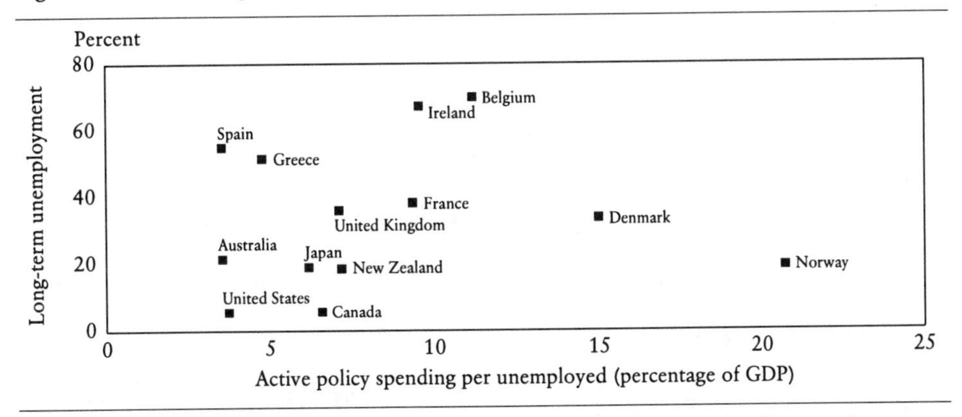

Note: Long-term unemployment is the percentage of unemployed who have been unemployed for more than one year. Data are for 1990, 1991, or 1992, depending on data availability. *Figure 1*—Maximum length of notice or severance pay is the sum of the maximum length of notice that has to be given before a dismissal can be brought into force and the number of months of pay that have to be given as severance payment at the time of dismissal. *Figure 2*—Maximum duration of benefit is the maximum number of weeks that an eligible worker is entitled to receive unemployment compenstion. *Figure 3*—The horizontal axis measures expenditure on active policy measures, as defined by the OECD, expressed first as a percentage of GDP and then divided by the proportion of unemployed workers.

Source: OECD 1993.

unemployment, especially for EU countries. Multiple regression analysis confirms the claim that active measures reduce both overall unemployment and the incidence of long-term unemployment (Jackman, Pissarides, and Savouri 1990; OECD 1993).

Lessons for Developing Countries

The labor market has to provide both a flexible framework to allow for the adoption of new technologies and growth and satisfactory incomes for people who committed to their skills at some time in the past. Even mature economies cannot cope with change without disadvantaging some sections of the labor force. In the United States the disadvantaged are those whose only access to the market is through unstable, low-income jobs; in most of Europe the disadvantaged are the long-term unemployed. What lessons can developing nations learn from this experience?

I concentrate here on the lessons that have been learned from policy. First, measures that support low-income groups can lead to rigidities at the unskilled end of the labor market and reduce the market's adaptability to new circumstances. A welfare policy has to pay attention to the incentives that firms have for job creation and those that unskilled workers have for seeking employment and acquiring new skills.

A second lesson is that an active labor market policy, such as the subsidization of training and job searches, helps remove the disincentives of a passive income support policy. The challenge for emerging labor markets is how to combine income support policies to avoid poverty with active measures that can remove the disincentives of the policy and provide the right incentives for disadvantaged groups to reenter regular employment. The experience of European countries in this respect, especially of the Scandinavian countries that pioneered active policy, can shed light on the design of such policies.

References

Bates, R.H. 1981. *Markets and States in Tropical Africa.* Berkeley: University of California Press.

Bevan, D.L., P. Collier, and J.W. Gunning. 1989. *Peasants and Governments: An Economic Analysis.* Oxford: Clarendon Press.

Birdsall, Nancy, and Richard Sabot. 1994. "Virtuous Circles: Human Capital, Equity, and Growth in East Asia."

Blanchard, Olivier, and Peter Diamond. 1994. "Ranking, Unemployment Duration and Wages." *Review of Economic Studies* 61 (October): 417–34.

Caballero, R.J., and E.M.R.A. Engel. 1993. "Microeconomic Adjustment Hazards and Aggregate Dynamics." *Quarterly Journal of Economics* 108: 359–84.

Collier, P. 1989. "Contractual Constraints on Labor Exchange in Rural Kenya." *International Labor Review* 128 (6): 745–68.

Collier, P., and J.W. Gunning. 1992. "Aid and Exchange Rate Adjustment in African Trade Liberalisations." *Economic Journal* 102: 925–39.

Collier, P., and D. Lal. 1986. *Labor and Poverty in Kenya.* Oxford: Clarendon Press.

Cox-Edwards, Alejandra. 1993. "Labor Market Legislation in Latin America and the Caribbean." Report 31. World Bank, Regional Studies Program, Latin America and the Caribbean Technical Department, Washington, D.C.

Dixit, A. 1989. "Inter-Sectoral Capital Reallocation under Price Uncertainty." *Journal of International Economics* 26: 309–25.

Feliciano, Zadia. 1994. "Workers and Trade Liberalization: The Impact of Trade Reforms in Mexico on Wages and Employment." Ph.D. diss., Harvard University, Cambridge, Mass.

Fields, Gary. 1974. "The Private Demand for Education in Relation to Labor Market Conditions in Less Developed Countries." *Economic Journal* 84: 906–25.

———. 1993. "Changing Labor Market Conditions and Economic Development in Hong Kong, Republic of Korea, Singapore, and Taiwan, China." *World Bank Economic Review* 8 (3): 395–414.

Freeman, Richard. 1993a. "Is Globalization Impoverishing Low-Skill American Workers?" Paper presented at the Forum on Policy Responses to an International Market, The Urban Institute, November 17, Washington, D.C.

———. 1993b. "Labor Market Institutions and Policies: Help or Hindrance to Economic Development?" In Lawrence H. Summers and Shekhar Shah, eds., *Proceedings of the World Bank Annual Conference on Development Economics 1992*. Washington, D.C.

———. 1994. "A Hard-Headed Look at Labor Standards." Paper presented at the U.S. Department of Labor conference on Standards and Global Economic Integration, April 25, Washington, D.C.

Harris, J., and M.P. Todaro. 1970. "Migration, Unemployment and Development: A Two-Sector Analysis." *American Economic Review* 60: 126–42.

Hoddinott, J. 1993. "Wages and Unemployment in Urban Côte d'Ivoire." Working Paper 93/3. Centre for the Study of African Economies, Oxford.

Jackman, Richard, Christopher Pissarides, and Savvas Savouri. 1990. "Labour Market Policy and Unemployment in the OECD." *Economic Policy* 11 (October): 449–90.

Jamal, V., and J. Weeks. 1993. *Africa Misunderstood*. London: MacMillan.

Jones, P. 1994. "Education and Labour Productivity in Ghana: An Applied Production Analysis." Working Paper 94/12. Centre for the Study of African Economies, Oxford.

Krishnan, P. 1994. "Getting By and Getting On." Centre for the Study of African Economies, Oxford.

Layard, Richard, Stephen Nickell, and Richard Jackman. 1991. *Unemployment: Macroeconomic Performance and the Labour Market*. Oxford: Oxford University Press.

Mazumdar, D. 1994. "Wages in Africa." World Bank, Africa Technical Department, Washington, D.C.

Nickell, Stephen. 1982. "The Determinants of Equilibrium Unemployment in Britain." *Economic Journal* 92: 555–75.

OECD (Organization for Economic Cooperation and Development). 1993. *Employment Outlook*. Paris.

Sachs, Jeffrey, and Howard Schatz. 1994. "Trade and Jobs in U.S. Manufacturing." Brookings Panel Paper. Brookings Institution, Washington, D.C.

Velenchik, A. 1994. "Labor Markets." In J.W. Gunning, ed., "Enterprise Survey of Zimbabwe: Final Report." Free University, Amsterdam.

Wood, Adrian. 1994. *North-South Trade, Employment, and Inequality*. Oxford: Clarendon Press.

World Bank. 1993. *The East Asian Miracle: Economic Growth and Public Policy*. A Policy Research Report. Washington, D.C.

Floor Discussion of the Roundtable Discussion on Employment and Development

Freeman, said a participant from the World Bank, has stated that demand for labor standards comes from workers, consumers, and groups seeking increased protection. What happened recently in Marrakesh, however, illustrates that Western countries also apply pressure for labor standards to protect their industries from labor-intensive exports from developing countries. High unemployment rates in the European Union, the participant felt, would only exacerbate the tendency toward this form of protectionism, and the newly emerging markets were unlikely to benefit from the globalization of labor markets.

Whether labor standards would hurt some countries' chances was a politically hot question, said Freeman, and in a sense it depended on where the demand for labor standards came from and how it operated. If it was workers demanding greater safety, the result might be lower wages, because the workers were effectively saying that they would rather take some of their compensation in the form of safer working conditions. If the demand for labor standards came from consumers, the consumers would be paying for the standard. Basically they would be saying, I'm willing to pay a nickel more for a shirt made in a country with decent standards rather than buy one from a country without them. It would be silly, even disastrous, to insist on U.S.-level minimum wages in developing countries, or European minimum wages in the United States. But many rights that elicit concern—the right for women not to be harassed, for example, or the right to decent working conditions—are not expensive to guarantee. Many employers, faced with the prospect of not selling their product, would instantly improve working conditions. The problem, then, is government demands that really reflect pressure from trade unions or textile lobbying groups, not out of concern for workers' rights but to keep competitive products from coming into their country. This problem can be phrased in a much better way if we grab control of the issue, said Freeman.

Alan Gelb (speaker in another session) asked Pissarides to summarize the current state of thinking about the efficiency of active labor market policies. To what extent do such policies facilitate improvements in the labor market and to what extent do

This session was chaired by Michael Bruno, chief economist and vice president, Development Economics, at the World Bank.

Proceedings of the World Bank Annual Conference on Development Economics 1994

they simply keep officially registered unemployment low while subsidizing jobs? Pissarides replied that there had been some exploitation of labor market policy for political reasons, to reduce the number of unemployed. But what he meant by active policy measures was measures that get unemployed workers working. Sweden, for example, subsidizes training in the private sector: after a year of unemployment the government converts what would have been an unemployment benefit (a direct subsidy to the worker) into a subsidy to a firm for employing the unemployed worker. That gives the unemployed worker some skills and facilitates the transition to a job. Another example was the RESTART program in the United Kingdom, in which the Department of Employment interviewed the long-term unemployed and tried to find them jobs. The program has been successful because it turned out that there were jobs for the long-term unemployed but that they had become discouraged and had stopped going out and applying for them.

A participant from the University of Massachusetts asked Collier for more details about firm-specific training. How significant was it as a proportion of firm costs? In Africa, did it matter what type of firm it was (multinational, public, or private)? Was there a difference in firm costs within an industry or across national boundaries or regions? Collier responded that they had just gotten data on whether firm training differed by type of firm. They would soon be able to provide a robust answer to that question from surveys conducted in the manufacturing sectors of half a dozen African countries.

A participant from Congressional Research asked Birdsall to compare prospects in Latin America with prospects in Asia. If the question was, where should you put your money, replied Birdsall, she would say that the potential returns were greater in Latin America, but so were the risks. It was a question of how much of a risk-taker you are. (She was speaking on that point as Nancy Birdsall, she reminded the audience, not as executive vice president of the Inter-American Development Bank.) The biggest challenge in Latin America, both politically and economically, was inequality, which was probably reducing household savings and investment in children's health and education. Inequality also threatened the social and political sustainability of difficult but essential ongoing economic reforms.

Another participant asked Birdsall how important labor market outputs and aggregate growth were to women's employment and investments in women's human capital. There is no question, responded Birdsall, that returns to labor and returns to education in the labor market affect parents' and people's choices about how much education to invest in and that in the long run labor market outcomes clearly affect women's welfare. Whether they affect women's employment in the formal sector, as Freeman implied in a different context, depends very much on institutional and other factors.

A participant asked Collier to what extent were demographic trends a factor in Africa's wage decline? Collier responded that the demand for labor had failed more than the supply; a successful economy can generate enough growth in labor demand to accommodate growth in the labor supply. In some countries the African labor supply has been endogenous to economic failure. In Ghana in the 1970s, for example, the labor supply didn't grow because people migrated out of the country. But the main factor was demand failure, in Collier's view, not demographics.

The Harris-Todaro model might not work for places like New Delhi, said a participant from the George Washington University, but there was some evidence that it helped to explain Botswana and South Africa (in the work by Robert Lucas, for example). Yes, responded Collier, South Africa was a distinctive labor market, by African standards; in particular, there was virtually no smallholder sector, so alternatives to wage employment in the formal sector were very different. Also, the political economy in South Africa was radically out of phase with the rest of Africa, so South Africa today looks somewhat like the rest of Africa did in the early 1960s.

A participant from the George Washington University asked Freeman if there were any lessons for developing countries on works councils, gain-sharing, and the like, which under certain conditions might boost efficiency and even human capital accumulation. Freeman did not know of any good examples from developing countries. The issue was, he said, what level of education and stage of development you must reach before you could move to that form of organization. In the United States Xerox and Texas Instruments do this kind of thing very well, but even in the United States most companies don't do it. It is a complicated question, and Freeman hoped someone would do more work on it.